## The Editor

CANDACE WAID is the author of *Edith Wharton's Letters from the Underworld: Fictions of Women and Writing* and the editor of Wharton's novels, short stories, and autobiography. In addition to teaching for a decade on the faculty of Yale University, where she worked extensively in the Wharton Collection, she also has taught as a visiting professor at the Institut du Monde Anglophone at the Université de Paris (III) of the Sorbonne and the École Normale Superieure. Currently Associate Professor of English at the University of California, Santa Barbara, Candace Waid teaches American literature with a focus on race and regional cultures.

## W. W. NORTON & COMPANY, INC.
### *Also Publishes*

ENGLISH RENAISSANCE DRAMA: A NORTON ANTHOLOGY
*edited by David Bevington et al.*

THE NORTON ANTHOLOGY OF AFRICAN AMERICAN LITERATURE
*edited by Henry Louis Gates Jr. and Nellie Y. McKay et al.*

THE NORTON ANTHOLOGY OF AMERICAN LITERATURE
*edited by Nina Baym et al.*

THE NORTON ANTHOLOGY OF CHILDREN'S LITERATURE
*edited by Jack Zipes et al.*

THE NORTON ANTHOLOGY OF ENGLISH LITERATURE
*edited by M. H. Abrams and Stephen Greenblatt et al.*

THE NORTON ANTHOLOGY OF LITERATURE BY WOMEN
*edited by Sandra M. Gilbert and Susan Gubar*

THE NORTON ANTHOLOGY OF MODERN AND CONTEMPORARY POETRY
*edited by Jahan Ramazani, Richard Ellmann, and Robert O'Clair*

THE NORTON ANTHOLOGY OF POETRY
*edited by Margaret Ferguson, Mary Jo Salter, and Jon Stallworthy*

THE NORTON ANTHOLOGY OF SHORT FICTION
*edited by R. V. Cassill and Richard Bausch*

THE NORTON ANTHOLOGY OF THEORY AND CRITICISM
*edited by Vincent B. Leitch et al.*

THE NORTON ANTHOLOGY OF WORLD LITERATURE
*edited by Sarah Lawall et al.*

THE NORTON FACSIMILE OF THE FIRST FOLIO OF SHAKESPEARE
*prepared by Charlton Hinman*

THE NORTON INTRODUCTION TO LITERATURE
*edited by Alison Booth, J. Paul Hunter, and Kelly J. Mays*

THE NORTON INTRODUCTION TO THE SHORT NOVEL
*edited by Jerome Beaty*

THE NORTON READER
*edited by Linda H. Peterson and John C. Brereton*

THE NORTON SAMPLER
*edited by Thomas Cooley*

THE NORTON SHAKESPEARE, BASED ON THE OXFORD EDITION
*edited by Stephen Greenblatt et al.*

For a complete list of Norton Critical Editions, visit
wwnorton.com/college/English/nce_home.htm

A NORTON CRITICAL EDITION

Edith Wharton

# THE AGE OF INNOCENCE

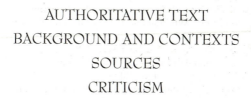

AUTHORITATIVE TEXT
BACKGROUND AND CONTEXTS
SOURCES
CRITICISM

*Edited by*

## CANDACE WAID

THE UNIVERSITY OF CALIFORNIA, SANTA BARBARA

W. W. NORTON & COMPANY • *New York* • *London*

for R. W. B. Lewis (1917–2002)

The text of this book is composed in Fairfield Medium
with the display set in Bernhard Modern.
Composition by PennSet, Inc.
Manufacturing by the Courier Companies.
Book design by Antonina Krass.

Library of Congress Cataloging-in-Publication Data
Wharton, Edith, 1862–1937.
The age of innocence : authoritative text, contexts, criticism / Edith
Wharton; edited by Candace Waid.—Norton critical ed.
    p. cm.
Includes historical documents and passages from other publications
contemporary with the featured work.
Includes bibliographical references.

**ISBN 0-393-96794-8 (pbk.)**

1. Upper class—Fiction.   2. Marriage—Fiction.   3. New York (N.Y.)—
Fiction.   4. Wharton, Edith, 1862–1937. Age of innocence.   I. Waid,
Candace.   II. Title.

PS3545 .H16 A7 2002
813'.52—dc21

                                                                    00-026408

W. W. Norton & Company, Inc., 500 Fifth Avenue, New York, N.Y. 10110
www.wwnorton.com
W. W. Norton & Company Ltd., Castle House, 75/76 Wells Street,
London W1T 3QT

7 8 9 0

# Contents

## Criticism

# Illustrations

# Acknowledgments

Much of the texture of this edition has been gathered over years of friendship with Wharton scholars as we shared our experiences of reading Edith Wharton's writing and benefiting from her expertise on so many diverse subjects. It is challenging to try to thank the large number of gifted and knowledgable people who have contributed to the success of this project. Significant information on sources and a sense of critical direction have been drawn from the work of R. W. B. Lewis, Elizabeth Ammons, Clare Colquitt, Susan Goodman, Helen Killoran, Cynthia Griffin Wolff, Sarah Bird Wright, and Patricia Willis. This project would not have been completed without the intellectual support and literary guidance of Carol Bemis, Brian Baker, Marian Johnson, Jane Carter, and Katharine Ings of W. W. Norton, the finest editors with whom I have worked. Julia Ehrhardt, after serving as a research assistant during the initial stage of this project, wrote an important article generated by her work that is included in this edition. Five individuals worked separately to locate the series of recipes that led to the inclusion of the formulas for Roman Punch, and more than a dozen scholars spent long periods trying to discover the historical identity of a French actress that Jennifer Rae Greeson finally located. Like Greeson, many others may have supplied the information for a single note or source, but their contributions to me and to the collective work of this project are finally incalculable.

Having carried this project through several geographic removes, I have the fortune of having many people to thank. As I acknowledge my debts to the scholarly communities that have helped me to excavate the layers of allusions that form and inform the art of *The Age of Innocence*, I am particularly grateful to experts on Edith Wharton, Old New York, legal historians specializing in marriage and divorce laws, and an ever-widening circle of consultants on interior decorating and material culture. In compiling the array of visual documents selected for this edition, Scott Marshall was a primary source, suggesting archival sources as well as volumes of published photographs. Eleanor Dwight's pictorial record (the most complete in relation to all phases of Wharton's life and work) led the way to several of the most beautiful photographs depicting the summer pastimes of the New York elite; many of these images were also suggested by the archivists of the Newport Historical Society. M. Joan Youngken of the Newport Historical Society was particularly helpful in researching the obscure history of "The Young Ladies Archery Society." Without exception, the most detailed and accurate source for historical information about the New York of the novel is *The Encyclopedia of New York City* edited by Kenneth T. Jackson.

While most of the photographs and all of the maps included here have never been used in relation to any Wharton project, others have become part of an iconic visual record representing Edith Wharton's life and her childhood in Old New York. Robert Bennett and Carly Andrews produced the maps, transforming lists and locations into publishable documents. Julia Ehrhardt, Jennifer Rae Greeson, and Sara Gerend offered important as-sistance in sifting through archives and published books to find particular images and secure permissions for their publication. The New York Historical Society, the Museum of the City of New York, the New York State Historical Archive in Albany, the Newington Cropsey Foundation, the Newport Historical Society, the Preservation Society of Newport County, the Special Collections of the University of California, Santa Barbara and Los Angeles, the Beinecke Rare Book and Manuscript Library of Yale University, the Schlesinger Library of Radcliffe University, the Tulane University Law Library, and the Lilly Collection of Indiana University made a significant contribution to this project by sharing their considerable resources and making their archival collections accessible. I am grateful for the research funds provided by the Academic Senate and the Interdisciplinary Humanities Center at the University of California, Santa Barbara.

A partial list of those who contributed information or identified sources for this edition includes: Jean-Christophe Agnew, Carly Andrews, Joseph Baldwin, Laura Baldwin, Valerie Baudier, Carol Bemis, Ann Bermingham, Robert Bennett, Emily Bernard, Elizabeth Blackmar, Cynthia Blakely, Karen Bowie, Rachel Bowlby, Christy A. Cannariato, Jane Carter, Andrea Carneiro, Linda Cirino, Ljilijana Coklin, Clare Colquitt, Elizabeth Heckendorn Cook, Kim Coonen, Stephanie Copeland, Gayane Demirchyan, Andrew S. Dolcart, Manina DuBroca, Heather Ecker, Brian T. Edwards, Julia Ehrhardt, Robert Erickson, Elizabeth Evans, Melissa Fanny, Jill Finsten, Paul Fry, James W. Gargano, Wendy Gamber, W. Randall Garr, Sara Gerend, Rose Gladney, Laure Goldstein, Susan Gosling, Rosibel Guzman, Mary Green, Michael Green, Jennifer Rae Greeson, Michael Grossman, Miriam Hansen, Hendrik Hartog, Richard Helgerson, Katharine Ings, Zia Isola, Laura Kalman, Marie-Christine Lemardeley, R. W. B. Lewis, Nancy Lewis, Joanna Lipking, Toni Mantych, Cindy Marshall, David Marshall, Karen Marshall, Scott Marshall, Rhoda McGraw, Michael Perry, Pierre-Yves Pétillon, Brigitte Peucker, Joe Rodriguez, Mark Rose, Roy Rosenzweig, Daniel Royot, Pat Saik, Brian Sciacca, Jolie Sheffer, Randy Schiff, Regina Schwartz, Carl Smith, Dana Spoonerow, Harriet Swift, Lyn Thompson, John Tschirch, Alan Trachtenberg, Allen Tullos, Anne Ullmo-Michel, Christina Vella, Jennifer Wicke, and the entire community of the English Department of the University of California, Santa Barbara. I thank Harriet Jones, Billie Fay Waid, Donna Waid, Donald Waid, Paula Ballard, Will Murray, Kathleen Tanner, Dawn Michelle, Augusta Harper Cunningham, Hannah Rose Blakely, Helene Marshall, Arthur Marshall, David Marshall and Daniel Waid Marshall for the personal support that has made this project possible. This edition of *The Age of Innocence* is dedicated to the memory of R. W. B. Lewis, whose writing, teaching, and generosity brought me and so many others to Edith Wharton.

# Introduction

In 1919, as the Allied forces plotted the future by remaking the map of Europe, Edith Wharton seemed compelled to plot the past, in particular the world of her own past located in the exclusive and excluding society of her childhood. Wharton returned to her life as a writer by drafting several outlines for what would become her Pulitzer Prize–winning novel, *The Age of Innocence* (1920), using "Old New York" as her working title. Aside from her brief and passionate novel, *Summer* (1917), and war-driven work such as editing *The Book of the Homeless* (1916), Wharton spent her days organizing institutions to feed, clothe, and shelter the refugees who were pouring into Paris. A permanent resident since 1909, Wharton's service to France was acknowledged when she was awarded the Cross of the Legion of Honor in 1915, the highest honor that can be bestowed on foreign-born heroes. In *Fighting France from Dunkerque to Belfort* (1915), Wharton described her many trips to the battlefront through the death she had seen along the roadways. Recognizing the threat to the communal body in a city that was likened to a "disemboweled corpse," Wharton mourned "the destruction of the obscurist human communities." Faced with "exposed interiors": "house fronts sliced . . . clean off," Wharton conveyed the poignancy of photographs still attached to exposed walls and "bundles of letters laboriously written and just as laboriously deciphered" lying in the ruins. To Wharton, these objects torn from their human settings were "the thousand and one bits of the past" that had once given "meaning and continuity to the present."[1]

While she would speak of the writing of *The Age of Innocence* as a retreat "to childish memories of a long-vanished America," a manifestation of her desire for "a momentary escape,"[2] Wharton characteristically escaped to a past that allowed her to critique America as she grieved over a fallen Europe. Less an escape to a distanced past than a return to the present, Wharton's novel set in the decade following the Civil War draws a great deal of its emotional force from the sense of loss associated with the Great War. In *The Age of Innocence*, Wharton created a novel distinguished by its almost surgical accuracy, composing an elegy for a lost world that is both a tribute to and a cutting analysis of the realm of her childhood. Piecing together her elegy for the shattered past, Wharton reflected on her own experience of history. In this "backward glance," Wharton did not see the "well traveled

1. Edith Wharton, *Fighting France from Dunkerque to Belfort* (New York: Scribner's, 1915), pp. 153, 158.
2. Edith Wharton, *A Backward Glance* (New York: Charles Scribner's Sons, 1934), p. 369.

roads" promised by Whitman; she saw instead a cataclysmic abyss, an irrevocable divide between "the pathetic picturesqueness"[3] of the America of her childhood and the unsettling modernity of a post-war world that had become "a roaring and discontinuous universe."[4]

Wharton's decision to write *The Age of Innocence* during the months following the armistice was driven by the same forces that later compelled her to publish a personal memoir: "If anyone had suggested to me before 1914, to write my reminiscences, I should have answered that my life had been too uneventful to be worth recording." Indeed, as Wharton would confess, it was "not until the successive upheavals which resulted in the catastrophe of 1914 had 'cut all likeness of the name' from my old New York did I see its pathetic picturesqueness."[5] By writing *The Age of Innocence*, Wharton evoked the era of her own childhood, documenting the customs she had observed when she returned in 1872 at age ten after six years in Europe to face the strange and estranging society of her origins. Wharton, who watched the models for her character, May, unveil themselves to draw back the bow in the newly fashionable sport of archery, also writes of a hidden realm in which the "Dark Ladies," the African American "artists," prepared feasts for these pale goddess figures.

Like May, as R. W. B. Lewis points out in his biography, Wharton knew what it meant to be sacrificed to an ideal that required women to suffer from what her protagonist Newland Archer reveres and condemns as "abysmal purity"(6).[6] The twenty-four-year-old Edith Jones had approached her wedding day with increasing horror because she still did not know where babies came from. Sexually ignorant, the young woman who would become Edith Wharton had long lived amid a social and familial ethos of silence, a world in which a hint of sexual scandal could cause a man's name, and by implication the story of his fall, to remain unspoken.

A few months after publishing her novel that begins by invoking "the early seventies" (3), Wharton wrote to her publisher justifying her decision to draw her "allusions rang[ing] from, say, 1875 to 1885. Any narrower field of evocation must necessarily reduce the novel to a piece of archeological pedantry instead of a living image of the times."[7] While Wharton chose to change some things, altering details that were not integral to her story, the fact that she chose to leave other questioned details as they were suggests that her position on the temporal latitude that was necessary for the writing of strong historical fiction was much more than a retrospectively conceived defensive posture. Indeed, the second manuscript plan for the novel documents the time frame for the novel as being from "1875–1885" while the

3. *Backward Glance*, p. 6.
4. Edith Wharton, "Preface," *The Ghost Stories of Edith Wharton* (New York: Popular Library, 1976), p. 9. Originally published as the preface to Edith Wharton's *Ghosts* (New York: Appleton-Century Co., 1937).
5. *Backward Glance*, pp. 5, 6.
6. References to *The Age of Innocence*, as well as to other selections included in this volume, will appear as page references in the text.
7. Letter from Edith Wharton to Rutger Jewett, Feb. 7, 1921, quoted by Julia Ehrhardt in "To Read These Pages is to Live Again," p. 411 in this edition. See also Greeson.

third manuscript outline that simply gives the year, "1875," confirms that the novel was always being located just beyond the time alluded to vaguely as "the early seventies" in the opening sentence of the published work. Wharton's novel has its most personal origins in 1872, the year "the young hawk" returned home to realize that she was "in exile in America."[8] In the most intimate of terms, this was the moment that the young Edith realized (without ever having "seen one in the flesh") that she wanted to become "an author."[9] At the age of fourteen, this aspiring writer of the mid-seventies worked in secret to complete her first novella, "Fast and Loose," the tale of a young woman who agrees to a mercenary marriage rather than marry the man she loves. This doomed female protagonist then dies an appropriately early and sentimental death, leaving her unrequited lover obsessed with her grave. Demonstrating her awareness of the consequences of publication, the precocious Edith wrote a series of scathing mock reviews. Penning a brutal assessment that she pretended had been published in *The Nation*, the astute writer turned critic concluded: "It is false charity to reader and writer to mince matters. The English of it is that every character is a failure, the plot a vacuum, the style spiritless, the dialogue vague, the sentiment weak & the whole thing a fiasco." Castigating the writer of "Fast and Loose" (to whom she had given a male pseudonym) for being "very, very like a sick-sentimental school-girl,"[1] the girl who would become Edith Wharton laid the groundwork for her future opus by writing a novella that established the decade of the seventies as a fertile location for a novel about failed marriages, sacrificial deaths, and the problem of uncongenial marital alliances with foreign aristocrats. In many ways, Wharton's *Age of Innocence* is most autobiographical because the very act of writing such a novel was in itself a return to her own primal scene as she spirited away paper to complete her secret novella in 1876.

Taking its title from Sir Joshua Reynolds's evocative portrait of the daughter of his favorite niece, *The Age of Innocence* is not the novel of a young girl. As Cynthia Griffin Wolff points out, invoking Wharton's reference to Henry James, it is not a novel concerned with drawing *The Portrait of a Lady*. Instead of focusing on a female figure such as James's Isabel Archer, Wharton's novel centers on the fate of Newland Archer, a man who is described as "the portrait of a gentleman" (79). While the central events of the novel take place in the period from the "early seventies" through the historical decade that closes in the mid-eighties, the concluding section describes the intervening years from the perspective of an aging Newland Archer who has remained a faithful father and husband, has contributed to the growth of institutions helping the needy, and has made a brief foray into politics after being

---

8. R. W. B. Lewis, *Edith Wharton: A Biography* (New York: Harper Colophon Books, 1975), p. 431. Edith Wharton, "Life and I," Wharton Collection, Beinecke Rare Book and Manuscript Library, Yale University, New Haven, Connecticut, p. 20.
9. *Backward Glance*, p. 76.
1. Edith Wharton, "Fast and Loose," in *Fast and Loose and The Buccaneers*, ed. Viola Winner Hopkins, (Charlottesville: University of Virginia Press, 1993), p. 117.

encouraged by his prominent friend, Wharton's actual friend, Theodore Roosevelt.

In the closing scene, modeled on the end of Wharton's *House of Mirth* (1905), Newland Archer, who is fifty-seven, the same age as Wharton herself when she began writing *The Age of Innocence*, sits on a park bench in Paris looking up at the window of the Countess Olenska. After walking through a series of sites known for their fallen monuments and places that recall fallen reigns, Newland Archer chooses to remain with his memories of the past he has lost and the past he continues to experience. Wharton, who was fond of saying that she and Teddy Roosevelt were "self-made men," clearly identifies with her male protagonist. Refusing to introduce her past to her present, Wharton has her character Newland Archer decide to remain with the memory of his Ellen rather than look into the eyes of the powerful, expatriot woman whom Wharton had in many ways become. The Countess Olenska may not be the "Gorgon" who has the power to blind those who look on her, but this mysterious American woman is a figure who has lived in "the golden light . . . the pervading illumination" of an art-infused life "spent in this rich atmosphere that [Newland Archer] already felt to be too dense and yet too stimulating for his lungs" (215).

*The Age of Innocence* is set in a time of great change and the entire novel is written with a consciousness of what this world is destined to become, from the anticipation of technological advances in travel and communication to the shifting mores in marriage and money. Despite its elegiac tone, this novel finally is not defined by a sense of nostalgia. Like Wharton's other works describing New York society, *The Age of Innocence* offers a profound critique of the world it describes, even as it finds value in the sacrifices made to ensure the stability of the quietly violent ranks of the "New York four hundred." This exclusive group, defined by the limits of Mrs. Astor's ballroom and the closest thing to an aristocracy that America had ever known, was the closely guarded world into which Wharton was born; her writing, despite her own repeated and explicit disclaimers, was from the outset assumed to have the force and authority of a social exposé. It was thought, and not without reason, that Wharton's society novels might be read as an insider's guide to what had long been an inaccessible realm of mysteries and manners. As Wharton's autobiographical writings suggest, the novel emerged from her intimate knowledge of the world that she (like the Countess Olenska) had to leave in order to fulfill herself through art.

For Edith Wharton, Old New York was an airless world she escaped to experience the ecstasy of breath she found in literary creation and the seductive call of words themselves. If art from the outset was part of a forbidden world for Wharton, her writing long continued to be her only means of understanding the power of erotic passion. (Wharton, who discovered sexual passion late in life, may never even have consummated her twenty-six year marriage to Teddy Wharton. The couple's efforts at sexual intimacy seem to have ceased after the harrowing experiments of the first three weeks of marriage.) Divorced in 1913, Wharton had reason to critique her culture's fetish of the ideal of female innocence, a life-blighting ignorance that she later argued "did more than anything else to falsify and misdirect my whole life."[2]

Known for her critiques of New York society in her first bestseller, *The House of Mirth* (1905) and in *The Custom of the Country* (1913) (both of which depicted the destruction of the society of Old New York as it was consumed by the appetite of a soulless materialism), Wharton from the outset had included participant observers in her novels. Aware of the forces of change, whether technological, economic, or sexual, these observers comment on the acts of carnivorous pleasure or passive denial that threaten to destroy this rigidly ritualized and moribund society. The denizens of Old New York, surrounded by change, inhabit what the ill-fated Ralph Marvell of *The Custom of the Country* calls "the 'Reservation'."[3] Educated through his passion for his wife's cousin, Newland Archer, who reads the new treatises on "Primitive Man," becomes the most sophisticated critic of the rituals concerning female purity and the brutal acts of purification that insist on the exclusion of foreign contaminants and the sacrifice of women. As *The Age of Innocence* suggests, female sexual experience itself is tainted with foreignness. Through her sexual attractiveness alone, the estranged Countess Olenska constitutes a threat to the sanctity of the tribe not only by giving the lie to the supposed inviolability of marriage, but also by embodying the possibility of female sexual desire and female sexual agency.

*The Age of Innocence* catalogues the ways in which Old New York divides the society of men from that of women. The cost of this story of sexual separation, the devastation that can be traced to a type of "factitious" and calculated innocence that takes the form of infantilization, is presented in Wharton's early story, "The Valley of Childish Things, and Other Emblems," as well as in her essay, "The New Frenchwoman," in *French Ways and Their Meaning* (1919), a group of cultural essays published as a book the year before *The Age of Innocence* appeared. Included in the "Sources" section of this edition, these evocative pieces suggest the ways in which Wharton drew on a life-long concern to articulate the pointed critique of female innocence she sets forth in her novel.

The modern critical essays included in this edition provide a variety of lenses through which to view Wharton's novel. In *The Age of Innocence*, as Nancy Bentley argues, the novel of manners must be understood by examining its connection to the ethnographic case study. Wharton's novel is obsessed with rituals of purity and the necessity of sacrifice, with the threat of contamination and the fierce (if bloodless) violence of being excluded from what is called the "tribe." Indeed, the

2. Quoted in Lewis, *Edith Wharton*, p. 54, from Wharton's "Life and I" in the Beinecke Rare Book and Manuscript Library, Yale University, New Haven, Connecticut.
3. Edith Wharton, *The Custom of the Country* (New York: Charles Scribner's Sons, 1913), p. 74.

contaminating foreignness that enters the novel in the form of the "kinswoman" (200), the Europeanized, experienced, and therefore corrupted Ellen Olenska, must be read in the context of the novel's informed and incisive disquisition on the problem of culture. The Countess Olenska represents at once the return of the repressed, an embodiment of art and sexuality that, as Elizabeth Ammons insists, must be exiled; and as Anne MacMaster and Dale Bauer conclude, this woman is a dark figure, an embodiment of otherness who in her evocation of "fear and desire" is both vulnerable and strangely powerful.

Indeed, the question of blood itself was a problem in this age of American isolationism, in which race- and class-based claims insisted on the ideal of a "factitious purity" (30), and were bred by values that insisted on breeding a stultifying sameness. Purity has other meanings here as the elite pursue an illusory whiteness at the core of what might be called the age of eugenics. While Newland is at once the primary figure articulating the novel's critique of female innocence and his culture's obsession with the ideal of female purity, he also, as Brian Edwards argues, occupies a walled world that insists on the harem-like separation of men and women. This ethos of the harem has international implications as Newland Archer becomes an increasingly impotent figure who represents American isolationism and the United States' reluctance to enter World War I.

Newland Archer's story of temptation and renunciation, as Cynthia Griffin Wolff points out, makes this hesitant gentleman the protagonist of Wharton's most impressive *Bildungsroman*. He is a man whose life is finally determined by the unannounced collaboration between the surprisingly innocent Ellen and the paradoxically experienced May. As Jennifer Rae Greeson argues, these categories of innocence and experience wavered for Wharton as she mapped out plans for the novel that was to be her parable of American culture.

*The Age of Innocence* reflects Wharton's growing obsession with an anthropological perspective. As Wharton delved into the complex layers of her social and material past, she wrote a historical novel that was not only an ethnographic *tour de force*, but also the recreation of a living structure, what R. W. B. Lewis calls "a strenuous act of revivification."[4] For Wharton, this historical novel could only be written through the unearthing of shards of memory, gathering pieces in a writing process that came to resemble an archaeological expedition. Writing about her desire to discover and recover the past through fiction and memoirs, Wharton concluded: "The compact world of my youth has receded into a past from which it can only be dug up in bits by the assiduous relic-hunter; and, its smallest fragments begin to be worth collecting and putting together before the last of those who knew the live structure are swept away with it."[5] As Julia Ehrhardt's account of the novel's generation reveals, not only Wharton, but her readers and reviewers were obsessed with the idea of historical accu-

---

4. Lewis, *Edith Wharton*, p. 430.
5. *Backward Glance*, p. 7.

racy, an accuracy that became more difficult to achieve with each added layer of cultural allusion.

Wharton's desire to bring the past to life through the accretion of words on the page, as well as her obsession as an artist with art and culture, is evoked again in Brigitte Peucker's analysis of Martin Scorcese's late-twentieth-century translation of the novel into film. Recalling the story of Galatea (the mythical statue who is brought to life in the arms of her creator, Pygmalion) and the still moments of the novel, Peucker suggests the ways in which Scorcese's film alludes to layers of film history and that medium's incorporation of the paradoxical aesthetic of motion and stillness. In Wharton's *Age of Innocence*, characters are framed in momentary stillness before being brought to life on the page itself, a transformation that is bodied forth even more forcefully through the medium of film.

Classified by Edmund Wilson as "[t]he poet of interior decoration,"[6] Wharton proved in *The Age of Innocence* that there is indeed life, and perhaps poetry, in the description of the objects that furnish and recreate a lost world. This poetry ranges from the archive of colonial history found in the list of place settings and serving plate used by the van der Luydens to the sense of the past conveyed through a list of types of carriages (including the vis-à-vis familiar to readers of Jane Austen) that were still to be seen in the fashionable resort town of Newport in the 1870s. Like everything about the novel, including the icon of female purity embodied in the complex figure of May, interiors of *The Age of Innocence* are finally not innocent. As the extensive notes to this edition demonstrate, the novel is comprised of layer upon layer of allusion that, taken together, create a world of great complexity where objects themselves—such as the seemingly inert books lifted at random from a table in Archer's study—are included to tell a story. Rich in the lyric poetry of sounds and lists, *The Age of Innocence* can be read without understanding the significance of objects mentioned on the page, but these details (histories of places, events, and objects) carry part of the deeper meaning of the narrative and, in many ways, function as keys to the interior and living world of the novel. Asked to read the manuscript, Wharton's close friend Walter Berry insisted, "Yes; it's good. But of course you and I are the only people who will ever read it." By "read,"[7] Berry may have meant that he and Wharton would be the only ones to understand the power of her creation and the meaning of the myriad allusions that she had hoped would bring art to life. The notes in this edition are designed to serve as a guide to the past world of Wharton's childhood, a world Berry felt might be lost even to the modern reader of 1920.

*The Age of Innocence* is a parable of America and its relationship to the Old World. While Newland seems compelled to marry one of "his own kind" (21), part of what he recognizes as "real life" (148, 159) is embodied in his love of art and books, a love that has the other

---

6. Edmund Wilson, "Justice to Edith Wharton," in *The Wound and the Bow* (New York, 1947), p. 163.
7. *Backward Glance*, p. 369.

woman, the exiled countess, as its muse. Although Ellen Olenska has
separated permanently from her husband, she remains married to
the Old World that this Polish count represents. Appreciative of the
hope, if not ignorance, that lies in the joining of a "Newland" with a
"Welland," the novel underlines the cultural significance of the
Countess Olenska whose ties with an "old land"[8] have long been heard
in the resonant syllables of her married name. As Wharton returns to
the scene of her own first effort to write a novel, she creates in stunning detail the world she had seen nearly a half century earlier when
her own eyes, sharpened by exile, had lost their innocence. If Ellen
Olenska must be driven out of New York society, Newland and May remain to sacrifice their lives to the orderly world of family and tradition
that forms the matrix of the insular and (as the novel already knows)
doomed society of Old New York. Wharton's novel is a profound refig-
uring of her own escape through the writing of a work that is itself obsessed with sacrifice and preoccupied with the problem of return.

Likening the lost world of her childhood to "the lowest layer of
Schliemann's Troy," Wharton writing in her autobiography insists that
"[n]othing but the Atlantis-fate of Old New York . . . which had slowly
and continuously developed from the early seventeenth century to
[her] own childhood" has made "that childhood worth recalling."[9]
Wharton concludes:

> Even negatively, these traditions have acquired with the passing
> of time, an unsuspected value. When I was young it used to seem
> to me that the group in which I grew up was like an empty vessel
> into which no new wine would ever again be poured. Now I see
> that one of its uses lay in preserving a few drops of an old vintage
> too rare to be savoured by a youthful palate; and I should like to
> atone for my unappreciativeness by trying to revive that faint fra-
> grance.[1]

Finally, The Age of Innocence must be read as the powerful rendering
of a paradox in which exile is represented as essential to the preservation of a culture while the recreation of the author's Old New York becomes desirable or perhaps even possible only after that enclosed
world has been violated and shattered. The same Edith Wharton who
became an artist through exile felt compelled to recreate the broken
world that once had had the power to destroy her. Returning through
imagination to the world of her childhood, Wharton wrote The Age of
Innocence to reverse time, to bring the past to life by recounting history from the intimate distance of art.

8. R. W. B. Lewis in conversation, New Haven, Connecticut, 1979.
9. Backward Glance, p. 55.
1. Backward Glance, p. 5.

The Text of
# THE AGE OF INNOCENCE

**Wharton's Outline for *The Age of Innocence*.** A photograph of the first page of the holographic manuscript of the third outline for *The Age of Innocence*, bearing the working title of "Old New York." For a discussion of the three outlines and Wharton's inscription in Arabic at the top of this manuscript, see Jennifer Rae Greeson's article and p. 416, *n.* 7.

# BOOK ONE

## I

On a January evening of the early seventies,[1] Christine Nilsson was singing in *Faust* at the Academy of Music in New York.[2]

Though there was already talk of the erection, in remote metropolitan distances "above the Forties," of a new Opera House[3] which should compete in costliness and splendor with those of the great European capitals, the world of fashion was still content to reassemble every winter in the shabby red and gold boxes of the sociable old Academy. Conservatives cherished it for being small and inconvenient, and thus keeping out the "new people" whom New York was beginning to dread and yet be drawn to; and the sentimental clung to it for its historic associations, and the musical for its excellent acoustics, always so problematic a quality in halls built for the hearing of music.

It was Madame Nilsson's first appearance that winter, and what the daily press had already learned to describe as "an exceptionally brilliant audience" had gathered to hear her, transported through the slippery, snowy streets in private broughams, in the spacious family landau, or in the humbler but more convenient "Brown *coupé*."[4] To come to the Opera in a Brown *coupé* was almost as honorable a way of arriving as in one's own carriage; and departure by the same means

1. By her own account, Wharton based this historical novel on events drawn from a full decade. Although many of the historical and cultural events that provide the factual sources for the novel take place beginning in "the early seventies," the textual detail proves that Wharton's decade begins in the mid-1880s and extends into the mid-1880s.
2. Christine Nilsson, a Swedish opera singer (1843–1921), was a soprano known for decades for her rendition of Marguerite in Gounod's *Faust*. She made her American debut in this role in 1870 at the Academy of Music in New York (14th Street and Irving Place), which, in the early 1870s, was the largest opera house in the world (capacity 4,500). *Faust* premiered in America at the Academy of Music in 1863. Based on Goethe's *Faust*, Gounod's opera tells the story of an aging and suicidal philosopher who in his despair accepts a youth potion from the devil, Mephistopheles, seduces the innocent Marguerite, and then abandons the distraught woman to her misery. Near the opera's close, the devil leads Faust back to the imprisoned Marguerite, who has been accused of killing their child. Although Mephistopheles insists that Marguerite is damned, a choir of angels proclaims her innocence as the fallen woman rises to heaven. (See also p. 6, *n*. 2.) The work sung here, Gounod's musically improved *Faust* of 1869, was the most popular opera in late nineteenth- and early twentieth-century America.
3. The Metropolitan Opera House, on Broadway between 39th and 40th Streets, opened in 1883 to the sounds of Christine Nilsson singing the role of Marguerite in Gounod's *Faust*. Mrs. William K. Vanderbilt, the leader of the wealthy interlopers whom members of the traditional aristocracy of old New York were "beginning to dread," is said to have organized the building of the Metropolitan Opera House when, despite her husband's tremendous wealth, she was unable to procure a box at the Academy of Music. Its proposed location "above the forties" would have been considered outside the boundaries of polite and settled society. Notorious for saloons, animal pens, and squatters (estimated to number in the thousands), this region of Manhattan was considered a wild world (a "wilderness," p. 9) by the New York elite.
4. broughams: Closed, four-wheeled carriages with seating for two or four; landau: A covered, four-wheeled carriage featuring a divided top, the back half of which can be thrown back; Brown *coupé*: A four-wheeled, covered carriage designed for two with an elevated seat outside for the driver. Isaac H. Brown was an entrepreneur who successfully introduced a fleet of these horse-drawn carriages for hire.

4 THE AGE OF INNOCENCE

had the immense advantage of enabling one (with a playful allusion to democratic principles) to scramble into the first Brown conveyance in the line, instead of waiting till the cold-and-gin congested nose of one's own coachman gleamed under the portico of the Academy. It was one of the great livery-stableman's most masterly intuitions to have discovered that Americans want to get away from amusement even more quickly than they want to get to it.

When Newland Archer opened the door at the back of the club box the curtain had just gone up on the garden scene. There was no reason why the young man should not have come earlier, for he had dined at seven, alone with his mother and sister, and had lingered afterward over a cigar in the Gothic library with glazed black-walnut bookcases and finial-topped chairs which was the only room in the house where Mrs. Archer allowed smoking. But, in the first place, New York was a metropolis, and perfectly aware that in metropolises it was "not the thing" to arrive early at the Opera; and what was or was not "the thing" played a part as important in Newland Archer's New York as the inscrutable totem terrors that had ruled the destinies of his forefathers thousands of years ago.

The second reason for his delay was a personal one. He had dawdled over his cigar because he was at heart a dilettante, and thinking over a pleasure to come often gave him a subtler satisfaction than its realization. This was especially the case when the pleasure was a delicate one, as his pleasures mostly were; and on this occasion the moment he looked forward to was so rare and exquisite in quality that—well, if he had timed his arrival in accord with the prima donna's stage-manager he could not have entered the Academy at a more significant moment than just as she was singing: "He loves me— he loves me not—_he loves me!_" and sprinkling the falling daisy petals with notes as clear as dew.

She sang, of course, "_M'ama!_" and not "He loves me,"[5] since an unalterable and unquestioned law of the musical world required that the German text of French operas sung by Swedish artists should be translated into Italian for the clearer understanding of English-speaking audiences. This seemed as natural to Newland Archer as all the other conventions on which his life was moulded: such as the duty of using two silver-backed brushes with his monogram in blue enamel to part his hair, and of never appearing in society without a flower (preferably a gardenia) in his buttonhole.

"_M'ama . . . non m'ama . . . ,_" the prima donna sang, and "_M'ama!_," with a final burst of love triumphant, as she pressed the dishevelled daisy to her lips and lifted her large eyes to the sophisticated countenance of the little brown Faust-Capoul,[6] who was vainly trying, in a tight purple velvet doublet and plumed cap, to look as pure and true as his artless victim.

Newland Archer, leaning against the wall at the back of the club

---

5. Marguerite's "_M'ama_" is a bilingual pun in which, to English speakers, the vulnerable maiden seems to call for her mother; in Italian "_M'ama_" means "He loves me."
6. Victor Capoul (1839–1924), opera singer performing the role of Faust.

box,[7] turned his eyes from the stage and scanned the opposite side of
the house. Directly facing him was the box of old Mrs. Manson Mingott, whose monstrous obesity had long since made it impossible for
her to attend the Opera, but who was always represented on fashionable nights by some of the younger members of the family. On this
occasion, the front of the box was filled by her daughter-in-law,
Mrs. Lovell Mingott, and her daughter, Mrs. Welland; and slightly
withdrawn behind these brocaded matrons sat a young girl in white
with eyes ecstatically fixed on the stage-lovers. As Madame Nilsson's
"M'ama!" thrilled out above the silent house (the boxes always stopped
talking during the Daisy Song) a warm pink mounted to the girl's
cheek, mantled her brow to the roots of her fair braids, and suffused
the young slope of her breast to the line where it met a modest tulle
tucker fastened with a single gardenia.[8] She dropped her eyes to the
immense bouquet of lilies-of-the-valley on her knee, and Newland
Archer saw her white-gloved finger tips touch the flowers softly. He
drew a breath of satisfied vanity and his eyes returned to the stage.

No expense had been spared on the setting, which was acknowledged to be very beautiful even by people who shared his acquaintance with the Opera houses of Paris and Vienna. The foreground, to
the footlights, was covered with emerald green cloth. In the middle
distance symmetrical mounds of woolly green moss bounded by croquet hoops formed the base of shrubs shaped like orange-trees but
studded with large pink and red roses. Gigantic pansies, considerably
larger than the roses, and closely resembling the floral penwipers
made by female parishioners for fashionable clergymen, sprang from
the moss beneath the rose-trees; and here and there a daisy grafted on
a rose-branch flowered with a luxuriance prophetic of Mr. Luther Bur-
bank's[9] far-off prodigies.

In the center of this enchanted garden Madame Nilsson, in white
cashmere slashed with pale blue satin, a reticule[1] dangling from a blue
girdle, and large yellow braids carefully disposed on each side of her
muslin chemisette, listened with downcast eyes to M. Capoul's impassioned wooing, and affected a guileless incomprehension of his designs whenever, by word or glance, he persuasively indicated the
ground floor window of the neat brick villa projecting obliquely from
the right wing.

"The darling!" thought Newland Archer, his glance flitting back to
the young girl with the lilies-of-the-valley. "She doesn't even guess
what it's all about." And he contemplated her absorbed young face
with a thrill of possessorship in which pride in his own masculine ini-

---

7. One of a series of small, draped, and walled enclosures occupying the first raised tier in a
   stylish theater. The right to certain boxes was part of a familially determined social legacy.
   Even the most elite men's clubs could not lease boxes in the old Academy of Music; this innovation became possible with the opening of the much larger Metropolitan Opera House.
8. Daisy Song: See p. 266 for a photograph of Christine Nilsson as Marguerite plucking the
   petals that according to the ancient game will reveal whether one is loved; tulle tucker: The
   yoke of net (*tulle* in French) or lace designed as a concession to modesty to cover the chest
   laid bare by a low-cut bodice.
9. American horticulturist (1849–1926) famous for his experiments in plant breeding.
1. A small drawstring pouch or purse used by fashionable women to carry personal items.

tiation was mingled with a tender reverence for her abysmal purity. "We'll read *Faust*[2] together . . . by the Italian lakes . . ." he thought, somewhat hazily confusing the scene of his projected honeymoon with the masterpieces of literature which it would be his manly privilege to reveal to his bride. It was only that afternoon that May Welland had let him guess that she "cared" (New York's consecrated phrase of maiden avowal), and already his imagination, leaping ahead of the engagement ring, the betrothal kiss and the march from *Lohengrin*,[3] pictured her at his side in some scene of old European witchery.

He did not in the least wish the future Mrs. Newland Archer to be a simpleton. He meant her (thanks to his enlightening companionship) to develop a social tact and readiness of wit enabling her to hold her own with the most popular married women of the "younger set," in which it was the recognized custom to attract masculine homage while playfully discouraging it. If he had probed to the bottom of his vanity (as he sometimes nearly did) he would have found there the wish that his wife should be as worldly-wise and as eager to please as the married lady whose charms had held his fancy through two mildly agitated years; without, of course, any hint of the frailty which had so nearly marred that unhappy being's life, and had disarranged his own plans for a whole winter.

How this miracle of fire and ice was to be created, and to sustain itself in a harsh world, he had never taken the time to think out; but he was content to hold his view without analyzing it, since he knew it was that of all the carefully-brushed, white-waistcoated, buttonhole-flowered gentlemen who succeeded each other in the club box, exchanged friendly greetings with him, and turned their opera glasses critically on the circle of ladies who were the product of the system. In matters intellectual and artistic Newland Archer felt himself distinctly the superior of these chosen specimens of old New York gentility; he had probably read more, thought more, and even seen a good deal more of the world, than any other man of the number. Singly they betrayed their inferiority; but grouped together they represented "New York," and the habit of masculine solidarity made him accept their doctrine on all the issues called moral. He instinctively felt that in this respect it would be troublesome—and also rather bad form—to strike out for himself.

"Well—upon my soul!" exclaimed Lawrence Lefferts, turning his opera glass abruptly away from the stage. Lawrence Lefferts was, on the whole, the foremost authority on "form" in New York. He had probably devoted more time than anyone else to the study of this intricate and fascinating question; but study alone could not account for

---

2. A dramatic epic in verse composed 1770–1832 by the German writer Johann Wolfgang von Goethe (1749–1832). This famous story of a man who sells his soul to the devil rose to prominence with the posthumous publication of *Doctor Faustus* (1604) by Christopher Marlowe (1564–1593). Unlike Marlowe's Faustus, Goethe's Faust is ultimately redeemed. In addition to drawing on preceding published works, the versions of the Faust narrative were also inspired by tales about the life of the legendary German conjurer, Johann Faust (1488–1541).
3. From an 1850 opera by the German composer Richard Wagner (1813–1883); the march was played during wedding processionals.

his complete and easy competence. One had only to look at him, from the slant of his bald forehead and the curve of his beautiful fair moustache to the long patent-leather feet at the other end of his lean and elegant person, to feel that the knowledge of "form" must be congenital in anyone who knew how to wear such good clothes so carelessly and carry such height with so much lounging grace. As a young admirer had once said of him: "If anybody can tell a fellow just when to wear a black tie with evening clothes and when not to, it's Larry Lefferts." And on the question of pumps versus patent-leather "Oxfords" his authority had never been disputed.

"My God!" he said; and silently handed his glass to old Sillerton Jackson.

Newland Archer, following Lefferts's glance, saw with surprise that his exclamation had been occasioned by the entry of a new figure into old Mrs. Mingott's box. It was that of a slim young woman, a little less tall than May Welland, with brown hair growing in close curls about her temples and held in place by a narrow band of diamonds. The suggestion of this headdress, which gave her what was then called a "Josephine look," was carried out in the cut of the dark blue velvet gown rather theatrically caught up under her bosom by a girdle with a large old-fashioned clasp.[4] The wearer of this unusual dress, who seemed quite unconscious of the attention it was attracting, stood a moment in the center of the box, discussing with Mrs. Welland the propriety of taking the latter's place in the front right-hand corner; then she yielded with a slight smile, and seated herself in line with Mrs. Welland's sister-in-law, Mrs. Lovell Mingott, who was installed in the opposite corner.

Mr. Sillerton Jackson had returned the opera glass to Lawrence Lefferts. The whole of the club turned instinctively, waiting to hear what the old man had to say; for old Mr. Jackson was as great an authority on "family" as Lawrence Lefferts was on "form." He knew all the ramifications of New York's cousinships; and could not only elucidate such complicated questions as that of the connection between the Mingotts (through the Thorleys) with the Dallases of South Carolina, and that of the relationship of the elder branch of Philadelphia Thorleys to the Albany Chiverses (on no account to be confused with the Manson Chiverses of University Place), but could also enumerate the leading characteristics of each family: as, for instance, the fabulous stinginess of the younger lines of Leffertses (the Long Island ones); or the fatal tendency of the Rushworths to make foolish matches; or the insanity recurring in every second generation of the Albany Chiverses, with whom their New York cousins had always refused to intermarry—with the disastrous exception of poor Medora Manson, who, as everybody knew . . . but then her mother was a Rushworth.

4. Josephine (1763–1814), empress of Napoleon Bonaparte, popularized a style that included decorative headbands and dresses that were belted under the bosom and worn over a sheer slip; the "Josephine look" contrasted sharply with the plunging, lace-covered necklines and accentuated bodices that characterized the dresses worn by fashionable American women in the 1870s.

In addition to this forest of family trees, Mr. Sillerton Jackson carried between his narrow hollow temples, and under his soft thatch of silver hair, a register of most of the scandals and mysteries that had smouldered under the unruffled surface of New York society within the last fifty years. So far indeed did his information extend, and so acutely retentive was his memory, that he was supposed to be the only man who could have told you who Julius Beaufort, the banker, really was, and what had become of handsome Bob Spicer, old Mrs. Manson Mingott's father, who had disappeared so mysteriously (with a large sum of trust money) less than a year after his marriage, on the very day that a beautiful Spanish dancer who had been delighting thronged audiences in the old Opera-house on the Battery[5] had taken ship for Cuba. But these mysteries, and many others, were closely locked in Mr. Jackson's breast; for not only did his keen sense of honor forbid his repeating anything privately imparted, but he was fully aware that his reputation for discretion increased his opportunities of finding out what he wanted to know.

The club box, therefore, waited in visible suspense while Mr. Sillerton Jackson handed back Lawrence Lefferts's opera glass. For a moment he silently scrutinized the attentive group out of his filmy blue eyes overhung by old veined lids; then he gave his moustache a thoughtful twist, and said simply: "I didn't think the Mingotts would have tried it on."

## II

Newland Archer, during this brief episode, had been thrown into a strange state of embarrassment.

It was annoying that the box which was thus attracting the undivided attention of masculine New York should be that in which his betrothed was seated between her mother and aunt; and for a moment he could not identify the lady in the Empire dress,[1] nor imagine why her presence created such excitement among the initiated. Then light dawned on him, and with it came a momentary rush of indignation. No, indeed; no one would have thought the Mingotts would have tried it on!

But they had; they undoubtedly had; for the low-toned comments behind him left no doubt in Archer's mind that the young woman was May Welland's cousin, the cousin always referred to in the family as "poor Ellen Olenska." Archer knew that she had suddenly arrived from Europe a day or two previously; he had even heard from Miss Welland

---

5. Built as a fort in anticipation of the War of 1812 with the British, Castle Garden was opened as a pleasure garden in 1824. By mid-century, after the addition of a roof, it became a venue for opera and other major musical events. Closed in 1854, "the old Opera-house" reopened the next year as a facility for processing arriving immigrants, a function that it served until 1890. During the time of the novel's central action Castle Garden was the site most associated with the influx of foreigners into New York, a city already distinguished by the fact that half of its population at mid-century had been foreign born. (See p. 307 for painting.)
1. Countess Olenska follows the fashion set by the Empress Josephine (see p. 7, *n.* 4).

(not disapprovingly) that she had been to see poor Ellen, who was staying with old Mrs. Mingott. Archer entirely approved of family solidarity, and one of the qualities he most admired in the Mingotts was their resolute championship of the few black sheep that their blameless stock had produced. There was nothing mean or ungenerous in the young man's heart, and he was glad that his future wife should not be restrained by false prudery from being kind (in private) to her unhappy cousin; but to receive Countess Olenska in the family circle was a different thing from producing her in public, at the Opera of all places, and in the very box with the young girl whose engagement to him, Newland Archer, was to be announced within a few weeks. No, he felt as old Sillerton Jackson felt; he did not think the Mingotts would have tried it on!

He knew, of course, that whatever man dared (within Fifth Avenue's[2] limits) that old Mrs. Manson Mingott, the Matriarch of the line, would dare. He had always admired the high and mighty old lady, who, in spite of having been only Catherine Spicer of Staten Island, with a father mysteriously discredited, and neither money nor position enough to make people forget it, had allied herself with the head of the wealthy Mingott line, married two of her daughters to "foreigners" (an Italian Marquis and an English banker), and put the crowning touch to her audacities by building a large house of pale cream-colored stone (when brown sandstone seemed as much the only wear as a frockcoat in the afternoon) in an inaccessible wilderness near the Central Park.[3]

Old Mrs. Mingott's foreign daughters had become a legend. They never came back to see their mother, and the latter being, like many persons of active mind and dominating will, sedentary and corpulent in her habit, had philosophically remained at home. But the cream-colored house (supposed to be modelled on the private hotels of the Parisian aristocracy) was there as a visible proof of her moral courage; and she throned in it, among pre-Revolutionary furniture and souvenirs of the Tuileries of Louis Napoleon (where she had shone in her middle age), as placidly as if there were nothing peculiar in living above Thirty-fourth Street, or in having French windows that opened like doors instead of sashes that pushed up.[4]

Everyone (including Mr. Sillerton Jackson) was agreed that old

---

2. Famous thoroughfare in Manhattan. Extending from the Harlem River south to Washington Square, Fifth Avenue, known in the late nineteenth century for its elegant mansions, had become synonymous by 1920 (the year of the publication of *The Age of Innocence*) with the world of fashion because of the department stores that dominated the Avenue between 34th and 59th Streets. During the historical period of the novel, the famous "Ladies Mile" between 14th and 23rd Streets, bounded by Broadway and Sixth Avenues, was the premier shopping district.

3. Located between Fifth Avenue and Central Park West, from 59th to 110th Streets, Central Park was the first landscaped urban park in America. Designed by Frederick Law Olmsted and Calvert Vaux, it was opened to the public in 1859. Wharton's aunt (a model for Mrs. Manson Mingott) actually built a mansion in this part of Manhattan with its farms, pastures, and quarries. (See p. 240 for photographs of this mansion, a structure which served as a source for the one described in the novel.)

4. Hotels: In the French of the period, "hotel" refers to the city mansion of a wealthy individual; Tuileries of Louis Napoleon: The French royal residence adjoining the Louvre in Paris; Louis-Napoleon, Bonaparte's nephew, inhabited the Tuileries and ruled France 1849–1870.

Catherine had never had beauty—a gift which, in the eyes of New York, justified every success, and excused a certain number of failings. Unkind people said that, like her Imperial namesake,[5] she had won her way to success by strength of will and hardness of heart, and a kind of haughty effrontery that was somehow justified by the extreme decency and dignity of her private life. Mr. Manson Mingott had died when she was only twenty-eight, and had "tied up" the money with an additional caution born of the general distrust of the Spicers; but his bold young widow went her way fearlessly, mingled freely in foreign society, married her daughters in heaven knew what corrupt and fashionable circles, hobnobbed with Dukes and Ambassadors, associated familiarly with Papists, entertained Opera singers, and was the intimate friend of Mme. Taglioni;[6] and all the while (as Sillerton Jackson was the first to proclaim) there had never been a breath on her reputation; the only respect, he always added, in which she differed from the earlier Catherine.

Mrs. Manson Mingott had long since succeeded in untying her husband's fortune, and had lived in affluence for half a century; but memories of her early straits had made her excessively thrifty, and though, when she bought a dress or a piece of furniture, she took care that it should be of the best, she could not bring herself to spend much on the transient pleasures of the table. Therefore, for totally different reasons, her food was as poor as Mrs. Archer's, and her wines did nothing to redeem it. Her relatives considered that the penury of her table discredited the Mingott name, which had always been associated with good living; but people continued to come to her in spite of the "made dishes"[7] and flat champagne, and in reply to the remonstrances of her son Lovell (who tried to retrieve the family credit by having the best *chef* in New York) she used to say laughingly: "What's the use of two good cooks in one family, now that I've married the girls and can't eat sauces?"

Newland Archer, as he mused on these things, had once more turned his eyes toward the Mingott box. He saw that Mrs. Welland and her sister-in-law were facing their semicircle of critics with the Mingottian *aplomb* which old Catherine had inculcated in all her tribe, and that only May Welland betrayed, by a heightened color (perhaps due to the knowledge that he was watching her), a sense of the gravity of the situation. As for the cause of the commotion, she sat gracefully in her corner of the box, her eyes fixed on the stage, and revealing, as she leaned forward, a little more shoulder and bosom than New York was accustomed to seeing, at least in ladies who had reasons for wishing to pass unnoticed.

Few things seemed to Newland Archer more awful than an offense against "Taste," that far-off divinity of whom "Form" was the mere vis-

---

5. Catherine the Great, Empress of Russia (1729–1796), a powerful ruler known for, among other things, her rapacious sexual appetite.
6. Papists: A disparaging term designating Roman Catholics (most members of New York Society would have been Protestant); Mme. Taglioni: Italian ballerina (1804–1884) known for introducing dancing on the point of the toe.
7. Food dishes, such as casseroles and stews, that could be prepared in advance.

ible representative and vicegerent. Madame Olenska's pale and serious face appealed to his fancy as suited to the occasion and to her unhappy situation; but the way her dress (which had no tucker) sloped away from her thin shoulders shocked and troubled him. He hated to think of May Welland's being exposed to the influence of a young woman so careless of the dictates of Taste.

"After all," he heard one of the younger men begin behind him (everybody talked through the Mephistopheles-and-Martha scenes),[8] "after all, just *what* happened?"

"Well—she left him; nobody attempts to deny that."

"He's an awful brute, isn't he?" continued the young enquirer, a candid Thorley, who was evidently preparing to enter the lists as the lady's champion.

"The very worst; I knew him at Nice," said Lawrence Lefferts with authority. "A half-paralyzed white sneering fellow—rather handsome head, but eyes with a lot of lashes. Well, I'll tell you the sort: when he wasn't with women he was collecting china. Paying any price for both, I understand."

There was a general laugh, and the young champion said: "Well, then——?"

"Well, then; she bolted with his secretary."

"Oh, I see." The champion's face fell.

"It didn't last long, though: I heard of her a few months later living alone in Venice. I believe Lovell Mingott went out to get her. He said she was desperately unhappy. That's all right—but this parading her at the Opera's another thing."

"Perhaps," young Thorley hazarded, "she's too unhappy to be left at home."

This was greeted with an irreverent laugh, and the youth blushed deeply, and tried to look as if he had meant to insinuate what knowing people called a "*double entendre.*"

"Well—it's queer to have brought Miss Welland, anyhow," someone said in a low tone, with a side glance at Archer.

"Oh, that's part of the campaign: Granny's orders, no doubt," Lefferts laughed. "When the old lady does a thing she does it thoroughly."

The act was ending, and there was a general stir in the box. Suddenly Newland Archer felt himself impelled to decisive action. The desire to be the first man to enter Mrs. Mingott's box, to proclaim to the waiting world his engagement to May Welland, and to see her through whatever difficulties her cousin's anomalous situation might involve her in; this impulse had abruptly overruled all scruples and hesitations, and sent him hurrying through the red corridors to the farther side of the house.

As he entered the box his eyes met Miss Welland's, and he saw that she had instantly understood his motive, though the family dignity which both considered so high a virtue would not permit her to tell

---

8. In a subplot of the opera, Mephistopheles courts Marguerite's companion, Martha, so that Faust can be alone with Marguerite.

him so. The persons of their world lived in an atmosphere of faint implications and pale delicacies, and the fact that he and she understood
each other without a word seemed to the young man to bring them
nearer than any explanation would have done. Her eyes said: "You see
why Mamma brought me," and his answered: "I would not for the
world have had you stay away."

"You know my niece Countess Olenska?" Mrs. Welland enquired as
she shook hands with her future son-in-law. Archer bowed without extending his hand, as was the custom on being introduced to a lady;
and Ellen Olenska bent her head slightly, keeping her own pale-gloved
hands clasped on her huge fan of eagle feathers. Having greeted Mrs.
Lovell Mingott, a large blonde lady in creaking satin, he sat down beside his betrothed, and said in a low tone: "I hope you've told Madame
Olenska that we're engaged? I want everybody to know—I want you to
let me announce it this evening at the ball."

Miss Welland's face grew rosy as the dawn, and she looked at him
with radiant eyes. "If you can persuade Mamma," she said; "but why
should we change what is already settled?" He made no answer but
that which his eyes returned, and she added, still more confidently
smiling: "Tell my cousin yourself: I give you leave. She says she used
to play with you when you were children."

She made way for him by pushing back her chair, and promptly, and
a little ostentatiously, with the desire that the whole house should see
what he was doing, Archer seated himself at the Countess Olenska's
side.

"We *did* use to play together, didn't we?" she asked, turning her
grave eyes to his. "You were a horrid boy, and kissed me once behind a
door; but it was your cousin Vandie Newland, who never looked at me,
that I was in love with." Her glance swept the horseshoe curve of
boxes. "Ah, how this brings it all back to me—I see everybody here in
knickerbockers and pantalettes,"[9] she said, with her trailing slightly
foreign accent, her eyes returning to his face.

Agreeable as their expression was, the young man was shocked that
they should reflect so unseemly a picture of the august tribunal before
which, at that very moment, her case was being tried. Nothing could
be in worse taste than misplaced flippancy; and he answered somewhat stiffly: "Yes, you have been away a very long time."

"Oh, centuries and centuries; so long," she said, "that I'm sure I'm
dead and buried, and this dear old place is heaven," which, for reasons
he could not define, struck Newland Archer as an even more disrespectful way of describing New York society.

---

9. horseshoe curve: the location of the van der Luyden box at the middle of this curve suggests
their acknowledged centrality in the hierarchically defined society of Old New York; knickerbockers and pantalettes: Garments worn by children; knickerbockers are short pants fastened at the knee and pantalettes are undergarments with divided legs that were worn
beneath young girls' skirts.

# III

It invariably happened in the same way.

Mrs. Julius Beaufort, on the night of her annual ball,[1] never failed to appear at the Opera; indeed, she always gave her ball on an Opera night in order to emphasize her complete superiority to household cares, and her possession of a staff of servants competent to organize every detail of the entertainment in her absence.

The Beauforts' house was one of the few in New York that possessed a ballroom (it antedated even Mrs. Manson Mingott's and the Headly Chiverses); and at a time when it was beginning to be thought "provincial" to put a "crash"[2] over the drawing-room floor and move the furniture upstairs, the possession of a ballroom that was used for no other purpose, and left for three-hundred-and-sixty-four days of the year to shuttered darkness, with its gilt chairs stacked in a corner and its chandelier in a bag; this undoubted superiority was felt to compensate for whatever was regrettable in the Beaufort past.

Mrs. Archer, who was fond of coining her social philosophy into axioms, had once said: "We all have our pet common people—" and though the phrase was a daring one, its truth was secretly admitted in many an exclusive bosom. But the Beauforts were not exactly common; some people said they were even worse. Mrs. Beaufort belonged indeed to one of America's most honored families; she had been the lovely Regina Dallas (of the South Carolina branch), a penniless beauty introduced to New York society by her cousin, the imprudent Medora Manson, who was always doing the wrong thing from the right motive. When one was related to the Mansons and the Rushworths one had a *"Droit de cité"*[3] (as Mr. Sillerton Jackson, who had frequented the Tuileries, called it) in New York society; but did one not forfeit it in marrying Julius Beaufort?

The question was: who *was* Beaufort?[4] He passed for an Englishman, was agreeable, handsome, ill-tempered, hospitable and witty. He had come to America with letters of recommendation from old Mrs. Manson Mingott's English son-in-law, the banker, and had speedily made himself an important position in the world of affairs; but his habits were dissipated, his tongue was bitter, his antecedents were mysterious; and when Medora Manson announced her cousin's en-

1. An allusion to Mrs. William Astor's annual opera ball. Considered the premier event of the New York social season, this ball was a social monument to Mrs. Astor's exclusivity. Indeed, the limits of the Astor ballroom—four hundred guests—were said to establish the boundaries of New York "society."
2. A rough fabric woven from yarns of uneven texture, used to protect floors from the scraping of dancers' feet. Crash became increasingly maligned as a dancing surface because its loosened fibers and dust were seen as health hazards.
3. Literally, "the right of the city," meaning the right to enter and to be accepted by "society."
4. Julius Beaufort may have been modeled on the powerful financier, August Belmont. Both first names are those of Roman emperors, and their last names have similar meanings in French: "Beaufort" meaning "beautiful stronghold" and "Belmont," "beautiful mountain." Said to have been an illegitimate son of the Jewish and aristocratic House of Rothschild, a rumor that had its source in Belmont's early work and meteoric rise in the Rothschild's financial empire, Belmont was at the center of talk that focused on his mysterious origins. (See pp. 402–3.)

gagement to him it was felt to be one more act of folly in poor
Medora's long record of imprudences.

But folly is as often justified of her children as wisdom, and two
years after young Mrs. Beaufort's marriage it was admitted that she
had the most distinguished house in New York. No one knew exactly
how the miracle was accomplished. She was indolent, passive, the
caustic even called her dull; but dressed like an idol, hung with pearls,
growing younger and blonder and more beautiful each year, she
throned in Mr. Beaufort's heavy brownstone palace, and drew all the
world there without lifting her jewelled little finger. The knowing people said it was Beaufort himself who trained the servants, taught the
*chef* new dishes, told the gardeners what hot-house flowers to grow for
the dinner-table and the drawing rooms, selected the guests, brewed
the after-dinner punch and dictated the little notes his wife wrote to
her friends. If he did, these domestic activities were privately performed, and he presented to the world the appearance of a careless
and hospitable millionaire strolling into his own drawing room with
the detachment of an invited guest, and saying: "My wife's gloxinias
are a marvel, aren't they? I believe she gets them out from Kew."[5]

Mr. Beaufort's secret, people were agreed, was the way he carried
things off. It was all very well to whisper that he had been "helped" to
leave England by the international banking-house in which he had
been employed; he carried off that rumor as easily as the rest—though
New York's business conscience was no less sensitive than its moral
standard—he carried everything before him, and all New York into his
drawing rooms, and for over twenty years now people had said they
were "going to the Beauforts'" with the same tone of security as if
they had said they were going to Mrs. Manson Mingott's, and with the
added satisfaction of knowing they would get hot canvasback ducks
and vintage wines, instead of tepid Veuve Cliquot without a year[6] and
warmed-up croquettes from Philadelphia.

Mrs. Beaufort, then, had as usual appeared in her box just before
the Jewel Song;[7] and when, again as usual, she rose at the end of the
third act, drew her opera cloak about her lovely shoulders, and disappeared, New York knew that meant that half an hour later the ball
would begin.

The Beaufort house was one that New Yorkers were proud to show
to foreigners, especially on the night of the annual ball. The Beauforts
had been among the first people in New York to own their own red velvet carpet and have it rolled down the steps by their own footmen,

5. Site of the Royal Botanic Gardens outside London.
6. Veuve Cliquot was among the most distinguished producers of champagne, ranked with
   Perrier-Jouet and Moet. Champagne from 1874 was the most distinguished vintage of the
   period and brought high prices at auction in the 1880s and 1890s. Champagne, which remained the most expensive wine, surpassed claret in 1874 to assume its current status as
   the favored celebratory wine. Here, a "tepid" offering "without a year," appears to allude to
   the years of inferior champagne that followed 1874. The absence of the named year refers to
   non-vintage wine. Champagne became an expensive and popular import in the latter half of
   the nineteenth century.
7. Sung by Marguerite while trying on jewels left by Mephistopheles as a gift from Faust. The
   reference indicates that Mrs. Beaufort arrived during the third act, approximately halfway
   through the opera.

under their own awning, instead of hiring it with the supper and the ballroom chairs. They had also inaugurated the custom of letting the ladies take their cloaks off in the hall, instead of shuffling up to the hostess's bedroom and recurling their hair with the aid of the gas-burner; Beaufort was understood to have said that he supposed all his wife's friends had maids who saw to it that they were properly *coiffées*[8] when they left home.

Then the house had been boldly planned with a ballroom, so that, instead of squeezing through a narrow passage to get to it (as at the Chiverses'), one marched solemnly down a vista of enfiladed drawing rooms (the sea-green, the crimson and the *bouton d'or*),[9] seeing from afar the many-candled lusters reflected in the polished parquetry, and beyond that the depths of a conservatory where camellias and tree ferns arched their costly foliage over seats of black and gold bamboo.

Newland Archer, as became a young man of his position, strolled in somewhat late. He had left his overcoat with the silk-stockinged footmen (the stockings were one of Beaufort's few fatuities), had dawdled a while in the library hung with Spanish leather and furnished with buhl and malachite,[1] where a few men were chatting and putting on their dancing-gloves, and had finally joined the line of guests whom Mrs. Beaufort was receiving on the threshold of the crimson drawing room.

Archer was distinctly nervous. He had not gone back to his club after the Opera (as the young bloods usually did), but, the night being fine, had walked for some distance up Fifth Avenue before turning back in the direction of the Beauforts' house. He was definitely afraid that the Mingotts might be going too far; that, in fact, they might have Granny Mingott's orders to bring the Countess Olenska to the ball.

From the tone of the club box he had perceived how grave a mistake that would be; and, though he was more than ever determined to "see the thing through," he felt less chivalrously eager to champion his betrothed's cousin than before their brief talk at the Opera.

Wandering on to the *bouton d'or* drawing room (where Beaufort had had the audacity to hang "Love Victorious," the much-discussed nude of Bouguereau)[2] Archer found Mrs. Welland and her daughter stand-

8. French, "with hair done."
9. enfiladed . . . rooms: A series of rooms that open into one another; *bouton d'or*: French, literally, "button of gold"—as an adjective, "buttercup colored."
1. buhl: Initially referring to French furniture with a dark finish. In England and the United States, buhl refers to furniture with inlaid patterns of tortoiseshell, ivory, and metals of various colors. malachite: A green stone, often marked by bands or striations of varied colors.
2. "Love Victorious": Actually a well-known painting by the Italian artist Caravaggio (1573–1610), featuring a boyish, winged, and naked Cupid holding a sheaf of arrows and surrounded by sheet music, a violin, and a bow; Caravaggio's painting of male rather than female nudity would have been considered somewhat risqué by New York society in the late nineteenth century. Bouguereau: William Adolphe Bouguereau (1825–1905), a French painter renowned for his voluptuous nudes. In her autobiography, *A Backward Glance*, Wharton recalls that allusions to William Astor's notorious acquisition of a Bouguereau Venus served as a staple of conversation in New York society when she was a child. August Belmont (see p. 13 *n.* 4) also owned a Bouguereau nude considered shocking. An expert in art history, Wharton, by joining historical fact to an art historical reference, makes a joke rather than a mistake. While "Love Victorious" could refer to an unknown painting of Venus by Bouguereau, the allusion gains meaning by using the actual title of a painting by Caravaggio featuring a nude male archer.

ing near the ballroom door. Couples were already gliding over the floor beyond: the light of the wax candles fell on revolving tulle skirts, on girlish heads wreathed with modest blossoms, on the dashing aigrettes and ornaments of the young married women's coiffures, and on the glitter of highly glazed shirtfronts and fresh glacé gloves.[3]

Miss Welland, evidently about to join the dancers, hung on the threshold, her lilies-of-the-valley in her hand (she carried no other bouquet), her face a little pale, her eyes burning with a candid excitement. A group of young men and girls were gathered about her, and there was much hand-clasping, laughing and pleasantry on which Mrs. Welland, standing slightly apart, shed the beam of a qualified approval. It was evident that Miss Welland was in the act of announcing her engagement, while her mother affected the air of parental reluctance considered suitable to the occasion.

Archer paused a moment. It was at his express wish that the announcement had been made, and yet it was not thus that he would have wished to have his happiness known. To proclaim it in the heat and noise of a crowded ballroom was to rob it of the fine bloom of privacy which should belong to things nearest the heart. His joy was so deep that this blurring of the surface left its essence untouched; but he would have liked to keep the surface pure too. It was something of a satisfaction to find that May Welland shared this feeling. Her eyes fled to his beseechingly, and their look said: "Remember, we're doing this because it's right."

No appeal could have found a more immediate response in Archer's breast; but he wished that the necessity of their action had been represented by some ideal reason, and not simply by poor Ellen Olenska. The group about Miss Welland made way for him with significant smiles, and after taking his share of the felicitations he drew his betrothed into the middle of the ballroom floor and put his arm about her waist.

"Now we shan't have to talk," he said, smiling into her candid eyes, as they floated away on the soft waves of the "Blue Danube."[4]

She made no answer. Her lips trembled into a smile, but the eyes remained distant and serious, as if bent on some ineffable vision. "Dear," Archer whispered, pressing her to him: it was borne in on him that the first hours of being engaged, even if spent in a ballroom, had in them something grave and sacramental. What a new life it was going to be, with this whiteness, radiance, goodness at one's side!

The dance over, the two, as became an affianced couple, wandered into the conservatory; and sitting behind a tall screen of tree ferns and camellias Newland pressed her gloved hand to his lips.

"You see I did as you asked me to," she said.

---

3. aigrettes: Sprays of egret feathers, diamonds, or other decorations worn as hair ornaments; glacé: Literally "iced" in French, here used to describe glossy gloves of kid leather that men put on just before beginning to dance.
4. A waltz by Johann Strauss (1825–1899) first performed in 1867; Strauss's American debut of this waltz in 1872 was a major cultural event.

"Yes: I couldn't wait," he answered smiling. After a moment he added: "Only I wish it hadn't had to be at a ball."

"Yes, I know." She met his glance comprehendingly. "But after all—even here we're alone together, aren't we?"

"Oh, dearest—always!" Archer cried.

Evidently she was always going to understand; she was always going to say the right thing. The discovery made the cup of his bliss over-flow, and he went on gaily: "The worst of it is that I want to kiss you and I can't." As he spoke he took a swift glance about the conservatory, assured himself of their momentary privacy, and catching her to him laid a fugitive pressure on her lips. To counteract the audacity of this proceeding he led her to a bamboo sofa in a less secluded part of the conservatory, and sitting down beside her broke a lily-of-the-valley from her bouquet. She sat silent, and the world lay like a sunlit valley at their feet.

"Did you tell my cousin Ellen?" she asked presently, as if she spoke through a dream.

He roused himself, and remembered that he had not done so. Some invincible repugnance to speak of such things to the strange foreign woman had checked the words on his lips.

"No—I hadn't the chance after all," he said, fibbing hastily.

"Ah." She looked disappointed, but gently resolved on gaining her point. "You must, then, for I didn't either; and I shouldn't like her to think—"

"Of course not. But aren't you, after all, the person to do it?"

She pondered on this. "If I'd done it at the right time, yes: but now that there's been a delay I think you must explain that I'd asked you to tell her at the Opera, before our speaking about it to everybody here. Otherwise she might think I had forgotten her. You see, she's one of the family, and she's been away so long that she's rather—sensitive."

Archer looked at her glowingly. "Dear and great angel! Of course I'll tell her." He glanced a trifle apprehensively toward the crowded ball-room. "But I haven't seen her yet. Has she come?"

"No; at the last minute she decided not to."

"At the last minute?" he echoed, betraying his surprise that she should ever have considered the alternative possible.

"Yes. She's awfully fond of dancing," the young girl answered simply. "But suddenly she made up her mind that her dress wasn't smart enough for a ball, though we thought it so lovely; and so my aunt had to take her home."

"Oh, well—" said Archer with happy indifference. Nothing about his betrothed pleased him more than her resolute determination to carry to its utmost limit that ritual of ignoring the "unpleasant" in which they had both been brought up.

"She knows as well as I do," he reflected, "the real reason of her cousin's staying away; but I shall never let her see by the least sign that I am conscious of there being a shadow of a shade on poor Ellen Olenska's reputation."

# IV

In the course of the next day the first of the usual betrothal visits were exchanged. The New York ritual was precise and inflexible in such matters; and in conformity with it Newland Archer first went with his mother and sister to call on Mrs. Welland, after which he and Mrs. Welland and May drove out to old Mrs. Manson Mingott's to receive the venerable ancestress' blessing.

A visit to Mrs. Manson Mingott was always an amusing episode to the young man. The house in itself was already an historic document, though not, of course, as venerable as certain other old family houses in University Place and lower Fifth Avenue.[1] Those were of the purest 1830, with a grim harmony of cabbage-rose-garlanded carpets, rosewood consoles, round-arched fireplaces with black marble mantels, and immense glazed bookcases of mahogany; whereas old Mrs. Mingott, who had built her house later, had bodily cast out the massive furniture of her prime, and mingled with the Mingott heirlooms the frivolous upholstery of the Second Empire.[2] It was her habit to sit in a window of her sitting room on the ground floor, as if watching calmly for life and fashion to flow northward to her solitary doors. She seemed in no hurry to have them come, for her patience was equalled by her confidence. She was sure that presently the hoardings, the quarries, the one-story saloons, the wooden greenhouses in ragged gardens, and the rocks from which goats surveyed the scene, would vanish before the advance of residences as stately as her own—perhaps (for she was an impartial woman) even statelier; and that the cobblestones over which the old clattering omnibuses bumped would be replaced by smooth asphalt, such as people reported having seen in Paris. Meanwhile, as everyone she cared to see came to *her* (and she could fill her rooms as easily as the Beauforts, and without adding a single item to the *menu* of her suppers), she did not suffer from her geographic isolation.

The immense accretion of flesh which had descended on her in middle life like a flood of lava on a doomed city had changed her from a plump active little woman with a neatly-turned foot and ankle into something as vast and august as a natural phenomenon. She had accepted this submergence as philosophically as all her other trials, and now, in extreme old age, was rewarded by presenting to her mirror an almost unwrinkled expanse of firm pink and white flesh, in the center of which the traces of a small face survived as if awaiting excavation. A flight of smooth double chins led down to the dizzy depths of a still-snowy bosom veiled in snowy muslins that were held in place by a miniature portrait of the late Mr. Mingott; and around and below, wave after wave of black silk surged away over the edges of a capacious armchair,

1. Near Washington Square in Greenwich Village. An early Manhattan settlement, this became the neighborhood where the most traditional of the New York elite lived.
2. Highly ornate, covered furniture; the Second Empire (1852–1870) in France took place during the reign of Louis-Napoleon.

with two tiny white hands poised like gulls on the surface of the billows.

The burden of Mrs. Manson Mingott's flesh had long since made it impossible for her to go up and down stairs, and with characteristic independence she had made her reception rooms upstairs and established herself (in flagrant violation of all the New York proprieties) on the ground floor of her house; so that, as you sat in her sitting room window with her, you caught (through a door that was always open, and a looped-back yellow damask portière) the unexpected vista of a bedroom with a huge low bed upholstered like a sofa, and a toilet-table with frivolous lace flounces and a gilt-framed mirror.

Her visitors were startled and fascinated by the foreignness of this arrangement, which recalled scenes in French fiction, and architectural incentives to immorality such as the simple American had never dreamed of. That was how women with lovers lived in the wicked old societies, in apartments with all the rooms on one floor, and all the indecent propinquities that their novels described. It amused Newland Archer (who had secretly situated the love-scenes of *Monsieur de Camors*[3] in Mrs. Mingott's bedroom) to picture her blameless life led in the stage-setting of adultery; but he said to himself, with considerable admiration, that if a lover had been what she wanted, the intrepid woman would have had him too.

To the general relief the Countess Olenska was not present in her grandmother's drawing room during the visit of the betrothed couple. Mrs. Mingott said she had gone out; which, on a day of such glaring sunlight, and at the "shopping hour," seemed in itself an indelicate thing for a compromised woman to do. But at any rate it spared them the embarrassment of her presence, and the faint shadow that her unhappy past might seem to shed on their radiant future. The visit went off successfully, as was to have been expected. Old Mrs. Mingott was delighted with the engagement, which, being long foreseen by watchful relatives, had been carefully passed upon in family council; and the engagement ring, a large thick sapphire set in invisible claws, met with her unqualified admiration.

"It's the new setting: of course it shows the stone beautifully, but it looks a little bare to old-fashioned eyes," Mrs. Welland had explained, with a conciliatory side glance at her future son-in-law.

"Old-fashioned eyes? I hope you don't mean mine, my dear? I like all the novelties," said the ancestress, lifting the stone to her small bright orbs, which no glasses had ever disfigured. "Very handsome," she added, returning the jewel, "very liberal. In my time a cameo set in pearls was thought sufficient. But it's the hand that sets off the ring, isn't it, my dear Mr. Archer?" and she waved one of her tiny hands, with small pointed nails and rolls of aged fat encircling the wrist like ivory bracelets. "Mine was modeled in Rome by the great Ferrigiani.[4]

---

3. A novel (1867) by the French author Octave Feuillet (1821–1890). Like other works by this prolific and popular author, *Monsieur de Camors* is about romantic passions and family honor. It has been likened to Laclos's more scandalous *Les Liaisons dangereuses* for its depiction of adultery.
4. In all likelihood a now-forgotten Roman sculptor. Like Ferrigiani, the popularity of carved likenesses of American women's hands has disappeared.

You should have May's done: no doubt he'll have it done, my child. Her hand is large—it's these modern sports that spread the joints—but the skin is white.—And when's the wedding to be?" she broke off, fixing her eyes on Archer's face.

"Oh—" Mrs. Welland murmured, while the young man, smiling at his betrothed, replied: "As soon as ever it can, if only you'll back me up, Mrs. Mingott."

"We must give them time to get to know each other a little better, mamma," Mrs. Welland interposed, with the proper affectation of reluctance; to which the ancestress rejoined: "Know each other? Fiddlesticks! Everybody in New York has always known everybody. Let the young man have his way, my dear; don't wait till the bubble's off the wine. Marry them before Lent; I may catch pneumonia any winter now, and I want to give the wedding breakfast."

These successive statements were received with the proper expressions of amusement, incredulity and gratitude; and the visit was breaking up in a vein of mild pleasantry when the door opened to admit the Countess Olenska, who entered in bonnet and mantle followed by the unexpected figure of Julius Beaufort.

There was a cousinly murmur of pleasure between the ladies, and Mrs. Mingott held out Ferrigiani's model to the banker. "Ha! Beaufort, this is a rare favor!" (She had an odd foreign way of addressing men by their surnames.)

"Thanks. I wish it might happen oftener," said the visitor in his easy arrogant way. "I'm generally so tied down; but I met the Countess Ellen in Madison Square,[5] and she was good enough to let me walk home with her."

"Ah—I hope the house will be gayer, now that Ellen's here!" cried Mrs. Mingott with a glorious effrontery. "Sit down—sit down, Beaufort: push up the yellow armchair; now I've got you I want a good gossip. I hear your ball was magnificent; and I understand you invited Mrs. Lemuel Struthers? Well—I've a curiosity to see the woman myself."

She had forgotten her relatives, who were drifting out into the hall under Ellen Olenska's guidance. Old Mrs. Mingott had always professed a great admiration for Julius Beaufort, and there was a kind of kinship in their cool domineering way and their short-cuts through the conventions. Now she was eagerly curious to know what had decided the Beauforts to invite (for the first time) Mrs. Lemuel Struthers, the widow of Struthers' Shoe-polish, who had returned the previous year from a long initiatory sojourn in Europe to lay siege to the tight little citadel of New York. "Of course if you and Regina invite her the thing is settled. Well, we need new blood and new money—and I hear she's still very good-looking," the carnivorous old lady declared.

In the hall, while Mrs. Welland and May drew on their furs, Archer saw that the Countess Olenska was looking at him with a faintly questioning smile.

---

5. On 23rd Street between Broadway and Madison Avenue; by the middle of the nineteenth century, the area around this square had become a center for fashionable society chosen by the newly wealthy as a place to build their magnificent mansions.

"Of course you know already—about May and me," he said, answering her look with a shy laugh. "She scolded me for not giving you the news last night at the Opera: I had her orders to tell you that we were engaged—but I couldn't, in that crowd."

The smile passed from Countess Olenska's eyes to her lips: she looked younger, more like the bold, brown Ellen Mingott of his boyhood. "Of course I know; yes. And I'm so glad. But one doesn't tell such things first in a crowd." The ladies were on the threshold and she held out her hand.

"Good-bye; come and see me some day," she said, still looking at Archer.

In the carriage, on the way down Fifth Avenue, they talked pointedly of Mrs. Mingott, of her age, her spirit, and all her wonderful attributes. No one alluded to Ellen Olenska; but Archer knew that Mrs. Welland was thinking: "It's a mistake for Ellen to be seen, the very day after her arrival, parading up Fifth Avenue at the crowded hour with Julius Beaufort—" and the young man himself mentally added: "And she ought to know that a man who's just engaged doesn't spend his time calling on married women. But I daresay in the set she's lived in they do—they never do anything else." And, in spite of the cosmopolitan views on which he prided himself, he thanked heaven that he was a New Yorker, and about to ally himself with one of his own kind.

## V

The next evening old Mr. Sillerton Jackson came to dine with the Archers.

Mrs. Archer was a shy woman and shrank from society; but she liked to be well informed as to its doings. Her old friend Mr. Sillerton Jackson applied to the investigation of his friends' affairs the patience of a collector and the science of a naturalist; and his sister, Miss Sophy Jackson, who lived with him, and was entertained by all the people who could not secure her much-sought-after brother, brought home bits of minor gossip that filled out usefully the gaps in his picture.

Therefore, whenever anything happened that Mrs. Archer wanted to know about, she asked Mr. Jackson to dine; and as she honored few people with her invitations, and as she and her daughter Janey were an excellent audience, Mr. Jackson usually came himself instead of sending his sister. If he could have dictated all the conditions, he would have chosen the evenings when Newland was out; not because the young man was uncongenial to him (the two got on capitally at their club) but because the old anecdotist sometimes felt, on Newland's part, a tendency to weigh his evidence that the ladies of the family never showed.

Mr. Jackson, if perfection had been attainable on earth, would also have asked that Mrs. Archer's food should be a little better. But then New York, as far back as the mind of man could travel, had been divided into the two great fundamental groups of the Mingotts and Mansons and all their clan, who cared about eating and clothes and money, and the Archer-Newland-van-der-Luyden tribe, who were devoted to travel, horticulture and the best fiction, and looked down on the grosser forms of pleasure.

You couldn't have everything, after all. If you dined with the Lovell Mingotts you got canvasback and terrapin and vintage wines; at Adeline Archer's you could talk about Alpine scenery and "The Marble Faun"; and luckily the Archer Madeira had gone round the Cape.[1] Therefore when a friendly summons came from Mrs. Archer, Mr. Jackson, who was a true eclectic, would usually say to his sister: "I've been a little gouty since my last dinner at the Lovell Mingotts'—it will do me good to diet at Adeline's."

Mrs. Archer, who had long been a widow, lived with her son and daughter in West Twenty-eighth Street. An upper floor was dedicated to Newland, and the two women squeezed themselves into narrower quarters below. In an unclouded harmony of tastes and interests they cultivated ferns in Wardian cases, made macramé lace and wool embroidery on linen, collected American Revolutionary glazed ware, subscribed to "Good Words," and read Ouida's novels for the sake of the Italian atmosphere. (They preferred those about peasant life, because of the descriptions of scenery and the pleasanter sentiments, though in general they liked novels about people in society, whose motives and habits were more comprehensible, spoke severely of Dickens, who "had never drawn a gentleman," and considered Thackeray less at home in the great world than Bulwer—who, however, was beginning to be thought old-fashioned.)[2]

Mrs. and Miss Archer were both great lovers of scenery. It was what they principally sought and admired on their occasional travels abroad; considering architecture and painting as subjects for men, and chiefly for learned persons who read Ruskin. Mrs. Archer had been born a Newland, and mother and daughter, who were as like as sisters, were both, as people said, "true Newlands"; tall, pale, and slightly

1. canvasback: A species of wild duck, especially abundant in the Chesapeake Bay during the period; terrapin: An edible freshwater turtle; "The Marble Faun": A novel (1860) by Nathaniel Hawthorne (1804–1864) in which the protagonist defends the female art student he loves by killing the man who is persecuting her; conversations would have been focused on the feelings of guilt that eventually lead the murderer to surrender; Madeira . . . round the Cape: A rich, strong white or amber wine resembling sherry that is imported from the Madeira islands, a possession of Portugal located off the northwest coast of Africa. Wharton's mother's family was famous for its "Newbold Madeira," a wine that retained its name even after an ancestor had sold the family's cellar. Since this Madeira would not have gone "round the Cape" (the southwestern tip of Africa) geographically, this phrase suggests that this historic wine has survived the storms of change. This was the expression Wharton's family actually used to describe their Madeira.
2. Wardian cases: Cases with glass sides and tops designed for growing and carrying live plants, named after the English inventor Nathan B. Ward (1791–1868); "Good Words": London literary periodical published monthly, 1860–1906; Ouida's novels: Novels of fashionable life by British-born author Marie Louise de la Ramée (1839–1908), whose pen name was Ouida; Dickens: Charles Dickens (1812–1870), English novelist noted for his depiction of the social conditions of the working class in England; Thackeray: William Makepeace Thackeray (1811–1863), English novelist noted for his realistic depictions of middle- and upper-class society; Bulwer: Edward George Earl Bulwer-Lytton (1803–1873), English novelist and playwright whose overwrought novels were often about the downfall of past civilizations.

round-shouldered, with long noses, sweet smiles and a kind of droop-ing distinction like that in certain faded Reynolds portraits. Their physical resemblance would have been complete if an elderly *embon-point* had not stretched Mrs. Archer's black brocade, while Miss Archer's brown and purple poplins hung, as the years went on, more and more slackly on her virgin frame.[3]

Mentally, the likeness between them, as Newland was aware, was less complete than their identical mannerisms often made it appear. The long habit of living together in mutually dependent intimacy had given them the same vocabulary, and the same habit of beginning their phrases "Mother thinks" or "Janey thinks," according as one or the other wished to advance an opinion of her own; but in reality, while Mrs. Archer's serene unimaginativeness rested easily in the accepted and familiar, Janey was subject to starts and aberrations of fancy welling up from springs of suppressed romance.

Mother and daughter adored each other and revered their son and brother; and Archer loved them with a tenderness made compunctious and uncritical by the sense of their exaggerated admiration, and by his secret satisfaction in it. After all, he thought it a good thing for a man to have his authority respected in his own house, even if his sense of humor sometimes made him question the force of his mandate.

On this occasion the young man was very sure that Mr. Jackson would rather have had him dine out; but he had his own reasons for not doing so.

Of course old Jackson wanted to talk about Ellen Olenska, and of course Mrs. Archer and Janey wanted to hear what he had to tell. All three would be slightly embarrassed by Newland's presence, now that his prospective relation to the Mingott clan had been made known; and the young man waited with an amused curiosity to see how they would turn the difficulty.

They began, obliquely, by talking about Mrs. Lemuel Struthers.

"It's a pity the Beauforts asked her," Mrs. Archer said gently. "But then Regina always does what he tells her; and *Beaufort*—"

"Certain *nuances* escape Beaufort," said Mr. Jackson, cautiously in-specting the broiled shad, and wondering for the thousandth time why Mrs. Archer's cook always burnt the roe to a cinder. (Newland, who had long shared his wonder, could always detect it in the older man's expression of melancholy disapproval.)

"Oh, necessarily; Beaufort is a vulgar man," said Mrs. Archer. "My grandfather Newland always used to say to my mother: 'Whatever you do, don't let that fellow Beaufort be introduced to the girls.' But at least he's had the advantage of associating with gentlemen; in England too, they say. It's all very mysterious—" She glanced at Janey and paused. She and Janey knew every fold of the Beaufort mystery, but in

---

3. Ruskin: John Ruskin (1819–1900), English critic of art and architecture; Reynolds: Sir Joshua Reynolds (1723–1792), prolific English portraitist who painted over 2,000 celebrities of his day. Reynolds called the 1788 portrait of the daughter of his favorite niece "The Age of Innocence," providing Wharton with the title for her novel; *embonpoint*: French, "plump-ness."

public Mrs. Archer continued to assume that the subject was not one for the unmarried.

"But this Mrs. Struthers," Mrs. Archer continued; "what did you say *she* was, Sillerton?"

"Out of a mine: or rather out of the saloon at the head of the pit. Then with Living Wax-Works,[4] touring New England. After the police broke *that* up, they say she lived—" Mr. Jackson in his turn glanced at Janey, whose eyes began to bulge from under her prominent lids. There were still hiatuses for her in Mrs. Struthers's past.

"Then," Mr. Jackson continued (and Archer saw he was wondering why no one had told the butler never to slice cucumbers with a steel knife), "then Lemuel Struthers came along. They say his advertiser used the girl's head for the shoe-polish posters; her hair's intensely black, you know—the Egyptian style. Anyhow, he—eventually—married her." There were volumes of innuendo in the way the "eventually" was spaced, and each syllable given its due stress.

"Oh, well—at the pass we've come to nowadays, it doesn't matter," said Mrs. Archer indifferently. The ladies were not really interested in Mrs. Struthers just then; the subject of Ellen Olenska was too fresh and too absorbing to them. Indeed, Mrs. Struthers's name had been introduced by Mrs. Archer only that she might presently be able to say: "And Newland's new cousin—Countess Olenska? Was *she* at the ball too?"

There was a faint touch of sarcasm in the reference to her son, and Archer knew it and had expected it. Even Mrs. Archer, who was seldom unduly pleased with human events, had been altogether glad of her son's engagement. ("Especially after that silly business with Mrs. Rushworth," as she had remarked to Janey, alluding to what had once seemed to Newland a tragedy of which his soul would always bear the scar.) There was no better match in New York than May Welland, look at the question from whatever point you chose. Of course such a marriage was only what Newland was entitled to; but young men are so foolish and incalculable—and some women so ensnaring and unscrupulous—that it was nothing short of a miracle to see one's only son safe past the Siren Isle[5] and in the haven of a blameless domesticity.

All this Mrs. Archer felt, and her son knew she felt; but he knew also that she had been perturbed by the premature announcement of his engagement, or rather by its cause; and it was for that reason—because on the whole he was a tender and indulgent master—that he

4. A type of itinerate entertainment based on Dickens's *The Old Curiosity Shop* (1841) that featured Mrs. Jarley and her traveling show displaying wax automatons. Here, the "Living Wax-Works" refers to a performance in which human actors dressed up as wax automatons based on famous historical and literary figures. In these plays living actors performing as Dickens's fictional automatons moved with jerky gestures until they gradually "wound down" and came to rest as if they were wax statues. These shows became popular as both community and home entertainment during the latter half of the nineteenth century. (See pp. 347–48.)

5. In Greek mythology, the Sirens were monsters with the faces of women and the bodies of birds who inhabited the island of Anthemoessa. Lured by the irresistible beauty of the Sirens' songs, sailors would wreck their boats on the rocks and die or remain forever in the thrall of these monsters' seductive voices.

had stayed at home that evening. "It's not that I don't approve of the Mingotts' *esprit de corps*; but why Newland's engagement should be mixed up with that Olenska woman's comings and goings I don't see," Mrs. Archer grumbled to Janey, the only witness of her slight lapses from perfect sweetness.

She had behaved beautifully—and in beautiful behavior she was unsurpassed—during the call on Mrs. Welland; but Newland knew (and his betrothed doubtless guessed) that all through the visit she and Janey were nervously on the watch for Madame Olenska's possible intrusion; and when they left the house together she had permitted herself to say to her son: "I'm thankful that Augusta Welland received us alone."

These indications of inward disturbance moved Archer the more that he too felt that the Mingotts had gone a little too far. But, as it was against all the rules of their code that the mother and son should ever allude to what was uppermost in their thoughts, he simply replied: "Oh, well, there's always a phase of family parties to be gone through when one gets engaged, and the sooner it's over the better." At which his mother merely pursed her lips under the lace veil that hung down from her gray velvet bonnet trimmed with frosted grapes.

Her revenge, he felt—her lawful revenge—would be to "draw" Mr. Jackson that evening on the Countess Olenska; and, having publicly done his duty as a future member of the Mingott clan, the young man had no objection to hearing the lady discussed in private—except that the subject was already beginning to bore him.

Mr. Jackson had helped himself to a slice of the tepid *filet* which the mournful butler had handed him with a look as skeptical as his own, and had rejected the mushroom sauce after a scarcely perceptible sniff. He looked baffled and hungry, and Archer reflected that he would probably finish his meal on Ellen Olenska.

Mr. Jackson leaned back in his chair, and glanced up at the candlelit Archers, Newlands and van der Luydens hanging in dark frames on the dark walls.

"Ah, how your grandfather Archer loved a good dinner, my dear Newland!" he said, his eyes on the portrait of a plump full-chested young man in a stock and a blue coat, with a view of a white-columned country house behind him. "Well—well—well . . . I wonder what he would have said to all these foreign marriages!"[6]

Mrs. Archer ignored the allusion to the ancestral *cuisine* and Mr. Jackson continued with deliberation: "No, she was *not* at the ball."

"Ah—" Mrs. Archer murmured, in a tone that implied: "She had that decency."

"Perhaps the Beauforts don't know her," Janey suggested, with her artless malice.

Mr. Jackson gave a faint sip, as if he had been tasting invisible Madeira. "Mrs. Beaufort may not—but Beaufort certainly does, for

6. Consuela Vanderbilt and the daughter of Mrs. Paran Stevens (the matriarch who is said to have forced her son to break his engagement to the young woman who would become Edith Wharton) were among the American women who married into the European aristocracy during the late nineteenth century. (See pp. 338–39.)

she was seen walking up Fifth Avenue this afternoon with him by the whole of New York."

"Mercy—" moaned Mrs. Archer, evidently perceiving the uselessness of trying to ascribe the actions of foreigners to a sense of delicacy.

"I wonder if she wears a round hat or a bonnet in the afternoon," Janey speculated. "At the Opera I know she had on dark blue velvet, perfectly plain and flat—like a nightgown."

"Janey!" said her mother; and Miss Archer blushed and tried to look audacious.

"It was, at any rate, in better taste not to go to the ball," Mrs. Archer continued.

A spirit of perversity moved her son to rejoin: "I don't think it was a question of taste with her. May said she meant to go, and then decided that the dress in question wasn't smart enough."

Mrs. Archer smiled at this confirmation of her inference. "Poor Ellen," she simply remarked; adding compassionately: "We must always bear in mind what an eccentric bringing-up Medora Manson gave her. What can you expect of a girl who was allowed to wear black satin at her coming-out ball?"[7]

"Ah—don't I remember her in it!" said Mr. Jackson; adding: "Poor girl!" in the tone of one who, while enjoying the memory, had fully understood at the time what the sight portended.

"It's odd," Janey remarked, "that she should have kept such an ugly name as Ellen. I should have changed it to Elaine." She glanced about the table to see the effect of this.

Her brother laughed. "Why Elaine?"

"I don't know; it sounds more—more Polish," said Janey, blushing.

"It sounds more conspicuous; and that can hardly be what she wishes," said Mrs. Archer distantly.

"Why not?" broke in her son, growing suddenly argumentative. "Why shouldn't she be conspicuous if she chooses? Why should she slink about as if it were she who had disgraced herself? She's 'poor Ellen' certainly, because she had the bad luck to make a wretched marriage; but I don't see that that's a reason for hiding her head as if she were the culprit."

"That, I suppose," said Mr. Jackson, speculatively, "is the line the Mingotts mean to take."

The young man reddened. "I didn't have to wait for their cue, if that's what you mean, sir. Madame Olenska has had an unhappy life: that doesn't make her an outcast."

"There are rumors," began Mr. Jackson, glancing at Janey.

"Oh, I know: the secretary," the young man took him up. "Nonsense, mother; Janey's grown-up. They say, don't they," he went on, "that the secretary helped her to get away from her brute of a husband, who kept her practically a prisoner? Well, what if he did? I hope there isn't a man among us who wouldn't have done the same in such a case."

---

7. Debutantes traditionally wear white to symbolize their purity.

Mr. Jackson glanced over his shoulder to say to the sad butler: "Perhaps . . . that sauce . . . just a little, after all—"; then, having helped himself, he remarked: "I'm told she's looking for a house. She means to live here."

"I hear she means to get a divorce," said Janey boldly.

"I hope she will!" Archer exclaimed.

The word had fallen like a bombshell in the pure and tranquil atmosphere of the Archer dining room. Mrs. Archer raised her delicate eyebrows in the particular curve that signified: "The butler—" and the young man, himself mindful of the bad taste of discussing such intimate matters in public, hastily branched off into an account of his visit to old Mrs. Mingott.

After dinner, according to immemorial custom, Mrs. Archer and Janey trailed their long silk draperies up to the drawing room, where, while the gentlemen smoked below stairs, they sat beside a Carcel lamp[8] with an engraved globe, facing each other across a rosewood work-table with a green silk bag under it, and stitched at the two ends of a tapestry band of field flowers destined to adorn an "occasional" chair in the drawing room of young Mrs. Newland Archer.

While this rite was in progress in the drawing room, Archer settled Mr. Jackson in an armchair near the fire in the Gothic library and handed him a cigar. Mr. Jackson sank into the armchair with satisfaction, lit his cigar with perfect confidence (it was Newland who bought them), and stretching his thin old ankles to the coals, said: "You say the secretary merely helped her to get away, my dear fellow? Well, he was still helping her a year later, then; for somebody met 'em living at Lausanne[9] together."

Newland reddened. "Living together? Well, why not? Who had the right to make her life over if she hadn't? I'm sick of the hypocrisy that would bury alive a woman of her age if her husband prefers to live with harlots."

He stopped and turned away angrily to light his cigar. "Women ought to be free—as free as we are," he declared, making a discovery of which he was too irritated to measure the terrific consequences.

Mr. Sillerton Jackson stretched his ankles nearer the coals and emitted a sardonic whistle.

"Well," he said after a pause, "apparently Count Olenski takes your view; for I never heard of his having lifted a finger to get his wife back."

# VI

That evening, after Mr. Jackson had taken himself away, and the ladies had retired to their chintz-curtained bedroom, Newland Archer mounted thoughtfully to his own study. A vigilant hand had, as usual,

---

8. Invented in France in 1798, the earliest mechanical lamp featuring a clockwork pump and rods.
9. City in Switzerland.

kept the fire alive and the lamp trimmed; and the room, with its rows and rows of books, its bronze and steel statuettes of "The Fencers" on the mantelpiece and its many photographs of famous pictures, looked singularly homelike and welcoming.

As he dropped into his armchair near the fire his eyes rested on a large photograph of May Welland, which the young girl had given him in the first days of their romance, and which had now displaced all the other portraits on the table. With a new sense of awe he looked at the frank forehead, serious eyes and gay innocent mouth of the young creature whose soul's custodian he was to be. That terrifying product of the social system he belonged to and believed in, the young girl who knew nothing and expected everything, looked back at him like a stranger through May Welland's familiar features; and once more it was borne in on him that marriage was not the safe anchorage he had been taught to think, but a voyage on uncharted seas.

The case of the Countess Olenska had stirred up old settled convictions and set them drifting dangerously through his mind. His own exclamation: "Women should be free—as free as we are," struck to the root of a problem that it was agreed in his world to regard as nonexistent. "Nice" women, however wronged, would never claim the kind of freedom he meant, and generous-minded men like himself were therefore—in the heat of argument—the more chivalrously ready to concede it to them. Such verbal generosities were in fact only a humbugging disguise of the inexorable conventions that tied things together and bound people down to the old pattern. But here he was pledged to defend, on the part of his betrothed's cousin, conduct that, on his own wife's part, would justify him in calling down on her all the thunders of Church and State.[1] Of course the dilemma was purely hypothetical; since he wasn't a blackguard Polish nobleman, it was absurd to speculate what his wife's rights[2] would be if he *were*. But Newland Archer was too imaginative not to feel that, in his case and May's, the tie might gall for reasons far less gross and palpable. What could he and she really know of each other, since it was his duty, as a "decent" fellow, to conceal his past from her, and hers, as a marriageable girl, to have no past to conceal? What if, for some one of the subtler reasons that would tell with both of them, they should tire of each

1. The conflict, particularly volatile in Catholic countries, over whether marriage was a sacred rite or a civil contract. Although the Episcopal denomination has long been associated in popular belief with the idea that its forebear, the Church of England, originated in a dispute over divorce that divided King Henry VIII and his state from the Roman Catholic Church, the Episcopal Church of the Mingott clan was strict in relation to divorce and even stricter in its prohibitions against remarriage. (See p. 69, *n*. 4.)

2. Even Newland, a practicing lawyer, despairs over the futility of speculating about his "wife's rights" if he were a "blackguard [a scoundrel] Polish nobleman." Countess Olenska would not have had a right to divorce in Poland or France. In these countries, even a woman who had attained a legal separation from her husband was considered married under the law and therefore had no right to enter contractual relations without her husband's consent. The minimal area of wife's rights usually entailed a limitation on the husband's right to dispose of his wife's dowry. While "wife's rights" were established in Britain by a series of nineteenth-century legislative measures known as the Married Women's Property Acts, laws in the United States concerning married women's rights to property and divorce differed state by state. In America, the issue of a "wife's rights," including rights to inheritance and divorce, were subsumed under the struggle to gain the right to vote, which was won for educated white women in 1921, the year after *The Age of Innocence* was published. (See pp. 374–76.)

other, misunderstand or irritate each other? He reviewed his friends' marriages—the supposedly happy ones—and saw none that answered, even remotely, to the passionate and tender comradeship which he pictured as his permanent relation with May Welland. He perceived that such a picture presupposed, on her part, the experience, the versatility, the freedom of judgment, which she had been carefully trained not to possess; and with a shiver of foreboding he saw his marriage becoming what most of the other marriages about him were: a dull association of material and social interests held together by ignorance on the one side and hypocrisy on the other. Lawrence Lefferts occurred to him as the husband who had most completely realized this enviable ideal. As became the high priest of form, he had formed a wife so completely to his own convenience that, in the most conspicuous moments of his frequent love affairs with other men's wives, she went about in smiling unconsciousness, saying that "Lawrence was so frightfully strict"; and had been known to blush indignantly, and avert her gaze, when someone alluded in her presence to the fact that Julius Beaufort (as became a "foreigner" of doubtful origin) had what was known in New York as "another establishment."

Archer tried to console himself with the thought that he was not quite such an ass as Larry Lefferts, nor May such a simpleton as poor Gertrude; but the difference was after all one of intelligence and not of standards. In reality they all lived in a kind of hieroglyphic world, where the real thing was never said or done or even thought, but only represented by a set of arbitrary signs; as when Mrs. Welland, who knew exactly why Archer had pressed her to announce her daughter's engagement at the Beaufort ball (and had indeed expected him to do no less), yet felt obliged to simulate reluctance, and the air of having had her hand forced, quite as, in the books on Primitive Man[3] that people of advanced culture were beginning to read, the savage bride is dragged with shrieks from her parents' tent.

The result, of course, was that the young girl who was the center of this elaborate system of mystification remained the more inscrutable for her very frankness and assurance. She was frank, poor darling, because she had nothing to conceal, assured because she knew of nothing to be on her guard against; and with no better preparation than this, she was to be plunged overnight into what people evasively called "the facts of life."

The young man was sincerely but placidly in love. He delighted in the radiant good looks of his betrothed, in her health, her horsemanship, her grace and quickness at games, and the shy interest in books and ideas that she was beginning to develop under his guidance. (She had advanced far enough to join him in ridiculing the "Idyls of the King," but not to feel the beauty of "Ulysses" and the "Lotus Eaters.")[4] She was

---

3. Prominent books on "Primitive Man" during the period would have been *The Descent of Man* (1871) by Charles Darwin (1809–1872), *Primitive Culture* (1871) by Sir Edward Burnett Tylor (1832–1917), and *A System of Synthetic Philosophy* (installments of which began to appear in 1860) by Herbert Spencer (1820–1903).

4. "Idyls of the King" (1859), "Ulysses" (1842), and "The Lotus Eaters" (1842) were all poems by Alfred, Lord Tennyson (1809–1892), the premier poet of Victorian England.

straightforward, loyal and brave; she had a sense of humor (chiefly proved by her laughing at *his* jokes); and he suspected, in the depths of her innocently-gazing soul, a glow of feeling that it would be a joy to waken. But when he had gone the brief round of her he returned discouraged by the thought that all this frankness and innocence were only an artificial product. Untrained human nature was not frank and innocent; it was full of the twists and defenses of an instinctive guile. And he felt himself oppressed by this creation of factitious purity, so cunningly manufactured by a conspiracy of mothers and aunts and grandmothers and long-dead ancestresses, because it was supposed to be what he wanted, what he had a right to, in order that he might exercise his lordly pleasure in smashing it like an image made of snow.

There was a certain triteness in these reflections: they were those habitual to young men on the approach of their wedding day. But they were generally accompanied by a sense of compunction and self-abasement of which Newland Archer felt no trace. He could not deplore (as Thackeray's heroes so often exasperated him by doing) that he had not a blank page to offer his bride in exchange for the unblemished one she was to give to him. He could not get away from the fact that if he had been brought up as she had they would have been no more fit to find their way about than the Babes in the Wood;[5] nor could he, for all his anxious cogitations, see any honest reason (any, that is, unconnected with his own momentary pleasure, and the passion of masculine vanity) why his bride should not have been allowed the same freedom of experience as himself.

Such questions, at such an hour, were bound to drift through his mind; but he was conscious that their uncomfortable persistence and precision were due to the inopportune arrival of the Countess Olenska. Here he was, at the very moment of his betrothal—a moment for pure thoughts and cloudless hopes—pitchforked into a coil of scandal which raised all the special problems he would have preferred to let lie. "Hang Ellen Olenska!" he grumbled, as he covered his fire and began to undress. He could not really see why her fate should have the least bearing on his; yet he dimly felt that he had only just begun to measure the risks of the championship which his engagement had forced upon him.

A few days later the bolt fell.

The Lovell Mingotts had sent out cards for what was known as "a formal dinner" (that is, three extra footmen, two dishes for each course, and a Roman punch[6] in the middle), and had headed their invitations with the words "To meet the Countess Olenska," in accordance with the hospitable American fashion, which treats strangers as if they were royalties, or at least as their ambassadors.

5. Two young children in an old English ballad and nursery tale who are abandoned and left to die in the woods by their avaricious uncle.
6. A frozen slush; rougher, looser, and more granular in its texture than sherbet, this concoction made with lemon juice, rum, sugar, and other ingredients was served to cleanse the palate between courses at formal dinner parties in nineteenth-century New York. (See p. 329.)

The guests had been selected with a boldness and discrimination in which the initiated recognized the firm hand of Catherine the Great. Associated with such immemorial standbys as the Selfridge Merrys, who were asked every where because they always had been, the Beauforts, on whom there was a claim of relationship, and Mr. Sillerton Jackson and his sister Sophy (who went wherever her brother told her to), were some of the most fashionable and yet most irreproachable of the dominant "young married" set; the Lawrence Leffertses, Mrs. Lefferts Rushworth (the lovely widow), the Harry Thorleys, the Reggie Chiverses and young Morris Dagonet and his wife (who was a van der Luyden). The company indeed was perfectly assorted, since all the members belonged to the little inner group of people who, during the long New York season, disported themselves together daily and nightly with apparently undiminished zest.

Forty-eight hours later the unbelievable had happened; everyone had refused the Mingotts' invitation except the Beauforts and old Mr. Jackson and his sister. The intended slight was emphasized by the fact that even the Reggie Chiverses, who were of the Mingott clan, were among those inflicting it; and by the uniform wording of the notes, in all of which the writers "regretted that they were unable to accept," without the mitigating plea of a "previous engagement" that ordinary courtesy prescribed.

New York society was, in those days, far too small, and too scant in its resources, for everyone in it (including livery-stablekeepers, butlers and cooks) not to know exactly on which evenings people were free; and it was thus possible for the recipients of Mrs. Lovell Mingott's invitations to make cruelly clear their determination not to meet the Countess Olenska.

The blow was unexpected; but the Mingotts, as their way was, met it gallantly. Mrs. Lovell Mingott confided the case to Mrs. Welland, who confided it to Newland Archer; who, aflame at the outrage, appealed passionately and authoritatively to his mother; who, after a painful period of inward resistance and outward temporizing, succumbed to his instances (as she always did), and immediately embracing his cause with an energy redoubled by her previous hesitations, put on her gray velvet bonnet and said: "I'll go and see Louisa van der Luyden."

The New York of Newland Archer's day was a small and slippery pyramid, in which, as yet, hardly a fissure had been made or a foothold gained. At its base was a firm foundation of what Mrs. Archer called "plain people"; an honorable but obscure majority of respectable families who (as in the case of the Spicers or the Leffertses or the Jacksons) had been raised above their level by marriage with one of the ruling clans. People, Mrs. Archer always said, were not as particular as they used to be; and with old Catherine Spicer ruling one end of Fifth Avenue, and Julius Beaufort the other, you couldn't expect the old traditions to last much longer.

Firmly narrowing upward from this wealthy but inconspicuous substratum was the compact and dominant group which the Mingotts,

Newlands, Chiverses and Mansons so actively represented. Most people imagined them to be the very apex of the pyramid; but they themselves (at least those of Mrs. Archer's generation) were aware that, in the eyes of the professional genealogist, only a still smaller number of families could lay claim to that eminence.

"Don't tell me," Mrs. Archer would say to her children, "all this modern newspaper rubbish about a New York aristocracy.[7] If there is one, neither the Mingotts nor the Mansons belong to it; no, nor the Newlands or the Chiverses either. Our grandfathers and great-grandfathers were just respectable English or Dutch merchants, who came to the colonies to make their fortune, and stayed here because they did so well. One of your great-grandfathers signed the Declaration, and another was a general on Washington's staff, and received General Burgoyne's[8] sword after the battle of Saratoga. These are things to be proud of, but they have nothing to do with rank or class. New York has always been a commercial community, and there are not more than three families in it who can claim an aristocratic origin in the real sense of the word."

Mrs. Archer and her son and daughter, like everyone else in New York, knew who these privileged beings were: the Dagonets of Washington Square, who came of an old English county family allied with the Pitts and Foxes; the Lannings, who had intermarried with the descendants of Count de Grasse; and the van der Luydens, direct descendants of the first Dutch governor of Manhattan,[9] and related by pre-Revolutionary marriages to several members of the French and British aristocracy.

The Lannings survived only in the person of two very old but lively Miss Lannings, who lived cheerfully and reminiscently among family portraits and Chippendale;[1] the Dagonets were a considerable clan, allied to the best names in Baltimore and Philadelphia; but the van der Luydens, who stood above all of them, had faded into a kind of super-

---

7. The "New York 400"; see p. 13, *n.* 1, and pp. 333–39.
8. General John Burgoyne (1722–1792), British officer during the American Revolution who captured Fort Ticonderoga in July 1777 and surrendered to General Horatio Gates after the Battle of Saratoga in October 1777.
9. Dagonets of Washington Square: An elite family of Old New York that appears in Edith Wharton's novel *The Custom of the Country* (1913); the name *Dagonet* is that of King Arthur's fool in Sir Thomas Malory's (d. 1471) *Le Morte D'Arthur* (composed 1469–70, published in 1485); Washington Square is an elite address at the southern end of Fifth Avenue. Pitts and Foxes: Aristocratic English families whose most noted members were the statesman and prime minister William Pitt, First Earl of Chatham (1708–1778), his son William Pitt the Younger (1759–1806), also a statesman and prime minister, and Charles James Fox (1749–1806), statesman and orator, third son of the first Lord Holland; Count de Grasse: François Joseph Paul, Comte de Grasse (1722–1788), French admiral who fought for the Continental forces during the American Revolution; the first Dutch governor of Manhattan: Peter Minuit (1580–1638), born in Germany to a French-speaking Belgian family that immigrated to the Netherlands, was the first director general of New Amsterdam, serving as the chief governing official 1626–1633. According to historical legend, Minuit represented the Dutch in a trade with the leaders of the local Algonquin tribe through which the Dutch acquired what is now Manhattan for trinkets and useful goods whose value was estimated at twenty-four dollars.
1. Furniture in the style of or, in this case, made by famous London furniture designer Thomas Chippendale (1718–1779). Codified in his *The Gentleman and Cabinet Makers Director* (1752), Chippendale's designs were associated with a move away from massiveness in objects and toward a lighter style associated with elegance.

terrestrial twilight, from which only two figures impressively emerged; those of Mr. and Mrs. Henry van der Luyden.

Mrs. Henry van der Luyden had been Louisa Dagonet, and her mother had been the granddaughter of Colonel du Lac, of an old Channel Island family, who had fought under Cornwallis[2] and had settled in Maryland, after the war, with his bride, Lady Angelica Trevenna, fifth daughter of the Earl of St. Austrey. The tie between the Dagonets, the du Lacs of Maryland, and their aristocratic Cornish kinfolk, the Trevennas, had always remained close and cordial. Mr. and Mrs. van der Luyden had more than once paid long visits to the present head of the house of Trevenna,[3] the Duke of St. Austrey, at his country-seat in Cornwall and at St. Austrey in Gloucestershire; and His Grace had frequently announced his intention of some day returning their visit (without the Duchess, who feared the Atlantic).

Mr. and Mrs. van der Luyden divided their time between Trevenna, their place in Maryland, and Skuytercliff, the great estate on the Hudson which had been one of the colonial grants of the Dutch government to the famous first governor, and of which Mr. van der Luyden was still "Patroon."[4] Their large solemn house in Madison Avenue was seldom opened, and when they came to town they received in it only their most intimate friends.

"I wish you would go with me, Newland," his mother said, suddenly pausing at the door of the Brown *coupé*. "Louisa is fond of you; and of course it's on account of dear May that I'm taking this step—and also because, if we don't all stand together, there'll be no such thing as Society left."

## VII

Mrs. Henry van der Luyden listened in silence to her cousin Mrs. Archer's narrative.

It was all very well to tell yourself in advance that Mrs. van der Luyden was always silent, and that, though noncommittal by nature and training, she was very kind to the people she really liked. Even personal experience of these facts was not always a protection from the chill that descended on one in the high-ceilinged white-walled Madison Avenue drawing room, with the pale brocaded armchairs so obviously uncovered for the occasion, and the gauze still veiling the ormolu mantel ornaments and the beautiful old carved frame of Gainsborough's "Lady Angelica du Lac."[1]

2. old Channel Island family: A family from a group of British islands ten miles off the coast of France; Cornwallis: General Lord George Cornwallis (1738–1805), British general who surrendered to Washington at Yorktown, Virginia, in 1781, marking the end of the American Revolution.
3. The van der Luydens' other country home is named for the site of the ruins of the castle of the legendary King Marc, who was betrayed by the adulterous desire of Tristan and Iseult.
4. An original Dutch settler of New Amsterdam.
1. Madison Avenue: Major thoroughfare that runs parallel to Fifth Avenue, one block east; ormolu: A finish used on metal to imitate gold associated with decorative techniques of the French eighteenth century; Gainsborough's "Lady Angelica du Lac": A fictitious portrait purportedly by the English painter Thomas Gainsborough (1727–1788); Lady Angelica is Mrs. van der Luyden's maternal great-grandmother.

Mrs. van der Luyden's portrait by Huntington (in black velvet and Venetian point) faced that of her lovely ancestress. It was generally considered "as fine as a Cabanel,"[2] and, though twenty years had elapsed since its execution, was still "a perfect likeness." Indeed the Mrs. van der Luyden who sat beneath it listening to Mrs. Archer might have been the twin-sister of the fair and still youngish woman drooping against a gilt armchair before a green rep[3] curtain. Mrs. van der Luyden still wore black velvet and Venetian point when she went into society—or rather (since she never dined out) when she threw open her own doors to receive it. Her fair hair, which had faded without turning gray, was still parted in flat overlapping points on her forehead, and the straight nose that divided her pale blue eyes was only a little more pinched about the nostrils than when the portrait had been painted. She always, indeed, struck Newland Archer as having been rather gruesomely preserved in the airless atmosphere of a perfectly irreproachable existence, as bodies caught in glaciers keep for years a rosy life-in-death.

Like all his family, he esteemed and admired Mrs. van der Luyden; but he found her gentle bending sweetness less approachable than the grimness of some of his mother's old aunts, fierce spinsters who said "No" on principle before they knew what they were going to be asked.

Mrs. van der Luyden's attitude said neither yes nor no, but always appeared to incline to clemency till her thin lips, wavering into the shadow of a smile, made the almost invariable reply: "I shall first have to talk this over with my husband."

She and Mr. van der Luyden were so exactly alike that Archer often wondered how, after forty years of the closest conjugality, two such merged identities ever separated themselves enough for anything as controversial as a talking-over. But as neither had ever reached a decision without prefacing it by this mysterious conclave, Mrs. Archer and her son, having set forth their case, waited resignedly for the familiar phrase.

Mrs. van der Luyden, however, who had seldom surprised anyone, now surprised them by reaching her long hand toward the bell-rope.

"I think," she said, "I should like Henry to hear what you have told me."

A footman appeared, to whom she gravely added: "If Mr. van der Luyden has finished reading the newspaper, please ask him to be kind enough to come."

She said "reading the newspaper" in the tone in which a Minister's wife might have said: "Presiding at a Cabinet meeting"—not from any arrogance of mind, but because the habit of a lifetime, and the attitude of her friends and relations, had led her to consider Mr. van der Luyden's least gesture as having an almost sacerdotal importance.

2. Huntington: Daniel P. Huntington (1816–1906), American portraitist; Venetian point: A type of lace made in the Italian city of Venice; Cabanel: Alexandre Cabanel (1823–1889), French painter.
3. Upholstery fabric in plain weave with rounded and prominent crosswise ribs, made by alternating fine and coarse yarns or varying the tension on the yarns during weaving.

Her promptness of action showed that she considered the case as pressing as Mrs. Archer; but, lest she should be thought to have committed herself in advance, she added, with the sweetest look: "Henry always enjoys seeing you, dear Adeline; and he will wish to congratulate Newland."

The double doors had solemnly reopened and between them appeared Mr. Henry van der Luyden, tall, spare and frock-coated, with faded fair hair, a straight nose like his wife's and the same look of frozen gentleness in eyes that were merely pale gray instead of pale blue.

Mr. van der Luyden greeted Mrs. Archer with cousinly affability, proffered to Newland low-voiced congratulations couched in the same language as his wife's, and seated himself in one of the brocade armchairs with the simplicity of a reigning sovereign.

"I had just finished reading *The Times*,"[4] he said, laying his long fingertips together. "In town my mornings are so much occupied that I find it more convenient to read the newspapers after luncheon."

"Ah, there's a great deal to be said for that plan—indeed I think my Uncle Egmont used to say he found it less agitating not to read the morning papers till after dinner," said Mrs. Archer responsively.

"Yes: my good father abhorred hurry. But now we live in a constant rush," said Mr. van der Luyden in measured tones, looking with pleasant deliberation about the large shrouded room which to Archer was so complete an image of its owners.

"But I hope you *had* finished your reading, Henry?" his wife interposed.

"Quite—quite," he reassured her.

"Then I should like Adeline to tell you—"

"Oh, it's really Newland's story," said his mother smiling; and proceeded to rehearse once more the monstrous tale of the affront inflicted on Mrs. Lovell Mingott.

"Of course," she ended, "Augusta Welland and Mary Mingott both felt that, especially in view of Newland's engagement, you and Henry *ought to know.*"

"Ah—" said Mr. van der Luyden, drawing a deep breath.

There was a silence during which the tick of the monumental ormolu clock on the white marble mantelpiece grew as loud as the boom of a minute-gun. Archer contemplated with awe the two slender faded figures, seated side by side in a kind of viceregal rigidity, mouthpieces of some remote ancestral authority which fate compelled them to wield, when they would so much rather have lived in simplicity and seclusion, digging invisible weeds out of the perfect lawns of Skuytercliff, and playing Patience together in the evenings.[5]

4. Founded in 1851, *The New York Times* rose to prominence with its investigative reporting of local news, particularly the exposure of politically based economic scandals.
5. minute-gun: Guns discharged every minute as signals of distress or mourning. This term is usually plural because at the time such rapidly repeated firing required more than one gun; Patience: An English card game that is often played by one person but that, like American Solitaire, can also be played by two people. While this scene remains ambiguous, it suggests that this couple is so united in their isolation that even if they are playing separately, they are playing together.

Mr. van der Luyden was the first to speak.

"You really think this is due to some—some intentional interference of Lawrence Lefferts's?" he enquired, turning to Archer.

"I'm certain of it, sir. Larry has been going it rather harder than usual lately—if Cousin Louisa won't mind my mentioning it—having rather a stiff affair with the postmaster's wife in their village, or someone of that sort; and whenever poor Gertrude Lefferts begins to suspect anything, and he's afraid of trouble, he gets up a fuss of this kind, to show how awfully moral he is, and talks at the top of his voice about the impertinence of inviting his wife to meet people he doesn't wish her to know. He's simply using Madame Olenska as a lightning-rod; I've seen him try the same thing often before."

"The *Leffertses!*—" said Mrs. van der Luyden.

"The *Leffertses!*—" echoed Mrs. Archer. "What would Uncle Egmont have said of Lawrence Lefferts's pronouncing on anybody's social position? It shows what Society has come to."

"We'll hope it has not quite come to that," said Mr. van der Luyden firmly.

"Ah, if only you and Louisa went out more!" sighed Mrs. Archer.

But instantly she became aware of her mistake. The van der Luydens were morbidly sensitive to any criticism of their secluded existence. They were the arbiters of fashion, the Court of Last Appeal, and they knew it, and bowed to their fate. But being shy and retiring persons, with no natural inclination for their part, they lived as much as possible in the sylvan solitude of Skuytercliff, and when they came to town, declined all invitations on the plea of Mrs. van der Luyden's health.

Newland Archer came to his mother's rescue. "Everybody in New York knows what you and Cousin Louisa represent. That's why Mrs. Mingott felt she ought not to allow this slight on Countess Olenska to pass without consulting you."

Mrs. van der Luyden glanced at her husband, who glanced back at her.

"It is the principle that I dislike," said Mr. van der Luyden. "As long as a member of a well-known family is backed up by that family it should be considered—final."

"It seems so to me," said his wife, as if she were producing a new thought.

"I had no idea," Mr. van der Luyden continued, "that things had come to such a pass." He paused, and looked at his wife again. "It occurs to me, my dear, that the Countess Olenska is already a sort of relation—through Medora Manson's first husband. At any rate, she will be when Newland marries." He turned toward the young man. "Have you read this morning's *Times*, Newland?"

"Why, yes, sir," said Archer, who usually tossed off half a dozen papers with his morning coffee.

Husband and wife looked at each other again. Their pale eyes clung together in prolonged and serious consultation; then a faint smile fluttered over Mrs. van der Luyden's face. She had evidently guessed and approved.

Mr. van der Luyden turned to Mrs. Archer. "If Louisa's health allowed her to dine out—I wish you would say to Mrs. Lovell Mingott— she and I would have been happy to—er—fill the places of the Lawrence Leffertses at her dinner." He paused to let the irony of this sink in. "As you know, this is impossible." Mrs. Archer sounded a sympathetic assent. "But Newland tells me he has read this morning's *Times*; therefore he has probably seen that Louisa's relative, the Duke of St. Austrey, arrives next week on the 'Russia.' He is coming to enter his new sloop, the 'Guinevere,' in next summer's International Cup Race;[6] and also to have a little canvasback shooting at Trevenna." Mr. van der Luyden paused again, and continued with increasing benevolence: "Before taking him down to Maryland we are inviting a few friends to meet him here—only a little dinner—with a reception afterward. I am sure Louisa will be as glad as I am if Countess Olenska will let us include her among our guests." He got up, bent his long body with a stiff friendliness toward his cousin, and added: "I think I have Louisa's authority for saying that she will herself leave the invitation to dine when she drives out presently: with our cards—of course with our cards."

Mrs. Archer, who knew this to be a hint that the seventeen-hand chestnuts which were never kept waiting were at the door, rose with a hurried murmur of thanks. Mrs. van der Luyden beamed on her with the smile of Esther interceding with Ahasuerus;[7] but her husband raised a protesting hand.

"There is nothing to thank me for, dear Adeline; nothing whatever. This kind of thing must not happen in New York; it shall not, as long as I can help it," he pronounced with sovereign gentleness as he steered his cousins to the door.

Two hours later, everyone knew that the great C-spring barouche[8] in which Mrs. van der Luyden took the air at all seasons had been seen at old Mrs. Mingott's door, where a large square envelope was handed in; and that evening at the Opera Mr. Sillerton Jackson was able to state that the envelope contained a card inviting the Countess Olenska to the dinner which the van der Luydens were giving the following week for their cousin, the Duke of St. Austrey.

Some of the younger men in the club box exchanged a smile at this announcement, and glanced sideways at Lawrence Lefferts, who sat carelessly in the front of the box, pulling his long fair moustache, and who remarked with authority, as the soprano paused: "No one but Patti ought to attempt the *Sonnambula*."[9]

6. 'Russia': See p. 200, n. 8. 'Guinevere': The name of the Duke's sailing sloop is taken from that of King Arthur's queen, who is blamed for destroying the utopian community of the Round Table as a result of her adulterous passion for Sir Lancelot. International Cup Race: Also called the America's Cup, the oldest and most prestigious international race for large sloops, begun in 1851.
7. Reference to the biblical story of Esther, wife of King Ahasuerus, who reveals her Jewish heritage to convince the king to spare the lives of her people after the king's adviser, Haman, has recommended killing all the Jews.
8. A four-wheeled carriage, with a folding top shaped like the letter C.
9. Patti: Adeline Patti (1843–1919), Italian soprano; *Sonnambula*: Italian Opera *La Sonnambula* (The Sleepwalking Girl), an 1831 work by Vincenzo Bellini (1801–1835); Patti made her debut in this opera in 1861.

# VIII

It was generally agreed in New York that the Countess Olenska had "lost her looks."

She had appeared there first, in Newland Archer's boyhood, as a brilliantly pretty little girl of nine or ten, of whom people said that she "ought to be painted." Her parents had been continental wanderers, and after a roaming babyhood she had lost them both, and been taken in charge by her aunt, Medora Manson, also a wanderer, who was herself returning to New York to "settle down."

Poor Medora, repeatedly widowed, was always coming home to settle down (each time in a less expensive house), and bringing with her a new husband or an adopted child; but after a few months she invariably parted from her husband or quarrelled with her ward, and, having got rid of her house at a loss, set out again on her wanderings. As her mother had been a Rushworth, and her last unhappy marriage had linked her to one of the crazy Chiverses, New York looked indulgently on her eccentricities; but when she returned with her little orphaned niece, whose parents had been popular in spite of their regrettable taste for travel, people thought it a pity that the pretty child should be in such hands.

Everyone was disposed to be kind to little Ellen Mingott, though her dusky red cheeks and tight curls gave her an air of gaiety that seemed unsuitable in a child who should still have been in black for her parents. It was one of the misguided Medora's many peculiarities to flout the unalterable rules that regulated American mourning, and when she stepped from the steamer her family were scandalized to see that the crepe veil she wore for her own brother was seven inches shorter than those of her sisters-in-law, while little Ellen was in crimson merino and amber beads, like a gipsy foundling.[1]

But New York had so long resigned itself to Medora that only a few old ladies shook their heads over Ellen's gaudy clothes, while her other relations fell under the charm of her high color and high spirits. She was a fearless and familiar little thing, who asked disconcerting questions, made precocious comments, and possessed outlandish arts, such as dancing a Spanish shawl dance and singing Neapolitan love-songs to a guitar. Under the direction of her aunt (whose real name was Mrs. Thorley Chivers, but who, having received a Papal title, had resumed her first husband's patronymic, and called herself the Marchioness Manson, because in Italy she could turn it into Manzoni) the little girl received an expensive but incoherent education, which included "drawing from the model," a thing never dreamed of before, and playing the piano in quintets with professional musicians.[2]

---

1. crimson merino: A finely textured fabric, resembling cashmere, made from the wool of merino sheep; gipsy foundling: A child lost or abandoned by her family and adopted by gypsies, a tightly bound ethnic group that migrated from India to Europe in the fourteenth century and was thought by nineteenth-century Americans to have come from Bohemia.
2. Papal title: Formal permission issued by the Pope or by the judicial offices of the Vatican. Here, Medora Manson's ecclesiastical dispensation allowing her to revert to her former husband's name, despite the fact that her current husband is still alive, suggests that this decree

Of course no good could come of this; and when, a few years later, poor Chivers finally died in a madhouse, his widow (draped in strange weeds)[3] again pulled up stakes and departed with Ellen, who had grown into a tall bony girl with conspicuous eyes. For some time no more was heard of them; then news came of Ellen's marriage to an immensely rich Polish nobleman of legendary fame, whom she had met at a ball at the Tuileries, and who was said to have princely establishments in Paris, Nice and Florence, a yacht at Cowes, and many square miles of shooting in Transylvania.[4] She disappeared in a kind of sulphurous apotheosis, and when a few years later Medora again came back to New York, subdued, impoverished, mourning a third husband, and in quest of a still smaller house, people wondered that her rich niece had not been able to do something for her. Then came the news that Ellen's own marriage had ended in disaster, and that she was herself returning home to seek rest and oblivion among her kinsfolk.

These things passed through Newland Archer's mind a week later as he watched the Countess Olenska enter the van der Luyden drawing room on the evening of the momentous dinner. The occasion was a solemn one, and he wondered a little nervously how she would carry it off. She came rather late, one hand still ungloved, and fastening a bracelet about her wrist; yet she entered without any appearance of haste or embarrassment the drawing room in which New York's most chosen company was somewhat awfully assembled.

In the middle of the room she paused, looking about her with a grave mouth and smiling eyes; and in that instant Newland Archer rejected the general verdict on her looks. It was true that her early radiance was gone. The red cheeks had paled; she was thin, worn, a little older-looking than her age, which must have been nearly thirty. But there was about her the mysterious authority of beauty, a sureness in the carriage of the head, the movement of the eyes, which, without being in the least theatrical, struck him as highly trained and full of a conscious power. At the same time she was simpler in manner than most of the ladies present, and many people (as he heard afterward from Janey) were disappointed that her appearance was not more "stylish"—for stylishness was what New York most valued. It was, perhaps, Archer reflected, because her early vivacity had disappeared; because she was so quiet—quiet in her movements, her voice, and the tones of her low-pitched voice. New York had expected something

---

may function as a type of annulment. While members of the New York elite were unlikely to be Catholic, the unorthodox Medora appears to have converted to the Roman Church while continuing to flirt with other religious ideas and movements. Manzoni: The name of Italian novelist and poet Alessandro Manzoni (1785–1873), best known for *The Betrothed* (1827), a depiction of life in sixteenth-century Milan that by 1875 had appeared in 118 editions. "drawing from the model": It would have been scandalous for an American girl to sketch or paint a nude model.

3. Widow's weeds, somber garments worn in mourning. Like everything else this eccentric character wears in the novel, there is something "strange" or inappropriate about her efforts to conform to well-known mourning rituals: the deceased is no longer her husband.

4. Cowes: City at the mouth of the Medina River on the Isle of Wight and site of an annual yachting regatta; Transylvania: Region in northwest and central Romania linked in the public imagination to the infamous fifteenth-century Baron Vlad Dracul, who was immortalized in Bram Stoker's novel *Dracula* (1897).

a good deal more resonant in a young woman with such a history.

The dinner was a somewhat formidable business. Dining with the van der Luydens was at best no light matter, and dining there with a Duke who was their cousin was almost a religious solemnity. It pleased Archer to think that only an old New Yorker could perceive the shade of difference (to New York) between being merely a Duke and being the van der Luydens' Duke. New York took stray noblemen calmly, and even (except in the Struthers set) with a certain distrustful *hauteur*; but when they presented such credentials as these they were received with an old-fashioned cordiality that they would have been greatly mistaken in ascribing solely to their standing in Debrett.[5] It was for just such distinctions that the young man cherished his old New York even while he smiled at it.

The van der Luydens had done their best to emphasize the importance of the occasion. The du Lac Sèvres and the Trevenna George II plate were out; so was the van der Luyden "Lowestoft" (East India Company) and the Dagonet Crown Derby. Mrs. van der Luyden looked more than ever like a Cabanel, and Mrs. Archer, in her grandmother's seed-pearls and emeralds, reminded her son of an Isabey miniature. All the ladies had on their handsomest jewels, but it was characteristic of the house and the occasion that these were mostly in rather heavy old-fashioned settings; and old Miss Lanning, who had been persuaded to come, actually wore her mother's cameos and a Spanish blonde shawl.[6]

The Countess Olenska was the only young woman at the dinner; yet, as Archer scanned the smooth plump elderly faces between their diamond necklaces and towering ostrich feathers, they struck him as curiously immature compared with hers. It frightened him to think what must have gone to the making of her eyes.

The Duke of St. Austrey, who sat at his hostess' right, was naturally the chief figure of the evening. But if the Countess Olenska was less conspicuous than had been hoped, the Duke was almost invisible. Being a well-bred man he had not (like another recent ducal visitor) come to the dinner in a shooting-jacket; but his evening clothes were so shabby and baggy, and he wore them with such an air of their being homespun, that (with his stooping way of sitting, and the vast beard spreading over his shirt-front) he hardly gave the appearance of being in dinner attire. He was short, round-shouldered, sunburnt, with a thick nose, small eyes and a sociable smile; but he seldom spoke, and

---

5. The definitive guide to British peerage, first published as *Peerage of England, Scotland, and Ireland, containing an Account of all the Peers* by John Debrett (1802).

6. du Lac Sèvres . . . Crown Derby: A list of fine china and serving plate passed down through generations from the reign of George II, grandfather of the last English king to rule the American colonies: du Lac Sèvres is highly decorated French porcelain produced in the town of Sèvres; Trevenna George II plate is serving ware in silver or gold made during the reign of George II (1727–1760) and inherited by Louisa van der Luyden from her grandmother, Lady Angelica Trevenna; "Lowestoft" is fine bone china named for Lowestoft, England, but imported from China to America by the colonial mercantile enterprise, the East India Company; Crown Derby is richly decorated, delicate china produced in Derby, England, in the royal name by permission of Queen Victoria in 1880. Isabey: Louis Gabriel Eugene Isabey (1803–1886), French sculptor; blonde shawl: A light-colored shawl of handmade silk lace featuring floral patterns in a heavy thread.

when he did it was in such low tones that, despite the frequent silences of expectation about the table, his remarks were lost to all but his neighbors.

When the men joined the ladies after dinner the Duke went straight up to the Countess Olenska, and they sat down in a corner and plunged into animated talk. Neither seemed aware that the Duke should first have paid his respects to Mrs. Lovell Mingott and Mrs. Headly Chivers, and the Countess have conversed with that amiable hypochondriac, Mr. Urban Dagonet of Washington Square, who, in order to have the pleasure of meeting her, had broken through his fixed rule of not dining out between January and April. The two chatted together for nearly twenty minutes; then the Countess rose and, walking alone across the wide drawing room, sat down at Newland Archer's side.

It was not the custom in New York drawing rooms for a lady to get up and walk away from one gentleman in order to seek the company of another. Etiquette required that she should wait, immovable as an idol, while the men who wished to converse with her succeeded each other at her side. But the Countess was apparently unaware of having broken any rule; she sat at perfect ease in a corner of the sofa beside Archer, and looked at him with the kindest eyes.

"I want you to talk to me about May," she said.

Instead of answering her he asked: "You knew the Duke before?"

"Oh, yes—we used to see him every winter at Nice. He's very fond of gambling—he used to come to the house a great deal." She said it in the simplest manner, as if she had said: "He's fond of wildflowers"; and after a moment she added candidly: "I think he's the dullest man I ever met."

This pleased her companion so much that he forgot the slight shock her previous remark had caused him. It was undeniably exciting to meet a lady who found the van der Luydens' Duke dull, and dared to utter the opinion. He longed to question her, to hear more about the life of which her careless words had given him so illuminating a glimpse; but he feared to touch on distressing memories, and before he could think of anything to say she had strayed back to her original subject.

"May is a darling; I've seen no young girl in New York so handsome and so intelligent. Are you very much in love with her?"

Newland Archer reddened and laughed. "As much as a man can be."

She continued to consider him thoughtfully, as if not to miss any shade of meaning in what he said, "Do you think, then, there is a limit?"

"To being in love? If there is, I haven't found it!"

She glowed with sympathy. "Ah—it's really and truly a romance?"

"The most romantic of romances!"

"How delightful! And you found it all out for yourselves—it was not in the least arranged for you?"

Archer looked at her incredulously. "Have you forgotten," he asked with a smile, "that in our country we don't allow our marriages to be arranged for us?"

A dusky blush rose to her cheek, and he instantly regretted his words.

"Yes," she answered, "I'd forgotten. You must forgive me if I sometimes make these mistakes. I don't always remember that everything here is good that was—that was bad where I've come from." She looked down at her Viennese fan of eagle feathers, and he saw that her lips trembled.

"I'm so sorry," he said impulsively; "but you *are* among friends here, you know."

"Yes—I know. Wherever I go I have that feeling. That's why I came home. I want to forget everything else, to become a complete American again, like the Mingotts and Wellands, and you and your delightful mother, and all the other good people here tonight. Ah, here's May arriving, and you will want to hurry away to her," she added, but without moving; and her eyes turned back from the door to rest on the young man's face.

The drawing rooms were beginning to fill up with after-dinner guests, and following Madame Olenska's glance Archer saw May Welland entering with her mother. In her dress of white and silver, with a wreath of silver blossoms in her hair, the tall girl looked like a Diana just alight from the chase.[7]

"Oh," said Archer, "I have so many rivals: you see she's already surrounded. There's the Duke being introduced."

"Then stay with me a little longer," Madame Olenska said in a low tone, just touching his knee with her plumed fan. It was the lightest touch, but it thrilled him like a caress.

"Yes, let me stay," he answered in the same tone, hardly knowing what he said; but just then Mr. van der Luyden came up, followed by old Mr. Urban Dagonet. The Countess greeted them with her grave smile, and Archer, feeling his host's admonitory glance on him, rose and surrendered his seat.

Madame Olenska held out her hand as if to bid him goodbye.

"Tomorrow, then, after five—I shall expect you," she said; and then turned back to make room for Mr. Dagonet.

"Tomorrow—" Archer heard himself repeating, though there had been no engagement, and during their talk she had given him no hint that she wished to see him again.

As he moved away he saw Lawrence Lefferts, tall and resplendent, leading his wife up to be introduced; and heard Gertrude Lefferts say, as she beamed on the Countess with her large unperceiving smile: "But I think we used to go to dancing-school together when we were children—." Behind her, waiting their turn to name themselves to the Countess, Archer noticed a number of the recalcitrant couples who had declined to meet her at Mrs. Lovell Mingott's. As Mrs. Archer remarked: when the van der Luydens chose, they knew how to give a lesson. The wonder was that they chose so seldom.

---

7. Diana, the Roman goddess of the hunt or the "chase"; often depicted with bow and arrows, this fierce virgin goddess was also responsible for overseeing the rites of childbirth.

The young man felt a touch on his arm and saw Mrs. van der Luyden looking down on him from the pure eminence of black velvet and
the family diamonds. "It was good of you, dear Newland, to devote
yourself so unselfishly to Madame Olenska. I told your Cousin Henry
he must really come to the rescue."

He was aware of smiling at her vaguely, and she added, as if condescending to his natural shyness: "I've never seen May looking lovelier.
The Duke thinks her the handsomest girl in the room."

# IX

The Countess Olenska had said "after five"; and at half after the
hour Newland Archer rang the bell of the peeling stucco house with a
giant wisteria throttling its feeble cast-iron balcony, which she had
hired, far down West Twenty-third Street, from the vagabond Medora.

It was certainly a strange quarter to have settled in. Small dressmakers, bird-stuffers and "people who wrote" were her nearest neighbors; and further down the disheveled street Archer recognized a
dilapidated wooden house, at the end of a paved path, in which a
writer and journalist called Winsett, whom he used to come across
now and then, had mentioned that he lived. Winsett did not invite
people to his house; but he had once pointed it out to Archer in the
course of a nocturnal stroll, and the latter had asked himself, with a
little shiver, if the humanities were so meanly housed in other capitals.

Madame Olenska's own dwelling was redeemed from the same ap-
pearance only by a little more paint about the window frames; and as
Archer mustered its modest front he said to himself that the Polish
Count must have robbed her of her fortune as well as of her illusions.

The young man had spent an unsatisfactory day. He had lunched
with the Wellands, hoping afterward to carry off May for a walk in the
Park. He wanted to have her to himself, to tell her how enchanting
she had looked the night before, and how proud he was of her, and to
press her to hasten their marriage. But Mrs. Welland had firmly reminded him that the round of family visits was not half over, and,
when he hinted at advancing the date of the wedding, had raised reproachful eyebrows and sighed out: "Twelve dozen of everything—
hand-embroidered—"[1]

Packed in the family landau they rolled from one tribal doorstep to
another, and Archer, when the afternoon's round was over, parted from
his betrothed with the feeling that he had been shown off like a wild
animal cunningly trapped. He supposed that his readings in anthropology caused him to take such a coarse view of what was after all a
simple and natural demonstration of family feeling; but when he remembered that the Wellands did not expect the wedding to take place

---

1. A reference to a well-to-do lady's standard trousseau and table linens finished with fancy
embroidery done by the women of the family. This type of sewing serves a ritualized as well
as a practical function by "tying the knots" that will provide the bride with a secure foundation.

till the following autumn, and pictured what his life would be till then, a dampness fell upon his spirit.

"Tomorrow," Mrs. Welland called after him, "we'll do the Chiverses and the Dallases"; and he perceived that she was going through their two families alphabetically, and that they were only in the first quarter of the alphabet.

He had meant to tell May of the Countess Olenska's request—her command, rather—that he should call on her that afternoon; but in the brief moments when they were alone he had had more pressing things to say. Besides, it struck him as a little absurd to allude to the matter. He knew that May most particularly wanted him to be kind to her cousin; was it not that wish which had hastened the announcement of their engagement? It gave him an odd sensation to reflect that, but for the Countess's arrival, he might have been, if not still a free man, at least a man less irrevocably pledged. But May had willed it so, and he felt himself somehow relieved of further responsibility—and therefore at liberty, if he chose, to call on her cousin without telling her.

As he stood on Madame Olenska's threshold curiosity was his uppermost feeling. He was puzzled by the tone in which she had summoned him; he concluded that she was less simple than she seemed.

The door was opened by a swarthy foreign-looking maid, with a prominent bosom under a gay neckerchief, whom he vaguely fancied to be Sicilian. She welcomed him with all her white teeth, and answering his enquiries by a head-shake of incomprehension led him through the narrow hall into a low firelit drawing room. The room was empty, and she left him, for an appreciable time, to wonder whether she had gone to find her mistress, or whether she had not understood what he was there for, and thought it might be to wind the clocks—of which he perceived that the only visible specimen had stopped. He knew that the southern races communicated with each other in the language of pantomime, and was mortified to find her shrugs and smiles so unintelligible. At length she returned with a lamp; and Archer, having meanwhile put together a phrase out of Dante and Petrarch,[2] evoked the answer: "*La signora è fuori; ma verrà subito*"; which he took to mean: "She's out—but you'll soon see."

What he saw, meanwhile, with the help of the lamp, was the faded shadowy charm of a room unlike any room he had known. He knew that the Countess Olenska had brought some of her possessions with her—bits of wreckage, she called them—and these, he supposed, were represented by some small slender tables of dark wood, a delicate little Greek bronze on the chimney-piece, and a stretch of red damask nailed on the discolored wallpaper behind a couple of Italian-looking pictures in old frames.

Newland Archer prided himself on his knowledge of Italian art. His boyhood had been saturated with Ruskin, and he had read all the latest books: John Addington Symonds, Vernon Lee's "Euphorion," the

2. Dante: Italian poet (1265–1321); Petrarch: Italian poet (1304–1374). Both were known for their love poetry addressed to unattainable women, Dante's to Beatrice and Petrarch's to Laura.

essays of P. G. Hamerton and a wonderful new volume called *The Renaissance* by Walter Pater. He talked easily of Botticelli, and spoke of Fra Angelico with a faint condescension.[3] But these pictures bewildered him, for they were like nothing that he was accustomed to look at (and therefore able to see) when he travelled in Italy; and perhaps, also, his powers of observation were impaired by the oddness of finding himself in this strange empty house, where apparently no one expected him. He was sorry that he had not told May Welland of Countess Olenska's request, and a little disturbed by the thought that his betrothed might come in to see her cousin. What would she think if she found him sitting there with the air of intimacy implied by waiting alone in the dusk at a lady's fireside?

But since he had come he meant to wait; and he sank into a chair and stretched his feet to the logs.

It was odd to have summoned him in that way, and then forgotten him; but Archer felt more curious than mortified. The atmosphere of the room was so different from any he had ever breathed that self-consciousness vanished in the sense of adventure. He had been before in drawing rooms hung with red damask, with pictures "of the Italian school"; what struck him was the way in which Medora Manson's shabby hired house, with its blighted background of pampas grass and Rogers statuettes, had, by a turn of the hand, and the skilful use of a few properties, been transformed into something intimate, "foreign," subtly suggestive of old romantic scenes and sentiments. He tried to analyze the trick, to find a clue to it in the way the chairs and tables were grouped, in the fact that only two Jacqueminot roses (of which nobody ever bought less than a dozen) had been placed in the slender vase at his elbow, and in the vague pervading perfume that was not what one put on handkerchiefs, but rather like the scent of some far-off bazaar, a smell made up of Turkish coffee and ambergris and dried roses.[4]

His mind wandered away to the question of what May's drawing

3. Ruskin: See p. 23, *n.* 3; John Addington Symonds: English scholar and historian (1840–1893), writer of *History of the Renaissance in Italy* (1875–76), a series of picturesque sketches. Vernon Lee: Pen name of Violet Paget (1856–1935), English novelist, essayist, critic, and author of *Euphorion*, a study of Renaissance art published in 1884. Although critics called the late publication date to Wharton's attention as a mistake, she made the decision to preserve this allusion to Faust audible in the name Euphorion, the ill-fated son of Helen of Troy and Faust in Goethe's *Faust*. Since Wharton based her novel on events which were drawn from a full decade, Lee's study of 1884 is within the period that Wharton established as the era that she drew upon for the sources of the novel. P. G. Hamerton: English art critic and essayist (1834–1894). Walter Pater: English essayist and critic (1839–1894) whose *Studies in the History of the Renaissance* (1873) inspired a revival of interest in the art and culture of that period. Botticelli: Florentine painter (1444–1510) best known for *The Birth of Venus*. Fra Angelico: Italian painter (1400–1485) famed for his murals at San Marco in Florence.

4. Rogers statuettes: The early work of Randolph Rogers, American sculptor (1825–1892), presented here as an example of poor taste, is exemplified by *Nydia, the Blind Flower Girl of Pompeii* and tended to be based on narrative subjects. His later commissions celebrated military and national figures, including Washington and Lincoln. Widely available in plaster, Rogers' work was devalued by mass production. Jacqueminot: A variety of red rose named after the French viscount Jean Jacqueminot, who died in 1865. ambergris: Taking its name from its color, this yellow and gray wax-like substance, found floating in tropical oceans and believed to come from the intestines of the sperm whale, was valued as an essential ingredient in the manufacture of fine perfumes.

room would look like. He knew that Mr. Welland, who was behaving "very handsomely," already had his eye on a newly built house in East Thirty-ninth Street. The neighborhood was thought remote, and the house was built in a ghastly greenish-yellow stone that the younger architects were beginning to employ as a protest against the brownstone of which the uniform hue coated New York like a cold chocolate sauce; but the plumbing was perfect. Archer would have liked to travel, to put off the housing question; but, though the Wellands approved of an extended European honeymoon (perhaps even a winter in Egypt), they were firm as to the need of a house for the returning couple. The young man felt that his fate was sealed: for the rest of his life he would go up every evening between the cast-iron railings of that greenish-yellow doorstep, and pass through a Pompeian vestibule into a hall with a wainscoting of varnished yellow wood. But beyond that his imagination could not travel. He knew the drawing room above had a bay window, but he could not fancy how May would deal with it. She submitted cheerfully to the purple satin and yellow tuftings of the Welland drawing room, to its sham buhl tables and gilt vitrines full of modern Saxe. He saw no reason to suppose that she would want anything different in her own house; and his only comfort was to reflect that she would probably let him arrange his library as he pleased—which would be, of course, with "sincere" Eastlake furniture, and the plain new bookcases without glass doors.[5]

The round-bosomed maid came in, drew the curtains, pushed back a log, and said consolingly: "*Verrà—verrà.*"[6] When she had gone Archer stood up and began to wander about. Should he wait any longer? His position was becoming rather foolish. Perhaps he had misunderstood Madame Olenska—perhaps she had not invited him after all.

Down the cobblestones of the quiet street came the ring of a stepper's hoofs; they stopped before the house, and he caught the opening of a carriage door. Parting the curtains he looked out into the early dusk. A street lamp faced him, and in its light he saw Julius Beaufort's compact English brougham, drawn by a big roan, and the banker descending from it, and helping out Madame Olenska.

5. Pompeian vestibule: A foyer or entry hall into a house decorated in the flamboyant style associated with what was the recently excavated Roman city of Pompeii. Preserved by volcanic ash and lava in 79 A.D., the Pompeii unearthed by mid-nineteenth-century archaeologists inspired one of the most dramatic trends in Victorian era's interior decoration. While columns and other classical details had long been popular, this style introduced brightly painted walls featuring bold colors, including the vibrant Victorian shade still known as "Pompeian red." gilt vitrines: Glass cabinets with gilded frames. Here, cases used for displaying valued objects, whether souvenirs or works of art; "modern Saxe": A French term for fine porcelain first produced near Dresden in the Saxony region of Germany around 1700. "Modern Saxe" is distinguished from "*vieux saxes,*" the "old Saxe" that had inspired important collections in Europe. Made by the same process, these reproductions displayed in glass cases mock American efforts to imitate European practices. Eastlake furniture: Furniture designed in the style described in Charles Locke Eastlake's *Hints on Household Taste* (1872), an extremely popular pattern book of the period. In her first book, *The Decoration of Houses* (1897, coauthored with Ogden Codman, 1863–1951) Wharton opposes Eastlake's focus on ornament, insisting that interior decoration should be based on structural principles that would make it a branch of architecture. In comparison with the highly ornate and overstuffed furniture popular in the 1870s, the gently scalloped sides and lathe-turned legs of Eastlake's furniture would have seemed modest and "sincere."
6. Italian, "She will come—she will come."

Beaufort stood, hat in hand, saying something which his companion seemed to negative; then they shook hands, and he jumped into his carriage while she mounted the steps.

When she entered the room she showed no surprise at seeing Archer there; surprise seemed the emotion that she was least addicted to.

"How do you like my funny house?" she asked. "To me it's like heaven."

As she spoke she untied her little velvet bonnet and tossing it away with her long cloak stood looking at him with meditative eyes.

"You've arranged it delightfully," he rejoined, alive to the flatness of the words, but imprisoned in the conventional by his consuming desire to be simple and striking.

"Oh, it's a poor little place. My relations despise it. But at any rate it's less gloomy than the van der Luydens'."

The words gave him an electric shock, for few were the rebellious spirits who would have dared to call the stately home of the van der Luydens gloomy. Those privileged to enter it shivered there, and spoke of it as "handsome." But suddenly he was glad that she had given voice to the general shiver.

"It's delicious—what you've done here," he repeated.

"I like the little house," she admitted; "but I suppose what I like is the blessedness of its being here, in my own country and my own town; and then, of being alone in it." She spoke so low that he hardly heard the last phrase; but in his awkwardness he took it up.

"You like so much to be alone?"

"Yes; as long as my friends keep me from feeling lonely." She sat down near the fire, said: "Nastasia will bring the tea presently," and signed to him to return to his armchair, adding: "I see you've already chosen your corner."

Leaning back, she folded her arms behind her head, and looked at the fire under drooping lids.

"This is the hour I like best—don't you?"

A proper sense of his dignity caused him to answer: "I was afraid you'd forgotten the hour. Beaufort must have been very engrossing."

She looked amused. "Why—have you waited long? Mr. Beaufort took me to see a number of houses—since it seems I'm not to be allowed to stay in this one." She appeared to dismiss both Beaufort and himself from her mind, and went on: "I've never been in a city where there seems to be such a feeling against living in *des quartiers excentriques*. What does it matter where one lives? I'm told this street is respectable."

"It's not fashionable."

"Fashionable! Do you all think so much of that? Why not make one's own fashions? But I suppose I've lived too independently; at any rate, I want to do what you all do—I want to feel cared for and safe."

He was touched, as he had been the evening before when she spoke of her need of guidance.

"That's what your friends want you to feel. New York's an awfully safe place," he added with a flash of sarcasm.

"Yes, isn't it? One feels that," she cried, missing the mockery. "Being here is like—like—being taken on a holiday when one has been a good little girl and done all one's lessons."

The analogy was well meant, but did not altogether please him. He did not mind being flippant about New York, but disliked to hear anyone else take the same tone. He wondered if she did not begin to see what a powerful engine it was, and how nearly it had crushed her. The Lovell Mingotts' dinner, patched up *in extremis*[7] out of all sorts of social odds and ends, ought to have taught her the narrowness of her escape; but either she had been all along unaware of having skirted disaster, or else she had lost sight of it in the triumph of the van der Luyden evening. Archer inclined to the former theory; he fancied that her New York was still completely undifferentiated, and the conjecture nettled him.

"Last night," he said, "New York laid itself out for you. The van der Luydens do nothing by halves."

"No: how kind they are! It was such a nice party. Everyone seems to have such an esteem for them."

The terms were hardly adequate; she might have spoken in that way of a tea-party at the dear old Miss Lannings'.

"The van der Luydens," said Archer, feeling himself pompous as he spoke, "are the most powerful influence in New York society. Unfortunately—owing to her health—they receive very seldom."

She unclasped her hands from behind her head, and looked at him meditatively.

"Isn't that perhaps the reason?"

"The reason—?"

"For their great influence; that they make themselves so rare."

He colored a little, stared at her—and suddenly felt the penetration of the remark. At a stroke she had pricked the van der Luydens and they collapsed. He laughed, and sacrificed them.

Nastasia brought the tea, with handleless Japanese cups and little covered dishes, placing the tray on a low table.

"But you'll explain these things to me—you'll tell me all I ought to know," Madame Olenska continued, leaning forward to hand him his cup.

"It's you who are telling me; opening my eyes to things I'd looked at so long that I'd ceased to see them."

She detached a small gold cigarette-case[8] from one of her bracelets, held it out to him, and took a cigarette herself. On the chimney were long spills for lighting them.

"Ah, then we can both help each other. But I want help so much more. You must tell me just what to do."

It was on the tip of his tongue to reply: "Don't be seen driving about

7. Latin, "in the extreme," an expression for being at the point of death.
8. cigarette: Associated with urban and Bohemian tastes and more libertine views in relation to female sexuality, the popularity of smoking what were called "Turkish cigarettes" in New York led to an influx of expert rollers from Europe during the years from 1865 to 1870. While the first American cigarette factory opened in 1864, the popularity of this form of tobacco use was limited before the invention in 1880 of a machine for rolling cigarettes.

the streets with Beaufort—" but he was being too deeply drawn into the atmosphere of the room, which was her atmosphere, and to give advice of that sort would have been like telling someone who was bargaining for attar-of-roses in Samarkand that one should always be provided with arctics for a New York winter.[9] New York seemed much farther off than Samarkand, and if they were indeed to help each other she was rendering what might prove the first of their mutual services by making him look at his native city objectively. Viewed thus, as through the wrong end of a telescope, it looked disconcertingly small and distant; but then from Samarkand it would.

A flame darted from the logs and she bent over the fire, stretching her thin hands so close to it that a faint halo shone about the oval nails. The light touched to russet the rings of dark hair escaping from her braids, and made her pale face paler.

"There are plenty of people to tell you what to do," Archer rejoined, obscurely envious of them.

"Oh—all my aunts? And my dear old Granny?" She considered the idea impartially. "They're all a little vexed with me for setting up for myself—poor Granny especially. She wanted to keep me with her; but I had to be free—" He was impressed by this light way of speaking of the formidable Catherine, and moved by the thought of what must have given Madame Olenska this thirst for even the loneliest kind of freedom. But the idea of Beaufort gnawed him.

"I think I understand how you feel," he said. "Still, your family can advise you; explain differences; show you the way."

She lifted her thin black eyebrows. "Is New York such a labyrinth? I thought it so straight up and down—like Fifth Avenue. And with all the cross streets numbered!" She seemed to guess his faint disapproval of this, and added, with the rare smile that enchanted her whole face: "If you know how I like it for just *that*—the straight-up-and-downness, and the big honest labels on everything!"[1]

He saw his chance. "Everything may be labeled—but everybody is not."

"Perhaps. I may simplify too much—but you'll warn me if I do." She turned from the fire to look at him. "There are only two people here who make me feel as if they understood what I mean and could explain things to me: you and Mr. Beaufort."

Archer winced at the joining of the names, and then, with a quick readjustment, understood, sympathized and pitied. So close to the powers of evil she must have lived that she still breathed more freely in their air. But since she felt that he understood her also, his business would be to make her see Beaufort as he really was, with all he represented—and abhor it.

He answered gently: "I understand. But just at first don't let go of

9. attar-of-roses: A fragrant essential oil distilled from rose petals, in particular the petals of the damask rose; Samarkand: an old market city of Uzbekistan. arctics: Fabric-lined, rubber overshoes reaching to the ankle or above, often fastened with buckles.
1. cross streets numbered . . . the straight-up-and-downness: The "grid plan" or grid iron plan was approved by New York state legislature in 1811 as the most practical and profitable design for Manhattan's streets.

your old friends' hands: I mean the older women, your Granny Mingott, Mrs. Welland, Mrs. van der Luyden. They like and admire you—
they want to help you."

She shook her head and sighed. "Oh, I know—I know! But on condition that they don't hear anything unpleasant. Aunt Welland put it in
those very words when I tried. . . . Does no one want to know the truth
here, Mr. Archer? The real loneliness is living among all these kind
people who only ask one to pretend!" She lifted her hands to her face,
and he saw her thin shoulders shaken by a sob.

"Madame Olenska!—Oh, don't, Ellen," he cried, starting up and
bending over her. He drew down one of her hands, clasping and chaf-
ing it like a child's while he murmured reassuring words; but in a moment she freed herself, and looked up at him with wet lashes.

"Does no one cry here, either? I suppose there's no need to, in
heaven," she said, straightening her loosened braids with a laugh, and
bending over the tea-kettle. It was burnt into his consciousness that
he had called her "Ellen"—called her so twice; and that she had not
noticed it. Far down the inverted telescope he saw the faint white figure of May Welland—in New York.

Suddenly Nastasia put her head in to say something in her rich Italian.

Madame Olenska, again with a hand at her hair, uttered an exclamation of assent—a flashing "Già—già"[2]—and the Duke of St. Austrey
entered, piloting a tremendous black-wigged and red-plumed lady in
overflowing furs.

"My dear Countess, I've brought an old friend of mine to see you—
Mrs. Struthers. She wasn't asked to the party last night, and she wants
to know you."

The Duke beamed on the group, and Madame Olenska advanced
with a murmur of welcome toward the queer couple. She seemed to
have no idea how oddly matched they were, nor what a liberty the
Duke had taken in bringing his companion—and to do him justice, as
Archer perceived, the Duke seemed as unaware of it himself.

"Of course I want to know you, my dear," cried Mrs. Struthers in a
round rolling voice that matched her bold feathers and her brazen wig. "I
want to know everybody who's young and interesting and charming. And
the Duke tells me you like music—didn't you, Duke? You're a pianist
yourself, I believe? Well, do you want to hear Sarasate[3] play tomorrow
evening at my house? You know I've something going on every Sunday
evening—it's the day when New York doesn't know what to do with itself,
and so I say to it: 'Come and be amused.' And the Duke thought you'd be
tempted by Sarasate. You'll find a number of your friends."

Madame Olenska's face grew brilliant with pleasure. "How kind!
How good of the Duke to think of me!" She pushed a chair up to the
tea-table and Mrs. Struthers sank into it delectably. "Of course I shall
be too happy to come."

"That's all right, my dear. And bring your young gentleman with

---

2. Italian, "I'm coming," "in a moment."
3. Spanish violinist (1844–1908) who embarked on a forty-year world tour in 1859.

you." Mrs. Struthers extended a hail-fellow hand to Archer. "I can't put a name to you—but I'm sure I've met you—I've met everybody, here, or in Paris or London. Aren't you in diplomacy? All the diplomatists come to me. You like music too? Duke, you must be sure to bring him."

The Duke said "Rather" from the depths of his beard, and Archer withdrew with a stiffly circular bow that made him feel as full of spine as a self-conscious schoolboy among careless and unnoticing elders.

He was not sorry for the *dénouement*[4] of his visit: he only wished it had come sooner, and spared him a certain waste of emotion. As he went out into the wintry night, New York again became vast and imminent, and May Welland the loveliest woman in it. He turned into his florist's to send her the daily box of lilies-of-the-valley which, to his confusion, he found he had forgotten that morning.

As he wrote a word on his card and waited for an envelope he glanced about the embowered shop, and his eye lit on a cluster of yellow roses.[5] He had never seen any as sun-golden before, and his first impulse was to send them to May instead of the lilies. But they did not look like her—there was something too rich, too strong, in their fiery beauty. In a sudden revulsion of mood, and almost without knowing what he did, he signed to the florist to lay the roses in another long box, and slipped his card into a second envelope, on which he wrote the name of the Countess Olenska; then, just as he was turning away, he drew the card out again, and left the empty envelope on the box.

"They'll go at once?" he enquired, pointing to the roses.

The florist assured him that they would.

# X

The next day he persuaded May to escape for a walk in the Park after luncheon. As was the custom in old-fashioned Episcopalian New York, she usually accompanied her parents to church on Sunday afternoons; but Mrs. Welland condoned her truancy, having that very morning won her over to the necessity of a long engagement, with time to prepare a hand-embroidered trousseau containing the proper number of dozens.

The day was delectable. The bare vaulting of trees along the Mall was ceiled with lapis lazuli,[1] and arched above snow that shone like splintered crystals. It was the weather to call out May's radiance, and

---

4. French, "unraveling," a transformative and telling crisis in a scene of literature or life.
5. In the traditional language of flowers, the meaning ascribed to yellow roses varies unusually widely in the lists that comprise nineteenth-century flower dictionaries. Yellow roses are associated variously with jealousy, infidelity, love that will not last, and friendship. (See pp. 349–74.)
1. "the Mall:" Originally called the "Promenade," "the Mall" that led into the pathway called the "Literary Walk" was designed to be the finest walkway in Central Park. Viewed as a coming-of-age for New York as a cultured city, this landscaped park was designed as a place for leisurely strolls by the fashionable elite, a pastime associated with the capitols of Europe. lapis lazuli: Rich blue of the semi-precious stone, often used in jewelry and decorative inlays.

she burned like a young maple in the frost. Archer was proud of the glances turned on her, and the simple joy of possessorship cleared away his underlying perplexities.

"It's so delicious—waking every morning to smell lilies-of-the-valley in one's room!" she said.

"Yesterday they came late. I hadn't time in the morning—"

"But your remembering each day to send them makes me love them so much more than if you'd given a standing order, and they came every morning on the minute, like one's music-teacher—as I know Gertrude Lefferts's did, for instance, when she and Lawrence were engaged."

"Ah—they would!" laughed Archer, amused at her keenness. He looked sideways at her fruit-like cheek and felt rich and secure enough to add: "When I sent your lilies yesterday afternoon I saw some rather gorgeous yellow roses and packed them off to Madame Olenska. Was that right?"

"How dear of you! Anything of that kind delights her. It's odd she didn't mention it: she lunched with us today, and spoke of Mr. Beaufort's having sent her wonderful orchids, and Cousin Henry van der Luyden a whole hamper of carnations from Skuytercliff. She seems so surprised to receive flowers. Don't people send them in Europe? She thinks it such a pretty custom."

"Oh, well, no wonder mine were overshadowed by Beaufort's," said Archer irritably. Then he remembered that he had not put a card with the roses, and was vexed at having spoken of them. He wanted to say: "I called on your cousin yesterday," but hesitated. If Madame Olenska had not spoken of his visit it might seem awkward that he should. Yet not to do so gave the affair an air of mystery that he disliked. To shake off the question he began to talk of their own plans, their future, and Mrs. Welland's insistence on a long engagement.

"If you call it long! Isabel Chivers and Reggie were engaged for two years:[2] Grace and Thorley for nearly a year and a half. Why aren't we very well off as we are?"

It was the traditional maidenly interrogation, and he felt ashamed of himself for finding it singularly childish. No doubt she simply echoed what was said for her; but she was nearing her twenty-second birthday, and he wondered at what age "nice" women began to speak for themselves.

"Never, if we won't let them, I suppose," he mused, and recalled his mad outburst to Mr. Sillerton Jackson: "Women ought to be as free as we are—"

It would presently be his task to take the bandage from this young woman's eyes, and bid her look forth on the world. But how many generations of the women who had gone to her making had descended bandaged to the family vault? He shivered a little, remembering some of the new ideas in his scientific books, and the much-cited instance

---

2. Traditionally an engagement was announced a year or more in advance. Part of the reason for long engagements was to make it clear that the bride-to-be was not pregnant and that neither party was obliged to marry in haste for any reason.

of the Kentucky cave-fish,[3] which had ceased to develop eyes because they had no use for them. What if, when he had bidden May Welland to open hers, they could only look out blankly at blankness?

"We might be much better off. We might be altogether together— we might travel."

Her face lit up. "That would be lovely," she owned: she would love to travel. But her mother would not understand their wanting to do things so differently.

"As if the mere 'differently' didn't account for it!" the wooer insisted.

"Newland! You're so original!" she exulted.

His heart sank, for he saw that he was saying all the things that young men in the same situation were expected to say, and that she was making the answers that instinct and tradition taught her to make—even to the point of calling him original.

"Original! We're all as like each other as those dolls cut out of the same folded paper. We're like patterns stencilled on a wall. Can't you and I strike out for ourselves, May?"

He had stopped and faced her in the excitement of their discussion, and her eyes rested on him with a bright unclouded admiration.

"Mercy—shall we elope?" she laughed.

"If you would—"

"You *do* love me, Newland! I'm so happy."

"But then—why not be happier?"

"We can't behave like people in novels, though, can we?"

"Why not—why not—why not?"

She looked a little bored by his insistence. She knew very well that they couldn't, but it was troublesome to have to produce a reason. "I'm not clever enough to argue with you. But that kind of thing is rather— vulgar, isn't it?" she suggested, relieved to have hit on a word that would assuredly extinguish the whole subject.

"Are you so much afraid, then, of being vulgar?"

She was evidently staggered by this. "Of course I should hate it—so would you," she rejoined, a trifle irritably.

He stood silent, beating his stick nervously against his boot-top; and feeling that she had indeed found the right way of closing the discussion, she went on lightheartedly: "Oh, did I tell you that I showed Ellen my ring? She thinks it the most beautiful setting she ever saw. There's nothing like it in the rue de la Paix,[4] she said. I do love you, Newland, for being so artistic!"

The next afternoon, as Archer, before dinner, sat smoking sullenly in his study, Janey wandered in on him. He had failed to stop at his club on the way up from the office where he exercised the profession of the

3. Strangely white in color and with vestigial markings in place of eyes, these fish evolved as a result of the perpetual darkness of the underground stream that flows through Mammoth Cave in Kentucky.
4. French, Street of the Peace. Located near the French opera house in Paris, this street, known for its fancy restaurants and theaters, was a favored destination for wealthy foreign visitors to Paris during the 1870s; this is also the street from which the well-dressed women of New York would bring back their fashionable Worth gowns. (See p. 118, *n.* 5.)

law in the leisurely manner common to well-to-do New Yorkers of his class. He was out of spirits and slightly out of temper, and a haunting horror of doing the same thing every day at the same hour besieged his brain.

"Sameness—sameness!" he muttered, the word running through his head like a persecuting tune as he saw the familiar tall-hatted figures lounging behind the plate glass; and because he usually dropped in at the club at that hour he had gone home instead. He knew not only what they were likely to be talking about, but the part each one would take in the discussion. The Duke of course would be their principal theme; though the appearance in Fifth Avenue of a golden-haired lady in a small canary-colored brougham with a pair of black cobs (for which Beaufort was generally thought responsible) would also doubtless be thoroughly gone into. Such "women"[5] (as they were called) were few in New York, those driving their own carriages still fewer, and the appearance of Miss Fanny Ring in Fifth Avenue at the fashionable hour had profoundly agitated society. Only the day before, her carriage had passed Mrs. Lovell Mingott's, and the latter had instantly rung the little bell at her elbow and ordered the coachman to drive her home. "What if it had happened to Mrs. van der Luyden?" people asked each other with a shudder. Archer could hear Lawrence Lefferts, at that very hour, holding forth on the disintegration of society.

He raised his head irritably when his sister Janey entered, and then quickly bent over his book (Swinburne's *Chastelard*—just out) as if he had not seen her. She glanced at the writing-table heaped with books, opened a volume of the *Contes Drôlatiques,* made a wry face over the archaic French, and sighed: "What learned things you read!"[6]

"Well—?" he asked, as she hovered Cassandra-like[7] before him.

"Mother's very angry."

"Angry? With whom? About what?"

"Miss Sophy Jackson has just been here. She brought word that her brother would come in after dinner: she couldn't say very much, because he forbade her to: he wishes to give all the details himself. He's with Cousin Louisa van der Luyden now."

"For heaven's sake, my dear girl, try a fresh start. It would take an omniscient Deity to know what you're talking about."

---

5. cobs: Strong, closely built ponies known for their hardiness. The word "women," particularly when placed in quotation marks, is a derogatory term that contrasts this group with those who were considered ladies.

6. Swinburne's *Chastelard*: A drama in verse (1860), by the English poet Algernon Charles Swinburne (1837–1909), known for his rebellion against Victorian social strictures. *Chastelard* tells the story of a man who, obsessed with Mary Queen of Scots, pursues her to her private rooms and is put to death for his quest. The story is based on the life of Pierre de Boscoselde Chastelard (1540–1563), who exchanged verses with the queen and was only executed after getting into her rooms a second time. *Contes Drôlatiques*: This French title, which could be translated as "Amusing Tales," was given to a series of three collections of short and humorous anecdotes published 1832–37 (see pp. 276–83 for excerpts). While Balzac based his tales on the bawdy literature of sixteenth-century France, Wharton based the humorous speculations on innocence in her early work "The Valley of Childish Things, and Other Emblems" (pp. 284–88) on Balzac's form.

7. Cassandra, a figure in Greek myth, had been given the gift of prophecy by Apollo but was then cursed for repulsing his amorous advances; her fate was to speak the truth only to have her warnings fall on unbelieving ears.

"It's not a time to be profane, Newland. . . . Mother feels badly enough about your not going to church. . . ."

With a groan he plunged back into his book.

"*Newland!* Do listen. Your friend Madame Olenska was at Mrs. Lemuel Struthers's party last night: she went there with the Duke and Mr. Beaufort."

At the last clause of this announcement a senseless anger swelled the young man's breast. To smother it he laughed. "Well, what of it? I knew she meant to."

Janey paled and her eyes began to project. "You knew she meant to—and you didn't try to stop her? To warn her?"

"Stop her? Warn her?" He laughed again. "I'm not engaged to be married to the Countess Olenska!" The words had a fantastic sound in his own ears.

"You're marrying into her family."

"Oh, family—family!" he jeered.

"Newland—don't you care about Family?"

"Not a brass farthing."

"Nor about what Cousin Louisa van der Luyden will think?"

"Not the half of one—if she thinks such old maid's rubbish."

"Mother is not an old maid," said his virgin sister with pinched lips.

He felt like shouting back: "Yes, she is, and so are the van der Luydens, and so we all are, when it comes to being so much as brushed by the wing-tip of Reality." But he saw her long gentle face puckering into tears, and felt ashamed of the useless pain he was inflicting.

"Hang Countess Olenska! Don't be a goose, Janey—I'm not her keeper."

"No; but you *did* ask the Wellands to announce your engagement sooner so that we might all back her up; and if it hadn't been for that Cousin Louisa would never have invited her to the dinner for the Duke."

"Well—what harm was there in inviting her? She was the best-looking woman in the room; she made the dinner a little less funereal than the usual van der Luyden banquet."

"You know Cousin Henry asked her to please you: he persuaded Cousin Louisa. And now they're so upset that they're going back to Skuytercliff tomorrow. I think, Newland, you'd better come down. You don't seem to understand how Mother feels."

In the drawing room Newland found his mother. She raised a troubled brow from her needlework to ask: "Has Janey told you?"

"Yes." He tried to keep his tone as measured as her own. "But I can't take it very seriously."

"Not the fact of having offended Cousin Louisa and Cousin Henry?"

"The fact that they can be offended by such a trifle as Countess Olenska's going to the house of a woman they consider common."

"*Consider—!*"

"Well, who is; but who has good music, and amuses people on Sunday evenings, when the whole of New York is dying of inanition."

"Good music? All I know is, there was a woman who got up on a table and sang the things they sing at the places you go to in Paris. There was smoking and champagne."

"Well—that kind of thing happens in other places, and the world still goes on."

"I don't suppose, dear, you're really defending the French Sunday?"

"I've heard you often enough, Mother, grumble at the English Sunday when we've been in London."

"New York is neither Paris nor London."

"Oh, no, it's not!" her son groaned.

"You mean, I suppose, that society here is not as brilliant? You're right, I daresay; but we belong here, and people should respect our ways when they come among us. Ellen Olenska especially: she came back to get away from the kind of life people lead in brilliant societies."

Newland made no answer, and after a moment his mother ventured: "I was going to put on my bonnet and ask you to take me to see Cousin Louisa for a moment before dinner." He frowned, and she continued: "I thought you might explain to her what you've just said: that society abroad is different . . . that people are not as particular, and that Madame Olenska may not have realized how we feel about such things. It would be, you know, dear," she added with an innocent adroitness, "in Madame Olenska's interests if you did."

"Dearest Mother, I really don't see how we're concerned in the matter. The Duke took Madame Olenska to Mrs. Struthers's—in fact he brought Mrs. Struthers to call on her. I was there when they came. If the van der Luydens want to quarrel with anybody, the real culprit is under their own roof."

"Quarrel? Newland, did you ever know of Cousin Henry's quarrelling? Besides, the Duke's his guest; and a stranger too. Strangers don't discriminate: how should they? Countess Olenska is a New Yorker, and should have respected the feelings of New York."

"Well, then, if they must have a victim, you have my leave to throw Madame Olenska to them," cried her son, exasperated. "I don't see myself—or you either—offering ourselves up to expiate her crimes."

"Oh, of course you see only the Mingott side," his mother answered, in the sensitive tone that was her nearest approach to anger.

The sad butler drew back the drawing-room portières[8] and announced: "Mr. Henry van der Luyden."

Mrs. Archer dropped her needle and pushed her chair back with an agitated hand.

"Another lamp," she cried to the retreating servant, while Janey bent over to straighten her mother's cap.

Mr. van der Luyden's figure loomed on the threshold, and Newland Archer went forward to greet his cousin.

"We were just talking about you, sir," he said.

Mr. van der Luyden seemed overwhelmed by the announcement.

8. French, "door curtains."

He drew off his glove to shake hands with the ladies, and smoothed his tall hat shyly, while Janey pushed an armchair forward, and Archer continued: "And the Countess Olenska."

Mrs. Archer paled.

"Ah—a charming woman. I have just been to see her," said Mr. van der Luyden, complacency restored to his brow. He sank into the chair, laid his hat and gloves on the floor beside him in the old-fashioned way, and went on: "She has a real gift for arranging flowers. I had sent her a few carnations from Skuytercliff, and I was astonished. Instead of massing them in big bunches as our head-gardener does, she had scattered them about loosely, here and there . . . I can't say how. The Duke had told me: he said: 'Go and see how cleverly she's arranged her drawing room.' And she has. I should really like to take Louisa to see her, if the neighborhood were not so—unpleasant."

A dead silence greeted this unusual flow of words from Mr. van der Luyden. Mrs. Archer drew her embroidery out of the basket into which she had nervously tumbled it, and Newland, leaning against the chimney-place and twisting a hummingbird-feather screen in his hand, saw Janey's gaping countenance lit up by the coming of the second lamp.

"The fact is," Mr. van der Luyden continued, stroking his long gray leg with a bloodless hand weighed down by the Patroon's great signet ring, "the fact is, I dropped in to thank her for the very pretty note she wrote me about my flowers; and also—but this is between ourselves, of course—to give her a friendly warning about allowing the Duke to carry her off to parties with him. I don't know if you've heard—"

Mrs. Archer produced an indulgent smile. "Has the Duke been carrying her off to parties?"

"You know what these English grandees are. They're all alike. Louisa and I are very fond of our cousin—but it's hopeless to expect people who are accustomed to the European courts to trouble themselves about our little republican distinctions. The Duke goes where he's amused." Mr. van der Luyden paused, but no one spoke. "Yes—it seems he took her with him last night to Mrs. Lemuel Struthers's. Sillerton Jackson has just been to us with the foolish story, and Louisa was rather troubled. So I thought the shortest way was to go straight to Countess Olenska and explain—by the merest hint, you know—how we feel in New York about certain things. I felt I might, without indelicacy, because the evening she dined with us she rather suggested . . . rather let me see that she would be grateful for guidance. And she *was*."

Mr. van der Luyden looked about the room with what would have been self-satisfaction on features less purged of the vulgar passions. On his face it became a mild benevolence which Mrs. Archer's countenance dutifully reflected.

"How kind you both are, dear Henry—always! Newland will particularly appreciate what you have done because of dear May and his new relations."

She shot an admonitory glance at her son, who said: "Immensely, sir. But I was sure you'd like Madame Olenska."

Mr. van der Luyden looked at him with extreme gentleness. "I never ask to my house, my dear Newland," he said, "anyone whom I do not like. And so I have just told Sillerton Jackson." With a glance at the clock he rose and added: "But Louisa will be waiting. We are dining early, to take the Duke to the Opera."

After the portières had solemnly closed behind their visitor a silence fell upon the Archer family.

"Gracious—how romantic!" at last broke explosively from Janey. No one knew exactly what inspired her elliptic comments, and her relations had long since given up trying to interpret them.

Mrs. Archer shook her head with a sigh. "Provided it all turns out for the best," she said, in the tone of one who knows how surely it will not. "Newland, you must stay and see Sillerton Jackson when he comes this evening: I really shan't know what to say to him."

"Poor mother! But he won't come—" her son laughed, stooping to kiss away her frown.

# XI

Some two weeks later, Newland Archer, sitting in abstracted idleness in his private compartment of the office of Letterblair, Lamson and Low, attorneys at law, was summoned by the head of the firm.

Old Mr. Letterblair, the accredited legal adviser of three generations of New York gentility, throned behind his mahogany desk in evident perplexity. As he stroked his closeclipped white whiskers and ran his hand through the rumpled gray locks above his jutting brows, his disrespectful junior partner thought how much he looked like the Family Physician annoyed with a patient whose symptoms refuse to be classified.

"My dear sir—" he always addressed Archer as "sir"—"I have sent for you to go into a little matter; a matter which, for the moment, I prefer not to mention either to Mr. Skipworth or Mr. Redwood." The gentlemen he spoke of were the other senior partners of the firm; for, as was always the case with legal associations of old standing in New York, all the partners named on the office letter-head were long since dead; and Mr. Letterblair, for example, was, professionally speaking, his own grandson.

He leaned back in his chair with a furrowed brow. "For family reasons—" he continued.

Archer looked up.

"The Mingott family," said Mr. Letterblair with an explanatory smile and bow. "Mrs. Manson Mingott sent for me yesterday. Her granddaughter the Countess Olenska wishes to sue her husband for divorce. Certain papers have been placed in my hands." He paused and drummed on his desk. "In view of your prospective alliance with the family I should like to consult you—to consider the case with you—before taking any further steps."

Archer felt the blood in his temples. He had seen the Countess

Olenska only once since his visit to her, and then at the Opera, in the Mingott box. During this interval she had become a less vivid and importunate image, receding from his foreground as May Welland resumed her rightful place in it. He had not heard her divorce spoken of since Janey's first random allusion to it, and had dismissed the tale as unfounded gossip. Theoretically, the idea of divorce was almost as distasteful to him as to his mother; and he was annoyed that Mr. Letterblair (no doubt prompted by old Catherine Mingott) should be so evidently planning to draw him into the affair. After all, there were plenty of Mingott men for such jobs, and as yet he was not even a Mingott by marriage.

He waited for the senior partner to continue. Mr. Letterblair unlocked a drawer and drew out a packet. "If you will run your eye over these papers—"

Archer frowned. "I beg your pardon, sir; but just because of the prospective relationship, I should prefer your consulting Mr. Skipworth or Mr. Redwood."

Mr. Letterblair looked surprised and slightly offended. It was unusual for a junior to reject such an opening.

He bowed. "I respect your scruple, sir; but in this case I believe true delicacy requires you to do as I ask. Indeed, the suggestion is not mine but Mrs. Manson Mingott's and her son's. I have seen Lovell Mingott; and also Mr. Welland. They all named you."

Archer felt his temper rising. He had been somewhat languidly drifting with events for the last fortnight, and letting May's fair looks and radiant nature obliterate the rather importunate pressure of the Mingott claims. But this behest of old Mrs. Mingott's roused him to a sense of what the clan thought they had the right to exact from a prospective son-in-law; and he chafed at the rôle.

"Her uncles ought to deal with this," he said.

"They have. The matter has been gone into by the family. They are opposed to the Countess's idea; but she is firm, and insists on a legal opinion."

The young man was silent: he had not opened the packet in his hand.

"Does she want to marry again?"

"I believe it is suggested; but she denies it."

"Then—"

"Will you oblige me, Mr. Archer, by first looking through these papers? Afterward, when we have talked the case over, I will give you my opinion."

Archer withdrew reluctantly with the unwelcome documents. Since their last meeting he had half-unconsciously collaborated with events in ridding himself of the burden of Madame Olenska. His hour alone with her by the firelight had drawn them into a momentary intimacy on which the Duke of St. Austrey's intrusion with Mrs. Lemuel Struthers, and the Countess's joyous greeting of them, had rather providentially broken. Two days later Archer had assisted at the comedy of her reinstatement in the van der Luydens' favor, and had said to himself, with a touch of tartness, that a lady who knew how to thank all-powerful elderly gentlemen to such good purpose for a bunch of flowers did not need either the private consolations or the public championship of a young man of his small compass. To look at the matter in this light simplified his own case and surprisingly furbished up all the dim domestic virtues. He could not picture May Welland, in whatever conceivable emergency, hawking about her private difficulties and lavishing her confidences on strange men; and she had never seemed to him finer or fairer than in the week that followed. He had even yielded to her wish for a long engagement, since she had found the one disarming answer to his plea for haste.

"You know, when it comes to the point, your parents have always let you have your way ever since you were a little girl," he argued; and she had answered, with her clearest look: "Yes; and that's what makes it so hard to refuse the very last thing they'll ever ask of me as a little girl."

That was the old New York note; that was the kind of answer he would like always to be sure of his wife's making. If one had habitually breathed the New York air there were times when anything less crystalline seemed stifling.

The papers he had retired to read did not tell him much in fact; but they plunged him into an atmosphere in which he choked and spluttered. They consisted mainly of an exchange of letters between Count Olenski's solicitors and a French legal firm to whom the Countess had applied for the settlement of her financial situation.[1] There was also a short letter from the Count to his wife: after reading it, Newland Archer rose, jammed the papers back into their envelope, and reentered Mr. Letterblair's office.

"Here are the letters, sir. If you wish I'll see Madame Olenska," he said in a constrained voice.

"Thank you—thank you, Mr. Archer. Come and dine with me tonight if you're free, and we'll go into the matter afterward: in case you wish to call on our client tomorrow."

Newland Archer walked straight home again that afternoon. It was a winter evening of transparent clearness, with an innocent young moon above the housetops; and he wanted to fill his soul's lungs with the pure radiance, and not exchange a word with anyone till he and Mr. Letterblair were closeted together after dinner. It was impossible to decide otherwise than he had done: he must see Madame Olenska himself rather than let her secrets be bared to other eyes. A great wave of compassion had swept away his indifference and impatience: she stood before him as an exposed and pitiful figure, to be saved at all costs from farther wounding herself in her mad plunges against fate.

He remembered what she had told him of Mrs. Welland's request to

---

1. While divorce itself was not legal in France, the Countess' legal position is further complicated by the husband's marital rights which include his authority to determine his and his wife's domicile. By having fled the Count's home and then later by explicitly refusing her husband's request that she return to sit at his table, Madame Olenska has unquestionably deserted her husband, thereby forfeiting her rights to her dowry. These rights, minimal as they were, limited a husband's power to dispose of his wife's dowry. (See p. 198, *n.* 5.)

be spared whatever was "unpleasant" in her history, and winced at the thought that it was perhaps this attitude of mind which kept the New York air so pure. "Are we only Pharisees[2] after all?" he wondered, puzzled by the effort to reconcile his instinctive disgust at human vileness with his equally instinctive pity for human frailty.

For the first time he perceived how elementary his own principles had always been. He passed for a young man who had not been afraid of risks, and he knew that his secret love-affair with poor silly Mrs. Thorley Rushworth had not been too secret to invest him with a becoming air of adventure. But Mrs. Rushworth was "that kind of woman"; foolish, vain, clandestine by nature, and far more attracted by the secrecy and peril of the affair than by such charms and qualities as he possessed. When the fact dawned on him it nearly broke his heart, but now it seemed the redeeming feature of the case. The affair, in short, had been of the kind that most of the young men of his age had been through, and emerged from with calm consciences and an undisturbed belief in the abysmal distinction between the women one loved and respected and those one enjoyed—and pitied. In this view they were sedulously abetted by their mothers, aunts and other elderly female relatives, who all shared Mrs. Archer's belief that when "such things happened" it was undoubtedly foolish of the man, but somehow always criminal of the woman. All the elderly ladies whom Archer knew regarded any woman who loved imprudently as necessarily unscrupulous and designing, and mere simple-minded man as powerless in her clutches. The only thing to do was to persuade him, as early as possible, to marry a nice girl, and then trust to her to look after him.

In the complicated old European communities, Archer began to guess, love-problems might be less simple and less easily classified. Rich and idle and ornamental societies must produce many more such situations; and there might even be one in which a woman naturally sensitive and aloof would yet, from the force of circumstances, from sheer defenselessness and loneliness, be drawn into a tie inexcusable by conventional standards.

On reaching home he wrote a line to the Countess Olenska, asking at what hour of the next day she could receive him, and despatched it by a messenger-boy, who returned presently with a word to the effect that she was going to Skuytercliff the next morning to stay over Sunday with the van der Luydens, but that he would find her alone that evening after dinner. The note was written on a rather untidy half-sheet, without date or address, but her hand was firm and free. He was amused at the idea of her week-ending in the stately solitude of Skuytercliff, but immediately afterward felt that there, of all places, she would most feel the chill of minds rigorously averted from the "unpleasant."

He was at Mr. Letterblair's punctually at seven, glad of the pretext for excusing himself soon after dinner. He had formed his own opinion

2. Members of an historic Jewish sect known for their strict adherence to written law. The narrative of the New Testament repeatedly shows Jesus revealing the hypocrisy of the Pharisees.

from the papers entrusted to him, and did not especially want to go into the matter with his senior partner. Mr. Letterblair was a widower, and they dined alone, copiously and slowly, in a dark shabby room hung with yellowing prints of "The Death of Chatham" and "The Coronation of Napoleon."[3] On the sideboard, between fluted Sheraton knife-cases, stood a decanter of Haut Brion,[4] and another of the old Lanning port (the gift of a client), which the wastrel Tom Lanning had sold off a year or two before his mysterious and discreditable death in San Francisco—an incident less publicly humiliating to the family than the sale of the cellar.

After a velvety oyster soup came shad and cucumbers, then a young broiled turkey with corn fritters, followed by a canvasback with currant jelly and a celery mayonnaise. Mr. Letterblair, who lunched on a sandwich and tea, dined deliberately and deeply, and insisted on his guest's doing the same. Finally, when the closing rites had been accomplished, the cloth was removed, cigars were lit, and Mr. Letterblair, leaning back in his chair and pushing the port westward, said, spreading his back agreeably to the coal fire behind him: "The whole family are against a divorce. And I think rightly."

Archer instantly felt himself on the other side of the argument. "But why, sir? If there ever was a case—"

"Well—what's the use? *She's* here—he's there; the Atlantic's between them. She'll never get back a dollar more of her money than what he's voluntarily returned to her: their damned heathen marriage settlements take precious good care of that. As things go over there, Olenski's acted generously: he might have turned her out without a penny."

The young man knew this and was silent.

"I understand, though," Mr. Letterblair continued, "that she attaches no importance to the money. Therefore, as the family say, why not let well enough alone?"

Archer had gone to the house an hour earlier in full agreement with Mr. Letterblair's view; but put into words by this selfish, well-fed and supremely indifferent old man it suddenly became the Pharisaic voice of a society wholly absorbed in barricading itself against the unpleasant.

"I think that's for her to decide."

"H'm—have you considered the consequences if she decides for divorce?"

"You mean the threat in her husband's letter? What weight would that carry? It's no more than the vague charge of an angry blackguard."

---

3. "The Death of Chatham": A painting (1779) by the American artist John Singleton Copley (1738–1815) depicting the death of William Pitt, the first Earl of Chatham, who died from a stroke during a debate about the revolutionaries in America; "The Coronation of Napoleon": A painting (1805–1807) by Jacques-Louis David (1748–1825), the first court painter of the Emperor Napoleon.
4. Sheraton: Thomas Sheraton (1751–1806), furniture maker and designer, author of *Cabinet-maker and Upholsterer's Drawing Book* (1791) and *Cabinet Dictionary* (1803); Haut Brion: A highly distinguished red Bordeaux from the Château Haut-Brion (1509). Shipped to England in 1666, this famous vintage was the first red wine to retain its name after being imported. Previously, red wines were referred to simply as "claret."

"Yes; but it might make some unpleasant talk if he really defends the suit."

"Unpleasant—!" said Archer explosively.

Mr. Letterblair looked at him from under enquiring eyebrows, and the young man, aware of the uselessness of trying to explain what was in his mind, bowed acquiescently while his senior continued: "Divorce is always unpleasant."

"You agree with me?" Mr. Letterblair resumed, after a waiting silence.

"Naturally," said Archer.

"Well, then, I may count on you; the Mingotts may count on you; to use your influence against the idea?"

Archer hesitated. "I can't pledge myself till I've seen the Countess Olenska," he said at length.

"Mr. Archer, I don't understand you. Do you want to marry into a family with a scandalous divorce-suit hanging over it?"

"I don't think that has anything to do with the case."

Mr. Letterblair put down his glass of port and fixed on his young partner a cautious and apprehensive gaze.

Archer understood that he ran the risk of having his mandate withdrawn, and for some obscure reason he disliked the prospect. Now that the job had been thrust on him he did not propose to relinquish it; and, to guard against the possibility, he saw that he must reassure the unimaginative old man who was the legal conscience of the Mingotts.

"You may be sure, sir, that I shan't commit myself till I've reported to you; what I meant was that I'd rather not give an opinion till I've heard what Madame Olenska has to say."

Mr. Letterblair nodded approvingly at an excess of caution worthy of the best New York tradition, and the young man, glancing at his watch, pleaded an engagement and took leave.

## XII

Old-fashioned New York dined at seven, and the habit of after-dinner calls, though derided in Archer's set, still generally prevailed. As the young man strolled up Fifth Avenue from Waverley Place, the long thoroughfare was deserted but for a group of carriages standing before the Reggie Chiverses' (where there was a dinner for the Duke), and the occasional figure of an elderly gentleman in heavy overcoat and muffler ascending a brownstone doorstep and disappearing into a gas-lit hall. Thus, as Archer crossed Washington Square, he remarked that old Mr. du Lac was calling on his cousins the Dagonets, and turning down the corner of West Tenth Street he saw Mr. Skipworth, of his own firm, obviously bound on a visit to the Miss Lannings. A little farther up Fifth Avenue, Beaufort appeared on his doorstep, darkly projected against a blaze of light, descended to his private brougham, and rolled away to a mysterious and probably unmentionable destination.

It was not an Opera night, and no one was giving a party, so that Beaufort's outing was undoubtedly of a clandestine nature. Archer connected it in his mind with a little house beyond Lexington Avenue in which beribboned window curtains and flower-boxes had recently appeared, and before whose newly painted door the canary-colored brougham of Miss Fanny Ring was frequently seen to wait.

Beyond the small and slippery pyramid which composed Mrs. Archer's world lay the almost unmapped quarter inhabited by artists, musicians and "people who wrote." These scattered fragments of humanity had never shown any desire to be amalgamated with the social structure. In spite of odd ways they were said to be, for the most part, quite respectable; but they preferred to keep to themselves. Medora Manson, in her prosperous days, had inaugurated a "literary salon"; but it had soon died out owing to the reluctance of the literary to frequent it.

Others had made the same attempt, and there was a household of Blenkers—an intense and voluble mother, and three blowsy daughters who imitated her—where one met Edwin Booth and Patti and William Winter, and the new Shakespearian actor George Rignold, and some of the magazine editors and musical and literary critics.[1]

Mrs. Archer and her group felt a certain timidity concerning these persons. They were odd, they were uncertain, they had things one didn't know about in the background of their lives and minds. Literature and art were deeply respected in the Archer set, and Mrs. Archer was always at pains to tell her children how much more agreeable and cultivated society had been when it included such figures as Washington Irving, Fitz-Greene Halleck and the poet of "The Culprit Fay."[2] The most celebrated authors of that generation had been "gentlemen"; perhaps the unknown persons who succeeded them had gentlemanly sentiments, but their origin, their appearance, their hair, their intimacy with the stage and the Opera, made any old New York criterion inapplicable to them.

"When I was a girl," Mrs. Archer used to say, "we knew everybody between the Battery and Canal Street; and only the people one knew had carriages. It was perfectly easy to place anyone then; now one can't tell, and I prefer not to try."

Only old Catherine Mingott, with her absence of moral prejudices and almost *parvenu* indifference to the subtler distinctions, might have bridged the abyss; but she had never opened a book or looked at a picture, and cared for music only because it reminded her of gala

---

1. Edwin Booth (1833–1893), renowned American tragedian; Patti: see p. 37, *n.* 9; William Winter (1836–1917), American drama columnist whose forty years of reviews in the *New York Tribune* established him as one of the most powerful critics of his day; George Rignold (1839–1912), English actor who appeared in *Henry V* and *Macbeth* at Booth's Theater in New York in 1875.
2. Washington Irving (1783–1859), American essayist, biographer, historian, and writer of tales. Wharton refers to Irving in her autobiography as a friend of the family. Fitz-Greene Halleck (1790–1867), American poet, banker, and secretary to John Jacob Astor; Halleck's *Poetical Works* was first published in 1847 and he cowrote the *Croaker Papers*, a series of light verses satirizing New York society, with American poet Joseph Rodman Drake (1795–1820), the author of *The Culprit Fay.*

nights at the *Italiens*,[3] in the days of her triumph at the Tuileries. Possibly Beaufort, who was her match in daring, would have succeeded in bringing about a fusion; but his grand house and silk-stockinged footmen were an obstacle to informal sociability. Moreover, he was as illiterate as old Mrs. Mingott, and considered "fellows who wrote" as the mere paid purveyors of rich men's pleasures; and no one rich enough to influence his opinion had ever questioned it.

Newland Archer had been aware of these things ever since he could remember, and had accepted them as part of the structure of his universe. He knew that there were societies where painters and poets and novelists and men of science, and even great actors, were as sought after as Dukes; he had often pictured to himself what it would have been to live in the intimacy of drawing rooms dominated by the talk of Mérimée (whose *Lettres à une Inconnue* was one of his inseparables), of Thackeray, Browning or William Morris.[4] But such things were inconceivable in New York, and unsettling to think of. Archer knew most of the "fellows who wrote," the musicians and the painters: he met them at the Century, or at the little musical and theatrical clubs that were  beginning to come into existence.[5] He enjoyed them there, and was bored with them at the Blenkers', where they were mingled with fervid and dowdy women who passed them about like captured curiosities; and even after his most exciting talks with Ned Winsett he always came away with the feeling that if his world was small, so was theirs, and that the only way to enlarge either was to reach a stage of manners where they would naturally merge.

He was reminded of this by trying to picture the society in which the Countess Olenska had lived and suffered, and also—perhaps—tasted mysterious joys. He remembered with what amusement she had told him that her grandmother Mingott and the Wellands objected to her living in a "Bohemian"[6] quarter given over to "people who wrote."

3. French adjective for Italian. Here, the repertory company that inherited the Italian theatrical tradition of the Commedia dell'Arte. This troupe was the major competitor to the government authorized *Comedie-Française*. Denied the right to perform what were considered the elite plays, the *Italiens* were more entertaining because they were less controlled by the French establishment's dictates concerning high culture.

4. Mérimée (1803–1870), French novelist and man of letters known for his vivid historical novels; his *Lettres à une inconnue* (French, *Letters to an Unknown*) was a volume of letters written to Mlle. Jenny Dacquin from 1831 until the author's death and published posthumously in 1873. Thackeray: see p. 22, *n.* 2; Browning: Robert Browning (1812–1889), English poet; William Morris (1834–1896), English artist, designer, poet, socialist, and social theorist whose interior decorating firm established British standards of taste during the late nineteenth century.

5. The Century: New York City's most prominent cultural club, located at 7 West 43rd Street, was founded in 1847 by the well-known nineteenth-century poet William Cullen Bryant and the painter Asher B. Durand as a place where authors and artists could convene; the Century Club was so named because its membership was initially limited to one hundred. the little musical and theatrical clubs: These clubs suggest the emergence of the city's first theater district in the 1860s and 1870s around Union Square. Music halls featuring variety shows, minstrel shows, and melodramas beginning in the 1830s were increasingly associated with the low-brow tastes of the Bowery, while venues associated with high-brow entertainments began to appear on Broadway extending to Astor Place and the Astor Place Opera House, eventually concentrating around Union Square. Once divided primarily by the expense of seats, nineteenth-century New Yorkers were increasingly divided by class as they pursued radically different forms of entertainment.

6. A term used in the latter half of the nineteenth century to refer to immigrants from central European countries such as Poland and Romania, the word Bohemian, placed in quotation

It was not the peril but the poverty that her family disliked; but that shade escaped her, and she supposed they considered literature compromising.

She herself had no fears of it, and the books scattered about her drawing room (a part of the house in which books were usually supposed to be "out of place"), though chiefly works of fiction, had whetted Archer's interest with such new names as those of Paul Bourget, Huysmans, and the Goncourt brothers.[7] Ruminating on these things as he approached her door, he was once more conscious of the curious way in which she reversed his values, and of the need of thinking himself into conditions incredibly different from any that he knew if he were to be of use in her present difficulty.

Nastasia opened the door, smiling mysteriously. On the bench in the hall lay a sable-lined overcoat, a folded opera hat of dull silk with a gold J. B. on the lining, and a white silk muffler: there was no mistaking the fact that these costly articles were the property of Julius Beaufort.

Archer was angry: so angry that he came near scribbling a word on his card and going away; then he remembered that in writing to Madame Olenska he had been kept by excess of discretion from saying that he wished to see her privately. He had therefore no one but himself to blame if she had opened her doors to other visitors; and he entered the drawing room with the dogged determination to make Beaufort feel himself in the way, and to outstay him.

The banker stood leaning against the mantelshelf, which was draped with an old embroidery held in place by brass candelabra containing church candles of yellowish wax. He had thrust his chest out, supporting his shoulders against the mantel and resting his weight on one large patent-leather foot. As Archer entered he was smiling and looking down on his hostess, who sat on a sofa placed at right angles to the chimney. A table banked with flowers formed a screen behind it, and against the orchids and azaleas which the young man recognized as tributes from the Beaufort hot-houses, Madame Olenska sat half-reclined, her head propped on a hand and her wide sleeve leaving the arm bare to the elbow.

It was usual for ladies who received in the evening to wear what were called "simple dinner dresses": a close-fitting armor of whale-boned silk, slightly open in the neck, with lace ruffles filling in the crack, and tight sleeves with a flounce uncovering just enough wrist to show an Etruscan gold bracelet[8] or a velvet band. But Madame Olen-

---

marks, gradually came to refer to those who defied the strictures of society, defining themselves through their pursuit of the arts and less limited definitions of sexuality.

7. Paul Bourget (1852–1935), French novelist and critic, and a personal friend of Edith Wharton; Huysmans (1848–1907), French novelist of Dutch descent; Edmond (1822–1896) and Jules (1830–1870) de Goncourt, French brothers who wrote, among other things, an influential treatise *L'art du dix-huitième siècle* (French *Eighteenth-century Art*), 1873–1874.

8. close-fitting armor of whale-boned silk: Undergarments, often tightly laced, were reinforced with vertical strips of whale bone in order to achieve the exacting silhouette known as an "hour-glass" figure with its fashionable "wasp-waist" of eighteen inches. Etruscan gold bracelet: A bangle fastened with a catch from or after the fashion of those worn in the ancient civilization of Etruria, located in what is now central Italy. Jewelry made in the Etruscan style became part of a fashion revival in the early and mid-1870s.

ska, heedless of tradition, was attired in a long robe of red velvet bordered about the chin and down the front with glossy black fur. Archer remembered, on his last visit to Paris, seeing a portrait by the new painter, Carolus Duran, whose pictures were the sensation of the Salon, in which the lady wore one of these bold sheath-like robes with her chin nestling in fur.[9] There was something perverse and provocative in the notion of fur worn in the evening in a heated drawing room, and in the combination of a muffled throat and bare arms; but the effect was undeniably pleasing.

"Lord love us—three whole days at Skuytercliff!" Beaufort was saying in his loud sneering voice as Archer entered. "You'd better take all your furs, and a hot water-bottle."

"Why? Is the house so cold?" she asked holding out her left hand to Archer in a way mysteriously suggesting that she expected him to kiss it.

"No; but the missus is," said Beaufort, nodding carelessly to the young man.

"But I thought her so kind. She came herself to invite me. Granny says I must certainly go."

"Granny would, of course. And *I* say it's a shame you're going to miss the little oyster supper I'd planned for you at Delmonico's next Sunday, with Campanini and Scalchi and a lot of jolly people."[1]

She looked doubtfully from the banker to Archer.

"Ah—that does tempt me! Except the other evening at Mrs. Struthers's, I've not met a single artist since I've been here."

"What kind of artists? I know one or two painters, very good fellows, that I could bring to see you if you'd allow me," said Archer boldly.

"Painters? Are there painters in New York?" asked Beaufort, in a tone implying that there could be none since he did not buy their pictures; and Madame Olenska said to Archer, with her grave smile: "That would be charming. But I was really thinking of dramatic artists, singers, actors, musicians. My husband's house was always full of them."

She said the words "my husband" as if no sinister associations were

9. Carolus Duran (1837–1917), French artist known primarily for his society portraits. the Salon: Refers to the official art exhibition first organized by the Academy in 1667 and then followed by sporadic exhibitions in Paris that became annual events after 1737. Having work shown in this exhibition was the primary measure of social success for artists in France for nearly two centuries. Responding to complaints that innovative art was not being accepted by the official salon, Emperor Napoleon III called for an alternative exhibit, the famous Salon des Refuses staged in 1863. After the Salon became notorious for rejecting innovative art (in particular paintings by Impressionists and Post-impressionists), another Salon des Refuses appeared in 1883. In the following year, the new Société des Artistes Independants organized what became known as the Salon des Independants, a yearly exhibition open to all artists.
1. Delmonico's: A fashionable New York restaurant founded in 1831 by Lorenzo Delmonico; the New York four hundred regularly held subscription balls known as assemblies as well as coming-out parties for debutantes at the restaurant, which occupied a number of different locations throughout the latter half of the nineteenth century. Campanini: Italo (1845–1896), Italian opera singer. Scalchi: Sofia (1850–1922) Italian contralto. Her American debut was in the role of Siebel, the honorable and displaced lover of Marguerite in Gounod's *Faust*, performed at the Metropolitan Opera House on October 22, 1883; as the performer of what were called "pants roles," Scalchi sang the male parts that in an earlier era would have been assigned to Castrati.

connected with them, and in a tone that seemed almost to sigh over the lost delights of her married life. Archer looked at her perplexedly, wondering if it were lightness or dissimulation that enabled her to touch so easily on the past at the very moment when she was risking her reputation in order to break with it.

"I do think," she went on, addressing both men, "that the *imprévu*[2] adds to one's enjoyment. It's perhaps a mistake to see the same people every day."

"It's confoundedly dull, anyhow; New York is dying of dullness," Beaufort grumbled. "And when I try to liven it up for you, you go back on me. Come—think better of it! Sunday is your last chance, for Campanini leaves next week for Baltimore and Philadelphia; and I've a private room, and a Steinway,[3] and they'll sing all night for me."

"How delicious! May I think it over, and write to you tomorrow morning?"

She spoke amiably, yet with the least hint of dismissal in her voice. Beaufort evidently felt it, and being unused to dismissals, stood staring at her with an obstinate line between his eyes.

"Why not now?"

"It's too serious a question to decide at this late hour."

"Do you call it late?"

She returned his glance coolly. "Yes; because I have still to talk business with Mr. Archer for a little while."

"Ah," Beaufort snapped. There was no appeal from her tone, and with a slight shrug he recovered his composure, took her hand, which he kissed with a practiced air, and calling out from the threshold: "I say, Newland, if you can persuade the Countess to stop in town of course you're included in the supper," left the room with his heavy important step.

For a moment Archer fancied that Mr. Letterblair must have told her of his coming; but the irrelevance of her next remark made him change his mind.

"You know painters, then? You live in their *milieu*?" she asked, her eyes full of interest.

"Oh, not exactly. I don't know that the arts have a *milieu* here, any of them; they're more like a very thinly settled outskirt."

"But you care for such things?"

"Immensely. When I'm in Paris or London I never miss an exhibition. I try to keep up."

She looked down at the tip of the little satin boot that peeped from her long draperies.

"I used to care immensely too: my life was full of such things. But now I want to try not to."

"You want to try not to?"

"Yes: I want to cast off all my old life, to become just like everybody else here."

2. French, the "unforeseen," "unexpected."
3. A piano made by the American firm founded by Heinrich Steinway (1797–1871).

Archer reddened. "You'll never be like everybody else," he said.

She raised her straight eyebrows a little. "Ah, don't say that. If you knew how I hate to be different!"

Her face had grown as somber as a tragic mask. She leaned forward, clasping her knee in her thin hands, and looking away from him into remote dark distances.

"I want to get away from it all," she insisted.

He waited a moment and cleared his throat. "I know. Mr. Letterblair has told me."

"Ah?"

"That's the reason I've come. He asked me to—you see I'm in the firm."

She looked slightly surprised, and then her eyes brightened. "You mean you can manage it for me? I can talk to you instead of Mr. Letterblair? Oh, that will be so much easier!"

Her tone touched him, and his confidence grew with his self-satisfaction. He perceived that she had spoken of business to Beaufort simply to get rid of him; and to have routed Beaufort was something of a triumph.

"I am here to talk about it," he repeated.

She sat silent, her head still propped by the arm that rested on the back of the sofa. Her face looked pale and extinguished, as if dimmed by the rich red of her dress. She struck Archer, of a sudden, as a pathetic and even pitiful figure.

"Now we're coming to hard facts," he thought, conscious in himself of the same instinctive recoil that he had so often criticized in his mother and her contemporaries. How little practice he had had in dealing with unusual situations! Their very vocabulary was unfamiliar to him, and seemed to belong to fiction and the stage. In face of what was coming he felt as awkward and embarrassed as a boy.

After a pause Madame Olenska broke out with unexpected vehemence: "I want to be free; I want to wipe out all the past."

"I understand that."

Her face warmed. "Then you'll help me?"

"First—" he hesitated—"perhaps I ought to know a little more."

She seemed surprised. "You know about my husband—my life with him?"

He made a sign of assent.

"Well—then—what more is there? In this country are such things tolerated? I'm a Protestant[4]—our church does not forbid divorce in such cases."

"Certainly not."

---

4. Although Protestants did not forbid divorce, the Mingott and Welland's denomination, the Episcopal Church, held conventions in 1868 and 1877 that produced strict edicts forbidding divorced parishioners from remarrying while the former spouse was still living. In a notable exception, the right to remarry was granted to the innocent party in a marriage that had been dissolved for reasons of adultery. Countess Olenska's passionate declaration that she is "a Protestant" raises the question of whether Ellen and her husband are married according to ecclesiastical as well as what is later called "French" or state law. Much about Ellen Olenska's status as a married woman, particularly a woman whose marriage crosses legal and national borders, remains pointedly vague in *The Age of Innocence*.

They were both silent again, and Archer felt the specter of Count Olenski's letter grimacing hideously between them. The letter filled only half a page, and was just what he had described it to be in speaking of it to Mr. Letterblair: the vague charge of an angry blackguard. But how much truth was behind it? Only Count Olenski's wife could tell.

"I've looked through the papers you gave to Mr. Letterblair," he said at length.

"Well—can there be anything more abominable?"

"No."

She changed her position slightly, screening her eyes with her lifted hand.

"Of course you know," Archer continued, "that if your husband chooses to fight the case—as he threatens to—"

"Yes—?"

"He can say things—things that might be unpl—might be disagreeable to you: say them publicly, so that they would get about, and harm you even if—"

"If—?"

"I mean: no matter how unfounded they were."

She paused for a long interval; so long that, not wishing to keep his eyes on her shaded face, he had time to imprint on his mind the exact shape of her other hand, the one on her knee, and every detail of the three rings on her fourth and fifth fingers; among which, he noticed, a wedding ring did not appear.

"What harm could such accusations, even if he made them publicly, do me here?"

It was on his lips to exclaim: "My poor child—far more harm than anywhere else!" Instead, he answered, in a voice that sounded in his ears like Mr. Letterblair's: "New York society is a very small world compared with the one you've lived in. And it's ruled, in spite of appearances, by a few people with—well, rather old-fashioned ideas."

She said nothing, and he continued: "Our ideas about marriage and divorce are particularly old-fashioned. Our legislation favors divorce—our social customs don't."[5]

"Never?"

"Well—not if the woman, however injured, however irreproachable, has appearances in the least degree against her, has exposed herself by any unconventional action to—to offensive insinuations—"

She drooped her head a little lower, and he waited again, intensely hoping for a flash of indignation, or at least a brief cry of denial. None came.

A little traveling clock ticked purringly at her elbow, and a log broke in two and sent up a shower of sparks. The whole hushed and brooding room seemed to be waiting silently with Archer.

---

5. There were liberal divorce states in the 1870s, such as Wisconsin and Indiana, but New York was not among them (see p. 71, *n.* 6). In the early 1870s, defense lawyers were successfully arguing that a woman accused of adultery must be found guilty beyond a "reasonable doubt," but publicly conceding that there was any doubt about Ellen's "virtue" would have constituted a nightmare for her respectable New York family. (See pp. 374–77.)

"Yes," she murmured at length, "that's what my family tell me."

He winced a little. "It's not unnatural—"

"*Our* family," she corrected herself; and Archer colored. "For you'll be my cousin soon," she continued gently.

"I hope so."

"And you take their view?"

He stood up at this, wandered across the room, stared with void eyes at one of the pictures against the old red damask, and came back irresolutely to her side. How could he say: "Yes, if what your husband hints is true, or if you've no way of disproving it?"

"Sincerely—" she interjected, as he was about to speak.

He looked down into the fire. "Sincerely, then—what should you gain that would compensate for the possibility—the certainty—of a lot of beastly talk?"

"But my freedom—is that nothing?"

It flashed across him at that instant that the charge in the letter was true, and that she hoped to marry the partner of her guilt. How was he to tell her that, if she really cherished such a plan, the laws of the State were inexorably opposed to it?[6] The mere suspicion that the thought was in her mind made him feel harshly and impatiently toward her. "But aren't you as free as air as it is?" he returned. "Who can touch you? Mr. Letterblair tells me the financial question has been settled—"

"Oh, yes," she said indifferently.

"Well, then: is it worth while to risk what may be infinitely disagreeable and painful? Think of the newspapers—their vileness! It's all stupid and narrow and unjust—but one can't make over society."

"No," she acquiesced; and her tone was so faint and desolate that he felt a sudden remorse for his own hard thoughts.

"The individual, in such cases, is nearly always sacrificed to what is supposed to be the collective interest: people cling to any convention that keeps the family together—protects the children, if there are any," he rambled on, pouring out all the stock phrases that rose to his lips in his intense desire to cover over the ugly reality which her silence seemed to have laid bare. Since she would not or could not say the one word that would have cleared the air, his wish was not to let her feel that he was trying to probe into her secret. Better keep on the surface, in the prudent old New York way, than risk uncovering a wound he could not heal.

"It's my business, you know," he went on, "to help you to see these things as the people who are fondest of you see them. The Mingotts, the Wellands, the van der Luydens, all your friends and relations: if I didn't show you honestly how they judge such questions, it wouldn't be fair of me, would it?" He spoke insistently, almost pleading with her in his eagerness to cover up that yawning silence.

6. New York had stringent laws forbidding the remarriage of a divorced person convicted of adultery, particularly preventing the divorced person from marrying the person with whom the party in question had had illicit sexual relations. This New York ruling was established in 1854 to support monogamy in marriage, a practice that was perceived as threatened by lax divorce laws. (See contemporary article on divorce, pp. 374–77.)

She said slowly: "No; it wouldn't be fair."

The fire had crumbled down to grayness, and one of the lamps made a gurgling appeal for attention. Madame Olenska rose, wound it up and returned to the fire, but without resuming her seat.

Her remaining on her feet seemed to signify that there was nothing more for either of them to say, and Archer stood up also.

"Very well; I will do what you wish," she said abruptly. The blood rushed to his forehead; and, taken aback by the suddenness of her surrender, he caught her two hands awkwardly in his.

"I—I do want to help you," he said.

"You do help me. Goodnight, my cousin."

He bent and laid his lips on her hands, which were cold and lifeless. She drew them away, and he turned to the door, found his coat and hat under the faint gaslight of the hall, and plunged out into the winter night bursting with the belated eloquence of the inarticulate.

# XIII

It was a crowded night at Wallack's Theater.[1]

The play was *The Shaughraun*, with Dion Boucicault in the title rôle and Harry Montague and Ada Dyas as the lovers.[2] The popularity of the admirable English company was at its height, and *The Shaughraun* always packed the house. In the galleries the enthusiasm was unreserved; in the stalls and boxes, people smiled a little at the hackneyed sentiments and claptrap situations, and enjoyed the play as much as the galleries did.

There was one episode, in particular, that held the house from floor to ceiling. It was that in which Harry Montague, after a sad, almost monosyllabic scene of parting with Miss Dyas, bade her good-bye, and turned to go. The actress, who was standing near the mantelpiece and looking down into the fire, wore a gray cashmere dress without fashionable loopings or trimmings, moulded to her tall figure and flowing in long lines about her feet. Around her neck was a narrow black velvet ribbon with the ends falling down her back.

When her wooer turned from her she rested her arms against the mantel-shelf and bowed her face in her hands. On the threshold he paused to look at her; then he stole back, lifted one of the ends of velvet ribbon, kissed it, and left the room without her hearing him or changing her attitude. And on this silent parting the curtain fell.[3]

1. The Star Theatre, managed by Lester Wallack.
2. A melodramatic comedy and romantic farce by theater manager and playwright Dion Boucicault (1820–1890), that debuted in the United States at the Star Theater on November 14, 1874. Harry Montague (1844–1878), an American actor, played Captain Molyneaux, an English officer sent to Ireland to arrest a convict, Robert Folliott. The convict's fiancée, Arte, his sister Claire (played by American actress Ada Dyas, 1844–1908), and his happy-go-lucky friend, Conn the Shaughraun, help Folliott to avoid arrest by distracting Molyneaux.
3. This kissing of the ribbon does not appear in the stage directions for the play but was indeed a part of the staging of the play (see p. 247 for a photograph of this memorable renunciation scene and p. 405, *n.* 5).

It was always for the sake of that particular scene that Newland Archer went to see *The Shaughraun*. He thought the adieux of Montague and Ada Dyas as fine as anything he had ever seen Croisette and Bressant do in Paris, or Madge Robertson and Kendal in London;[4] in its reticence; its dumb sorrow, it moved him more than the most famous histrionic outpourings.

On the evening in question the little scene acquired an added poignancy by reminding him—he could not have said why—of his leave-taking from Madame Olenska after their confidential talk a week or ten days earlier.

It would have been as difficult to discover any resemblance between the two situations as between the appearance of the persons concerned. Newland Archer could not pretend to anything approaching the young English actor's romantic good looks, and Miss Dyas was a tall redhaired woman of monumental build whose pale and pleasantly ugly face was utterly unlike Ellen Olenska's vivid countenance. Nor were Archer and Madame Olenska two lovers parting in heartbroken silence; they were client and lawyer separating after a talk which had given the lawyer the worst possible impression of the client's case. Wherein, then, lay the resemblance that made the young man's heart beat with a kind of retrospective excitement? It seemed to be in Madame Olenska's mysterious faculty of suggesting tragic and moving possibilities outside the daily run of experience. She had hardly ever said a word to him to produce this impression, but it was a part of her, either a projection of her mysterious and outlandish background or of something inherently dramatic, passionate and unusual in herself. Archer had always been inclined to think that chance and circumstance played a small part in shaping people's lots compared with their innate tendency to have things happen to them. This tendency he had felt from the first in Madame Olenska. The quiet, almost passive young woman struck him as exactly the kind of person to whom things were bound to happen, no matter how much she shrank from them and went out of her way to avoid them. The exciting fact was her having lived in an atmosphere so thick with drama that her own tendency to provoke it had apparently passed unperceived. It was precisely the odd absence of surprise in her that gave him the sense of her having been plucked out of a very maelstrom: the things she took for granted gave the measure of those she had rebelled against.

Archer had left her with the conviction that Count Olenski's accusation was not unfounded. The mysterious person who figured in his wife's past as "the secretary" had probably not been unrewarded for his share in her escape. The conditions from which she had fled were

4. Croisette and Bressant: Born in 1847 in St. Petersburg, Sophie Croizette (spelled with a "z"), an early rival of Sarah Bernhardt, married a rich American banker named Stern after retiring from the Comédie Française in 1883. Jean-Baptiste Prosper Bressant (1815–1886), a French actor primarily known for giving his name to a popular haircut, a *coupe à la Bressant* (better known in America as a crew cut). Madge Robertson and Kendal: Madge (Sholto) Robertson (1848–1935), English actress, and her husband William Hunter Kendal (1843–1917), English actor and theatre manager; married in 1874 and acted together in many productions.

intolerable, past speaking of, past believing: she was young, she was frightened, she was desperate—what more natural than that she should be grateful to her rescuer? The pity was that her gratitude put her, in the law's eyes and the world's, on a par with her abominable husband. Archer had made her understand this, as he was bound to do; he had also made her understand that simple-hearted kindly New York, on whose larger charity she had apparently counted, was precisely the place where she could least hope for indulgence.

To have to make this fact plain to her—and to witness her resigned acceptance of it—had been intolerably painful to him. He felt himself drawn to her by obscure feelings of jealousy and pity, as if her dumbly-confessed error had put her at his mercy, humbling yet endearing her. He was glad it was to him she had revealed her secret, rather than to the cold scrutiny of Mr. Letterblair, or the embarrassed gaze of her family. He immediately took it upon himself to assure them both that she had given up her idea of seeking a divorce, basing her decision on the fact that she had understood the uselessness of the proceeding; and with infinite relief they had all turned their eyes from the "unpleasantness" she had spared them.

"I was sure Newland would manage it," Mrs. Welland had said proudly of her future son-in-law; and old Mrs. Mingott, who had summoned him for a confidential interview, had congratulated him on his cleverness, and added impatiently: "Silly goose! I told her myself what nonsense it was. Wanting to pass herself off as Ellen Mingott and an old maid, when she has the luck to be a married woman and a Countess!"

These incidents had made the memory of his last talk with Madame Olenska so vivid to the young man that as the curtain fell on the parting of the two actors his eyes filled with tears, and he stood up to leave the theater.

In doing so, he turned to the side of the house behind him, and saw the lady of whom he was thinking seated in a box with the Beauforts, Lawrence Lefferts and one or two other men. He had not spoken with her alone since their evening together, and had tried to avoid being with her in company; but now their eyes met, and as Mrs. Beaufort recognized him at the same time, and made her languid little gesture of invitation, it was impossible not to go into the box.

Beaufort and Lefferts made way for him, and after a few words with Mrs. Beaufort, who always preferred to look beautiful and not have to talk, Archer seated himself behind Madame Olenska. There was no one else in the box but Mr. Sillerton Jackson, who was telling Mrs. Beaufort in a confidential undertone about Mrs. Lemuel Struthers's last Sunday reception (where some people reported that there had been dancing). Under cover of this circumstantial narrative, to which Mrs. Beaufort listened with her perfect smile, and her head at just the right angle to be seen in profile from the stalls, Madame Olenska turned and spoke in a low voice.

"Do you think," she asked, glancing toward the stage, "he will send her a bunch of yellow roses tomorrow morning?"

Archer reddened, and his heart gave a leap of surprise. He had called only twice on Madame Olenska, and each time he had sent her a box of yellow roses, and each time without a card. She had never before made any allusion to the flowers, and he supposed she had never thought of him as the sender. Now her sudden recognition of the gift, and her associating it with the tender leave-taking on the stage, filled him with an agitated pleasure.

"I was thinking of that too—I was going to leave the theater in order to take the picture away with me," he said.

To his surprise her color rose, reluctantly and duskily. She looked down at the mother-of-pearl opera glass in her smoothly gloved hands, and said, after a pause: "What do you do while May is away?"

"I stick to my work," he answered, faintly annoyed by the question.

In obedience to a long-established habit, the Wellands had left the previous week for St. Augustine,[5] where, out of regard for the supposed susceptibility of Mr. Welland's bronchial tubes, they always spent the latter part of the winter. Mr. Welland was a mild and silent man, with no opinions but with many habits. With these habits none might interfere; and one of them demanded that his wife and daughter should always go with him on his annual journey to the south. To preserve an unbroken domesticity was essential to his peace of mind; he would not have known where his hair-brushes were, or how to provide stamps for his letters, if Mrs. Welland had not been there to tell him.

As all the members of the family adored each other, and as Mr. Welland was the central object of their idolatry, it never occurred to his wife and May to let him go to St. Augustine alone; and his sons, who were both in the law, and could not leave New York during the winter, always joined him for Easter and traveled back with him.

It was impossible for Archer to discuss the necessity of May's accompanying her father. The reputation of the Mingotts' family physician was largely based on the attack of pneumonia which Mr. Welland had never had; and his insistence on St. Augustine was therefore inflexible. Originally, it had been intended that May's engagement should not be announced till her return from Florida, and the fact that it had been made known sooner could not be expected to alter Mr. Welland's plans. Archer would have liked to join the travelers and have a few weeks of sunshine and boating with his betrothed; but he too was bound by custom and conventions. Little arduous as his professional duties were, he would have been convicted of frivolity by the whole Mingott clan if he had suggested asking for a holiday in midwinter; and he accepted May's departure with the resignation which he perceived would have to be one of the principal constituents of married life.

He was conscious that Madame Olenska was looking at him under

5. A resort city in northeast Florida founded in 1565 by Spanish settlers. This popular post–Civil War destination for Northern visitors was promoted by Harriet Beecher Stowe in a collection of essays entitled *Palmetto Leaves* (1873). Stowe's book emphasizing the charms of the area was so adulatory that readers accused the author of having betrayed the spirit of her earlier abolitionist writings.

lowered lids. "I have done what you wished—what you advised," she said abruptly.

"Ah—I'm glad," he returned, embarrassed by her broaching the subject at such a moment.

"I understand—that you were right," she went on a little breathlessly; "but sometimes life is difficult . . . perplexing. . . ."

"I know."

"And I wanted to tell you that I *do* feel you were right; and that I'm grateful to you," she ended, lifting her opera glass quickly to her eyes as the door of the box opened and Beaufort's resonant voice broke in on them.

Archer stood up, and left the box and the theater.

Only the day before he had received a letter from May Welland in which, with characteristic candor, she had asked him to "be kind to Ellen" in their absence. "She likes you and admires you so much—and you know, though she doesn't show it, she's still very lonely and unhappy. I don't think Granny understands her, or Uncle Lovell Mingott either; they really think she's much worldlier and fonder of society than she is. And I can quite see that New York must seem dull to her, though the family won't admit it. I think she's been used to lots of things we haven't got; wonderful music, and picture shows, and celebrities—artists and authors and all the clever people you admire. Granny can't understand her wanting anything but lots of dinners and clothes—but I can see that you're almost the only person in New York who can talk to her about what she really cares for."

His wise May—how he had loved her for that letter! But he had not meant to act on it; he was too busy, to begin with, and he did not care, as an engaged man, to play too conspicuously the part of Madame Olenska's champion. He had an idea that she knew how to take care of herself a good deal better than the ingenuous May imagined. She had Beaufort at her feet, Mr. van der Luyden hovering above her like a protecting deity, and any number of candidates (Lawrence Lefferts among them) waiting their opportunity in the middle distance. Yet he never saw her, or exchanged a word with her, without feeling that, after all, May's ingenuousness almost amounted to a gift of divination. Ellen Olenska was lonely and she was unhappy.

## XIV

As he came out into the lobby Archer ran across his friend Ned Winsett, the only one among what Janey called his "clever people" with whom he cared to probe into things a little deeper than the average level of club and chop-house banter.

He had caught sight, across the house, of Winsett's shabby round-shouldered back, and had once noticed his eyes turned toward the Beaufort box. The two men shook hands, and Winsett proposed a bock at a little German restaurant around the corner. Archer, who was not in the mood for the kind of talk they were likely to get there, declined on the plea that he had work to do at home; and Winsett said: "Oh, well, so have I for that matter, and I'll be the Industrious Apprentice too."[1]

They strolled along together, and presently Winsett said: "Look here, what I'm really after is the name of the dark lady in that swell box of yours—with the Beauforts, wasn't she? The one your friend Lefferts seems so smitten by."

Archer, he could not have said why, was slightly annoyed. What the devil did Ned Winsett want with Ellen Olenska's name? And above all, why did he couple it with Lefferts's? It was unlike Winsett to manifest such curiosity; but after all, Archer remembered, he was a journalist.

"It's not for an interview, I hope?" he laughed.

"Well—not for the press; just for myself," Winsett rejoined. "The fact is she's a neighbor of mine—queer quarter for such a beauty to settle in—and she's been awfully kind to my little boy, who fell down her area chasing his kitten, and gave himself a nasty cut. She rushed in bareheaded, carrying him in her arms, with his knee all beautifully bandaged, and was so sympathetic and beautiful that my wife was too dazzled to ask her name."

A pleasant glow dilated Archer's heart. There was nothing extraordinary in the tale: any woman would have done as much for a neighbor's child. But it was just like Ellen, he felt, to have rushed in bareheaded, carrying the boy in her arms, and to have dazzled poor Mrs. Winsett into forgetting to ask who she was.

"That is the Countess Olenska—a granddaughter of old Mrs. Mingott's."

"Whew—a Countess!" whistled Ned Winsett. "Well, I didn't know Countesses were so neighborly. Mingotts ain't."

"They would be, if you'd let them."

"Ah, well—" It was their old interminable argument as to the obstinate unwillingness of the "clever people" to frequent the fashionable, and both men knew that there was no use in prolonging it.

"I wonder," Winsett broke off, "how a Countess happens to live in our slum?"

"Because she doesn't care a hang about where she lives—or about any of our little social sign-posts," said Archer, with a secret pride in his own picture of her.

"H'm—been in bigger places, I suppose," the other commented. "Well, here's my corner."

He slouched off across Broadway, and Archer stood looking after him and musing on his last words.

Ned Winsett had those flashes of penetration; they were the most interesting thing about him, and always made Archer wonder why they

---

1. bock: A strong, dark, sweet lager made for spring. Industrious Apprentice: A character in a series of twelve related etchings called "Industry and Idleness" (1747) by William Hogarth (1697–1764). In these works designed to encourage wayward apprentices to become more industrious, the character of the Industrious Apprentice becomes the Lord Mayor of London while his idle counterpart is hung as a murderer.

had allowed him to accept failure so stolidly at an age when most men are still struggling.

Archer had known that Winsett had a wife and child, but he had never seen them. The two men always met at the Century, or at some haunt of journalists and theatrical people, such as the restaurant where Winsett had proposed to go for a bock. He had given Archer to understand that his wife was an invalid; which might be true of the poor lady, or might merely mean that she was lacking in social gifts or in evening clothes, or in both. Winsett himself had a savage abhorrence of social observances: Archer, who dressed in the evening because he thought it cleaner and more comfortable to do so, and who had never stopped to consider that cleanliness and comfort are two of the costliest items in a modest budget, regarded Winsett's attitude as part of the boring "Bohemian" pose that always made fashionable people who changed their clothes without talking about it, and were not forever harping on the number of servants one kept, seem so much simpler and less self-conscious than the others. Nevertheless, he was always stimulated by Winsett, and whenever he caught sight of the journalist's lean bearded face and melancholy eyes he would rout him out of his corner and carry him off for a long talk.

Winsett was not a journalist by choice. He was a pure man of letters, untimely born in a world that had no need of letters; but after publishing one volume of brief and exquisite literary appreciations, of which one hundred and twenty copies were sold, thirty given away, and the balance eventually destroyed by the publishers (as per contract) to make room for more marketable material, he had abandoned his real calling, and taken a sub-editorial job on a women's weekly, where fashion-plates and paper patterns alternated with New England love-stories and advertisements of temperance drinks.

On the subject of "Hearth-fires" (as the paper was called) he was inexhaustibly entertaining; but beneath his fun lurked the sterile bitterness of the still young man who has tried and given up. His conversation always made Archer take the measure of his own life, and feel how little it contained; but Winsett's, after all, contained still less, and though their common fund of intellectual interests and curiosities made their talks exhilarating, their exchange of views usually remained within the limits of a pensive dilettantism.

"The fact is, life isn't much a fit for either of us," Winsett had once said. "I'm down and out; nothing to be done about it. I've got only one ware to produce, and there's no market for it here, and won't be in my time. But you're free and you're well-off. Why don't *you* get into touch? There's only one way to do it: to go into politics."

Archer threw his head back and laughed. There one saw at a flash the unbridgeable difference between men like Winsett and the others—Archer's kind. Everyone in polite circles knew that, in America, "a gentleman couldn't go into politics." But, since he could hardly put it in that way to Winsett, he answered evasively: "Look at the career of the honest man in American politics! They don't want us."

"Who's 'they'? Why don't you all get together and be 'they' your-selves?"

Archer's laugh lingered on his lips in a slightly condescending smile. It was useless to prolong the discussion: everybody knew the melan-choly fate of the few gentlemen who had risked their clean linen in municipal or state politics in New York. The day was past when that sort of thing was possible: the country was in possession of the bosses and the emigrant,[2] and decent people had to fall back on sport or cul-ture.

"Culture! Yes—if we had it! But there are just a few little local patches, dying out here and there for lack of—well, hoeing and cross-fertilizing: the last remnants of the old European tradition that your forebears brought with them. But you're in a pitiful little minority: you've got no center, no competition, no audience. You're like the pic-tures on the walls of a deserted house: 'The Portrait of a Gentleman.'[3] You'll never amount to anything, any of you, till you roll up your sleeves and get right down into the muck. That, or emigrate . . . God! If I could emigrate. . . ."

Archer mentally shrugged his shoulders and turned the conversa-tion back to books, where Winsett, if uncertain, was always interest-ing. Emigrate! As if a gentleman could abandon his own country! One could no more do that than one could roll up one's sleeves and go down into the muck. A gentleman simply stayed at home and ab-stained. But you couldn't make a man like Winsett see that; and that was why the New York of literary clubs and exotic restaurants, though a first shake made it seem more of a kaleidoscope, turned out, in the end, to be a smaller box, with a more monotonous pattern, than the assembled atoms of Fifth Avenue.

The next morning Archer scoured the town in vain for more yellow roses. In consequence of this search he arrived late at the office, per-ceived that his doing so made no difference whatever to anyone, and was filled with sudden exasperation at the elaborate futility of his life. Why should he not be, at that moment, on the sands of St. Augustine with May Welland? No one was deceived by his pretense of profes-sional activity. In old-fashioned legal firms like that of which Mr. Letterblair was the head, and which were mainly engaged in the man-agement of large estates and "conservative" investments, there were always two or three young men, fairly well-off, and without profes-sional ambition, who, for a certain number of hours of each day, sat at

2. The type of the political boss was defined by the flamboyant William M. "Boss" Tweed, the most powerful (but by no means the only) political boss in nineteenth-century America. Tweed rose to power in New York by providing food, clothing, and shelter to the poor and immigrants ("emigrants") in exchange for their votes. Boss Tweed, through his position at Tammany Hall, controlled the judicial system, municipal and county governments, and other financially lucrative public trusts from 1866 to 1871. The degree of financial corrup-tion is suggested by the fact that the debt of New York City tripled in just three years, 1869–1871. Tweed was indicted and convicted for graft in the early 1870s.
3. A play on the title of Henry James's novel, *The Portrait of a Lady* (1881), which tells of the American Isabel Archer's emigration to England and her subsequent unhappy marriage to an expatriate American in Italy.

their desks accomplishing trivial tasks, or simply reading the newspapers. Though it was supposed to be proper for them to have an
occupation, the crude fact of money-making was still regarded as
derogatory, and the law, being a profession, was accounted a more
gentlemanly pursuit than business. But none of these young men had
much hope of really advancing in his profession, or any earnest desire
to do so; and over many of them the green mould of the perfunctory
was already perceptibly spreading.

It made Archer shiver to think that it might be spreading over him
too. He had, to be sure, other tastes and interests; he spent his vaca-
tions in European travel, cultivated the "clever people" May spoke of,
and generally tried to "keep up," as he had somewhat wistfully put it to
Madame Olenska. But once he was married, what would become of
this narrow margin of life in which his real experiences were lived? He
had seen enough of other young men who had dreamed his dream,
though perhaps less ardently, and who had gradually sunk into the
placid and luxurious routine of their elders.

From the office he sent a note by messenger to Madame Olenska,
asking if he might call that afternoon, and begging her to let him find
a reply at his club; but at the club he found nothing, nor did he receive any letter the following day. This unexpected silence mortified
him beyond reason, and though the next morning he saw a glorious
cluster of yellow roses behind a florist's window-pane, he left it there.
It was only on the third morning that he received a line by post from
the Countess Olenska. To his surprise it was dated from Skuytercliff,
whither the van der Luydens had promptly retreated after putting the
Duke on board his steamer.

"I ran away," the writer began abruptly (without the usual prelimi-
naries), "the day after I saw you at the play, and these kind friends
have taken me in. I wanted to be quiet, and think things over. You
were right in telling me how kind they were; I feel myself so safe here.
I wish that you were with us." She ended with a conventional "Yours
sincerely," and without any allusion to the date of her return.

The tone of the note surprised the young man. What was Madame
Olenska running away from, and why did she feel the need to be safe?
His first thought was of some dark menace from abroad; then he reflected that he did not know her epistolary style, and that it might run
to picturesque exaggeration. Women always exaggerated; and moreover she was not wholly at her ease in English, which she often spoke
as if she were translating from the French. "Je me suis évadée—" put
in that way, the opening sentence immediately suggested that she
might merely have wanted to escape from a boring round of engagements; which was very likely true, for he judged her to be capricious,
and easily wearied of the pleasure of the moment.

It amused him to think of the van der Luydens' having carried her
off to Skuytercliff on a second visit, and this time for an indefinite period. The doors of Skuytercliff were rarely and grudgingly opened to
visitors, and a chilly weekend was the most ever offered to the few
thus privileged. But Archer had seen, on his last visit to Paris, the de-

licious play of Labiche, *Le Voyage de M. Perrichon*,[4] and he remembered M. Perrichon's dogged and undiscouraged attachment to the
young man whom he had pulled out of the glacier. The van der Luydens had rescued Madame Olenska from a doom almost as icy; and
though there were many other reasons for being attracted to her,
Archer knew that beneath them all lay the gentle and obstinate determination to go on rescuing her.

He felt a distinct disappointment on learning that she was away; and
almost immediately remembered that, only the day before, he had refused an invitation to spend the following Sunday with the Reggie Chiverses at their house on the Hudson, a few miles below Skuytercliff.

He had had his fill long ago of the noisy friendly parties at Highbank, with coasting, ice-boating, sleighing, long tramps in the snow,
and a general flavor of mild flirting and milder practical jokes. He had
just received a box of new books from his London bookseller, and had
preferred the prospect of a quiet Sunday at home with his spoils. But
he now went into the club writing-room, wrote a hurried telegram,
and told the servant to send it immediately. He knew that Mrs. Reggie
didn't object to her visitors' suddenly changing their minds, and that
there was always a room to spare in her elastic house.

# XV

Newland Archer arrived at the Chiverses' on Friday evening, and on
Saturday went conscientiously through all the rites appertaining to a
weekend at Highbank.

In the morning he had a spin in the ice-boat with his hostess and a
few of the hardier guests; in the afternoon he "went over the farm"
with Reggie, and listened, in the elaborately appointed stables, to long
and impressive disquisitions on the horse; after tea he talked in a corner of the firelit hall with a young lady who had professed herself
broken-hearted when his engagement was announced, but was now
eager to tell him of her own matrimonial hopes; and finally, about midnight, he assisted in putting a goldfish in one visitor's bed, dressed up
a burglar in the bathroom of a nervous aunt, and saw in the small
hours by joining in a pillow-fight that ranged from the nurseries to the
basement. But on Sunday after luncheon he borrowed a cutter,[1] and
drove over to Skuytercliff.

People had always been told that the house at Skuytercliff was an
Italian villa. Those who had never been to Italy believed it; so did
some who had. The house had been built by Mr. van der Luyden in his
youth, on his return from the "grand tour,"[2] and in anticipation of his
approaching marriage with Miss Louisa Dagonet. It was a large square

4. Eugene Labiche (1815–1888), French dramatist known for his light comedies of which *Le
   Voyage de M. Perrichon* (1860) was one of his most popular.
1. A one-horse sleigh.
2. A rite of passage in which young men of the privileged classes traveled throughout Europe
   visiting well-known cultural sites to imbibe European sophistication and the spirit of the
   past.

wooden structure, with tongued and grooved walls painted pale green and white, a Corinthian portico, and fluted pilasters between the windows. From the high ground on which it stood a series of terraces bordered by balustrades and urns descended in the steel-engraving style to a small irregular lake with an asphalt edge overhung by rare weeping conifers. To the right and left, the famous weedless lawns studded with "specimen" trees[3] (each of a different variety) rolled away to long ranges of grass crested with elaborate cast-iron ornaments; and below, in a hollow, lay the four-roomed stone house which the first Patroon had built on the land granted him in 1612.

Against the uniform sheet of snow and the grayish winter sky the Italian villa loomed up rather grimly; even in summer it kept its distance, and the boldest coleus bed had never ventured nearer than thirty feet from its awful front. Now, as Archer rang the bell, the long tinkle seemed to echo through a mausoleum; and the surprise of the butler who at length responded to the call was as great as though he had been summoned from his final sleep.

Happily Archer was of the family, and therefore, irregular though his arrival was, entitled to be informed that the Countess Olenska was out, having driven to afternoon service with Mrs. van der Luyden exactly three quarters of an hour earlier.

"Mr. van der Luyden," the butler continued, "is in, sir; but my impression is that he is either finishing his nap or else reading yesterday's *Evening Post*.[4] I heard him say, sir, on his return from church this morning, that he intended to look through the *Evening Post* after luncheon; if you like, sir, I might go to the library door and listen—"

But Archer, thanking him, said that he would go and meet the ladies; and the butler, obviously relieved, closed the door on him majestically.

A groom took the cutter to the stables, and Archer struck through the park to the high-road. The village of Skuytercliff was only a mile and a half away, but he knew that Mrs. van der Luyden never walked, and that he must keep to the road to meet the carriage. Presently, however, coming down a footpath that crossed the highway, he caught sight of a slight figure in a red cloak, with a big dog running ahead. He hurried forward, and Madame Olenska stopped short with a smile of welcome.

"Ah, you've come!" she said, and drew her hand from her muff.

The red cloak made her look gay and vivid, like the Ellen Mingott of old days; and he laughed as he took her hand, and answered: "I came to see what you were running away from."

Her face clouded over, but she answered: "Ah, well—you will see, presently."

The answer puzzled him. "Why—do you mean that you've been overtaken?"

---

3. steel-engraving style: A structure consisting of steel-engraved pillars; "specimen" trees: Since trees require significant land and take long periods of time to reach maturity, the hobby of developing a tree collection known for its wide variety is one of the most elite horticultural endeavors.

4. Boston newspaper founded by Thomas Fleet (1685–1758) as the *Weekly Rehearsal*, renamed the *Evening Post* in 1735.

She shrugged her shoulders, with a little movement like Nastasia's, and rejoined in a lighter tone: "Shall we walk on? I'm so cold after the sermon. And what does it matter, now you're here to protect me?"

The blood rose to his temples and he caught a fold of her cloak. "Ellen—what is it? You must tell me."

"Oh, presently—let's run a race first: my feet are freezing to the ground," she cried; and gathering up the cloak she fled away across the snow, the dog leaping about her with challenging barks. For a moment Archer stood watching, his gaze delighted by the flash of the red meteor against the snow; then he started after her, and they met, panting and laughing, at a wicket that led into the park.

She looked up at him and smiled. "I knew you'd come!"

"That shows you wanted me to," he returned, with a disproportionate joy in their nonsense. The white glitter of the trees filled the air with its own mysterious brightness, and as they walked on over the snow the ground seemed to sing under their feet.

"Where did you come from?" Madame Olenska asked.

He told her, and added: "It was because I got your note."

After a pause she said, with a just perceptible chill in her voice: "May asked you to take care of me."

"I didn't need any asking."

"You mean—I'm so evidently helpless and defenseless? What a poor thing you must all think me! But women here seem not—seem never to feel the need: any more than the blessed in heaven."

He lowered his voice to ask: "What sort of a need?"

"Ah, don't ask me! I don't speak your language," she retorted petulantly.

The answer smote him like a blow, and he stood still in the path, looking down at her.

"What did I come for, if I don't speak yours?"

"Oh, my friend—!" She laid her hand lightly on his arm, and he pleaded earnestly: "Ellen—why won't you tell me what's happened?"

She shrugged again. "Does anything ever happen in heaven?"

He was silent, and they walked on a few yards without exchanging a word. Finally she said: "I will tell you—but where, where, where? One can't be alone for a minute in that great seminary of a house, with all the doors wide open, and always a servant bringing tea, or a log for the fire, or the newspaper! Is there nowhere in an American house where one may be by one's self? You're so shy, and yet you're so public. I always feel as if I were in the convent again—or on the stage, before a dreadfully polite audience that never applauds."

"Ah, you don't like us!" Archer exclaimed.

They were walking past the house of the old Patroon, with its squat walls and small square windows compactly grouped about a central chimney. The shutters stood wide, and through one of the newly-washed windows Archer caught the light of a fire.

"Why—the house is open!" he said.

She stood still. "No; only for today, at least. I wanted to see it, and Mr. van der Luyden had the fire lit and the windows opened, so that we might stop there on the way back from church this morning." She ran up the steps and tried the door. "It's still unlocked—what luck! Come in and we can have a quiet talk. Mrs. van der Luyden has driven over to see her old aunts at Rhinebeck and we shan't be missed at the house for another hour."

He followed her into the narrow passage. His spirits, which had dropped at her last words, rose with an irrational leap. The homely little house stood there, its panels and brasses shining in the firelight, as if magically created to receive them. A big bed of embers still gleamed in the kitchen chimney, under an iron pot hung from an ancient crane. Rush-bottomed armchairs faced each other across the tiled hearth, and rows of Delft plates[5] stood on shelves against the walls. Archer stooped over and threw a log upon the embers.

Madame Olenska, dropping her cloak, sat down in one of the chairs. Archer leaned against the chimney and looked at her.

"You're laughing now; but when you wrote me you were unhappy," he said.

"Yes." She paused. "But I can't feel unhappy when you're here."

"I shan't be here long," he rejoined, his lips stiffening with the effort to say just so much and no more.

"No; I know. But I'm improvident: I live in the moment when I'm happy."

The words stole through him like a temptation, and to close his senses to it he moved away from the hearth and stood gazing out at the black tree-boles against the snow. But it was as if she too had shifted her place, and he still saw her, between himself and the trees, drooping over the fire with her indolent smile. Archer's heart was beating insubordinately. What if it were from him that she had been running away, and if she had waited to tell him so till they were here alone together in this secret room?

"Ellen, if I'm really a help to you—if you really wanted me to come—tell me what's wrong, tell me what it is you're running away from," he insisted.

He spoke without shifting his position, without even turning to look at her: if the thing was to happen, it was to happen in this way, with the whole width of the room between them, and his eyes still fixed on the outer snow.

For a long moment she was silent; and in that moment Archer imagined her, almost heard her, stealing up behind him to throw her light arms about his neck. While he waited, soul and body throbbing with the miracle to come, his eyes mechanically received the image of a heavily-coated man with his fur collar turned up who was advancing along the path to the house. The man was Julius Beaufort.

"Ah—!" Archer cried, bursting into a laugh.

Madame Olenska had sprung up and moved to his side, slipping her hand into his; but after a glance through the window her face paled and she shrank back.

5. Blue-and-white glazed pottery manufactured in the Netherlands and England; named after a Dutch city.

"So that was it?" Archer said derisively.

"I didn't know he was here," Madame Olenska murmured. Her hand still clung to Archer's; but he drew away from her, and walking out into the passage threw open the door of the house.

"Hallo, Beaufort—this way! Madame Olenska was expecting you," he said.

During his journey back to New York the next morning, Archer re-lived with a fatiguing vividness his last moments at Skuytercliff.

Beaufort, though clearly annoyed at finding him with Madame Olenska, had, as usual, carried off the situation high-handedly. His way of ignoring people whose presence inconvenienced him actually gave them, if they were sensitive to it, a feeling of invisibility, of non-existence. Archer, as the three strolled back through the park, was aware of this odd sense of disembodiment; and humbling as it was to his vanity it gave him the ghostly advantage of observing unobserved.

Beaufort had entered the little house with his usual easy assurance; but he could not smile away the vertical line between his eyes. It was fairly clear that Madame Olenska had not known that he was coming, though her words to Archer had hinted at the possibility; at any rate, she had evidently not told him where she was going when she left New York, and her unexplained departure had exasperated him. The osten-sible reason of his appearance was the discovery, the very night before, of a "perfect little house," not in the market, which was really just the thing for her, but would be snapped up instantly if she didn't take it; and he was loud in mock-reproaches for the dance she had led him in running away just as he had found it.

"If only this new dodge for talking along a wire[6] had been a little bit nearer perfection I might have told you all this from town, and been toasting my toes before the club fire at this minute, instead of tramp-ing after you through the snow," he grumbled, disguising a real irrita-tion under the pretense of it; and at this opening Madame Olenska twisted the talk away to the fantastic possibility that they might one day actually converse with each other from street to street, or even— incredible dream!—from one town to another. This struck from all three allusions to Edgar Poe and Jules Verne,[7] and such platitudes as naturally rise to the lips of the most intelligent when they are talking against time, and dealing with a new invention in which it would seem ingenuous to believe too soon; and the question of the telephone car-ried them safely back to the big house.

Mrs. van der Luyden had not yet returned; and Archer took his leave and walked off to fetch the cutter, while Beaufort followed the Countess Olenska indoors. It was probable that, little as the van der Luydens encouraged unannounced visits, he could count on being

6. The telephone was patented by Alexander Graham Bell in 1876.
7. Edgar Allan Poe (1809–1849), American poet, short-story writer, and critic, famous for his tales of horror; Jules Verne (1828–1905), French novelist known for his narratives of adven-ture based on ideas associated with popular science, including *Journey to the Center of the Earth* (1864), *Twenty Thousand Leagues under the Sea* (1869), and *Around the World in Eighty Days* (1873).

asked to dine, and sent back to the station to catch the nine o'clock train; but more than that he would certainly not get, for it would be inconceivable to his hosts that a gentleman traveling without luggage should wish to spend the night, and distasteful to them to propose it to a person with whom they were on terms of such limited cordiality as Beaufort.

Beaufort knew all this, and must have foreseen it; and his taking the long journey for so small a reward gave the measure of his impatience. He was undeniably in pursuit of the Countess Olenska; and Beaufort had only one object in view in his pursuit of pretty women. His dull and childless home had long since palled on him; and in addition to more permanent consolations he was always in quest of amorous adventures in his own set. This was the man from whom Madame Olenska was avowedly flying: the question was whether she had fled because his importunities displeased her, or because she did not wholly trust herself to resist them; unless, indeed, all her talk of flight had been a blind, and her departure no more than a maneuver.

Archer did not really believe this. Little as he had actually seen of Madame Olenska, he was beginning to think that he could read her face, and if not her face, her voice; and both had betrayed annoyance, and even dismay, at Beaufort's sudden appearance. But, after all, if this were the case, was it not worse than if she had left New York for the express purpose of meeting him? If she had done that, she ceased to be an object of interest, she threw in her lot with the vulgarest of dissemblers: a woman engaged in a love affair with Beaufort "classed" herself irretrievably.

No, it was worse a thousand times if, judging Beaufort, and probably despising him, she was yet drawn to him by all that gave him an advantage over the other men about her: his habit of two continents and two societies, his familiar association with artists and actors and people generally in the world's eye, and his careless contempt for local prejudices. Beaufort was vulgar, he was uneducated, he was purseproud; but the circumstances of his life, and a certain native shrewdness, made him better worth talking to than many men, morally and socially his betters, whose horizon was bounded by the Battery and the Central Park. How should anyone coming from a wider world not feel the difference and be attracted by it?

Madame Olenska, in a burst of irritation, had said to Archer that he and she did not talk the same language; and the young man knew that in some respects this was true. But Beaufort understood every turn of her dialect, and spoke it fluently: his view of life, his tone, his attitude, were merely a coarser reflection of those revealed in Count Olenski's letter. This might seem to be to his disadvantage with Count Olenski's wife; but Archer was too intelligent to think that a young woman like Ellen Olenska would necessarily recoil from everything that reminded her of her past. She might believe herself wholly in revolt against it; but what had charmed her in it would still charm her, even though it were against her will.

Thus, with a painful impartiality, did the young man make out the case for Beaufort, and for Beaufort's victim. A longing to enlighten her was strong in him; and there were moments when he imagined that all she asked was to be enlightened.

That evening he unpacked his books from London. The box was full of things he had been waiting for impatiently; a new volume of Herbert Spencer, another collection of the prolific Alphonse Daudet's brilliant tales, and a novel called *Middlemarch*, as to which there had lately been interesting things said in the reviews.[8] He had declined three dinner invitations in favor of this feast; but though he turned the pages with the sensuous joy of the book-lover, he did not know what he was reading, and one book after another dropped from his hand. Suddenly, among them, he lit on a small volume of verse which he had ordered because the name had attracted him: *The House of Life*.[9] He took it up, and found himself plunged in an atmosphere unlike any he had ever breathed in books; so warm, so rich, and yet so ineffably tender, that it gave a new and haunting beauty to the most elementary of human passions. All through the night he pursued through those enchanted pages the vision of a woman who had the face of Ellen Olenska; but when he woke the next morning, and looked out at the brownstone houses across the street, and thought of his desk in Mr. Letterblair's office, and the family pew in Grace Church, his hour in the park of Skuytercliff became as far outside the pale of probability as the visions of the night.

"Mercy, how pale you look, Newland!" Janey commented over the coffee cups at breakfast; and his mother added: "Newland, dear, I've noticed lately that you've been coughing; I do hope you're not letting yourself be overworked?" For it was the conviction of both ladies that, under the iron despotism of his senior partners, the young man's life was spent in the most exhausting professional labors—and he had never thought it necessary to undeceive them.

The next two or three days dragged by heavily. The taste of the usual was like cinders in his mouth, and there were moments when he felt as if he were being buried alive under his future. He heard nothing of the Countess Olenska, or of the perfect little house, and though he met Beaufort at the club they merely nodded at each other across the whist-tables. It was not till the fourth evening that he found a note awaiting him on his return home. "Come late tomorrow: I must explain to you. Ellen." These were the only words it contained.

The young man, who was dining out, thrust the note into his pocket, smiling a little at the Frenchness of the "to you." After dinner he went to a play; and it was not until his return home, after midnight, that he drew Madame Olenska's missive out again and re-read it slowly a number of times. There were several ways of answering it,

8. Herbert Spencer: English philosopher and social scientist (1820–1903) known for his application of the scientific doctrines of evolution to ethics and philosophy. Alphonse Daudet: French novelist of the naturalist school (1840–1897); Archer is probably referring to Daudet's tales of village life in Provence. *Middlemarch: A Study of Provincial Life* (1871–72) by the English author George Eliot (1819–1880).

9. A sonnet sequence by the poet and painter Dante Gabriel Rossetti (1828–1882). These love poems published in 1870 were dedicated to the poet's wife.

and he gave considerable thought to each one during the watches of an agitated night. That on which, when morning came, he finally decided was to pitch some clothes into a portmanteau and jump on board a boat that was leaving that very afternoon for St. Augustine.

# XVI

When Archer walked down the sandy main street of St. Augustine to the house which had been pointed out to him as Mr. Welland's, and saw May Welland standing under a magnolia with the sun in her hair, he wondered why he had waited so long to come.

Here was truth, here was reality, here was the life that belonged to him; and he, who fancied himself so scornful of arbitrary restraints, had been afraid to break away from his desk because of what people might think of his stealing a holiday!

Her first exclamation was: "Newland—has anything happened?" and it occurred to him that it would have been more "feminine" if she had instantly read in his eyes why he had come. But when he answered: "Yes—I found I had to see you," her happy blushes took the chill from her surprise, and he saw how easily he would be forgiven, and how soon even Mr. Letterblair's mild disapproval would be smiled away by a tolerant family.

Early as it was, the main street was no place for any but formal greetings, and Archer longed to be alone with May, and to pour out all his tenderness and his impatience. It still lacked an hour to the late Welland breakfast-time, and instead of asking him to come in she proposed that they should walk out to an old orange-garden beyond the town. She had just been for a row on the river, and the sun that netted the little waves with gold seemed to have caught her in its meshes. Across the warm brown of her cheek her blown hair glittered like silver wire; and her eyes too looked lighter, almost pale in their youthful limpidity. As she walked beside Archer with her long swinging gait her face wore the vacant serenity of a young marble athlete.

To Archer's strained nerves the vision was as soothing as the sight of the blue sky and the lazy river. They sat down on a bench under the orange-trees and he put his arm about her and kissed her. It was like drinking at a cold spring with the sun on it; but his pressure may have been more vehement than he had intended, for the blood rose to her face and she drew back as if he had startled her.

"What is it?" he asked, smiling; and she looked at him with surprise, and answered: "Nothing."

A slight embarrassment fell on them, and her hand slipped out of his. It was the only time that he had kissed her on the lips except for their fugitive embrace in the Beaufort conservatory, and he saw that she was disturbed, and shaken out of her cool boyish composure.

"Tell me what you do all day," he said, crossing his arms under his tilted-back head, and pushing his hat forward to screen the sun-dazzle. To let her talk about familiar and simple things was the easiest way of carrying on his own independent train of thought; and he sat listening to her simple chronicle of swimming, sailing and riding, varied by an occasional dance at the primitive inn when a man-of-war came in. A few pleasant people from Philadelphia and Baltimore were picnicking at the inn, and the Selfridge Merrys had come down for three weeks because Kate Merry had had bronchitis. They were planning to lay out a lawn tennis[1] court on the sands; but no one but Kate and May had racquets, and most of the people had not even heard of the game.

All this kept her very busy, and she had not had time to do more than look at the little vellum book that Archer had sent her the week before (the *Sonnets from the Portuguese*); but she was learning by heart "How They Brought the Good News from Ghent to Aix," because it was one of the first things he had ever read to her; and it amused her to be able to tell him that Kate Merry had never even heard of a poet called Robert Browning.[2]

Presently she started up, exclaiming that they would be late for breakfast; and they hurried back to the tumbledown house with its paintless porch and unpruned hedge of plumbago and pink geraniums where the Wellands were installed for the winter. Mr. Welland's sensitive domesticity shrank from the discomforts of the slovenly southern hotel, and at immense expense, and in face of almost insuperable difficulties, Mrs. Welland was obliged, year after year, to improvise an establishment partly made up of discontented New York servants and partly drawn from the local African supply.[3]

"The doctors want my husband to feel that he is in his own home; otherwise he would be so wretched that the climate would not do him any good," she explained, winter after winter, to the sympathizing Philadelphians and Baltimoreans; and Mr. Welland, beaming across a breakfast table miraculously supplied with the most varied delicacies, was presently saying to Archer: "You see, my dear fellow, we camp—we literally camp. I tell my wife and May that I want to teach them how to rough it."

Mr. and Mrs. Welland had been as much surprised as their daughter by the young man's sudden arrival; but it had occurred to him to explain that he had felt himself on the verge of a nasty cold, and this seemed to Mr. Welland an all-sufficient reason for abandoning any duty.

"You can't be too careful, especially toward spring," he said, heap-

---

1. Derived around 1874 from what is sometimes called "real" tennis, lawn tennis is played on a surface with marked boundaries, but without the walls that characterized court tennis in America. The first national competition in lawn tennis was held in the United States in 1880; the British national competition in the sport dates from 1888.
2. A collection of poems by the English poet Elizabeth Barrett Browning (1806–1861) addressed to her husband Robert Browning. This collection, which asks the famous question "How do I love thee? Let me count the ways," stands in sharp contrast to the unromantic poem "How They Brought the Good News from Ghent to Aix."
3. The servant population of St. Augustine was largely comprised of former slaves. While Northern visitors were being welcomed, the 1870s were a time of explicit repression for recently freed African Americans. Florida in 1876 was one of the last states to use violence to end Reconstruction by revoking the briefly acquired rights of citizenship from the newly free.

ing his plate with straw-colored griddle-cakes and drowning them in golden syrup. "If I'd only been as prudent at your age May would have been dancing at the Assemblies[4] now, instead of spending her winters in a wilderness with an old invalid."

"Oh, but I love it here, Papa; you know I do. If only Newland could stay I should like it a thousand times better than New York."

"Newland must stay till he has quite thrown off his cold," said Mrs. Welland indulgently; and the young man laughed, and said he supposed there was such a thing as one's profession.

He managed, however, after an exchange of telegrams with the firm, to make his cold last a week; and it shed an ironic light on the situation to know that Mr. Letterblair's indulgence was partly due to the satisfactory way in which his brilliant young junior partner had settled the troublesome matter of the Olenski divorce. Mr. Letterblair had let Mrs. Welland know that Mr. Archer had "rendered an invaluable service" to the whole family, and that old Mrs. Manson Mingott had been particularly pleased; and one day when May had gone for a drive with her father in the only vehicle the place produced Mrs. Welland took occasion to touch on a topic which she always avoided in her daughter's presence.

"I'm afraid Ellen's ideas are not at all like ours. She was barely eighteen when Medora Manson took her back to Europe—you remember the excitement when she appeared in black at her coming-out ball? Another of Medora's fads—really this time it was almost prophetic! That must have been at least twelve years ago; and since then Ellen has never been to America. No wonder she is completely Europeanized."

"But European society is not given to divorce: Countess Olenska thought she would be conforming to American ideas[5] in asking for her freedom." It was the first time that the young man had pronounced her name since he had left Skuytercliff, and he felt the color rise to his cheek.

Mrs. Welland smiled compassionately. "That is just like the extraordinary things that foreigners invent about us. They think we dine at two o'clock and countenance divorce! That is why it seems to me so foolish to entertain them when they come to New York. They accept our hospitality, and then they go home and repeat the same stupid stories."

Archer made no comment on this, and Mrs. Welland continued: "But we do most thoroughly appreciate your persuading Ellen to give up the idea. Her grandmother and her Uncle Lovell could do nothing with her; both of them have written that her changing her mind was

---

4. Formal social gatherings, in particular fancy dress balls organized through subscriptions by members of the upper class. The most prestigious series of these annual events in the society of Old New York were called the Patriarchs' Balls (see pp. 314–15; 320–28).
5. France and England were known for their legal statutes forbidding or severely limiting divorce. In England until 1858, divorce required an act of Parliament. Of the thirty-six divorces obtained through these petitions, only five were granted to women. If divorce was an affair of state in England, it was legal for neither men nor women in the France of the 1870s. (See p. 198, *n.* 5.)

entirely due to your influence—in fact she said so to her grandmother. She has an unbounded admiration for you. Poor Ellen—she was always a wayward child. I wonder what her fate will be?"

"What we've all contrived to make it," he felt like answering. "If you'd all of you rather she should be Beaufort's mistress than some decent fellow's wife you've certainly gone the right way about it."

He wondered what Mrs. Welland would have said if he had uttered the words instead of merely thinking them. He could picture the sudden decomposure of her firm placid features, to which a lifelong mastery over trifles had given an air of factitious authority. Traces still lingered on them of a fresh beauty like her daughter's; and he asked himself if May's face was doomed to thicken into the same middle-aged image of invincible innocence.

Ah, no, he did not want May to have that kind of innocence, the innocence that seals the mind against imagination and the heart against experience!

"I verily believe," Mrs. Welland continued, "that if the horrible business had come out in the newspapers it would have been my husband's death-blow. I don't know any of the details; I only ask not to, as I told poor Ellen when she tried to talk to me about it. Having an invalid to care for, I have to keep my mind bright and happy. But Mr. Welland was terribly upset; he had a slight temperature every morning while we were waiting to hear what had been decided. It was the horror of his girl's learning that such things were possible—but of course, dear Newland, you felt that too. We all knew that you were thinking of May."

"I'm always thinking of May," the young man rejoined, rising to cut short the conversation.

He had meant to seize the opportunity of his private talk with Mrs. Welland to urge her to advance the date of his marriage. But he could think of no arguments that would move her, and with a sense of relief he saw Mr. Welland and May driving up to the door.

His only hope was to plead again with May, and on the day before his departure he walked with her to the ruinous garden of the Spanish Mission. The background lent itself to allusions to European scenes; and May, who was looking her loveliest under a wide-brimmed hat that cast a shadow of mystery over her too-clear eyes, kindled into eagerness as he spoke of Granada and the Alhambra.[6]

"We might be seeing it all this spring—even the Easter ceremonies at Seville,"[7] he urged, exaggerating his demands in the hope of a larger concession.

"Easter in Seville? And it will be Lent next week!" she laughed.

"Why shouldn't we be married in Lent?"[8] he rejoined; but she looked so shocked that he saw his mistake.

6. City in southern Spain in which the Moorish kings built their famed palace, the Alhambra, during the thirteenth and fourteenth centuries.
7. A city in southwestern Spain, capital of the province of Seville and the chief city of Andalusia, widely known for the extravagance and color of its week-long festival at Easter.
8. Marriage during Lent was considered inappropriate because this forty day period of mourning leading up to Easter was a time to focus on foregoing, rather than celebrating, earthly pleasures.

"Of course I didn't mean that, dearest; but soon after Easter—so that we could sail at the end of April. I know I could arrange it at the office."

She smiled dreamily upon the possibility; but he perceived that to dream of it sufficed her. It was like hearing him read aloud out of his poetry books the beautiful things that could not possibly happen in real life.

"Oh, do go on, Newland; I do love your descriptions."

"But why should they be only descriptions? Why shouldn't we make them real?"

"We shall, dearest, of course; next year." Her voice lingered over it.

"Don't you want them to be real sooner? Can't I persuade you to break away now?"

She bowed her head, vanishing from him under her conniving hat-brim.

"Why should we dream away another year? Look at me, dear! Don't you understand how I want you for my wife?"

For a moment she remained motionless; then she raised on him eyes of such despairing clearness that he half-released her waist from his hold. But suddenly her look changed and deepened inscrutably. "I'm not sure if I *do* understand," she said. "Is it—is it because you're not certain of continuing to care for me?"

Archer sprang up from his seat. "My God—perhaps—I don't know," he broke out angrily.

May Welland rose also; as they faced each other she seemed to grow in womanly stature and dignity. Both were silent for a moment, as if dismayed by the unforeseen trend of their words: then she said in a low voice: "If that is it—is there someone else?"

"Someone else—between you and me?" He echoed her words slowly, as though they were only half-intelligible and he wanted time to repeat the question to himself. She seemed to catch the uncertainty of his voice, for she went on in a deepening tone: "Let us talk frankly, Newland. Sometimes I've felt a difference in you; especially since our engagement has been announced."

"Dear—what madness!" he recovered himself to exclaim.

She met his protest with a faint smile. "If it is, it won't hurt us to talk about it." She paused, and added, lifting her head with one of her noble movements: "Or even if it's true: why shouldn't we speak of it? You might so easily have made a mistake."

He lowered his head, staring at the black leaf-pattern on the sunny path at their feet. "Mistakes are always easy to make; but if I had made one of the kind you suggest, is it likely that I should be imploring you to hasten our marriage?"

She looked downward too, disturbing the pattern with the point of her sunshade while she struggled for expression. "Yes," she said at length. "You might want—once for all—to settle the question: it's one way."

Her quiet lucidity startled him, but did not mislead him into thinking her insensible. Under her hat-brim he saw the pallor of her profile, and a slight tremor of the nostril above her resolutely steadied lips.

"Well—?" he questioned, sitting down on the bench, and looking up at her with a frown that he tried to make playful.

She dropped back into her seat and went on: "You mustn't think that a girl knows as little as her parents imagine. One hears and one notices—one has one's feelings and ideas. And of course, long before you told me that you cared for me, I'd known that there was someone else you were interested in; everyone was talking about it two years ago at Newport. And once I saw you sitting together on the verandah at a dance—and when she came back into the house her face was sad, and I felt sorry for her; I remembered it afterward, when we were engaged."

Her voice had sunk almost to a whisper, and she sat clasping and unclasping her hands about the handle of her sunshade. The young man laid his upon them with a gentle pressure; his heart dilated with an inexpressible relief.

"My dear child—was *that* it? If you only knew the truth!"

She raised her head quickly. "Then there is a truth I don't know?"

He kept his hand over hers. "I meant, the truth about the old story you speak of."

"But that's what I want to know, Newland—what I ought to know. I couldn't have my happiness made out of a wrong—an unfairness—to somebody else. And I want to believe that it would be the same with you. What sort of a life could we build on such foundations?"

Her face had taken on a look of such tragic courage that he felt like bowing himself down at her feet. "I've wanted to say this for a long time," she went on. "I've wanted to tell you that, when two people really love each other, I understand that there may be situations which make it right that they should—should go against public opinion. And if you feel yourself in any way pledged . . . pledged to the person we've spoken of . . . and if there is any way . . . any way in which you can fulfill your pledge . . . even by her getting a divorce . . . Newland, don't give her up because of me!"

His surprise at discovering that her fears had fastened upon an episode so remote and so completely of the past as his love affair with Mrs. Thorley Rushworth gave way to wonder at the generosity of her view. There was something superhuman in an attitude so recklessly unorthodox, and if other problems had not pressed on him he would have been lost in wonder at the prodigy of the Wellands' daughter urging him to marry his former mistress. But he was still dizzy with the glimpse of the precipice they had skirted, and full of a new awe at the mystery of young-girlhood.

For a moment he could not speak; then he said: "There is no pledge—no obligation whatever—of the kind you think. Such cases don't always—present themselves quite as simply as . . . But that's no matter . . . I love your generosity, because I feel as you do about those things . . . I feel that each case must be judged individually, on its own merits . . . irrespective of stupid conventionalities . . . I mean, each woman's right to her liberty—" He pulled himself up, startled by the turn his thoughts had taken, and went on, looking at her with a smile: "Since you understand so many things, dearest, can't you go a little farther, and understand the uselessness of our submitting to another form of the same foolish conventionalities? If there's no one and nothing between us, isn't that an argument for marrying quickly, rather than for more delay?"

She flushed with joy and lifted her face to his; as he bent to it he saw that her eyes were full of happy tears. But in another moment she seemed to have descended from her womanly eminence to helpless and timorous girlhood; and he understood that her courage and initiative were all for others, and that she had none for herself. It was evident that the effort of speaking had been much greater than her studied composure betrayed, and that at his first word of reassurance she had dropped back into the usual, as a too adventurous child takes refuge in its mother's arms.

Archer had no heart to go on pleading with her; he was too much disappointed at the vanishing of the new being who had cast that one deep look at him from her transparent eyes. May seemed to be aware of his disappointment, but without knowing how to alleviate it; and they stood up and walked silently home.

# XVII

"Your cousin the Countess called on Mother while you were away," Janey Archer announced to her brother on the evening of his return.

The young man, who was dining alone with his mother and sister, glanced up in surprise and saw Mrs. Archer's gaze demurely bent on her plate. Mrs. Archer did not regard her seclusion from the world as a reason for being forgotten by it; and Newland guessed that she was slightly annoyed that he should be surprised by Madame Olenska's visit.

"She had on a black velvet polonaise with jet buttons, and a tiny green monkey muff;[1] I never saw her so stylishly dressed," Janey continued. "She came alone, early on Sunday afternoon; luckily the fire was lit in the drawing room. She had one of those new card-cases. She said she wanted to know us because you'd been so good to her."

Newland laughed. "Madame Olenska always takes that tone about her friends. She's very happy at being among her own people again."

"Yes, so she told us," said Mrs. Archer. "I must say she seems thankful to be here."

"I hope you liked her, mother."

Mrs. Archer drew her lips together. "She certainly lays herself out to please, even when she is calling on an old lady."

"Mother doesn't think her simple," Janey interjected, her eyes screwed upon her brother's face.

1. polonaise: A dress associated with eighteenth-century Polish fashion (*polonaise* is French for "Polish") with a fitted bodice, low-cut neck, and an elaborate outerdress with a cutaway overskirt draped at the hips. monkey muff: A tubular hand-warmer made from monkey fur.

"It's just my old-fashioned feeling; dear May is my ideal," said Mrs. Archer.

"Ah," said her son, "they're not alike."

Archer had left St. Augustine charged with many messages for old Mrs. Mingott; and a day or two after his return to town he called on her.

The old lady received him with unusual warmth; she was grateful to him for persuading the Countess Olenska to give up the idea of a divorce; and when he told her that he had deserted the office without leave, and rushed down to St. Augustine simply because he wanted to see May, she gave an adipose chuckle and patted his knee with her puff-ball hand.

"Ah, ah—so you kicked over the traces,[2] did you? And I suppose Augusta and Welland pulled long faces, and behaved as if the end of the world had come? But little May—she knew better, I'll be bound?"

"I hoped she did; but after all she wouldn't agree to what I'd gone down to ask for."

"Wouldn't she indeed? And what was that?"

"I wanted to get her to promise that we should be married in April. What's the use of our wasting another year?"

Mrs. Manson Mingott screwed up her little mouth into a grimace of mimic prudery and twinkled at him through malicious lids. " 'Ask Mamma,' I suppose—the usual story. Ah, these Mingotts—all alike! Born in a rut, and you can't root 'em out of it. When I built this house you'd have thought I was moving to California! Nobody ever *had* built above Fortieth Street—no, says I, nor above the Battery either, before Christopher Columbus discovered America. No, no; not one of them wants to be different; they're as scared of it as the smallpox. Ah, my dear Mr. Archer, I thank my stars I'm nothing but a vulgar Spicer; but there's not one of my own children that takes after me but my little Ellen." She broke off, still twinkling at him, and asked, with the casual irrelevance of old age: "Now, why in the world didn't you marry my little Ellen?"

Archer laughed. "For one thing, she wasn't there to be married."

"No—to be sure; more's the pity. And now it's too late; her life is finished." She spoke with the cold-blooded complacency of the aged throwing earth into the grave of young hopes. The young man's heart grew chill, and he said hurriedly: "Can't I persuade you to use your influence with the Wellands, Mrs. Mingott? I wasn't made for long engagements."

Old Catherine beamed on him approvingly. "No; I can see that. You've got a quick eye. When you were a little boy I've no doubt you liked to be helped first." She threw back her head with a laugh that made her chins ripple like little waves. "Ah, here's my Ellen now!" she exclaimed, as the portières parted behind her.

Madame Olenska came forward with a smile. Her face looked vivid

---

2. An idiom suggesting that a work horse has escaped from the restraints that have tied it to its burden.

and happy, and she held out her hand gaily to Archer while she stooped to her grandmother's kiss.

"I was just saying to him, my dear: 'Now, why didn't you marry my little Ellen?' "

Madame Olenska looked at Archer, still smiling. "And what did he answer?"

"Oh, my darling, I leave you to find that out! He's been down to Florida to see his sweetheart."

"Yes, I know." She still looked at him. "I went to see your mother, to ask where you'd gone. I sent a note that you never answered, and I was afraid you were ill."

He muttered something about leaving unexpectedly, in a great hurry, and having intended to write to her from St. Augustine.

"And of course once you were there you never thought of me again!" She continued to beam on him with a gaiety that might have been a studied assumption of indifference.

"If she still needs me, she's determined not to let me see it," he thought, stung by her manner. He wanted to thank her for having been to see his mother, but under the ancestress's malicious eye he felt himself tongue-tied and constrained.

"Look at him—in such hot haste to get married that he took French leave[3] and rushed down to implore the silly girl on his knees! That's something like a lover—that's the way handsome Bob Spicer carried off my poor mother; and then got tired of her before I was weaned—though they only had to wait eight months for me![4] But there—you're not a Spicer, young man; luckily for you and for May. It's only my poor Ellen that has kept any of their wicked blood; the rest of them are all model Mingotts," cried the old lady scornfully.

Archer was aware that Madame Olenska, who had seated herself at her grandmother's side, was still thoughtfully scrutinizing him. The gaiety had faded from her eyes, and she said with great gentleness: "Surely, Granny, we can persuade them between us to do as he wishes."

Archer rose to go, and as his hand met Madame Olenska's he felt that she was waiting for him to make some allusion to her unanswered letter.

"When can I see you?" he asked, as she walked with him to the door of the room.

"Whenever you like; but it must be soon if you want to see the little house again. I am moving next week."

A pang shot through him at the memory of his lamplit hours in the low-studded drawing room. Few as they had been, they were thick with memories.

"Tomorrow evening?"

3. Leaving a social event without the courtesy of informing the host or hostess. This term gets its name from an actual French custom meant to free the host and hostess from the responsibility of excessive leave takings.
4. The reference to eight months suggests that either she was born eight months after her parents were married (i.e., that she was premature or conceived out of wedlock) or that she was weaned eight months after birth.

She nodded. "Tomorrow; yes; but early. I'm going out."

The next day was a Sunday, and if she were "going out" on a Sunday evening it could, of course, be only to Mrs. Lemuel Struthers's. He felt a slight movement of annoyance, not so much at her going there (for he rather liked her going where she pleased in spite of the van der Luydens), but because it was the kind of house at which she was sure to meet Beaufort, where she must have known beforehand that she would meet him—and where she was probably going for that purpose.

"Very well; tomorrow evening," he repeated, inwardly resolved that he would not go early, and that by reaching her door late he would either prevent her from going to Mrs. Struthers's, or else arrive after she had started—which, all things considered, would no doubt be the simplest solution.

It was only half-past eight, after all, when he rang the bell under the wisteria; not as late as he had intended by half an hour—but a singular restlessness had driven him to her door. He reflected, however, that Mrs. Struthers's Sunday evenings were not like a ball, and that her guests, as if to minimize their delinquency, usually went early.

The one thing he had not counted on, in entering Madame Olenska's hall, was to find hats and overcoats there. Why had she bidden him to come early if she was having people to dine? On a closer inspection of the garments besides which Nastasia was laying his own, his resentment gave way to curiosity. The overcoats were in fact the very strangest he had ever seen under a polite roof; and it took but a glance to assure himself that neither of them belonged to Julius Beaufort. One was a shaggy yellow ulster of "reach-me-down" cut,[5] the other a very old and rusty cloak with a cape—something like what the French called a "Macfarlane." This garment, which appeared to be made for a person of prodigious size, had evidently seen long and hard wear, and its greenish-black folds gave out a moist sawdusty smell suggestive of prolonged sessions against barroom walls.[6] On it lay a ragged gray scarf and an odd felt hat of semi-clerical shape.

Archer raised his eyebrows enquiringly at Nastasia, who raised hers in return with a fatalistic "Già!" as she threw open the drawing-room door.

The young man saw at once that his hostess was not in the room; then, with surprise, he discovered another lady standing by the fire. This lady, who was long, lean and loosely put together, was clad in raiment intricately looped and fringed, with plaids and stripes and bands of plain color disposed in a design to which the clue seemed missing. Her hair, which had tried to turn white and only succeeded in fading, was surmounted by a Spanish comb and black lace scarf, and silk mittens, visibly darned, covered her rheumatic hands.

Beside her, in a cloud of cigar-smoke, stood the owners of the two

5. ulster: A long overcoat made of frieze, a blend of coarse wool and shoddy, original to Ireland; reach-me-down: British equivalent of "hand-me-down" (i.e., second-hand).
6. Barrooms scattered sawdust on the floor to soak up the various forms of spillage from a raucous crowd; these shavings could be swept out and replaced at intervals with fresh sawdust.

overcoats, both in morning clothes that they had evidently not taken off since morning. In one of the two, Archer, to his surprise, recognized Ned Winsett; the other and older, who was unknown to him, and whose gigantic frame declared him to be the wearer of the "Macfarlane," had a feebly leonine head with crumpled gray hair, and moved his arms with large pawing gestures, as though he were distributing lay blessings to a kneeling multitude.

These three persons stood together on the hearth-rug, their eyes fixed on an extraordinarily large bouquet of crimson roses, with a knot of purple pansies at their base, that lay on the sofa where Madame Olenska usually sat.

"What they must have cost at this season—though of course it's the sentiment one cares about!" The lady was saying in a sighing staccato as Archer came in.

The three turned with surprise at his appearance, and the lady, advancing, held out her hand.

"Dear Mr. Archer—almost my nephew Newland!" she said. "I am the Marchioness Manson."

Archer bowed, and she continued: "My Ellen has taken me in for a few days. I came from Cuba, where I have been spending the winter with Spanish friends—such delightful distinguished people: the highest nobility of old Castile—how I wish you could know them! But I was called away by our dear great friend here, Dr. Carver. You don't know Dr. Agathon Carver, founder of the Valley of Love Community?"[7]

Dr. Carver inclined his leonine head, and the Marchioness continued: "Ah, New York—New York—how little the life of the spirit has reached it! But I see you do know Mr. Winsett."

"Oh, yes—I reached him some time ago; but not by that route," Winsett said with his dry smile.

The Marchioness shook her head reprovingly. "How do you know, Mr. Winsett? The spirit bloweth where it listeth."

"List—oh, list!" interjected Dr. Carver in a stentorian murmur.

"But do sit down, Mr. Archer. We four have been having a delightful little dinner together, and my child has gone up to dress. She expects you; she will be down in a moment. We were just admiring these marvelous flowers, which will surprise her when she reappears."

Winsett remained on his feet. "I'm afraid I must be off. Please tell Madame Olenska that we shall all feel lost when she abandons our street. This house has been an oasis."

"Ah, but she won't abandon you. Poetry and art are the breath of life to her. It is poetry you write, Mr. Winsett?"

---

7. A society (here a fictional creation) that recalls the numerous nineteenth-century utopian communities organized around ideals of Christian socialism. New York state was home to several of these utopian experiments, most notably the Oneida Community, begun in 1848 and reconfigured in 1872 when former members became shareholders in a capitalist enterprise. With their belief in "complex marriage" (that all of the men and women of their community were husband and wife), members of the Oneida Community were part of a spiritually driven social experiment that considered traditional marriage and private property as impediments to spiritual development and earthly perfection.

"Well, no; but I sometimes read it," said Winsett, including the group in a general nod and slipping out of the room.

"A caustic spirit—*un peu sauvage.*[8] But so witty; Dr. Carver, you *do* think him witty?"

"I never think of wit," said Dr. Carver severely.

"Ah—ah—you never think of wit! How merciless he is to us weak mortals, Mr. Archer! But he lives only in the life of the spirit; and tonight he is mentally preparing the lecture he is to deliver presently at Mrs. Blenker's. Dr. Carver, would there be time, before you start for the Blenkers' to explain to Mr. Archer your illuminating discovery of the Direct Contact?[9] But no; I see it is nearly nine o'clock, and we have no right to detain you while so many are waiting for your message."

Dr. Carver looked slightly disappointed at this conclusion, but, having compared his ponderous gold timepiece with Madame Olenska's little traveling-clock, he reluctantly gathered up his mighty limbs for departure.

"I shall see you later, dear friend?" he suggested to the Marchioness, who replied with a smile: "As soon as Ellen's carriage comes I will join you; I do hope the lecture won't have begun."

Dr. Carver looked thoughtfully at Archer. "Perhaps, if this young gentleman is interested in my experiences, Mrs. Blenker might allow you to bring him with you?"

"Oh, dear friend, if it were possible—I am sure she would be too happy. But I fear my Ellen counts on Mr. Archer herself."

"That," said Dr. Carver, "is unfortunate—but here is my card." He handed it to Archer, who read on it, in Gothic characters:

𝔄𝔤𝔞𝔱𝔥𝔬𝔫 𝔠𝔞𝔯𝔳𝔢𝔯
𝔗𝔥𝔢 𝔙𝔞𝔩𝔩𝔢𝔶 𝔬𝔣 𝔩𝔬𝔳𝔢
𝔎𝔦𝔱𝔱𝔞𝔰𝔮𝔲𝔞𝔱𝔱𝔞𝔪𝔶, 𝔑. 𝔜.

Dr. Carver bowed himself out, and Mrs. Manson, with a sigh that might have been either of regret or relief, again waved Archer to a seat.

"Ellen will be down in a moment; and before she comes, I am so glad of this quiet moment with you."

Archer murmured his pleasure at their meeting, and the Marchioness continued, in her low sighing accents: "I know everything, dear Mr. Archer—my child has told me all you have done for her. Your wise advice: your courageous firmness—thank heaven it was not too late!"

The young man listened with considerable embarrassment. Was there anyone, he wondered, to whom Madame Olenska had not proclaimed his intervention in her private affairs?

---

8. French, literally, "a little savage," here an unsocialized person.
9. The belief in the ability to communicate with the dead which was essential to spreading the spiritualist movement from mid-nineteenth-century England to America. Some famed mediums of the period claimed to hear voices. The dead either spoke to them directly through sounds ("rappings") or by guiding their hands in acts of "automatic writing" or by contacting them through the assistance of long-dead spirit guides.

"Madame Olenska exaggerates; I simply gave her a legal opinion, as she asked me to."

"Ah, but in doing it—in doing it you were the unconscious instrument of—of—what word have we moderns for Providence, Mr. Archer?" cried the lady, tilting her head on one side and drooping her lids mysteriously. "Little did you know that at that very moment I was being appealed to: being approached, in fact—from the other side of the Atlantic!"

She glanced over her shoulder, as though fearful of being overheard, and then, drawing her chair nearer, and raising a tiny ivory fan to her lips, breathed behind it: "By the Count himself—my poor, mad, foolish Olenski; who asks only to take her back on her own terms."

"Good God!" Archer exclaimed, springing up.

"You are horrified? Yes, of course; I understand. I don't defend poor Stanislas,[1] though he has always called me his best friend. He does not defend himself—he casts himself at her feet: in my person." She tapped her emaciated bosom. "I have his letter here."

"A letter?—Has Madame Olenska seen it?" Archer stammered, his brain whirling with the shock of the announcement.

The Marchioness Manson shook her head softly. "Time—time; I must have time. I know my Ellen—haughty, intractable; shall I say, just a shade unforgiving?"

"But, good heavens, to forgive is one thing; to go back into that hell—"

"Ah, yes," the Marchioness acquiesced. "So she describes it—my sensitive child! But on the material side, Mr. Archer, if one may stoop to consider such things; do you know what she is giving up? Those roses there on the sofa—acres like them, under glass and in the open, in his matchless terraced gardens at Nice! Jewels—historic pearls: the Sobieski[2] emeralds—sables—but she cares nothing for all these! Art and beauty, those she does care for, she lives for, as I always have; and those also surrounded her. Pictures, priceless furniture, music, brilliant conversation—ah, that, my dear young man, if you'll excuse me, is what you've no conception of here! And she had it all; and the homage of the greatest. She tells me she is not thought handsome in New York—good heavens! Her portrait has been painted nine times; the greatest artists in Europe have begged for the privilege. Are these things nothing? And the remorse of an adoring husband?"

As the Marchioness Manson rose to her climax her face assumed an expression of ecstatic retrospection which would have moved Archer's mirth had he not been numb with amazement.

He would have laughed if anyone had foretold to him that his first sight of poor Medora Manson would have been in the guise of a messenger of Satan; but he was in no mood for laughing now, and she

1. Named for St. Stanislaus (1031–1079), the religious figure most associated with Polish nationalism, the Saint who supported the Catholic Church and defied the King. The Count's Christian name suggests that he, like most titled Poles (and unlike his explicitly "Protestant" wife), is Catholic and limited by his religion's well-known opposition to divorce.
2. Famed jewels associated with John III (1624–1696), King of Poland 1674–1696.

seemed to him to come straight out of the hell from which Ellen Olenska had just escaped.

"She knows nothing yet—of all this?" he asked abruptly.

Mrs. Manson laid a purple finger on her lips. "Nothing directly—
but does she suspect? Who can tell? The truth is, Mr. Archer, I have
been waiting to see you. From the moment I heard of the firm stand
you had taken, and of your influence over her, I hoped it might be possible to count on your support—to convince you. . . ."

"That she ought to go back? I would rather see her dead!" cried the
young man violently.

"Ah," the Marchioness murmured, without visible resentment. For a
while she sat in her armchair, opening and shutting the absurd ivory
fan between her mittened fingers; but suddenly she lifted her head
and listened.

"Here she comes," she said in a rapid whisper; and then, pointing to
the bouquet[3] on the sofa: "Am I to understand that you prefer *that*,
Mr. Archer? After all, marriage is marriage . . . and my niece is still a
wife. . . ."

# XVIII

What are you two plotting together, Aunt Medora?" Madame Olenska cried as she came into the room.

She was dressed as if for a ball. Everything about her shimmered
and glimmered softly, as if her dress had been woven out of candle
beams; and she carried her head high, like a pretty woman challenging
a roomful of rivals.

"We were saying, my dear, that here was something beautiful to surprise you with," Mrs. Manson rejoined, rising to her feet and pointing
archly to the flowers.

Madame Olenska stopped short and looked at the bouquet. Her
color did not change, but a sort of white radiance of anger ran over
her like summer lightning. "Ah," she exclaimed, in a shrill voice that
the young man had never heard, "who is ridiculous enough to send me
a bouquet? Why a bouquet? And why tonight of all nights? I am not
going to a ball; I am not a girl engaged to be married. But some people
are always ridiculous."

She turned back to the door, opened it, and called out: "Nastasia!"

The ubiquitous handmaiden promptly appeared, and Archer heard
Madame Olenska say, in an Italian that she seemed to pronounce with
intentional deliberateness in order that he might follow it: "Here—
throw this into the dustbin!" and then, as Nastasia stared protestingly:
"But no—it's not the fault of the poor flowers. Tell the boy to carry
them to the house three doors away, the house of Mr. Winsett, the
dark gentleman who dined here. His wife is ill—they may give her

---

3. While bouquets were associated with the rituals of courtship, this bouquet would have been
   considered scandalous even as an offering from an engaged man to his fiancée. (See
   pp. 342–43 for a reading of this floral message.)

pleasure. . . . The boy is out, you say? Then, my dear one, run yourself; here, put my cloak over you and fly. I want the thing out of the house immediately! And, as you live, don't say they come from me!"

She flung her velvet opera cloak over the maid's shoulders and turned back into the drawing room, shutting the door sharply. Her bosom was rising high under its lace, and for a moment Archer thought she was about to cry; but she burst into a laugh instead, and looking from the Marchioness to Archer, asked abruptly: "And you two—have you made friends!"

"It's for Mr. Archer to say, darling; he has waited patiently while you were dressing."

"Yes—I gave you time enough: my hair wouldn't go," Madame Olenska said, raising her hand to the heaped-up curls of her *chignon*.[1] "But that reminds me: I see Dr. Carver is gone, and you'll be late at the Blenkers'. Mr. Archer, will you put my aunt in the carriage?"

She followed the Marchioness into the hall, saw her fitted into a miscellaneous heap of overshoes, shawls and tippets,[2] and called from the doorstep: "Mind, the carriage is to be back for me at ten!" Then she returned to the drawing room, where Archer, on re-entering it, found her standing by the mantelpiece, examining herself in the mirror. It was not usual, in New York society, for a lady to address her parlor-maid as "my dear one," and send her out on an errand wrapped in her own opera cloak; and Archer, through all his deeper feelings, tasted the pleasurable excitement of being in a world where action followed on emotion with such Olympian speed.

Madame Olenska did not move when he came up behind her, and for a second their eyes met in the mirror; then she turned, threw herself into her sofa-corner, and sighed out: "There's time for a cigarette."

He handed her the box and lit a spill for her; and as the flame flashed up into her face she glanced at him with laughing eyes and said: "What do you think of me in a temper?"

Archer paused a moment; then he answered with sudden resolution: "It makes me understand what your aunt has been saying about you."

"I knew she'd been talking about me. Well?"

"She said you were used to all kinds of things—splendors and amusements and excitements—that we could never hope to give you here."

Madame Olenska smiled faintly into the circle of smoke about her lips.

"Medora is incorrigibly romantic. It has made up to her for so many things!"

Archer hesitated again, and again took his risk. "Is your aunt's romanticism always consistent with accuracy?"

"You mean: does she speak the truth?" Her niece considered. "Well, I'll tell you: in almost everything she says, there's something true and

---

1. Hair bun.
2. Lengthy black scarves worn in their singular form over the robe of an Episcopal clergyman, these tippets have a debased clerical association as part of a collation of random winter garments worn by people other than ordained ministers.

something untrue. But why do you ask? What has she been telling you?"

He looked away into the fire, and then back at her shining presence. His heart tightened with the thought that this was their last evening by that fireside, and that in a moment the carriage would come to carry her away.

"She says—she pretends that Count Olenski has asked her to persuade you to go back to him."

Madame Olenska made no answer. She sat motionless, holding her cigarette in her half-lifted hand. The expression of her face had not changed; and Archer remembered that he had before noticed her apparent incapacity for surprise.

"You knew, then?" he broke out.

She was silent for so long that the ash dropped from her cigarette. She brushed it to the floor. "She has hinted about a letter: poor darling! Medora's hints—"

"Is it at your husband's request that she has arrived here suddenly?"

Madame Olenska seemed to consider this question also. "There again: one can't tell. She told me she had had a 'spiritual summons,' whatever that is, from Dr. Carver. I'm afraid she's going to marry Dr. Carver . . . poor Medora, there's always someone she wants to marry. But perhaps the people in Cuba just got tired of her! I think she was with them as a sort of paid companion. Really, I don't know why she came."

"But you do believe she has a letter from your husband?"

Again Madame Olenska brooded silently; then she said: "After all, it was to be expected."

The young man rose and went to lean against the fireplace. A sudden restlessness possessed him, and he was tongue-tied by the sense that their minutes were numbered, and that at any moment he might hear the wheels of the returning carriage.

"You know that your aunt believes you will go back?"

Madame Olenska raised her head quickly. A deep blush rose to her face and spread over her neck and shoulders. She blushed seldom and painfully, as if it hurt her like a burn.

"Many cruel things have been believed of me," she said.

"Oh, Ellen—forgive me; I'm a fool and a brute!"

She smiled a little. "You are horribly nervous; you have your own troubles. I know you think the Wellands are unreasonable about your marriage, and of course I agree with you. In Europe people don't understand our long American engagements; I suppose they are not as calm as we are." She pronounced the "we" with a faint emphasis that gave it an ironic sound.

Archer felt the irony but did not dare to take it up. After all, she had perhaps purposely deflected the conversation from her own affairs, and after the pain his last words had evidently caused her he felt that all he could do was to follow her lead. But the sense of the waning hour made him desperate: he could not bear the thought that a barrier of words should drop between them again.

"Yes," he said abruptly; "I went south to ask May to marry me after Easter. There's no reason why we shouldn't be married then."

"And May adores you—and yet you couldn't convince her? I thought her too intelligent to be the slave of such absurd superstitions."

"She *is* too intelligent—she's not their slave."

Madame Olenska looked at him. "Well, then—I don't understand."

Archer reddened, and hurried on with a rush. "We had a frank talk—almost the first. She thinks my impatience is a bad sign."

"Merciful heavens—a bad sign?"

"She thinks it means that I can't trust myself to go on caring for her. She thinks, in short, I want to marry her at once to get away from someone that I—care for more."

Madame Olenska examined this curiously. "But if she thinks that— why isn't she in a hurry too?"

"Because she's not like that: she's so much nobler. She insists all the more on the long engagement, to give me time—"

"Time to give her up for the other woman?"

"If I want to."

Madame Olenska leaned toward the fire and gazed into it with fixed eyes. Down the quiet street Archer heard the approaching trot of her horses.

"That *is* noble," she said, with a slight break in her voice.

"Yes. But it's ridiculous."

"Ridiculous? Because you don't care for anyone else?"

"Because I don't mean to marry anyone else."

"Ah." There was another long interval. At length she looked up at him and asked: "This other woman—does she love you?"

"Oh, there's no other woman; I mean, the person that May was thinking of is—was never—"

"Then, why, after all, are you in such haste?"

"There's your carriage," said Archer.

She half-rose and looked about her with absent eyes. Her fan and gloves lay on the sofa beside her and she picked them up mechanically.

"Yes; I suppose I must be going."

"You're going to Mrs. Struthers's?"

"Yes." She smiled and added; "I must go where I am invited, or I should be too lonely. Why not come with me?"

Archer felt that at any cost he must keep her beside him, must make her give him the rest of her evening. Ignoring her question, he continued to lean against the chimneypiece, his eyes fixed on the hand in which she held her gloves and fan, as if watching to see if he had the power to make her drop them.

"May guessed the truth," he said. "There is another woman—but not the one she thinks."

Ellen Olenska made no answer, and did not move. After a moment he sat down beside her, and, taking her hand, softly unclasped it, so that the gloves and fan fell on the sofa between them.

She started up, and freeing herself from him moved away to the other side of the hearth. "Ah, don't make love to me! Too many people have done that," she said, frowning.

Archer, changing color, stood up also: it was the bitterest rebuke she could have given him. "I have never made love to you," he said, "and I never shall. But you are the woman I would have married if it had been possible for either of us."

"Possible for either of us?" She looked at him with unfeigned astonishment. "And you say that—when it's you who've made it impossible?"

He stared at her, groping in a blackness through which a single arrow of light tore its blinding way.

"*I've* made it impossible—?"

"You, you, *you!*" she cried, her lip trembling like a child's on the verge of tears. "Isn't it you who made me give up divorcing—give it up because you showed me how selfish and wicked it was, how one must sacrifice one's self to preserve the dignity of marriage . . . and to spare one's family the publicity, the scandal? And because my family was going to be your family—for May's sake and for yours—I did what you told me, what you proved to me that I ought to do. Ah," she broke out with a sudden laugh, "I've made no secret of having done it for you!"

She sank down on the sofa again, crouching among the festive ripples of her dress like a stricken masquerader; and the young man stood by the fireplace and continued to gaze at her without moving.

"Good God," he groaned. "When I thought—"

"You thought?"

"Ah, don't ask me what I thought!"

Still looking at her, he saw the same burning flush creep up her neck to her face. She sat upright, facing him with a rigid dignity.

"I do ask you."

"Well, then: there were things in that letter you asked me to read—"

"My husband's letter?"

"Yes."

"I had nothing to fear from that letter: absolutely nothing! All I feared was to bring notoriety, scandal, on the family—on you and May."

"Good God," he groaned again, bowing his face in his hands.

The silence that followed lay on them with the weight of things final and irrevocable. It seemed to Archer to be crushing him down like his own grave-stone; in all the wide future he saw nothing that would ever lift that load from his heart. He did not move from his place, or raise his head from his hands; his hidden eyeballs went on staring into utter darkness.

"At least I loved you—" he brought out.

On the other side of the hearth, from the sofa-corner where he supposed that she still crouched, he heard a faint stifled crying like a child's. He started up and came to her side.

"Ellen! What madness! Why are you crying? Nothing's done that can't be undone. I'm still free, and you're going to be." He had her in his arms, her face like a wet flower at his lips, and all their vain terrors shrivelling up like ghosts at sunrise. The one thing that astonished him now was that he should have stood for five minutes arguing with her across the width of the room, when just touching her made everything so simple.

She gave him back all his kiss, but after a moment he felt her stiffening in his arms, and she put him aside and stood up.

"Ah, my poor Newland—I suppose this had to be. But it doesn't in the least alter things," she said, looking down at him in her turn from the hearth.

"It alters the whole of life for me."

"No, no—it mustn't, it can't. You're engaged to May Welland; and I'm married."

He stood up too, flushed and resolute. "Nonsense! It's too late for that sort of thing. We've no right to lie to other people or to ourselves. We won't talk of your marriage; but do you see me marrying May after this?"

She stood silent, resting her thin elbows on the mantelpiece, her profile reflected in the glass behind her. One of the locks of her *chignon* had become loosened and hung on her neck; she looked haggard and almost old.

"I don't see you," she said at length, "putting that question to May. Do you?"

He gave a reckless shrug. "It's too late to do anything else."

"You say that because it's the easiest thing to say at this moment—not because it's true. In reality it's too late to do anything but what we'd both decided on."

"Ah, I don't understand you!"

She forced a pitiful smile that pinched her face instead of smoothing it. "You don't understand because you haven't yet guessed how you've changed things for me: oh, from the first—long before I knew all you'd done."

"All I'd done?"

"Yes. I was perfectly unconscious at first that people here were shy of me—that they thought I was a dreadful sort of person. It seems they had even refused to meet me at dinner. I found that out afterward; and how you'd made your mother go with you to the van der Luydens'; and how you'd insisted on announcing your engagement at the Beaufort ball, so that I might have two families to stand by me instead of one—"

At that he broke into a laugh.

"Just imagine," she said, "how stupid and unobservant I was! I knew nothing of all this till Granny blurted it out one day. New York simply meant peace and freedom to me: it was coming home. And I was so happy at being among my own people that everyone I met seemed kind and good, and glad to see me. But from the very beginning," she continued, "I felt there was no one as kind as you; no one who gave me reasons that I understood for doing what at first seemed so hard and—unnecessary. The very good people didn't convince me; I felt they'd never been tempted. But you knew; you understood; you had felt the world outside tugging at one with all its golden hands—and yet you hated the things it asks of one; you hated happiness bought by disloyalty and cruelty and indifference. That was what I'd never known before—and it's better than anything I've known."

She spoke in a low even voice, without tears or visible agitation; and each word, as it dropped from her, fell into his breast like burning lead. He sat bowed over, his head between his hands, staring at the hearth-rug, and at the tip of the satin shoe that showed under her dress. Suddenly he knelt down and kissed the shoe.

She bent over him, laying her hands on his shoulders, and looking at him with eyes so deep that he remained motionless under her gaze.

"Ah, don't let us undo what you've done!" she cried. "I can't go back now to that other way of thinking. I can't love you unless I give you up."

His arms were yearning up to her; but she drew away, and they remained facing each other, divided by the distance that her words had created. Then, abruptly, his anger overflowed.

"And Beaufort? Is he to replace me?"

As the words sprang out he was prepared for an answering flare of anger; and he would have welcomed it as fuel for his own. But Madame Olenska only grew a shade paler, and stood with her arms hanging down before her, and her head slightly bent, as her way was when she pondered a question.

"He's waiting for you now at Mrs. Struthers's; why don't you go to him?" Archer sneered.

She turned to ring the bell. "I shall not go out this evening; tell the carriage to go and fetch the Signora Marchesa," she said when the maid came.

After the door had closed again Archer continued to look at her with bitter eyes. "Why this sacrifice? Since you tell me that you're lonely I've no right to keep you from your friends."

She smiled a little under her wet lashes. "I shan't be lonely now. I *was* lonely; I *was* afraid. But the emptiness and the darkness are gone; when I turn back into myself now I'm like a child going at night into a room where there's always a light."

Her tone and her look still enveloped her in a soft inaccessibility, and Archer groaned out again: "I don't understand you!"

"Yet you understand May!"

He reddened under the retort, but kept his eyes on her. "May is ready to give me up."

"What! Three days after you've entreated her on your knees to hasten your marriage?"

"She's refused; that gives me the right—"

"Ah, you've taught me what an ugly word that is," she said.

He turned away with a sense of utter weariness. He felt as though he had been struggling for hours up the face of a steep precipice, and now, just as he had fought his way to the top, his hold had given way and he was pitching down headlong into darkness.

If he could have got her in his arms again he might have swept away her arguments; but she still held him at a distance by something inscrutably aloof in her look and attitude, and by his own awed sense of her sincerity. At length he began to plead again.

"If we do this now it will be worse afterward—worse for everyone—"

"No—no—no!" she almost screamed, as if he frightened her.

At that moment the bell sent a long tinkle through the house. They had heard no carriage stopping at the door, and they stood motionless, looking at each other with startled eyes.

Outside, Nastasia's step crossed the hall, the outer door opened, and a moment later she came in carrying a telegram which she handed to the Countess Olenska.

"The lady was very happy at the flowers," Nastasia said, smoothing her apron. "She thought it was her *signor marito*[3] who had sent them, and she cried a little and said it was a folly."

Her mistress smiled and took the yellow envelope. She tore it open and carried it to the lamp; then, when the door had closed again, she handed the telegram to Archer.

It was dated from St. Augustine, and addressed to the Countess Olenska. In it he read: "Granny's telegram successful. Papa and Mamma agree marriage after Easter. Am telegraphing Newland. Am too happy for words and love you dearly. Your grateful May."

Half an hour later, when Archer unlocked his own frontdoor, he found a similar envelope on the hall-table on top of his pile of notes and letters. The message inside the envelope was also from May Welland, and ran as follows: "Parents consent wedding Tuesday after Easter at twelve Grace Church[4] eight bridesmaids please see Rector so happy love May."

Archer crumpled up the yellow sheet as if the gesture could annihilate the news it contained. Then he pulled out a small pocket-diary and turned over the pages with trembling fingers; but he did not find what he wanted, and cramming the telegram into his pocket he mounted the stairs.

A light was shining through the door of the little hall room which served Janey as a dressing room and boudoir, and her brother rapped impatiently on the panel. The door opened, and his sister stood before him in her immemorial purple flannel dressing-gown, with her hair "on pins." Her face looked pale and apprehensive.

"Newland! I hope there's no bad news in that telegram? I waited on purpose, in case—" (No item of his correspondence was safe from Janey.)

He took no notice of her question. "Look here—what day is Easter this year?"

She looked shocked at such unchristian ignorance. "Easter? Newland! Why, of course, the first week in April. Why?"

3. Italian term used to refer to someone else's husband.
4. Gothic revival church, built 1843–1846, located at Broadway and 10th St., and supported by an elite congregation.

"The first week?" He turned again to the pages of his diary, calculating rapidly under his breath. "The first week, did you say?" He threw back his head with a long laugh.

"For mercy's sake what's the matter?"

"Nothing's the matter, except that I'm going to be married in a month."

Janey fell upon his neck and pressed him to her purple flannel breast. "Oh Newland, how wonderful! I'm so glad! But, dearest, why do you keep on laughing? Do hush, or you'll wake Mamma."

# BOOK TWO

# XIX

The day was fresh, with a lively spring wind full of dust. All the old ladies in both families had got out their faded sables and yellowing ermines, and the smell of camphor from the front pews almost smothered the faint spring scent of the lilies banking the altar.

Newland Archer, at a signal from the sexton, had come out of the vestry and placed himself with his best man on the chancel step of Grace Church.

The signal meant that the brougham bearing the bride and her father was in sight; but there was sure to be a considerable interval of adjustment and consultation in the lobby, where the bridesmaids were already hovering like a cluster of Easter blossoms. During this unavoidable lapse of time the bridegroom, in proof of his eagerness, was expected to expose himself alone to the gaze of the assembled company; and Archer had gone through this formality as resignedly as through all the others which made of a nineteenth-century New York wedding a rite that seemed to belong to the dawn of history. Everything was equally easy—or equally painful, as one chose to put it—in the path he was committed to tread, and he had obeyed the flurried injunctions of his best man as piously as other bridegrooms had obeyed his own, in the days when he had guided them through the same labyrinth.

So far he was reasonably sure of having fulfilled all his obligations. The bridesmaids' eight bouquets of white lilac and lilies-of-the-valley had been sent in due time, as well as the gold and sapphire sleevelinks of the eight ushers and the best man's cat's-eye scarf-pin;[1] Archer had sat up half the night trying to vary the wording of his thanks for the last batch of presents from men friends and ex-lady-loves; the fees for the Bishop and the Rector were safely in the pocket of his best

---

1. Part of the established ritual of giving mementos to members of the wedding party, this particular object provides evidence of the detailed research into social customs that informed the writing of the novel. Mrs. Mary Elizabeth Sherwood's *Manners and Social Usages* (1887) recalls "[t]he groom at a recent wedding [who] gave cat's-eyes set round with diamonds to his ushers for scarf pins, the cat's-eye being considered a very lucky stone" (112). (See also pp. 317–29 of this volume.)

man; his own luggage was already at Mrs. Manson Mingott's, where the wedding-breakfast was to take place, and so were the traveling clothes into which he was to change; and a private compartment had been engaged in the train that was to carry the young couple to their unknown destination—concealment of the spot in which the bridal night was to be spent being one of the most sacred taboos of the prehistoric ritual.

"Got the ring all right?" whispered young van der Luyden Newland, who was inexperienced in the duties of a best man, and awed by the weight of his responsibility.

Archer made the gesture which he had seen so many bridegrooms make: with his ungloved right hand he felt in the pocket of his dark gray waistcoat, and assured himself that the little gold circlet (engraved inside: *Newland to May, April——, 187—*) (was in its place; then, resuming his former attitude, his tall hat and pearl-gray gloves with black stitchings grasped in his left hand, he stood looking at the door of the church.

Overhead, Handel's March[2] swelled pompously through the imitation stone vaulting, carrying on its waves the faded drift of the many weddings at which, with cheerful indifference, he had stood on the same chancel step[3] watching other brides float up the nave toward other bridegrooms.

"How like a first night at the Opera!" he thought, recognizing all the same faces in the same boxes (no, pews), and wondering if, when the Last Trump[4] sounded, Mrs. Selfridge Merry would be there with the same towering ostrich feathers in her bonnet, and Mrs. Beaufort with the same diamond earrings and the same smile—and whether suitable proscenium seats were already prepared for them in another world.

After that there was still time to review, one by one, the familiar countenances in the first rows; the women's sharp with curiosity and excitement, the men's sulky with the obligation of having to put on their frock-coats before luncheon, and fight for food at the weddingbreakfast.

"Too bad the breakfast is at old Catherine's," the bridegroom could fancy Reggie Chivers saying. "But I'm told that Lovell Mingott insisted on its being cooked by his own *chef*, so it ought to be good if one can only get at it." And he could imagine Sillerton Jackson adding with authority: "My dear fellow, haven't you heard? It's to be served at small tables, in the new English fashion."

Archer's eyes lingered a moment on the left-hand pew, where his mother, who had entered the church on Mr. Henry van der Luyden's arm, sat weeping softly under her Chantilly veil, her hands in her grandmother's ermine muff.

"Poor Janey!" he thought, looking at his sister, "even by screwing her

2. Composed by George Frederick Handel (1685–1759), German-English composer.
3. Near the altar, usually a place reserved for church officials.
4. A reference to the trumpet blast that will initiate the Day of Judgment, according to Paul (1 Cor 15); also a crucial moment in the card game Bridge: when the last trump is pulled and players have no surprises to fear or anticipate.

head around she can see only the people in the few front pews; and they're mostly dowdy Newlands and Dagonets."

On the hither side of the white ribbon dividing off the seats reserved for the families he saw Beaufort, tall and redfaced, scrutinizing the women with his arrogant stare. Beside him sat his wife, all silvery chinchilla and violets; and on the far side of the ribbon, Lawrence Lefferts's sleekly brushed head seemed to mount guard over the invisible deity of "Good Form" who presided at the ceremony.

Archer wondered how many flaws Lefferts's keen eyes would discover in the ritual of his divinity; then he suddenly recalled that he too had once thought such questions important. The things that had filled his days seemed now like a nursery parody of life, or like the wrangles of medieval schoolmen over metaphysical terms that nobody had ever understood. A stormy discussion as to whether the wedding presents should be "shown" had darkened the last hours before the wedding; and it seemed inconceivable to Archer that grown-up people should work themselves into a state of agitation over such trifles, and that the matter should have been decided (in the negative) by Mrs. Welland's saying, with indignant tears: "I should as soon turn the reporters loose in my house." Yet there was a time when Archer had had definite and rather aggressive opinions on all such problems, and when everything concerning the manners and customs of his little tribe had seemed to him fraught with world-wide significance.

"And all the while, I suppose," he thought, "real people were living somewhere, and real things happening to them . . ."

"*There they come!*" breathed the best man excitedly; but the bridegroom knew better.

The cautious opening of the door of the church meant only that Mr. Brown the livery-stable keeper (gowned in black in his intermittent character of sexton)[5] was taking a preliminary survey of the scene before marshaling his forces. The door was softly shut again; then after another interval it swung majestically open, and a murmur ran through the church: "The family!"

Mrs. Welland came first, on the arm of her eldest son. Her large pink face was appropriately solemn, and her plum-colored satin with pale blue side-panels, and blue ostrich plumes in a small satin bonnet, met with general approval; but before she had settled herself with a stately rustle in the pew opposite Mrs. Archer's the spectators were craning their necks to see who was coming after her. Wild rumors had been abroad the day before to the effect that Mrs. Manson Mingott, in spite of her physical disabilities, had resolved on being present at the ceremony; and the idea was so much in keeping with her sporting character that bets ran high at the clubs as to her being able to walk up the nave and squeeze into a seat. It was known that she had insisted on sending her own carpenter to look into the possibility of taking down the end panel of the front pew, and to measure the space

---

5. Brown (see p. 3, *n.* 4) is shown here to have achieved the honorable position of sexton, a respected official in charge of the church building and the church grounds.

between the seat and the front; but the result had been discouraging, and for one anxious day her family had watched her dallying with the plan of being wheeled up the nave in her enormous Bath chair[6] and sitting enthroned in it at the foot of the chancel.

The idea of this monstrous exposure of her person was so painful to her relations that they could have covered with gold the ingenious person who suddenly discovered that the chair was too wide to pass between the iron uprights of the awning which extended from the church door to the curbstone. The idea of doing away with this awning, and revealing the bride to the mob of dressmakers and newspaper reporters who stood outside fighting to get near the joints of the canvas, exceeded even old Catherine's courage, though for a moment she had weighed the possibility. "Why, they might take a photograph of my child *and put it in the papers!*" Mrs. Welland exclaimed when her mother's last plan was hinted to her; and from this unthinkable indecency the clan recoiled with a collective shudder. The ancestress had had to give in; but her concession was bought only by the promise that the wedding-breakfast should take place under her roof, though (as the Washington Square connection said) with the Wellands' house in easy reach it was hard to have to make a special price with Brown to drive one to the other end of nowhere.

Though all these transactions had been widely reported by the Jacksons a sporting minority still clung to the belief that old Catherine would appear in church, and there was a distinct lowering of the temperature when she was found to have been replaced by her daughter-in-law. Mrs. Lovell Mingott had the high color and glassy stare induced in ladies of her age and habit by the effort of getting into a new dress; but once the disappointment occasioned by her mother-in-law's non-appearance had subsided, it was agreed that her black Chantilly over lilac satin, with a bonnet of Parma violets,[7] formed the happiest contrast to Mrs. Welland's blue and plum-color. Far different was the impression produced by the gaunt and mincing lady who followed on Mr. Mingott's arm, in a wild dishevelment of stripes and fringes and floating scarves; and as this last apparition glided into view Archer's heart contracted and stopped beating.

He had taken it for granted that the Marchioness Manson was still in Washington, where she had gone some four weeks previously with her niece, Madame Olenska. It was generally understood that their abrupt departure was due to Madame Olenska's desire to remove her aunt from the baleful eloquence of Dr. Agathon Carver, who had nearly succeeded in enlisting her as a recruit for the Valley of Love; and in the circumstances no one had expected either of the ladies to return for the wedding. For a moment Archer stood with his eyes fixed on Medora's fantastic figure, straining to see who came behind her;

---

6. Named for the resort city in England, a large chair encased in glass or other materials, moved on wheels and pulled by a horse or pushed by an attendant.
7. Chantilly: Lace made with a heavy linen or silk thread, named for the city in France where it was first produced; Parma violets: Known for their distinctively light lavender color, this type of violet is native to Parma, a city in northern Italy.

but the little procession was at an end, for all the lesser members of the family had taken their seats, and the eight tall ushers, gathering themselves together like birds or insects preparing for some migratory maneuver, were already slipping through the side doors into the lobby.

"Newland—I say: *she's here!*" the best man whispered.

Archer roused himself with a start.

A long time had apparently passed since his heart had stopped beating, for the white and rosy procession was in fact half-way up the nave, the Bishop, the Rector and two white-winged assistants were hovering about the flower-banked altar, and the first chords of the Spohr symphony[8] were strewing their flower-like notes before the bride.

Archer opened his eyes (but could they really have been shut, as he imagined?), and felt his heart beginning to resume its usual task. The music, the scent of the lilies on the altar, the vision of the cloud of tulle and orange-blossoms floating nearer and nearer, the sight of Mrs. Archer's face suddenly convulsed with happy sobs, the low benedictory murmur of the Rector's voice, the ordered evolutions of the eight pink bridesmaids and the eight black ushers: all these sights, sounds and sensations, so familiar in themselves, so unutterably strange and meaningless in his new relation to them, were confusedly mingled in his brain.

"My God," he thought, "*have* I got the ring?"—and once more he went through the bridegroom's convulsive gesture.

Then, in a moment, May was beside him, such radiance streaming from her that it sent a faint warmth through his numbness, and he straightened himself and smiled into her eyes.

"Dearly beloved, we are gathered together here,"[9] the Rector began . . .

The ring was on her hand, the Bishop's benediction had been given, the bridesmaids were apoise to resume their place in the procession, and the organ was showing preliminary symptoms of breaking out into the Mendelssohn March,[1] without which no newly-wedded couple had ever emerged upon New York.

"Your arm—*I say, give her your arm!*" young Newland nervously hissed; and once more Archer became aware of having been adrift far off in the unknown. What was it that had sent him there, he wondered? Perhaps the glimpse, among the anonymous spectators in the transept, of a dark coil of hair under a hat which, a moment later, revealed itself as belonging to an unknown lady with a long nose, so laughably unlike the person whose image she had evoked that he asked himself if he were becoming subject to hallucinations.

8. Symphony by Louis Spohr (1784–1859), German composer, violinist, and conductor whose music was marked by a combination of both conservative and progressive strains.
9. This opening, the familiar greeting that begins the Episcopalian wedding ceremony, was added in the third printing and it replaced the most telling mistake in the first edition, which began the wedding with the ritualized greeting reserved for funeral services: "Forasmuch as it hath pleased Almighty God—."
1. "The Wedding March"—by Felix Mendelssohn-Bartholdy (1809–1847), German pianist, violinist, conductor, and composer—was composed in the mid-1840s as part of his *Overture to a Midsummer Night's Dream.*

And now he and his wife were pacing slowly down the nave, carried
forward on the light Mendelssohn ripples, the spring day beckoning to
them through widely opened doors, and Mrs. Welland's chestnuts,
with big white favors on their frontlets, curvetting and showing off at
the far end of the canvas tunnel.[2]

The footman, who had a still bigger white favor on his lapel,
wrapped May's white cloak about her, and Archer jumped into the
brougham at her side. She turned to him with a triumphant smile and
their hands clasped under her veil.

"Darling!" Archer said—and suddenly the same black abyss yawned
before him and he felt himself sinking into it, deeper and deeper,
while his voice rambled on smoothly and cheerfully: "Yes, of course I
thought I'd lost the ring; no wedding would be complete if the poor
devil of a bridegroom didn't go through that. But you *did* keep me
waiting, you know! I had time to think of every horror that might possibly happen."

She surprised him by turning, in full Fifth Avenue, and flinging her
arms about his neck. "But none ever *can* happen now, can it, Newland, as long as we two are together?"

Every detail of the day had been so carefully thought out that the
young couple, after the wedding-breakfast, had ample time to put on
their traveling clothes, descend the wide Mingott stairs between
laughing bridesmaids and weeping parents, and get into the brougham
under the traditional shower of rice and satin slippers; and there was
still half an hour left in which to drive to the station, buy the last
weeklies at the bookstall with the air of seasoned travellers, and settle
themselves in the reserved compartment in which May's maid had
already placed her dove-colored traveling cloak and glaringly new
dressing-bag from London.

The old du Lac aunts at Rhinebeck had put their house at the dis-
posal of the bridal couple, with a readiness inspired by the prospect of
spending a week in New York with Mrs. Archer; and Archer, glad to escape the usual "bridal suite" in a Philadelphia or Baltimore hotel, had
accepted with an equal alacrity.

May was enchanted at the idea of going to the country, and child-
ishly amused at the vain efforts of the eight bridesmaids to discover
where their mysterious retreat was situated. It was thought "very English" to have a country-house lent to one, and the fact gave a last
touch of distinction to what was generally conceded to be the most
brilliant wedding of the year; but where the house was no one was permitted to know, except the parents of bride and groom, who, when
taxed with the knowledge, pursed their lips and said mysteriously: "Ah,
they didn't tell us—" which was manifestly true, since there was no
need to.

Once they were settled in their compartment, and the train, shaking

2. curvetting: The prancing of a horse during which all four legs are off the ground at the same
time; chestnuts: Chestnut-colored horses; favors: Ornaments; frontlets: Foreheads.

off the endless wooden suburbs, had pushed out into the pale land-scape of spring, talk became easier than Archer had expected. May was still, in look and tone, the simple girl of yesterday, eager to com-pare notes with him as to the incidents of the wedding, and discussing them as impartially as a bridesmaid talking it all over with an usher. At first Archer had fancied that this detachment was the disguise of an inward tremor; but her clear eyes revealed only the most tranquil un-awareness. She was alone for the first time with her husband; but her husband was only the charming comrade of yesterday. There was no one whom she liked as much, no one whom she trusted as completely, and the culminating "lark" of the whole delightful adventure of en-gagement and marriage was to be off with him alone on a journey, like a grown-up person, like a "married woman," in fact.

It was wonderful that—as he had learned in the Mission garden at St. Augustine—such depths of feeling could coexist with such absence of imagination. But he remembered how, even then, she had surprised him by dropping back to inexpressive girlishness as soon as her conscience had been eased of its burden; and he saw that she would probably go through life dealing to the best of her ability with each ex-perience as it came, but never anticipating any by so much as a stolen glance.

Perhaps that faculty of unawareness was what gave her eyes their transparency, and her face the look of representing a type rather than a person; as if she might have been chosen to pose for a Civic Virtue[3] or a Greek goddess. The blood that ran so close to her fair skin might have been a preserving fluid rather than a ravaging element; yet her look of indestructible youthfulness made her seem neither hard nor dull, but only primitive and pure. In the thick of this medita-tion Archer suddenly felt himself looking at her with the startled gaze of a stranger, and plunged into a reminiscence of the wedding-breakfast and of Granny Mingott's immense and triumphant pervasion of it.

May settled down to frank enjoyment of the subject. "I was sur-prised, though—weren't you?—that Aunt Medora came after all. Ellen wrote that they were neither of them well enough to take the journey; I do wish it had been she who had recovered! Did you see the exqui-site old lace she sent me?"

He had known that the moment must come sooner or later, but he had somewhat imagined that by force of willing he might hold it at bay.

"Yes—I—no: yes, it was beautiful," he said, looking at her blindly, and wondering if, whenever he heard those two syllables, all his care-fully built-up world would tumble about him like a house of cards.

"Aren't you tired? It will be good to have some tea when we arrive—I'm sure the aunts have got everything beautifully ready," he rattled on, taking her hand in his; and her mind rushed away instantly to

3. Larger-than-life female figures painted in murals of the period representing the fundamental values of the city, state, or nation; a secular replacement for the Greek goddesses of the clas-sical pantheon.

the magnificent tea and coffee service of Baltimore silver[4] which the Beauforts had sent, and which "went" so perfectly with Uncle Lovell Mingott's trays and side-dishes.

In the spring twilight the train stopped at the Rhinebeck station, and they walked along the platform to the waiting carriage.

"Ah, how awfully kind of the van der Luydens—they've sent their man over from Skuytercliff to meet us," Archer exclaimed, as a sedate person out of livery approached them and relieved the maid of her bags.

"I'm extremely sorry, sir," said this emissary, "that a little accident has occurred at the Miss du Lacs': a leak in the water-tank. It happened yesterday, and Mr. van der Luyden, who heard of it this morning, sent a housemaid up by the early train to get the Patroon's house ready. It will be quite comfortable, I think you'll find, sir; and the Miss du Lacs have sent their cook over, so that it will be exactly the same as if you'd been at Rhinebeck."

Archer stared at the speaker so blankly that he repeated in still more apologetic accents: "It'll be exactly the same, sir, I do assure you—" and May's eager voice broke out, covering the embarrassed silence: "The same as Rhinebeck? The Patroon's house? But it will be a hundred thousand times better—won't it, Newland? It's too dear and kind of Mr. van der Luyden to have thought of it."

And as they drove off, with the maid beside the coachman, and their shining bridal bags on the seat before them, she went on excitedly: "Only fancy, I've never been inside it—have you? The van der Luydens show it to so few people. But they opened it for Ellen, it seems, and she told me what a darling little place it was: she says it's the only house she's seen in America that she could imagine being perfectly happy in."

"Well—that's what we're going to be, isn't it?" cried her husband gaily; and she answered with her boyish smile: "Ah, it's just our luck beginning—the wonderful luck we're always going to have together!"

# XX

"Of course we must dine with Mrs. Carfry, dearest," Archer said; and his wife looked at him with an anxious frown across the monumental Britannia ware[1] of their lodging house breakfast-table.

In all the rainy desert of autumnal London there were only two people whom the Newland Archers knew; and these two they had sedulously avoided, in conformity with the old New York tradition that it

---

4. Part of a rococo revival in mid-nineteenth-century Baltimore led by master silversmiths Samuel Kirk and William Warner, these ornate vessels and decorative objects featured complex raised designs made by pushing the structures from within, filling these inner indentations with resin, and then working from the exterior with fine tools to articulate the elaborate patterns.
1. Durable tableware made from an alloy of tin, copper, antimony, and possibly bismuth and zinc.

was not "dignified" to force one's self on the notice of one's acquaintances in foreign countries.

Mrs. Archer and Janey, in the course of their visits to Europe, had
so unflinchingly lived up to this principle, and met the friendly advances of their fellow-travelers with an air of such impenetrable reserve, that they had almost achieved the record of never having
exchanged a word with a "foreigner" other than those employed in hotels and railway-stations. Their own compatriots—save those previously known or properly accredited—they treated with an even more
pronounced disdain; so that, unless they ran across a Chivers, a
Dagonet or a Mingott, their months abroad were spent in an unbroken
*tête-à-tête.*[2] But the utmost precautions are sometimes unavailing; and
one night at Botzen[3] one of the two English ladies in the room across
the passage (whose names, dress and social situation were already intimately known to Janey) had knocked on the door and asked if Mrs.
Archer had a bottle of liniment. The other lady—the intruder's sister,
Mrs. Carfry—had been seized with a sudden attack of bronchitis; and
Mrs. Archer, who never traveled without a complete family pharmacy,
was fortunately able to produce the required remedy.

Mrs. Carfry was very ill, and as she and her sister Miss Harle were
traveling alone they were profoundly grateful to the Archer ladies, who
supplied them with ingenious comforts and whose efficient maid
helped to nurse the invalid back to health.

When the Archers left Botzen they had no idea of ever seeing Mrs.
Carfry and Miss Harle again. Nothing, to Mrs. Archer's mind, would
have been more "undignified" than to force one's self on the notice of
a "foreigner" to whom one had happened to render an accidental service. But Mrs. Carfry and her sister, to whom this point of view was
unknown, and who would have found it utterly incomprehensible, felt
themselves linked by an eternal gratitude to the "delightful Americans"
who had been so kind at Botzen. With touching fidelity they seized
every chance of meeting Mrs. Archer and Janey in the course of their
continental travels, and displayed a supernatural acuteness in finding
out when they were to pass through London on their way to or from
the States. The intimacy became indissoluble, and Mrs. Archer and
Janey, whenever they alighted at Brown's Hotel, found themselves
awaited by two affectionate friends who, like themselves, cultivated
ferns in Wardian cases, made macramé lace, read the memoirs of
the Baroness Bunsen[4] and had views about the occupants of the leading London pulpits. As Mrs. Archer said, it made "another thing of
London" to know Mrs. Carfry and Miss Harle; and by the time that
Newland became engaged the tie between the families was so firmly
established that it was thought "only right" to send a wedding invitation to the two English ladies, who sent, in return, a pretty bouquet of

2. French, literally "head-to-head"; a private conversation, here suggesting that Mrs. Archer
   and Janey converse only with each other.
3. Another name for Bolzano, a city in northeastern Italy.
4. Brown's Hotel: A fashionable London hotel established in 1837 on Albemarle Street in
   Mayfair near the Royal Academy of Arts; Baroness Bunsen: Frances Waddington Bunsen
   (1791–1876), whose memoirs were published 1868–79.

pressed Alpine flowers under glass. And on the dock, when Newland and his wife sailed for England, Mrs. Archer's last word had been: "You must take May to see Mrs. Carfry."

Newland and his wife had had no idea of obeying this injunction; but Mrs. Carfry, with her usual acuteness, had run them down and sent them an invitation to dine; and it was over this invitation that May Archer was wrinkling her brows across the tea and muffins.

"It's all very well for you, Newland; you *know* them. But I shall feel so shy among a lot of people I've never met. And what shall I wear?"

Newland leaned back in his chair and smiled at her. She looked handsomer and more Diana-like than ever. The moist English air seemed to have deepened the bloom of her cheeks and softened the slight hardness of her virginal features; or else it was simply the inner glow of happiness, shining through like a light under ice.

"Wear, dearest? I thought a trunkful of things had come from Paris last week."

"Yes, of course. I meant to say that I shan't know *which* to wear." She pouted a little. "I've never dined out in London; and I don't want to be ridiculous."

He tried to enter into her perplexity. "But don't Englishwomen dress just like everybody else in the evening?"

"Newland! How can you ask such funny questions? When they go to the theater in old ball-dresses and bare heads."

"Well, perhaps they wear new ball-dresses at home; but at any rate Mrs. Carfry and Miss Harle won't. They'll wear caps like my mother's—and shawls; very soft shawls."

"Yes; but how will the other women be dressed?"

"Not as well as you, dear," he rejoined, wondering what had suddenly developed in her Janey's morbid interest in clothes.

She pushed back her chair with a sigh. "That's dear of you, Newland; but it doesn't help me much."

He had an inspiration. "Why not wear your wedding-dress? That can't be wrong, can it?"

"Oh, dearest! If I only had it here! But it's gone to Paris to be made over for next winter, and Worth[5] hasn't sent it back."

"Oh, well—" said Archer, getting up. "Look here—the fog's lifting. If we made a dash for the National Gallery[6] we might manage to catch a glimpse of the pictures."

The Newland Archers were on their way home, after a three months' wedding-tour which May, in writing to her girl friends, vaguely summarized as "blissful."

They had not gone to the Italian Lakes: on reflection, Archer had not been able to picture his wife in that particular setting. Her own inclination (after a month with the Paris dressmakers) was for mountaineering

5. Charles Frederick Worth (1826–1895), British-born, premier fashion designer whose clients included noblewomen and celebrities. Worth's shop was located on the Rue de la Paix. (See also p. 53, *n.* 4.)
6. Founded in 1824 and located since 1838 on Trafalgar Square in London.

in July and swimming in August. This plan they punctually fulfilled, spending July at Interlaken and Grindelwald, and August at a little place called Etretat, on the Normandy coast, which someone had recommended as quaint and quiet. Once or twice, in the mountains, Archer had pointed southward and said: "There's Italy"; and May, her feet in a gentian-bed, had smiled cheerfully, and replied: "It would be lovely to go there next winter, if only you didn't have to be in New York."

But in reality traveling interested her even less than he had expected. She regarded it (once her clothes were ordered) as merely an enlarged opportunity for walking, riding, swimming, and trying her hand at the fascinating new game of lawn tennis; and when they finally got back to London (where they were to spend a fortnight while he ordered *his* clothes) she no longer concealed the eagerness with which she looked forward to sailing.

In London nothing interested her but the theaters and the shops; and she found the theaters less exciting than the Paris *cafés chantants* where, under the blossoming horse-chestnuts of the Champs Élysées, she had had the novel experience of looking down from the restaurant terrace on an audience of "cocottes," and having her husband interpret to her as much of the songs as he thought suitable for bridal ears.[7]

Archer had reverted to all his old inherited ideas about marriage. It was less trouble to conform with the tradition and treat May exactly as all his friends treated their wives than to try to put into practice the theories with which his untrammeled bachelorhood had dallied. There was no use in trying to emancipate a wife who had not the dimmest notion that she was not free; and he had long since discovered that May's only use of the liberty she supposed herself to possess would be to lay it on the altar of her wifely adoration. Her innate dignity would always keep her from making the gift abjectly; and a day might even come (as it once had) when she would find strength to take it altogether back if she thought she were doing it for his own good. But with a conception of marriage so uncomplicated and incurious as hers such a crisis could be brought about only by something visibly outrageous in his own conduct; and the fineness of her feeling for him made that unthinkable. Whatever happened, he knew, she would always be loyal, gallant and unresentful; and that pledged him to the practice of the same virtues.

All this tended to draw him back into his old habits of mind. If her simplicity had been the simplicity of pettiness he would have chafed and rebelled; but since the lines of her character, though so few, were on the same fine mould as her face, she became the tutelary divinity of all his old traditions and reverences.

Such qualities were scarcely of the kind to enliven foreign travel, though they made her so easy and pleasant a companion; but he saw

7. *café chantants*: A cafe where concerts take place. Champs Élysées: An avenue in Paris (known for its cafés, theaters, and shops) that leads from the Place de la Concorde to the Arc de Triomphe. "cocottes": Literally, "stewpots," in France this word is a term of familiarity meaning "little chick." In the late-nineteenth century, "cocotte" was a slang word used by Americans to refer to women who were considered "sex pots," flirts whose behavior suggested the openness of their sexual interest and their availability.

at once how they would fall into place in their proper setting. He had no fear of being oppressed by them, for his artistic and intellectual life would go on, as it always had, outside the domestic circle; and within it there would be nothing small and stifling—coming back to his wife would never be like entering a stuffy room after a tramp in the open. And when they had children the vacant corners in both their lives would be filled.

All these things went through his mind during their long, slow drive from Mayfair to South Kensington,[8] where Mrs. Carfry and her sister lived. Archer too would have preferred to escape their friends' hospitality: in conformity with the family tradition he had always traveled as a sight-seer and looker-on, affecting a haughty unconsciousness of the presence of his fellow-beings. Once only, just after Harvard, he had spent a few gay weeks at Florence with a band of queer Europeanized Americans, dancing all night with titled ladies in palaces, and gambling half the day with the rakes and dandies of the fashionable club; but it had all seemed to him, though the greatest fun in the world, as unreal as a carnival. These queer cosmopolitan women, deep in complicated love affairs which they appeared to feel the need of retailing to everyone they met, and the magnificent young officers and elderly dyed wits who were the subjects or the recipients of their confidences, were too different from the people Archer had grown up among, too much like expensive and rather malodorous hot-house exotics, to detain his imagination long. To introduce his wife into such a society was out of the question; and in the course of his travels no other had shown any marked eagerness for his company.

Not long after their arrival in London he had run across the Duke of St. Austrey, and the Duke, instantly and cordially recognizing him, had said: "Look me up, won't you?"—but no proper-spirited American would have considered that a suggestion to be acted on, and the meeting was without a sequel. They had even managed to avoid May's English aunt, the banker's wife, who was still in Yorkshire; in fact, they had purposely postponed going to London till the autumn in order that their arrival during the season might not appear pushing and snobbish to these unknown relatives.

"Probably there'll be nobody at Mrs. Carfry's—London's a desert at this season, and you've made yourself much too beautiful," Archer said to May, who sat at his side in the hansom so spotlessly splendid in her sky-blue cloak edged with swansdown that it seemed wicked to expose her to the London grime.

"I don't want them to think that we dress like savages," she replied, with a scorn that Pocahontas[9] might have resented; and he was struck again by the religious reverence of even the most unwordly American women for the social advantages of dress.

8. Newland and May are traveling from one of the most fashionable sections of London to a more rural area that had been encompassed by the growing city.
9. Native American princess of an Algonquin tribe (1595/6–1616/17) best known for her role in the popular, if historically unfounded, legend of John Smith's rescue from Indian captivity.

"It's their armor," he thought, "their defense against the unknown, and their defiance of it." And he understood for the first time the earnestness with which May, who was incapable of tying a ribbon in her hair to charm him, had gone through the solemn rite of selecting and ordering her extensive wardrobe.

He had been right in expecting the party at Mrs. Carfry's to be a small one. Besides their hostess and her sister, they found, in the long chilly drawing room, only another shawled lady, a genial Vicar who was her husband, a silent lad whom Mrs. Carfry named as her nephew, and a small dark gentleman with lively eyes whom she introduced as his tutor, pronouncing a French name as she did so.

Into this dimly-lit and dim-featured group May Archer floated like a swan with the sunset on her: she seemed larger, fairer, more voluminously rustling than her husband had ever seen her; and he perceived that the rosiness and rustlingness were the tokens of an extreme and infantile shyness.

"What on earth will they expect me to talk about?" her helpless eyes implored him, at the very moment that her dazzling apparition was calling forth the same anxiety in their own bosoms. But beauty, even when distrustful of itself, awakens confidence in the manly heart; and the Vicar and the French-named tutor were soon manifesting to May their desire to put her at her ease.

In spite of their best efforts, however, the dinner was a languishing affair. Archer noticed that his wife's way of showing herself at her ease with foreigners was to become more uncompromisingly local in her references, so that, though her loveliness was an encouragement to admiration, her conversation was a chill to repartee. The Vicar soon abandoned the struggle; but the tutor, who spoke the most fluent and accomplished English, gallantly continued to pour it out to her until the ladies, to the manifest relief of all concerned, went up to the drawing room.

The Vicar, after a glass of port, was obliged to hurry away to a meeting, and the shy nephew, who appeared to be an invalid, was packed off to bed. But Archer and the tutor continued to sit over their wine, and suddenly Archer found himself talking as he had not done since his last symposium with Ned Winsett. The Carfry nephew, it turned out, had been threatened with consumption, and had had to leave Harrow for Switzerland, where he had spent two years in the milder air of Lake Léman.[1] Being a bookish youth, he had been entrusted to M. Rivière, who had brought him back to England, and was to remain with him till he went up to Oxford the following spring; and M. Rivière added with simplicity that he should then have to look out for another job.

It seemed impossible, Archer thought, that he should be long without one, so varied were his interests and so many his gifts. He was a man of about thirty, with a thin ugly face (May would certainly have

---

1. Harrow: A prestigious secondary school for boys in Middlesex, England; the French name for Lake Geneva.

called him common-looking) to which the play of his ideas gave an in-tense expressiveness; but there was nothing frivolous or cheap in his animation.

His father, who had died young, had filled a small diplomatic post, and it had been intended that the son should follow the same ca-reer; but an insatiable taste for letters had thrown the young man into journalism, then into authorship (apparently unsuccessful), and at length—after other experiments and vicissitudes which he spared his listener—into tutoring English youths in Switzerland. Before that, however, he had lived much in Paris, frequented the Goncourt *grenier*, been advised by Maupassant not to attempt to write (even that seemed to Archer a dazzling honor!), and had often talked with Mérimée in his mother's house.[2] He had obviously always been desperately poor and anxious (having a mother and an unmarried sister to provide for), and it was apparent that his literary ambitions had failed. His situation, in fact, seemed, materially speaking, no more brilliant than Ned Win-sett's; but he had lived in a world in which, as he said, no one who loved ideas need hunger mentally. As it was precisely of that love that poor Winsett was starving to death, Archer looked with a sort of vicar-ious envy at this eager impecunious young man who had fared so richly in his poverty.

"You see, Monsieur, it's worth everything, isn't it, to keep one's in-tellectual liberty, not to enslave one's powers of appreciation, one's critical independence? It was because of that that I abandoned jour-nalism, and took to so much duller work: tutoring and private secre-taryship. There is a good deal of drudgery, of course; but one preserves one's moral freedom, what we call in French one's *quant à soi*. And when one hears good talk one can join in it without compromising any opinions but one's own; or one can listen, and answer it inwardly. Ah, good conversation—there's nothing like it, is there? The air of ideas is the only air worth breathing. And so I have never regretted giving up either diplomacy or journalism—two different forms of the same self-abdication." He fixed his vivid eyes on Archer as he lit another ciga-rette. "*Voyez-vous,*[3] Monsieur, to be able to look life in the face: that's worth living in a garret for, isn't it? But, after all, one must earn enough to pay for the garret; and I confess that to grow old as a private tutor—or a 'private' anything—is almost as chilling to the imagination as a second secretaryship at Bucharest. Sometimes I feel I must make a plunge: an immense plunge. Do you suppose, for instance, there would be any opening for me in America—in New York?"

Archer looked at him with startled eyes. New York, for a young man who had frequented the Goncourts and Flaubert,[4] and who thought

2. *grenier*: French, literally "loft," "garret", or "attic." The Goncourt *grenier* was a salon organ-ized around the presence of the famous Goncourt brothers (see p. 66, *n.* 7). Maupassant: Famous French short-story writer and novelist of the naturalist school (1850–1893). Mérimée: (1803–1870) French writer of novellas and essays; one of his novellas formed the basis of the opera *Carmen* (see p. 65, *n.* 4).
3. French, "Look" or more colloquially "Look here."
4. Gustave Flaubert (1821–1880), nineteenth-century French writer, best known for his novel *Madame Bovary* (1856), a biting critique of bourgeois life.

the life of ideas the only one worth living! He continued to stare at M. Rivière perplexedly, wondering how to tell him that his very superiorities and advantages would be the surest hindrance to success.

"New York—New York—but must it be especially New York?" he stammered, utterly unable to imagine what lucrative opening his native city could offer to a young man to whom good conversation appeared to be the only necessity.

A sudden flush rose under M. Rivière's sallow skin. "I—I thought it your metropolis: is not the intellectual life more active there?" he rejoined; then, as if fearing to give his hearer the impression of having asked a favor, he went on hastily: "One throws out random suggestions—more to one's self than to others. In reality, I see no immediate prospect—" and rising from his seat he added, without a trace of constraint: "But Mrs. Carfry will think that I ought to be taking you upstairs."

During the homeward drive Archer pondered deeply on this episode. His hour with M. Rivière had put new air into his lungs, and his first impulse had been to invite him to dine the next day; but he was beginning to understand why married men did not always immediately yield to their first impulses.

"That young tutor is an interesting fellow: we had some awfully good talk after dinner about books and things," he threw out tentatively in the hansom.

May roused herself from one of the dreamy silences into which he had read so many meanings before six months of marriage had given him the key to them.

"The little Frenchman? Wasn't he dreadfully common?" she questioned coldly; and he guessed that she nursed a secret disappointment at having been invited out in London to meet a clergyman and a French tutor. The disappointment was not occasioned by the sentiment ordinarily defined as snobbishness, but by old New York's sense of what was due to it when it risked its dignity in foreign lands. If May's parents had entertained the Carfrys in Fifth Avenue they would have offered them something more substantial than a parson and a schoolmaster.

But Archer was on edge, and took her up.

"Common—common *where?*" he queried; and she returned with unusual readiness: "Why, I should say anywhere but in his schoolroom. Those people are always awkward in society. But then," she added disarmingly, "I suppose I shouldn't have known if he was clever."

Archer disliked her use of the word "clever" almost as much as her use of the word "common"; but he was beginning to fear his tendency to dwell on the things he disliked in her. After all, her point of view had always been the same. It was that of all the people he had grown up among, and he had always regarded it as necessary but negligible. Until a few months ago he had never known a "nice" woman who looked at life differently; and if a man married it must necessarily be among the nice.

"Ah—then I won't ask him to dine!" he concluded with a laugh; and May echoed, bewildered: "Goodness—ask the Carfrys' tutor?"

"Well, not on the same day with the Carfrys, if you prefer I shouldn't. But I did rather want another talk with him. He's looking for a job in New York."

Her surprise increased with her indifference: he almost fancied that she suspected him of being tainted with "foreignness."

"A job in New York? What sort of a job? People don't have French tutors: what does he want to do?"

"Chiefly to enjoy good conversation, I understand," her husband retorted perversely; and she broke into an appreciative laugh. "Oh, Newland, how funny! Isn't that *French?*"

On the whole, he was glad to have the matter settled for him by her refusing to take seriously his wish to invite M. Rivière. Another after-dinner talk would have made it difficult to avoid the question of New York; and the more Archer considered it the less he was able to fit M. Rivière into any conceivable picture of New York as he knew it.

He perceived with a flash of chilling insight that in future many problems would be thus negatively solved for him; but as he paid the hansom and followed his wife's long train into the house he took refuge in the comforting platitude that the first six months were always the most difficult in marriage. "After that I suppose we shall have pretty nearly finished rubbing off each other's angles," he reflected; but the worst of it was that May's pressure was already bearing on the very angles whose sharpness he most wanted to keep.

# XXI

The small bright lawn stretched away smoothly to the big bright sea.

The turf was hemmed with an edge of scarlet geranium and coleus, and cast-iron vases painted in chocolate color, standing at intervals along the winding path that led to the sea, looped their garlands of petunia and ivy geranium above the neatly raked gravel.

Halfway between the edge of the cliff and the square wooden house (which was also chocolate-colored, but with the tin roof of the veran-dah striped in yellow and brown to represent an awning) two large targets had been placed against a background of shrubbery. On the other side of the lawn, facing the targets, was pitched a real tent, with benches and garden-seats about it. A number of ladies in summer dresses and gentlemen in gray frock-coats and tall hats stood on the lawn or sat upon the benches; and every now and then a slender girl in starched muslin would step from the tent, bow in hand, and speed her shaft at one of the targets, while the spectators interrupted their talk to watch the result.

Newland Archer, standing on the verandah of the house, looked curiously down upon this scene. On each side of the shiny painted steps was a large blue china flower-pot on a bright yellow china stand. A spiky green plant filled each pot, and below the verandah ran a wide border of blue hydrangeas edged with more red geraniums. Behind him, the French windows of the drawing rooms through which he had passed gave glimpses, between swaying lace curtains, of glassy parquet floors islanded with chintz *poufs*,[1] dwarf armchairs, and velvet tables covered with trifles in silver.

The Newport Archery Club always held its August meeting at the Beauforts'.[2] The sport, which had hitherto known no rival but croquet, was beginning to be discarded in favor of lawn tennis; but the latter game was still considered too rough and inelegant for social occasions, and as an opportunity to show off pretty dresses and graceful attitudes the bow and arrow held their own.

Archer looked down with wonder at the familiar spectacle. It surprised him that life should be going on in the old way when his own reactions to it had so completely changed. It was Newport that had first brought home to him the extent of the change. In New York, during the previous winter, after he and May had settled down in the new greenish-yellow house with the bow-window and the Pompeian vestibule, he had dropped back with relief into the old routine of the office, and the renewal of this daily activity had served as a link with his former self. Then there had been the pleasurable excitement of choosing a showy gray stepper for May's brougham (the Wellands had given the carriage), and the abiding occupation and interest of arranging his new library, which, in spite of family doubts and disapprovals, had been carried out as he had dreamed, with a dark embossed paper, Eastlake bookcases and "sincere" armchairs and tables. At the Century he had found Winsett again, and at the Knickerbocker[3] the fashionable young men of his own set; and what with the hours dedicated to the law and those given to dining out or entertaining friends at home, with an occasional evening at the Opera or the play, the life he was living had still seemed a fairly real and inevitable sort of business.

But Newport represented the escape from duty into an atmosphere of unmitigated holiday-making. Archer had tried to persuade May to spend the summer on a remote island off the coast of Maine (called, appropriately enough, Mount Desert),[4] where a few hardy Bostonians and Philadelphians were camping in "native" cottages, and whence came reports of enchanting scenery and a wild, almost trapper-like existence amid woods and waters.

1. Stuffed cushions.
2. In her autobiography (see pp. 248–59), Wharton recalled that the archery party at the Belmonts was a staple feature of Newport entertainment. Archery was becoming a popular sport in the late nineteenth century for young women of the elite. See pp. 343–47 as well as the illustrations on pp. 254 and 345. Newport, to which Wharton's family (the Joneses) returned in 1872 after six years in Europe, was a quietly fashionable seaside village in Rhode Island and the center of the summer social season for the elite of New York and Boston. By the 1890s, the extravagant mansions called "cottages" built by the Astors and Vanderbilts had begun to transform the scale of the social and architectural landscape.
3. A fashionable New York men's club founded in 1871 by John Jacob Astor and John L. Cadwalader in response to the perceived relaxation of membership standards at the Union Club.
4. An increasingly popular destination for summer visitors in the late nineteenth century. Even after mansions had been built here by the wealthy, the landscape of this seasonal colony continued to be sought out for its rugged beauty and sublime vistas, providing an alternative to the intensely social pursuits of Newport.

But the Wellands always went to Newport, where they owned one of the square boxes on the cliffs,[5] and their son-in-law could adduce no good reason why he and May should not join them there. As Mrs. Welland rather tartly pointed out, it was hardly worth while for May to have worn herself out trying on summer clothes in Paris if she was not to be allowed to wear them; and this argument was of a kind to which Archer had as yet found no answer.

May herself could not understand his obscure reluctance to fall in with so reasonable and pleasant a way of spending the summer. She reminded him that he had always liked Newport in his bachelor days, and as this was indisputable he could only profess that he was sure he was going to like it better than ever now that they were to be there together. But as he stood on the Beaufort verandah and looked out on the brightly peopled lawn it came home to him with a shiver that he was not going to like it at all.

It was not May's fault, poor dear. If, now and then, during their travels, they had fallen slightly out of step, harmony had been restored by their return to the conditions she was used to. He had always foreseen that she would not disappoint him; and he had been right. He had married (as most young men did) because he had met a perfectly charming girl at the moment when a series of rather aimless sentimental adventures were ending in premature disgust; and she had represented peace, stability, comradeship, and the steadying sense of an unescapable duty.

He could not say that he had been mistaken in his choice, for she had fulfilled all that he had expected. It was undoubtedly gratifying to be the husband of one of the handsomest and most popular young married women in New York, especially when she was also one of the sweetest-tempered and most reasonable of wives; and Archer had never been insensible to such advantages. As for the momentary madness which had fallen upon him on the eve of his marriage, he had trained himself to regard it as the last of his discarded experiments. The idea that he could ever, in his senses, have dreamed of marrying the Countess Olenska had become almost unthinkable, and she remained in his memory simply as the most plaintive and poignant of a line of ghosts.

But all these abstractions and eliminations made of his mind a rather empty and echoing place, and he supposed that was one of the reasons why the busy animated people on the Beaufort lawn shocked him as if they had been children playing in a graveyard.

He heard a murmur of skirts beside him, and the Marchioness Manson fluttered out of the drawing-room window. As usual, she was extraordinarily festooned and bedizened, with a limp Leghorn hat[6] an-

---

5. Rising at times to a level of seventy feet, this high bank on the eastern shore of Newport provided a scenic perch for the ornate mansions of the elite, including the summer residences of the Vanderbilts and the Belmonts. Demarcated by the Cliff Walk, the famed path that extends along the bank for three and a half miles from Easton's Beach to Bailey's Beach, the Cliffs was the most fashionable and exclusive section of Newport. (See the map of Newport, p. 252.)
6. A large hat plaited from straw grown in Tuscany, Italy.

chored to her head by many windings of faded gauze, and a little black velvet parasol on a carved ivory handle absurdly balanced over her much larger hat-brim.

"My dear Newland, I had no idea that you and May had arrived! You yourself came only yesterday, you say? Ah, business—business—professional duties . . . I understand. Many husbands, I know, find it impossible to join their wives here except for the weekend." She cocked her head on one side and languished at him through screwed-up eyes. "But marriage is one long sacrifice, as I used often to remind my Ellen—"

Archer's heart stopped with the queer jerk which it had given once before, and which seemed suddenly to slam a door between himself and the outer world; but this break of continuity must have been of the briefest, for he presently heard Medora answering a question he had apparently found voice to put.

"No, I am not staying here, but with the Blenkers, in their delicious solitude at Portsmouth. Beaufort was kind enough to send his famous trotters for me this morning, so that I might have at least a glimpse of one of Regina's garden-parties; but this evening I go back to rural life. The Blenkers, dear original beings, have hired a primitive old farm-house at Portsmouth where they gather about them representative people. . . ."[7] She drooped slightly beneath her protecting brim, and added with a faint blush: "This week Dr. Agathon Carver is holding a series of Inner Thought meetings there. A contrast indeed to this gay scene of worldly pleasure—but then I have always lived on contrasts! To me the only death is monotony. I always say to Ellen: Beware of monotony; it's the mother of all the deadly sins. But my poor child is going through a phase of exaltation, of abhorrence of the world. You know, I suppose, that she has declined all invitations to stay at Newport, even with her grandmother Mingott? I could hardly persuade her to come with me to the Blenkers', if you believe it! The life she leads is morbid, unnatural. Ah, if she had only listened to me when it was still possible . . . When the door was still open. . . . But shall we go down and watch this absorbing match? I hear your May is one of the competitors."

Strolling toward them from the tent Beaufort advanced over the lawn, tall, heavy, too tightly buttoned into a London frock-coat, with one of his own orchids in its buttonhole. Archer, who had not seen him for two or three months, was struck by the change in his appearance. In the hot summer light his floridness seemed heavy and bloated, and but for his erect square-shouldered walk he would have looked like an over-fed and over-dressed old man.

7. Portsmouth: Originally Pocasset, this village four miles north of Newport was founded by Anne Hutchinson in 1638 after her exile from the Massachusetts Bay Colony for religious heresy. The first community in America to codify ideals of religious and civil freedom, the Portsmouth of the novel, which still provides a place for unorthodox thinkers, was best known for its horse-breeding farms owned by racing enthusiasts such as August Belmont. famous trotters: Horses bred for harness racing; this sport, a descendant of chariot racing, emerged as a popular pastime in America during the years following the Civil War. representative people: The idea of people as types, specimens of humanity embodying differing ideas and ideals that can be brought together for cross-fertilization.

There were all sorts of rumors afloat about Beaufort. In the spring he had gone off on a long cruise to the West Indies in his new steam-yacht, and it was reported that, at various points where he had touched, a lady resembling Miss Fanny Ring had been seen in his company. The steam-yacht, built in the Clyde,[8] and fitted with tiled bathrooms and other unheard-of luxuries, was said to have cost him half a million; and the pearl necklace which he had presented to his wife on his return was as magnificent as such expiatory offerings are apt to be. Beaufort's fortune was substantial enough to stand the strain; and yet the disquieting rumors persisted, not only in Fifth Avenue but in Wall Street.[9] Some people said he had speculated unfortunately in railways, others that he was being bled by one of the most insatiable members of her profession; and to every report of threatened insolvency Beaufort replied by a fresh extravagance: the building of a new row of orchid-houses, the purchase of a new string of racehorses, or the addition of a new Meissonnier or Cabanel to his picture gallery.[1]

He advanced toward the Marchioness and Newland with his usual half-sneering smile. "Hullo, Medora! Did the trotters do their business? Forty minutes,[2] eh? . . . Well, that's not so bad, considering your nerves had to be spared." He shook hands with Archer, and then, turning back with them, placed himself on Mrs. Manson's other side, and said, in a low voice, a few words which their companion did not catch.

The Marchioness replied by one of her queer foreign jerks, and a "*Que voulez-vous?*"[3] which deepened Beaufort's frown; but he produced a good semblance of a congratulatory smile as he glanced at Archer to say: "You know May's going to carry off the first prize."

"Ah, then it remains in the family," Medora rippled; and at that moment they reached the tent and Mrs. Beaufort met them in a girlish cloud of mauve muslin and floating veils.

May Welland was just coming out of the tent. In her white dress, with a pale green ribbon about the waist and a wreath of ivy on her hat, she had the same Diana-like aloofness as when she had entered the Beaufort ballroom on the night of her engagement. In the interval not a thought seemed to have passed behind her eyes or a feeling through her heart; and though her husband knew that she had the capacity for both he marveled afresh at the way in which experience dropped away from her.

She had her bow and arrow in her hand, and placing herself on the chalk-mark traced on the turf she lifted the bow to her shoulder and took aim. The attitude was so full of a classic grace that a murmur of

8. A river in Scotland in the center of a shipbuilding region.
9. Financial district, named for a wooden wall built in 1653 by the Dutch to stave off attacks by New Englanders and the British as well as local tribes.
1. Meissonnier: French artist (1852–1917) of the Academic movement, characterized by its depiction of history and mythology; Cabanel: See p. 34, n. 2.
2. Making this trip at about six miles per hour, Beaufort's trotters are going nearly twice as fast as ordinary horses would be expected to travel while pulling a buggy.
3. French, for "What do you want?" "What can I do for you?" or "What can you expect?"

appreciation followed her appearance, and Archer felt the glow of proprietorship that so often cheated him into momentary well-being. Her rivals—Mrs. Reggie Chivers, the Merry girls, and divers rosy Thorleys, Dagonets and Mingotts, stood behind her in a lovely anxious group, brown heads and golden bent above the scores, and pale muslins and flower-wreathed hats mingled in a tender rainbow. All were young and pretty, and bathed in summer bloom; but not one had the nymph-like ease of his wife, when, with tense muscles and happy frown, she bent her soul upon some feat of strength.

"Gad," Archer heard Lawrence Lefferts say, "not one of the lot holds the bow as she does"; and Beaufort retorted: "Yes; but that's the only kind of target she'll ever hit."

Archer felt irrationally angry. His host's contemptuous tribute to May's "niceness" was just what a husband should have wished to hear said of his wife. The fact that a coarse-minded man found her lacking in attraction was simply another proof of her quality; yet the words sent a faint shiver through his heart. What if "niceness" carried to that supreme degree were only a negation, the curtain dropped before an emptiness? As he looked at May, returning flushed and calm from her final bull's-eye, he had the feeling that he had never yet lifted that curtain.

She took the congratulations of her rivals and of the rest of the company with the simplicity that was her crowning grace. No one could ever be jealous of her triumphs because she managed to give the feeling that she would have been just as serene if she had missed them. But when her eyes met her husband's her face glowed with the pleasure she saw in his.

Mrs. Welland's basket-work pony-carriage was waiting for them, and they drove off among the dispersing carriages, May handling the reins and Archer sitting at her side.

The afternoon sunlight still lingered upon the bright lawns and shrubberies, and up and down Bellevue Avenue rolled a double line of victorias, dog-carts, landaus and "vis-à-vis," carrying well-dressed ladies and gentlemen away from the Beaufort garden-party, or homeward from their daily afternoon turn along the Ocean Drive.[4]

"Shall we go to see Granny?" May suddenly proposed. "I should like to tell her myself that I've won the prize. There's lots of time before dinner."

Archer acquiesced, and she turned the ponies down Narragansett Avenue, crossed Spring Street and drove out toward the rocky moorland beyond. In this unfashionable region Catherine the Great, always indifferent to precedent and thrifty of purse, had built herself in her youth a

---

4. Bellevue Avenue: Running on a north-south vector through Newport, Bellevue Avenue is the major street that forms the inland boundary for a number of the estates that occupy the land which extends to the Cliffs. victorias: Low, four-wheeled carriages with hooded tops; dog-carts: Light, two-wheeled carriages, usually drawn by one horse, with two back-to-back seats; landaus: See p. 4, *n.* 4; "vis-à-vis": From the French for "face-to-face," a carriage with two seats in which the passengers face each other. Ocean Drive: A fashionable and scenic route that makes a circuit of the southwestern tip of Newport connecting at its eastern conclusion to a small road to Land's End, Newport's easternmost point. (See the map of Newport, p. 252.)

many-peaked and cross-beamed *cottage orné*[5] on a bit of cheap land overlooking the bay. Here, in a thicket of stunted oaks, her verandahs spread themselves above the island-dotted waters. A winding drive led up between iron stags and blue glass balls embedded in mounds of geraniums to a front door of highly-varnished walnut under a striped verandah-roof; and behind it ran a narrow hall with a black and yellow star-patterned parquet floor, upon which opened four small square rooms with heavy flock-papers under ceilings on which an Italian house-painter had lavished all the divinities of Olympus. One of these rooms had been turned into a bedroom by Mrs. Mingott when the burden of flesh descended on her, and in the adjoining one she spent her days, enthroned in a large armchair between the open door and window, and perpetually waving a palm-leaf fan which the prodigious projection of her bosom kept so far from the rest of her person that the air it set in motion stirred only the fringe of the antimacassars[6] on the chair-arms.

Since she had been the means of hastening his marriage old Catherine had shown to Archer the cordiality which a service rendered excites toward the person served. She was persuaded that irrepressible passion was the cause of his impatience; and being an ardent admirer of impulsiveness (when it did not lead to the spending of money) she always received him with a genial twinkle of complicity and a play of allusion to which May seemed fortunately impervious.

She examined and appraised with much interest the diamond-tipped arrow which had been pinned on May's bosom at the conclusion of the match, remarking that in her day a filigree brooch would have been thought enough, but that there was no denying that Beaufort did things handsomely.

"Quite an heirloom, in fact, my dear," the old lady chuckled. "You must leave it in fee to your eldest girl." She pinched May's white arm and watched the color flood her face. "Well, well, what have I said to make you shake out the red flag? Ain't there going to be any daughters—only boys, eh? Good gracious, look at her blushing again all over her blushes! What—can't I say that either? Mercy me—when my children beg me to have all those gods and goddesses painted out overhead I always say I'm too thankful to have somebody about me that *nothing* can shock!"

Archer burst into a laugh, and May echoed it, crimson to the eyes.

"Well, now tell me all about the party, please, my dears, for I shall never get a straight word about it out of that silly Medora," the ancestress continued; and, as May exclaimed: "Aunt Medora? But I thought she was going back to Portsmouth?" she answered placidly: "So she is—but she's got to come here first to pick up Ellen. Ah—you didn't know Ellen had come to spend the day with me? Such fol-de-rol,[7] her not coming for the

5. French for "ornate cottage." The word cottage in the parlance of the elite of Newport refers to summer homes that range from rambling wooden castles to enormous limestone and marble-covered mansions.
6. Crocheted doilies and other washable coverings used to protect the backs and arms of upholstered furniture from the stains left by Macassar Oil, a popular pomade for men invented and marketed by Charles Macassar.
7. A refrain in an old song; impractical, unnecessary, or excessive trimming or effects.

summer; but I gave up arguing with young people about fifty years ago. Ellen—*Ellen!*" she cried in her shrill old voice, trying to bend forward far enough to catch a glimpse of the lawn beyond the verandah.

There was no answer, and Mrs. Mingott rapped impatiently with her stick on the shiny floor. A mulatto[8] maid-servant in a bright turban, replying to the summons, informed her mistress that she had seen "Miss Ellen" going down the path to the shore; and Mrs. Mingott turned to Archer.

"Run down and fetch her, like a good grandson; this pretty lady will describe the party to me," she said; and Archer stood up as if in a dream.

He had heard the Countess Olenska's name pronounced often enough during the year and a half since they had last met, and was even familiar with the main incidents of her life in the interval. He knew that she had spent the previous summer at Newport, where she appeared to have gone a great deal into society, but that in the autumn she had suddenly sub-let the "perfect house" which Beaufort had been at such pains to find for her, and decided to establish herself in Washington. There, during the winter, he had heard of her (as one always heard of pretty women in Washington) as shining in the "brilliant diplomatic society" that was supposed to make up for the social short-comings of the Administration.[9] He had listened to these accounts, and to various contradictory reports on her appearance, her conversation, her point of view and her choice of friends, with the detachment with which one listens to reminiscences of someone long since dead; not till Medora suddenly spoke her name at the archery match had Ellen Olenska become a living presence to him again. The Marchioness's foolish lisp had called up a vision of the little fire-lit drawing room and the sound of the carriage-wheels returning down the deserted street. He thought of a story he had read, of some peasant children in Tuscany lighting a bunch of straw in a wayside cavern, and revealing old silent images in their painted tomb. . . .

The way to the shore descended from the bank on which the house was perched to a walk above the water planted with weeping willows. Through their veil Archer caught the glint of the Lime Rock, with its white-washed turret and the tiny house in which the heroic lighthouse keeper, Ida Lewis,[1] was living her last venerable years. Beyond it lay the flat reaches and ugly government chimneys of Goat Island, the bay

---

8. An individual of mixed Caucasian and African racial heritage.
9. "brilliant diplomatic society": As a result of its diplomatic history, Washington society oper-ated under a different set of social rules than the older and more prominent cities to the north along the eastern seaboard. Unlike newcomers to New York, Boston, and Philadelphia who had to wait to be visited by society, those arriving in the national capitol were expected to take the initiative, announcing their presence in the city by making the rounds to leave cards. The Administration: While Ulysses S. Grant was called the "butcher" and accused of being an alcoholic by his detractors, the "social shortcomings" of the Grant administration were less the fault of Grant than the legislators who had been bribed in 1867 and 1868 by the Union Pacific Railroad in what came to be known as the Credit Mobilier scandal. The revelation of this corruption cast a pall on the election of 1872 and the Washington social scene of the period.
1. Ida Lewis, 1842–1911, was keeper of the lighthouse on Lime Rock in Newport Harbor for over fifty years. In 1866, she rescued a valuable sheep belonging to August Belmont from the waters off Newport. Lewis gained a national reputation for valor in 1869, the year when her rescues of soldiers and others in danger made her a figure in the popular press.

spreading northward in a shimmer of gold to Prudence Island with its low growth of oaks, and the shores of Conanicut faint in the sunset haze.[2]

From the willow walk projected a slight wooden pier ending in a sort of pagoda-like summer-house; and in the pagoda a lady stood, leaning against the rail, her back to the shore. Archer stopped at the sight as if he had waked from sleep. That vision of the past was a dream, and the reality was what awaited him in the house on the bank overhead: was Mrs. Welland's pony-carriage circling around and around the oval at the door, was May sitting under the shameless Olympians and glowing with secret hopes, was the Welland villa at the far end of Bellevue Avenue, and Mr. Welland, already dressed for dinner, and pacing the drawing-room floor, watch in hand, with dyspeptic impatience—for it was one of the houses in which one always knew exactly what is happening at a given hour.

"What am I? A son-in-law—" Archer thought.

The figure at the end of the pier had not moved. For a long moment the young man stood halfway down the bank, gazing at the bay furrowed with the coming and going of sailboats, yacht-launches, fishing-craft and the trailing black coal-barges hauled by noisy tugs. The lady in the summer-house seemed to be held by the same sight. Beyond the gray bastions of Fort Adams a long-drawn sunset was splintering up into a thousand fires, and the radiance caught the sail of a catboat as it beat out through the channel between the Lime Rock and the shore.[3] Archer, as he watched, remembered the scene in *The Shaughraun*,[4] and Montague lifting Ada Dyas's ribbon to his lips without her knowing that he was in the room.

"She doesn't know—she hasn't guessed. Shouldn't I know if she came up behind me; I wonder?" he mused; and suddenly he said to himself: "If she doesn't turn before that sail crosses the Lime Rock light I'll go back."

The boat was gliding out on the receding tide. It slid before the Lime Rock, blotted out Ida Lewis's little house, and passed across the turret in which the light was hung. Archer waited till a wide space of water sparkled between the last reef of the island and the stern of the boat; but still the figure in the summer-house did not move.

He turned and walked up the hill.

"I'm sorry you didn't find Ellen—I should have liked to see her again," May said as they drove home through the dusk. "But perhaps she wouldn't have cared—she seems so changed."

"Changed?" echoed her husband in a colorless voice, his eyes fixed on the ponies' twitching ears.

2. Goat, Prudence, and Conanicut islands all lie in Narragansett Bay beyond the lighthouse warning sailors of the rocky coast. (The location of some of these islands as well as other places named in the novel are indicated on the map of Newport, p. 252.)
3. Fort Adams: Named for President Adams and begun in 1824, this structure built to guard the entry into Narragansett Bay was part of a plan to fortify the U.S. seacoast; catboat: See photograph, p. 253.
4. See p. 247 for a photograph of this scene.

"So indifferent to her friends, I mean; giving up New York and her house, and spending her time with such queer people. Fancy how hideously uncomfortable she must be at the Blenkers'! She says she does it to keep Aunt Medora out of mischief: to prevent her marrying dreadful people. But I sometimes think we've always bored her."

Archer made no answer, and she continued, with a tinge of hardness that he had never before noticed in her frank fresh voice: "After all, I wonder if she wouldn't be happier with her husband."

He burst into a laugh. "*Sancta simplicitas!*"[5] he exclaimed; and as she turned a puzzled frown on him he added: "I don't think I ever heard you say a cruel thing before."

"Cruel?"

"Well—watching the contortions of the damned is supposed to be a favorite sport of the angels; but I believe even they don't think people happier in hell."

"It's a pity she ever married abroad then," said May, in the placid tone with which her mother met Mr. Welland's vagaries; and Archer felt himself gently relegated to the category of unreasonable husbands.

They drove down Bellevue Avenue and turned in between the chamfered[6] wooden gate-posts surmounted by cast-iron lamps which marked the approach to the Welland villa. Lights were already shining through its windows, and Archer, as the carriage stopped, caught a glimpse of his father-in-law, exactly as he had pictured him, pacing the drawing room, watch in hand and wearing the pained expression that he had long since found to be much more efficacious than anger.

The young man, as he followed his wife into the hall, was conscious of a curious reversal of mood. There was something about the luxury of the Welland house and the density of the Welland atmosphere, so charged with minute observances and exactions, that always stole into his system like a narcotic. The heavy carpets, the watchful servants, the perpetually reminding tick of disciplined clocks, the perpetually renewed stack of cards and invitations on the hall table, the whole chain of tyrannical trifles binding one hour to the next, and each member of the household to all the others, made any less systematized and affluent existence seem unreal and precarious. But now it was the Welland house, and the life he was expected to lead in it, that had become unreal and irrelevant, and the brief scene on the shore, when he had stood irresolute, halfway down the bank, was as close to him as the blood in his veins.

All night he lay awake in the big chintz[7] bedroom at May's side, watching the moonlight slant along the carpet, and thinking of Ellen Olenska driving home across the gleaming beaches behind Beaufort's trotters.

---

5. Latin, literally, "Holy simplicity"; here, an expression of exasperation that takes the place of a profanity.
6. Posts with edges cut off, beveled. The process of being chamfered also refers to decorative cutting, a channeling that effects a grooved or fluted design.
7. See photograph of "chintz" interior in Wharton's mother's home, p. 237. References to this glossy floral fabric appear throughout the novel.

# XXII

"A party for the Blenkers—the Blenkers?"

Mr. Welland laid down his knife and fork and looked anxiously and incredulously across the luncheon table at his wife, who, adjusting her gold eye-glasses, read aloud, in the tone of high comedy: "Professor and Mrs. Emerson Sillerton request the pleasure of Mr. and Mrs. Welland's company at the meeting of the Wednesday Afternoon Club on August 25th at 3 o'clock punctually. To meet Mrs. and the Misses Blenker.

Red Gables, Catherine Street.                                    R. S. V. P."

"Good gracious—" Mr. Welland gasped, as if a second reading had been necessary to bring the monstrous absurdity of the thing home to him.

"Poor Amy Sillerton—you never can tell what her husband will do next," Mrs. Welland sighed. "I suppose he's just discovered the Blenkers."

Professor Emerson Sillerton was a thorn in the side of Newport society; and a thorn that could not be plucked out, for it grew on a venerable and venerated family tree. He was, as people said, a man who had had "every advantage." His father was Sillerton Jackson's uncle, his mother a Pennilow of Boston; on each side there was wealth and position, and mutual suitability. Nothing—as Mrs. Welland had often remarked—nothing on earth obliged Emerson Sillerton to be an archeologist, or indeed a Professor of any sort, or to live in Newport in winter, or do any of the other revolutionary things that he did. But at least, if he was going to break with tradition and flout society in the face, he need not have married poor Amy Dagonet, who had a right to expect "something different," and money enough to keep her own carriage.

No one in the Mingott set could understand why Amy Sillerton had submitted so tamely to the eccentricities of a husband who filled the house with long-haired men and short-haired women, and, when he traveled, took her to explore tombs in Yucatan instead of going to Paris or Italy. But there they were, set in their ways, and apparently unaware that they were different from other people; and when they gave one of their dreary annual garden-parties every family on the Cliffs, because of the Sillerton-Pennilow-Dagonet connection, had to draw lots and send an unwilling representative.

"It's a wonder," Mrs. Welland remarked, "that they didn't choose the Cup Race day! Do you remember, two years ago, their giving a party for a black man on the day of Julia Mingott's *thé dansant*?[1] Luckily this time there's nothing else going on that I know of—for of course some of us will have to go."

---

1. French, a tea party with dancing. The British custom of afternoon tea (without the French extravagance of dancing) became increasingly popular among elite New Yorkers during the 1870s. Since society demanded social reciprocity, less intimate teas held for larger groups provided an affordable alternative for those who had suffered financial reverses during this mercurial decade, most notably in the aftermath of the Panic of 1873.

Mr. Welland sighed nervously. " 'Some of us,' my dear—more than one? Three o'clock is such a very awkward hour. I have to be here at half-past three to take my drops: it's really no use trying to follow Bencomb's new treatment if I don't do it systematically; and if I join you later, of course I shall miss my drive." At the thought he laid down his knife and fork again, and a flush of anxiety rose to his finely-wrinkled cheek.

"There's no reason why you should go at all, my dear," his wife answered with a cheerfulness that had become automatic. "I have some cards to leave at the other end of Bellevue Avenue, and I'll drop in at about half-past three and stay long enough to make poor Amy feel that she hasn't been slighted." She glanced hesitatingly at her daughter. "And if Newland's afternoon is provided for perhaps May can drive you out with the ponies, and try their new russet harness."

It was a principle in the Welland family that people's days and hours should be what Mrs. Welland called "provided for." The melancholy possibility of having to "kill time" (especially for those who did not care for whist or solitaire) was a vision that haunted her as the specter of the unemployed haunts the philanthropist. Another of her principles was that parents should never (at least visibly) interfere with the plans of their married children; and the difficulty of adjusting this respect for May's independence with the exigency of Mr. Welland's claims could be overcome only by the exercise of an ingenuity which left not a second of Mrs. Welland's own time unprovided for.

"Of course I'll drive with Papa—I'm sure Newland will find something to do," May said, in a tone that gently reminded her husband of his lack of response. It was a cause of constant distress to Mrs. Welland that her son-in-law showed so little foresight in planning his days. Often already, during the fortnight that he had passed under her roof, when she enquired how he meant to spend his afternoon, he had answered paradoxically: "Oh, I think for a change I'll just save it instead of spending it—" and once, when she and May had had to go on a long-postponed round of afternoon calls, he had confessed to having lain all the afternoon under a rock on the beach below the house.

"Newland never seems to look ahead," Mrs. Welland once ventured to complain to her daughter; and May answered serenely: "No; but you see it doesn't matter, because when there's nothing particular to do he reads a book."

"Ah, yes—like his father!" Mrs. Welland agreed, as if allowing for an inherited oddity; and after that the question of Newland's unemployment was tacitly dropped.

Nevertheless, as the day for the Sillerton reception approached, May began to show a natural solicitude for his welfare, and to suggest a tennis match at the Chiverses', or a sail on Julius Beaufort's cutter,[2] as a means of atoning for her temporary desertion. "I shall be back by six, you know, dear: Papa never drives later than that—" and she was not reassured till Archer said that he thought of hiring a run-about

2. A single-masted boat with sails suspended fore and aft.

and driving up the island to a stud-farm to look at a second horse for her brougham. They had been looking for this horse for some time, and the suggestion was so acceptable that May glanced at her mother as if to say: "You see he knows how to plan out his time as well as any of us."

The idea of the stud-farm and the brougham horse had germinated in Archer's mind on the very day when the Emerson Sillerton invitation had first been mentioned; but he had kept it to himself as if there were something clandestine in the plan, and discovery might prevent its execution. He had, however, taken the precaution to engage in advance a run-about with a pair of old livery-stable trotters that could still do their eighteen miles[3] on level roads; and at two o'clock, hastily deserting the luncheon-table, he sprang into the light carriage and drove off.

The day was perfect. A breeze from the north drove little puffs of white cloud across an ultramarine sky, with a bright sea running under it. Bellevue Avenue was empty at that hour, and after dropping the stable-lad at the corner of Mill Street Archer turned down the Old Beach Road and drove across Eastman's Beach.[4]

He had the feeling of unexplained excitement with which, on half-holidays at school, he used to start off into the unknown. Taking his pair at an easy gait, he counted on reaching the stud-farm, which was not far beyond Paradise Rocks,[5] before three o'clock; so that, after looking over the horse (and trying him if he seemed promising) he would still have four golden hours to dispose of.

As soon as he heard of the Sillertons' party he had said to himself that the Marchioness Manson would certainly come to Newport with the Blenkers, and that Madame Olenska might again take the opportunity of spending the day with her grandmother. At any rate, the Blenker habitation would probably be deserted, and he would be able, without indiscretion, to satisfy a vague curiosity concerning it. He was not sure that he wanted to see the Countess Olenska again; but ever since he had looked at her from the path above the bay he had wanted, irrationally and indescribably, to see the place she was living in, and to follow the movements of her imagined figure as he had watched the real one in the summer-house. The longing was with him day and night, an incessant undefinable craving, like the sudden whim of a sick man for food or drink once tasted and long since forgotten. He could not see beyond the craving, or picture what it might lead to, for he was not conscious of any wish to speak to Madame Olenska or to hear her voice. He simply felt that if he could carry away the vision of the spot of earth she walked on, and the way the sky and sea enclosed it, the rest of the world might seem less empty.

3. The expected distance that could be traversed in a day by a team of horses pulling a wheeled conveyance over level roads. Begun in the mid-afternoon, Newland's entire journey to Portsmouth and back is about eight miles.
4. The actual name, Easton's Beach, was taken from the adjacent Easton Farm, which ends at the steep, rocky embankment of the Cliffs that rise southward to form Newport's eastern shore (see map, p. 252).
5. One of several distinctive and suggestively named conglomerate rocks (including Hanging Rock and Purgatory Chasm) which signal the change in the shoreline as it rises to form the steep embankment called "the Cliffs" (see map, p. 252).

When he reached the stud-farm a glance showed him that the horse was not what he wanted; nevertheless he took a turn behind it in order to prove to himself that he was not in a hurry. But at three o'clock he shook out the reins over the trotters and turned into the by-roads leading to Portsmouth. The wind had dropped and a faint haze on the horizon showed that a fog was waiting to steal up the Saconnet[6] on the turn of the tide; but all about him fields and woods were steeped in golden light.

He drove past gray-shingled farm-houses in orchards, past hay-fields and groves of oak, past villages with white steeples rising sharply into the fading sky; and at last, after stopping to ask the way of some men at work in a field, he turned down a lane between high banks of golden-rod and brambles. At the end of the lane was the blue glimmer of the river; to the left, standing in front of a clump of oaks and maples, he saw a long tumbledown house with white paint peeling from its clapboards.

On the road-side facing the gateway stood one of the open sheds in which the New Englander shelters his farming implements and visitors "hitch" their "teams." Archer, jumping down, led his pair into the shed, and after tying them to a post turned toward the house. The patch of lawn before it had relapsed into a hay-field; but to the left an overgrown box-garden full of dahlias and rusty rose-bushes encircled a ghostly summer-house of trellis-work that had once been white, surmounted by a wooden Cupid who had lost his bow and arrow but continued to take ineffectual aim.

Archer leaned for a while against the gate. No one was in sight, and not a sound came from the open windows of the house: a grizzled Newfoundland[7] dozing before the door seemed as ineffectual a guardian as the arrowless Cupid. It was strange to think that this place of silence and decay was the home of the turbulent Blenkers; yet Archer was sure that he was not mistaken.

For a long time he stood there, content to take in the scene, and gradually falling under its drowsy spell; but at length he roused himself to the sense of the passing time. Should he look his fill and then drive away? He stood irresolute, wishing suddenly to see the inside of the house, so that he might picture the room that Madame Olenska sat in. There was nothing to prevent his walking up to the door and ringing the bell; if, as he supposed, she was away with the rest of the party, he could easily give his name, and ask permission to go into the sitting room to write a message.

But instead, he crossed the lawn and turned toward the box-garden. As he entered it he caught sight of something bright-colored in the summer-house, and presently made it out to be a pink parasol. The parasol drew him like a magnet: he was sure it was hers. He went into

---

6. The Saconnet River flows southward, dividing Aquidneck Island from the mainland of Rhode Island and forms the eastern boundary of Middletown, a village located one mile north of Newport.
7. A breed of intelligent, very large, black dogs reputed to have originated from the breeding of European dogs to native stock.

the summer-house, and sitting down on the rickety seat picked up the silken thing and looked at its carved handle, which was made of some rare wood that gave out an aromatic scent. Archer lifted the handle to his lips.

He heard a rustle of skirts against the box, and sat motionless, leaning on the parasol handle with clasped hands, and letting the rustle come nearer without lifting his eyes. He had always known that this must happen. . . .

"Oh, Mr. Archer!" exclaimed a loud young voice; and looking up he saw before him the youngest and largest of the Blenker girls, blonde and blowsy, in bedraggled muslin. A red blotch on one of her cheeks seemed to show that it had recently been pressed against a pillow, and her half-awakened eyes stared at him hospitably but confusedly.

"Gracious—where did you drop from? I must have been sound asleep in the hammock. Everybody else has gone to Newport. Did you ring?" she incoherently enquired.

Archer's confusion was greater than hers. "I—no—that is, I was just going to. I had to come up the island to see about a horse, and I drove over on a chance of finding Mrs. Blenker and your visitors. But the house seemed empty—so I sat down to wait."

Miss Blenker, shaking off the fumes of sleep, looked at him with increasing interest. "The house *is* empty. Mother's not here, or the Marchioness—or anybody but me." Her glance became faintly reproachful. "Didn't you know that Professor and Mrs. Sillerton are giving a garden-party for mother and all of us this afternoon? It was too unlucky that I couldn't go; but I've had a sore throat, and mother was afraid of the drive home this evening. Did you ever know anything so disappointing? Of course," she added gaily, "I shouldn't have minded half as much if I'd known you were coming."

Symptoms of a lumbering coquetry became visible in her, and Archer found the strength to break in: "But Madame Olenska—has she gone to Newport too?"

Miss Blenker looked at him with surprise. "Madame Olenska—didn't you know she'd been called away?"

"Called away?—"

"Oh, my best parasol! I lent it to that goose of a Katie, because it matched her ribbons, and the careless thing must have dropped it here. We Blenkers are all like that . . . real Bohemians!" Recovering the sunshade with a powerful hand she unfurled it and suspended its rosy dome above her head. "Yes, Ellen was called away yesterday: she lets us call her Ellen, you know. A telegram came from Boston: she said she might be gone for two days. I do *love* the way she does her hair, don't you?" Miss Blenker rambled on.

Archer continued to stare through her as though she had been transparent. All he saw was the trumpery parasol that arched its pinkness above her giggling head.

After a moment he ventured: "You don't happen to know why Madame Olenska went to Boston? I hope it was not on account of bad news?"

Miss Blenker took this with a cheerful incredulity. "Oh, I don't believe so. She didn't tell us what was in the telegram. I think she didn't want the Marchioness to know. She's so romantic-looking, isn't she? Doesn't she remind you of Mrs. Scott-Siddons when she reads *Lady Geraldine's Courtship*?[8] Did you never hear her?"

Archer was dealing hurriedly with crowding thoughts. His whole future seemed suddenly to be unrolled before him; and passing down its endless emptiness he saw the dwindling figure of a man to whom nothing was ever to happen. He glanced about him at the unpruned garden, the tumbledown house, and the oak-grove under which the dusk was gathering. It had seemed so exactly the place in which he ought to have found Madame Olenska; and she was far away, and even the pink sunshade was not hers. . . .

He frowned and hesitated. "You don't know, I suppose—I shall be in Boston tomorrow. If I could manage to see her—"

He felt that Miss Blenker was losing interest in him, though her smile persisted. "Oh, of course; how lovely of you! She's staying at the Parker House;[9] it must be horrible there in this weather."

After that Archer was but intermittently aware of the remarks they exchanged. He could only remember stoutly resisting her entreaty that he should await the returning family and have high tea with them before he drove home. At length, with his hostess still at his side, he passed out of range of the wooden Cupid, unfastened his horses and drove off. At the turn of the lane he saw Miss Blenker standing at the gate and waving the pink parasol.

# XXIII

The next morning, when Archer got out of the Fall River train, he emerged upon a steaming mid-summer Boston. The streets near the station were full of the smell of beer and coffee and decaying fruit, and a shirt-sleeved populace moved through them with the intimate abandon of boarders going down the passage to the bathroom.

Archer found a cab and drove to the Somerset Club[1] for breakfast. Even the fashionable quarters had the air of untidy domesticity to which no excess of heat ever degrades the European cities. Caretakers in calico lounged on the doorsteps of the wealthy, and the Common looked like a pleasure-ground on the morrow of a Masonic picnic.[2] If Archer had tried to imagine Ellen Olenska in improbable scenes he

---

8. Mrs. Scott-Siddons: Mary Frances Scott-Siddons (1744–1796), English actress; painted by Sir Joshua Reynolds in *Sara Siddons as the Tragic Muse* (1784); *Lady Geraldine's Courtship*: An 1844 poem by Elizabeth Barrett that contained a tribute to the work of Robert Browning; this poem led to the meeting of the two poets, who eventually married.
9. The oldest continuously operated hotel in Boston, built in 1854 and located on School Street.
1. The first men's club in Boston, founded 1851 and located at the corner of Beacon and Somerset Streets.
2. Common: A park in downtown Boston that was originally a common pasture; Masonic picnic: Public and lively gathering of members of the secret society of Free Masonry, an international fraternal organization.

could not have called up any into which it was more difficult to fit her than this heat-prostrated and deserted Boston.

He breakfasted with appetite and method, beginning with a slice of melon, and studying a morning paper while he waited for his toast and scrambled eggs. A new sense of energy and activity had possessed him ever since he had announced to May the night before that he had business in Boston, and should take the Fall River boat[3] that night and go on to New York the following evening. It had always been understood that he would return to town early in the week, and when he got back from his expedition to Portsmouth a letter from the office, which fate had conspicuously placed on a corner of the hall table, sufficed to justify his sudden change of plan. He was even ashamed of the ease with which the whole thing had been done: it reminded him, for an uncomfortable moment, of Lawrence Lefferts's masterly contrivances for securing his freedom. But this did not long trouble him, for he was not in an analytic mood.

After breakfast he smoked a cigarette and glanced over the *Commercial Advertiser*.[4] While he was thus engaged two or three men he knew came in, and the usual greetings were exchanged: it was the same world after all, though he had such a queer sense of having slipped through the meshes of time and space.

He looked at his watch, and finding that it was half-past nine got up and went into the writing room. There he wrote a few lines, and ordered a messenger to take a cab to the Parker House and wait for the answer. He then sat down behind another newspaper and tried to calculate how long it would take a cab to get to the Parker House.

"The lady was out, sir," he suddenly heard a waiter's voice at his elbow; and he stammered: "Out?—" as if it were a word in a strange language.

He got up and went into the hall. It must be a mistake: she could not be out at that hour. He flushed with anger at his own stupidity: why had he not sent the note as soon as he arrived?

He found his hat and stick and went forth into the street. The city had suddenly become as strange and vast and empty as if he were a traveler from distant lands. For a moment he stood on the doorstep hesitating; then he decided to go to the Parker House. What if the messenger had been misinformed, and she were still there?

He started to walk across the Common; and on the first bench, under a tree, he saw her sitting. She had a gray silk sunshade over her head—how could he ever have imagined her with a pink one? As he approached he was struck by her listless attitude: she sat there as if she had nothing else to do. He saw her drooping profile, and the knot

---

3. A steamship line that connected New York to seaside resorts to the north, such as Newport. From Fall River passengers would have to switch to the railroad to continue north to Boston. Together, this popular route combining travel by rail and boat was known as the Fall River Line (see p. 233).
4. A type of newspaper that specialized in announcements for goods being sold and schedules for travel by stagecoach, train, and boat. This particular paper is, in all likelihood, the *Weekly Commercial Advertiser*, an offshoot of the *New York Spectator*, printed only on Thursday mornings under the bold claim that it was "The Largest and Cheapest Weekly . . . published in the World."

of hair fastened low in the neck under her dark hat, and the long wrinkled glove on the hand that held the sunshade. He came a step or two nearer, and she turned and looked at him.

"Oh"—she said; and for the first time he noticed a startled look on her face; but in another moment it gave way to a slow smile of wonder and contentment.

"Oh"—she murmured again, on a different note, as he stood looking down at her; and without rising she made a place for him on the bench.

"I'm here on business—just got here," Archer explained; and, without knowing why, he suddenly began to feign astonishment at seeing her. "But what on earth are *you* doing in this wilderness?" He had really no idea what he was saying: he felt as if he were shouting at her across endless distances, and she might vanish again before he could overtake her.

"I? Oh, I'm here on business too," she answered, turning her head toward him so that they were face to face. The words hardly reached him: he was aware only of her voice, and of the startling fact that not an echo of it had remained in his memory. He had not even remembered that it was low-pitched, with a faint roughness on the consonants.

"You do your hair differently," he said, his heart beating as if he had uttered something irrevocable.

"Differently? No—it's only that I do it as best I can when I'm without Nastasia."

"Nastasia; but isn't she with you?"

"No; I'm alone. For two days it was not worthwhile to bring her."

"You're alone—at the Parker House?"

She looked at him with a flash of her old malice. "Does it strike you as dangerous?"

"No; not dangerous—"

"But unconventional? I see; I suppose it is." She considered a moment. "I hadn't thought of it, because I've just done something so much more unconventional." The faint tinge of irony lingered in her eyes. "I've just refused to take back a sum of money—that belonged to me."

Archer sprang up and moved a step or two away. She had furled her parasol and sat absently drawing patterns on the gravel. Presently he came back and stood before her.

"Someone—has come here to meet you?"

"Yes."

"With this offer?"

She nodded.

"And you refused—because of the conditions?"

"I refused," she said after a moment.

He sat down by her again. "What were the conditions?"

"Oh, they were not onerous: just to sit at the head of his table now and then."

There was another interval of silence. Archer's heart had slammed itself shut in the queer way it had, and he sat vainly groping for a word.

"He wants you back—at any price?"

"Well—a considerable price. At least the sum is considerable for me."

He paused again, beating about the question he felt he must put.

"It was to meet him here that you came?"

She stared, and then burst into a laugh. "Meet him—my husband? *Here*? At this season he's always at Cowes or Baden."[5]

"He sent someone?"

"Yes."

"With a letter?"

She shook her head. "No; just a message. He never writes. I don't think I've had more than one letter from him." The allusion brought the color to her cheek, and it reflected itself in Archer's vivid blush.

"Why does he never write?"

"Why should he? What does one have secretaries for?"

The young man's blush deepened. She had pronounced the word as if it had no more significance than any other in her vocabulary. For a moment it was on the tip of his tongue to ask: "Did he send his secretary, then?" But the remembrance of Count Olenski's only letter to his wife was too present to him. He paused again, and then took another plunge.

"And the person?"—

"The emissary? The emissary," Madame Olenska rejoined, still smiling, "might, for all I care, have left already; but he has insisted on waiting till this evening . . . in case . . . on the chance. . . ."

"And you came out here to think the chance over?"

"I came out to get a breath of air. The hotel's too stifling. I'm taking the afternoon train back to Portsmouth."

They sat silent, not looking at each other, but straight ahead at the people passing along the path. Finally she turned her eyes again to his face and said: "You're not changed."

He felt like answering: "I was, till I saw you again"; but instead he stood up abruptly and glanced about him at the untidy sweltering park.

"This is horrible. Why shouldn't we go out a little on the bay? There's a breeze, and it will be cooler. We might take the steamboat down to Point Arley." She glanced up at him hesitatingly and he went on: "On a Monday morning there won't be anybody on the boat. My train doesn't leave till evening: I'm going back to New York. Why shouldn't we?" he insisted, looking down at her; and suddenly he broke out: "Haven't we done all we could?"

"Oh"—she murmured again. She stood up and reopened her sunshade, glancing about her as if to take counsel of the scene, and assure herself of the impossibility of remaining in it. Then her eyes returned to his face. "You mustn't say things like that to me," she said.

5. A resort city in Switzerland.

"I'll say anything you like; or nothing. I won't open my mouth unless you tell me to. What harm can it do to anybody? All I want is to listen to you," he stammered.

She drew out a little gold-faced watch on an enameled chain. "Oh, don't calculate," he broke out; "give me the day! I want to get you away from that man. At what time was he coming?"

Her color rose again. "At eleven."

"Then you must come at once."

"You needn't be afraid—if I don't come."

"Nor you either—if you do. I swear I only want to hear about you, to know what you've been doing. It's a hundred years since we've met—it may be another hundred before we meet again."

She still wavered, her anxious eyes on his face. "Why didn't you come down to the beach to fetch me, the day I was at Granny's?" she asked.

"Because you didn't look round—because you didn't know I was there. I swore I wouldn't unless you looked round." He laughed as the childishness of the confession struck him.

"But I didn't look round on purpose."

"On purpose?"

"I knew you were there; when you drove in I recognized the ponies. So I went down to the beach."

"To get away from me as far as you could?"

She repeated in a low voice: "To get away from you as far as I could."

He laughed out again, this time in boyish satisfaction. "Well, you see it's no use. I may as well tell you," he added, "that the business I came here for was just to find you. But, look here, we must start or we shall miss our boat."

"Our boat?" She frowned perplexedly, and then smiled. "Oh, but I must go back to the hotel first: I must leave a note—"

"As many notes as you please. You can write here." He drew out a note-case and one of the new stylographic pens.[6] "I've even got an envelope—you see how everything's predestined! There—steady the thing on your knee, and I'll get the pen going in a second. They have to be humored; wait—" He banged the hand that held the pen against the back of the bench. "It's like jerking down the mercury in a ther-mometer: just a trick. Now try—"

She laughed, and bending over the sheet of paper which he had laid on his note-case, began to write. Archer walked away a few steps, star-ing with radiant unseeing eyes at the passers-by, who, in their turn, paused to stare at the unwonted sight of a fashionably-dressed lady writing a note on her knee on a bench in the Common.

Madame Olenska slipped the sheet into the envelope, wrote a name on it, and put it into her pocket. Then she too stood up.

They walked back toward Beacon Street, and near the club Archer

---

6. Patented in Canada (1875) and in the United States (1876), a stylographic pen is a fountain pen in which ink is released through a steel tube when a needle in the nib is pressed down; traditional fountain pens needed to be dipped in ink before writing.

caught sight of the plush-lined "herdic"[7] which had carried his note to the Parker House, and whose driver was reposing from this effort by bathing his brow at the corner hydrant.

"I told you everything was predestined! Here's a cab for us. You see!" They laughed, astonished at the miracle of picking up a public conveyance at that hour, and in that unlikely spot, in a city where cabstands were still a "foreign" novelty.

Archer, looking at his watch, saw that there was time to drive to the Parker House before going to the steamboat landing. They rattled through the hot streets and drew up at the door of the hotel.

Archer held out his hand for the letter. "Shall I take it in?" he asked; but Madame Olenska, shaking her head, sprang out and disappeared through the glazed doors. It was barely half-past ten; but what if the emissary, impatient for her reply, and not knowing how else to employ his time, were already seated among the travelers with cooling drinks at their elbows of whom Archer had caught a glimpse as she went in?

He waited, pacing up and down before the herdic. A Sicilian youth with eyes like Nastasia's offered to shine his boots, and an Irish matron to sell him peaches; and every few moments the doors opened to let out hot men with straw hats tilted far back, who glanced at him as they went by. He marveled that the door should open so often, and that all the people it let out should look so like each other, and so like all the other hot men who, at that hour, through the length and breadth of the land, were passing continuously in and out of the swinging doors of hotels.

And then, suddenly, came a face that he could not relate to the other faces. He caught but a flash of it, for his pacings had carried him to the farthest point of his beat, and it was in turning back to the hotel that he saw, in a group of typical countenances—the lank and weary, the round and surprised, the lantern-jawed and mild—this other face that was so many more things at once, and things so different. It was that of a young man, pale too, and half-extinguished by the heat, or worry, or both, but somehow, quicker, vivider, more conscious; or perhaps seeming so because he was so different. Archer hung a moment on a thin thread of memory, but it snapped and floated off with the disappearing face—apparently that of some foreign business man, looking doubly foreign in such a setting. He vanished in the stream of passers-by, and Archer resumed his patrol.

He did not care to be seen watch in hand within view of the hotel, and his unaided reckoning of the lapse of time led him to conclude that, if Madame Olenska was so long in reappearing, it could only be because she had met the emissary and been waylaid by him. At the thought Archer's apprehension rose to anguish.

"If she doesn't come soon I'll go in and find her," he said.

The doors swung open again and she was at his side. They got into the herdic, and as it drove off he took out his watch and saw that she

7. A small horse-drawn omnibus of late nineteenth-century America, featuring side seats and typically entered from the back.

had been absent just three minutes. In the clatter of loose windows that made talk impossible they bumped over the disjointed cobblestones to the wharf.

Seated side by side on a bench of the half-empty boat they found that they had hardly anything to say to each other, or rather that what they had to say communicated itself best in the blessed silence of their release and their isolation.

As the paddle-wheels began to turn, and wharves and shipping to recede through the veil of heat, it seemed to Archer that everything in the old familiar world of habit was receding also. He longed to ask Madame Olenska if she did not have the same feeling: the feeling that they were starting on some long voyage from which they might never return. But he was afraid to say it, or anything else that might disturb the delicate balance of her trust in him. In reality he had no wish to betray that trust. There had been days and nights when the memory of their kiss had burned and burned on his lips; the day before even, on the drive to Portsmouth, the thought of her had run through him like fire; but now that she was beside him, and they were drifting forth into this unknown world, they seemed to have reached the kind of deeper nearness that a touch may sunder.

As the boat left the harbor and turned seaward a breeze stirred about them and the bay broke up into long oily undulations, then into ripples tipped with spray. The fog of sultriness still hung over the city, but ahead lay a fresh world of ruffled waters, and distant promontories with lighthouses in the sun. Madame Olenska, leaning back against the boat-rail, drank in the coolness between parted lips. She had wound a long veil about her hat, but it left her face uncovered, and Archer was struck by the tranquil gaiety of her expression. She seemed to take their adventure as a matter of course, and to be neither in fear of unexpected encounters nor (what was worse) unduly elated by their possibility.

In the bare dining room of the inn, which he had hoped they would have to themselves, they found a strident party of innocent-looking young men and women—school-teachers on a holiday, the landlord told them—and Archer's heart sank at the idea of having to talk through their noise.

"This is hopeless—I'll ask for a private room," he said; and Madame Olenska, without offering any objection, waited while he went in search of it. The room opened on a long wooden verandah, with the sea coming in at the windows. It was bare and cool, with a table covered with a coarse checkered cloth and adorned by a bottle of pickles and a blueberry pie under a cage. No more guileless-looking *cabinet particulier*[8] ever offered its shelter to a clandestine couple: Archer fancied he saw the sense of its reassurance in the faintly amused smile with which Madame Olenska sat down opposite to him. A woman who had run away from her husband—and reputedly with another man—

8. French, "private room."

was likely to have mastered the art of taking things for granted; but something in the quality of her composure took the edge from his irony. By being so quiet, so unsurprised, and so simple she had managed to brush away the conventions and make him feel that to seek to be alone was the natural thing for two old friends who had so much to say to each other. . . .

## XXIV

They lunched slowly and meditatively, with mute intervals between rushes of talk; for, the spell once broken, they had much to say, and yet moments when saying became the mere accompaniment to long duologues of silence. Archer kept the talk from his own affairs, not with conscious intention but because he did not want to miss a word of her history; and leaning on the table, her chin resting on her clasped hands, she talked to him of the year and a half since they had met.

She had grown tired of what people called "society"; New York was kind, it was almost oppressively hospitable; she should never forget the way in which it had welcomed her back; but after the first flush of novelty she had found herself, as she phrased it, too "different" to care for the things it cared about—and so she had decided to try Washington, where one was supposed to meet more varieties of people and of opinion. And on the whole she should probably settle down in Washington, and make a home there for poor Medora, who had worn out the patience of all her other relations just at the time when she most needed looking after and protecting from matrimonial perils.

"But Dr. Carver—aren't you afraid of Dr. Carver? I hear he's been staying with you at the Blenkers'."

She smiled. "Oh, the Carver danger is over. Dr. Carver is a very clever man. He wants a rich wife to finance his plans, and Medora is simply a good advertisement as a convert."

"A convert to what?"

"To all sorts of new and crazy social schemes. But, do you know, they interest me more than the blind conformity to tradition—somebody else's tradition—that I see among our own friends. It seems stupid to have discovered America only to make it into a copy of another country." She smiled across the table. "Do you suppose Christopher Columbus would have taken all that trouble just to go to the Opera with the Selfridge Merrys?"

Archer changed color. "And Beaufort—do you say these things to Beaufort?" he asked abruptly.

"I haven't seen him for a long time. But I used to; and he understands."

"Ah, it's what I've always told you; you don't like us. And you like Beaufort because he's so unlike us." He looked about the bare room and out at the bare beach and the row of stark white village houses strung along the shore. "We're damnably dull. We've no character, no color, no variety—I wonder," he broke out, "why you don't go back?"

Her eyes darkened, and he expected an indignant rejoinder. But she sat silent, as if thinking over what he had said, and he grew frightened lest she should answer that she wondered too.

At length she said: "I believe it's because of you."

It was impossible to make the confession more dispassionately, or in a tone less encouraging to the vanity of the person addressed. Archer reddened to the temples, but dared not move or speak: it was as if her words had been some rare butterfly that the least motion might drive off on startled wings, but that might gather a flock about it if it were left undisturbed.

"At least," she continued, "it was you who made me understand that under the dullness there are things so fine and sensitive and delicate that even those I most cared for in my other life look cheap in comparison. I don't know how to explain myself"—she drew together her troubled brows—"but it seems as if I'd never before understood with how much that is hard and shabby and base the most exquisite pleasures may be paid."

"Exquisite pleasures—it's something to have had them!" he felt like retorting; but the appeal in her eyes kept him silent.

"I want," she went on, "to be perfectly honest with you—and with myself. For a long time I've hoped this chance would come: that I might tell you how you've helped me, what you've made of me—"

Archer sat staring beneath frowning brows. He interrupted her with a laugh. "And what do you make out that you've made of me?"

She paled a little. "Of you?"

"Yes: for I'm of your making much more than you ever were of mine. I'm the man who married one woman because another one told him to."

Her paleness turned to a fugitive flush. "I thought—you promised—you were not to say such things today."

"Ah—how like a woman! None of you will ever see a bad business through!"

She lowered her voice. "*Is* it a bad business—for May?"

He stood in the window, drumming against the raised sash, and feeling in every fiber the wistful tenderness with which she had spoken her cousin's name.

"For that's the thing we've always got to think of—haven't we—by your own showing?" she insisted.

"My own showing?" he echoed, his blank eyes still on the sea.

"Or if not," she continued, pursuing her own thought with a painful application, "if it's not worthwhile to have given up, to have missed things, so that others may be saved from disillusionment and misery—then everything I came home for, everything that made my other life seem by contrast so bare and so poor because no one there took account of them—all these things are a sham or a dream—"

He turned around without moving from his place. "And in that case there's no reason on earth why you shouldn't go back?" he concluded for her.

Her eyes were clinging to him desperately. "Oh, *is* there no reason?"

"Not if you staked your all on the success of my marriage. My marriage," he said savagely, "isn't going to be a sight to keep you here." She made no answer, and he went on: "What's the use? You gave me my first glimpse of a real life, and at the same moment you asked me to go on with a sham one. It's beyond human enduring—that's all."

"Oh, don't say that; when I'm enduring it!" she burst out, her eyes filling.

Her arms had dropped along the table, and she sat with her face abandoned to his gaze as if in the recklessness of a desperate peril. The face exposed her as much as if it had been her whole person, with the soul behind it: Archer stood dumb, overwhelmed by what it suddenly told him.

"You too—oh, all this time, you too?"

For answer, she let the tears on her lids overflow and run slowly downward.

Half the width of the room was still between them, and neither made any show of moving. Archer was conscious of a curious indifference to her bodily presence: he would hardly have been aware of it if one of the hands she had flung out on the table had not drawn his gaze as on the occasion when, in the little Twenty-third Street house, he had kept his eye on it in order not to look at her face. Now his imagination spun about the hand as about the edge of a vortex; but still he made no effort to draw nearer. He had known the love that is fed on caresses and feeds them; but this passion that was closer than his bones was not to be superficially satisfied. His one terror was to do anything which might efface the sound and impression of her words; his one thought, that he should never again feel quite alone.

But after a moment the sense of waste and ruin overcame him. There they were, close together and safe and shut in; yet so chained to their separate destinies that they might as well have been half the world apart.

"What's the use—when you will go back?" he broke out, a great hopeless *How on earth can I keep you?* crying out to her beneath his words.

She sat motionless, with lowered lids. "Oh—I shan't go yet!"

"Not yet? Some time, then? Some time that you already foresee?"

At that she raised her clearest eyes. "I promise you: not as long as you hold out. Not as long as we can look straight at each other like this."

He dropped into his chair. What her answer really said was: "If you lift a finger you'll drive me back: back to all the abominations you know of, and all the temptations you half guess." He understood it as clearly as if she had uttered the words, and the thought kept him anchored to his side of the table in a kind of moved and sacred submission.

"What a life for you!—" he groaned.

"Oh—as long as it's a part of yours."

"And mine a part of yours?"

She nodded.

"And that's to be all—for either of us?"

"Well; it *is* all, isn't it?"

At that he sprang up, forgetting everything but the sweetness of her face. She rose too, not as if to meet him or to flee from him, but quietly, as though the worst of the task were done and she had only to wait; so quietly that, as he came close, her outstretched hands acted not as a check but as a guide to him. They fell into his, while her arms, extended but not rigid, kept him far enough off to let her surrendered face say the rest.

They may have stood in that way for a long time, or only for a few moments; but it was long enough for her silence to communicate all she had to say, and for him to feel that only one thing mattered. He must do nothing to make this meeting their last; he must leave their future in her care, asking only that she should keep fast hold of it.

"Don't—don't be unhappy," she said, with a break in her voice, as she drew her hands away; and he answered: "You won't go back—you won't go back?" as if it were the one possibility he could not bear.

"I won't go back," she said; and turning away she opened the door and led the way into the public dining room.

The strident school-teachers were gathering up their possessions preparatory to a straggling flight to the wharf; across the beach lay the white steam-boat at the pier; and over the sunlit waters Boston loomed in a line of haze.

# XXV

Once more on the boat, and in the presence of others, Archer felt a tranquillity of spirit that surprised as much as it sustained him.

The day, according to any current valuation, had been a rather ridiculous failure; he had not so much as touched Madame Olenska's hand with his lips, or extracted one word from her that gave promise of further opportunities. Nevertheless, for a man sick with unsatisfied love, and parting for an indefinite period from the object of his passion, he felt himself almost humiliatingly calm and comforted. It was the perfect balance she had held between their loyalty to others and their honesty to themselves that had so stirred and yet tranquillized him; a balance not artfully calculated, as her tears and her falterings showed, but resulting naturally from her unabashed sincerity. It filled him with a tender awe, now the danger was over, and made him thank the fates that no personal vanity, no sense of playing a part before sophisticated witnesses, had tempted him to tempt her. Even after they had clasped hands for good-bye at the Fall River station, and he had turned away alone, the conviction remained with him of having saved out of their meeting much more than he had sacrificed.

He wandered back to the club, and went and sat alone in the deserted library, turning and turning over in his thoughts every separate second of their hours together. It was clear to him, and it grew more

clear under closer scrutiny, that if she should finally decide on returning to Europe—returning to her husband—it would not be because
her old life tempted her, even on the new terms offered. No: she
would go only if she felt herself becoming a temptation to Archer, a
temptation to fall away from the standard they had both set up. Her
choice would be to stay near him as long as he did not ask her to come
nearer; and it depended on himself to keep her just there, safe but
secluded.

In the train these thoughts were still with him. They enclosed him
in a kind of golden haze, through which the faces about him looked
remote and indistinct: he had a feeling that if he spoke to his fellow-
travelers they would not understand what he was saying. In this state
of abstraction he found himself, the following morning, waking to the
reality of a stifling September day in New York. The heat-withered
faces in the long train streamed past him, and he continued to stare at
them through the same golden blur; but suddenly, as he left the station, one of the faces detached itself, came closer and forced itself
upon his consciousness. It was, as he instantly recalled, the face of the
young man he had seen, the day before, passing out of the Parker
House, and had noted as not conforming to type, as not having an
American hotel face.

The same thing struck him now; and again he became aware of a
dim stir of former associations. The young man stood looking about
him with the dazed air of the foreigner flung upon the harsh mercies
of American travel; then he advanced toward Archer, lifted his hat, and
said in English: "Surely, Monsieur, we met in London?"

"Ah, to be sure: in London!" Archer grasped his hand with curiosity
and sympathy. "So you *did* get here, after all?" he exclaimed, casting a
wondering eye on the astute and haggard little countenance of young
Carfry's French tutor.

"Oh, I got here—yes," M. Rivière smiled with drawn lips. "But not
for long; I return the day after tomorrow." He stood grasping his light
valise in one neatly gloved hand, and gazing anxiously, perplexedly, almost appealingly, into Archer's face.

"I wonder, Monsieur, since I've had the good luck to run across you,
if I might—"

"I was just going to suggest it: come to luncheon, won't you? Down
town, I mean: if you'll look me up in my office I'll take you to a very
decent restaurant in that quarter."

M. Rivière was visibly touched and surprised. "You're too kind. But I
was only going to ask if you would tell me how to reach some sort of
conveyance. There are no porters, and no one here seems to listen—"

"I know: our American stations must surprise you. When you ask for
a porter they give you chewing-gum. But if you'll come along I'll extri-
cate you; and you must really lunch with me, you know."

The young man, after a just perceptible hesitation, replied, with
profuse thanks, and in a tone that did not carry complete conviction,
that he was already engaged; but when they had reached the comparative reassurance of the street he asked if he might call that afternoon.

Archer, at ease in the midsummer leisure of the office, fixed an hour and scribbled his address, which the Frenchman pocketed with reiterated thanks and a wide flourish of his hat. A horse-car received him, and Archer walked away.

Punctually at the hour M. Rivière appeared, shaved, smoothed-out, but still unmistakably drawn and serious. Archer was alone in his office, and the young man, before accepting the seat he proffered, began abruptly: "I believe I saw you, sir, yesterday in Boston."

The statement was insignificant enough, and Archer was about to frame an assent when his words were checked by something mysterious yet illuminating in his visitor's insistent gaze.

"It is extraordinary, very extraordinary," M. Rivière continued, "that we should have met in the circumstances in which I find myself."

"What circumstances?" Archer asked, wondering a little crudely if he needed money.

M. Rivière continued to study him with tentative eyes. "I have come, not to look for employment, as I spoke of doing when we last met, but on a special mission—"

"Ah—!" Archer exclaimed. In a flash the two meetings had connected themselves in his mind. He paused to take in the situation thus suddenly lighted up for him, and M. Rivière also remained silent, as if aware that what he had said was enough.

"A special mission," Archer at length repeated.

The young Frenchman, opening his palms, raised them slightly, and the two men continued to look at each other across the office-desk till Archer roused himself to say: "Do sit down"; whereupon M. Rivière bowed, took a distant chair, and again waited.

"It was about this mission that you wanted to consult me?" Archer finally asked.

M. Rivière bent his head. "Not in my own behalf: on that score I—I have fully dealt with myself. I should like—if I may—to speak to you about the Countess Olenska."

Archer had known for the last few minutes that the words were coming; but when they came they sent the blood rushing to his temples as if he had been caught by a bent-back branch in a thicket.

"And on whose behalf," he said, "do you wish to do this?"

M. Rivière met the question sturdily. "Well—I might say *hers*, if it did not sound like a liberty. Shall I say instead: on behalf of abstract justice?"

Archer considered him ironically. "In other words: you are Count Olenski's messenger?"

He saw his blush more darkly reflected in M. Rivière's sallow countenance. "Not to *you*, Monsieur. If I come to you, it is on quite other grounds."

"What right have you, in the circumstances, to *be* on any other ground?" Archer retorted. "If you're an emissary, you're an emissary."

The young man considered. "My mission is over: as far as the Countess Olenska goes, it has failed."

"I can't help that," Archer rejoined on the same note of irony.

"No: but you can help—" M. Rivière paused, turned his hat about in his still carefully gloved hands, looked into its lining and then back at Archer's face. "You can help, Monsieur, I am convinced, to make it equally a failure with her family."

Archer pushed back his chair and stood up. "Well—and by God I will!" he exclaimed. He stood with his hands in his pockets, staring down wrathfully at the little Frenchman, whose face, though he too had risen, was still an inch or two below the line of Archer's eyes.

M. Rivière paled to his normal hue: paler than that his complexion could hardly turn.

"Why the devil," Archer explosively continued, "should you have thought—since I suppose you're appealing to me on the ground of my relationship to Madame Olenska—that I should take a view contrary to the rest of her family?"

The change of expression in M. Rivière's face was for a time his only answer. His look passed from timidity to absolute distress: for a young man of his usually resourceful mien it would have been difficult to appear more disarmed and defenseless. "Oh, Monsieur—"

"I can't imagine," Archer continued, "why you should have come to me when there are others so much nearer to the Countess; still less why you thought I should be more accessible to the arguments I suppose you were sent over with."

M. Rivière took this onslaught with a disconcerting humility. "The arguments I want to present you, Monsieur, are my own and not those I was sent over with."

"Then I see still less reason for listening to them."

M. Rivière again looked into his hat, as if considering whether these last words were not a sufficiently broad hint to put it on and be gone. Then he spoke with sudden decision. "Monsieur—will you tell me one thing? Is it my right to be here that you question? Or do you perhaps believe the whole matter to be already closed?"

His quiet insistence made Archer feel the clumsiness of his own bluster. M. Rivière had succeeded in imposing himself: Archer, reddening slightly, dropped into his chair again, and signed to the young man to be seated.

"I beg your pardon: but why isn't the matter closed?"

M. Rivière gazed back at him with anguish. "You do, then, agree with the rest of the family that, in face of the new proposals I have brought, it is hardly possible for Madame Olenska not to return to her husband?"

"Good God!" Archer exclaimed; and his visitor gave out a low murmur of confirmation.

"Before seeing her, I saw—at Count Olenski's request—Mr. Lovell Mingott, with whom I had several talks before going to Boston. I understand that he represents his mother's view; and that Mrs. Manson Mingott's influence is great throughout her family."

Archer sat silent, with the sense of clinging to the edge of a sliding precipice. The discovery that he had been excluded from a share in these negotiations, and even from the knowledge that they were on foot, caused him a surprise hardly dulled by the acuter wonder of what he was learning. He saw in a flash that if the family had ceased to consult him it was because some deep tribal instinct warned them that he was no longer on their side; and he recalled, with a start of comprehension, a remark of May's during their drive home from Mrs. Manson Mingott's on the day of the Archery Meeting: "Perhaps, after all, Ellen would be happier with her husband."

Even in the tumult of new discoveries Archer remembered his indignant exclamation, and the fact that since then his wife had never named Madame Olenska to him. Her careless allusion had no doubt been the straw held up to see which way the wind blew; the result had been reported to the family, and thereafter Archer had been tacitly omitted from their counsels. He admired the tribal discipline which made May bow to this decision. She would not have done so, he knew, had her conscience protested; but she probably shared the family view that Madame Olenska would be better off as an unhappy wife than as a separated one, and that there was no use in discussing the case with Newland, who had an awkward way of suddenly not seeming to take the most fundamental things for granted.

Archer looked up and met his visitor's anxious gaze. "Don't you know, Monsieur—is it possible you don't know—that the family begin to doubt if they have the right to advise the Countess to refuse her husband's last proposals?"

"The proposals you brought?"

"The proposals I brought."

It was on Archer's lips to exclaim that whatever he knew or did not know was no concern of M. Rivière's; but something in the humble and yet courageous tenacity of M. Rivière's gaze made him reject this conclusion, and he met the young man's question with another. "What is your object in speaking to me of this?"

He had not to wait a moment for the answer. "To beg you, Monsieur—to beg you with all the force I'm capable of—not to let her go back.—Oh, don't let her!" M. Rivière exclaimed.

Archer looked at him with increasing astonishment. There was no mistaking the sincerity of his distress or the strength of his determination: he had evidently resolved to let everything go by the board but the supreme need of thus putting himself on record. Archer considered.

"May I ask," he said at length, "if this is the line you took with the Countess Olenska?"

M. Rivière reddened, but his eyes did not falter. "No, Monsieur: I accepted my mission in good faith. I really believed—for reasons I need not trouble you with—that it would be better for Madame Olenska to recover her situation, her fortune, the social consideration that her husband's standing gives her."

"So I supposed: you could hardly have accepted such a mission otherwise."

"I should not have accepted it."

"Well, then—?" Archer paused again, and their eyes met in another protracted scrutiny.

"Ah, Monsieur, after I had seen her, after I had listened to her, I knew she was better off here."

"You knew—?"

"Monsieur, I discharged my mission faithfully: I put the Count's arguments, I stated his offers, without adding any comment of my own. The Countess was good enough to listen patiently; she carried her goodness so far as to see me twice; she considered impartially all I had come to say. And it was in the course of these two talks that I changed my mind, that I came to see things differently."

"May I ask what led to this change?"

"Simply seeing the change in *her*," M. Rivière replied.

"The change in her? Then you knew her before?"

The young man's color again rose. "I used to see her in her husband's house. I have known Count Olenski for many years. You can imagine that he would not have sent a stranger on such a mission."

Archer's gaze, wandering away to the blank walls of the office, rested on a hanging calendar surmounted by the rugged features of the President of the United States.[1] That such a conversation should be going on anywhere within the millions of square miles subject to his rule seemed as strange as anything that the imagination could invent.

"The change—what sort of a change?"

"Ah, Monsieur, if I could tell you!" M. Rivière paused. "*Tenez*[2]—the discovery, I suppose, of what I'd never thought of before: that she's an American. And that if you're an American of *her* kind—of your kind—things that are accepted in certain other societies, or at least put up with as part of a general convenient give-and-take—become unthinkable, simply unthinkable. If Madame Olenska's relations understood what these things were, their opposition to her returning would no doubt be as unconditional as her own; but they seem to regard her husband's wish to have her back as proof of an irresistible longing for domestic life." M. Rivière paused, and then added: "Whereas it's far from being as simple as that."

Archer looked back to the President of the United States, and then down at his desk and at the papers scattered on it. For a second or two he could not trust himself to speak. During this interval he heard M. Rivière's chair pushed back, and was aware that the young man had risen. When he glanced up again he saw that his visitor was as moved as himself.

1. While four presidents govern during the roughly ten years from which the central events of the novel are drawn, this description recalls the distinctively craggy features of Ulysses S. Grant rather than the comparatively smooth faces of his successors: Rutherford B. Hayes, James Garfield, and Chester B. Arthur. Grant was president from 1869 to 1877.
2. French, "Take this to heart," "Listen," "Look here," "Pay attention."

"Thank you," Archer said simply.

"There's nothing to thank me for, Monsieur: it is I, rather—" M. Rivière broke off, as if speech for him too were difficult. "I should like, though," he continued in a firmer voice, "to add one thing. You asked me if I was in Count Olenski's employ. I am at this moment: I returned to him, a few months ago, for reasons of private necessity such as may happen to anyone who has persons, ill and older persons, dependent on him. But from the moment that I have taken the step of coming here to say these things to you I consider myself discharged, and I shall tell him so on my return, and give him the reasons. That's all, Monsieur."

M. Rivière bowed and drew back a step.

"Thank you," Archer said again, as their hands met.

# XXVI

Every year on the fifteenth of October Fifth Avenue opened its shutters, unrolled its carpets and hung up its triple layer of window-curtains.

By the first of November this household ritual was over, and society had begun to look about and take stock of itself. By the fifteenth the season was in full blast, Opera and theaters were putting forth their new attractions, dinner-engagements were accumulating, and dates for dances being fixed. And punctually at about this time Mrs. Archer always said that New York was very much changed.

Observing it from the lofty standpoint of a non-participant, she was able, with the help of Mr. Sillerton Jackson and Miss Sophy, to trace each new crack in its surface, and all the strange weeds pushing up between the ordered rows of social vegetables. It had been one of the amusements of Archer's youth to wait for this annual pronouncement of his mother's, and to hear her enumerate the minute signs of disintegration that his careless gaze had overlooked. For New York, to Mrs. Archer's mind, never changed without changing for the worse; and in this view Miss Sophy Jackson heartily concurred.

Mr. Sillerton Jackson, as became a man of the world, suspended his judgment and listened with an amused impartiality to the lamentations of the ladies. But even he never denied that New York had changed; and Newland Archer, in the winter of the second year of his marriage, was himself obliged to admit that if it had not actually changed it was certainly changing.

These points had been raised, as usual, at Mrs. Archer's Thanksgiving dinner. At the date when she was officially enjoined to give thanks for the blessings of the year it was her habit to take a mournful though not embittered stock of her world, and wonder what there was to be thankful for. At any rate, not the state of society; society, if it could be said to exist, was rather a spectacle on which to call down Biblical imprecations—and in fact, everyone knew what the Reverend Dr. Ashmore meant when he chose a text from Jeremiah (chap. ii., verse 25)[1] for his Thanksgiving sermon. Dr. Ashmore, the new Rector of St. Matthew's, had been chosen because he was very "advanced": his sermons were considered bold in thought and novel in language. When he fulminated against fashionable society he always spoke of its "trend"; and to Mrs. Archer it was terrifying and yet fascinating to feel herself part of a community that was trending.

"There's no doubt that Dr. Ashmore is right: there *is* a marked trend," she said, as if it were something visible and measurable, like a crack in a house.

"It was odd, though, to preach about it on Thanksgiving," Miss Jackson opined; and her hostess drily rejoined: "Oh, he means us to give thanks for what's left."

Archer had been wont to smile at these annual vaticinations[2] of his mother's; but this year even he was obliged to acknowledge, as he listened to an enumeration of the changes, that the "trend" was visible.

"The extravagance in dress—" Miss Jackson began. "Sillerton took me to the first night of the Opera, and I can only tell you that Jane Merry's dress was the only one I recognized from last year; and even that had had the front panel changed. Yet I know she got it out from Worth only two years ago, because my seamstress always goes in to make over her Paris dresses before she wears them."

"Ah, Jane Merry is one of *us*," said Mrs. Archer sighing, as if it were not such an enviable thing to be in an age when ladies were beginning to flaunt abroad their Paris dresses as soon as they were out of the Custom House,[3] instead of letting them mellow under lock and key, in the manner of Mrs. Archer's contemporaries.

"Yes; she's one of the few. In my youth," Miss Jackson rejoined, "it was considered vulgar to dress in the newest fashions; and Amy Sillerton has always told me that in Boston the rule was to put away one's Paris dresses for two years. Old Mrs. Baxter Pennilow, who did everything handsomely, used to import twelve a year, two velvet, two satin, two silk, and the other six of poplin and the finest cashmere. It was a standing order, and as she was ill for two years before she died they found forty-eight Worth dresses that had never been taken out of tissue paper; and when the girls left off their mourning they were able to wear the first lot at the Symphony concerts without looking in advance of the fashion."

"Ah, well, Boston is more conservative than New York; but I always think it's a safe rule for a lady to lay aside her French dresses for one season," Mrs. Archer conceded.

"It was Beaufort who started the new fashion by making his wife clap her new clothes on her back as soon as they arrived: I must say at

---

1. "Withhold thy foot from being unshod, and thy throat from thirst: but thou saidst, there is no hope: no; for I have loved strangers, and after them I will go." This is one of several warnings against adultery in relation to individuals as well as in relation to philanderings of the tribe of Israel, which Jeremiah fears is becoming contaminated or adulterated by incorporating foreign ways.
2. Dire phrophecies.
3. The site on Wall Street where duties were imposed on goods imported from Europe.

times it takes all Regina's distinction not to look like . . . like . . ." Miss Jackson glanced around the table, caught Janey's bulging gaze, and took refuge in an unintelligible murmur.

"Like her rivals," said Mr. Sillerton Jackson, with the air of producing an epigram.

"Oh,—" the ladies murmured; and Mrs. Archer added, partly to distract her daughter's attention from forbidden topics: "Poor Regina! Her Thanksgiving hasn't been a very cheerful one, I'm afraid. Have you heard the rumors about Beaufort's speculations, Sillerton?"

Mr. Jackson nodded carelessly. Everyone had heard the rumors in question, and he scorned to confirm a tale that was already common property.

A gloomy silence fell upon the party. No one really liked Beaufort, and it was not wholly unpleasant to think the worst of his private life; but the idea of his having brought financial dishonor on his wife's family was too shocking to be enjoyed even by his enemies. Archer's New York tolerated hypocrisy in private relations; but in business matters it exacted a limpid and impeccable honesty. It was a long time since any well-known banker had failed discreditably; but everyone remembered the social extinction visited on the heads of the firm when the last event of the kind had happened. It would be the same with the Beauforts, in spite of his power and her popularity; not all the leagued strength of the Dallas connection would save poor Regina if there were any truth in the reports of her husband's unlawful speculations.[4]

The talk took refuge in less ominous topics; but everything they touched on seemed to confirm Mrs. Archer's sense of an accelerated trend.

"Of course, Newland, I know you let dear May go to Mrs. Struthers's Sunday evenings—" she began; and May interposed gaily: "Oh, you know, everybody goes to Mrs. Struthers's now; and she was invited to Granny's last reception."

It was thus, Archer reflected, that New York managed its transitions: conspiring to ignore them till they were well over, and then, in all good faith, imagining that they had taken place in a preceding age. There was always a traitor in the citadel; and after he (or generally she) had surrendered the keys, what was the use of pretending that it was impregnable? Once people had tasted of Mrs. Struthers's easy Sunday hospitality they were not likely to sit at home remembering that her champagne was transmuted Shoe-Polish.

"I know, dear, I know," Mrs. Archer sighed. "Such things have to be, I suppose, as long as *amusement* is what people go out for; but I've never quite forgiven your cousin Madame Olenska for being the first person to countenance Mrs. Struthers."

A sudden blush rose to young Mrs. Archer's face; it surprised her husband as much as the other guests about the table. "Oh, *Ellen*—"

---

4. Unscrupulous financial gambling with other people's money, taking place outside of the protective regulations established by the government or outside the code of financial probity practiced by gentlemen.

she murmured, much in the same accusing and yet deprecating tone in which her parents might have said: "Oh, *the Blenkers*—."

It was the note which the family had taken to sounding on the mention of the Countess Olenska's name, since she had surprised and inconvenienced them by remaining obdurate to her husband's advances; but on May's lips it gave food for thought, and Archer looked at her with the sense of strangeness that sometimes came over him when she was most in the tone of her environment.

His mother, with less than her usual sensitiveness to atmosphere, still insisted: "I've always thought that people like the Countess Olenska, who have lived in aristocratic societies, ought to help us to keep up our social distinctions, instead of ignoring them."

May's blush remained permanently vivid: it seemed to have a significance beyond that implied by the recognition of Madame Olenska's social bad faith.

"I've no doubt we all seem alike to foreigners," said Miss Jackson tartly.

"I don't think Ellen cares for society; but nobody knows exactly what she does care for," May continued, as if she had been groping for something noncommittal.

"Ah, well—" Mrs. Archer sighed again.

Everybody knew that the Countess Olenska was no longer in the good graces of her family. Even her devoted champion, old Mrs. Manson Mingott, had been unable to defend her refusal to return to her husband. The Mingotts had not proclaimed their disapproval aloud: their sense of solidarity was too strong. They had simply, as Mrs. Welland said, "let poor Ellen find her own level"—and that, mortifyingly and incomprehensibly, was in the dim depths where the Blenkers prevailed, and "people who wrote" celebrated their untidy rites. It was incredible, but it was a fact, that Ellen, in spite of all her opportunities and her privileges, had become simply "Bohemian." The fact enforced the contention that she had made a fatal mistake in not returning to Count Olenski. After all, a young woman's place was under her husband's roof, especially when she had left it in circumstances that . . . well . . . if one had cared to look into them. . . .

"Madame Olenska is a great favorite with the gentlemen," said Miss Sophy, with her air of wishing to put forth something conciliatory when she knew that she was planting a dart.

"Ah, that's the danger that a young woman like Madame Olenska is always exposed to," Mrs. Archer mournfully agreed; and the ladies, on this conclusion, gathered up their trains to seek the carcel globes of the drawing room, while Archer and Mr. Sillerton Jackson withdrew to the Gothic library.

Once established before the grate, and consoling himself for the inadequacy of the dinner by the perfection of his cigar, Mr. Jackson became portentous and communicable.

"If the Beaufort smash comes," he announced, "there are going to be disclosures."

Archer raised his head quickly: he could never hear the name without the sharp vision of Beaufort's heavy figure, opulently furred and shod, advancing through the snow at Skuytercliff.

"There's bound to be," Mr. Jackson continued, "the nastiest kind of a cleaning up. He hasn't spent all his money on Regina."

"Oh, well—that's discounted, isn't it? My belief is he'll pull out yet," said the young man, wanting to change the subject.

"Perhaps—perhaps. I know he was to see some of the influential people today. Of course," Mr. Jackson reluctantly conceded, "it's to be hoped they can tide him over—this time anyhow. I shouldn't like to think of poor Regina's spending the rest of her life in some shabby foreign watering-place for bankrupts."

Archer said nothing. It seemed to him so natural—however tragic—that money ill-gotten should be cruelly expiated, that his mind, hardly lingering over Mrs. Beaufort's doom, wandered back to closer questions. What was the meaning of May's blush when the Countess Olenska had been mentioned:

Four months had passed since the midsummer day that he and Madame Olenska had spent together; and since then he had not seen her. He knew that she had returned to Washington, to the little house which she and Medora Manson had taken there: he had written to her once—a few words, asking when they were to meet again—and she had even more briefly replied: "Not yet."

Since then there had been no farther communication between them, and he had built up within himself a kind of sanctuary in which she throned among his secret thoughts and longings. Little by little it became the scene of his real life, of his only rational activities; thither he brought the books he read, the ideas and feelings which nourished him, his judgments and his visions. Outside it, in the scene of his actual life, he moved with a growing sense of unreality and insufficiency, blundering against familiar prejudices and traditional points of view as an absent-minded man goes on bumping into the furniture of his own room. Absent—that was what he was: so absent from everything most densely real and near to those about him that it sometimes startled him to find they still imagined he was there.

He became aware that Mr. Jackson was clearing his throat preparatory to farther revelations.

"I don't know, of course, how far your wife's family are aware of what people say about—well, about Madame Olenska's refusal to accept her husband's latest offer."

Archer was silent, and Mr. Jackson obliquely continued: "It's a pity—it's certainly a pity—that she refused it."

"A pity? In God's name, why?"

Mr. Jackson looked down his leg to the unwrinkled sock that joined it to a glossy pump.

"Well—to put it on the lowest ground—what's she going to live on now?"

"Now—?"

"If Beaufort—"

Archer sprang up, his fist banging down on the black walnut-edge of the writing-table. The wells of the brass double inkstand danced in their sockets.

"What the devil do you mean, sir?"

Mr. Jackson, shifting himself slightly in his chair, turned a tranquil gaze on the young man's burning face.

"Well—I have it on pretty good authority—in fact, on old Catherine's herself—that the family reduced Countess Olenska's allowance considerably when she definitely refused to go back to her husband; and as, by this refusal, she also forfeits the money settled on her when she married—which Olenski was ready to make over to her if she returned—why, what the devil do *you* mean, my dear boy, by asking me what *I* mean?" Mr. Jackson good-humoredly retorted.

Archer moved toward the mantelpiece and bent over to knock his ashes into the grate.

"I don't know anything of Madame Olenska's private affairs; but I don't need to, to be certain that what you insinuate—"

"Oh, *I* don't: it's Lefferts, for one," Mr. Jackson interposed.

"Lefferts—who made love to her and got snubbed for it!" Archer broke out contemptuously.

"Ah—*did* he?" snapped the other, as if this were exactly the fact he had been laying a trap for. He still sat sideways from the fire, so that his hard old gaze held Archer's face as if in a spring of steel.

"Well, well: it's a pity she didn't go back before Beaufort's cropper,"[5] he repeated. "If she goes *now*, and if he fails, it will only confirm the general impression: which isn't by any means peculiar to Lefferts, by the way."

"Oh, she won't go back now: less than ever!" Archer had no sooner said it than he had once more the feeling that it was exactly what Mr. Jackson had been waiting for.

The old gentleman considered him attentively. "That's your opinion, eh? Well, no doubt you know. But everybody will tell you that the few pennies Medora Manson has left are all in Beaufort's hands; and how the two women are to keep their heads above water unless he does, I can't imagine. Of course, Madame Olenska may still soften old Catherine, who's been the most inexorably opposed to her staying; and old Catherine could make her any allowance she chooses. But we all know that she hates parting with good money; and the rest of the family have no particular interest in keeping Madame Olenska here."

Archer was burning with unavailing wrath: he was exactly in the state when a man is sure to do something stupid, knowing all the while that he is doing it.

He saw that Mr. Jackson had been instantly struck by the fact that Madame Olenska's differences with her grandmother and her other relations were not known to him, and that the old gentleman had

5. An unexpected fall or crash, commonly used to describe a fall from a horse. Here, a financial disaster, an unexpected crash that has wide-reaching effects. The Panic of 1873, the most devastating financial crash of the period, took place at the beginning of the decade covered by the novel but has been relocated near the end as actual events are rearranged to construct the plot. For contemporary accounts of the Panic of 1873, see pp. 300–307.

drawn his own conclusions as to the reasons for Archer's exclusion from the family councils. This fact warned Archer to go warily; but the insinuations about Beaufort made him reckless. He was mindful, however, if not of his own danger, at least of the fact that Mr. Jackson was under his mother's roof, and consequently his guest. Old New York scrupulously observed the etiquette of hospitality, and no discussion with a guest was ever allowed to degenerate into a disagreement.

"Shall we go up and join my mother?" he suggested curtly, as Mr. Jackson's last cone of ashes dropped into the brass ash-tray at his elbow.

On the drive homeward May remained oddly silent; through the darkness, he still felt her enveloped in her menacing blush. What its menace meant he could not guess: but he was sufficiently warned by the fact that Madame Olenska's name had evoked it.

They went upstairs, and he turned into the library. She usually followed him; but he heard her passing down the passage to her bedroom.

"May!" he called out impatiently; and she came back, with a slight glance of surprise at his tone.

"This lamp is smoking again; I should think the servants might see that it's kept properly trimmed," he grumbled nervously.

"I'm so sorry: it shan't happen again," she answered, in the firm bright tone she had learned from her mother; and it exasperated Archer to feel that she was already beginning to humor him like a younger Mr. Welland. She bent over to lower the wick, and as the light struck up on her white shoulders and the clear curves of her face he thought: "How young she is! For what endless years this life will have to go on!"

He felt, with a kind of horror, his own strong youth and the bounding blood in his veins. "Look here," he said suddenly, "I may have to go to Washington for a few days—soon; next week perhaps."

Her hand remained on the key of the lamp as she turned to him slowly. The heat from its flame had brought back a glow to her face, but it paled as she looked up.

"On business?" she asked, in a tone which implied that there could be no other conceivable reason, and that she had put the question automatically, as if merely to finish his own sentence.

"On business, naturally. There's a patent case coming up before the Supreme Court—" He gave the name of the inventor, and went on furnishing details with all Lawrence Lefferts's practiced glibness, while she listened attentively, saying at intervals: "Yes, I see."

"The change will do you good," she said simply, when he had finished; "and you must be sure to go and see Ellen," she added, looking him straight in the eyes with her cloudless smile, and speaking in the tone she might have employed in urging him not to neglect some irksome family duty.

It was the only word that passed between them on the subject; but in the code in which they had both been trained it meant: "Of course you understand that I know all that people have been saying about

Ellen, and heartily sympathize with my family in their effort to get her to return to her husband. I also know that, for some reason you have not chosen to tell me, you have advised her against this course, which all the older men of the family, as well as our grandmother, agree in approving; and that it is owing to your encouragement that Ellen defies us all, and exposes herself to the kind of criticism of which Mr. Sillerton Jackson probably gave you, this evening, the hint that has made you so irritable. . . . Hints have indeed not been wanting; but since you appear unwilling to take them from others, I offer you this one myself, in the only form in which well-bred people of our kind can communicate unpleasant things to each other: by letting you understand that I know you mean to see Ellen when you are in Washington, and are perhaps going there expressly for that purpose; and that, since you are sure to see her, I wish you to do so with my full and explicit approval—and to take the opportunity of letting her know what the course of conduct you have encouraged her in is likely to lead to."

Her hand was still on the key of the lamp when the last word of this mute message reached him. She turned the wick down, lifted off the globe, and breathed on the sulky flame.

"They smell less if one blows them out," she explained, with her bright housekeeping air. On the threshold she turned and paused for his kiss.

# XXVII

Wall Street, the next day, had more reassuring reports of Beaufort's situation. They were not definite, but they were hopeful. It was generally understood that he could call on powerful influences in case of emergency, and that he had done so with success; and that evening, when Mrs. Beaufort appeared at the Opera wearing her old smile and a new emerald necklace, society drew a breath of relief.

New York was inexorable in its condemnation of business irregularities. So far there had been no exception to its tacit rule that those who broke the law of probity must pay; and everyone was aware that even Beaufort and Beaufort's wife would be offered up unflinchingly to this principle. But to be obliged to offer them up would be not only painful but inconvenient. The disappearance of the Beauforts would leave a considerable void in their compact little circle; and those who were too ignorant or too careless to shudder at the moral catastrophe bewailed in advance the loss of the best ballroom in New York.

Archer had definitely made up his mind to go to Washington. He was waiting only for the opening of the lawsuit of which he had spoken to May, so that its date might coincide with that of his visit; but on the following Tuesday he learned from Mr. Letterblair that the case might be postponed for several weeks. Nevertheless, he went home that afternoon determined in any event to leave the next evening. The chances were that May, who knew nothing of his professional life, and had never shown any interest in it, would not learn of the postponement, should it take place, nor remember the names of the litigants if they were mentioned before her; and at any rate he could no longer put off seeing Madame Olenska. There were too many things that he must say to her.

On the Wednesday morning, when he reached his office, Mr. Letterblair met him with a troubled face. Beaufort, after all, had not managed to "tide over"; but by setting afloat the rumor that he had done so he had reassured his depositors, and heavy payments had poured into the bank till the previous evening, when disturbing reports again began to predominate. In consequence, a run on the bank had begun, and its doors were likely to close before the day was over. The ugliest things were being said of Beaufort's dastardly maneuver, and his failure promised to be one of the most discreditable in the history of Wall Street.[1]

The extent of the calamity left Mr. Letterblair white and incapacitated. "I've seen bad things in my time; but nothing as bad as this. Everybody we know will be hit, one way or another. And what will be done about Mrs. Beaufort? What *can* be done about her? I pity Mrs. Manson Mingott as much as anybody: coming at her age, there's no knowing what effect this affair may have on her. She always believed in Beaufort—she made a friend of him! And there's the whole Dallas connection: poor Mrs. Beaufort is related to everyone of you. Her only chance would be to leave her husband—yet how can anyone tell her so? Her duty is at his side; and luckily she seems always to have been blind to his private weaknesses."

There was a knock, and Mr. Letterblair turned his head sharply. "What is it? I can't be disturbed."

A clerk brought in a letter for Archer and withdrew. Recognizing his wife's hand, the young man opened the envelope and read: "Won't you please come up town as early as you can? Granny had a slight stroke last night. In some mysterious way she found out before anyone else this awful news about the bank. Uncle Lovell is away shooting, and the idea of the disgrace has made poor Papa so nervous that he has a temperature and can't leave his room. Mamma needs you dreadfully, and I do hope you can get away at once and go straight to Granny's."

Archer handed the note to his senior partner, and a few minutes later was crawling northward in a crowded horsecar,[2] which he exchanged at Fourteenth Street for one of the high staggering omnibuses of the Fifth Avenue line. It was after twelve o'clock when this laborious vehicle dropped him at old Catherine's. The sitting-room window on the ground floor, where she usually throned, was tenanted by the inadequate figure of her daughter, Mrs. Welland, who signed a haggard welcome as she caught sight of Archer; and at the door he was met by May. The hall wore the unnatural appearance peculiar to well-kept houses suddenly invaded by illness: wraps and furs lay in

---

1. The prospect of Beaufort's financial ruin recalls the details of the Panic of 1873, which occurred following a bank crash that ruined some of New York's richest financiers (see pp. 300–307).
2. A forerunner of the trolley, this horse-drawn vehicle was guided along rails.

heaps on the chairs, a doctor's bag and overcoat were on the table, and beside them letters and cards had already piled up unheeded.

May looked pale but smiling: Dr. Bencomb, who had just come for the second time, took a more hopeful view, and Mrs. Mingott's daunt- less determination to live and get well was already having an effect on her family. May led Archer into the old lady's sitting room, where the sliding doors opening into the bedroom had been drawn shut, and the heavy yellow damask portières dropped over them; and here Mrs. Welland communicated to him in horrified undertones the details of the catastrophe. It appeared that the evening before something dread- ful and mysterious had happened. At about eight o'clock, just after Mrs. Mingott had finished the game of solitaire that she always played after dinner, the door-bell had rung, and a lady so thickly veiled that the servants did not immediately recognize her had asked to be re- ceived.

The butler, hearing a familiar voice, had thrown open the sitting- room door, announcing: "Mrs. Julius Beaufort"—and had then closed it again on the two ladies. They must have been together, he thought, about an hour. When Mrs. Mingott's bell rang Mrs. Beaufort had al- ready slipped away unseen, and the old lady, white and vast and terri- ble, sat alone in her great chair, and signed to the butler to help her into her room. She seemed, at that time, though obviously distressed, in complete control of her body and brain. The mulatto maid put her to bed, brought her a cup of tea as usual, laid everything straight in the room, and went away; but at three in the morning the bell rang again, and the two servants, hastening in at this unwonted summons (for old Catherine usually slept like a baby), had found their mistress sitting up against her pillows with a crooked smile on her face and one little hand hanging limp from its huge arm.

The stroke had clearly been a slight one, for she was able to articu- late and to make her wishes known; and soon after the doctor's first visit she had begun to regain control of her facial muscles. But the alarm had been great; and proportionately great was the indignation when it was gathered from Mrs. Mingott's fragmentary phrases that Regina Beaufort had come to ask her—incredible effrontery!—to back up her husband, see them through—not to "desert" them, as she called it—in fact to induce the whole family to cover and condone their monstrous dishonor.

"I said to her: 'Honor's always been honor, and honesty honesty, in Manson Mingott's house, and will be till I'm carried out of it feet first,' " the old woman had stammered into her daughter's ear, in the thick voice of the partly paralyzed. "And when she said: 'But my name, Auntie—my name's Regina Dallas,' I said: 'It was Beaufort when he covered you with jewels, and it's got to stay Beaufort now that he's covered you with shame.' "

So much, with tears and gasps of horror, Mrs. Welland imparted, blanched and demolished by the unwonted obligation of having at last to fix her eyes on the unpleasant and the discreditable. "If only I could keep it from your father-in-law: he always says: 'Augusta, for pity's sake, don't destroy my last illusions'—and how am I to prevent his knowing these horrors?" the poor lady wailed.

"After all, Mamma, he won't have *seen* them," her daughter suggested; and Mrs. Welland sighed: "Ah, no; thank heaven he's safe in bed. And Dr. Bencomb has promised to keep him there till poor Mamma is better, and Regina has been got away somewhere."

Archer had seated himself near the window and was gazing out blankly at the deserted thoroughfare. It was evident that he had been summoned rather for the moral support of the stricken ladies than because of any specific aid that he could render. Mr. Lovell Mingott had been telegraphed for, and messages were being despatched by hand to the members of the family living in New York; and meanwhile there was nothing to do but to discuss in hushed tones the consequences of Beaufort's dishonor and of his wife's unjustifiable action.

Mrs. Lovell Mingott, who had been in another room writing notes, presently reappeared, and added her voice to the discussion. In *their* day, the elder ladies agreed, the wife of a man who had done anything disgraceful in business had only one idea: to efface herself, to disappear with him. "There was the case of poor Grandmamma Spicer; your great-grandmother, May. Of course," Mrs. Welland hastened to add, "your great-grandfather's money difficulties were private—losses at cards, or signing a note for somebody—I never quite knew, because Mamma would never speak of it. But she was brought up in the country because her mother had to leave New York after the disgrace, whatever it was: they lived up the Hudson alone, winter and summer, till Mamma was sixteen. It would never have occurred to Grandmamma Spicer to ask the family to 'countenance' her, as I understand Regina calls it; though a private disgrace is nothing compared to the scandal of ruining hundreds of innocent people."

"Yes, it would be more becoming in Regina to hide her own countenance than to talk about other people's," Mrs. Lovell Mingott agreed. "I understand that the emerald necklace she wore at the Opera last Friday had been sent on approval from Ball and Black's[3] in the afternoon. I wonder if they'll ever get it back?"

Archer listened unmoved to the relentless chorus. The idea of absolute financial probity as the first law of a gentleman's code was too deeply ingrained in him for sentimental considerations to weaken it. An adventurer like Lemuel Struthers might build up the millions of his Shoe Polish on any number of shady dealings; but unblemished honesty was the *noblesse oblige*[4] of old financial New York. Nor did Mrs. Beaufort's fate greatly move Archer. He felt, no doubt, more sorry for her than her indignant relatives; but it seemed to him that the tie between husband and wife, even if breakable in prosperity, should be indissoluble in misfortune. As Mr. Letterblair had said, a wife's place was at her husband's side when he was in trouble; but society's place was not at his side, and Mrs. Beaufort's cool assumption that it was

---

3. New York jewelry firm, founded in 1810, later Black, Starr, and Frost.
4. French for the obligations of rank, which include the assumed responsibility for those considered under one's purview who are less fortunate.

seemed almost to make her his accomplice. The mere idea of a
woman's appealing to her family to screen her husband's business dishonor was inadmissible, since it was the one thing that the Family, as
an institution, could not do.

The mulatto maid called Mrs. Lovell Mingott into the hall, and the
latter came back in a moment with a frowning brow.

"She wants me to telegraph for Ellen Olenska. I had written to
Ellen, of course, and to Medora; but now it seems that's not enough.
I'm to telegraph to her immediately, and to tell her that she's to come
alone."

The announcement was received in silence. Mrs. Welland sighed resignedly, and May rose from her seat and went to gather up some
newspapers that had been scattered on the floor.

"I suppose it must be done," Mrs. Lovell Mingott continued, as if
hoping to be contradicted; and May turned back toward the middle of
the room.

"Of course it must be done," she said. "Granny knows what she
wants, and we must carry out all her wishes. Shall I write the telegram
for you, Auntie? If it goes at once Ellen can probably catch tomorrow
morning's train." She pronounced the syllables of the name with a peculiar clearness, as if she had tapped on two silver bells.

"Well, it can't go at once. Jasper and the pantry-boy are both out
with notes and telegrams."

May turned to her husband with a smile. "But here's Newland,
ready to do anything. Will you take the telegram, Newland? There'll be
just time before luncheon."

Archer rose with a murmur of readiness, and she seated herself at
old Catherine's rosewood bonheur du jour,[5] and wrote out the message in her large immature hand. When it was written she blotted it
neatly and handed it to Archer.

"What a pity," she said, "that you and Ellen will cross each other on
the way!—Newland," she added, turning to her mother and aunt, "is
obliged to go to Washington about a patent law-suit that is coming up
before the Supreme Court. I suppose Uncle Lovell will be back by tomorrow night, and with Granny improving so much it doesn't seem
right to ask Newland to give up an important engagement for the
firm—does it?"

She paused, as if for an answer, and Mrs. Welland hastily declared:
"Oh, of course not, darling. Your Granny would be the last person to
wish it." As Archer left the room with the telegram, he heard his
mother-in-law add, presumably to Mrs. Lovell Mingott: "But why on
earth she should make you telegraph for Ellen Olenska—" and May's
clear voice rejoin: "Perhaps it's to urge on her again that after all her
duty is with her husband."

The outer door closed on Archer and he walked hastily away toward
the telegraph office.

5. Literally, "happiness of the day" in French; here, a small writing table with drawers.

# XXVIII

"Ol—ol—howjer spell it, anyhow?" asked the tart young lady to whom Archer had pushed his wife's telegram across the brass ledge of the Western Union office.

"Olenska—O-len-ska," he repeated, drawing back the message in order to print out the foreign syllables above May's rambling script.

"It's an unlikely name for a New York telegraph office; at least in this quarter," an unexpected voice observed; and turning around Archer saw Lawrence Lefferts at his elbow, pulling an imperturbable moustache and affecting not to glance at the message.

"Hallo, Newland: thought I'd catch you here. I've just heard of old Mrs. Mingott's stroke; and as I was on my way to the house I saw you turning down this street and nipped after you. I suppose you've come from there?"

Archer nodded, and pushed his telegram under the lattice.

"Very bad, eh?" Lefferts continued. "Wiring to the family, I suppose. I gather it *is* bad, if you're including Countess Olenska."

Archer's lips stiffened; he felt a savage impulse to dash his fist into the long, vain, handsome face at his side.

"Why?" he questioned.

Lefferts, who was known to shrink from discussion, raised his eyebrows with an ironic grimace that warned the other of the watching damsel behind the lattice. Nothing could be worse "form" the look reminded Archer, than any display of temper in a public place.

Archer had never been more indifferent to the requirements of form; but his impulse to do Lawrence Lefferts a physical injury was only momentary. The idea of bandying Ellen Olenska's name with him at such a time, and on whatsoever provocation, was unthinkable. He paid for his telegram, and the two young men went out together into the street. There Archer, having regained his self-control, went on: "Mrs. Mingott is much better: the doctor feels no anxiety whatever"; and Lefferts, with profuse expressions of relief, asked him if he had heard that there were beastly bad rumors again about Beaufort. . . .

That afternoon the announcement of the Beaufort failure was in all the papers. It overshadowed the report of Mrs. Manson Mingott's stroke, and only the few who had heard of the mysterious connection between the two events thought of ascribing old Catherine's illness to anything but the accumulation of flesh and years.

The whole of New York was darkened by the tale of Beaufort's dishonor. There had never, as Mr. Letterblair said, been a worse case in his memory, nor, for that matter, in the memory of the far-off Letterblair who had given his name to the firm. The bank had continued to take in money for a whole day after its failure was inevitable; and as many of its clients belonged to one or another of the ruling clans, Beaufort's duplicity seemed doubly cynical. If Mrs. Beaufort had not taken the tone that such misfortunes (the word was her own) were "the test of friendship," compassion for her might have tempered the general indignation against her husband. As it was—and especially after the object of her nocturnal visit to Mrs. Manson Mingott had become known—her cynicism was held to exceed his; and she had not the excuse—nor her detractors the satisfaction—of pleading that she was "a foreigner." It was some comfort (to those whose securities were not in jeopardy) to be able to remind themselves that Beaufort *was*; but, after all, if a Dallas of South Carolina took his view of the case, and glibly talked of his soon being "on his feet again," the argument lost its edge, and there was nothing to do but to accept this awful evidence of the indissolubility of marriage. Society must manage to get on without the Beauforts, and there was an end of it—except indeed for such hapless victims of the disaster as Medora Manson, the poor old Miss Lannings, and certain other misguided ladies of good family who, if only they had listened to Mr. Henry van der Luyden. . . .

"The best thing the Beauforts can do," said Mrs. Archer, summing it up as if she were pronouncing a diagnosis and prescribing a course of treatment, "is to go and live at Regina's little place in North Carolina. Beaufort has always kept a racing stable, and he had better breed trotting horses. I should say he had all the qualities of a successful horse-dealer." Everyone agreed with her, but no one condescended to enquire what the Beauforts really meant to do.

The next day Mrs. Manson Mingott was much better: she recovered her voice sufficiently to give orders that no one should mention the Beauforts to her again, and asked—when Dr. Bencomb appeared—what in the world her family meant by making such a fuss about her health.

"If people of my age *will* eat chicken salad in the evening what are they to expect?" she enquired; and, the doctor having opportunely modified her dietary, the stroke was transformed into an attack of indigestion. But in spite of her firm tone old Catherine did not wholly recover her former attitude toward life. The growing remoteness of old age, though it had not diminished her curiosity about her neighbors, had blunted her never very lively compassion for their troubles; and she seemed to have no difficulty in putting the Beaufort disaster out of her mind. But for the first time she became absorbed in her own symptoms, and began to take a sentimental interest in certain members of her family to whom she had hitherto been contemptuously indifferent.

Mr. Welland, in particular, had the privilege of attracting her notice. Of her sons-in-law he was the one she had most consistently ignored; and all his wife's efforts to represent him as a man of forceful character and marked intellectual ability (if he had only "chosen") had been met with a derisive chuckle. But his eminence as a valetudinarian now made him an object of engrossing interest, and Mrs. Mingott issued an imperial summons to him to come and compare diets as soon as his temperature permitted; for old Catherine was now the first to recognize that one could not be too careful about temperatures.

Twenty-four hours after Madame Olenska's summons a telegram announced that she would arrive from Washington on the evening of the following day. At the Wellands', where the Newland Archers chanced to be lunching, the question as to who should meet her at Jersey City was immediately raised; and the material difficulties amid which the Welland household struggled as if it had been a frontier outpost, lent animation to the debate. It was agreed that Mrs. Welland could not possibly go to Jersey City because she was to accompany her husband to old Catherine's that afternoon, and the brougham could not be spared, since, if Mr. Welland were "upset" by seeing his mother-in-law for the first time after her attack, he might have to be taken home at a moment's notice. The Welland sons would of course be "down town," Mr. Lovell Mingott would be just hurrying back from his shooting, and the Mingott carriage engaged in meeting him; and one could not ask May, at the close of a winter afternoon, to go alone across the ferry to Jersey City, even in her own carriage. Nevertheless, it might appear inhospitable—and contrary to old Catherine's express wishes—if Madame Olenska were allowed to arrive without any of the family being at the station to receive her. It was just like Ellen, Mrs. Welland's tired voice implied, to place the family in such a dilemma. "It's always one thing after another," the poor lady grieved, in one of her rare revolts against fate; "the only thing that makes me think Mamma must be less well than Dr. Bencomb will admit is this morbid desire to have Ellen come at once, however inconvenient it is to meet her."

The words had been thoughtless, as the utterances of impatience often are; and Mr. Welland was upon them with a pounce.

"Augusta," he said, turning pale and laying down his fork, "have you any other reason for thinking that Bencomb is less to be relied on than he was? Have you noticed that he has been less conscientious than usual in following up my case or your mother's?"

It was Mrs. Welland's turn to grow pale as the endless consequences of her blunder unrolled themselves before her; but she managed to laugh, and take a second helping of scalloped oysters, before she said, struggling back into her old armor of cheerfulness: "My dear, how could you imagine such a thing? I only meant that, after the decided stand Mamma took about its being Ellen's duty to go back to her husband, it seems strange that she should be seized with this sudden whim to see her, when there are half a dozen other grandchildren that she might have asked for. But we must never forget that Mamma, in spite of her wonderful vitality, is a very old woman."

Mr. Welland's brow remained clouded, and it was evident that his perturbed imagination had fastened at once on this last remark. "Yes: your mother's a very old woman; and for all we know Bencomb may not be as successful with very old people. As you say, my dear, it's always one thing after another; and in another ten or fifteen years I suppose I shall have the pleasing duty of looking about for a new doctor. It's always better to make such a change before it's absolutely necessary." And having arrived at this Spartan decision Mr. Welland firmly took up his fork.

"But all the while," Mrs. Welland began again, as she rose from the luncheon table, and led the way into the wilderness of purple satin and malachite known as the back drawing room, "I don't see how Ellen's to be got here tomorrow evening; and I do like to have things settled for at least twenty-four hours ahead."

Archer turned from the fascinated contemplation of a small painting representing two Cardinals carousing, in an octagonal ebony frame set with medallions of onyx.

"Shall I fetch her?" he proposed. "I can easily get away from the office in time to meet the brougham at the ferry, if May will send it there." His heart was beating excitedly as he spoke.

Mrs. Welland heaved a sigh of gratitude, and May, who had moved away to the window, turned to shed on him a beam of approval. "So you see, Mamma, everything *will* be settled twenty-four hours in advance," she said, stooping over to kiss her mother's troubled forehead.

May's brougham awaited her at the door, and she was to drive Archer to Union Square, where he could pick up a Broadway car to carry him to the office. As she settled herself in her corner she said: "I didn't want to worry Mamma by raising fresh obstacles; but how can you meet Ellen tomorrow, and bring her back to New York, when you're going to Washington?"

"Oh, I'm not going," Archer answered.

"Not going? Why, what's happened?" Her voice was as clear as a bell, and full of wifely solicitude.

"The case is off—postponed."

"Postponed? How odd! I saw a note this morning from Mr. Letterblair to Mamma saying that he was going to Washington tomorrow for the big patent case that he was to argue before the Supreme Court. You said it was a patent case, didn't you?"

"Well—that's it: the whole office can't go. Letterblair decided to go this morning."

"Then it's *not* postponed?" she continued, with an insistence so unlike her that he felt the blood rising to his face, as if he were blushing for her unwonted lapse from all the traditional delicacies.

"No: but my going is," he answered, cursing the unnecessary explanations that he had given when he had announced his intention of going to Washington, and wondering where he had read that clever liars give details, but that the cleverest do not. It did not hurt him half as much to tell May an untruth as to see her trying to pretend that she had not detected him.

"I'm not going till later on: luckily for the convenience of your family," he continued, taking base refuge in sarcasm. As he spoke he felt that she was looking at him, and he turned his eyes to hers in order not to appear to be avoiding them. Their glances met for a second, and perhaps let them into each other's meanings more deeply than either cared to go.

"Yes; it *is* awfully convenient," May brightly agreed, "that you should be able to meet Ellen after all; you saw how much Mamma appreciated your offering to do it."

"Oh, I'm delighted to do it." The carriage stopped, and as he jumped out she leaned to him and laid her hand on his. "Good-bye, dearest," she said, her eyes so blue that he wondered afterward if they had shone on him through tears.

He turned away and hurried across Union Square, repeating to himself, in a sort of inward chant: "It's all of two hours from Jersey City to old Catherine's. It's all of two hours—and it may be more."

# XXIX

His wife's dark blue brougham (with the wedding varnish still on it) met Archer at the ferry, and conveyed him luxuriously to the Pennsylvania terminus in Jersey City.

It was a somber snowy afternoon, and the gas-lamps were lit in the big reverberating station. As he paced the platform, waiting for the Washington express, he remembered that there were people who thought there would one day be a tunnel under the Hudson through which the trains of the Pennsylvania railway would run straight into New York. They were of the brotherhood of visionaries who likewise predicted the building of ships that would cross the Atlantic in five days, the invention of a flying machine, lighting by electricity, telephonic communication without wires, and other Arabian Night marvels.[1]

"I don't care which of their visions comes true," Archer mused, "as long as the tunnel isn't built yet." In his senseless schoolboy happiness he pictured Madame Olenska's descent from the train, his discovery of her a long way off, among the throngs of meaningless faces, her clinging to his arm as he guided her to the carriage, their slow approach to the wharf among slipping horses, laden carts, vociferating teamsters, and then the startling quiet of the ferry-boat, where they would sit side by side under the snow, in the motionless carriage, while the earth seemed to glide away under them, rolling to the other side of the sun. It was incredible, the number of things he had to say to her, and in what eloquent order they were forming themselves on his lips. . . .

The clanging and groaning of the train came nearer, and it staggered slowly into the station like a prey-laden monster into its lair. Archer pushed forward, elbowing through the crowd, and staring blindly into window after window of the high-hung carriages. And then, suddenly, he saw Madame Olenska's pale and surprised face close at hand, and had again the mortified sensation of having forgotten what she looked like.

They reached each other, their hands met, and he drew her arm through his. "This way—I have the carriage," he said.

1. The British ship *Mauretania*, which won the blue ribbon for speed in 1906, was the first ship to cross the Atlantic in under five days; the first tunnel under the Hudson was opened 1904–5; the first powered airplane flight took place in 1903; electric lighting was established in New York when the Edison Illuminating Company opened its Pearl Street power station in 1882; Marconi patented the first system of radio telegraphy (without wires) in 1896; the first translation into English of the Persian-Indian-Arabian tales known as *The Arabian Nights* appeared in 1885–86.

After that it all happened as he had dreamed. He helped her into the brougham with her bags, and had afterward the vague recollection of having properly reassured her about her grandmother and given her a summary of the Beaufort situation (he was struck by the softness of her: "Poor Regina!"). Meanwhile the carriage had worked its way out of the coil about the station, and they were crawling down the slippery incline to the wharf, menaced by swaying coal-carts, bewildered horses, dishevelled express-wagons, and an empty hearse—ah, that hearse! She shut her eyes as it passed, and clutched at Archer's hand.

"If only it doesn't mean—poor Granny!"

"Oh, no, no—she's much better—she's all right, really. There—we've passed it!" he exclaimed, as if that made all the difference. Her hand remained in his, and as the carriage lurched across the gangplank onto the ferry he bent over, unbuttoned her tight brown glove, and kissed her palm as if he had kissed a relic. She disengaged herself with a faint smile, and he said: "You didn't expect me today?"

"Oh, no."

"I meant to go to Washington to see you. I'd made all my arrangements—I very nearly crossed you in the train."

"Oh—" she exclaimed, as if terrified by the narrowness of their escape.

"Do you know—I hardly remembered you?"

"Hardly remembered me?"

"I mean: how shall I explain? I—it's always so. *Each time you happen to me all over again.*"

"Oh, yes: I know! I know!"

"Does it—do I too: to you?" he insisted.

She nodded, looking out of the window.

"Ellen—Ellen—Ellen!"

She made no answer, and he sat in silence, watching her profile grow indistinct against the snow-streaked dusk beyond the window. What had she been doing in all those four long months, he wondered? How little they knew of each other, after all! The precious moments were slipping away, but he had forgotten everything that he had meant to say to her and could only helplessly brood on the mystery of their remoteness and their proximity, which seemed to be symbolized by the fact of their sitting so close to each other, and yet being unable to see each other's faces.

"What a pretty carriage! Is it May's?" she asked, suddenly turning her face from the window.

"Yes."

"It was May who sent you to fetch me, then? How kind of her!"

He made no answer for a moment; then he said explosively: "Your husband's secretary came to see me the day after we met in Boston."

In his brief letter to her he had made no allusion to M. Rivière's visit, and his intention had been to bury the incident in his bosom. But her reminder that they were in his wife's carriage provoked him to an impulse of retaliation. He would see if she liked his reference to

Rivière any better than he liked hers to May! As on certain other occasions when he had expected to shake her out of her usual composure, she betrayed no sign of surprise: and at once he concluded: "He writes to her, then."

"M. Rivière went to see you?"

"Yes: didn't you know?"

"No," she answered simply.

"And you're not surprised?"

She hesitated. "Why should I be? He told me in Boston that he knew you; that he'd met you in England I think."

"Ellen—I must ask you one thing."

"Yes."

"I wanted to ask it after I saw him, but I couldn't put it in a letter. It was Rivière who helped you to get away—when you left your husband?"

His heart was beating suffocatingly. Would she meet this question with the same composure?

"Yes: I owe him a great debt," she answered, without the least tremor in her quiet voice.

Her tone was so natural, so almost indifferent, that Archer's turmoil subsided. Once more she had managed, by her sheer simplicity, to make him feel stupidly conventional just when he thought he was flinging convention to the winds.

"I think you're the most honest woman I ever met!" he exclaimed.

"Oh, no—but probably one of the least fussy," she answered, a smile in her voice.

"Call it what you like: you look at things as they are."

"Ah—I've had to. I've had to look at the Gorgon."[2]

"Well—it hasn't blinded you! You've seen that she's just an old bogey like all the others."

"She doesn't blind one; but she dries up one's tears."

The answer checked the pleading on Archer's lips: it seemed to come from depths of experience beyond his reach. The slow advance of the ferry-boat had ceased, and her bows bumped against the piles of the slip with a violence that made the brougham stagger, and flung Archer and Madame Olenska against each other. The young man, trembling, felt the pressure of her shoulder, and passed his arm about her.

"If you're not blind, then, you must see that this can't last."

"What can't?"

"Our being together—and not together."

"No. You ought not to have come today," she said in an altered voice; and suddenly she turned, flung her arms about him and pressed her lips to his. At the same moment the carriage began to move, and a gas-lamp at the head of the slip flashed its light into the window. She drew away, and they sat silent and motionless while the brougham

---

2. One of three female monsters in Greek mythology, often depicted with writhing snakes for hair; according to myth, anyone who looks at these figures directly is turned into stone. In the singular, "the Gorgon" refers to Medusa.

struggled through the congestion of carriages about the ferry-landing. As they gained the street Archer began to speak hurriedly.

"Don't be afraid of me: you needn't squeeze yourself back into your corner like that. A stolen kiss isn't what I want. Look: I'm not even trying to touch the sleeve of your jacket. Don't suppose that I don't understand your reasons for not wanting to let this feeling between us dwindle into an ordinary hole-and-corner love affair. I couldn't have spoken like this yesterday, because when we've been apart, and I'm looking forward to seeing you, every thought is burnt up in a great flame. But then you come; and you're so much more than I remembered, and what I want of you is so much more than an hour or two every now and then, with wastes of thirsty waiting between, that I can sit perfectly still beside you, like this, with that other vision in my mind, just quietly trusting to it to come true."

For a moment she made no reply; then she asked, hardly above a whisper: "What do you mean by trusting to it to come true?"

"Why—you know it will, don't you?"

"Your vision of you and me together?" She burst into a sudden hard laugh. "You choose your place well to put it to me!"

"Do you mean because we're in my wife's brougham? Shall we get out and walk, then? I don't suppose you mind a little snow?"

She laughed again, more gently. "No; I shan't get out and walk, because my business is to get to Granny's as quickly as I can. And you'll sit beside me, and we'll look, not at visions, but at realities."

"I don't know what you mean by realities. The only reality to me is this."

She met the words with a long silence, during which the carriage rolled down an obscure side-street and then turned into the searching illumination of Fifth Avenue.

"Is it your idea, then, that I should live with you as your mistress— since I can't be your wife?" she asked.

The crudeness of the question startled him: the word was one that women of his class fought shy of, even when their talk flitted closest about the topic. He noticed that Madame Olenska pronounced it as if it had a recognized place in her vocabulary, and he wondered if it had been used familiarly in her presence in the horrible life she had fled from. Her question pulled him up with a jerk, and he floundered.

"I want—I want somehow to get away with you into a world where words like that—categories like that—won't exist. Where we shall be simply two human beings who love each other, who are the whole of life to each other; and nothing else on earth will matter."

She drew a deep sigh that ended in another laugh. "Oh, my dear— where is that country? Have you ever been there?" she asked; and as he remained sullenly dumb she went on: "I know so many who've tried to find it; and, believe me, they all got out by mistake at wayside stations: at places like Boulogne, or Pisa, or Monte Carlo[3]—and it wasn't

3. An inland port in Northern Italy, the site of the oldest university in Europe; Pisa: A village in northwestern Italy; Monte Carlo: A city in Monaco famous for its gambling resorts.

at all different from the old world they'd left, but only rather smaller and dingier and more promiscuous."

He had never heard her speak in such a tone, and he remembered the phrase she had used a little while before.

"Yes, the Gorgon *has* dried your tears," he said.

"Well, she opened my eyes too; it's a delusion to say that she blinds people. What she does is just the contrary—she fastens their eyelids open, so that they're never again in the blessed darkness. Isn't there a Chinese torture like that? There ought to be. Ah, believe me, it's a miserable little country!"

The carriage had crossed Forty-second Street: May's sturdy brougham-horse was carrying them northward as if he had been a Kentucky trotter. Archer choked with the sense of wasted minutes and vain words.

"Then what, exactly, is your plan for us?" he asked.

"For *us*? But there's no *us* in that sense! We're near each other only if we stay far from each other. Then we can be ourselves. Otherwise we're only Newland Archer, the husband of Ellen Olenska's cousin, and Ellen Olenska, the cousin of Newland Archer's wife, trying to be happy behind the backs of the people who trust them."

"Ah, I'm beyond that," he groaned.

"No, you're not! You've never been beyond. And *I* have," she said, in a strange voice, "and I know what it looks like there."

He sat silent, dazed with inarticulate pain. Then he groped in the darkness of the carriage for the little bell that signaled orders to the coachman. He remembered that May rang twice when she wished to stop. He pressed the bell, and the carriage drew up beside the curbstone.

"Why are we stopping? This is not Granny's," Madame Olenska exclaimed.

"No: I shall get out here," he stammered, opening the door and jumping to the pavement. By the light of a street-lamp he saw her startled face, and the instinctive motion she made to detain him. He closed the door, and leaned for a moment in the window.

"You're right: I ought not to have come today," he said, lowering his voice so that the coachman should not hear. She bent forward, and seemed about to speak; but he had already called out the order to drive on, and the carriage rolled away while he stood on the corner. The snow was over, and a tingling wind had sprung up, that lashed his face as he stood gazing. Suddenly he felt something stiff and cold on his lashes, and perceived that he had been crying, and that the wind had frozen his tears.

He thrust his hands in his pockets, and walked at a sharp pace down Fifth Avenue to his own house.

## XXX

That evening when Archer came down before dinner he found the drawing room empty.

He and May were dining alone, all the family engagements having been postponed since Mrs. Manson Mingott's illness; and as May was the more punctual of the two he was surprised that she had not preceded him. He knew that she was at home, for while he dressed he had heard her moving about in her room; and he wondered what had delayed her.

He had fallen into the way of dwelling on such conjectures as a means of tying his thoughts fast to reality. Sometimes he felt as if he had found the clue to his father-in-law's absorption in trifles; perhaps even Mr. Welland, long ago, had had escapes and visions, and had conjured up all the hosts of domesticity to defend himself against them.

When May appeared he thought she looked tired. She had put on the low-necked and tightly-laced dinner-dress which the Mingott ceremonial exacted on the most informal occasions, and had built her fair hair into its usual accumulated coils; and her face, in contrast, was wan and almost faded. But she shone on him with her usual tenderness, and her eyes had kept the blue dazzle of the day before.

"What became of you, dear?" she asked. "I was waiting at Granny's, and Ellen came alone, and said she had dropped you on the way because you had to rush off on business. There's nothing wrong?"

"Only some letters I'd forgotten, and wanted to get off before dinner."

"Ah—" she said; and a moment afterward: "I'm sorry you didn't come to Granny's—unless the letters were urgent."

"They were," he rejoined, surprised at her insistence. "Besides, I don't see why I should have gone to your grandmother's. I didn't know you were there."

She turned and moved to the looking-glass above the mantelpiece. As she stood there, lifting her long arm to fasten a puff that had slipped from its place in her intricate hair, Archer was struck by something languid and inelastic in her attitude, and wondered if the deadly monotony of their lives had laid its weight on her also. Then he remembered that, as he had left the house that morning, she had called over the stairs that she would meet him at her grandmother's so that they might drive home together. He had called back a cheery "Yes!" and then, absorbed in other visions, had forgotten his promise. Now he was smitten with compunction, yet irritated that so trifling an omission should be stored up against him after nearly two years of marriage. He was weary of living in a perpetual tepid honeymoon, without the temperature of passion yet with all its exactions. If May had spoken out her grievances (he suspected her of many) he might have laughed them away; but she was trained to conceal imaginary wounds under a Spartan smile.

To disguise his own annoyance he asked how her grandmother was, and she answered that Mrs. Mingott was still improving, but had been rather disturbed by the last news about the Beauforts.

"What news?"

"It seems they're going to stay in New York. I believe he's going into an insurance business, or something. They're looking about for a small house."

The preposterousness of the case was beyond discussion, and they went in to dinner. During dinner their talk moved in its usual limited circle; but Archer noticed that his wife made no allusion to Madame Olenska, nor to old Catherine's reception of her. He was thankful for the fact, yet felt it to be vaguely ominous.

They went up to the library for coffee, and Archer lit a cigar and took down a volume of Michelet.[1] He had taken to history in the evenings since May had shown a tendency to ask him to read aloud whenever she saw him with a volume of poetry: not that he disliked the sound of his own voice, but because he could always foresee her comments on what he read. In the days of their engagement she had simply (as he now perceived) echoed what he told her; but since he had ceased to provide her with opinions she had begun to hazard her own, with results destructive to his enjoyment of the works commented on.

Seeing that he had chosen history she fetched her work-basket, drew up an armchair to the green-shaded student lamp, and uncovered a cushion she was embroidering for his sofa. She was not a clever needlewoman; her large capable hands were made for riding, rowing and open-air activities; but since other wives embroidered cushions for their husbands she did not wish to omit this last link in her devotion.

She was so placed that Archer, by merely raising his eyes, could see her bent above her work-frame, her ruffled elbow-sleeves slipping back from her firm round arms, the betrothal sapphire shining on her left hand above her broad gold wedding-ring, and the right hand slowly and laboriously stabbing the canvas. As she sat thus, the lamplight full on her clear brow, he said to himself with a secret dismay that he would always know the thoughts behind it, that never, in all the years to come, would she surprise him by an unexpected mood, by a new idea, a weakness, a cruelty or an emotion. She had spent her poetry and romance on their short courting: the function was exhausted because the need was past. Now she was simply ripening into a copy of her mother, and mysteriously, by the very process, trying to turn him into a Mr. Welland. He laid down his book and stood up impatiently; and at once she raised her head.

1. Jules Michelet (1798–1874), a distinguished nineteenth-century French historian, known for his *Histoire de France* (1833–1867). He completed his *History of the French Revolution* (1847–1853), a celebratory account of the rise of the French people against the abuses of the aristocracy and the established Catholic Church, at the same time that Karl Marx was writing *Das Kapital*. Criticized for romanticizing "the people" as he focused on the formation of the modern French nation, Michelet's history has also been criticized for its failure to understand social class as a force behind the revolution.

"What's the matter?"

"The room is stifling: I want a little air."

He had insisted that the library curtains should draw backward and forward on a rod, so that they might be closed in the evening, instead of remaining nailed to a gilt cornice, and immovably looped up over layers of lace, as in the drawing room; and he pulled them back and pushed up the sash, leaning out into the icy night. The mere fact of not looking at May, seated beside his table, under his lamp, the fact of seeing other houses, roofs, chimneys, of getting the sense of other lives outside his own, other cities beyond New York, and a whole world beyond his world, cleared his brain and made it easier to breathe.

After he had leaned out into the darkness for a few minutes he heard her say: "Newland! Do shut the window. You'll catch your death."

He pulled the sash down and turned back. "Catch my death!" he echoed; and he felt like adding: "But I've caught it already. I *am* dead—I've been dead for months and months."

And suddenly the play of the word flashed up a wild suggestion. What if it were *she* who was dead! If she were going to die—to die soon—and leave him free! The sensation of standing there, in that warm familiar room, and looking at her, and wishing her dead, was so strange, so fascinating and overmastering, that its enormity did not immediately strike him. He simply felt that chance had given him a new possibility to which his sick soul might cling. Yes, May might die—people did: young people, healthy people like herself: she might die, and set him suddenly free.

She glanced up, and he saw by her widening eyes that there must be something strange in his own.

"Newland! Are you ill?"

He shook his head and turned toward his armchair. She bent over her work-frame, and as he passed he laid his hand on her hair. "Poor May!" he said.

"Poor? Why poor?" she echoed with a strained laugh.

"Because I shall never be able to open a window without worrying you," he rejoined, laughing also.

For a moment she was silent; then she said very low, her head bowed over her work: "I shall never worry if you're happy."

"Ah, my dear; and I shall never be happy unless I can open the windows!"

"In *this* weather?" she remonstrated; and with a sigh he buried his head in his book.

Six or seven days passed. Archer heard nothing from Madame Olenska, and became aware that her name would not be mentioned in his presence by any member of the family. He did not try to see her; to do so while she was at old Catherine's guarded bedside would have been almost impossible. In the uncertainty of the situation he let himself drift, conscious, somewhere below the surface of his thoughts, of a resolve which had come to him when he had leaned out from his library window into the icy night. The strength of that resolve made it easy to wait and make no sign.

Then one day May told him that Mrs. Manson Mingott had asked to see him. There was nothing surprising in the request, for the old lady was steadily recovering, and she had always openly declared that she preferred Archer to any of her other grandsons-in-law. May gave the message with evident pleasure: she was proud of old Catherine's appreciation of her husband.

There was a moment's pause, and then Archer felt it incumbent on him to say: "All right. Shall we go together this afternoon?"

His wife's face brightened, but she instantly answered: "Oh, you'd much better go alone. It bores Granny to see the same people too often."

Archer's heart was beating violently when he rang old Mrs. Mingott's bell. He had wanted above all things to go alone, for he felt sure the visit would give him the chance of saying a word in private to the Countess Olenska. He had determined to wait till the chance presented itself naturally; and here it was, and here he was on the doorstep. Behind the door, behind the curtains of the yellow damask room next to the hall, she was surely awaiting him; in another moment he should see her, and be able to speak to her before she led him to the sickroom.

He wanted only to put one question: after that his course would be clear. What he wished to ask was simply the date of her return to Washington; and that question she could hardly refuse to answer.

But in the yellow sitting room it was the mulatto maid who waited. Her white teeth shining like a keyboard, she pushed back the sliding doors and ushered him into old Catherine's presence.

The old woman sat in a vast throne-like armchair near her bed. Beside her was a mahogany stand bearing a cast bronze lamp with an engraved globe, over which a green paper shade had been balanced. There was not a book or a newspaper in reach, nor any evidence of feminine employment: conversation had always been Mrs. Mingott's sole pursuit, and she would have scorned to feign an interest in fancywork.

Archer saw no trace of the slight distortion left by her stroke. She merely looked paler, with darker shadows in the folds and recesses of her obesity; and, in the fluted mob-cap tied by a starched bow between her first two chins, and the muslin kerchief crossed over her billowing purple dressing-gown, she seemed like some shrewd and kindly ancestress of her own who might have yielded too freely to the pleasures of the table.

She held out one of the little hands that nestled in a hollow of her huge lap like pet animals, and called to the maid: "Don't let in anyone else. If my daughters call, say I'm asleep."

The maid disappeared, and the old lady turned to her grandson.

"My dear, am I perfectly hideous?" she asked gaily, launching out one hand in search of the folds of muslin on her inaccessible bosom. "My daughters tell me it doesn't matter at my age—as if hideousness didn't matter all the more the harder it gets to conceal!"

"My dear, you're handsomer than ever!" Archer rejoined in the same tone; and she threw back her head and laughed.

"Ah, but not as handsome as Ellen!" she jerked out, twinkling at him maliciously; and before he could answer she added: "Was she so awfully handsome the day you drove her up from the ferry?"

He laughed, and she continued: "Was it because you told her so that she had to put you out on the way? In my youth young men didn't desert pretty women unless they were made to!" She gave another chuckle, and interrupted it to say almost querulously: "It's a pity she didn't marry you; I always told her so. It would have spared me all this worry. But who ever thought of sparing their grandmother worry?"

Archer wondered if her illness had blurred her faculties; but suddenly she broke out: "Well, it's settled, anyhow: she's going to stay with me, whatever the rest of the family say! She hadn't been here five minutes before I'd have gone down on my knees to keep her—if only, for the last twenty years, I'd been able to see where the floor was!"

Archer listened in silence, and she went on: "They'd talked me over, as no doubt you know: persuaded me, Lovell, and Letterblair, and Augusta Welland, and all the rest of them, that I must hold out and cut off her allowance, till she was made to see that it was her duty to go back to Olenski. They thought they'd convinced me when the secretary, or whatever he was, came out with the last proposals: handsome proposals I confess they were. After all, marriage is marriage, and money's money—both useful things in their way . . . and I didn't know what to answer—" She broke off and drew a long breath, as if speaking had become an effort. "But the minute I laid eyes on her, I said: 'You sweet bird, you! Shut you up in that cage again? Never!' And now it's settled that she's to stay here and nurse her Granny as long as there's a Granny to nurse. It's not a gay prospect, but she doesn't mind; and of course I've told Letterblair that she's to be given her proper allowance."

The young man heard her with veins aglow; but in his confusion of mind he hardly knew whether her news brought joy or pain. He had so definitely decided on the course he meant to pursue that for the moment he could not readjust his thoughts. But gradually there stole over him the delicious sense of difficulties deferred and opportunities miraculously provided. If Ellen had consented to come and live with her grandmother it must surely be because she had recognized the impossibility of giving him up. This was her answer to his final appeal of the other day: if she would not take the extreme step he had urged, she had at last yielded to half-measures. He sank back into the thought with the involuntary relief of a man who has been ready to risk everything, and suddenly tastes the dangerous sweetness of security.

"She couldn't have gone back—it was impossible!" he exclaimed.

"Ah, my dear, I always knew you were on her side; and that's why I sent for you today, and why I said to your pretty wife, when she proposed to come with you: 'No, my dear, I'm pining to see Newland, and

I don't want anybody to share our transports.' For you see, my dear—"
she drew her head back as far as its tethering chins permitted, and
looked him full in the eyes—"you see, we shall have a fight yet. The
family don't want her here, and they'll say it's because I've been ill, because I'm a weak old woman, that she's persuaded me. I'm not well
enough yet to fight them one by one, and you've got to do it for me."

"I?" he stammered.

"You. Why not?" she jerked back at him, her round eyes suddenly as
sharp as pen-knives. Her hand fluttered from its chair-arm and lit on
his with a clutch of little pale nails like bird-claws. "Why not?" she
searchingly repeated.

Archer, under the exposure of her gaze, had recovered his self-
possession.

"Oh, I don't count—I'm too insignificant."

"Well, you're Letterblair's partner, ain't you? You've got to get at
them through Letterblair. Unless you've got a reason," she insisted.

"Oh, my dear, I back you to hold your own against them all without
my help; but you shall have it if you need it," he reassured her.

"Then we're safe!" she sighed; and smiling on him with all her ancient cunning she added, as she settled her head among the cushions:
"I always knew you'd back us up, because they never quote you when
they talk about its being her duty to go home."

He winced a little at her terrifying perspicacity, and longed to ask:
"And May—do they quote her?" But he judged it safer to turn the
question.

"And Madame Olenska? When am I to see her?" he said.

The old lady chuckled, crumpled her lids, and went through the
pantomime of archness. "Not today. One at a time, please. Madame
Olenska's gone out."

He flushed with disappointment, and she went on: "She's gone out,
my child: gone in my carriage to see Regina Beaufort."

She paused for this announcement to produce its effect. "That's
what she's reduced me to already. The day after she got here she put
on her best bonnet, and told me, as cool as a cucumber, that she was
going to call on Regina Beaufort. 'I don't know her; who is she?' says I.
'She's your grand-niece, and a most unhappy woman,' she says. 'She's
the wife of a scoundrel,' I answered. 'Well,' she says, 'and so am I, and
yet all my family want me to go back to him.' Well, that floored me,
and I let her go; and finally one day she said it was raining too hard to
go out on foot, and she wanted me to lend her my carriage. 'What for?'
I asked her; and she said: 'To go and see Cousin Regina'—*cousin!*
Now, my dear, I looked out of the window, and saw it wasn't raining a
drop; but I understood her, and I let her have the carriage. . . . After
all, Regina's a brave woman, and so is she; and I've always liked
courage above everything."

Archer bent down and pressed his lips on the little hand that still lay
on his.

"Eh—eh—eh! Whose hand did you think you were kissing, young

man—your wife's, I hope?" the old lady snapped out with her mocking cackle; and as he rose to go she called out after him: "Give her her Granny's love; but you'd better not say anything about our talk."

# XXXI

Archer had been stunned by old Catherine's news. It was only natural that Madame Olenska should have hastened from Washington in response to her grandmother's summons; but that she should have decided to remain under her roof—especially now that Mrs. Mingott had almost regained her health—was less easy to explain.

Archer was sure that Madame Olenska's decision had not been influenced by the change in her financial situation. He knew the exact figure of the small income which her husband had allowed her at their separation. Without the addition of her grandmother's allowance it was hardly enough to live on, in any sense known to the Mingott vocabulary; and now that Medora Manson, who shared her life, had been ruined, such a pittance would barely keep the two women clothed and fed. Yet Archer was convinced that Madame Olenska had not accepted her grandmother's offer from interested motives.

She had the heedless generosity and the spasmodic extravagance of persons used to large fortunes, and indifferent to money; but she could go without many things which her relations considered indispensable, and Mrs. Lovell Mingott and Mrs. Welland had often been heard to deplore that anyone who had enjoyed the cosmopolitan luxuries of Count Olenski's establishments should care so little about "how things were done." Moreover, as Archer knew, several months had passed since her allowance had been cut off; yet in the interval she had made no effort to regain her grandmother's favor. Therefore if she had changed her course it must be for a different reason.

He did not have far to seek for that reason. On the way from the ferry she had told him that he and she must remain apart; but she had said it with her head on his breast. He knew that there was no calculated coquetry in her words; she was fighting her fate as he had fought his, and clinging desperately to her resolve that they should not break faith with the people who trusted them. But during the ten days which had elapsed since her return to New York she had perhaps guessed from his silence, and from the fact of his making no attempt to see her, that he was meditating a decisive step, a step from which there was no turning back. At the thought, a sudden fear of her own weakness might have seized her, and she might have felt that, after all, it was better to accept the compromise usual in such cases, and follow the line of least resistance.

An hour earlier, when he had rung Mrs. Mingott's bell, Archer had fancied that his path was clear before him. He had meant to have a word alone with Madame Olenska, and failing that, to learn from her grandmother on what day, and by which train, she was returning to Washington. In that train he intended to join her, and travel with her to Washington, or as much farther as she was willing to go. His own fancy inclined to Japan. At any rate she would understand at once that, wherever she went, he was going. He meant to leave a note for May that should cut off any other alternative.

He had fancied himself not only nerved for this plunge but eager to take it; yet his first feeling on hearing that the course of events was changed had been one of relief. Now, however, as he walked home from Mrs. Mingott's, he was conscious of a growing distaste for what lay before him. There was nothing unknown or unfamiliar in the path he was presumably to tread; but when he had trodden it before it was as a free man, who was accountable to no one for his actions, and could lend himself with an amused detachment to the game of precautions and prevarications, concealments and compliances, that the part required. This procedure was called "protecting a woman's honor"; and the best fiction, combined with the after-dinner talk of his elders, had long since initiated him into every detail of its code.

Now he saw the matter in a new light, and his part in it seemed singularly diminished. It was, in fact, that which, with a secret fatuity, he had watched Mrs. Thorley Rushworth play toward a fond and unperceiving husband: a smiling, bantering, humoring, watchful, and incessant lie. A lie by day, a lie by night, a lie in every touch and every look; a lie in every caress and every quarrel; a lie in every word and in every silence.

It was easier, and less dastardly on the whole, for a wife to play such a part toward her husband. A woman's standard of truthfulness was tacitly held to be lower: she was the subject creature, and versed in the arts of the enslaved. Then she could always plead moods and nerves, and the right not to be held too strictly to account; and even in the most strait-laced societies the laugh was always against the husband.

But in Archer's little world no one laughed at a wife deceived, and a certain measure of contempt was attached to men who continued their philandering after marriage. In the rotation of crops there was a recognized season for wild oats; but they were not to be sown more than once.

Archer had always shared this view: in his heart he thought Lefferts despicable. But to love Ellen Olenska was not to become a man like Lefferts: for the first time Archer found himself face to face with the dread argument of the individual case. Ellen Olenska was like no other woman, he was like no other man: their situation, therefore, resembled no one else's, and they were answerable to no tribunal but that of their own judgment.

Yes, but in ten minutes more he would be mounting his own doorstep; and there were May, and habit, and honor, and all the old decencies that he and his people had always believed in. . . .

At his corner he hesitated, and then walked on down Fifth Avenue.

Ahead of him, in the winter night, loomed a big unlit house. As he drew near he thought how often he had seen it blazing with lights, its steps awninged and carpeted, and carriages waiting in double line to draw up at the curbstone. It was in the conservatory that stretched its dead-black bulk down the side street that he had taken his first kiss from May; it was under the myriad candles of the ballroom that he had seen her appear, tall and silver-shining as a young Diana.

Now the house was as dark as the grave, except for a faint flare of gas in the basement, and a light in one upstairs room where the blind had not been lowered. As Archer reached the corner he saw that the carriage standing at the door was Mrs. Manson Mingott's. What an opportunity for Sillerton Jackson, if he should chance to pass! Archer had been greatly moved by old Catherine's account of Madame Olenska's attitude toward Mrs. Beaufort; it made the righteous reprobation of New York seem like a passing-by on the other side. But he knew well enough what construction the clubs and drawing rooms would put on Ellen Olenska's visits to her cousin.

He paused and looked up at the lighted window. No doubt the two women were sitting together in that room: Beaufort had probably sought consolation elsewhere. There were even rumors that he had left New York with Fanny Ring; but Mrs. Beaufort's attitude made the report seem improbable.

Archer had the nocturnal perspective of Fifth Avenue almost to himself. At that hour most people were indoors, dressing for dinner; and he was secretly glad that Ellen's exit was likely to be unobserved. As the thought passed through his mind the door opened, and she came out. Behind her was a faint light, such as might have been carried down the stairs to show her the way. She turned to say a word to someone; then the door closed, and she came down the steps.

"Ellen," he said in a low voice, as she reached the pavement.

She stopped with a slight start, and just then he saw two young men of fashionable cut approaching. There was a familiar air about their overcoats and the way their smart silk mufflers were folded over their white ties; and he wondered how youths of their quality happened to be dining out so early. Then he remembered that the Reggie Chiverses, whose house was a few doors above, were taking a large party that evening to see Adelaide Neilson[1] in *Romeo and Juliet,* and guessed that the two were of the number. They passed under a lamp, and he recognized Lawrence Lefferts and a young Chivers.

A mean desire not to have Madame Olenska seen at the Beauforts' door vanished as he felt the penetrating warmth of her hand.

"I shall see you now—we shall be together," he broke out, hardly knowing what he said.

"Ah," she answered, "Granny has told you?"

While he watched her he was aware that Lefferts and Chivers, on reaching the farther side of the street corner, had discreetly struck away across Fifth Avenue. It was the kind of masculine solidarity that he himself often practiced; now he sickened at their connivance. Did

---

1. English actress (1846–1880) renowned for her portrayal of Shakespeare's Juliet; Neilson toured the United States in 1872.

she really imagine that he and she could live like this? And if not, what else did she imagine?

"Tomorrow I must see you—somewhere where we can be alone," he said, in a voice that sounded almost angry to his own ears.

She wavered, and moved toward the carriage.

"But I shall be at Granny's—for the present that is," she added, as if conscious that her change of plans required some explanation.

"Somewhere where we can be alone," he insisted.

She gave a faint laugh that grated on him.

"In New York? But there are no churches . . . no monuments."

"There's the Art Museum—in the Park,"[2] he explained, as she looked puzzled. "At half-past two. I shall be at the door. . . ."

She turned away without answering and got quickly into the carriage. As it drove off she leaned forward, and he thought she waved her hand in the obscurity. He stared after her in a turmoil of contradictory feelings. It seemed to him that he had been speaking not to the woman he loved but to another, a woman he was indebted to for pleasures already wearied of: it was hateful to find himself the prisoner of this hackneyed vocabulary.

"She'll come!" he said to himself, almost contemptuously.

Avoiding the popular "Wolfe collection," whose anecdotic canvases filled one of the main galleries of the queer wilderness of cast-iron and encaustic tiles known as the Metropolitan Museum, they had wandered down a passage to the room where the "Cesnola antiquities" mouldered in unvisited loneliness.[3]

They had this melancholy retreat to themselves, and seated on the divan enclosing the central steam-radiator, they were staring silently at the glass cabinets mounted in ebonized wood which contained the recovered fragments of Ilium.[4]

"It's odd," Madame Olenska said, "I never came here before."

"Ah, well—. Some day, I suppose, it will be a great Museum."

"Yes," she assented absently.

She stood up and wandered across the room. Archer, remaining seated, watched the light movements of her figure, so girlish even under its heavy furs, the cleverly planted heron wing in her fur cap, and the way a dark curl lay like a flattened vine spiral on each cheek above the ear. His mind, as always when they first met, was wholly absorbed

2. The Metropolitan Museum of Art, originally located on Fifth Avenue between 53rd and 54th Streets, did not move to its current location on Fifth Avenue between 82nd and 85th Streets bordering Central Park until 1880. There was no "Art Museum—in the Park" in the early 1870s. Among Wharton's most criticized "errors," the time of the opening of the new museum at the beginning of the 1880s was well within the decade-long period beginning in "the early seventies" that marks the temporal limits for the sources of the novel.
3. Wolfe collection: The 143 paintings owned by Catharine Lorillard Wolfe and donated to the Metropolitan Museum of Art beginning in the 1870s; cast iron and encaustic tiles: Tiles made from cast iron (an alloy of iron, carbon, and silicon) and colored with fired clays; "Cesnola antiquities": Over 10,000 Egyptian, Assyrian, Phoenician, and early Greek antiquities excavated from the island of Cyprus by the American consul, General Luigi Palma di Cesnola (1832–1904), and donated to the museum in 1876; elected in 1879, Cesnola was the first director of the museum.
4. Ilium: Greek, Troy.

in the delicious details that made her herself and no other. Presently
he rose and approached the case before which she stood. Its glass
shelves were crowded with small broken objects—hardly recognizable
domestic utensils, ornaments and personal trifles—made of glass, of
clay, of discolored bronze and other time-blurred substances.

"It seems cruel," she said, "that after a while nothing matters . . .
any more than these little things, that used to be necessary and important to forgotten people, and now have to be guessed at under a
magnifying glass and labeled: 'Use unknown.' "

"Yes; but meanwhile—"

"Ah, meanwhile—"

As she stood there, in her long sealskin coat, her hands thrust in
a small round muff, her veil drawn down like a transparent mask to
the tip of her nose, and the bunch of violets he had brought her stir-
ring with her quickly-taken breath, it seemed incredible that this
pure harmony of line and color should ever suffer the stupid law of
change.

"Meanwhile everything matters—that concerns you," he said.

She looked at him thoughtfully, and turned back to the divan. He
sat down beside her and waited; but suddenly he heard a step echoing
far off down the empty rooms, and felt the pressure of the minutes.

"What is it you wanted to tell me?" she asked, as if she had received
the same warning.

"What I wanted to tell you?" he rejoined. "Why, that I believe you
came to New York because you were afraid."

"Afraid?"

"Of my coming to Washington."

She looked down at her muff, and he saw her hands stir in it un-
easily.

"Well—?"

"Well—yes," she said.

"You *were* afraid? You knew—?"

"Yes: I knew. . . ."

"Well, then?" he insisted.

"Well, then: this is better, isn't it?" she returned with a long questioning sigh.

"Better—?"

"We shall hurt others less. Isn't it, after all, what you always
wanted?"

"To have you here, you mean—in reach and yet out of reach? To
meet you in this way, on the sly? It's the very reverse of what I want. I
told you the other day what I wanted."

She hesitated. "And you still think this—worse?"

"A thousand times!" He paused. "It would be easy to lie to you; but
the truth is I think it detestable."

"Oh, so do I!" she cried with a deep breath of relief.

He sprang up impatiently. "Well, then—it's my turn to ask: what is
it, in God's name, that you think better?"

She hung her head and continued to clasp and unclasp her hands in her muff. The step drew nearer, and a guardian in a braided cap walked listlessly through the room like a ghost stalking through a necropolis. They fixed their eyes simultaneously on the case opposite them, and when the official figure had vanished down a vista of mummies and sarcophagi Archer spoke again.[5]

"What do you think better?"

Instead of answering she murmured: "I promised Granny to stay with her because it seemed to me that here I should be safer."

"From me?"

She bent her head slightly, without looking at him.

"Safer from loving me?"

Her profile did not stir, but he saw a tear overflow on her lashes and hang in a mesh of her veil.

"Safer from doing irreparable harm. Don't let us be like all the others!" she protested.

"What others? I don't profess to be different from my kind. I'm consumed by the same wants and the same longings."

She glanced at him with a kind of terror, and he saw a faint color steal into her cheeks.

"Shall I—once come to you; and then go home?" she suddenly hazarded in a low clear voice.

The blood rushed to the young man's forehead. "Dearest!" he said, without moving. It seemed as if he held his heart in his hands, like a full cup that the least motion might overbrim.

Then her last phrase struck his ear and his face clouded. "Go home? What do you mean by going home?"

"Home to my husband."

"And you expect me to say yes to that?"

She raised her troubled eyes to his. "What else is there? I can't stay here and lie to the people who've been good to me."

"But that's the very reason why I ask you to come away!"

"And destroy their lives, when they've helped me to remake mine?"

Archer sprang to his feet and stood looking down on her in inarticulate despair. It would have been easy to say: "Yes, come; come once." He knew the power she would put in his hands if she consented; there would be no difficulty then in persuading her not to go back to her husband.

But something silenced the word on his lips. A sort of passionate honesty in her made it inconceivable that he should try to draw her into that familiar trap. "If I were to let her come," he said to himself, "I should have to let her go again." And that was not to be imagined.

But he saw the shadow of the lashes on her wet cheek, and wavered.

"After all," he began again, "we have lives of our own. . . . There's no use attempting the impossible. You're so unprejudiced about some things, so used, as you say, to looking at the Gorgon, that I don't know

---

5. Necropolis. Ancient cemetery with above-ground tombs, Greek for "city of the dead"; sarcophagi: Limestone coffins, from the Greek for "flesh-eating stone"—limestone was thought to disintegrate the flesh of dead bodies.

why you're afraid to face our case, and see it as it really is—unless you think the sacrifice is not worth making."

She stood up also, her lips tightening under a rapid frown.

"Call it that, then—I must go," she said, drawing her little watch from her bosom.

She turned away, and he followed and caught her by the wrist. "Well, then: come to me once," he said, his head turning suddenly at the thought of losing her; and for a second or two they looked at each other almost like enemies.

"When?" he insisted. "Tomorrow?"

She hesitated. "The day after."

"Dearest—!" he said again.

She had disengaged her wrist; but for a moment they continued to hold each other's eyes, and he saw that her face, which had grown very pale, was flooded with a deep inner radiance. His heart beat with awe: he felt that he had never before beheld love visible.

"Oh, I shall be late—good-bye. No, don't come any farther than this," she cried, walking hurriedly away down the long room, as if the reflected radiance in his eyes had frightened her. When she reached the door she turned for a moment to wave a quick farewell.

Archer walked home alone. Darkness was falling when he let himself into his house, and he looked about at the familiar objects in the hall as if he viewed them from the other side of the grave.

The parlormaid, hearing his step, ran up the stairs to light the gas on the upper landing.

"Is Mrs. Archer in?"

"No, sir; Mrs. Archer went out in the carriage after luncheon, and hasn't come back."

With a sense of relief he entered the library and flung himself down in his armchair. The parlormaid followed, bringing the student lamp and shaking some coals onto the dying fire. When she left he continued to sit motionless, his elbows on his knees, his chin on his clasped hands, his eyes fixed on the red grate.

He sat there without conscious thoughts, without sense of the lapse of time, in a deep and grave amazement that seemed to suspend life rather than quicken it. "This was what had to be, then . . . this was what had to be," he kept repeating to himself, as if he hung in the clutch of doom. What he had dreamed of had been so different that there was a mortal chill in his rapture.

The door opened and May came in.

"I'm dreadfully late—you weren't worried, were you?" she asked, laying her hand on his shoulder with one of her rare caresses.

He looked up astonished. "Is it late?"

"After seven. I believe you've been asleep!" She laughed, and drawing out her hatpins tossed her velvet hat on the sofa. She looked paler than usual, but sparkling with an unwonted animation.

"I went to see Granny, and just as I was going away Ellen came in from a walk; so I stayed and had a long talk with her. It was ages since we'd had a real talk. . . ." She had dropped into her usual armchair, facing his, and was running her fingers through her rumpled hair. He fancied she expected him to speak.

"A really good talk," she went on, smiling with what seemed to Archer an unnatural vividness. "She was so dear—just like the old Ellen. I'm afraid I haven't been fair to her lately. I've sometimes thought—"

Archer stood up and leaned against the mantelpiece, out of the radius of the lamp.

"Yes, you've thought—?" he echoed as she paused.

"Well, perhaps I haven't judged her fairly. She's so different—at least on the surface. She takes up such odd people—she seems to like to make herself conspicuous. I suppose it's the life she's led in that fast European society; no doubt we seem dreadfully dull to her. But I don't want to judge her unfairly."

She paused again, a little breathless with the unwonted length of her speech, and sat with her lips slightly parted and a deep blush on her cheeks.

Archer, as he looked at her, was reminded of the glow which had suffused her face in the Mission Garden at St. Augustine. He became aware of the same obscure effort in her, the same reaching out toward something beyond the usual range of her vision.

"She hates Ellen," he thought, "and she's trying to overcome the feeling, and to get me to help her to overcome it."

The thought moved him, and for a moment he was on the point of breaking the silence between them, and throwing himself on her mercy.

"You understand, don't you," she went on, "why the family have sometimes been annoyed? We all did what we could for her at first; but she never seemed to understand. And now this idea of going to see Mrs. Beaufort, of going there in Granny's carriage! I'm afraid she's quite alienated the van der Luydens. . . ."

"Ah," said Archer with an impatient laugh. The open door had closed between them again.

"It's time to dress; we're dining out, aren't we?" he asked, moving from the fire.

She rose also, but lingered near the hearth. As he walked past her she moved forward impulsively, as though to detain him: their eyes met, and he saw that hers were of the same swimming blue as when he had left her to drive to Jersey City.

She flung her arms about his neck and pressed her cheek to his.

"You haven't kissed me today," she said in a whisper; and he felt her tremble in his arms.

# XXXII

At the Court of the Tuileries," said Mr. Sillerton Jackson with his reminiscent smile, "such things were pretty openly tolerated."

The scene was the van der Luydens' black walnut dining room in Madison Avenue, and the time the evening after Newland Archer's visit to the Museum of Art. Mr. and Mrs. van der Luyden had come to town for a few days from Skuytercliff, whither they had precipitately fled at the announcement of Beaufort's failure. It had been represented to them that the disarray into which society had been thrown by this deplorable affair made their presence in town more necessary than ever. It was one of the occasions when, as Mrs. Archer put it, they "owed it to society" to show themselves at the Opera, and even to open their own doors.

"It will never do, my dear Louisa, to let people like Mrs. Lemuel Struthers think they can step into Regina's shoes. It is just at such times that new people push in and get a footing. It was owing to the epidemic of chicken-pox in New York the winter Mrs. Struthers first appeared that the married men slipped away to her house while their wives were in the nursery. You and dear Henry, Louisa, must stand in the breach as you always have."

Mr. and Mrs. van der Luyden could not remain deaf to such a call, and reluctantly but heroically they had come to town, unmuffled the house, and sent out invitations for two dinners and an evening reception.

On this particular evening they had invited Sillerton Jackson, Mrs. Archer and Newland and his wife to go with them to the Opera, where *Faust*[1] was being sung for the first time that winter. Nothing was done without ceremony under the van der Luyden roof, and though there were but four guests the repast had begun at seven punctually, so that the proper sequence of courses might be served without haste before the gentlemen settled down to their cigars.

Archer had not seen his wife since the evening before. He had left early for the office, where he had plunged into an accumulation of unimportant business. In the afternoon one of the senior partners had made an unexpected call on his time; and he had reached home so late that May had preceded him to the van der Luydens', and sent back the carriage.

Now, across the Skuytercliff carnations and the massive plate, she struck him as pale and languid; but her eyes shone, and she talked with exaggerated animation.

The subject which had called forth Mr. Sillerton Jackson's favorite allusion had been brought up (Archer fancied not without intention) by their hostess. The Beaufort failure, or rather the Beaufort attitude since the failure, was still a fruitful theme for the drawing-room moralist; and after it had been thoroughly examined and condemned Mrs. van der Luyden had turned her scrupulous eyes on May Archer.

"Is it possible, dear, that what I hear is true? I was told your Grandmother Mingott's carriage was seen standing at Mrs. Beaufort's door."

---

1. See p. 3, *n.* 2. Gounod's *Faust*, the most popular opera in late nineteenth- and early twentieth-century America, was performed annually.

It was noticeable that she no longer called the offending lady by her Christian name.

May's color rose, and Mrs. Archer put in hastily: "If it was, I'm convinced it was there without Mrs. Mingott's knowledge."

"Ah, you think——?" Mrs. van der Luyden paused, sighed, and glanced at her husband.

"I'm afraid," Mr. van der Luyden said, "that Madame Olenska's kind heart may have led her into the imprudence of calling on Mrs. Beaufort."

"Or her taste for peculiar people," put in Mrs. Archer in a dry tone, while her eyes dwelt innocently on her son's.

"I'm sorry to think it of Madame Olenska," said Mrs. van der Luyden; and Mrs. Archer murmured: "Ah, my dear—and after you'd had her twice at Skuytercliff!"

It was at this point that Mr. Jackson seized the chance to place his favorite allusion.

"At the Tuileries," he repeated, seeing the eyes of the company expectantly turned on him, "the standard was excessively lax in some respects; and if you'd asked where Morny's money[2] came from—! Or who paid the debts of some of the Court beauties. . . ."

"I hope, dear Sillerton," said Mrs. Archer, "you are not suggesting that we should adopt such standards?"

"I never suggest," returned Mr. Jackson imperturbably. "But Madame Olenska's foreign bringing-up may make her less particular—"

"Ah," the two elder ladies sighed.

"Still, to have kept her grandmother's carriage at a defaulter's door!" Mr. van der Luyden protested; and Archer guessed that he was remembering, and resenting, the hampers of carnations he had sent to the little house in Twenty-third Street.

"Of course I've always said that she looks at things quite differently," Mrs. Archer summed up.

A flush rose to May's forehead. She looked across the table at her husband, and said precipitately: "I'm sure Ellen meant it kindly."

"Imprudent people are often kind," said Mrs. Archer, as if the fact were scarcely an extenuation; and Mrs. van der Luyden murmured: "If only she had consulted someone—"

"Ah, that she never did!" Mrs. Archer rejoined.

At this point Mr. van der Luyden glanced at his wife, who bent her head slightly in the direction of Mrs. Archer; and the glimmering trains of the three ladies swept out of the door while the gentlemen settled down to their cigars. Mr. van der Luyden supplied short ones on Opera nights; but they were so good that they made his guests deplore his inexorable punctuality.

Archer, after the first act, had detached himself from the party and made his way to the back of the club box. From there he watched, over various Chivers, Mingott and Rushworth shoulders, the same scene

2. Charles-Auguste Louis-Joseph Morny (1811–1865), who made a fortune in speculation and in the beet-sugar business, used his wealth and influence among financiers after being elected Deputy of France in 1842 to support the coup that toppled Louis Napoleon in 1848.

that he had looked at, two years previously, on the night of his first meeting with Ellen Olenska. He had half-expected her to appear again in old Mrs. Mingott's box, but it remained empty; and he sat motionless, his eyes fastened on it, till suddenly Madame Nilsson's pure soprano broke out into "*M'ama, non m'ama. . . .*"

Archer turned to the stage, where, in the familiar setting of giant roses and pen-wiper pansies, the same large blonde victim was succumbing to the same small brown seducer.

From the stage his eyes wandered to the point of the horseshoe where May sat between two older ladies, just as, on that former evening, she had sat between Mrs. Lovell Mingott and her newly-arrived "foreign" cousin. As on that evening, she was all in white; and Archer, who had not noticed what she wore, recognized the blue-white satin and old lace of her wedding dress.

It was the custom, in old New York, for brides to appear in this costly garment during the first year or two of marriage: his mother, he knew, kept hers in tissue paper in the hope that Janey might some day wear it, though poor Janey was reaching the age when pearl gray poplin and no bridesmaids would be thought more "appropriate."

It struck Archer that May, since their return from Europe, had seldom worn her bridal satin, and the surprise of seeing her in it made him compare her appearance with that of the young girl he had watched with such blissful anticipations two years earlier.

Though May's outline was slightly heavier, as her goddess-like build had foretold, her athletic erectness of carriage, and the girlish transparency of her expression, remained unchanged: but for the slight languor that Archer had lately noticed in her she would have been the exact image of the girl playing with the bouquet of lilies-of-the-valley on her betrothal evening. The fact seemed an additional appeal to his pity: such innocence was as moving as the trustful clasp of a child. Then he remembered the passionate generosity latent under that incurious calm. He recalled her glance of understanding when he had urged that their engagement should be announced at the Beaufort ball; he heard the voice in which she had said, in the Mission garden: "I couldn't have my happiness made out of a wrong—a wrong to someone else"; and an uncontrollable longing seized him to tell her the truth, to throw himself on her generosity, and ask for the freedom he had once refused.

Newland Archer was a quiet and self-controlled young man. Conformity to the discipline of a small society had become almost his second nature. It was deeply distasteful to him to do anything melodramatic and conspicuous, anything Mr. van der Luyden would have deprecated and the club box condemned as bad form. But he had become suddenly unconscious of the club box, of Mr. van der Luyden, of all that had so long enclosed him in the warm shelter of habit. He walked along the semi-circular passage at the back of the house, and opened the door of Mrs. van der Luyden's box as if it had been a gate into the unknown.

"*M'ama!*" thrilled out the triumphant Marguerite; and the occupants of the box looked up in surprise at Archer's entrance. He had already broken one of the rules of his world, which forbade the entering of a box during a solo.

Slipping between Mr. van der Luyden and Sillerton Jackson, he leaned over his wife.

"I've got a beastly headache; don't tell anyone, but come home, won't you?" he whispered.

May gave him a glance of comprehension, and he saw her whisper to his mother, who nodded sympathetically; then she murmured an excuse to Mrs. van der Luyden, and rose from her seat just as Marguerite fell into Faust's arms. Archer, while he helped her on with her opera cloak, noticed the exchange of a significant smile between the older ladies.

As they drove away May laid her hand shyly on his. "I'm so sorry you don't feel well. I'm afraid they've been over-working you again at the office."

"No—it's not that: do you mind if I open the window?" he returned confusedly, letting down the pane on his side. He sat staring out into the street, feeling his wife beside him as a silent watchful interrogation, and keeping his eyes steadily fixed on the passing houses. At their door she caught her skirt in the step of the carriage, and fell against him.

"Did you hurt yourself?" he asked, steadying her with his arm.

"No; but my poor dress—see how I've torn it!" she exclaimed. She bent to gather up a mud-stained breadth, and followed him up the steps into the hall. The servants had not expected them so early, and there was only a glimmer of gas on the upper landing.

Archer mounted the stairs, turned up the light, and put a match to the brackets on each side of the library mantelpiece. The curtains were drawn, and the warm friendly aspect of the room smote him like that of a familiar face met during an unavowable errand.

He noticed that his wife was very pale, and asked if he should get her some brandy.

"Oh, no," she exclaimed with a momentary flush, as she took off her cloak. "But hadn't you better go to bed at once?" she added, as he opened a silver box on the table and took out a cigarette.

Archer threw down the cigarette and walked to his usual place by the fire.

"No; my head is not as bad as that." He paused. "And there's something I want to say; something important—that I must tell you at once."

She had dropped into an armchair, and raised her head as he spoke. "Yes, dear?" she rejoined, so gently that he wondered at the lack of wonder with which she received this preamble.

"May—" he began, standing a few feet from her chair, and looking over at her as if the slight distance between them were an unbridgeable abyss. The sound of his voice echoed uncannily through the homelike hush, and he repeated: "There is something I've got to tell you . . . about myself. . . ."

She sat silent, without a movement or a tremor of her lashes. She was still extremely pale, but her face had a curious tranquility of expression that seemed drawn from some secret inner source.

Archer checked the conventional phrases of self-accusal that were crowding to his lips. He was determined to put the case baldly, without vain recrimination or excuse.

"Madame Olenska—" he said; but at the name his wife raised her hand as if to silence him. As she did so the gas-light struck on the gold of her wedding-ring.

"Oh, why should we talk about Ellen tonight?" she asked, with a slight pout of impatience.

"Because I ought to have spoken before."

Her face remained calm. "Is it really worthwhile, dear? I know I've been unfair to her at times—perhaps we all have. You've understood her, no doubt, better than we did: you've always been kind to her. But what does it matter, now it's all over?"

Archer looked at her blankly. Could it be possible that the sense of unreality in which he felt himself imprisoned had communicated itself to his wife?

"All over—what do you mean?" he asked in an indistinct stammer.

May still looked at him with transparent eyes. "Why—since she's going back to Europe so soon; since Granny approves and understands, and has arranged to make her independent of her husband—"

She broke off, and Archer, grasping the corner of the mantelpiece in one convulsed hand, and steadying himself against it, made a vain effort to extend the same control to his reeling thoughts.

"I supposed," he heard his wife's even voice go on, "that you had been kept at the office this evening about the business arrangements. It was settled this morning, I believe." She lowered her eyes under his unseeing stare, and another fugitive flush passed over her face.

He understood that his own eyes must be unbearable, and turning away, rested his elbows on the mantel-shelf and covered his face. Something drummed and clanged furiously in his ears; he could not tell if it were the blood in his veins, or the tick of the clock on the mantel.

May sat without moving or speaking while the clock slowly measured out five minutes. A lump of coal fell forward in the grate, and hearing her rise to push it back, Archer at length turned and faced her.

"It's impossible," he exclaimed.

"Impossible—?"

"How do you know—what you've just told me?"

"I saw Ellen yesterday—I told you I'd seen her at Granny's."

"It wasn't then that she told you?"

"No; I had a note from her this afternoon.—Do you want to see it?"

He could not find his voice, and she went out of the room, and came back almost immediately.

"I thought you knew," she said simply.

She laid a sheet of paper on the table, and Archer put out his hand and took it up. The letter contained only a few lines.

"May dear, I have at last made Granny understand that my visit to her could be no more than a visit; and she has been as kind and generous as ever. She sees now that if I return to Europe I must live by myself, or rather with poor Aunt Medora, who is coming with me. I am hurrying back to Washington to pack up, and we sail next week. You must be very good to Granny when I'm gone—as good as you've always been to me, Ellen.

"If any of my friends wish to urge me to change my mind, please tell them it would be utterly useless."

Archer read the letter over two or three times; then he flung it down and burst out laughing.

The sound of his laugh startled him. It recalled Janey's midnight fright when she had caught him rocking with incomprehensible mirth over May's telegram announcing that the date of their marriage had been advanced.

"Why did she write this?" he asked, checking his laugh with a supreme effort.

May met the question with her unshaken candor. "I suppose because we talked things over yesterday—"

"What things?"

"I told her I was afraid I hadn't been fair to her—hadn't always understood how hard it must have been for her here, alone among so many people who were relations and yet strangers; who felt the right to criticize, and yet didn't always know the circumstances." She paused. "I knew you'd been the one friend she could always count on; and I wanted her to know that you and I were the same—in all our feelings."

She hesitated, as if waiting for him to speak, and then added slowly: "She understood my wishing to tell her this. I think she understands everything."

She went up to Archer, and taking one of his cold hands pressed it quickly against her cheek.

"My head aches too; good-night, dear," she said, and turned to the door, her torn and muddy wedding-dress dragging after her across the room.

# XXXIII

It was, as Mrs. Archer smilingly said to Mrs. Welland, a great event for a young couple to give their first big dinner.

The Newland Archers, since they had set up their household, had received a good deal of company in an informal way. Archer was fond of having three or four friends to dine, and May welcomed them with the beaming readiness of which her mother had set her the example in conjugal affairs. Her husband questioned whether, if left to herself, she would ever have asked anyone to the house; but he had long given up trying to disengage her real self from the shape into which tradition and training had moulded her. It was expected that well-off young couples in New York should do a good deal of informal entertaining, and a Welland married to an Archer was doubly pledged to the tradition.

But a big dinner, with a hired *chef* and two borrowed footmen, with Roman punch, roses from Henderson's,[1] and *menus* on gilt-edged cards, was a different affair, and not to be lightly undertaken. As Mrs. Archer remarked, the Roman punch made all the difference; not in itself but by its manifold implications—since it signified either canvasbacks or terrapin, two soups, a hot and a cold sweet, full *décolletage*[2] with short sleeves, and guests of a proportionate importance.

It was always an interesting occasion when a young pair launched their first invitations in the third person, and their summons was seldom refused even by the seasoned and sought-after. Still, it was admittedly a triumph that the van der Luydens, at May's request, should have stayed over in order to be present at her farewell dinner for the Countess Olenska.

The two mothers-in-law sat in May's drawing room on the afternoon of the great day, Mrs. Archer writing out the *menus* on Tiffany's thickest gilt-edged bristol,[3] while Mrs. Welland superintended the placing of the palms and standard lamps.

Archer, arriving late from his office, found them still there. Mrs. Archer had turned her attention to the name-cards for the table, and Mrs. Welland was considering the effect of bringing forward the large gilt sofa, so that another "corner" might be created between the piano and the window.

May, they told him, was in the dining room inspecting the mound of Jacqueminot roses and maidenhair in the center of the long table, and the placing of the Maillard bonbons in openwork silver baskets between the candelabra.[4] On the piano stood a large basket of orchids which Mr. van der Luyden had had sent from Skuytercliff. Everything was, in short, as it should be on the approach of so considerable an event.

Mrs. Archer ran thoughtfully over the list, checking off each name with her sharp gold pen.

"Henry van der Luyden—Louisa—the Lovell Mingotts—the Reggie Chiverses—Lawrence Lefferts and Gertrude—(yes, I suppose May was right to have them)—the Selfridge Merrys, Sillerton Jackson, Van Newland and his wife. (How time passes! It seems only yesterday that he was your best man, Newland)—and Countess Olenska—yes, I think that's all. . . ."

1. A florist shop owned by David Henderson, located at 112 W. 15th Street.
2. Roman punch: see pp. 328–29. French, low neckline of a dress.
3. Tiffany's: Founded by Charles Tiffany in 1837, this New York stationery and jewelry store was located on the west side of Union Square at 15th Street in the 1870s; gilt-edged bristol: Cardboard with a smooth surface for writing (also known as bristol board), decorated with gold trim.
4. maidenhair: A delicate type of fern with very fine fronds; Maillard bonbons: Confections produced by the Maillard reaction, or nonenzymatic browning, a method of producing a brown color and roasted flavor through the chemical reaction caused by heating sugars.

Mrs. Welland surveyed her son-in-law affectionately. "No one can say, Newland, that you and May are not giving Ellen a handsome send-off."

"Ah, well," said Mrs. Archer, "I understand May's wanting her cousin to tell people abroad that we're not quite barbarians."

"I'm sure Ellen will appreciate it. She was to arrive this morning, I believe. It will make a most charming last impression. The evening before sailing is usually so dreary," Mrs. Welland cheerfully continued.

Archer turned toward the door, and his mother-in-law called to him: "Do go in and have a peep at the table. And don't let May tire herself too much." But he affected not to hear, and sprang up the stairs to his library. The room looked at him like an alien countenance composed into a polite grimace; and he perceived that it had been ruthlessly "tidied," and prepared, by a judicious distribution of ashtrays and cedarwood boxes, for the gentlemen to smoke in.

"Ah, well," he thought, "it's not for long—" and he went on to his dressing room.

Ten days had passed since Madame Olenska's departure from New York. During those ten days Archer had had no sign from her but that conveyed by the return of a key wrapped in tissue paper, and sent to his office in a sealed envelope addressed in her hand. This retort to his last appeal might have been interpreted as a classic move in a familiar game; but the young man chose to give it a different meaning. She was still fighting against her fate; but she was going to Europe, and she was not returning to her husband. Nothing, therefore, was to prevent his following her; and once he had taken the irrevocable step, and had proved to her that it was irrevocable, he believed she would not send him away.

This confidence in the future had steadied him to play his part in the present. It had kept him from writing to her, or betraying, by any sign or act, his misery and mortification. It seemed to him that in the deadly silent game between them the trumps were still in his hands; and he waited.

There had been, nevertheless, moments sufficiently difficult to pass; as when Mr. Letterblair, the day after Madame Olenska's departure, had sent for him to go over the details of the trust which Mrs. Manson Mingott wished to create for her granddaughter. For a couple of hours Archer had examined the terms of the deed with his senior, all the while obscurely feeling that if he had been consulted it was for some reason other than the obvious one of his cousinship; and that the close of the conference would reveal it.

"Well, the lady can't deny that it's a handsome arrangement," Mr. Letterblair had summed up, after mumbling over a summary of the settlement. "In fact I'm bound to say she's been treated pretty handsomely all round."

"All round?" Archer echoed with a touch of derision. "Do you refer to her husband's proposal to give her back her own money?"

Mr. Letterblair's bushy eyebrows went up a fraction of an inch. "My dear sir, the law's the law; and your wife's cousin was married under the French law.[5] It's to be presumed she knew what that meant."

"Even if she did, what happened subsequently—." But Archer paused. Mr. Letterblair had laid his pen-handle against his big corrugated nose, and was looking down it with the expression assumed by virtuous elderly gentlemen when they wish their youngers to understand that virtue is not synonymous with ignorance.

"My dear sir, I've no wish to extenuate the Count's transgressions; but—but on the other side . . . I wouldn't put my hand in the fire . . . well, that there hadn't been tit for tat . . . with the young champion. . . ." Mr. Letterblair unlocked a drawer and pushed a folded paper toward Archer. "This report, the result of discreet enquiries. . . ." And then, as Archer made no effort to glance at the paper or to repudiate the suggestion, the lawyer somewhat flatly continued: "I don't say it's conclusive, you observe; far from it. But straws show . . . and on the whole it's eminently satisfactory for all parties that this dignified solution has been reached."

"Oh, eminently," Archer assented, pushing back the paper.

A day or two later, on responding to a summons from Mrs. Manson Mingott, his soul had been more deeply tried.

He had found the old lady depressed and querulous.

"You know she's deserted me?" she began at once; and without waiting for his reply: "Oh, don't ask me why! She gave so many reasons that I've forgotten them all. My private belief is that she couldn't face the boredom. At any rate that's what Augusta and my daughters-in-law think. And I don't know that I altogether blame her. Olenski's a finished scoundrel; but life with him must have been a good deal gayer than it is in Fifth Avenue. Not that the family would admit that: they think Fifth Avenue is Heaven with the rue de la Paix thrown in. And poor Ellen, of course, has no idea of going back to her husband. She held out as firmly as ever against that. So she's to settle down in Paris with that fool Medora. . . . Well, Paris is Paris; and you can keep a carriage there on next to nothing. But she was as gay as a bird, and I shall miss her." Two tears, the parched tears of the old, rolled down her puffy cheeks and vanished in the abysses of her bosom.

"All I ask is," she concluded, "that they shouldn't bother me any more. I must really be allowed to digest my gruel. . . ." And she twinkled a little wistfully at Archer.

It was that evening, on his return home, that May announced her intention of giving a farewell dinner to her cousin. Madame Olenska's name had not been pronounced between them since the night of her flight to Washington; and Archer looked at his wife with surprise.

"A dinner—why?" he interrogated.

---

5. Divorce was outlawed in France from 1816 to 1886 and replaced by legal separation for men whose wives were convicted of adultery. Such a conviction carried a mandatory sentence in prison of from three months to two years. While men could not commit adultery under French law, men could be punished for having illicit conjugal relations within the confines of the family home by being forced to pay a fine and by giving their wives the right to ask for a legal separation (see pp. 374–77 for a contemporary article on divorce in New York).

Her color rose. "But you like Ellen—I thought you'd be pleased."

"It's awfully nice—your putting it in that way. But I really don't see—"

"I mean to do it, Newland," she said, quietly rising and going to her desk. "Here are the invitations all written. Mother helped me—she agrees that we ought to." She paused, embarrassed and yet smiling, and Archer suddenly saw before him the embodied image of the Family.

"Oh, all right," he said, staring with unseeing eyes at the list of guests that she had put in his hand.

When he entered the drawing room before dinner May was stooping over the fire and trying to coax the logs to burn in their unaccustomed setting of immaculate tiles.

The tall lamps were all lit, and Mr. van der Luyden's orchids had been conspicuously disposed in various receptacles of modern porcelain and knobby silver. Mrs. Newland Archer's drawing room was generally thought a great success. A gilt bamboo *jardinière*, in which the primulas and cinerarias were punctually renewed, blocked the access to the bay window (where the old-fashioned would have preferred a bronze reduction of the Venus of Milo);[6] the sofas and armchairs of pale brocade were cleverly grouped about little plush tables densely covered with silver toys, porcelain animals and efflorescent photograph frames; and tall rosy-shaded lamps shot up like tropical flowers among the palms.

"I don't think Ellen has ever seen this room lighted up," said May, rising flushed from her struggle, and sending about her a glance of pardonable pride. The brass tongs which she had propped against the side of the chimney fell with a crash that drowned her husband's answer; and before he could restore them Mr. and Mrs. van der Luyden were announced.

The other guests quickly followed, for it was known that the van der Luydens liked to dine punctually. The room was nearly full, and Archer was engaged in showing to Mrs. Selfridge Merry a small highly-varnished Verbeckhoven[7] "Study of Sheep," which Mr. Welland had given May for Christmas, when he found Madame Olenska at his side.

She was excessively pale, and her pallor made her dark hair seem denser and heavier than ever. Perhaps that, or the fact that she had wound several rows of amber beads about her neck, reminded him suddenly of the little Ellen Mingott he had danced with at children's parties, when Medora Manson had first brought her to New York.

The amber beads were trying to her complexion, or her dress was perhaps unbecoming: her face looked lusterless and almost ugly, and he had never loved it as he did at that minute. Their hands met, and

6. *jardinière*: French, "window box," "planter"; primulas and cinerarias: herbs with flowers of various colors; Venus of Milo: A famous marble statue of Venus found on the island of Melos in 1820 and later displayed prominently in Paris at the Louvre.
7. Dutch painter (1798–1881).

he thought he heard her say: "Yes, we're sailing tomorrow in the *Russia*—";[8] then there was an unmeaning noise of opening doors, and after an interval May's voice: "Newland! Dinner's been announced. Won't you please take Ellen in?"

Madame Olenska put her hand on his arm, and he noticed that the hand was ungloved, and remembered how he had kept his eyes fixed on it the evening that he had sat with her in the little Twenty-third Street drawing room. All the beauty that had forsaken her face seemed to have taken refuge in the long pale fingers and faintly dimpled knuckles on his sleeve, and he said to himself: "If it were only to see her hand again I should have to follow her—."

It was only at an entertainment ostensibly offered to a "foreign visitor" that Mrs. van der Luyden could suffer the diminution of being placed on her host's left. The fact of Madame Olenska's "foreignness"[9] could hardly have been more adroitly emphasized than by this farewell tribute; and Mrs. van der Luyden accepted her displacement with an affability which left no doubt as to her approval. There were certain things that had to be done, and if done at all, done handsomely and thoroughly; and one of these, in the old New York code, was the tribal rally around a kinswoman about to be eliminated from the tribe. There was nothing on earth that the Wellands and Mingotts would not have done to proclaim their unalterable affection for the Countess Olenska now that her passage for Europe was engaged; and Archer, at the head of his table, sat marveling at the silent untiring activity with which her popularity had been retrieved, grievances against her silenced, her past countenanced, and her present irradiated by the family approval. Mrs. van der Luyden shone on her with the dim benevolence which was her nearest approach to cordiality, and Mr. van der Luyden, from his seat at May's right, cast down the table glances plainly intended to justify all the carnations he had sent from Skuytercliff.

Archer, who seemed to be assisting at the scene in a state of odd imponderability, as if he floated somewhere between chandelier and ceiling, wondered at nothing so much as his own share in the proceedings. As his glance traveled from one placid well-fed face to another he saw all the harmless-looking people engaged upon May's canvasbacks as a band of dumb conspirators, and himself and the pale woman on his right as the center of their conspiracy. And then it came over him, in a vast flash made up of many broken gleams, that to all of them he and Madame Olenska were lovers, lovers in the extreme sense peculiar to "foreign" vocabularies. He guessed himself to have been, for months, the center of countless silently observing eyes and

---

8. First propeller-driven ship to win the blue riband for fastest Atlantic crossing, making the trip in 1867 between New York and Queenstown, Ireland, in just over eight days. Renamed the *Waesland* in 1880, the former *Russia* sank in 1903, close to the time in which the concluding segment of the novel is set.

9. Rules for formal seating at dinner parties are determined by strict principles of hierarchy established by court etiquette. A foreigner (because of the history of diplomacy) is generally understood to outrank all others. Otherwise Mrs. van der Luyden, who is understood to be the pinnacle of the aristocracy of Old New York, would have been placed at her host's right. In recognition of the van der Luydens' social stature, Mr. van der Luyden is seated at May's right.

patiently listening ears, he understood that, by means as yet unknown to him, the separation between himself and the partner of his guilt had been achieved, and that now the whole tribe had rallied about his wife on the tacit assumption that nobody knew anything, or had ever imagined anything, and that the occasion of the entertainment was simply May Archer's natural desire to take an affectionate leave of her friend and cousin.

It was the old New York way of taking life "without effusion of blood": the way of people who dreaded scandal more than disease, who placed decency above courage, and who considered that nothing was more ill-bred than "scenes," except the behavior of those who gave rise to them.

As these thoughts succeeded each other in his mind Archer felt like a prisoner in the center of an armed camp. He looked about the table, and guessed at the inexorableness of his captors from the tone in which, over the asparagus from Florida, they were dealing with Beaufort and his wife. "It's to show me," he thought, "what would happen to *me*—" and a deathly sense of the superiority of implication and analogy over direct action, and of silence over rash words, closed in on him like the doors of the family vault.

He laughed, and met Mrs. van der Luyden's startled eyes.

"You think it laughable?" she said with a pinched smile. "Of course poor Regina's idea of remaining in New York has its ridiculous side, I suppose"; and Archer muttered: "Of course."

At this point, he became conscious that Madame Olenska's other neighbor had been engaged for some time with the lady on his right. At the same moment he saw that May, serenely enthroned between Mr. van der Luyden and Mr. Selfridge Merry, had cast a quick glance down the table. It was evident that the host and the lady on his right could not sit through the whole meal in silence. He turned to Madame Olenska, and her pale smile met him. "Oh, do let's see it through," it seemed to say.

"Did you find the journey tiring?" he asked in a voice that surprised him by its naturalness; and she answered that, on the contrary, she had seldom traveled with fewer discomforts.

"Except, you know, the dreadful heat in the train," she added; and he remarked that she would not suffer from that particular hardship in the country she was going to.

"I never," he declared with intensity, "was more nearly frozen than once, in April, in the train between Calais[1] and Paris."

She said she did not wonder, but remarked that, after all, one could always carry an extra rug, and that every form of travel had its hardships; to which he abruptly returned that he thought them all of no account compared with the blessedness of getting away. She changed color, and he added, his voice suddenly rising in pitch: "I mean to do a lot of traveling myself before long." A tremor crossed her face, and leaning over to Reggie Chivers, he cried out: "I say, Reggie, what do you say to a trip

1. The French port of entry for travelers crossing the Channel by ferry from Britain.

round the world: now, next month, I mean? I'm game if you are—" at which Mrs. Reggie piped up that she could not think of letting Reggie go till after the Martha Washington Ball she was getting up for the Blind Asylum in Easter week; and her husband placidly observed that by that time he would have to be practicing for the International Polo match.[2]

But Mr. Selfridge Merry had caught the phrase "round the world," and having once circled the globe in his steamyacht, he seized the opportunity to send down the table several striking items concerning the shallowness of the Mediterranean ports. Though, after all, he added, it didn't matter; for when you'd seen Athens and Smyrna and Constantinople, what else was there? And Mrs. Merry said she could never be too grateful to Dr. Bencomb for having made them promise not to go to Naples on account of the fever.

"But you must have three weeks to do India properly," her husband conceded, anxious to have it understood that he was no frivolous globe-trotter.

And at this point the ladies went up to the drawing room.

In the library, in spite of weightier presences, Lawrence Lefferts predominated.

The talk, as usual, had veered around to the Beauforts, and even Mr. van der Luyden and Mr. Selfridge Merry, installed in the honorary armchairs tacitly reserved for them, paused to listen to the younger man's philippic.

Never had Lefferts so abounded in the sentiments that adorn Christian manhood and exalt the sanctity of the home. Indignation lent him a scathing eloquence, and it was clear that if others had followed his example, and acted as he talked, society would never have been weak enough to receive a foreign upstart like Beaufort—no, sir, not even if he'd married a van der Luyden or a Lanning instead of a Dallas. And what chance would there have been, Lefferts wrathfully questioned, of his marrying into such a family as the Dallases, if he had not already wormed his way into certain houses, as people like Mrs. Lemuel Struthers had managed to worm theirs in his wake? If society chose to open its doors to vulgar women the harm was not great, though the gain was doubtful; but once it got in the way of tolerating men of obscure origin and tainted wealth the end was total disintegration—and at no distant date.

"If things go on at this pace," Lefferts thundered, looking like a young prophet dressed by Poole,[3] and who had not yet been stoned,

2. An ancient game which originated in what is now India, polo is played by teams of mounted men, swinging wooden mallets at a contested ball as each group aims for an opposing goal. Emerging as a sport in Calcutta and Punjab in the early 1860s, this equestrian sport, first played in England in July of 1871, began to be a defining pastime for the men of the American elite near the close of the 1870s. Polo in the late-nineteenth century was limited in its international appeal to the wealthiest men in Britain, her colonies, and former colonies.

3. After inheriting the family business on Old Burlington Street in 1846, Henry Poole became the tailor for the courts of Emperor Napoleon III and Queen Victoria. Henry Poole & Co. made a smoking jacket for the Prince of Wales in 1860 and a similar short evening jacket for James Potter of Tuxedo Park, New York in 1886. Long before this shop with its showroom on Saville Row was credited with inventing what Americans call the tuxedo, Poole's set the standard for custom-made clothing for men of the aristocracy and the elite.

"we shall see our children fighting for invitations to swindlers' houses, and marrying Beaufort's bastards."

"Oh, I say—draw it mild!" Reggie Chivers and young Newland protested, while Mr. Selfridge Merry looked genuinely alarmed, and an expression of pain and disgust settled on Mr. van der Luyden's sensitive face.

"Has he got any?" cried Mr. Sillerton Jackson, pricking up his ears; and while Lefferts tried to turn the question with a laugh, the old gentleman twittered into Archer's ear: "Queer, those fellows who are always wanting to set things right. The people who have the worst cooks are always telling you they're poisoned when they dine out. But I hear there are pressing reasons for our friend Lawrence's diatribe:—typewriter[4] this time, I understand. . . ."

The talk swept past Archer like some senseless river running and running because it did not know enough to stop. He saw, on the faces about him, expressions of interest, amusement and even mirth. He listened to the younger men's laughter, and to the praise of the Archer Madeira, which Mr. van der Luyden and Mr. Merry were thoughtfully celebrating. Through it all he was dimly aware of a general attitude of friendliness toward himself, as if the guard of the prisoner he felt himself to be were trying to soften his captivity; and the perception increased his passionate determination to be free.

In the drawing room, where they presently joined the ladies, he met May's triumphant eyes, and read in them the conviction that everything had "gone off" beautifully. She rose from Madame Olenska's side, and immediately Mrs. van der Luyden beckoned the latter to a seat on the gilt sofa where she throned. Mrs. Selfridge Merry bore across the room to join them, and it became clear to Archer that here also a conspiracy of rehabilitation and obliteration was going on. The silent organization which held his little world together was determined to put itself on record as never for a moment having questioned the propriety of Madame Olenska's conduct, or the completeness of Archer's domestic felicity. All these amiable and inexorable persons were resolutely engaged in pretending to each other that they had never heard of, suspected, or even conceived possible, the least hint to the contrary; and from this tissue of elaborate mutual dissimulation Archer once more disengaged the fact that New York believed him to be Madame Olenska's lover. He caught the glitter of victory in his wife's eyes, and for the first time understood that she shared the belief. The discovery roused a laughter of inner devils that reverberated through all his efforts to discuss the Martha Washington Ball with Mrs. Reggie Chivers and little Mrs. Newland; and so the evening swept on, running and running like a senseless river that did not know how to stop.

4. The typewriter was invented by Christopher Latham Scholes in 1867, a practical model was devised in 1868, and the first machine was marketed in 1874. The word "typewriter" here refers to the person who uses it—a (female) typist. The presence of this woman in the workplace suggests the beginning of a radical shift in the sexual composition of the clerical workforce.

At length he saw that Madame Olenska had risen and was saying good-bye. He understood that in a moment she would be gone, and tried to remember what he had said to her at dinner; but he could not recall a single word they had exchanged.

She went up to May, the rest of the company making a circle about her as she advanced. The two young women clasped hands; then May bent forward and kissed her cousin.

"Certainly our hostess is much the handsomer of the two," Archer heard Reggie Chivers say in an undertone to young Mrs. Newland; and he remembered Beaufort's coarse sneer at May's ineffectual beauty.

A moment later he was in the hall, putting Madame Olenska's cloak about her shoulders.

Through all his confusion of mind he had held fast to the resolve to say nothing that might startle or disturb her. Convinced that no power could now turn him from his purpose he had found strength to let events shape themselves as they would. But as he followed Madame Olenska into the hall he thought with a sudden hunger of being for a moment alone with her at the door of her carriage.

"Is your carriage here?" he asked; and at that moment Mrs. van der Luyden, who was being majestically inserted into her sables, said gently: "We are driving dear Ellen home."

Archer's heart gave a jerk, and Madame Olenska, clasping her cloak and fan with one hand, held out the other to him. "Good-bye," she said.

"Good-bye—but I shall see you soon in Paris," he answered aloud—it seemed to him that he had shouted it.

"Oh," she murmured, "if you and May could come—!"

Mr. van der Luyden advanced to give her his arm, and Archer turned to Mrs. van der Luyden. For a moment, in the billowy darkness inside the big landau, he caught the dim oval of a face, eyes shining steadily—and she was gone.

As he went up the steps he crossed Lawrence Lefferts coming down with his wife. Lefferts caught his host by the sleeve, drawing back to let Gertrude pass.

"I say, old chap: do you mind just letting it be understood that I'm dining with you at the club tomorrow night? Thanks so much, you old brick! Good-night."

"It *did* go off beautifully, didn't it?" May questioned from the threshold of the library.

Archer roused himself with a start. As soon as the last carriage had driven away, he had come up to the library and shut himself in, with the hope that his wife, who still lingered below, would go straight to her room. But there she stood, pale and drawn, yet radiating the factitious energy of one who has passed beyond fatigue.

"May I come and talk it over?" she asked.

"Of course, if you like. But you must be awfully sleepy—"

"No, I'm not sleepy. I should like to sit with you a little."

"Very well," he said, pushing her chair near the fire.

She sat down and he resumed his seat; but neither spoke for a long time. At length Archer began abruptly: "Since you're not tired, and want to talk, there's something I must tell you. I tried to the other night—."

She looked at him quickly. "Yes, dear. Something about yourself?"

"About myself. You say you're not tired: well, I am. Horribly tired. . . ."

In an instant she was all tender anxiety. "Oh, I've seen it coming on, Newland! You've been so wickedly overworked—"

"Perhaps it's that. Anyhow, I want to make a break—"

"A break? To give up the law?"

"To go away, at any rate—at once. On a long trip, ever so far off— away from everything—"

He paused, conscious that he had failed in his attempt to speak with the indifference of a man who longs for a change, and is yet too weary to welcome it. Do what he would, the chord of eagerness vibrated. "Away from everything—" he repeated.

"Ever so far? Where, for instance?" she asked.

"Oh, I don't know. India—or Japan."

She stood up, and as he sat with bent head, his chin propped on his hands, he felt her warmly and fragrantly hovering over him.

"As far as that? But I'm afraid you can't, dear . . ." she said in an unsteady voice. "Not unless you'll take me with you." And then, as he was silent, she went on, in tones so clear and evenly-pitched that each separate syllable tapped like a little hammer on his brain: "That is, if the doctors will let me go . . . but I'm afraid they won't. For you see, Newland, I've been sure since this morning of something I've been so longing and hoping for—"

He looked up at her with a sick stare, and she sank down, all dew and roses, and hid her face against his knee.

"Oh, my dear," he said, holding her to him while his cold hand stroked her hair.

There was a long pause, which the inner devils filled with strident laughter; then May freed herself from his arms and stood up.

"You didn't guess—?"

"Yes—I; no. That is, of course I hoped—"

They looked at each other for an instant and again fell silent; then, turning his eyes from hers, he asked abruptly: "Have you told anyone else?"

"Only Mamma and your mother." She paused, and then added hurriedly, the blood flushing up to her forehead: "That is—and Ellen. You know I told you we'd had a long talk one afternoon—and how dear she was to me."

"Ah—" said Archer, his heart stopping.

He felt that his wife was watching him intently. "Did you *mind* my telling her first, Newland?"

"Mind? Why should I?" He made a last effort to collect himself. "But that was a fortnight ago, wasn't it? I thought you said you weren't sure till today."

Her color burned deeper, but she held his gaze. "No; I wasn't sure then—but I told her I was. And you see I was right!" she exclaimed, her blue eyes wet with victory.

# XXXIV

Newland Archer sat at the writing-table in his library in East Thirty-ninth Street.

He had just got back from a big official reception for the inauguration of the new galleries at the Metropolitan Museum, and the spectacle of those great spaces crowded with the spoils of the ages, where the throng of fashion circulated through a series of scientifically catalogued treasures, had suddenly pressed on a rusted spring of memory.

"Why, this used to be one of the old Cesnola rooms," he heard someone say; and instantly everything about him vanished, and he was sitting alone on a hard leather divan against a radiator, while a slight figure in a long sealskin cloak moved away down the meagerly-fitted vistas of the old Museum.

The vision had roused a host of other associations, and he sat looking with new eyes at the library which, for over thirty years, had been the scene of his solitary musings and of all the family confabulations.

It was the room in which most of the real things of his life had happened. There his wife, nearly twenty-six years ago, had broken to him, with a blushing circumlocution that would have caused the young women of the new generation to smile, the news that she was to have a child; and there their eldest boy, Dallas, too delicate to be taken to church in midwinter, had been christened by their old friend the Bishop of New York, the ample magnificent irreplaceable Bishop, so long the pride and ornament of his diocese. There Dallas had first staggered across the floor shouting "Dad," while May and the nurse laughed behind the door; there their second child, Mary (who was so like her mother), had announced her engagement to the dullest and most reliable of Reggie Chivers's many sons; and there Archer had kissed her through her wedding veil before they went down to the motor which was to carry them to Grace Church—for in a world where all else had reeled on its foundations the "Grace Church wedding" remained an unchanged institution.

It was in the library that he and May had always discussed the future of the children: the studies of Dallas and his young brother Bill, Mary's incurable indifference to "accomplishments," and passion for sport and philanthropy, and the vague leanings toward "art" which had finally landed the restless and curious Dallas in the office of a rising New York architect.

The young men nowadays were emancipating themselves from the law and business and taking up all sorts of new things. If they were not absorbed in state politics or municipal reform, the chances were that they were going in for Central American archeology, for architecture or landscape-engineering; taking a keen and learned interest in the pre-Revolutionary buildings of their own country, studying and adapting Georgian types, and protesting at the meaningless use of the word "Colonial." Nobody nowadays had "Colonial" houses except the millionaire grocers of the suburbs.

But above all—sometimes Archer put it above all—it was in that library that the Governor of New York, coming down from Albany one evening to dine and spend the night, had turned to his host, and said, banging his clenched fist on the table and gnashing his eye-glasses: "Hang the professional politician! You're the kind of man the country wants, Archer. If the stable's ever to be cleaned out,[1] men like you have got to lend a hand in the cleaning."

"Men like you—" how Archer had glowed at the phrase! How eagerly he had risen up at the call! It was an echo of Ned Winsett's old appeal to roll his sleeves up and get down into the muck; but spoken by a man who set the example of the gesture, and whose summons to follow him was irresistible.

Archer, as he looked back, was not sure that men like himself *were* what his country needed, at least in the active service to which Theodore Roosevelt[2] had pointed; in fact, there was reason to think it did not, for after a year in the State Assembly he had not been reelected, and had dropped back thankfully into obscure if useful municipal work, and from that again to the writing of occasional articles in one of the reforming weeklies that were trying to shake the country out of its apathy. It was little enough to look back on; but when he remembered to what the young men of his generation and his set had looked forward—the narrow groove of money-making, sport and society to which their vision had been limited—even his small contribution to the new state of things seemed to count, as each brick counts in a well-built wall. He had done little in public life; he would always be by nature a contemplative and a dilettante; but he had had high things to contemplate, great things to delight in; and one great man's friendship to be his strength and pride.

He had been, in short, what people were beginning to call "a good citizen." In New York, for many years past, every new movement, philanthropic, municipal or artistic, had taken account of his opinion and wanted his name. People said: "Ask Archer" when there was a question of starting the first school for crippled children, reorganizing the Museum of Art, founding the Grolier Club, inaugurating the new Library,[3] or getting up a new society of chamber music. His days were full, and they were filled decently. He supposed it was all a man ought to ask.

1. An allusion to one of the seemingly impossible tasks assigned to Hercules, the cleaning out of the Augean stables.
2. Roosevelt (1858–1919) was governor of New York (1898–1900), William McKinley's vice president (1900–1901), and president of the United States (1901–1909); he split off from the Republican Party to found the Progressive Party in 1912.
3. Grolier Club: Founded in 1884 and housed at 47 East 60th Street, the Grolier Club, named for the sixteenth-century French bibliophile Jean Grolier de Sevier (1479–1565), promoted bibliophily and the bookmaking craft. new Library: the New York Public Library, founded in 1895 by a merger of three earlier libraries—the Astor Library (founded in 1848), the Lenox Library (founded in 1875), and the Tilden Trust (established in 1886).

Something he knew he had missed: the flower of life. But he thought of it now as a thing so unattainable and improbable that to have repined would have been like despairing because one had not drawn the first prize in a lottery. There were a hundred million tickets in *his* lottery, and there was only one prize; the chances had been too decidedly against him. When he thought of Ellen Olenska it was abstractly, serenely, as one might think of some imaginary beloved in a book or a picture: she had become the composite vision of all that he had missed. That vision, faint and tenuous as it was, had kept him from thinking of other women. He had been what was called a faithful husband; and when May had suddenly died—carried off by the infectious pneumonia through which she had nursed their youngest child—he had honestly mourned her. Their long years together had shown him that it did not so much matter if marriage was a dull duty, as long as it kept the dignity of a duty: lapsing from that, it became a mere battle of ugly appetites. Looking about him, he honored his own past, and mourned for it. After all, there was good in the old ways.

His eyes, making the round of the room—done over by Dallas with English mezzotints,[4] Chippendale cabinets, bits of chosen blue-and-white and pleasantly shaded electric lamps—came back to the old Eastlake writing-table that he had never been willing to banish, and to his first photograph of May, which still kept its place beside his inkstand.

There she was, tall, round-bosomed and willowy, in her starched muslin and flapping Leghorn, as he had seen her under the orange-trees in the Mission garden. And as he had seen her that day, so she had remained; never quite at the same height, yet never far below it: generous, faithful, unwearied; but so lacking in imagination, so incapable of growth, that the world of her youth had fallen into pieces and rebuilt itself without her ever being conscious of the change. This hard bright blindness had kept her immediate horizon apparently unaltered. Her incapacity to recognize change made her children conceal their views from her as Archer concealed his; there had been, from the first, a joint pretense of sameness, a kind of innocent family hypocrisy, in which father and children had unconsciously collaborated. And she had died thinking the world a good place, full of loving and harmonious households like her own, and resigned to leave it because she was convinced that, whatever happened, Newland would continue to inculcate in Dallas the same principles and prejudices which had shaped his parents' lives, and that Dallas in turn (when Newland followed her) would transmit the sacred trust to little Bill. And of Mary she was sure as of her own self. So, having snatched little Bill from the grave, and given her life in the effort, she went contentedly to her place in the Archer vault in St. Mark's,[5] where Mrs. Archer already lay

---

4. Engravings printed from figures scratched on copperplates, achieving the visual effect of drawings done in India ink.
5. The second-oldest church in Manhattan. Built in 1795, the edifice stands at the corner of Tenth Street and Second Avenue on the site of Peter Stuyvesant's family chapel where the descendants of leading Dutch families were interred.

safe from the terrifying "trend" which her daughter-in-law had never even become aware of.

Opposite May's portrait stood one of her daughter. Mary Chivers was as tall and fair as her mother, but large-waisted, flat-chested and slightly slouching, as the altered fashion required. Mary Chivers's mighty feats of athleticism could not have been performed with the twenty-inch waist that May Archer's azure sash so easily spanned. And the difference seemed symbolic; the mother's life had been as closely girt as her figure. Mary, who was no less conventional, and no more intelligent, yet led a larger life and held more tolerant views. There was good in the new order too.

The telephone clicked, and Archer, turning from the photographs, unhooked the transmitter at his elbow. How far they were from the days when the legs of the brass-buttoned messenger boy had been New York's only means of quick communication!

"Chicago wants you."

Ah—it must be a long-distance from Dallas, who had been sent to Chicago by his firm to talk over the plan of the Lakeside palace[6] they were to build for a young millionaire with ideas. The firm always sent Dallas on such errands.

"Hallo, Dad—Yes: Dallas. I say—how do you feel about sailing on Wednesday? *Mauretania*: Yes, next Wednesday as ever is. Our client wants me to look at some Italian gardens before we settle anything, and has asked me to nip over on the next boat. I've got to be back on the first of June—" the voice broke into a joyful conscious laugh—"so we must look alive. I say, Dad, I want your help: do come."

Dallas seemed to be speaking in the room: the voice was as nearby and natural as if he had been lounging in his favorite armchair by the fire. The fact would not ordinarily have surprised Archer, for long-distance telephoning[7] had become as much a matter of course as electric lighting and five-day Atlantic voyages. But the laugh did startle him; it still seemed wonderful that across all those miles and miles of country—forest, river, mountain, prairie, roaring cities and busy indifferent millions—Dallas's laugh should be able to say: "Of course, whatever happens, I must get back on the first, because Fanny Beaufort and I are to be married on the fifth."

The voice began again: "Think it over? No, sir: not a minute. You've got to say yes now. Why not, I'd like to know? If you can allege a single reason—no; I knew it. Then it's a go, eh? Because I count on you to ring up the Cunard office first thing tomorrow; and you'd better book a return on a boat from Marseilles. I say, Dad; it'll be our last time together, in this kind of way—. Oh, good! I knew you would."

Chicago rang off, and Archer rose and began to pace up and down the room.

It would be their last time together in this kind of way: the boy was

---

6. Like the Cliffs of Newport, the western shore of Lake Michigan along Lakeshore Drive was lined with palatial residences designed and built for their wealthy owners.
7. Pioneered and proven possible in the early 1890s, long-distance calling across the United States was still considered novel in the first decade of the twentieth century.

right. They would have lots of other "times" after Dallas's marriage, his father was sure; for the two were born comrades, and Fanny Beaufort, whatever one might think of her, did not seem likely to interfere with their intimacy. On the contrary, from what he had seen of her, he thought she would be naturally included in it. Still, change was change, and differences were differences, and much as he felt himself drawn toward his future daughter-in-law, it was tempting to seize this last chance of being alone with his boy.

There was no reason why he should not seize it, except the profound one that he had lost the habit of travel. May had disliked to move except for valid reasons, such as taking the children to the sea or in the mountains: she could imagine no other motive for leaving the house in Thirty-ninth Street or their comfortable quarters at the Wellands' in Newport. After Dallas had taken his degree she had thought it her duty to travel for six months; and the whole family had made the old-fashioned tour through England, Switzerland and Italy. Their time being limited (no one knew why) they had omitted France. Archer remembered Dallas's wrath at being asked to contemplate Mont Blanc instead of Rheims and Chartres.[9] But Mary and Bill wanted mountain-climbing, and had already yawned their way in Dallas's wake through the English cathedrals; and May, always fair to her children, had insisted on holding the balance evenly between their athletic and artistic proclivities. She had indeed proposed that her husband should go to Paris for a fortnight, and join them on the Italian lakes after they had "done" Switzerland; but Archer had declined. "We'll stick together," he said; and May's face had brightened at his setting such a good example to Dallas.

Since her death, nearly two years before, there had been no reason for his continuing in the same routine. His children had urged him to travel: Mary Chivers had felt sure it would do him good to go abroad and "see the galleries." The very mysteriousness of such a cure made her the more confident of its efficacy. But Archer had found himself held fast by habit, by memories, by a sudden startled shrinking from new things.

Now, as he reviewed his past, he saw into what a deep rut he had sunk. The worst of doing one's duty was that it apparently unfitted one for doing anything else. At least that was the view that the men of his generation had taken. The trenchant divisions between right and wrong, honest and dishonest, respectable and the reverse, had left so little scope for the unforeseen. There are moments when a man's imagination, so easily subdued to what it lives in, suddenly rises above its daily level, and surveys the long windings of destiny. Archer hung there and wondered. . . .

What was left of the little world he had grown up in, and whose

---

9. Mont Blanc: The highest peak in the Alps, associated with the sublime in nature and the subject of noted poems and meditations; Rheims and Chartres: Famous medieval French cathedrals. The interior and stained glass windows of Rheims were destroyed during World War I.

standards had bent and bound him? He remembered a sneering prophecy of poor Lawrence Lefferts's, uttered years ago in that very room: "If things go on at this rate, our children will be marrying Beaufort's bastards."

It was just what Archer's eldest son, the pride of his life, was doing; and nobody wondered or reproved. Even the boy's Aunt Janey, who still looked so exactly as she used to in her elderly youth, had taken her mother's emeralds and seed-pearls out of their pink cotton-wool, and carried them with her own twitching hands to the future bride; and Fanny Beaufort, instead of looking disappointed at not receiving a "set" from a Paris jeweller, had exclaimed at their old-fashioned beauty, and declared that when she wore them she should feel like an Isabey miniature.

Fanny Beaufort, who had appeared in New York at eighteen, after the death of her parents, had won its heart much as Madame Olenska had won it thirty years earlier; only instead of being distrustful and afraid of her, society took her joyfully for granted. She was pretty, amusing and accomplished: what more did anyone want? Nobody was narrow-minded enough to rake up against her the half-forgotten facts of her father's past and her own origin. Only the older people remembered so obscure an incident in the business life of New York as Beaufort's failure, or the fact that after his wife's death he had been quietly married to the notorious Fanny Ring, and had left the country with his new wife, and a little girl who inherited her beauty. He was subsequently heard of in Constantinople, then in Russia; and a dozen years later American travelers were handsomely entertained by him in Buenos Aires, where he represented a large insurance agency. He and his wife died there in the odor of prosperity; and one day their orphaned daughter had appeared in New York in charge of May Archer's sister-in-law, Mrs. Jack Welland, whose husband had been appointed the girl's guardian. The fact threw her into almost cousinly relationship with Newland Archer's children, and nobody was surprised when Dallas's engagement was announced.

Nothing could more clearly give the measure of the distance that the world had traveled. People nowadays were too busy—busy with reforms and "movements," with fads and fetishes and frivolities[1]—to

1. reforms and "movements": Sometimes called the Progressive Era, this age has gone beyond innocence to insist on a measure of public guilt and responsibility for the problems of a flawed society. Late nineteenth- and early twentieth-century movements for reform focused on a variety of issues, including the need for child labor laws, birth control education, the regulation of sanitation (from assuring the purity of drinking water to cleaning up food processing plants), and the extension of the vote to educated white women. fads and fetishes and frivolities: Detailed in the novel through the changes in female atheticism that reconfigured the desired shapes of the female body, the word "fads" (from nineteenth-century American slang) had a much more specific resonance for elite New York at the time of Archer's reverie. The privately printed volume called *Fads and Fancies* (the full title was *Fads and Fancies of Representative Americans at the Beginning of the Twentieth Century, Being a Portrayal of Tastes, Diversions, and Achievements*) consisted of brief biographies of society figures purchased by their subjects for between $1,500 and $9,000. This payment was a form of tasteful blackmail paid to ensure that these individuals would not have their more questionable habits exposed in Colonel Mann's widely circulated New York weekly, *Town Topics* (see p. 329, *n.* 1).

bother much about their neighbors. And of what account was any-body's past, in the huge kaleidoscope where all the social atoms spun around on the same plane?

Newland Archer, looking out of his hotel window at the stately gai-ety of the Paris streets, felt his heart beating with the confusion and eagerness of youth.

It was long since it had thus plunged and reared under his widening waistcoat, leaving him, the next minute, with an empty breast and hot temples. He wondered if it was thus that his son's conducted itself in the presence of Miss Fanny Beaufort—and decided that it was not. "It functions as actively, no doubt, but the rhythm is different," he re-flected, recalling the cool composure with which the young man had announced his engagement, and taken for granted that his family would approve.

"The difference is that these young people take it for granted that they're going to get whatever they want, and that we almost always took it for granted that we shouldn't. Only, I wonder—the thing one's so certain of in advance: can it ever make one's heart beat as wildly?"

It was the day after their arrival in Paris, and the spring sunshine held Archer in his open window, above the wide silvery prospect of the Place Vendôme.[2] One of the things he had stipulated—almost the only one—when he had agreed to come abroad with Dallas, was that, in Paris, he shouldn't be made to go to one of the new-fangled "palaces."

"Oh, all right—of course," Dallas goodnaturedly agreed. "I'll take you to some jolly old-fashioned place—the Bristol say—" leaving his father speechless at hearing that the century-long home of kings and emperors was now spoken of as an old-fashioned inn, where one went for its quaint inconveniences and lingering local color.[3]

Archer had pictured often enough, in the first impatient years, the scene of his return to Paris; then the personal vision had faded, and he had simply tried to see the city as the setting of Madame Olenska's life. Sitting alone at night in his library, after the household had gone to bed, he had evoked the radiant outbreak of spring down the av-enues of horse-chestnuts, the flowers and statues in the public gar-dens, the whiff of lilacs from the flower-carts, the majestic roll of the river under the great bridges, and the life of art and study and pleasure that filled each mighty artery to bursting. Now the spectacle was be-fore him in its glory, and as he looked out on it he felt shy, old-fashioned, inadequate: a mere gray speck of a man compared with the ruthless magnificent fellow he had dreamed of being. . . .

Dallas's hand came down cheerily on his shoulder. "Hullo, father:

2. A famous square with arcades and facades designed by the great French architect, Jules Hardouin Mansart (1645–1708), principal architect of the palace and chapel at Versailles. Known as Pikes' Square during the revolution because aristocrats' heads were displayed there on pikes, Place Vendôme was once known for its column made from the bronze of melted cannons taken by Napoleon. This emblem of imperialism was pulled down by rioters in 1871.

3. This "quaint" inn does not appear to be a reference to the famous hotel of the same name located on the Rue du Faubourg Saint Honoré near the Ritz. This structure became the Bristol in the early 1930s, approximately twelve years after the publication of the novel.

this is something like, isn't it?" They stood for a while looking out in silence, and then the young man continued: "By the way, I've got a message for you: the Countess Olenska expects us both at half-past five."

He said it lightly, carelessly, as he might have imparted any casual item of information, such as the hour at which their train was to leave for Florence the next evening. Archer looked at him, and thought he saw in his gay young eyes a gleam of his great-grandmother Mingott's malice.

"Oh, didn't I tell you?" Dallas pursued. "Fanny made me swear to do three things while I was in Paris: get her the score of the last Debussy songs, go to the Grand-Guignol and see Madame Olenska.[4] You know she was awfully good to Fanny when Mr. Beaufort sent her over from Buenos Aires to the Assomption.[5] Fanny hadn't any friends in Paris, and Madame Olenska used to be kind to her and trot her about on holidays. I believe she was a great friend of the first Mrs. Beaufort's. And she's our cousin, of course. So I rang her up this morning before I went out, and told her you and I were here for two days and wanted to see her."

Archer continued to stare at him. "You told her I was here?"

"Of course—why not?" Dallas's eyebrows went up whimsically. Then, getting no answer, he slipped his arm through his father's with a confidential pressure.

"I say, Father: what was she like?"

Archer felt his color rise under his son's unabashed gaze. "Come, own up: you and she were great pals, weren't you? Wasn't she most awfully lovely?"

"Lovely? I don't know. She was different."

"Ah—there you have it! That's what it always comes to, doesn't it? When she comes, *she's different*—and one doesn't know why. It's exactly what I feel about Fanny."

His father drew back a step, releasing his arm. "About Fanny? But, my dear fellow—I should hope so! Only I don't see—"

"Dash it, Dad, don't be prehistoric. Wasn't she—once—your Fanny?"

Dallas belonged body and soul to the new generation. He was the first-born of Newland and May Archer, yet it had never been possible to inculcate in him even the rudiments of reserve. "What's the use of making mysteries? It only makes people want to nose 'em out," he always objected when enjoined to discretion. But Archer, meeting his eyes, saw the filial light under their banter.

"My Fanny—?"

---

4. Debussy: French composer (1862–1918). Grand-Guignol: A cabaret in the Montmartre district of Paris that specialized in violent short plays, often with plots involving murder, rape, and suicide.

5. French for "Assumption," Catholic doctrine that holds that the Virgin Mary ascended whole into Heaven with body and soul intact; here referring to an actual convent school located on the Rue St. Honoré in Paris and founded by Les Filles de L'Assomption. This order of Augustinian sisters was established at this location in September 1622 by Cardinal de la Rochefoucauld.

"Well, the woman you'd have chucked everything for: only you didn't," continued his surprising son.

"I didn't," echoed Archer with a kind of solemnity.

"No: you date, you see, dear old boy. But Mother said—"

"Your mother?"

"Yes: the day before she died. It was when she sent for me alone—you remember? She said she knew we were safe with you, and always would be, because once, when she asked you to, you'd given up the thing you most wanted."

Archer received this strange communication in silence. His eyes remained unseeingly fixed on the thronged sunlit square below the window. At length he said in a low voice: "She never asked me."

"No. I forgot. You never did ask each other anything, did you? And you never told each other anything. You just sat and watched each other, and guessed at what was going on underneath. A deaf-and-dumb asylum, in fact. Well, I back your generation for knowing more about each other's private thoughts than we ever have time to find out about our own.—I say, Dad," Dallas broke off, "you're not angry with me? If you are, let's make it up and go and lunch at Henri's. I've got to rush out to Versailles[6] afterward."

Archer did not accompany his son to Versailles. He preferred to spend the afternoon in solitary roamings through Paris. He had to deal all at once with the packed regrets and stifled memories of an inarticulate lifetime.

After a little while he did not regret Dallas's indiscretion. It seemed to take an iron band from his heart to know that, after all, someone had guessed and pitied. . . . And that it should have been his wife moved him indescribably. Dallas, for all his affectionate insight, would not have understood that. To the boy, no doubt, the episode was only a pathetic instance of vain frustration, of wasted forces. But was it really no more? For a long time Archer sat on a bench in the Champs Elysées and wondered, while the stream of life rolled by. . . .

A few streets away, a few hours away, Ellen Olenska waited. She had never gone back to her husband, and when he had died, some years before, she had made no change in her way of living. There was nothing now to keep her and Archer apart—and that afternoon he was to see her.

He got up and walked across the Place de la Concorde and the Tuileries gardens to the Louvre.[7] She had once told him that she often went there, and he had a fancy to spend the intervening time in a place where he could think of her as perhaps having lately been. For

6. The opulent palace of Louis XIV, which dates from 1661; completed in 1711, the palace once housed over 1,000 noblemen, and the grounds cover 250 acres.

7. Place de la Concorde: A major circle in Paris where a number of streets and avenues come together; known as the location of the guillotine that beheaded Marie Antoinette and others during the revolution, it was renamed "Concorde" to overcome the sense of raging discord associated with this site. Louvre: The foremost art museum in France; the structure was built in the late twelfth century as a royal fortress, was greatly expanded through the years, and was attached to the Tuileries in 1606; the Louvre was opened to the public in 1793.

an hour or more he wandered from gallery to gallery through the dazzle of afternoon light, and one by one the pictures burst on him in their half-forgotten splendor, filling his soul with the long echoes of beauty. After all, his life had been too starved. . . .

Suddenly, before an effulgent Titian,[8] he found himself saying: "But I'm only fifty-seven—" and then he turned away. For such summer dreams it was too late; but surely not for a quiet harvest of friendship, of comradeship, in the blessed hush of her nearness.

He went back to the hotel, where he and Dallas were to meet; and together they walked again across the Place de la Concorde and over the bridge that leads to the Chamber of Deputies.[9]

Dallas, unconscious of what was going on in his father's mind, was talking excitedly and abundantly of Versailles. He had had but one previous glimpse of it, during a holiday trip in which he had tried to pack all the sights he had been deprived of when he had had to go with the family to Switzerland; and tumultuous enthusiasm and cocksure criticism tripped each other up on his lips.

As Archer listened, his sense of inadequacy and inexpressiveness increased. The boy was not insensitive, he knew; but he had the facility and self-confidence that came of looking at fate not as a master but as an equal. "That's it: they feel equal to things—they know their way about," he mused, thinking of his son as the spokesman of the new generation which had swept away all the old landmarks, and with them the sign-posts and the danger-signal.

Suddenly Dallas stopped short, grasping his father's arm. "Oh, by Jove," he exclaimed.

They had come out into the great tree-planted space before the Invalides.[1] The dome of Mansart[2] floated ethereally above the budding trees and the long gray front of the building: drawing up into itself all the rays of afternoon light, it hung there like the visible symbol of the race's glory.

Archer knew that Madame Olenska lived in a square near one of the avenues radiating from the Invalides; and he had pictured the quarter as quiet and almost obscure, forgetting the central splendor that lit it up. Now, by some queer process of association, that golden light became for him the pervading illumination in which she lived. For nearly thirty years, her life—of which he knew so strangely little—had been spent in this rich atmosphere that he already felt to be too dense and yet too stimulating for his lungs. He thought of the theaters she must have been to, the pictures she must have looked at, the sober and splendid old houses she must have frequented, the people she must have talked with, the incessant stir of ideas, curiosities, images and associations thrown out by an intensely social race in a setting of immemorial manners; and suddenly he remembered the young Frenchman

8. Italian painter (1477–1576).
9. Historic structure built for the lower house of parliament in the Third Republic of France; together, the Chamber of Deputies and the Senate constituted the National Assembly.
1. Eighteenth-century Parisian complex originally built to house wounded or invalid veterans.
2. The Église du Dôme at the Invalides designed by Jules Hardouin-Mansart (see p. 212, *n.* 2).

who had once said to him: "Ah, good conversation—there is nothing like it, is there?"

Archer had not seen M. Rivière, or heard of him, for nearly thirty years; and that fact gave the measure of his ignorance of Madame Olenska's existence. More than half a lifetime divided them, and she had spent the long interval among people he did not know, in a society he but faintly guessed at, in conditions he would never wholly understand. During that time he had been living with his youthful memory of her; but she had doubtless had other and more tangible companionship. Perhaps she too had kept her memory of him as something apart; but if she had, it must have been like a relic in a small dim chapel, where there was not time to pray every day. . . .

They had crossed the Place des Invalides, and were walking down one of the thoroughfares flanking the building. It was a quiet quarter, after all, in spite of its splendor and its history; and the fact gave one an idea of the riches Paris had to draw on, since such scenes as this were left to the few and the indifferent.

The day was fading into a soft sun-shot haze, pricked here and there by a yellow electric light, and passers were rare in the little square into which they had turned. Dallas stopped again, and looked up.

"It must be here," he said, slipping his arm through his father's with a movement from which Archer's shyness did not shrink; and they stood together looking up at the house.

It was a modern building, without distinctive character, but many-windowed, and pleasantly balconied up its wide cream-colored front. On one of the upper balconies, which hung well above the rounded tops of the horse-chestnuts in the square, the awnings were still lowered, as though the sun had just left it.

"I wonder which floor—?" Dallas conjectured; and moving toward the *porte-cochère*[3] he put his head into the porter's lodge, and came back to say: "The fifth. It must be the one with the awnings."

Archer remained motionless, gazing at the upper windows as if the end of their pilgrimage had been attained.

"I say, you know, it's nearly six," his son at length reminded him.

The father glanced away at an empty bench under the trees.

"I believe I'll sit there a moment," he said.

"Why—aren't you well?" his son exclaimed.

"Oh, perfectly. But I should like you, please, to go up without me."

Dallas paused before him, visibly bewildered. "But, I say, Dad: do you mean you won't come up at all?"

"I don't know," said Archer slowly.

"If you don't she won't understand."

"Go, my boy; perhaps I shall follow you."

Dallas gave him a long look through the twilight.

"But what on earth shall I say?"

"My dear fellow, don't you always know what to say?" his father rejoined with a smile.

---

3. French, "carriage door."

"Very well. I shall say you're old-fashioned, and prefer walking up the five flights because you don't like lifts."

His father smiled again. "Say I'm old-fashioned: that's enough."

Dallas looked at him again, and then, with an incredulous gesture, passed out of sight under the vaulted doorway.

Archer sat down on the bench and continued to gaze at the awninged balcony. He calculated the time it would take his son to be carried up in the lift to the fifth floor, to ring the bell, and be admitted to the hall, and then ushered into the drawing room. He pictured Dallas entering that room with his quick assured step and his delightful smile, and wondered if the people were right who said that his boy "took after him."

Then he tried to see the persons already in the room—for probably at that sociable hour there would be more than one—and among them a dark lady, pale and dark, who would look up quickly, half rise, and hold out a long thin hand with three rings on it. . . . He thought she would be sitting in a sofa-corner near the fire, with azaleas banked behind her on a table.

"It's more real to me here than if I went up," he suddenly heard himself say; and the fear lest that last shadow of reality should lose its edge kept him rooted to his seat as the minutes succeeded each other.

He sat for a long time on the bench in the thickening dusk, his eyes never turning from the balcony. At length a light shone through the windows, and a moment later a man-servant came out on the balcony, drew up the awnings, and closed the shutters.

At that, as if it had been the signal he waited for, Newland Archer got up slowly and walked back alone to his hotel.

# BACKGROUND AND CONTEXTS

# Autobiography and Biography

*The Age of Innocence* was written from a combination of Wharton's personal memories, the memories of her friends, and old fashioned historical research. Wharton asked her sister-in-law, Mary Cadwalader Jones, to confirm and to add to her own memories of social practices, to check on particular dates for holidays and theatrical performances (see Julia Ehrhardt's essay in this volume). This section opens with a selection of Wharton's letters. By definition autobiographical, these letters have been included because of the insights they provide into the history of the writing of the novel as well as the reactions to *The Age of Innocence*. Serving as a biography of the novel, these letters record the Pulitzer Prize controversy and Wharton's concerns over her novel's translation into other mediums (see Brigitte Peucker's essay in this volume). Following a brief biographical overview of Wharton's life written by the editor, the series of autobiographical and biographical accounts included here concern Wharton's youth, the time period in which she set *The Age of Innocence*. "A Little Girl's New York," Wharton's most explicit memoir of her childhood published posthumously in *Harper's* in 1938, reads as if it were written to provide a historical guide to the authenticity of the sources that inspired the novel.

Wharton's *Age of Innocence* is grounded in an authentic time and place, a fictional realm that has been mapped onto memories of an actual world. Indeed, what has been defined as memorable in Wharton's childhood memoir suggests that this essay may have been designed to locate the novel in an undeniably personal past. The church sexton named Brown with his pioneer fleet of horse-drawn carriages for hire did exist and, perhaps, more important, the young Edith actually saw the woman that her mother forbade her to see, the figure in the shockingly yellow carriage who becomes the model for the scandalous character "Fanny Ring." While this memoir may have been conceived as a companion piece to *The Age of Innocence*, the excerpts from Wharton's 1934 autobiography, *A Backward Glance*, have been selected because they reveal some of the other ways in which Wharton transformed her experience of the past by rearranging historical materials into a compelling work of fiction.

Excerpts from R. W. B. Lewis's Pulitzer Prize–winning biography have been incorporated here to speak to the silences. These are the stories that Wharton chose not to tell about her painful coming-of-age and the publicity surrounding her broken engagement. Providing a telling counterpoint to Wharton's characteristically reticent representation of her early life, Lewis's biography describes the social customs of Old New York as they shaped and misshaped the lives of marriageable young women. *The Age of Innocence* as a work of fiction is by definition a complex translation of fragments of life into the illusion of wholeness made possible by art. Reading Lewis's analyses of Wharton's traumas, including her bitterness about the consequences of her own sexual innocence at the time of her marriage, reveals Wharton's profound understanding of what was at stake as she plotted possible turns in this historical novel (see Jennifer Rae Greeson's essay in this volume). These scenes from the life of Edith Wharton suggest that the author of *The Age of Innocence* understood the fears and dangers inherent in Old New York's cultural fetish that celebrated "abysmal purity" (6). This obsession leads to the cunning innocence that characterizes the deceptively complex May.

# LETTERS†

## To Rutger B. Jewett[1]

Paris
January 5, 1920

Dear Mr. Jewett,

I am sending you by hand by tomorrow's steamer another 25,000 words of "The Age of Innocence," and also the final revision of Book I. Two or three details important for the holding together of the story have been inserted in this revision and I have written my sister-in-law[2] that you will be kind enough to send it to her at once so that she can make the necessary changes in the proofs. They are all slight but nevertheless important.

I was very much surprised to hear from my sister-in-law the other day that when she called at the Pictorial Review Office for proofs the lady representing Mr. Vance[3] told her that the book was evidently to be a long one and that the editor would evidently have to cut out some passages.

As you know, it was stipulated that the novel furnished to the Pictorial Review should not be less than 100,000 words long. I see no reason to expect that it will exceed this length and it may even fall short by 3 or 4,000 words. In any case as I am prepared to keep my part of the agreement I shall expect the Magazine to do the same and not to tamper with the text of my novel.

I have done really a super-human piece of work in writing, within a year, the best part of two long novels, entirely different in subject and treatment, simply to suit the convenience of the Editor of the Pictorial and I cannot consent to have my work treated as if it were prose-by-the-yard.

\*　　\*　　\*

† The letters included here (with the single exception of the one written to Bernard Berenson) are housed in the Wharton Collection of the Beinecke Rare Book and Manuscript Library of Yale University. For the most complete published record of Wharton's correspondence, see R. W. B. and Nancy Lewis's extensively annotated volume, *The Letters of Edith Wharton* (New York: Scribners, 1988).

1. Wharton's editor and advisor at D. Appleton and Co.
2. Mary ("Minnie") Cadwalader Jones (1850–1935), Wharton's sister-in-law, intimate friend, and literary agent in America. Minnie Cadwalader married Wharton's brother Frederic R. Jones in 1870. Wharton continued to consider her former sister-in-law and her niece as her closest relatives even after that marriage ended in divorce in 1896.
3. Arthur Vance, editor of the *Pictorial Review*, the literary magazine in which *The Age of Innocence* appeared in monthly installments starting in July 1920.

# To Bernard Berenson[1]

Château Ste Claire[2]
Hyères
December 12, 1920

Glowing indeed, dearest B.B., & fragrant as incense, are the coals you have heaped on my unworthy head! I had sworn to have a letter on its way the week after you sailed; & here have I sat, mute & unresponsive, while you were storing up kind thoughts of me, & finding time to put them on paper.

The reason is the natural one: my tiresome heart (pump, not affective organ) "flanched" again, as it does now whenever I over-exert, & I got down here really dead-beat. My little secretary was taking a holiday, & business letters kept piling up on me at such a rate, after I arrived, that I only deal with them by abandoning my friends—which I did!

All this time, I was yearning over you both, & longing for news of you, & knowing that I didn't deserve it. * * *

And then came your dear letter, & nearly drew tears from these flinty eyes! I *did* so want "The Age" to be taken not as a "costume piece" but as a "simple & grave" story of two people trying to live up to something that was still "felt in the blood" at that time; & you, & the few other people whose opinion I care about, have made me feel that perhaps I have. Thank you so much for taking the trouble to tell me your impressions of the book.

\*        \*        \*

# To Mary Cadwalader Jones

Sainte Claire
February 17, 1921

Dearest Minnie,

Your letter announcing the signature of the contract with Shubert[1] has just come, & I must give you an immediate hug.—Did ever any lucky author have such a business-manager before, I wonder? As you know, I had no hopes of anything of the kind coming my way; & your news was a real surprise.

I am particularly pleased that Miss Akins[2] intends to dramatize the book. I hope you will tell her so; & also that she will send me "Déclassée" if it has been published.

1. Prominent American art critic (1865–1959) whose first book, *Venetian Painters of the Renaissance* (1894) established his expertise in the art of the Italian Renaissance. Berenson was a close friend and occasional traveling companion of Edith Wharton who shared his interest in painting. This letter is housed in the Villa I Tatti, Berenson's former home, the Center for Italian Renaissance Culture administered by Harvard University.
2. A former convent in Hyères on the French Riviera, which Wharton leased from the years following the war until her death in 1937.
1. The most powerful family of theater owners in America. The Shuberts owned several theaters in Manhattan as well as in other cities in the Northeast and became the leading managers and producers of legitimate theater in America during the first half of the twentieth century.
2. Known for her play, *The Greeks Had a Word for It*, Zoë Akins (1886–1958) did not adapt *The Age of Innocence* for the stage. Rather, she wrote a Pulitzer Prize–winning adaptation of Wharton's novella, *The Old Maid* (1924) set in the New York of the 1850s. *The Old Maid* is

I am very anxious about the staging & dressing. I could do every stick of furniture & every rag of clothing myself, for every detail of that far-off scene was indelibly stamped on my infant brain. I am so much afraid that the young actors will be "Summit Collar" athletes, with stern jaws & shaven lips, instead of gentlemen. Of course they ought all to have moustaches, & not tooth brush ones, but curved & slightly twisted at the ends. They should wear dark grey frock-coats & tall hats,[3] & always buttonhole-violets by day, a gardenia in evening dress. White waistcoats with their evening clothes, & pumps, *I think*. But you will remember all this as well as I do.—As for their "façons" & their language, since you say that Miss Akins knows European society, please tell her that a N.Y. drawing-room of my childhood was far more like a London one—a du Maurier[4] one of old-fashioned gentlefolk— than anything that modern N.Y. can give her. Above all, beg her to avoid slang & Americanisms, & tell her that English was then the lan- guage spoken by American ladies & gentlemen—since she is too young, I'm sure, to have known those happy days herself. Few people nowadays know that many of the young men of our day (in N.Y.) were educated in English Universities, & that English tutors & governesses were frequent & that *no* girl went to a school!* If she does not know this—& does not (equally) keep away from that grotesque stage inven- tion of "Southern chivalry"—she will never get the right atmosphere.

How thrilling if Doris Keane[5] should do Ellen! How I wish I had seen her act. Have you any idea when they mean to bring it out? And, oh, how odd that no one should know that there is a play in "The Reef[6] all ready to be pulled out!—

Thanks for the revised copy of "The Age." I have written to Jewett suggesting that I should write a preface for the next edition,[7] explain- ing under what difficulties the book was written, as regards revising & proof-correcting, & also stating my theory as to the writing of "histori- cal" novels, & the small importance of anachronisms.—

*   *   *

Best love, & all gratitude again.
  E.W.

* And that older women did not wear pince-nez & white false fronts—

*   *   *

one of four novellas collected and published as *Old New York*, a working title Wharton had used to refer to the novel that would become *The Age of Innocence*. The stage adaptation of *The Age of Innocence* was done by Margaret Barnes.
3. See Butterick Fashions, p. 319.
4. Sir Gerald Busson Du Maurier (1873–1934), celebrated British actor now best known as the father of Daphné Du Maurier, the popular twentieth-century novelist who wrote *Re- becca* (1938) and other Gothic thrillers.
5. American actress (1881–1945) considered for the role of Ellen because of her long-standing and successful performance as a European heroine in *Romance*, a popular play by Edward Sheldon. Ultimately, the distinguished actress Katherine Cornell was chosen to play Count- ess Olenska.
6. Edith Wharton's 1912 novel about the ill-fated romance between a dignified American widow and her fiancé. The widow living in France realizes that her fiancé has had a sexual relationship with a would-be actress, who, after becoming the governess for the widow's step-daughter, has become engaged to the widow's beloved step-son.
7. See Julia Ehrhardt's essay in this volume, pp. 401–412.

# To Sinclair Lewis[1]

Pavillon Colombe[2]
August 6, 1921

My dear Mr. Lewis,

Your letter touched me very deeply; & I should have told you so sooner if it hadn't gone to America (where I have not been since the war), & then travelled back to me here.

What you say is so kind, so generous & so unexpected, that I don't know where to begin to answer. It is the first sign I have ever had—literally—that "les jeunes"[3] at home had ever read a word of me. I had long since resigned myself to the idea that I was regarded by you all as the—say the Mrs. Humphry Ward[4] of the Western Hemisphere; though at times I wondered why. Your book & *Susan Lenox*[5] (unexpurgated) have been the only things out of America that have made me cease to despair of the republic—of letters; so you can imagine what a pleasure it is to know that you have read *me*, & cared, & understood. It gives me a "Nunc Dimittis"[6] feeling—or would, if I hadn't still about a hundred subjects to deal with!

As for the Columbia Prize,[7] the kind Appletons have smothered me in newspaper commentary; & when I discovered that I was being rewarded—by one of our leading Universities—for uplifting American morals, I confess I *did* despair.

Subsequently, when I found the prize shd really have been yours, but was withdrawn because your book (I quote from memory) had "offended a number of prominent persons in the Middle West," disgust was added to despair.—Hope returns to me, however, with your letter, & with the enclosed article, just received.—Some sort of standard *is*

1. American novelist (1885–1951) best known for *Main Street* (1920), which received the most votes for the Pulitzer Prize in 1921 but was rejected because a vocal lobby was offended by its critical representation of the Midwest and the mores of small-town America. Instead, Wharton's *Age of Innocence* was awarded this prize. Lewis dedicated *Babbitt* (1922) to Edith Wharton, signaling his respect for Wharton, who had preceded him in writing sharp critiques of the Midwest in novels such as *The Custom of the Country* (1913). When Lewis was awarded the 1926 Pulitzer Prize for *Arrowsmith* (1925), he chose to decline.
2. The villa Wharton purchased after World War I and where she lived while writing *The Age of Innocence*. Returning the house to its original name, Wharton recalled that this villa had been built by the lovers of two sisters, former actresses at the *Italiens* (see p. 65, n. 3.) who became noted courtesans. As R. W. B. Lewis notes, the slang word "cocottes," which appears in *The Age of Innocence*, entered the French language as a term used to describe these sisters. (See p. 119, n. 7.)
3. French, "the youths," "the young people."
4. Prolific British novelist (1851–1920) whose work emphasized the social responsibility of Christianity. As a political activist, Mrs. Humphry Ward was best known for her vociferous opposition to the women's suffrage movement.
5. A posthumously published novel (1917) by David Graham Phillips (1867–1911), that tells of a young woman who falls into prostitution before rising to become a noted actress on the New York stage.
6. "Nunc Dimittis" feeling: Having been promised that he would see Christ before his own death, St. Simeon's prayer of thanks, uttered when the infant Jesus is presented at the Temple, begins "Now thou dost dismiss [Nunc dimittis] Thy servant, O Lord" (*Luke*: 2, 29–31). Here Wharton jokingly acknowledges the feeling that she (identifying with the grateful and superseded St. Simeon) is being dismissed by God as a former servant who has been rewarded by seeing the new (if infant) gods of American literature arrive. Here, there is the sense that Wharton's departure and death are linked to the ascension of the new gods to their rightful places of honor. Ezra Pound, among the newly arriving, uses this Latin phrase in his "Cantico Del Sole," a commentary that appeared before the publication of Wharton's novel.
7. The trustees of Columbia University oversaw the selection of the Pulitzer Prize–winners.

emerging from the welter of cant & sentimentality, & if two or three of us are gathered together, I believe we can still save fiction in America.

I wish I could talk to you of all this. Is there no chance of your coming to Paris? I'm only half an hour away— If not, let me at least tell you again how many hopes your book & your letter have waked in me. Believe me, Yrs very sincerely

E. Wharton

Ms:BL

## To Mary Cadwalader Jones

> Sainte-Claire
> Hyères
> April 11, 1927

Dearest Minnie— Just a line to say that yr letter of April 1, enclosing the "Old Maid" scenario, has just come.[1]

The scenario seems to me excellent. I noted not only the kitchen, which is *perhaps* wrong—though the good housekeeper of those days did go into the kitchen, especially on the eve of festivities. At any rate, Charlotte wd certainly go to interview the cook somewhere—she does in my story.—What is radically wrong is afternoon tea! They would have a light port & cookies, or a dry sherry, wouldn't they?—These little touches are important in a "costume" play.

I am cabling that I like the scenario, as it may hasten matters.

*    *    *

Yrs ever
  E.W.

What has happened to "The Age of Innocence"? It seems to be dead—[2] My best remembrance to Sheldon—

Ms:BL

## CANDACE WAID

## [A Biographical Note on Edith Wharton]†

Edith Wharton (1862–1937), novelist and writer of short fiction, was born into the carefully guarded upper ranks of New York society. Both her father's and mother's lineage secured her a place in the New York Four Hundred (the size of which was determined by the capacity of

---

1. Zoë Akins's adaptation appeared on Broadway in 1935. (See also *n.* 2, p. 224).
2. Wharton is referring here to the stage version of *The Age of Innocence.*
† From *Oxford Companion to Women's Writing in the United States*, eds. Cathy N. Davidson and Linda Wagner-Martin (New York: Oxford University Press, 1994), pp. 916–919.

Mrs. Astor's ballroom). Wharton would publish over thirty-five book-length works in her career as a writer, including eighty-six short stories, eleven collections of short fiction, twenty-two works of longer fiction (both novels and novellas), three collections of poetry, books on architecture and gardens, travel books (including an account of the destruction along the French front while World War I was still being fought), a critical study called *The Writing of Fiction*, and an autobiography, *A Backward Glance*. The rumors spread by some of her contemporaries that her brother's tutor had really been her father were part of a family romance invented to explain how such a remarkable novelist and intellectual could have been produced by such unimaginative parents and the New York aristocracy. The idea that a daughter of this set would become a writer was perhaps too bizarre to be imagined. Aside from Washington Irving, the chronicler of early New York and its Dutch settlers, few writers of fiction emerged from the nineteenth-century elite society into which Edith Newbold Jones made her debut.

Wharton was distantly related to Herman Melville, but he was considered a bohemian by the socially conservative denizens of Wharton's Old New York, where writing was considered to be somewhere between manual labor and the occult arts. In the nineteenth century, novelists—especially the growing number of influential female novelists—came from the settled ranks of the middle classes. Literature seemed to be the province of clergymen's daughters in particular—for example, Jane Austen, the Brontë sisters, and Harriet Beecher Stowe. The privileged world of Wharton's family devoted its leisure time to social rituals, which (in novels such as *The Custom of the Country* and *The Age of Innocence*) Wharton would describe as tribal practices incompatible with art. In the years following the Civil War, a financial crisis caused the Joneses (like other families of their set) to move abroad, where they could live more cheaply. Between the ages of four and ten, in Paris and Florence, in German watering places and a still exotic Spain, Wharton was transformed by European culture and traditions. She would later insist that after she returned to New York at the age of ten, she "never felt otherwise than as in exile in America."

Wharton's mother, Lucretia Jones, represented the most repressive aspects of the American aristocratic class code. Yet despite her disapproval of her child's narrative aspirations, she did try to transcribe the stories that her precocious young daughter invented in an obsessive ritual called "making-up" in which the young Edith, although unable to read, would improvise stories as she stood holding a book. Wharton would later recall having had only two ambitions when she was a child: to be, like her mother, the best-dressed woman in New York, and to be a writer. She describes being caught between two opposing impulses, the desire "to make . . . pictures prettier" and the necessity of telling the truth, which she increasingly associated with books. Intellectually isolated during the "moral tortures" of her childhood, Wharton balanced her fears and attenuated her loneliness through the reading and writing that became the basis for what she would later describe as her "real life."

These conflicting polarities were intensely gendered. The world of decorative surfaces and politeness was ruled by her mother, whom she saw as standing in direct opposition to a darker masculine power called "God," which demanded the revelation of painful truths. These powerful oppositions between surface and depth, concealment and revelation, became in Wharton's work the codes for distinguishing between what she saw as the prettiness of sentimentalist fiction and the structural clarity of realist writing. At the age of fifteen she secretly wrote a thirty-thousand-word novella called *Fast and Loose* under the pseudonym of Mr. Oliveieri, accompanied by a savage review conceived for *The Nation* that compared the author to "a sick sentimental school-girl who has begun her work with a fierce and bloody resolve to make it as bad as Wilhelm Meister, Consuelo, and 'Goodbye Sweetheart' together."

When Wharton was sixteen, her mother had her poetry printed anonymously in a gesture that may have been meant to mark an end to such youthful pursuits. Fearing that she was becoming unattractively bookish, her parents hastened her debut into New York society just prior to her seventeenth birthday. When she married the sports-loving Teddy Wharton in 1885 at the age of twenty-three, Edith Wharton assumed the role of a young society matron. In 1889, she published three poems, and her first story appeared in *Scribner's* in 1891. In 1897 (with the architect Ogden Codman), she published *The Decoration of Houses*, which sought to elevate this field from the demeaning realm of dressmaking and ally it instead with architecture. In 1898, Wharton had a nervous breakdown; the prescribed cure, which required four months in almost complete isolation, released her from her exhausting life in society and resulted in a creative breakthrough that culminated in the publication of her first collection of stories, *The Greater Inclination* in 1899. She described this as an event that broke "the chains that had held me for so long in a kind of torpor. For nearly twelve years, I had tried to adjust myself to my marriage; but now I was overmastered by the longing to meet people who shared my interests." Determined to write every day, Wharton began to live the life of a disciplined writer.

Wharton set her first novel, *The Valley of Decision* (1902), in eighteenth-century Italy. Critics complained that the characters were wooden and less important than the rich details about architecture, art, and religious and philosophical controversies. Henry James recommended that Wharton should "Do New York!," that she "must be tethered in native pastures, even if it reduces her to a backyard in New York." Wharton subsequently "did New York" in *The House of Mirth*. The serial publication of this best-selling novel taught Wharton the discipline of writing for deadlines and offered encouragement from a public impatient for each installment. Wharton's most powerful work as a novelist began with the publication of *The House of Mirth* in 1905 and closed with the publication of her Pulitzer Prize-winning novel, *The Age of Innocence* in 1920. With *The Custom of the Country* (1913), the bitterly satirical novel that Wharton would call her "masterpiece," these novels contain Wharton's most devastating critiques of New York society. Declaring that a frivolous society may be judged by the value of what it destroys, Wharton chronicled in *The House of Mirth* the commodification and destruction of her heroine, Lily Bart.

In *The Custom of the Country*, Wharton shifted the source of destruction to a marauding heroine from the interior of America as the devouring Undine Spragg invades Old New York, an embattled world of tradition that Wharton calls "the Reservation." With her silver initials U.S. emblazoned on her pigeon-blood-colored stationary, Undine represents the nationalist and predatory aspects of her native country as she moves east from Manhattan to threaten the culture of the French aristocracy. Ellen Olenska of *The Age of Innocence* returns home from the old world of Europe to what she imagines is the more straightforward world represented by the allegorically named characters Newland Archer and May Welland. A historical novel that treats the world of Wharton's childhood, an "age of innocence" prior to the Great War, this novel reveals the tribal rituals of New York society as its members confirm their bonds by excluding a cousin who seems to bear the taint of European knowledge and experience.

These years in which Wharton produced her finest novels were also a difficult period of her life. Wharton had ceased having sexual relations with her husband after the first few weeks of their marriage—she would later admit that she had not known about sexual intercourse before she was married. At the age of forty-six, in the midst of a series of changes in her life, she began a passionate, yet finally unfulfilling, love affair with the journalist Morton Fullerton. In 1911, she separated from her husband and America, selling the New England home which she had built in 1902. Wharton, whom James had called "the great and glorious pendulum" because of her habitual trans-Atlantic crossings, became a permanent resident of France, where she would remain until her death twenty-six years later, returning to America only twice (in 1913, the year of her French divorce, and briefly in 1923, when she received an honorary degree from Yale). During the war in France, Wharton organized relief efforts for the refugees and orphans displaced by the advancing German army. In 1916, Wharton was named a Chevalier of the Legion of Honor, the highest honor given to a foreigner in France.

In 1912, Wharton published *The Reef*, a novel about Americans living in France. Yet during this period she also wrote her New England novels *Ethan Frome* (1911) and *Summer* (1917). In these related works—*Ethan Frome* in its earliest version written in French was called "Hiver," and she referred to *Summer* as the "Hot Ethan"— Wharton explored a psychic landscape ruled by primal forces. One of her most autobiographical works, *Ethan Frome* can be seen as a terrifying description of what her life might have been like if she had not divorced her invalid husband. This purgatory, where a wounded man seems trapped in a New England farmhouse burdened by sickly and complaining women, is transformed in *Summer*, which Wharton wrote while surrounded by the destruction of the Great War. In her most lyrical and erotic novel, Wharton rewrites the story of virgin death, which destroyed the attractive female figures in *The House of Mirth* and *Ethan Frome*. Although troubling because the heroine ends up marrying the man who adopted her, *Summer* tells the story of inevitable fertility and the struggle to preserve human life. *Ethan Frome* and *Summer* also represent Wharton's ambivalent dialogue with the best of the domestic realists and the female local colorists, including Sarah Orne Jewett and Mary Wilkins Freeman, as she tried to imagine the fate of women and women's stories in America. In the 1920s, Wharton wrote a number of novels concerned with maternal questions, the best of which are *The Mother's Recompense* (1925) and *The Children* (1928). This group of novels is generally regarded as Wharton's weakest work; its subjects are criticized for seeming tailored to the tastes of the women's magazines of the period.

In her last completed novels, *Hudson River Bracketed* (1929) and *The Gods Arrive* (1932), Wharton attempts to tell the story of the American artist by chronicling the career of the writer Vance Weston who comes East to encounter both the past and fashionable literary movements. Although Wharton included this two volume opus among her personal favorites, these novels are most interesting in the context of her ongoing effort to imagine the place and story of the American writer. From the publication of *The Touchstone* (1900), her first longer work of fiction, Wharton was concerned with the fate of the woman writer. In "Copy" (1901) a successful woman novelist describes herself as "a monster manufactured out of newspaper paragraphs, with ink in its veins" whose "keen sense of copyright is my nearest approach to an emotion." Both of these works depict the isolation of successful women novelists; both, like Wharton, have authored works called "Pomegranate Seed," evoking Wharton's lifelong identification of the woman writer with Persephone. The association of the woman writer with death is also apparent in Wharton's ghost stories, which include some of her finest work in her last years. *Ghosts*, published posthumously in 1937, the year of Wharton's death, depicts female figures who are abandoned or imprisoned. Although many of the stories focus on strangling and silencing, some tell of women who are rescued from isolation and silence long after their deaths by people who discover and decode their stories from written texts. The ghost stories provide a profound and psychically revealing account of Wharton's understanding of the place of the woman and the woman writer.

When Wharton published *The Reef*, James congratulated her by calling it Racinean, but others commended the novel by calling it Jamesian. From the beginning of her career, Wharton suffered in near silence praise from critics who could place her only as a female Henry James. Judged according to her class background and condescended to because of her sex, Wharton has only recently begun to be appreciated as one of the most productive and gifted American writers of her generation. Deeply influenced by both American and European literature, including the classics, Wharton during her lifetime was a powerful presence to her contemporaries. Elizabeth Ammons argues that women "like Wharton, Cather, and Stein" were "the real giants against whom" writers such as Fitzgerald and Hemingway "needed to define themselves;" Wharton must also be considered among those Ammons refers to as the "turn-of-the century women writers [who] were imitated by Theodore Dreiser, Sherwood Anderson, and Sinclair Lewis." Categories such as realist, naturalist, or even sentimentalist describe different aspects of her work, but these terms are not adequate to describe her writing. By birth and inclination, Wharton was fated to occupy two worlds: not only Europe and America, but also, and perhaps equally dramatically, the nineteenth and twentieth centuries. Her life began with the Civil War and ended on the eve of World War II. A culminating figure associated with the traditional and the past, Wharton is also particularly modern in her efforts to understand the place of women, artists, and America in the twentieth century.

# EDITH WHARTON

## A Little Girl's New York†

When four years ago I wrote the closing lines of my reminiscences, *A Backward Glance*, I thought of myself as an old woman laying a handful of rue on the grave of an age which had finished in storm and destruction. Now that I am older by only four years, I realize that my view was that of the sentimentalist watching the slow downward flutter of the first autumn leaves in still blue air, and talking with a shudder of forests stripped by winter gales. For the succeeding years have witnessed such convulsions, social and political, that those earlier disturbances now seem no more than a premonitory tremor; and the change between the customs of my youth and the world of even ten years ago a mere crack in the ground compared with the chasm now dividing that world from the present one.

All elderly people feel the shock of changes barely perceptible to the generation that has had a hand in their making; but even centenarians can seldom have had to look back across such a barrier of new towers of Babel (or their ruins) as divides my contemporaries from the era of the New Deal;[1] and I need no other excuse for beginning my old story over again than the growing mass of these obstructions. Everything that used to form the fabric of our daily life has been torn in shreds, trampled on, destroyed; and hundreds of little incidents, habits, traditions which, when I began to record my past, seemed too insignificant to set down, have acquired the historical importance of fragments of dress and furniture dug up in a Babylonian tomb.

† From *Harper's Magazine* CLXXVI (March, 1938): 356–64.
1. towers of Babel: Biblical story of a time when all the people on earth spoke the same language and began to build a tower to heaven. Consequently, God scattered the people and divided them by causing them to speak in different languages (see Genesis 11:1–9). the New Deal: Program initiated during the presidency of Franklin D. Roosevelt in an effort to bring about economic recovery and social reform in the United States during the international depression of the 1930s [Editor].

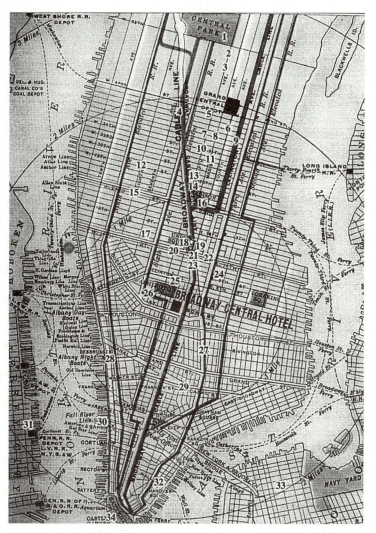

**Map of Manhattan.** (Based on a business map from the early 1890s.)

1. Central Park
2. Mrs. Manson Mingott's mansion (5th Ave. and 57th St.)
3. Temporary location of the Metropolitan Museum of Art (681 5th Ave.), relocated in 1880 to 5th Ave., between 80th and 84th Streets
4. Metropolitan Opera House (Broadway and 7th Ave.)
5. New York Public Library (5th Ave. and 42nd St.)
6. East 39th St. (The Archers' home after marriage)
7. Fifth Ave.
8. Madison Ave. (The Van der Luyden's mansion)
9. Lexington Ave.
10. Caroline Astor's Mansion (350 5th Ave.)
11. Grolier Club (29 East 32nd St.)
12. West 28th St. (The Archer ancestral home)
13. Knickerbocker Club (5th Ave. and 28th St.)
14. Delmonico's (after 1876)
15. West 23rd St. (Ellen Olenska's house, also Wharton's family home)
16. Madison Square
17. Henderson's Florist (112 West 15th St.)
18. Tiffany's (Union Square at 15th St.)
19. The Century Club (109 East 15th St.)
20. Delmonico's (between 1861 and 1876)
21. The Academy of Music (14th St. and Irving Place)
22. Grace Church
23. Wallack's Theater (844 Broadway)
24. St. Mark's (site of Archer vault, East 10th St.)
25. University Place
26. Washington Square
27. The Bowery
28. Ferry between Debrosses St. in NY, and Exchange Place in Jersey City
29. Canal Street
30. Fall River Line
31. Pennsylvania Station Terminus in Jersey City
32. Wall Street
33. Brooklyn
34. The Battery and Castle Garden, ("the old Opera-house")

It is these fragments that I should like to assemble and make into a little memorial like the boxes formed of exotic shells which sailors used to fabricate between voyages. And I must forestall my critics by adding that I already foresee how small will be the shells I shall collect, how ordinary their varieties, and the box, when it is made, what a mere joke of a thing—unless one should put one's ear to the shells; but how many will?

## II

In those days the little "brownstone" houses (I never knew the technical name of that geological horror) marched up Fifth Avenue (still called "*the* Fifth Avenue" by purists) in an almost unbroken procession from Washington Square to the Central Park. Between them there passed up and down, in a leisurely double line, every variety of horse-drawn vehicle, from Mrs. Belmont's or Mrs. Astor's C-spring barouche to a shabby little covered cart drawn by a discouraged old horse and labelled in large letters: *Universal Exterminator*—which suggested collecting souls for the *Dies Irae*,[2] but in reality designated a patent appliance for ridding kitchens of cockroaches.

The little brownstone houses, all with Dutch "stoops" (the five or six steps leading to the front door), and all not more than three stories high, marched Parkward in an orderly procession, like a young ladies' boarding school taking its daily exercise. The façades varied in width from twenty to thirty feet, and here and there, but rarely, the line was broken by a brick house with brownstone trimmings; but otherwise they were all so much alike that one could understand how easy it would be for a dinner guest to go to the wrong house—as once befell a timid young girl of eighteen, to whom a vulgar *nouveau-riche* hostess revealed her mistake, turning her out carriageless into the snow—a horrid adventure which was always used to point the rule that one must *never* allow a guest, even totally unknown, to discover such a mistake, but most immediately include him or her in the party. Imagine the danger of entertaining gangsters to which such social rules would expose the modern hostess! But I am probably the last person to remember that Arcadian code of hospitality.

Those were the days—à propos of Fifth Avenue—when my mother used to say: "Society is completely changed nowadays. When I was first married we knew everyone who kept a carriage."

And this tempts me to another digression, sending me forward to my seventeenth year, when there suddenly appeared in Fifth Avenue a very small canary-yellow brougham with dark trimmings, drawn by a big high-stepping bay and driven by a coachman who matched the brougham in size and the high-stepper in style. In this discreet yet brilliant equipage one just caught a glimpse of a lady whom I faintly remember as dark-haired, quietly dressed, and enchantingly pale, with a hat-brim lined with cherry color, which shed a lovely glow on her

2. Latin, "The Day of Wrath"; refers to the portion of the Catholic Requiem Mass dealing with the judgment associated with the Apocalypse, the end of the world.

cheeks. It was an apparition surpassing in elegance and mystery any that Fifth Avenue had ever seen; but when our dark-blue brougham encountered the yellow one, and I cried: "Oh, Mamma, look—what a smart carriage! Do you know the lady?" I was hurriedly drawn back with the stern order not to stare at strange people and to remember that whenever our carriage passed the yellow one I was to turn my head away and look out of the other window.

For the lady in the canary-colored carriage was New York's first fashionable hetaera.[3] Her name and history were known in all the clubs, and the name of her proud proprietor was no secret in New York drawing-rooms. I may add that, being an obedient daughter, I always thereafter *did* look out of the other window when the forbidden brougham passed; but that one and only glimpse of the loveliness within it peopled my imagination with images of enchantment from Broceliande and Shalott (we were all deep in the "Idylls of the King"), and from the Cornwall of Yseult.[4] She was, in short, sweet unsuspecting creature, my first doorway to romance, destined to become for me successively Guinevere and Francesca da Rimini, Beatrix Esmond and the *Dame aux Camélias*.[5] And in the impoverished emotional atmosphere of old New York such a glimpse was like the mirage of palm trees in the desert.

I have often sighed, in looking back at my childhood, to think how pitiful a provision was made for the life of the imagination behind those uniform brownstone façades, and then have concluded that since, for reasons which escape us, the creative mind thrives best on a reduced diet, I probably had the fare best suited to me. But this is not to say that the average well-to-do New Yorker of my childhood was not starved for a sight of the high gods. Beauty, passion, and danger were automatically excluded from his life (for the men were almost as starved as the women); and the average human being deprived of air from the heights is likely to produce other lives equally starved— which was what happened in old New York, where the tepid sameness of the moral atmosphere resulted in a prolonged immaturity of mind.

But we must return to the brownstone houses, and penetrate from the vestibule (painted in Pompeian red, and frescoed with a frieze of stencilled lotus-leaves, taken from Owen Jones's *Grammar of Ornament*)[6] into the carefully guarded interior. What would the New Yorker

3. Courtesan, or "kept" woman, originally a member of a class of cultivated prostitutes of ancient Greece.
4. Broceliande: Forest in Brittany, in northwestern France, traditionally held to be the place where Merlin, Arthur's magician, was magically entombed by the fairy Vivian; Shalott: Faerie realm of the poem "Lady of Shalott" by Alfred Lord Tennyson (1809–1892); "Idylls of the King": Series of poems (1842, final version published 1872) recounting the stories of Arthurian myth by Tennyson; Cornwall of Yseult: Celtic mythical traditions of Cornwall, in southwest England, such as the famed love story of Tristan and Yseult, whose adulterous passion was thwarted by Yseult's husband, King Mark of Cornwall.
5. Francesca da Rimini: Wife of Gianciotto Malatesta, killed by her husband when he learned of her love affair with his brother, Paolo in 1289; Beatrix Esmond: Wife of the title character of William Makepeace Thackeray's *Henry Esmond* (1852), who torments that military and political hero; *Dame aux Camélias*: Novel by Alexandre Dumas (1824–1895).
6. Published in 1856 by Welsh architect Owen Jones (1809–1874), this influential work based on his extensive international research, featured Jones's thirty-seven axioms of design with color plates depicting historical styles of ornamentation.

of the present day say to those interiors, and the lives lived in them? Both would be equally unintelligible to any New Yorker under fifty.

Beyond the vestibule (in the average house) was a narrow drawing-room. Its tall windows were hung with three layers of curtains: sash-curtains through which no eye from the street could possibly penetrate, and next to these draperies of lace or embroidered tulle, richly beruffled, and looped back under the velvet or damask hangings which were drawn in the evening. This window garniture always seemed to me to symbolize the superimposed layers of under-garments worn by the ladies of the period—and even, alas, by the little girls. They were in fact almost purely a symbol, for in many windows even the inner "sash-curtains" were looped back far enough to give the secluded dwellers a narrow glimpse of the street; but no self-respecting mistress of a house (a brownstone house) could dispense with this triple display of window-lingerie, and among the many things I did which pained and scandalized my Bostonian mother-in-law, she was not least shocked by the banishment from our house in the country of all the thicknesses of muslin which should have intervened between ourselves and the robins on the lawn.

The brownstone drawing-room was likely to be furnished with monumental pieces of modern Dutch marquetry, among which there was almost always a cabinet with glazed doors for the display of "bric-à-brac." Oh, that bric-à-brac! Our mothers, who prided themselves on the contents of these cabinets, really knew about only two artistic productions—old lace and old painted fans. With regard to these the eighteenth-century tradition was still alive, and in nearly every family there were yards and yards of precious old lace and old fans of ivory, chicken-skin, or pale tortoise-shell, exquisitely carved and painted. But as to the other arts a universal ignorance prevailed, and the treasures displayed in the wealthiest houses were no better than those of the average brownstone-dweller.

My mother had a collection of old lace which was famous among her friends, and a few fragments of it still remain to me, piously pinned up in the indigo-blue paper supposed (I have never known why) to be necessary to the preservation of fine lace. But the yards are few, alas; for true to my conviction that what was made to be used should be used, and not locked up, I have outlived many and many a yard of noble *point de Milan*, of stately Venetian point, of shadowy Mechlin, and exquisitely flowered *point de Paris*, not to speak of the delicate Valenciennes which ruffled the tiny handkerchiefs and incrusted and edged the elaborate *lingerie* of my youth. Nor do I regret having worn out what was meant to be worn out. I know few sadder sights than Museum collections of these Arachne-webs that were designed to borrow life and color from the nearness of young flesh and blood. Museums are cemeteries, as unavoidable, no doubt, as the other kind, but just as unrelated to the living beauty of what we have loved.

**Photograph of the Interior of Lucretia Rhinelander Jones's Home in New York.** This typical late-nineteenth-century interior, dominated by floral patterns, is a photograph of Wharton's mother's house on Twenty-fifth Street, where she moved with her daughter Edith after her husband's death in 1882.

*III*

I have said that the little brown houses, marching up Fifth Avenue like disciplined schoolgirls, now and then gave way to a more important façade, sometimes of their own chocolate hue, but with occasional pleasing alternatives in brick. Many successive Fifth Avenues have since been erected on the site of the one I first knew, and it is hard to remember that none of the "new" millionaire houses which, ten or fifteen years later, were to invade that restless thoroughfare (and all of which long ago joined the earlier layers of ruins) had been dreamed of by the boldest innovator. Even the old families, who were subsequently to join the newcomers in transforming Fifth Avenue into a street of would-be palaces, were still content with plain wide-fronted houses, mostly built in the 'forties or 'fifties. In those simple days one could count on one's two hands the New York houses with ballrooms: to the best of my recollection, only the Goelets, Astors, Butler Duncans, Belmonts, Schermerhorns, and Mason Joneses possessed these frivolous appendages; though a few years later, by the time I made my first curtsy at the "Assemblies," several rich couples, the Mortons, Waterburys, Coleman Draytons, and Francklyns among them, had added ballrooms to their smart establishments.

In the smaller houses a heavy linen called "crash," laid on the floors of two adjoining drawing-rooms, and gilt chairs hired from "old Brown" (the Grace Church sexton, who so oddly combined ecclesiastical and worldly duties) created temporary ballrooms for small dances; but the big balls of the season (from January to Lent) were held at Delmonico's, then, if I am not mistaken, at the corner of Twenty-eighth Street and Fifth Avenue.

The Assemblies were the most important of these big balls—if the word "big" as now understood could be applied to any social event in our old New York! There were, I think, three Assemblies in the winter, presided over by a committee of ladies who delegated three of their number to receive the guests at the ballroom door. The evening always opened with a quadrille, in which the ladies of the committee and others designated by them took part; and there followed other square dances, waltzes and polkas, which went on until the announcement of supper. A succulent repast of canvasback ducks, terrapin, foie-gras, and the best champagnes was served at small tables below stairs, in what was then New York's only fashionable restaurant; after which we re-ascended to the ballroom (in a shaky little lift) to begin the complicated maneuvers of the cotillion.

The "Thursday Evening Dances," much smaller and more exclusive, were managed by a committee of the younger married women—and how many young and pretty ones there were in our little society! I cannot, oddly enough, remember where these dances were held—and who is left, I wonder, to refresh my memory? There was no Sherry's restaurant as yet, and no Waldorf-Astoria, or any kind of modern hotel with a suite for entertaining; yet I am fairly sure we did not meet at "Del's"[7] for the "Thursday Evenings."

At all dances, large or small, a custom prevailed which caused untold misery to the less popular girls. This was the barbarous rule that if a young man asked a girl for a dance or, between dances, for a turn about the ballroom, he was obliged to keep her on his arm until another candidate replaced him; with the natural result that "to him (or rather *her*) that hath shall be given," and the wily young men risked themselves only in the vicinity of young women already provided with attendant swains. To remedy this embarrassing situation the more tactful girls always requested their partners, between dances, to bring them back to their mothers or "chaperons," a somnolent row of stout ladies in velvet and ostrich feathers enthroned on a row of settees against the ballroom walls.

The custom persisted for some years, and spoilt the enjoyment of many a "nice" girl not attractive enough to be perpetually surrounded by young men, and too proud to wish to chain at her side a dancer who might have risked captivity out of kindness of heart. I do not know when the fashion changed, and the young men were set free, for we went back to Europe when I was nineteen, and I had only brief glimpses of New York until I returned to it as a married woman.

The most conspicuous architectural break in the brownstone procession occurred where its march ended, at the awkwardly shaped entrance to the Central Park. Two of my father's cousins, Mrs. Mason Jones and Mrs. Colford Jones, bought up the last two blocks on the east side of Fifth Avenue, facing the so-called "Plaza" at the Park gates, and built thereon their houses and their children's houses; a bold move which surprised and scandalized society. Fifty-seventh Street was then a desert, and ball-goers anxiously wondered whether even the ubiquitous "Brown coupés" destined to carry home belated dancers would risk themselves so far a-field. But old Mrs. Mason Jones and her submissive cousin laughed at such apprehensions, and presently there rose before our astonished eyes a block of palegreenish limestone houses (almost uglier than the brownstone ones) for the Colford Jones cousins, adjoining which our audacious Aunt Mary, who had known life at the Court of the Tuileries, erected her own white marble residence and a row of smaller dwellings of the same marble to lodge her progeny. The "Jones blocks" were so revolutionary that I doubt whether any subsequent architectural upheavals along that historic thoroughfare have produced a greater impression. In our little provincial town (without electricity, telephones, taxis, or cab-stands) it had seemed inconceivable that houses or habits should ever change; whereas by the time the new millionaires arrived with their palaces in their pockets Fifth Avenue had become cosmopolitan, and was prepared for anything.

7. Delmonico's (see p. 67, *n.* 1).

**Mary Mason Jones's Home (1875).** (*Top*) Newly dug basements occupy the foreground of this photograph, featuring a distant view of the home of Edith Wharton's aunt, Mrs. Mary Mason Jones, the primary model for Mrs. Manson Mingott. These lots were designed for expensive housing near Central Park. This photograph of Mrs. Jones's isolated mansion, in a stretch that would later become known as "Marble Row," illustrates the boldness of her vision in moving beyond the boundaries of polite society. (*Bottom*) A close-up view of Mary Mason Jones's home on Fifth Avenue (between Fifty-seventh and Fifty-eighth Streets).

*IV*

The lives led behind the brownstone fronts were, with few exceptions, as monotonous as their architecture. European travel was growing more frequent, though the annual holiday abroad did not become general until I grew up. In the brownstone era, when one crossed the Atlantic it was for a longer stay; and the returned traveler arrived with a train of luggage too often heavy with works of art and "antiques." Our mothers, not always aware of their æsthetic limitations, seldom restricted their purchases to lace and fans; it was almost a point of honor to bring back an "Old Master" or two and a few monsters in the way of modern Venetian furniture. For the traveler of moderate means, who could not soar to Salvator Rosa, Paul Potter, or Carlo Dolci[8] (prime favorites of the day), facsimiles were turned out by the million by the industrious copyists of Florence, Rome, or Amsterdam; and seldom did the well-to-do New Yorker land from a European tour unaccompanied by a Mary Magdalen cloaked in carefully waved hair, or a swarthy group of plumed and gaitered gamblers doing a young innocent out of his last sequin. One of these "awful warnings," a Do-menichino,[9] I think, darkened the walls of our dining room, and Mary Magdalen, minutely reproduced on copper, graced the drawing-room table (which was of Louis Philippe *buhl*, with ornate brass heads at the angles).

In our country houses, collections of faïence, in which our mothers also flattered themselves that they were expert, were thought more suitable than pictures. Urbino, Gubbio, and various Italian luster wares, mostly turned out by the industrious Ginori of Florence,[1] abounded in Newport drawing-rooms. I shall never forget my mother's mortification when some ill-advised friend arranged for a newly arrived Italian Minister—Count Corti, I think—to visit her supposed "collection" of "china" (as all forms of porcelain and pottery were then indifferently called). The diplomatist happened to be a collector of some repute, and after one glance at the Ginori output crowding every cabinet and table, he hurriedly draped his surprise in a flow of compliments which did not for a moment deceive my mother. I still burn with the humiliation inflicted by that salutary visit, which had the happy effect of restricting her subsequent purchases to lace fans, or old silver—about which, incidentally, she also knew a good deal, partly, no doubt, because she and my father had inherited some very good examples of Colonial silver from their respective forebears.

This fine silver and Sheffield plate may have called her attention,

8. Salvator Rosa: Italian painter and etcher (1615–1673), of the Neapolitan school; Paul Potter: Dutch animal and landscape painter (1625–1654); Carlo Dolci: Florentine painter (1616–1686), best known for paintings of the suffering Christ and Mary.
9. Mary Magdalen: Mary Magdalene, the New Testament figure of the fallen woman who is redeemed by Jesus, was (with Venus and the Virgin Mary) among the three most popular female subjects for European painters through the nineteenth century. Like "the gamblers," this shamed woman with her famed hair provided an evocative portrayal of sin by framing the subject as a monitory image. Domenichino: Italian painter (1581–1641), also known as Domenico Zampiseri.
1. Urbino: Town in the Marche, central Italy, noted for its majolica ware; Gubbio: Town in Umbria, central Italy, noted for its ceramics; Ginori of Florence: manufacturer of elegant, glossily finished, and decorative porcelines founded by the Marchese Ginori in 1753.

earlier than most people's, to the Colonial furniture that could then be had almost for the asking in New England. At all events, our house at Newport was provided, chiefly through old Mr. Vernon, the Newport antiquarian, with a fine lot of highboys and lowboys, and with sets of the graceful Colonial Hepplewhite chairs. It is a pity she did not develop this branch of her collecting mania and turn a deaf ear to the purveyors of sham Fra Angelicos and Guido Renis,[2] who besieged the artless traveler from every shop door of the Lungarno and the Via Babuino. But even great critics go notoriously wrong in judging contemporary art and letters, and there was, as far as I know, only one Lord Hertford to gather up the matchless treasures of French eighteenth-century furniture in the arid days of the Empire.

Most of the little brownstone houses in which the Salvator Rosas and Domenichinos gloomed so incongruously on friendly drawing-room walls still possessed the surviving fragments of "a gentleman's library"—that is, the collection of good books, well written, well printed, well bound, with which the aboriginal New Yorkers had beguiled their long and dimly lit leisure. In a world of little music and no painting, there was time to read; and I grieve to think of the fate of the treasures to be found in the "libraries" of my childhood—which still belonged to gentlemen, though no longer, as a rule, to readers. Where have they gone, I wonder, all those good books, so inevitably scattered in a country without entail or primogeniture? The rarest, no doubt, have long since been captured by dealers and resold, at soaring prices, to the bibliophiles of two continents, and unexpurgated Hogarths splendidly bound in crushed Levant are no longer outspread on the nursery floor on rainy days, as they used to be for the delectation of my little Rhinelander cousins and myself. (I may add that, though Hogarth was accessible to infants, *Leaves of Grass*,[3] then just beginning to circulate among the most advanced intellectuals, was kept under lock and key, and brought out, like tobacco, only in the absence of "the ladies," to whom the name of Walt Whitman was unmentionable, if not utterly unknown.)

In our New York house, a full-blown specimen of Second Empire decoration, the creation of the fashionable French upholsterer, Marcotte, the books were easily accommodated in a small room on the ground floor which my father used as his study. This room was lined with low bookcases where, behind glass doors, languished the younger son's meager portion of a fine old family library. The walls were hung with a handsome wallpaper imitating the green damask of the curtains, and as the Walter Scott[4] tradition still lingered, and there was felt to be some obscure (perhaps Faustian) relation between the Middle Ages and

2. Fra Angelico: Florentine painter (c. 1400–55), also known as Guido, Guidolino di Pietro, and Giovanaida da Fiesole; Guido Reni: Italian painter and engraver (1575–1642).
3. Hogarth: William Hogarth (1697–1764), known for his engravings of politically satirical subjects. *Leaves of Grass*: Collection of poems (published and expanded from 1855 to 1892) by American poet Walt Whitman (1819–92); Whitman's poems celebrating the body and sexuality were considered so scandalous during Wharton's childhood that, as Wharton recalls, they were kept in locked drawers.
4. Sir Walter Scott (1771–1832), popular Scottish writer known as the originator of the historical novel.

culture, this sixteen-foot-square room in a New York house was furnished with a huge oak mantelpiece sustained by vizored knights, who
repeated themselves at the angles of a monumental writing table,
where I imagine little writing was done except the desperate calcula-
tions over which I seem to see my poor father always bent, in the vain
effort to squeeze my mother's expenditure into his narrowing income.

Luckily, once the unhappy consequences of the Civil War had worn
off, prosperity returned to us, as it did to the greater number of old
New Yorkers. To New York, in especial, it came with a rush; but in the
difficult years between my father must have had many anxious hours.
My mother was far worse than a collector—she was a born "shopper";
and the born shopper can never resist a bargain if the object is in itself
"good value," no matter how little the purchaser may need it. Perhaps
it was for this reason that my mother's houses were always unfinished
and that, for instance, a stately conservatory, opening out of the
billiard-room in our Twenty-third Street house, remained an empty
waste, unheated and flowerless, because the money gave out with the
furnishing of the billiard-room.

## V

We had returned when I was ten years old from a long sojourn in
Europe, so that the New York from which I received my most vivid impressions was only that tiny fraction of a big city which came within
the survey of a much governessed and guarded little girl—hardly less
of a little girl when she "came out" (at seventeen) than when she first
arrived on the scene, at ten.

Perhaps the best way of recapturing the atmosphere of my little corner of the metropolis is to try to remember what our principal interests were—I say "our" because, being virtually an only child, since my
big brothers had long since gone forth into the world, I shared either
directly or indirectly in most of the household goings-on.

My father and mother entertained a great deal and dined out a great
deal; but in these diversions I shared only to the extent of hanging
over the stair-rail to see the guests sweeping up to our drawing-room
or, conversely, my mother sweeping down to her carriage, resplendent
in train, aigrette, and opera cloak. But though my parents were much
invited, and extremely hospitable, the *tempo* of New York society was
so moderate that not infrequently they remained at home in the
evening. After-dinner visits were still customary, and on these occasions old family friends would drop in, ceremoniously arrayed in white
gloves and white tie, with a tall hat, always carried up to the drawing
room and placed on the floor beside the chair of the caller—who, in
due course, was regaled with the ten o'clock cup of tea which followed
the heavy repast at seven-thirty. On these occasions the lonely little
girl that I was remained in the drawing-room later than her usual bed-
time, and the kindly whiskered gentlemen encouraged her to join in
the mild talk. It was all very simple and friendly, and the conversation
ranged safely from Langdons, Van Rensselaers, and Lydigs to Riveses,

The Old Academy of Music (*top*) and the Metropolitan Opera House (*bottom*).

Duers, and Schermerhorns, with an occasional allusion to the Opera
(which there was some talk of transplanting from the old Academy of
Music to a "real" Opera House, like Covent Garden or the Scala),[5] or
to Mrs. Scott-Siddons's readings from Shakespeare, or Aunt Mary
Jones's evening receptions, or my uncle Fred Rhinelander's ambitious
dream of a Museum of Art in the Central Park, or cousin John King's[6]
difficulty in housing in the exiguous quarters of the New York Historical Society a rather burdensome collection of pictures bequeathed to
it by an eccentric young man whose family one did not wish to offend—a collection which Berenson, visiting it many years later, found
to be replete with treasures, both French and Italian.

But the events in which I took an active part were going to
church—and going to the theater. I venture to group them together
because, looking back across the blurred expanse of a long life, I see
them standing up side by side, like summits catching the light when
all else is in shadow. Going to church on Sunday mornings was, I fear,
no more than an unescapable family duty; but in the afternoon my father and I used to return alone together to the second service. Calvary
Church, at the corner of Gramercy Park, was our parish church, and
probably even in that day of hideous religious edifices, few less æs-
thetically pleasing could have been found. The service was "low," the
music indifferent, and the fuliginous chancel window of the Crucifix-
ion a horror to alienate any imaginative mind from all Episcopal forms
of ritual; but the Rector, the Reverend Dr. Washburn, was a man of
great learning, and possessed of a singularly beautiful voice—and I
fear it was chiefly to hear Dr. Washburn read the Evening Lessons
that my father and I were so regular in our devotions. Certainly it is to
Dr. Washburn that I owe the discovery of the matchless beauty of
English seventeenth-century prose; and the organ-roll of Isaiah, Job,
and above all, of the lament of David over the dead Absalom, always
come back to me in the accents of that voice, of which I can only say
that it was worthy to interpret the English Bible.

The other great emotion of my childhood was connected with the
theater. Not that I was, even at a tender age, an indiscriminate
theater-lover. On the contrary, something in me has always resisted
the influence of crowds and shows, and I have hardly ever been able to
yield myself unreservedly to a spectacle shared with a throng of people. But my distrust of theatrical representation goes deeper than that.
I am involuntarily hypercritical of any impersonation of characters already so intensely visible to my imagination that anyone else's conception of them interferes with that inward vision. And this applies not
only to plays already familiar to me by reading, but to any stage representation—for, five minutes after I have watched the actors in a new
play, I have formed an inner picture of what they ought to look like

5. Covent Garden: Royal Opera House, London (first built in 1732, present structure built
    1858); Scala: Opera house in Milan, Italy (built 1776).
6. Mrs. Scott-Siddons: See p. 139, *n.* 8; Aunt Mary Jones's evening receptions: See photo-
    graphs of Mrs. Jones's house, p. 237; John King: Governor of New York, 1857–59; possibly a
    reference to John Kings's father, Rufus King (1755–1827), senator and diplomat, instru-
    mental in developing the New–York Historical Society.

and speak like, and as I once said, in my rash youth, to someone who had asked me if I enjoyed the theater: "Well, I always want to get up on the stage and show them how they ought to act"—a reply naturally interpreted as a proof of intolerable self-assurance.

However, in spite of my inability to immerse myself in the play, I *did* enjoy the theater in my childhood, partly because it was something new, a window opening on the foam of faëryland (or at least I always hoped to see faëryland through that window), and partly, I still believe, because most of the acting I saw in those early days in New York was really much better than any I have seen since. The principal theaters were, in fact, still in possession of good English companies, of whom the elders had played together for years, and preserved and handed on the great tradition of well-trained repertory companies, versus the evil "star" system which was so soon to crowd them out of business.

At Wallack's Theatre, still ruled by the deeply dyed and undoubtedly absurd Lester Wallack, there were such first-rate actors as old Mrs. Ponisi, Beckett, Harry Montague, and Ada Dyas; and when they deserted the classic repertory (Sheridan, Goldsmith, etc.)[7] for the current drama, the average play they gave was about as good as the same type of play now acted by one or more out-of-focus stars with a fringe of obscure satellites.

But our most exciting evenings came when what the Germans call "guest-players" arrived from London, Berlin, or Rome with good repertory companies. Theater-going, for me, was in fact largely a matter of *listening to voices,* and never shall I forget the rapture of first hearing

>      And gentlemen in England now abed
>      Shall think themselves accursed they were not here,

in George Rignold's[8] vibrant baritone, when he brought Henry V to New York.

\*    \*    \*

In the way of other spectacles New York did not as yet provide much. There was in fact only the old Academy of Music, where Campanini, in his prime, warbled to an audience still innocently following the eighteenth-century tradition that the Opera was a social occasion, invented to stimulate conversation; but my recollection of those performances is not clear, for, by the time I was judged old enough to be taken to them, the new Opera House was inaugurated, and with it came Wagner, and with Wagner a cultivated and highly musical German audience in the stalls, which made short work of the chatter in the boxes. I well remember the astonishment with which we learned

7. Wallack's Theatre: See p. 72, *n.* 1; Mrs. Ponisi: Elizabeth Ponisi (1818–1899), best known for her roles as elderly women and aristocratic ladies, performed at Wallack's Theater for seventeen years; Harry Montague, and Ada Dyas: See p. 72, *n.* 2; Sheridan: Richard Brinsley Sheridan (1751–1816), playwright and theater owner best known for his masterpiece *School for Scandal* (1777); Goldsmith: Oliver Goldsmith (1730–74) Irish-born man of letters best known for his novel *The Vicar of Wakefield* (serialized, 1761–1762; published, 1766) and for his acclaimed stage comedy *She Stoops to Conquer* (1773).
8. See p. 64, *n.* 1.

"The Shaughraun" (1874). The Ribbon-Kissing Scene with H. J. Montague and Ada Dyas.

that it was "bad form" to talk during the acts, and the almost immediate compliance of the box-audience with this new rule of politeness, which thereafter was broken only by two or three thick-skinned newcomers in the social world.

Apart from the Opera, the only popular entertainments I can recall were Barnum's three-ring circus (a sort of modern ocean liner before the letter)—and Moody and Sankey's revivalist meetings. I group the two in no spirit of disrespect to the latter, but because both were new and sensational, and both took place in the old Madison Square Garden,[9] at that time New York's only large auditorium, where prize fights and circuses placidly alternated with religious revivals, without any sign of public disapproval. But I must add that, sincere as no doubt the protagonists were, there was a theatrical element in their call to religion which, in those pre-Eddyan[1] days, deeply offended the taste of many people; and certainly, among the throngs frequenting their meetings many avowedly went for the sake of Sankey's singing rather than of his companion's familiar chats with the Almighty. Though America has always been the chosen field of sensational religious performances, the New York of my childhood was still averse to any sort of pious exhibitionism; but as I was never allowed to assist at the Moody and Sankey meetings, my impression of them is gathered entirely from the comments of my father's friends, from whom I fear Saint Francis of Assisi and Savonarola[2] would have received small encouragement. * * *

*    *    *

# EDITH WHARTON

## From *A Backward Glance*†

### [*The Background*]

*    *    *

* * * The customs of the day were simple, and in my father's set the chief diversions were sea-fishing, boat-racing and wild-fowl shooting. There were no clubs as yet in New York, and my mother, whose view of

9. Barnum's three ring circus . . . Madison Square Garden: The already famous showman P. T. Barnum (1810–1891) founded his circus in 1870, performing in the former railroad shed at 26th Street and Madison Avenue for the first time in 1874; initially known as Barnum's Monster Classical and Geological Hippodrome and later The Great Roman Hippodrome, the structure was named Madison Square Garden in 1879 after William Vanderbilt regained control of the site. Moody and Sankey's revivalist meetings: American evangelists Dwight Lyman Moody (1837–1899) and Ira David Sankey (1840–1908) organized religious meetings that featured hymns and focused on God's love and mercy rather than on damnation.
1. Antedating the rise in power of the Christian Science movement, founded c. 1866 by Mary Baker Eddy (1821–1910). Opposed to medical intervention, this movement put its faith in divine healing.
2. Saint Francis of Assisi (1181/82–1226), founder of the Franciscan order, left his successful family, embracing a life of poverty fomenting a religious movement within Catholicism that focused on the spiritual needs of the poor and the illiterate. Fra Girolamo Savanarola (1452–1498), politically powerful Florentine monk who was hanged and burned for heresy after defying Papal orders that he cease preaching against the corruption of the church.
† New York: Charles Scribner's Sons, 1934, pp. 20–25, 44–47, 53–62.

life was incurably prosaic, always said that this accounted for the early marriages, as the young men of that day "had nowhere else to go". The young married couples, Langdons, Hones, Newbolds, Edgars, Joneses, Gallatins, etc., entertained each other a good deal, and my mother's sloping shoulders were often displayed above the elegant fringed and ruffled "berthas"[1] of her Parisian dinner gowns. The amusing diary of Mr. Philip Hone gives a good idea of the simple but incessant exchange of hospitality between the young people who ruled New York society before the Civil War.

My readers, by this time, may be wondering what were the particular merits, private or civic, of these amiable persons. Their lives, as one looks back, certainly seem lacking in relief; but I believe their value lay in upholding two standards of importance in any community, that of education and good manners, and of scrupulous probity in business and private affairs. New York has always been a commercial community, and in my infancy the merits and defects of its citizens were those of a mercantile middle class. The first duty of such a class was to maintain a strict standard of uprightness in affairs; and the gentlemen of my father's day did maintain it, whether in the law, in banking, shipping or wholesale commercial enterprises. I well remember the horror excited by any irregularity in affairs, and the relentless social ostracism inflicted on the families of those who lapsed from professional or business integrity. In one case, where two or three men of high social standing were involved in a discreditable bank failure, their families were made to suffer to a degree that would seem merciless to our modern judgment. But perhaps the New Yorkers of that day were unconsciously trying to atone for their culpable neglect of state and national politics, from which they had long disdainfully held aloof, by upholding the sternest principles of business probity, and inflicting the severest social penalties on whoever lapsed from them. At any rate I should say that the qualities justifying the existence of our old society were social amenity and financial incorruptibility; and we have travelled far enough from both to begin to estimate their value.

The weakness of the social structure of my parents' day was a blind dread of innovation, an instinctive shrinking from responsibility. In 1824 (or thereabouts) a group of New York gentlemen who were appointed to examine various plans for the proposed laying-out of the city, and whose private sympathies were notoriously anti-Jeffersonian and undemocratic, decided against reproducing the beautiful system of squares, circles and radiating avenues which Major L'Enfant, the brilliant French engineer, had designed for Washington, because it was thought "undemocratic" for citizens of the new republic to own building-plots which were not all of exactly the same shape, size—and *value!* This naïf document, shown to me by Robert Minturn, a descendant of a member of the original committee, and doubtless often since published, typified the prudent attitude of a society of prosperous business men who have no desire to row against the current.

---

1. Wide collars that cover the shoulders.

A little world so well-ordered and well-to-do does not often produce either eagles or fanatics, and both seem to have been conspicuously absent from the circle in which my forbears moved. In old-established and powerful societies originality of character is smiled at, and even encouraged to assert itself; but conformity is the bane of middle-class communities, and as far as I can recall, only two of my relations stepped out of the strait path of the usual. One was a mild and inoffensive old bachelor cousin, very small and frail, and reputed of immense wealth and morbid miserliness, who built himself a fine house in his youth, and lived in it for fifty or sixty years, in a state of negativeness and insignificance which made him proverbial even in our conforming class—and then, in his last years (so we children were told) *sat on a marble shelf, and thought he was a bust of Napoleon.*

Cousin Edmund's final illusion was not without pathos, but as a source of inspiration to my childish fancy he was a poor thing compared with George Alfred. George Alfred was another cousin, but one whom I had never seen, and could never hope to see, because years before he had—vanished. Vanished, that is, out of society, out of respectability, out of the safe daylight world of "nice people" and reputable doings. Before naming George Alfred my mother altered her expression and lowered her voice. Thank heaven *she* was not responsible for him—he belonged to my father's side of the family! But they too had long since washed their hands of George Alfred—had ceased even to be aware of his existence. If my mother pronounced his name it was solely, I believe, out of malice, out of the child's naughty desire to evoke some nursery hobgoblin by muttering a dark incantation like *Eena Meena Mina Mo,* and then darting away with affrighted backward looks to see if there is anything there.

My mother always darted away from George Alfred's name after pronouncing it, and it was not until I was grown up, and had acquired greater courage and persistency, that one day I drove her to the wall by suddenly asking: "But, Mamma, *what did he do?*" "Some woman"—my mother muttered; and no one accustomed to the innocuous word as now used can imagine the shades of disapproval, scorn and yet excited curiosity, that "some" could then connote on the lips of virtue.

George Alfred—and some woman! Who was she? From what heights had she fallen with him, to what depths dragged him down? For in those simple days it was always a case of "the woman tempted me". To her respectable sisters her culpability was as certain in advance as Predestination to the Calvinist. But I was not fated to know more—thank heaven I was not! For our shadowy Paolo and Francesca, circling together on the "accursèd air", somewhere outside the safe boundaries of our old New York, gave me, I verily believe, my earliest glimpse of the poetry that Goethe missed in the respectable world of the Hirschgraben,[2] and that my ancestors assuredly failed to find, or to cre-

---

2. Predestination to the Calvinist: The doctrine that all events are foreordained by God's decree; Paolo and Francesca: Lovers in Canto V of the *Inferno* by Dante Alghieri (1265–1321) who were condemned for their adulterous acts to whirl through the air in the second circle of Hell. Hirschgraben: Location of Goethe's childhood home in Frankfurt Am Main.

ate, between the Battery and Union Square. The vision of poor feature-less unknown Alfred and his siren, lurking in some cranny of my imag-ination, hinted at regions perilous, dark and yet lit with mysterious fires, just outside the world of copy-book axioms, and the old obedi-ences that were in my blood; and the hint was useful—for a novelist.

## Little Girl

I

\* \* \*

I remember once asking an old New Yorker why he never went abroad, and his answering: "Because I can't bear to cross Murray Street." It was indeed an unsavoury experience, and the shameless squalor of the purlieus of the New York docks in the 'seventies dis-mayed my childish eyes, stored with the glories of Rome and the ar-chitectural majesty of Paris. But it was summer; we were soon at Newport, under the friendly gables of Pencraig;[1] and to a little girl long pent up in hotels and flats there was inexhaustible delight in the freedom of a staircase to run up and down, of lawns and trees, a meadow full of clover and daisies, a pony to ride, terriers to romp with, a sheltered cove to bathe in, flower-beds spicy with "carnation, lily, rose", and a kitchen-garden crimson with strawberries and sweet as honey with Seckel pears.

The roomy and pleasant house of Pencraig was surrounded by a ve-randah wreathed in clematis and honeysuckle, and below it a lawn sloped to a deep daisied meadow, beyond which were a private bathing-beach and boat-landing. From the landing we used to fish for "scup-pers" and "porgies", succulent little fish that were grilled or fried for high tea; and off the rocky point lay my father's and brothers' "cat-boats", the graceful wide-sailed craft that flecked the bay like sea-gulls.

\* \* \*

Most vivid is my memory of the picturesque archery club meetings of which the grown daughters of the house, Margaret [Rutherford] (afterward Mrs. Henry White) and her sister Louisa were among the most brilliant performers. When the club met we children were al-lowed to be present, and to circulate among the grown-ups (usually all three of us astride of one patient donkey); and a pretty sight the meet-ing was, with parents and elders seated in a semicircle on the turf be-hind the lovely archeresses in floating silks or muslins, with their wide leghorn hats, and heavy veils flung back only at the moment of aiming. These veils are associated with all the summer festivities of my child-hood. In that simple society there was an almost pagan worship of physical beauty, and the first question asked about any youthful new-comer on the social scene was invariably: "Is she pretty?" or: "Is he handsome?"—for good looks were as much prized in young men as in maidens. For the latter no grace was rated as high as "a complexion". It is hard to picture nowadays the shell-like transparence, the lumi-

1. The name of Edith Wharton's parents' home in Newport.

Bird's-Eye Map of Newport (1888).

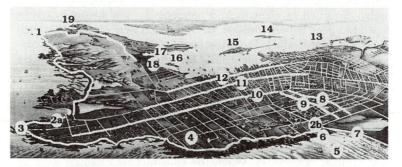

**Map to Sites of Interest for** *The Age of Innocence.* The map key locates places named in the novel as well as Edith Wharton's parents' house, Pencraig (no longer standing), and her own first house at Land's End.

1.  Ocean Drive
2a. Cliff Walk, North End
2b. Cliff Walk, South End
3.  Land's End, Wharton's first home after marriage
4.  The Breakers, August Belmont's estate
5.  The Atlantic
6.  Paradise Rock
7.  Easton's Beach
8.  Catherine Road
9.  Old Beach Road
10. Bellevue Road
11. Spring Street
12. Thames Street
13. Narragansett Bay
14. Rose Island
15. Goat Island
16. Lime Rock, Ida Lewis's light house
17. Fort Adams
18. Pencraig, Wharton's childhood home
19. Castle Hill Light

**Watching the Regatta at Castle Hill (1890s).** Spectators watch the races from the western shore of Newport as catboats ply the waters of Narragansett Bay.

**The Newport Young Ladies' Archery Society** (ca. 1872). The Archery Society, referred to locally as the Edgerston Club, was founded in 1872 by Lewis Rutherford, a neighbor of Edith Wharton's parents. Originally, twenty-four members competed yearly for the honor of wearing the club's gold bracelet. In *The Age of Innocence*, May Welland Archer competes in such a tournament for a diamond tipped arrow that will be passed down as a family heirloom.

nous red-and-white, of those young cheeks untouched by paint or pow-
der, in which the blood came and went like the lights of an aurora.
Beauty was unthinkable without "a complexion", and to defend that
treasure against sun and wind, and the arch-enemy sea air, veils as
thick as curtains (some actually of woollen barège)[2] were habitually
worn. It must have been very uncomfortable for the wearers, who could
hardly see or breathe; but even to my childish eyes the effect was dazzling when the curtain was drawn, and young beauty shone forth. My
dear friend Howard Sturgis used to laugh at the "heavily veiled" heroines who lingered on so late in Victorian fiction, and were supposed to
preserve their incognito until they threw back their veils; but if he had
known fashionable Newport in my infancy he would have seen that
the novelists' formula was based on what was once a reality.

Those archery meetings greatly heightened my infantile desire to
"tell a story", and the young gods and goddesses I used to watch
strolling across the Edgerston lawn were the prototypes of my first
novels. The spectacle was a charming one to an imaginative child already caught in the toils of romance; no wonder I remember it better
than my studies. * * *

*   *   *

To the modern child my little-girl life at Pencraig would seem sadly
tame and uneventful, for its chief distractions were the simple ones of
swimming and riding. My mother, like most married women of her
day, had long since given up exercise, my father's only active pursuits
were boating and shooting, and there was no one to ride with me but
the coachman—nor was our end of the island a happy place for eques-
trianism. I enjoyed scampering on my pony over the hard dull roads;
but it was better fun to swim in our own cove, in the jolly company of
brothers, cousins and young neighbours. There were always two or
three "cat-boats" moored off our point, but I never shared the passion
of my father and brothers for sailing. To be a passenger was too sedentary, and I felt no desire to sail the boat myself, being too wrapt in
dreams to burden my mind with so exact a science. Best of all I liked
our weekly walks with Mr. Rutherfurd over what we called the
Rocks—the rough moorland country, at that time without roads or
houses, extending from the placid blue expanse of Narragansett bay to
the gray rollers of the Atlantic. Every Sunday he used to collect the
children of the few friends living near us, and take them, with his
own, for a tramp across this rugged country to the sea.

Yet what I recall of those rambles is not so much the comradeship of
the other children, or the wise and friendly talk of our guide, as my secret sensitiveness to the landscape—something in me quite incommu-
nicable to others, that was tremblingly and inarticulately awake to
every detail of wind-warped fern and wide-eyed briar rose, yet more
profoundly alive to a unifying magic beneath the diversities of the visible scene—a power with which I was in deep and solitary communion
whenever I was alone with nature. It was the same tremor that had

2. A sheer fabric, made of a wool blend with either silk or cotton, used for women's apparel.

stirred in me in the spring woods of Mamaroneck, when I heard the whisper of the arbutus and the starry choir of the dogwood; and it has never since been still.

2

The old New York to which I came back as a little girl meant to me chiefly my father's library. Now for the first time I had my fill of books. Out of doors, in the mean monotonous streets, without architecture, without great churches or palaces, or any visible memorials of an historic past, what could New York offer to a child whose eyes had been filled with shapes of immortal beauty and immemorial significance? One of the most depressing impressions of my childhood is my recollection of the intolerable ugliness of New York, of its untended streets and the narrow houses so lacking in external dignity, so crammed with smug and suffocating upholstery. How could I understand that people who had seen Rome and Seville, Paris and London, could come back to live contentedly between Washington Square and the Central Park? What I could not guess was that this little low-studded rectangular New York, cursed with its universal chocolate-coloured coating of the most hideous stone ever quarried, this cramped horizontal gridiron of a town without towers, porticoes, fountains or perspectives, hide-bound in its deadly uniformity of mean ugliness, would fifty years later be as much a vanished city as Atlantis or the lowest layer of Schliemann's Troy,[3] or that the social organization which that prosaic setting had slowly secreted would have been swept to oblivion with the rest. Nothing but the Atlantis-fate of old New York, the New York which had slowly but continuously developed from the early seventeenth century to my own childhood, makes that childhood worth recalling now.

Looking back at that little world, and remembering the "hoard of petty maxims" with which its elders preached down every sort of initiative, I have often wondered at such lassitude in the descendants of the men who first cleared a place for themselves in a new world, and then fought for the right to be masters there. What had become of the spirit of the pioneers and the revolutionaries? Perhaps the very violence of their effort had caused it to exhaust itself in the next generation, or the too great prosperity succeeding on almost unexampled hardships had produced, if not inertia, at least indifference in all matters except business or family affairs.

Even the acquiring of wealth had ceased to interest the little society into which I was born. In the case of some of its members, such as the Astors and Goelets, great fortunes, originating in a fabulous increase of New York real estate values, had been fostered by judicious investments and prudent administration; but of feverish money-making, in Wall Street or in railway, shipping or industrial enterprises, I heard

3. Atlantis: A legendary civilization supposed by Plato and Arab geographers to have been enveloped by the sea after an earthquake around 1500 B.C.; Schliemann's Troy: Reference to the discovery in 1871 of the ruins of Troy—previously believed to be no more than a Homeric myth—by the German archaeologist Heinrich von Schliemann (1822–1890) at Hissarlik, Turkey.

nothing in my youth. Some of my father's friends may have been bankers, others have followed one of the liberal professions, usually the law; in fact almost all the young men I knew read law for a while after leaving college, though comparatively few practised it in after years. But for the most part my father's contemporaries, and those of my brothers also, were men of leisure—a term now almost as obsolete as the state it describes. It will probably seem unbelievable to present-day readers that only one of my own near relations, and not one of my husband's, was "in business". The group to which we belonged was composed of families to whom a middling prosperity had come, usually by the rapid rise in value of inherited real estate, and none of whom, apparently, aspired to be more than moderately well-off. I never in my early life came in contact with the gold-fever in any form, and when I hear that nowadays business life in New York is so strenuous that men and women never meet socially before the dinner hour, I remember the delightful week-day luncheons of my early married years, where the men were as numerous as the women.

*      *      *

The child of the well-to-do, hedged in by nurses and governesses, seldom knows much of its parents' activities. I have only the vaguest recollection of the way in which my father and mother spent their days. I know that my father was a director on the principal charitable boards of New York—the Blind Asylum and the Bloomingdale Insane Asylum among others; and that during Lent a ladies' "sewing class" met at our house to work with my mother for the poor. I also recall frequent drives with my mother, when the usual afternoon round of card-leaving was followed by a walk in the Central Park, and a hunt for violets and hepaticas in the secluded dells of the Ramble. In the evenings my parents went occasionally to the theatre, but never, as far as I remember, to a concert, or any kind of musical performance, until the Opera, then only sporadic, became an established entertainment, to which one went (as in eighteenth century Italy) chiefly if not solely for the pleasure of conversing with one's friends. Their most frequent distraction was dining out or dinner giving. Sometimes the dinners were stately and ceremonious (with engraved invitations issued three weeks in advance, soups, "thick" and "clear", and a Roman punch[4] half way through the *menu*), but more often they were intimate and sociable, though always the occasion of much excellent food and old wine being admirably served, and discussed with suitable gravity.

My father had inherited from his family a serious tradition of good cooking, with a cellar of vintage clarets, and of Madeira which had rounded the Cape. The "Jones" Madeira (my father's) and the "Newbold" (my uncle's) enjoyed a particular celebrity even in that day of noted cellars. The following generation, interested only in champagne and claret, foolishly dispersed these precious stores. My brothers sold my father's cellar soon after his death; and after my marriage, dining in a *nouveau riche* house of which the master was unfamiliar with old

4. See pp. 328–29.

New York cousinships, I had pressed on me, as a treat not likely to
have come the way of one of my modest condition, a glass of "the famous Newbold Madeira."

My mother, if left to herself, would probably not have been much
interested in the pleasures of the table. My father's Dutch blood accounted for his gastronomic enthusiasm; his mother, who was a
Schermerhorn, was reputed to have the best cook in New York. But to
know about good cooking was a part of every young wife's equipment,
and my mother's favourite cookery books (Francatelli's and Mrs.
Leslie's) are thickly interleaved with sheets of yellowing note paper, on
which, in a script of ethereal elegance, she records the making of
"Mrs. Joshua Jones's scalloped oysters with cream", "Aunt Fanny Gal-
latin's fried chicken", "William Edgar's punch", and the special recipes
of our two famous negro cooks, Mary Johnson and Susan Minneman.
These great artists stand out, brilliantly turbaned and ear-ringed, from
a Snyders-like[5] background of game, fish and vegetables transformed
into a succession of succulent repasts by their indefatigable blue-
nailed hands: Mary Johnson, a gaunt towering woman of a rich bronzy
black, with huge golden hoops in her ears, and crisp African crinkles
under vividly patterned kerchiefs; Susan Minneman, a small smiling
mulatto, more quietly attired, but as great a cook as her predecessor.

Ah, what artists they were! How simple yet sure were their methods—the mere perfection of broiling, roasting and basting—and what
an unexampled wealth of material, vegetable and animal, their genius
had to draw upon! Who will ever again taste anything in the whole
range of gastronomy to equal their corned beef, their boiled turkeys
with stewed celery and oyster sauce, their fried chickens, broiled red-
heads, corn fritters, stewed tomatoes, rice griddle cakes, strawberry
short-cake and vanilla ices? I am now enumerating only our daily fare,
that from which even my tender years did not exclude me; but when
my parents "gave a dinner", and terrapin and canvas-back ducks, or (in
their season) broiled Spanish mackerel, soft-shelled crabs with a mayonnaise of celery, and peach-fed Virginia hams cooked in champagne
(I am no doubt confusing all the seasons in this allegoric evocation of
their riches), lima-beans in cream, corn soufflés and salads of oyster-
crabs, poured in varied succulence from Mary Johnson's lifted cornu-
copia—ah, then, the *gourmet* of that long-lost day, when cream was
cream and butter butter and coffee coffee, and meat fresh every day,
and game hung just for the proper number of hours, might lean back
in his chair and murmur "Fate cannot harm me" over his cup of Moka
and his glass of authentic Chartreuse.[6]

*        *        *

And what of the guests who gathered at my father's table to enjoy the
achievements of the Dark Ladies? I remember a mild blur of rosy and

5. A background of animals and woodland hunting scenes like those of Flemish painter Frans
   Snyders (1579–1657).
6. Moka: Named for Arabian seaport near a famous coffee growing area, this drink (usually
   "mocha") is made from an infusion of strong coffee and chocolate; Chartreuse: a bright
   green herbal liqueur created as a curative by a Carthusian monk in early eighteenth-century
   France.

white-whiskered gentlemen, of ladies with bare sloping shoulders rising flower-like from voluminous skirts, peeped at from the stair-top while wraps were removed in the hall below. A great sense of leisure emanated from their kindly faces and voices. No motors waited to rush them on to ball or opera; balls were few and widely spaced, the opera just beginning; and "Opera night" would not have been chosen for one of my mother's big dinners. There being no haste, and a prodigious amount of good food to be disposed of, the guests sat long at table; and when my mother bowed slightly to the lady facing her on my father's right, and flounces and trains floated up the red velvet stair-carpet to the white-and-gold drawing-room with tufted purple satin arm-chairs, and voluminous purple satin curtains festooned with buttercup yellow fringe, the gentlemen settled down again to claret and Madeira, sent duly westward, and followed by coffee and Havana cigars.

My parents' guests ate well, and drank good wine with discernment; but a more fastidious taste had shortened the enormous repasts and deep bumpers of colonial days, and in twenty minutes the whiskered gentlemen had joined the flounced ladies on the purple settees for another half hour of amiable chat, accompanied by the cup of tea which always rounded off the evening. How mild and leisurely it all seems in the glare of our new century! Small parochial concerns no doubt formed the staple of the talk. Art and music and literature were rather timorously avoided (unless Trollope's last novel were touched upon, or a discreet allusion made to Mr. William Astor's audacious acquisition of a Bouguereau Venus),[7] and the topics chiefly dwelt on were personal: the thoughtful discussion of food, wine, horses ("high steppers" were beginning to be much sought after), the laying out and planting of country-seats, the selection of "specimen" copper beeches and fern-leaved maples for lawns just beginning to be shorn smooth by the new hand-mowers, and those plans of European travel which filled so large a space in the thought of old New Yorkers. From my earliest infancy I had always seen about me people who were either just arriving from "abroad" or just embarking on a European tour. The old New Yorker was in continual contact with the land of his fathers, and it was not until I went to Boston on my marriage that I found myself in a community of wealthy and sedentary people seemingly too lacking in intellectual curiosity to have any desire to see the world.

\*   \*   \*

7. See p. 15, *n*. 2.

# R. W. B. LEWIS

## From *Edith Wharton: A Biography*†

### [*Entry into Society*]

\* \* \*

Until about 1870 the social emergence of a young New York lady
had consisted in assembling in her own home assorted relatives and
family friends and solemnly introducing the girl to them. But in 1870,
Archibald Gracie King had the idea of hiring the largest room in the
fashionable Delmonico's—then situated on Fifth Avenue where Broadway and Twenty-sixth Street transected it—for a ball and supper in
honor of his daughter's entrance into society. Thereafter the first appearance of debutantes became increasingly a public affair.

When it came time for Edith's debut, however, Lucretia[1] refused to
countenance so vulgar a display. The affair took place late in 1879 in
the private ballroom—one of the few in the city—of Mrs. Levi Morton, wife of the well-known millionaire, on Fifth Avenue near Forty-
second Street. Edith apprehensively accompanied her parents there,
clad in a low-necked bodice of pale green brocade and a white muslin
skirt, carrying a bouquet of lilies of the valley. The event was not as
terrible for Edith as her mother's coming-out had been for Lucretia,
but Edith would recall it as "a long cold agony of shyness"; nothing
paralyzed her more than to be the object of attention by scores of people. She huddled next to Lucretia, unable to accept the many invitations to dance, and scarcely able to exchange greetings with the young
men who had so often dined in her home. It was a memorably painful
initiation for one whose social life in later years on two continents
would be so full and not infrequently so extravagant, but for whom
shyness, variously caused and variously disguised, would be a permanent feature in her character.

At the time Edith Jones was edging into it, New York society was
contradictory in nature, and it had upon her a contradictory but lasting effect. Much of that social world was subject to incessant change
and movement, as fortunes sprang up and ever larger mansions were
built. The Joneses and their kin, however, belonged to the narrowest
and stablest portion of society: an enclave of sorts within—in their
view, *above*—the broader, looser, and much more conspicuous element. The latter was made up of exceedingly wealthy and often recently arrived commercial folk, with homes on Fifth Avenue; and it
was their children, in a phrase of the 1880s, who filled the ranks of
"the ultra-fashionable dancing people," and who indeed constituted
society for the outsider or the visitor. There was of course considerable
mingling between the two sets and a partial sharing of mores. But they
tended to look askance at each other, to measure breeding against

† New York: Harper Colophon Books, 1975, pp. 33–36, 37–42, 44–46, 51–54.
1. Lucretia Rhinelander Jones (1824–1901), Edith Wharton's mother.

wealth and tradition against display. We shall shortly see a characteristic episode of social war between them—one of enduring importance for Edith Wharton.

She was acutely watchful of the entire social spectrum, from aristocrat to *arriviste*, but it was the narrowest segment that went into the early shaping of her. Looking back upon it, she was to think that its ideals were small, cautious, and essentially middle class. Yet they struck her in retrospect as "singularly coherent and respectable as contrasted with the chaos of indiscriminate appetites which made up [New York society's] modern tendencies." Moral coherence, restraint, dignity, integrity, and fidelity to the domestic pieties: these were among the values to be prized.

\*    \*    \*

It was not a world that encouraged literary leanings. Edith Wharton retained the impression that the intellectuals and artists who might be encountered amid the wholly masculine company at the Century Club were on the whole a boring lot. \* \* \*

It was amid such circumstances and attitudes that Edith Jones completed her adolescence and entered womanhood. Beneath her quietly watchful exterior, she was absorbing and combining, rejecting and no doubt mentally reaching beyond the assorted qualities of the life around her. She could not, anywhere in her old New York, have been the easiest of company. She was clothes-conscious and money-conscious, but she was also addicted to books and ideas and the world of the imagination. There was, indeed, no one quite like her in her New York generation. A growing awareness of the fact deepened her sense of loneliness and gave her an air of unpredictability. She was everything that was right and regular, someone was to say about her, but the young hawk looked out of her eyes.

In the phrase Edith Wharton used about it, it was an age of innocence. The word applied in particular to the young girl, the debutante, whose single-minded purpose, her elders constantly reminded her, was to make a suitable marriage. To this end her mother's function was to supply her with elegant clothes and make every arrangement to launch her upon a proper worldly career. It was not her mother's function, Edith Jones had to learn, to supply any hints about the real relationship between married men and women. About all that, the maternal contribution was an elaborate pattern of mystification, something which the mature Edith Wharton regarded with rancorous regret.

But the age was innocent in larger and more appreciable ways. If social engagements were all-absorbing, the pace was leisurely and the atmosphere decorous. One associated social life with the arrival of winter—the "season" began around the first of December—and one saw it, in retrospect, through a haze of snow. It seemed to snow more often in those New York winters, and the snow seemed to lie in cleaner heaps on the sidewalks than in later years. One of the regular diversions was to walk along Fifth Avenue or Broadway, well muffled, while snow swept down silently onto the roofs of the horsecars and the steps of the basement entryways. Snow could also provide difficulties. Edith Jones seems to have been the girl she herself referred to in a memoir who turned up at the wrong brownstone front door one evening in a driving snowstorm. Informed of her mistake and turned back, she stood amid the swirling snow uncertain which of the other indistinguishable brownstones was her correct destination.

When the ultrafashionable young were not dancing, they could be found tobogganing, sleigh riding, and ice skating in Central Park. But of dancing there was no end. At the series of great balls between December and April, all of them held at Delmonico's, there was dancing—waltzes, quadrilles, "germans," square dances—sometimes until three in the morning, with time out for a midnight supper and champagne. Under the yellow light that shone in soothing dimness at the Family Circle Dancing Class, some two hundred people followed the steps of the two leaders of the cotillion. There was holly on the mirrors and evergreen on the walls at the First Cotillion, just before New Year's, and the ballroom was lit by candles and gaslight. Dance orchestras also played evening after evening in the ballrooms of private homes; fancy-dress balls were revived, and the guests wore their elaborate costumes to dinners before the event.[2]

It was discovered that the number of people who could be fitted comfortably into Mrs. Astor's ballroom at Fifth Avenue and Thirty-fourth Street was about four hundred; Ward McAllister, Mrs. Astor's social entrepreneur, declared that number to represent the maximum size of the whole of genuine New York society. "The 400" turned out pretty much en masse for the three Patriarchs' Balls, the first of which took place a week before Christmas. Delmonico's was more than usually festive for these occasions (also organized by McAllister),[3] the most prestigious ones of the New York season. The music balcony was hidden behind thick hemlock boughs; poinsettia leaves and evergreen adorned the walls, and floral bells made of red and white carnations hung from the chandeliers.

\*     \*     \*

## [A Broken Engagement]

Soon after her coming-out party at Mrs. Levi Morton's, Edith made the acquaintance of a young man named Henry Leyden Stevens. He was a popular member of New York society, and with his glamorous sister Minnie—there is no other adjective for the tall, lovely Mary Fisk Stevens, with her graceful carriage and her rather hard green eyes—he had been coming to Newport for many summers. Their mother, Mrs. Paran Stevens, belonged to what the Joneses and their circle regarded as the pushy and ostentatious new element of society with whom Lucretia Jones did not encourage her children to mix. One imagines that if Lucretia and Marietta Stevens passed one another in their carriages on Bellevue Avenue in Newport, they would exchange only the barest of nods.

2. See pp. 320–28.
3. See pp. 313–17.

Harry Stevens was born in Boston in 1859. He entered St. Mark's School, but left there in 1873 before graduating, probably because of illness. It was at this time, apparently, that he contracted the disease which we have come to recognize as tuberculosis. He went on to Oxford for a stint, less to pursue academic study than (as a newspaper story would put it) to "learn the manly arts and elegances," and thence to Switzerland, the most healthful country in Europe for anyone suffering an affliction of throat or lungs. He made what seemed a complete recovery, and back in Newport he rapidly became known as a leader in sporting events and an expert organizer of games and social outings. It was said to be Harry Stevens who, after visiting his sister in England, brought back sufficient equipment to lay out, on the grounds of his mother's big cottage at Bellevue and Jones Avenues, the first lawn-tennis court in Newport.

Harry must have pursued Edith most assiduously during the winter and spring (1880) after they met. It was certainly the New York season that Edith Wharton would most enjoy remembering. Thanks in particular to her amiable brother Harry's great popularity, she received a swarm of invitations to dinner parties with the young married set and to informal Sunday lunches. Harry Stevens, one supposes, managed to penetrate this tightly knit little group, perhaps to escort Edith to the opera and to meet her in those houses where the drawing rooms were large enough for impromptu dances.

In Newport in June and July, Edith could watch Harry among the other young gentlemen in tail coats playing tennis with the young ladies in tight whaleboned dresses—tennis had replaced archery as Newport's favorite pastime—and no doubt he joined her at bathing parties and took her for an excursion up Narragansett Bay in his mother's white steam yacht. Society's habits were loosening a little, and the old requirement of ladies spending most of their time calling on other ladies had pretty much been given up by Edith's generation. She was free to be driven by her brother or her suitor along the newly built Ocean Drive, which circled down from the bay around to the Atlantic.

One surmises these things with some confidence since before the summer of 1880 was half over, Newporters were beginning to wonder whether Pussy Jones and Harry Stevens might not already be engaged. In fact, they were not. But Harry was probably the young man observed one evening that summer by Daisy Terry holding "animated conversation" with Edith in what looked like a "possibly important tête-à-tête." * * *

In late July, Edith, with her parents and with Harry Stevens in close attendance, turned up at Bar Harbor, that burgeoning resort on the northeast shore of Mount Desert Island, just off the coast of Maine. Mary Cadwalader Jones was already there, in a cottage next to that of the Lewis Rutherfords. * * *

* * *

One of the advantages of Bar Harbor over Newport for Harry and Edith was that it removed them from the sphere of Mrs. Paran Stevens. That somewhat overwhelming woman was not eyeing the courtship with much approval, and given her strength of character she would have the determining voice as to its outcome.

Mrs. Stevens was in the midst of one of the most remarkable and telling social careers in the New York history of the time. The former Marietta Reed was the daughter of a well-to-do grocer of Lowell, Massachusetts. While still in school she attracted the attention of the father of one of her friends, Paran Stevens of Boston, a wealthy widower in his late forties. Stevens fell immediately in love with the gray-eyed, spirited, and rather voluptuous young woman of nineteen, and they were married in 1846.

Stevens had begun his own impressive career by working in a Boston "cook house." Showing a certain genius at hotel management, he built or purchased a string of hotels in several cities and a row of shops and other property. The most luxurious and successful of his ventures was the Fifth Avenue Hotel, of which he had been a part owner since its construction in 1858, on Madison Square, where Broadway and Fifth Avenue divided. Here the Prince of Wales came to indulge in youthful misbehavior; Brazilian, French, and Siamese royalty appeared; and the leaders of New York's Republican party came to discuss, over excellent meals, how to enlarge their share in the city's political and financial future.

Paran Stevens was far more interested in buying fine race horses than in the social life of the day, and it was not until after his death in 1872 that Marietta Stevens felt free to launch her attack upon New York society. The first step took her, with her daughter Minnie, to England, where she met up again with the Prince of Wales and elicited invitations to Sandringham and Marlborough House. The Stevens ladies made a very handsome pair and were the best of company; they were warmly received on all sides. Before the season was over, Minnie Stevens, after rejecting the proposal of a duke, became engaged to Lord Arthur Paget, a captain in the Guards and the second son of Lord Clarence Paget.

The Duchess of Argyll, wife of the Secretary for India under Gladstone, could echo the resentful rumor that the Paget boy was marrying an American inn-keeper's daughter, and express her patrician understanding that all Americans were innkeepers or tradesmen. But by overseeing the match, Mrs. Paran Stevens moved at a stroke close to the forefront of the New York social scene. For this was the social epoch characterized by the marriage of American girls into the British aristocracy; social eminence in New York was partly measured by the distinction of one's noble in-law in London. Minnie Stevens had grown up with Consuelo Yznaga, who became the Duchess of Manchester, and she would later use her wiles to promote the marriage between the reluctant Consuelo Vanderbilt and the Duke of Marlborough. She also knew the Jerome sisters, one of whom, Jennie, made the seemingly brilliant marriage with Lord Randolph Churchill, while another, Leonie, was more happily wed to an Irish baronet, Sir John Leslie. With all these women, and especially Leonie Leslie, Edith Wharton would be on terms of friendship; and to the cluster of comely transatlantic invaders in the 1870s, she would devote her last and re-markable, though unfinished, novel, *The Buccaneers.*

A main sign of society's surrender to the former grocer's daughter was the moment in the late 1870s when Mrs. August Belmont drove up all conspicuously one morning to pay a call at 244 Fifth Avenue. Part of Mrs. Stevens' success was due to her combative character, which landed her in court on a number of occasions, but it was due also to the increasing and confusing fluidity of the New York social world, at a time when wealth was becoming as powerful an entrée as birth. The constituency of the old guard, the good old families, could be detected easily enough by the knowing. They were characterized by a long American ancestry, a cautious evasion of publicity, imper-turbable social assurance, and a slowly diminishing energy. But the members of the new breed seemed to spring up out of nowhere.

"How many of the swellest of the swell today were anything at all twenty years ago—fifteen years ago even?" asked an editorial in the gossipy *Town Topics* in 1877.[1] "Where were the Vanderbilts, socially, even five years ago? The Astors had just fifteen years the social start." One recognized these phenomena by their display of wealth, their hearty enjoyment of publicity, and the number of dinners and balls they attended and concerts they gave. The struggle between the two social elements came to something of a climax on an evening in late October 1883, at the opening of the Metropolitan Opera House.

The new breed had attempted to buy into the old Academy of Mu-sic, offering as much as thirty thousand dollars for a box. The old guard indignantly resisted, and the younger millionaires decided to build a house of their own, on Broadway between Thirty-ninth and Fortieth Streets. At the opening—with the Swedish soprano Christine Nilsson singing the role of Marguerite in *Faust* (as she would be heard doing in *The Age of Innocence*)—"all the nouveau riche were on hand," as one reporter wrote with some contempt. "The Goulds and Vanderbilts and people of that ilk perfumed the air with the odor of crisp greenbacks." Downtown that same evening, the writer contin-ued, the people who truly represented New York society, and who were "distinguished by their brilliant social altitude and by the identifica-tion of their names with Manhattan's history," crowded the Academy of Music "to show their willingness to support an opera season backed by something more than the money bags of indiscreet speculation." Mrs. Paran Stevens, who owned boxes in both places, sized up the sit-uation perfectly and divided her evening between them.

She had, meanwhile, inaugurated a series of Sunday evening musi-cal teas, where talented American and foreign musicians performed and tea was served from one of the only two samovars in New York. The genial William Travers, who was encouraged to say such things, was heard to remark to Mrs. Stevens that the music must indeed be good, since certainly no one would come to eat the food she served. She entertained foreign nobility; she arranged dazzling international

---

1. For a description of *Town Topics* as it developed as a scandal sheet, see p. 211, *n*.1 and
    p. 329, *n*.1.

**Christine Nilsson (1871).** The famous Swedish diva holding the flower as she sings the "Daisy Song" (M'ama . . . non m'ama . . . ) in Gounod's *Faust*.

marriages; her stately figure was photographed in the costume of Queen Elizabeth at the Vanderbilts' enormous fancy-dress ball. "Everybody goes to Mrs. Stevens'," said a social columnist, "and she is acknowledged to be one of the cleverest and most accomplished women in society."

The word "everybody" was an exaggeration. Many in the old guard continued to look at her with uneasy resentment, one of them voicing his displeasure at even having been invited to dine at the Washburns in order to meet her. Unfortunately for Edith Jones and Marietta Stevens' son Harry, a number of those hostile to Mrs. Stevens belonged to the Joneses' social contingent. Emelyn Washburn noticed the Rhinelanders,[2] among others, coming to pay their New Year's Day call and behaving with studied rudeness to Mrs. Paran Stevens, who had arrived, full of vitality and charm, on the same formal errand.

                    *    *    *

Lucretia and Edith returned to Newport, Harry Stevens either accompanying them or arriving shortly afterward. The courtship went forward amid walks and drives, tennis parties, and dancing till late hours at the Newport Casino. That capacious assembly of entertainments had been recently built by James Gordon Bennett of the New York *Herald* and equipped with club quarters, dance floor, restaurant, theater, and what quickly became the most famous tennis courts in the country.

This time, the persistent rumors about Harry Stevens and Pussy Jones were approaching truth. On a stiflingly hot Sunday in August, Edith appeared at the home on Redwood Street of her Uncle Fred Rhinelander, bearing a note from her mother.

> My dear Fred—
>
> I had hoped to go to you today with Pussie to announce her engagement to Mr. Stevens, but the heat has made me feel so wretchedly for the last day or two that I was afraid even to venture to Church today. So she must tell her own story—as I wished you and Fanny to know before it is announced to her friends tomorrow.
>
> I shall hope soon to be able to tell you how pleased we all are, notwithstanding this other loss to me within these last months, which naturally is hard for she has always been so very, very dear to me in all the years we have had together, friend and loving child in one. Love to all—
>
> > Affectionately yours,
> > L.S.J.

The incoherence of the second paragraph and the faintness of the handwriting can probably be attributed to heat, as well as to the "other loss" Lucretia had suffered with the death of her husband. One is skeptical at the description of Edith as a "friend and loving child in one," but it is easy to imagine that Lucretia was genuinely pleased to have her oddly difficult daughter off her hands, and in so excellent a match.

---

2. Edith Wharton's mother's maiden name and the patronym of some of her most distinguished forebears.

On August 19, *Town Topics* in Newport told its readers that "Mr. Henry Stevens, only son of Mrs. Paran Stevens, is reported to be engaged to Miss Edith Jones, daughter of the late George F. Jones, Esq." Despite such revelations, Harry's mother was ominously withholding her approval. She could almost be said not to have acknowledged that an engagement had taken place. Mrs. Paran Stevens appeared regularly at the Monday evening dances at the Casino: she made one of a small dinner party given by Julia Ward Howe for Oscar Wilde, who had booked in at Ocean House in Newport on his well-publicized tour of the United States; in early September she gave a huge reception for President Chester Arthur.[3] It is not recorded that she arranged a single event in honor of her son's forthcoming nuptials and of her prospective daughter-in-law.

The marriage, according to *Town Topics,* was scheduled to be held at All Saints Church in New York in the middle of October. Then on October 28 the same paper reported, with an air of quietly rubbing its hands, "The marriage of Mr. Henry Stevens, Mrs. Paran Stevens's son, to Miss Edith Jones, which was announced for the latter part of this month, has been postponed, it is said, indefinitely."

Rumors and counterrumors flew across the island. As Emelyn Washburn would remember it in her old age, Lucretia Jones told her that Mrs. Stevens was intensely resentful of the coldness shown her by members of the Joneses' set and had refused, as it were, to allow her son to marry into the enemy camp. The fifteen-year-old Helen Rhinelander, Edith's first cousin, gave a rather different story in a letter to her brother Tom:

> Is it not sad about Pussy's engagement being broken? I have only seen her once and then she did not appear particularly sad. It is evidently Mrs. S's fault, or rather she is the cause. We have not heard much about it, only Mrs. S behaved insultingly to Aunt Lu! Don't repeat this for the world. Aunt Lu told this to Mamma! I doubt Pussy and H have changed in their feeling for one another, but that Mrs. S is at the bottom of it all.

The Newport *Daily News* provided still another speculation:

> The only reason assigned for the breaking of the engagement hitherto existing between Harry Stevens and Miss Edith Jones is an alleged preponderance of intellectuality on the part of the intended bride. Miss Jones is an ambitious authoress, and it is said that, in the eyes of Mr. Stevens, ambition is a grievous fault.

What is not to be doubted is that Marietta Stevens was the one to bring the engagement to an end; her son, however gallant a courtier,

3. Julia Ward Howe: Writer and social reformer (1819–1910) known for her anti-slavery work and her advocacy of women's rights, Howe is best remembered as the author of the war poem "The Battle Hymn of the Republic" (1862), which provided the lyrics for the Civil War song. Oscar Wilde: Irish-born writer (1854–1900) whose best-known works include the plays *Lady Windermere's Fan* (1892) and *The Importance of Being Earnest* (1895), the novel *The Picture of Dorian Gray* (1891), and the poem *The Ballad of Reading Gaol* (1898), which draws on his experience of prison after he had been convicted of sodomy in 1895. Chester Arthur: (1829–1886), president of the United States, 1881–85.

did not have the strength of character, and perhaps not the will, to stand up to her. Yet from all that one knows of her, it seems unlikely that Mrs. Stevens was moved primarily by a spirit of social revenge, though that probably played some part. For all her forcefulness and flashes of temper, Mrs. Stevens was essentially a kind woman, and one more apt to abet than to oppose the marital desires of the young. A more serious consideration had to do with property.

*　　*　　*

Edith wrote Emelyn Washburn a short flat note, saying only that she had *had* to break the engagement; Marietta Stevens evidently allowed Edith to make the formal gesture. Four weeks later, toward the end of November, Edith was in Paris with her mother and her brother Harry. She called on Margaret Rutherford White, whose husband was attached to the American Embassy, and wrote young Lewis Rutherford cheerfully enough that his sister looked lovely and that the new baby was delightful.

She was probably less in love with Harry Stevens than he was with her. But the experience, while highly educational for the future social historian of New York in the 1870s and 1880s, was for the moment a deeply wounding one. Early in 1883 she was back in New York, and went to the second Patriarchs' Ball of the season on the arm of Julian White, Henry White's younger brother. As they entered Delmonico's, Julian could feel her begin to tremble, and he confided to his family how brave and shaken Pussy Jones had seemed under the watchful and knowing eyes of the other guests.

### [Marriage and Sexual Ignorance]

*　　*　　*

The months drifted by. In February 1884, Teddy came to New York to escort Edith to the second Patriarchs' Ball, an affair attended also by Mrs. Paran Stevens and her daughter and son-in-law, though not by Harry; by the Freddy Joneses and a variety of Schermerhorns and Van Rensselaers; not to mention Mrs. Astor and Ward McAllister, the Lorillards, the Cornelius Vanderbilts, and hordes of others. Following it, Edith and Teddy went their own ways.

It was not until the end of March a year later (1885) that *Town Topics* could announce the engagement of Miss Edith Jones to Mr. Edward Wharton of Boston. According to the paper's Boston correspondent, the news was a chief topic of conversation in the city: "The lady," he said, "is not generally known here," but Mr. Wharton's great popularity made his "good fortune" a matter for rejoicing. To an abbreviated list of relatives and friends, Lucretia Jones sent an engraved wedding invitation which failed to mention Edith's name: "Mrs. George Frederic Jones requests the honour of your presence at the marriage of her daughter to Mr. Edward R. Wharton, at Trinity Chapel, on Wednesday April Twenty-ninth at twelve o'clock."

The ceremony was performed by the Reverend Morgan Dix, the rec-

**Edith Newbold Jones (1884).** This photograph was taken the year before her marriage to Teddy Wharton.

tor of Trinity. "The wedding was a quiet one," *The New York Times* reported, in a column which also detailed the lavish arrangements and vast attendance at a marriage of two other socialites the same day. *Town Topics* raised its eyebrows at the absence of any bridesmaids— "which many people," it murmured, "expected there would have been." There were four ushers, including one of Edith's Rhinelander cousins; Teddy's best man was Percival Lowell.

Edith appeared in a white satin dress, with a court train covered with puffs of white silk mull; there was more drapery of mull and lace at her throat, and a cluster of lilies of the valley. Her veil, which was of tulle, was fastened by a glittering diamond tiara: some of the diamonds had been worn by Lucretia when she married George Frederic Jones more than forty years before; the rest were a gift from Teddy. Instead of the usual bouquet, Edith carried a gilt-bound prayer book. After the wedding, breakfast was served for an even more select group in Lucretia's new home at 28 West Twenty-fifth Street.

The bride and groom went directly to Pencraig ("Mr. and Mrs. Alfred Wharton have arrived in Newport," *Town Topics* observed conscientiously). They began at once to take part in social activities rather more energetically than Edith was accustomed to. On Memorial Day the Whartons were noticed among the fashionable crowd around the clubhouse in Jerome Park—it was the opening day of the spring races—in company with the Perry Belmonts, the Goelets, the Marquis of Queensbury, and James and Sara Roosevelt.

Six weeks later Edith heard that Harry Stevens had died in Newport Hospital. Since the breaking of his engagement to Edith Jones, Harry had been as visible as ever in New York and Newport society. But he fell ill in the midst of the season, and the doctors were unable to diagnose the cause. There was some talk of an abdominal tumor; one member of the Rutherford household put it about that Harry had gone insane after being jilted by Edith. In the Stevens family memory, it was an unexpected eruption of his youthful illness, tuberculosis. Harry died on July 18, just twenty-six years old.

*    *    *

A quarter of a century later Henry James would say that in marrying Teddy Wharton, Edith had done "an almost—or rather an utterly—inconceivable thing." By that time most of Edith's friends felt much the same way; and yet, considering her situation in 1885, her acceptance of Teddy is understandable enough. There had been the bruising termination of her engagement to Harry Stevens, followed all too quickly by the damage to her emotions and her self-confidence by the bewildering silence of Walter Berry.[1] As 1884 gave way to 1885, moreover, Edith found herself entering her twenty-fourth year, dangerously close to the age beyond which the young women of her set became steadily less marriageable. And whatever her innermost opinion of the ways of

---

1. This mention alludes to a relatively charged and finally disappointing first meeting between Edith Wharton and Walter Berry (1859–1927); in Bar Harbor, Maine, in 1883. Berry remained Wharton's most intimate, lifelong friend and was the person Wharton chose to read her fiction (including *The Age of Innocence*) in manuscript form.

New York social life, it had been drilled into her that marriage was the only real goal of the debutante.

If Emelyn Washburn's old-age memory is to be trusted, Edith felt herself during the brief engagement to be really in love for the first time; and in a memoir of her own in the 1930s, Edith repeated much the same thing. Teddy's attractions, it should also be remembered, were genuine ones.

He was extremely good-looking, he had the best of dispositions, he was a man of taste, and he was thoroughly devoted in a winningly subservient way. There was no suggestion, for example, that the married couple should settle in Boston and create their social world out of Teddy's family and friends. Their different financial situations may have affected the decision; in any event they took up their married life in Edith's New York and Newport. Teddy, like Edith, was fond of the out-of-doors and of horses; and if his literary sophistication lagged far behind his gourmet habits, there was some recompense, from his wife's point of view, in his affectionate and intimate manner with small dogs.

\*    \*    \*

There is no question that the sexual side of the marriage was a disaster. Edith entered into it in almost complete ignorance of sex and a blind dread of what was in store for her. Lucretia adamantly refused to enlighten her. A few days before the wedding, Edith plucked up her courage and went to her mother, her heart beating wildly, to ask "what marriage was really like." Lucretia's face instantly took on the look of icy disapproval which Edith most feared, and she answered with impatience: "I never heard such a ridiculous question!"

Edith's tormented anxiety spurred her to continue. "I'm afraid, Mamma—I want to know what will happen to me." After an awful silence, during which Lucretia's expression changed to disgust, she said with a distinct effort: "You've seen enough pictures and statues in your life. Haven't you noticed that men are . . . made differently from women?" Edith faltered out an uncomprehending "Yes." "Well, then—?" Edith stood staring blankly at her mother, quite unable to grasp her meaning, until Lucretia brought the conversation to an abrupt end: "Then for heaven's sake don't ask me any more silly questions. You can't be as stupid as you pretend."

The marriage was not consummated for three weeks. Whatever happened on those first occasions, it had the effect of sealing off Edith's vibrant but untutored erotic nature for an indefinite period, with far-reaching consequences for her psychological makeup and her very practice of life. She would in fact say that the failure of her mother to supply her with even the rudiments of sexual education—a failure Lucretia shared, of course, with most other New York society mothers of the day—"did more than anything else to falsify and misdirect my whole life." The falsity and misdirection were in fact overcome in time, but she always felt that the wilfully obtuse parental treatment of young women like herself with regard to sex contained the seeds of tragedy.

\*    \*    \*

# SOURCES

# Literary Sources

To understand Edith Wharton's sources for *The Age of Innocence*, and indeed, the most powerful forces shaping her life, it is essential to acknowledge that Wharton both defined and knew her world through her experience of art. When Newland's aging and unmarried sister Janey lifts Balzac's *Contes drôlatiques* from her brother's table, Wharton's novel calls attention to the importance of the appearance in 1874 of the English translation of Balzac that included illustrations by Gustave Doré. Balzac's series of humorous tales in the form of anecdotes and parables include strangely apt commentaries on the tragedy of Edith Wharton's own sexual ignorance. In a tale that must have been particularly poignant to Wharton, whose mother claimed that her daughter must know about the mysteries of life from having seen statues, Balzac's "Innocence" tells of two children who, like Edith Wharton, were unable to figure out the complexities of sexuality by looking at works of art. Here, the children standing before a painting by Titian cannot tell who is whom because Adam and Eve do not have their clothes on. The second tale from Balzac included here, "The Danger of Being Too Innocent," introduces adultery as part of the necessary education for a sexually ignorant bride and groom who have spent their wedding night praying. Again, this parable about innocence would have been painfully familiar to Wharton, who at the time of her marriage believed that babies came from God (after he saw the couple being married through the roof of the church), and who learned about adult passion through adultery late in life.

In form and content, these tales from Balzac were the impetus for Wharton's early work, "The Valley of Childish Things, and Other Emblems." This brief collation of parables opens with Wharton's first and most explicit anticipation of a blonde and infantile May-figure as she is seen through the eyes of a dark woman, an Ellen-figure who has matured by leaving "the Valley of Childish Things." This title parable takes the form of a morality tale, anticipating a component of *The Age of Innocence* that had already risen to the level of a motif in Wharton's fiction: a desired male prefers the child-woman to the experienced woman of the world. While Balzac's tales and Wharton's related emblems are clearly significant as archetypal antecedents to this novel, these brief works only begin to suggest Wharton's delight in literary allusion and the ways in which other volumes merely mentioned in the novel provide a texture of telling counterpoints. In addition to alluding to fallen cultures, many of the poems, plays, and novels referred to in *The Age of Innocence* include famous and ill-fated tales of adultery.

Wharton's critique of social mores, in particular the cultural emphasis on preserving the innocence of the child-woman who dwells in the "Valley of Childish Things," remained a staple element of her gendered analyses of American culture in her fiction and nonfiction. Just three years before she published *The Age of Innocence,* Wharton began to write a series of essays in 1917 designed to introduce American soldiers to French culture. Wharton's views on the tragic innocence of American women are recounted in her essay "The New Frenchwoman," incorporated into *French Ways and Their Meaning* (1919). Reprinted at the close of this section, this essay argues that French women are engaged in the living of "real life" while their American counterparts have remained infantilized, educated in what she calls a "baby school." Significantly, this oppositional construction once again anticipates the counterposing of May and Ellen as figures representing innocence and experience. Although Ellen Olenska is an American who has made her home in France, this woman of experience appears to have been drawn along the lines of Wharton's valorized depiction of the "new Frenchwoman."

# HONORÉ DE BALZAC

## From *Contes drôlatiques*†

### *Innocence*

By the double red crest of my fowl, and by the rose lining of my sweetheart's slipper! By all the horns of well-beloved cuckolds, and by the virtue of their blessed wives! the finest work of man is neither poetry, nor painted pictures, nor music, nor castles, nor statues, be they carved never so well, nor rowing, nor sailing galleys, but children. Understand me, children up to the age of ten years, for after that they become men or women, and cutting their wisdom teeth, are not worth what they cost: the worst are the best. Watch them playing, prettily and innocently, with slippers; above all, cancellated ones, with the household utensils, leaving that which displeases them, crying after that which pleases them, munching the sweets and confectionery in the house, nibbling at the stores, and always laughing as soon as their teeth are cut, and you will agree with me that they are in every way lovable; besides which they are flower and fruit—the fruit of love, the flower of life. Before their minds have been unsettled by the disturbances of life, there is nothing in this world more blessed or more pleasant than their sayings, which are naïve beyond description. This is as true as the double chewing machine of a cow. Do not expect a man to be innocent after the manner of children, because there is an, I know not what, ingredient of reason in the naïveté of a man, while the naïveté of children is candid, immaculate, and has all the finesse of the mother, which is plainly proved in this tale.

Queen Catherine was at that time Dauphine, and to make herself welcome to the king, her father-in-law, who at that time was very ill indeed, presented him, from time to time, with Italian pictures, knowing that he liked them much, being a friend of the Sieur Raphaël

† From Honoré de Balzac, *Contes drôlatiques* (London: Chatto and Windus, 1874), pp. 312–22, 614–16.

d'Urbin and of the Sieurs Primatice and Leonardo da Vinci, to whom he sent large sums of money. She obtained from her family—who had the pick of these works, because at that time the Duke of Medicis governed Tuscany—a precious picture, painted by a Venetian named Titian (artist to the Emperor Charles, and in very high favour), in which there were portraits of Adam and Eve at the moment when God left them to wander about the terrestial Paradise, and were painted their full height, in the costume of the period, in which it is difficult to make a mistake, because they were attired in their ignorance, and caparisoned with the divine grace which enveloped them—a difficult thing to execute on account of the colour, but one in which the said Sieur Titian excelled. The picture was put into the room of the poor king, who was then ill with the disease of which he eventually died. It had a great success at the Court of France, where every one wished to see it; but no one was able to until after the king's death, since at his desire it was allowed to remain in his room as long as he lived.

One day Madame Catherine took with her to the king's room her son Francis and little Margot, who began to talk at random, as children will. Now here, now there, these children had heard this picture of Adam and Eve spoken about, and had tormented their mother to take them there. Since the two little ones at times amused the old king, Madame the Dauphine consented to their request.

"You wished to see Adam and Eve, who were our first parents; there they are," said she.

Then she left them in great astonishment before Titian's picture, and seated herself by the bedside of the king, who delighted to watch the children.

"Which of the two is Adam?" said Francis, nudging his sister Margaret's elbow.

"You silly!" replied she, "to know that, they would have to be dressed!"

This reply, which delighted the poor king and the mother, was mentioned in a letter written in Florence by Queen Catherine.

No writer having brought it to light, it will remain, like a sweet flower, in a corner of these Tales, although it is in no way droll, and there is no other moral to be drawn from it except that to hear these pretty speeches of infancy one must beget the children.

### The Danger of Being Too Innocent

The lord of Moncontour was a brave soldier of Tours, who, in honour of the battle gained by the Duke of Anjou, afterwards our right glorious king, caused to be built at Vouvray the castle thus named, for he had borne himself most bravely in that affair, where he overcame the greatest of heretics, and from that was authorized to take the name. Now this said captain had two sons, good Catholics, of whom the eldest was in favour at court. After the peace, which was concluded before the stratagem arranged for St. Bartholomew's day, the good man returned to his manor, which was not ornamented as it is at the present day.

There he received the sad announcement of the death of his son, slain
in a duel by the lord of Villequier. The poor father was the more cut up
at this, as he had arranged a capital marriage for this said son with a
young lady of the male branch of Amboise. Now, by this death most
piteously inopportune, vanished all the future and advantages of his
family, of which he wished to make a great and noble house. With this
idea, he had put his other son in a monastery, under the guidance and
government of a man renowned for his holiness, who brought him up
in a Christian manner, according to the desire of his father, who wished
from high ambition to make of him a cardinal of renown. For this the
good abbot kept the young man in a private house, had him to sleep by
his side in his cell, allowed no evil weeds to grow in his mind, brought
him up in purity of soul and true contrition, as all priests should be.
This said clerk, when turned nineteen years, knew no other love than
the love of God, no other nature than that of the angels who have not
our carnal properties, in order that they may live in purity, seeing that
otherwise they would make good use of them. The which[,] the King
on High, who wished to have His pages always proper, was afraid of.
He has done well, because his good little people cannot drink in dram
shops or riot in brothels as ours do. He is divinely served; but then, remember, He is Lord of all. Now in this plight the lord of Moncontour
determined to withdraw his second son from the cloister, and invest
him with the purple of the soldier and the courtier, in the place of the
ecclesiastical purple; and determined to give him in marriage to the
maiden, affianced to the dead man, which was wisely determined, because wrapped round with continence and sobriety in all ways as was
the little monk, the bride would be as well used and happier than she
would have been with the elder, already well hauled over, upset, and
spoilt by the ladies of the court. The befrocked unfrocked, and very
sheepish in his ways, followed the sacred wishes of his father, and consented to the said marriage without knowing what a wife, and—what is
more curious—what a girl was. By chance, his journey having been
hindered by the troubles and marches of conflicting parties, this innocent—more innocent than it is lawful for a man to be innocent—only
came to the castle of Moncontour the evening before the wedding,
which was performed with dispensations bought in the archbishopric
of Tours. It is necessary here to describe the bride. Her mother, long
time a widow, lived in the house of M. de Braguelongne, civil lieutenant of the Chatelet de Paris, whose wife lived with the lord of Lig-
nieres, to the great scandal of the period. But every one then had so
many joists in his own eye that he had no right to notice the rafters in
the eyes of others. Now, in all families people go to perdition, without
noticing their neighbours, some at an amble, others at a gentle trot,
many at a gallop, and a small number walking, seeing that the road is
all down hill. Thus in these times the devil had many a good orgie in all
things, since that misconduct was fashionable. The poor old lady Virtue
had retired trembling, no one knew whither, but now here, now there,
lived miserably in company with honest women.
In the most noble house of Amboise there still lived the dowager of

Chaumont, an old woman of well proved virtue, in whom had retired all the religion and good conduct of this fine family. The said lady had taken to her bosom, from the age of ten years, the little maiden who is concerned in this adventure, and who never caused Madame Amboise the least anxiety, but left her free in her movements, and she came to see her daughter once a year, when the court passed that way. In spite of this high maternal reserve, Madame Amboise was invited to her daughter's wedding, and also the lord of Braguelongne, by the good old soldier, who knew his people. But the dear dowager came not to Moncontour, because she could not obtain leave from her sciatica, her cold, nor the state of her legs, which gambolled no longer. Over this the good woman cried copiously. It hurt her much to let go into the dangers of the court and of life this gentle maiden, as pretty as it was possible for a pretty girl to be, but she was obliged to give her her wings. But it was not without promising her many masses and orisons every evening for her happiness. And comforted a little, the good old lady began to think that the staff of her old age was passing into the hands of a quasi-saint, brought up to do good by the above-mentioned abbot, with whom she was acquainted, the which had aided considerably in the prompt exchange of spouses. At length, embracing her with tears, the virtuous dowager made those last recommendations to her that ladies make to young brides, as that she ought to be respectful to his mother, and obey her husband in everything.

Then the maid arrived with a great noise, conducted by servants, chamberlains, grooms, gentlemen, and people of the house of Chaumont, so that you would have imagined her suite to be that of a cardinal legate. So arrived the two spouses the evening before their marriage. Then, the feasting over, they were married with great pomp on the Lord's Day, a mass being said at the castle by the Bishop of Blois, who was a great friend of the lord of Moncontour; in short, the feasting, the dancing, and the festivities of all sorts lasted till the morning. But on the stroke of midnight the bridesmaids went to put the bride to bed, according to the custom of Touraine; and during this time they kept quarrelling with the innocent husband, to prevent him going to this innocent wife, who sided with them from ignorance. However, the good lord of Moncontour interrupted the jokers and the wits, because it was necessary that his son should occupy himself in well-doing. Then went the innocent into the chamber of his wife, whom he thought more beautiful than the Virgin Marys painted in Italian, Flemish, and other pictures, at whose feet he had said his prayers. But you may be sure he felt very much embarrassed at having so soon become a husband, because he knew nothing of his business, and saw that certain forms had to be gone through concerning which, from great and modest reserve, he had not time to question even his father, who had said sharply to him—

"You know what you have to do; be valiant therein."

Then he saw the gentle girl who was given him, comfortably tucked up in the bedclothes, terribly curious, her head buried under, but hazarding a glance as at the point of a halberd, and saying to herself—

"I must obey him."

And knowing nothing, she awaited the will of this slightly ecclesiastical gentleman, to whom, in fact, she belonged. Seeing which, the Chevalier de Moncontour came close to the bed, scratched his ear, and knelt down, a thing in which he was expert.

"Have you said your prayers?" said he.

"No," said she; "I have forgotten them. Do you wish me to say them?"

Then the young couple commenced the business of housekeeping by imploring God, which was not at all out of place. But unfortunately the devil heard, and at once replied to their requests, God being much occupied at that time with the new and abominable reformed religion.

"What did they tell you to do?" said the husband.

"To love you," said she, in perfect innocence.

"That has not been told to me; but I love you, I am ashamed to say, better than I love God."

This speech did not at all alarm the bride.

"I should like," said the husband, "to repose myself in your bed, if it will not disturb you."

"I will make room for you willingly, because I am to submit myself to you."

"Well," said he, "don't look at me, then. I'm going to take my clothes off, and come."

At this virtuous speech, the young damsel turned herself towards the wall in great expectation, seeing that it was for the very first time that she was about to find herself separated from a man by the confines of a shirt only. Then came the innocent, gliding into the bed, and thus they found themselves, so to speak, united, but far from you can imagine what. Did you ever see a monkey brought from across the seas, who for the first time is given a nut to crack? This ape, knowing by high apish imagination how delicious is the food hidden under the shell, sniffs and twists himself about in a thousand apish ways, saying, I know not what, between his chattering jaws. Ah! with what affection he studies it, with what study he examines it, in what examination he holds it, then throws it, rolls and tosses it about with passion, and often, when it is an ape of low extraction and intelligence, leaves the nut. As much did the poor innocent who, towards the dawn, was obliged to confess to his dear wife that, not knowing how to perform his office, or what that office was, or where to obtain the said office, it would be necessary for him to inquire concerning it, to have help and aid.

"Yes," said she; "since, unhappily, I cannot instruct you."

In fact, in spite of their efforts, essays of all kinds—in spite of a thousand things which the innocents invent, and which the wise in matters of love know nothing about—the pair dropped off to sleep, wretched at having been unable to discover the secret of marriage. But they wisely agreed to say that they had done so. When the wife got up, still a maiden, seeing that she had not been crowned, she boasted of her night, and said she had the king of husbands, and went on with her chattering and repartees as briskly as those who know nothing of these things. Then every one found the maiden a little too sharp, since for a two-edged joke a lady of Roche-Corbon having incited a young maiden, de la Bourdaisière, who knew nothing of such things, to ask the bride—

"How many loaves did your husband put in the oven?"

"Twenty-four," she replied.

Now, as the bridegroom was roaming sadly about, thereby distressing his wife, who followed him with her eyes, hoping to see his state of innocence come to an end, the ladies believed that the joy of that night had cost him dear, and that the said bride was already regretting having so quickly ruined him. And at breakfast came the bad jokes, which at that time were relished as excellent. One said that the bride had an open expression; another, that there had been some good strokes of business done that night in the castle; this one, that the oven had been burned; that one, that the two families had lost something that night that they would never find again. And a thousand other jokes, stupidities, and double meanings that, unfortunately, the husband did not understand. But on account of the great affluence of the relations, neighbours, and others, no one had been to bed; all had danced, rollicked, and frolicked, as is the custom at noble weddings.

At this was quite contented my said Sieur de Braguelongne, upon whom my lady of Amboise, excited by the thought of the good things which were happening to her daughter, cast the glances of a falcon in matters of gallant assignation. The poor lieutenant civil, learned in bailiffs' men and serjeants, and who nabbed all the pickpockets and scamps of Paris, pretended not to see his good fortune, although his good lady required him to. You may be sure this great lady's love weighed heavily upon him, so he only kept to her from a spirit of justice, because it was not seeming in a lieutenant criminal to change his mistresses as often as a man at court, because he had under his charge morals, the police, and religion. This notwithstanding his rebellion must come to an end. On the day after the wedding a great number of the guests departed; then Madame d'Amboise and Monsieur de Braguelongne could go to bed, their guests having decamped. Sitting down to supper, the lieutenant received a half-verbal summons to which it was not becoming, as in legal matters, to oppose any reasons for delay.

During supper the said lady d'Amboise made more than a hundred little signs in order to draw the good Braguelongne from the room where he was with the bride, but out came instead of the lieutenant[,] the husband, to walk about in company with the mother of his sweet wife. Now, in the mind of this innocent there had sprung up like a mushroom an expedient—namely, to interrogate this good lady, whom he considered discreet, for remembering the religious precepts of his abbot, who had told him to inquire concerning all things of old people expert in the ways of life, he thought of confiding his case to my said lady d'Amboise. But he made first awkwardly and shyly certain twists and turns, finding no terms in which to unfold his case. And the lady was also perfectly silent, since she was outrageously struck with the blindness, deafness, and voluntary paralysis of the lord of Braguelongne; and said to herself, walking by the side of this delicate morsel, a young innocent of whom she did not think, little imagining that this cat so well provided with young bacon could think of old—

"This Ho, Ho, with a beard of flies' legs, a flimsy, old, grey, ruined, shaggy beard—a beard without comprehension, beard without shame, without any feminine respect—beard which pretends neither to feel nor to hear nor to see, a pared away beard, a beaten down, disordered, gutted beard. May the Italian sickness deliver me from this vile joker with a squashed nose, fiery nose, frozen nose, nose without religion, nose dry as a lute table, pale nose, nose without a soul, nose which is nothing but a shadow; nose which sees not, nose wrinkled like the leaf of the vine; nose that I hate, old nose, nose full of mud—dead nose. Where have my eyes been to attach myself to this truffle nose, to this old hulk that no longer knows his way? I give my share to the devil of this old juiceless beard, of this old grey beard, of this monkey face, of these old tatters, of this old rag of a man, of this—I know not what; and I'll take a young husband who'll marry me properly, and . . . and often—every day—and well——"

In this wise train of thought was she when the innocent began his anthem to this woman, so warmly excited, who at the first paraphrase took fire in her understanding, like a piece of old touchwood from the carbine of a soldier; and finding it wise to try her son-in-law, said to herself—

"Ah! young beard, sweet scented! ah! pretty new nose—fresh beard—innocent nose—virgin beard—nose full of joy—beard of springtime, small key of love!"

She kept on talking the round of the garden, which was long, and then arranged with the Innocent that, night come, he should sally forth from his room and get into hers, where she engaged to render him more learned than ever was his father. And the husband was well content, and thanked Madame d'Amboise, begging her to say nothing of this arrangement.

During this time the good old Braguelongne had been growling and saying to himself, "Old ha, ha! old ho, ho! may the plague take thee! may a cancer eat thee!—worthless old currycomb! old slipper, too big for the foot! old arquebus! ten year old codfish! old spider that spins no more! old death with open eyes! old devil's cradle! vile lantern of an old town-crier! old wretch whose look kills! old moustache of an old theriacler! old wretch to make dead men weep! old organ-pedal! old sheath with a hundred knives! old church porch, worn out by the knees! old poor-box in which every one has dropped. I'll give all my future to be quit of thee!" As he finished these gentle thoughts the pretty bride, who was thinking of her young husband's great sorrow at not knowing the particulars of that essential item of marriage, and not having the slightest idea what it was, thought to save him much tribulation, shame, and labour by instructing herself. And she counted upon much astonishing and rejoicing him the next night when she should say to him, teaching him his duty, "That's the thing, my love!" Brought up in great respect of old people by her dear dowager, she thought of inquiring of this good man in her sweetest manner to distil for her the sweet mysteries of the commerce. Now, the lord of Braguelongne, ashamed of being lost in sad contemplation of his evening's work, and of saying nothing to his gay companion, put this summary interrogation to the fair bride—"If she was not happy with so good a young husband——"

"He is very good," said she.

"Too good, perhaps," said the lieutenant, smiling.

To be brief, matters were so well arranged between them that the lord of Braguelongne engaged to spare no pains to enlighten the understanding of Madame d'Amboise's daughter-in-law, who promised to come and study her lesson in his room. The said lady d'Amboise pretended after supper to play terrible music in a high key to Monsieur de Braguelongne, saying that he had no gratitude for the blessings she had brought him—her position, her wealth, her fidelity, &c. In fact, she talked for half an hour without having exhausted a quarter of her ire. From this a hundred knives were drawn between them, but they kept the sheaths. Meanwhile the spouses in bed were arranging to themselves how to get away, in order to please each other. Then the innocent began to say he felt quite giddy, he knew not from what, and wanted to go into the open air. And his maiden wife told him to take a stroll in the moonlight. And then the good fellow began to pity his wife in being left alone a moment. At her desire, both of them at different times left their conjugal couch and came to their preceptors, both very impatient, as you can well believe; and good instruction was given to them. How? I cannot say, because every one has his own method and practice, and of all sciences this is the most variable in principle. You may be sure that never did scholars receive more gaily the precepts of any language, grammar, or lessons whatsoever. And the two spouses returned to their nest, delighted at being able to communicate to each other the discoveries of their scientific peregrinations.

"Ah, my dear," said the bride, "you already know more than my master!"

From these curious tests came their domestic joy and perfect fidelity; because immediately after their entry into the married state they found out how much better each of them was adapted for love than any one else, their masters included. Thus for the remainder of their days they kept to the legitimate substance of their own persons; and the lord of Moncontour said in old age to his friends—

"Do like me, be cuckolds in the blade, and not in the sheaf."

Which is the true morality of the conjugal condition.

# EDITH WHARTON

## The Valley of Childish Things, and Other Emblems†

Once upon a time a number of children lived together in the Valley of Childish Things, playing all manner of delightful games, and studying the same lesson books. But one day a little girl, one of their number, decided that it was time to see something of the world about which the lesson books had taught her; and as none of the other children cared to leave their games, she set out alone to climb the pass which led out of the valley.

It was a hard climb, but at length she reached a cold, bleak table-land beyond the mountains. Here she saw cities and men, and learned many useful arts, and in so doing grew to be a woman. But the table-land was bleak and cold, and when she had served her apprenticeship she decided to return to her old companions in the Valley of Childish Things, and work with them instead of with strangers.

It was a weary way back, and her feet were bruised by the stones, and her face was beaten by the weather; but halfway down the pass she met a man, who kindly helped her over the roughest places. Like herself, he was lame and weather-beaten; but as soon as he spoke she recognized him as one of her old playmates. He too had been out in the world, and was going back to the valley; and on the way they talked together of the work they meant to do there. He had been a dull boy, and she had never taken much notice of him; but as she listened to his plans for building bridges and draining swamps and cutting roads through the jungle, she thought to herself, "Since he has grown into such a fine fellow, what splendid men and women my other play-mates must have become!"

But what was her surprise to find, on reaching the valley, that her former companions, instead of growing into men and women, had all remained little children. Most of them were playing the same old games, and the few who affected to be working were engaged in such strenuous occupations as building mudpies and sailing paper boats in basins. As for the lad who had been the favorite companion of her studies, he was playing marbles with all the youngest boys in the valley.

At first the children seemed glad to have her back, but soon she saw that her presence interfered with their games; and when she tried to tell them of the great things that were being done on the tableland beyond the mountains, they picked up their toys and went farther down the valley to play.

Then she turned to her fellow traveler, who was the only grown man in the valley; but he was on his knees before a dear little girl with blue eyes and a coral necklace, for whom he was making a garden out of cockleshells and bits of glass and broken flowers stuck in sand.

---

† From "The Valley of Childish Things, and Other Emblems." *The Century*, Vol. 52, Issue 3, July 1896.

The little girl was clapping her hands and crowing (she was too young to speak articulately); and when she who had grown to be a woman laid her hand on the man's shoulder, and asked him if he did not want to set to work with her building bridges, draining swamps, and cutting roads through the jungle, he replied that at that particular moment he was too busy.

And as she turned away, he added in the kindest possible way, "Really, my dear, you ought to have taken better care of your complexion."

## II

There was once a maiden lady who lived alone in a commodious brick house facing north and south. The lady was very fond of warmth and sunshine, but unfortunately her room was on the north side of the house, so that in winter she had no sun at all.

This distressed her so much that, after long deliberation, she sent for an architect, and asked him if it would be possible to turn the house around so that her room should face the south. The architect replied that anything could be done for money; but the estimated cost of turning the house around was so high that the lady, who enjoyed a handsome income, was obliged to reduce her way of living and sell her securities at a sacrifice to raise money enough for the purpose. At length, however, the house was turned around, and she felt almost consoled for her impoverishment by the first ray of sunlight which stole through her shutters the next morning.

That very day she received a visit from an old friend who had been absent a year; and this friend, finding her seated at her window in a flood of sunlight, immediately exclaimed:

"My dear, how sensible of you to have moved into a south room! I never could understand why you persisted so long in living on the north side of the house."

And the following day the architect sent in his bill.

## III

There was once a little girl who was so very intelligent that her parents feared that she would die.

But an aged aunt, who had crossed the Atlantic in a sailing vessel, said, "My dears, let her marry the first man she falls in love with, and she will make such a fool of herself that it will probably save her life."

## IV

A thinly clad man, who was trudging afoot through a wintry and shelterless region, met another wrapped in a big black cloak. The cloak hung heavily on its wearer, and seemed to drag him back, but at least it kept off the cold.

"That's a fine warm cloak you've got," said the first man through his chattering teeth.

"Oh," said the other, "it's none of my choosing, I promise you. It's only my old happiness dyed black and made over into a sorrow; but in this weather a man must wear what he's got."

"To think of some people's luck!" muttered the first man, as the other passed on. "Now I never had enough happiness to make a sorrow out of."

## V

There was once a man who married a sweet little wife; but when he set out with her from her father's house, he found that she had never been taught to walk. They had a long way to go, and there was nothing for him to do but to carry her; and as he carried her she grew heavier and heavier.

Then they came to a wide, deep river, and he found that she had never been taught to swim. So he told her to hold fast to his shoulder, and started to swim with her across the river. And as he swam she grew frightened, and dragged him down in her struggles. And the river was deep and wide, and the current ran fast; and once or twice she nearly had him under. But he fought his way through, and landed her safely on the other side; and behold, he found himself in a strange country, beyond all imagining delightful. And as he looked about him and gave thanks, he said to himself:

"Perhaps if I hadn't had to carry her over, I shouldn't have kept up long enough to get here myself."

## VI

A soul once cowered in a gray waste, and a mighty shape came by. Then the soul cried out for help, saying, "Shall I be left to perish alone in this desert of Unsatisfied Desires?"

"But you are mistaken," the shape replied; "this is the land of Gratified Longings. And, moreover, you are not alone, for the country is full of people; but whoever tarries here grows blind."

## VII

There was once a very successful architect who made a great name for himself. At length he built a magnificent temple, to which he devoted more time and thought than to any of the other buildings he had erected; and the world pronounced it his masterpiece. Shortly afterward he died, and when he came before the judgment angel he was not asked how many sins he had committed, but how many houses he had built.

He hung his head and said, more than he could count.

The judgment angel asked what they were like, and the architect said that he was afraid they were pretty bad.

"And are you sorry?" asked the angel.

"Very sorry," said the architect, with honest contrition.

"And how about that famous temple that you built just before you died?" the angel continued. "Are you satisfied with that?"

"Oh, no," the architect exclaimed. "I really think it has some good points about it—I did try my best, you know—but there's one dreadful mistake that I'd give my soul to go back and rectify."

"Well," said the angel, "you can't go back and rectify it, but you can take your choice of the following alternatives: either we can let the world go on thinking your temple a masterpiece and you the greatest architect that ever lived, or we can send to earth a young fellow we've got here who will discover your mistake at a glance, and point it out so clearly to posterity that you'll be the laughingstock of all succeeding generations of architects. Which do you choose?"

"Oh, well," said the architect, "if it comes to that, you know—as long as it suits my clients as it is, I really don't see the use of making such a fuss."

## VIII

A man once married a charming young person who agreed with him on every question. At first they were very happy, for the man thought his wife the most interesting companion he had ever met, and they spent their days telling each other what wonderful people they were. But by and by the man began to find his wife rather tiresome. Wherever he went she insisted upon going; whatever he did, she was sure to tell him that it would have been better to do the opposite; and moreover, it gradually dawned upon him that his friends had never thought so highly of her as he did. Having made this discovery, he naturally felt justified in regarding himself as the aggrieved party; she took the same view of her situation, and their life was one of incessant recrimination.

Finally, after years spent in violent quarrels and short-lived reconciliations, the man grew weary, and decided to divorce his wife.

He engaged an able lawyer, who assured him that he would have no difficulty in obtaining a divorce; but to his surprise, the judge refused to grant it.

"But—" said the man, and he began to recapitulate his injuries.

"That's all very true," said the judge, "and nothing would be easier than for you to obtain a divorce if you had only married another person."

"What do you mean by another person?" asked the man in astonishment.

"Well," replied the judge, "it appears that you inadvertently married yourself; that is a union no court has the power to dissolve."

"Oh," said the man; and he was secretly glad, for in his heart he was already longing to make it up again with his wife.

## IX

There was once a gentleman who greatly disliked to assume any responsibility. Being possessed of ample means and numerous poor relatives, he might have indulged a variety of tastes and even a few virtues;

but since there is no occupation that does not bring a few cares in its train, this gentleman resolutely refrained from doing anything.

He ceased to visit his old mother, who lived in the country, because it made him nervous to catch the train; he subscribed to no charities because it was a bother to write the checks; he received no visits because he did not wish to be under the obligation of returning them; he invited no guests to stay with him, for fear of being bored before they left; he gave no presents because it was so troublesome to choose them; finally, he even gave up asking his friends to dine because it was such a nuisance to tell the cook that they were coming.

This gentleman took an honest pride in his complete detachment from the trivial importunities of life, and was never tired of ridiculing those who complained of the weight of their responsibilities, justly remarking that if they really wished to be their own masters they had only to follow his example.

One day, however, one of his servants carelessly left the front door open, and Death walked in unannounced, and begged the gentleman to come along as quickly as possible, as there were a good many more people to be called for that afternoon.

"But I can't," cried the gentleman, in dismay. "I really can't, you know. I—why, I've asked some people to dine with me this evening."

"That's a little too much," said Death. And the devil carried the gentleman off in a big black bag.

## X

There was once a man who had seen the Parthenon, and he wished to build his god a temple like it.

But he was not a skillful man, and, try as he would, he could produce only a mud hut thatched with straw; and he sat down and wept because he could not build a temple for his god.

But one who passed by said to him:

"There are two worse plights than yours. One is to have no god; the other is to build a mud hut and mistake it for the Parthenon."

# EDITH WHARTON

## The New Frenchwoman†

There is no new Frenchwoman; but the real Frenchwoman is new to America, and it may be of interest to American women to learn something of what she is really like.

In saying that the real Frenchwoman is new to America I do not intend to draw the old familiar contrast between the so-called "real Frenchwoman" and the Frenchwoman of fiction and the stage. Ameri-

† From *French Ways and Their Meaning* (New York: D. Appleton and Company, 1919), pp. 98–121.

cans have been told a good many thousand times in the last four years that the real Frenchwoman is totally different from the person depicted under that name by French novelists and dramatists; but in truth every literature, in its main lines, reflects the chief characteristics of the people for whom, and about whom, it is written—and none more so than French literature, the freest and frankest of all.

The statement that the real Frenchwoman is new to America simply means that America has never before taken the trouble to look at her and try to understand her. She has always been there, waiting to be understood, and a little tired, perhaps, of being either caricatured or idealised. It would be easy enough to palm her off as a "new" Frenchwoman because the war has caused her to live a new life and do unfamiliar jobs; but one need only look at the illustrated papers to see what she looks like as a tram-conductor, a taxi-driver or a munition-maker. It is certain, even now, that all these new experiences are going to modify her character, and to enlarge her view of life; but that is not the point with which these papers are concerned. The first thing for the American woman to do is to learn to know *the Frenchwoman* as she has always been; to try to find out what she is, and why she is what she is. After that it will be easy to see why the war has developed in her certain qualities rather than others, and what its aftereffects on her are likely to be.

First of all, she is, in nearly all respects, as different as possible from the average American woman. That proposition is fairly evident, though not always easy to explain. Is it because she dresses better, or knows more about cooking, or is more "coquettish," or more "feminine," or more excitable, or more emotional, or more immoral? All these reasons have been often suggested, but none of them seems to furnish a complete answer. Millions of American women are, to the best of their ability (which is not small), coquettish, feminine, emotional, and all the rest of it; a good many dress as well as Frenchwomen; some even know a little about cooking—and the real reason is quite different, and not nearly as flattering to our national vanity. It is simply that, like the men of her race, the Frenchwoman is *grown up*.

Compared with the women of France the average American woman is still in the kindergarten. The world she lives in is exactly like the most improved and advanced and scientifically equipped Montessori-method baby-school.[1] At first sight it may seem preposterous to compare the American woman's independent and resonant activities—her "boards" and clubs and sororities, her public investigation of everything under the heavens from "the social evil" to baking-powder, and from "physical culture" to the newest esoteric religion—to compare such free and busy and seemingly influential lives with the artless exercises of an infant class. But what is the fundamental principle of the Montessori system? It is the development of the child's individuality,

---

1. Kindergarten or elementary school based on the Montessori Method. Developed in the early twentieth century by Maria Montessori (1870–1952), Italy's first female physician, this method was based on Montessori's observation that children learn by manipulating actual materials.

unrestricted by the traditional nursery discipline: a Montessori school is a baby world where, shut up together in the most improved hygienic surroundings, a number of infants noisily develop their individuality.

The reason why American women are not really "grown up" in comparison with the women of the most highly civilised countries—such as France—is that all their semblance of freedom, activity and authority bears not much more likeness to real living than the exercises of the Montessori infant. Real living, in any but the most elementary sense of the word, is a deep and complex and slowly-developed thing, the outcome of an old and rich social experience. It cannot be "got up" like gymnastics, or a proficiency in foreign languages; it has its roots in the fundamental things, and above all in close and constant and interesting and important relations between men and women.

It is because American women are each other's only audience, and to a great extent each other's only companions, that they seem, compared to women who play an intellectual and social part in the lives of men, like children in a baby-school. They are "developing their individuality," but developing it in the void, without the checks, the stimulus, and the discipline that comes of contact with the stronger masculine individuality. And it is not only because the man is the stronger and the closer to reality that his influence is necessary to develop woman to real womanhood; it is because the two sexes complete each other mentally as well as physiologically that no modern civilisation has been really rich or deep, or stimulating to other civilisations, which has not been based on the recognised interaction of influences between men and women.

There are several ways in which the Frenchwoman's relations with men may be called more important than those of her American sister. In the first place, in the commercial class, the Frenchwoman is always her husband's business partner. The lives of the French bourgeois couple are based on the primary necessity of getting enough money to live on, and of giving their children educational and material advantages. In small businesses the woman is always her husband's book-keeper or clerk, or both; above all, she is his business adviser. France, as you know, is held up to all other countries as a model of thrift, of wise and prudent saving and spending. No other country in the world has such immense financial vitality, such powers of recuperation from national calamity. After the Franco-Prussian war of 1870, when France, beaten to earth, her armies lost, half her territory occupied, and with all Europe holding aloof, and not a single ally to defend her interests—when France was called on by her conquerors to pay an indemnity of five thousand million francs in order to free her territory of the enemy, she raised the sum, and paid it off, *eighteen months sooner than the date agreed upon*: to the rage and disappointment of Germany, and the amazement and admiration of the rest of the world.

Every economist knows that if France was able to make that incredible effort it was because, all over the country, millions of Frenchwomen, labourers' wives, farmers' wives, small shopkeepers' wives, wives of big manufacturers and commission-merchants and bankers, were to all intents and purposes their husbands' business-partners, and had had a direct interest in saving and investing the millions and millions piled up to pay France's ransom in her day of need. At every stage in French history, in war, in politics, in literature, in art and in religion, women have played a splendid and a decisive part; but none more splendid or more decisive than the obscure part played by the millions of wives and mothers whose thrift and prudence silently built up her salvation in 1872.

When it is said that the Frenchwoman of the middle class is her husband's business partner the statement must not be taken in too literal a sense. The French wife has less legal independence than the American or English wife, and is subject to a good many legal disqualifications from which women have freed themselves in other countries. That is the technical situation; but what is the practical fact? That the Frenchwoman has gone straight through these theoretical restrictions to the heart of reality, and become her husband's associate, because, for her children's sake if not for her own, her heart is in his job, and because he has long since learned that the best business partner a man can have is one who has the same interests at stake as himself.

It is not only because she saves him a salesman's salary, or a bookkeeper's salary, or both, that the French tradesman associates his wife with his business; it is because he has the sense to see that no hired assistant will have so keen a perception of his interests, that none will receive his customers so pleasantly, and that none will so patiently and willingly work over hours when it is necessary to do so. There is no drudgery in this kind of partnership, because it is voluntary, and because each partner is stimulated by exactly the same aspirations. And it is this practical, personal and daily participation in her husband's job that makes the Frenchwoman more grown up than others. She has a more interesting and more living life, and therefore she develops more quickly.

It may be objected that money-making is not the most interesting thing in life, and that the "higher ideals" seem to have little place in this conception of feminine efficiency. The answer to such a criticism is to be found by considering once more the difference between the French and the American views as to the main object of money-making—a point to which any study of the two races inevitably leads one back.

Americans are too prone to consider money-making as interesting in itself: they regard the fact that a man has made money as something intrinsically meritorious. But money-making is interesting only in proportion as its object is interesting. If a man piles up millions in order to pile them up, having already all he needs to live humanly and decently, his occupation is neither interesting in itself, nor conducive to any sort of real social development in the money-maker or in those about him. No life is more sterile than one into which nothing enters to balance such an output of energy. To see how different is the French view of the object of money-making one must put one's self in the place of the average French household. For the immense majority of the French it is a far more modest ambition, and consists simply in the effort to earn one's living and put by enough for sickness, old age, and a good start in life for the children.

This conception of "business" may seem a tame one to Americans; but its advantages are worth considering. In the first place, it has the immense superiority of leaving time for living, time for men and women both. The average French business man at the end of his life may not have made as much money as the American; but meanwhile he has had, every day, something the American has not had: Time. Time, in the middle of the day, to sit down to an excellent luncheon, to eat it quietly with his family, and to read his paper afterward; time to go off on Sundays and holidays on long pleasant country rambles; time, almost any day, to feel fresh and free enough for an evening at the theatre, after a dinner as good and leisurely as his luncheon. And there is one thing certain: the great mass of men and women grow up and reach real maturity only through their contact with the material realities of living, with business, with industry, with all the great bread-winning activities; but the growth and the maturing take place *in the intervals between these activities:* and in lives where there are no such intervals there will be no real growth.

That is why the "slow" French business methods so irritating to the American business man produce, in the long run, results which he is often the first to marvel at and admire. Every intelligent American who has seen something of France and French life has had a first moment of bewilderment on trying to explain the seeming contradiction between the slow, fumbling, timid French business methods and the rounded completeness of French civilisation. How is it that a country which seems to have almost everything to learn in the way of "up-to-date" business has almost everything to teach, not only in the way of art and literature, and all the graces of life, but also in the way of municipal order, state administration, agriculture, forestry, engineering, and the whole harmonious running of the vast national machine? The answer is the last the American business man is likely to think of until he has had time to study France somewhat closely: it is that France is what she is because every Frenchman and every Frenchwoman takes time to live, and has an extraordinarily clear and sound sense of what constitutes *real living.*

We are too ready to estimate business successes by their individual results: a point of view revealed in our national awe of large fortunes. That is an immature and even childish way of estimating success. In terms of civilisation it is the total and ultimate result of a nation's business effort that matters, not the fact of Mr. Smith's being able to build a marble villa in place of his wooden cottage. If the collective life which results from our individual money-making is not richer; more interesting and more stimulating than that of countries where the individual effort is less intense, then it looks as if there were something wrong about our method.

This parenthesis may seem to have wandered rather far from the Frenchwoman who heads the chapter; but in reality she is at its very heart. For if Frenchmen care too much about other things to care as much as we do about making money, the chief reason is largely because their relations with women are more interesting. The Frenchwoman rules French life, and she rules it under a triple crown, as a business woman, as a mother, and above all as an artist. To explain the sense in which the last word is used it is necessary to go back to the contention that the greatness of France lies in her sense of the beauty and importance of living. As life is an art in France, so woman is an artist. She does not teach man, but she inspires him. As the Frenchwoman of the bread-winning class influences her husband, and inspires in him a respect for her judgment and her wishes, so the Frenchwoman of the rich and educated class is admired and held in regard for other qualities. But in this class of society her influence naturally extends much farther. The more civilised a society is, the wider is the range of each woman's influence over men, and of each man's influence over women. Intelligent and cultivated people of either sex will never limit themselves to communing with their own households. Men and women equally, when they have the range of interests that real cultivation gives, need the stimulus of different points of view, the refreshment of new ideas as well as of new faces. The long hypocrisy which Puritan England handed on to America concerning the danger of frank and free social relations between men and women has done more than anything else to retard real civilisation in America.

Real civilisation means an education that extends to the whole of life, in contradistinction to that of school or college: it means an education that forms speech, forms manners, forms taste, forms ideals, and above all forms judgment. This is the kind of civilisation of which France has always been the foremost model: it is because she possesses its secret that she has led the world so long not only in art and taste and elegance, but in ideas and in ideals. For it must never be forgotten that if the fashion of our note-paper and the cut of our dresses come from France, so do the conceptions of liberty and justice on which our republican institutions are based. No nation can have grown-up ideas till it has a ruling caste of grown-up men and women; and it is possible to have a ruling caste of grown-up men and women only in a civilisation where the power of each sex is balanced by that of the other.

It may seem strange to draw precisely this comparison between France, the country of all the old sex-conventions, and America, which is supposedly the country of the greatest sex-freedom; and the American reader may ask: "But where is there so much freedom of intercourse between men and women as in America?" The misconception arises from the confusion between two words, and two states of being that are fundamentally different. In America there is complete freedom of intercourse between boys and girls, but not between men and women; and there is a general notion that, in essentials, a girl and a woman are the same thing. It is true, in essentials, that a boy and a man are very much the same thing; but a girl and a woman—a married woman—are totally different beings. Marriage, union with a man, completes and transforms a woman's character, her point of view, her sense of the relative importance of things, far more thoroughly than a boy's nature is changed by the same experience. A girl is only a sketch; a married woman is the finished picture. And it is only the married woman who counts as a social factor.

Now it is precisely at the moment when her experience is rounded by marriage, motherhood, and the responsibilities, cares and interests of her own household, that the average American woman is, so to speak, "withdrawn from circulation." It is true that this does not apply to the small minority of wealthy and fashionable women who lead an artificial cosmopolitan life, and therefore represent no particular national tendency. It is not to them that the country looks for the development of its social civilisation, but to the average woman who is sufficiently free from bread-winning cares to act as an incentive to other women and as an influence upon men. In America this woman, in the immense majority of cases, has roamed through life in absolute freedom of communion with young men until the day when the rounding-out of her own experience by marriage puts her in a position to become a social influence; and from that day she is cut off from men's society in all but the most formal and intermittent ways. On her wedding-day she ceases, in any open, frank and recognised manner, to be an influence in the lives of the men of the community to which she belongs.

In France, the case is just the contrary. France, hitherto, has kept young girls under restrictions at which Americans have often smiled, and which have certainly, in some respects, been a bar to their growth. The doing away of these restrictions will be one of the few benefits of the war: the French young girl, even in the most exclusive and most tradition-loving society, will never again be the prisoner she has been in the past. But this is relatively unimportant, for the French have always recognised that, as a social factor, a woman does not count till she is married; and in the well-to-do classes girls marry extremely young, and the married woman has always had extraordinary social freedom. The famous French "Salon," the best school of talk and of ideas that the modern world has known, was based on the belief that the most stimulating conversation in the world is that between intelligent men and women who see each other often enough to be on terms of frank and easy friendship. The great wave of intellectual and social liberation that preceded the French revolution and prepared the way, not for its horrors but for its benefits, originated in the drawing-rooms of French wives and mothers, who received every day the most thoughtful and the most brilliant men of the time, who shared their talk, and often directed it. Think what an asset to the mental life of any country such a group of women forms! And in France they were not then, and they are not now, limited to the small class of the wealthy and fashionable. In France, as soon as a woman has a personality, social circumstances permit her to make it felt. What does it matter if she had spent her girlhood in seclusion, provided she is free to emerge from it at the moment when she is fitted to become a real factor in social life?

It may, of course, be asked at this point, how the French freedom of intercourse between married men and women affects domestic life, and the happiness of a woman's husband and children. It is hard to say what kind of census could be devised to ascertain the relative percentage of happy marriages in the countries where different social systems prevail. Until such a census can be taken, it is, at any rate, rash to assert that the French system is less favourable to domestic happiness than the Anglo-Saxon. At any rate, it acts as a greater incentive to the husband, since it rests with him to keep his wife's admiration and affection by making himself so agreeable to her, and by taking so much trouble to appear at an advantage in the presence of her men friends, that no rival shall supplant him. It would not occur to any Frenchman of the cultivated class to object to his wife's friendship with other men, and the mere fact that he has the influence of other men to compete with is likely to conduce to considerate treatment of his wife, and courteous relations in the household.

It must also be remembered that a man who comes home to a wife who has been talking with intelligent men will probably find her companionship more stimulating than if she has spent all her time with other women. No matter how intelligent women are individually, they tend, collectively, to narrow down their interests, and take a feminine, or even a female, rather than a broadly human view of things. The woman whose mind is attuned to men's minds has a much larger view of the world, and attaches much less importance to trifles, because men, being usually brought by circumstances into closer contact with reality, insensibly communicate their breadth of view to women. A "man's woman" is never fussy and seldom spiteful, because she breathes too free an air, and is having too good a time.

If, then, being "grown up" consists in having a larger and more liberal experience of life, in being less concerned with trifles, and less afraid of strong feelings, passions and risks, then the French woman is distinctly more grown up than her American sister; and she is so because she plays a much larger and more interesting part in men's lives.

It may, of course, also be asked whether the fact of playing this part—which implies all the dangers implied by taking the open seas instead of staying in port—whether such a fact is conducive to the eventual welfare of woman and of society. Well—the answer today is: *France!* Look at her as she has stood before the world for the last four years and a half, uncomplaining, undiscouraged, undaunted, holding up the banner of liberty: liberty of speech, liberty of thought, liberty of conscience, all the liberties that we of the western world have been taught to revere as the only things worth living for—look at her, as the world has beheld her since August, 1914, fearless, tearless, indestructible, in face of the most ruthless and formidable enemy the world has ever known, determined to fight on to the end for the principles she has always lived for. Such she is to-day; such are the millions of men who have spent their best years in her trenches, and the millions of brave, uncomplaining, self-denying mothers and wives and sisters who sent them forth smiling, who waited for them patiently and courageously, or who are mourning them silently and unflinchingly, and not one of whom, at the end of the most awful struggle in history, is ever heard to say that the cost has been too great or the trial too bitter to be borne.

No one who has seen Frenchwomen since the war can doubt that their great influence on French life, French thought, French imagination and French sensibility, is one of the strongest elements in the attitude that France holds before the world to-day.

# Time and Money: Economic Contexts and the Shifting Narratives of Ethnic Power

As Edith Wharton took what might be called literary license in writing *The Age of Innocence*, she came to terms with the literary necessity of changing the times of actual events. Both minor social details and major economic upheavals are rearranged to construct a compelling historical account. Drawing from the drama of a full decade, Wharton calibrated her subject with "measuring-worm exactness" (see Ehrhardt). After inquiring about the date of the month that Easter Sunday fell on in a particular year, Wharton appears to have realized that setting a precise date for Newland and May's wedding would raise questions about the timing of other events in the narrative. The inscription in May's wedding ring reads "187—," because of the need for greater flexibility in the temporal frame of the novel. To state the obvious, *The Age of Innocence* is a novel, albeit a painstakingly detailed and accurate novel, meant to recreate a particular historical period.

The demands of such an ambitious work of fiction cannot be girded by the minutiae of sequence, because the making of strong fiction means that the raw materials of history must be condensed and rearranged to support the demands of plot. This is the heightened truth made possible through fiction—what William Faulkner in *Absalom! Absalom!* called "the might-have-been which is more true than truth" (New York: Vintage Edition, 1986 [1936], 115). In *The Age of Innocence*, individual experiences are used to reveal the inner workings of society, and a single character, such as Julius Beaufort, can represent national and international economic forces that have the power to transform families and communities. This age, which increasingly located its innocence in the purity of its women and by extension in the conservative havens of the past preserved in the drawing rooms of the elite, saw the emergence of those called "robber barons." Some of the more disreputable of these men, the historical models for Beaufort, violated the gentleman's code in their rash speculations with other people's money and in their pursuit of what might be called other people's women.

Beaufort represents the power of money as fortunes changed hands amid the wildly fluctuating economy of the post–Civil War United States. During the decades following the war, profiteers from that lucrative venture were joined by those who rose to power or fell to bankruptcy as they laid the tracks to build and connect a modern nation. Completed in 1869, the transcontinental railroad opened vast lands in the west for economic development. This boom in stock companies built on economic possibilities that are in themselves best described as fictions explains the necessity for the economic term "inflation" that appeared in American English as early as 1864. In 1866, Edith Wharton's father took advantage of inflation, the high rents that meant that the Jones family could let their homes and other properties in America while living off that income in less expensive and elegant capitals of Europe. The young Edith came back in 1872 to the era that she would use as the background for her historical novel, returning to a United States where the economy was increasingly volatile and fragile.

Significantly, the most recognizable event that Wharton rearranged for dramatic effect in *The Age of Innocence* was the financial failure known as the Panic of 1873. Her decision to shift this financial crisis from the early seventies to near the close of the central action of the novel was clearly motivated by the demands of the plot. Here, the economic crash, personalized as "Beaufort's cropper" (160), is linked to the fall that results from the invasion of foreign financiers and other foreigners who are seen as contaminating influences. By joining sexuality with the love of high art, the novel underlines the danger associated with figures such as Julius Beaufort, Mrs. Lemuel Struthers, and even the Countess Olenska. The threat of a fall, based on sexual as well as financial seductions, is audible in the novel's monitory sermons and rumored liaisons, evidence of scandal that signals the end of the dangerously innocent and no longer insular society of Old New York.

The nightmare of the Panic of 1873 as experienced by the investors of New York was recorded in contemporary accounts documenting the rising tenor of emotional terror. Two sequential articles reporting the daily excitement in the *New York Times* and an equally timely but more contemplative analysis from *The Nation* have been included here. Written at the distance of a week and framed as a national rather than a local account, the article from *The Nation* discusses the phenomena of panics, in particular the significance of financial panics as they reveal the growing distrust of foreign investors amid the emergence of an international economy.

"Beaufort's situation" (162) with its intimations of "unlawful speculations" (157) remains somewhat mysterious in *The Age of Innocence*, but like the Panic of 1873, the financial crisis in Wharton's novel is experienced locally in relation to New York banks and individually in the financial ruin of respected members of the traditional elite. While Julius Beaufort, with his resonant name, his mysterious foreign past, and his taste for fast horses and fast women, was immediately associated with the prominent financier, August Belmont, the Panic of 1873 was based on the economic machinations of Jay Gould and Jim Fiske. Gould and Fiske, in their efforts to wrest control of the Erie Railroad from Commodore Cornelius Vanderbilt, colluded with Boss Tweed[1] and others to dilute the value of this stock by increasing the number of shares. Frightened by the volatility associated with this financial disaster, Europeans who had invested heavily in the railroads contributed to the economic failure by withdrawing their support.

While Gould made a profit in this risky venture and Fiske lost money, Commodore Vanderbilt used the difficulties to distinguish himself as a figure noted for his fiduciary responsibility. As runs were being made on the major banks, Vanderbilt announced that he would honor all requests from those who wanted to retrieve their money from his bank. The Commodore's act, along with Mrs. Vanderbilt's efforts that led to the building

1. See p. 79, *n.* 2.

of the Metropolitan Opera House, established the Vanderbilts as pillars of New York. When the novel suggests that the social world of the current administration in Washington has been dampened by earlier scandals, this vague allusion encompasses the Credit Mobilier scandal as well as the financial conspiracy of 1869 that saw the brother-in-law of President Ulysses S. Grant joining forces with the increasingly infamous Gould and Fiske as they tried and nearly succeeded in their plot to corner the U.S. gold market.

The financial depression that continued throughout the decade of the 1870s and into the 1880s had a widespread effect that could be measured in the increasing numbers of the destitute and the widening gap between the wealthy and those who comprised the lower classes. From the outset the foreign threat was not just that of foreign investors or, more intimately, outsiders with mysterious pasts who were making successful entries into the social enclave of Old New York. The foreign threat from mid-century forward was clearly located in the successive waves of immigrants who were being processed in a structure that the novel calls "the old Opera-house"—Castle Garden, the former fort and pleasure palace (p. 307). The 1869 woodcut "Squatters Near Central Park" (p. 308) depicts the agriculturally based subsistence economy still found in mixed race and mixed ethnic settlements such as Seneca Village. By the time of the concluding chapter, set just after the century's turn some thirty years later, the scene of poverty has shifted to the densely occupied tenements seen in the photograph by Jacob Riis (p. 309). This sense of an increasing crisis among the urban poor is acknowledged in the account of Newland Archer's brief role in progressive politics and his work to establish institutions for the public good.

Threatened by this influx of immigrants entering New York through Castle Garden to live in ethnically identified neighborhoods, the settled elite of Old New York experienced the threat of foreignness intimately as they themselves began to occupy islands within a Manhattan that was dominated by poor and aspiring new New Yorkers. At mid-century, over half the population of New York City was foreign born. These newcomers were the "bosses and the emigrant" (p. 79), the shifting political base that produced the Democratic political machine of Tammany Hall. By 1920, the year of the publication of The Age of Innocence, the fear of foreignness had gone beyond local political struggles to include nativist fears concerning class and manners, a province that for Henry James and Edith Wharton included the threat of foreign tongues sullying the English language. The Age of Innocence reveals these fears of New Yorkers at the time that the novel was written as well as the time in which it is set. As "The Lusk Committee Map" of 1920 (p. 310) demonstrates, ethnic neighborhoods were associated with the threat of communism, a perceived peril that is explicitly linked to the red areas, the color chosen for the neighborhoods dominated by Russian Jews. Revealing class-based and ideologically charted fears, this mapping of the "red scare" illustrates the defining presence of ethnic and racial groups that were redrawing the boundaries within New York and America.

# [The Source for the Beaufort Scandal]

## *The Panic: Excitement in Wall Street*

### SUSPENSION OF JAY COOKE AND CO.—WHAT IS THOUGHT OF IT EVERYWHERE—TROUBLE IN OTHER FIRMS†

It was a wild day in Wall street yesterday. The announcements of *The Times* in the morning prepared the public in a certain degree for the trouble which was to ensue, and many parties were enabled to go in the market early in the morning and protect themselves from loss. While many did this, and so saved themselves from ruin, there were others, and by far the majority, who thought that the trouble was solely brought about by machinations of the bears, and that there would be only a small-sized panic, which would result in a sudden rebound in prices. Those who took this view of the situation held on to their investments as long as possible, and as soon as their margins gave out, were compelled to go under. Of course, there were many who, by superior strength, were enabled to hold on to their purchases, and so escaped being sold out, at least for the time.

The first opening of the market was altogether in favor of the bull clique. The prices of the Vanderbilt, and nearly all other stocks, advanced. Parties who were frightened the night before by the marked decline in prices became sanguine and predicted an altogether better state of the market. This continued, however, but for a short time. The first intimation which came into the Stock Exchange of any change in the programme was contained in a brief notice, which said authoritatively that Jay Cooke and Co. had suspended payment. To say that the street became excited would only give a feeble view of the expressions of feeling. The brokers stood perfectly thunderstruck for a moment, and then there was a general run to notify the different houses in Wall street of the failure.

The brokers surged out of the Exchange, tumbling pell-mell over each other in the general confusion, and reached their respective offices in race-horse time. The members of firms who were surprised by this announcement had no time to deliberate. The bear clique was already selling the market down in the Exchange, and prices were declining frightfully.

Of course every one gave orders to sell out holdings as quick as possible, in order to obtain the best prices, and in this way when the brokers returned from the Long Room a fresh impetus was given to the decline, which brought about a fearful panic. There was no one on hand with nerve and money to arrest it either, and so the bear clique,[1]

---

† From *New York Times*, September 19, 1873: 1.
1. "bull clique . . . bear clique": Animal totems associated with business behaviors and types of markets in relation to the Stock Market or Stock Exchange. "Bulls" in what is known as a "bull market" are charging ahead and buying stock in an economy that is characterized by economic growth. "Bears," whether hoarding, hibernating, fleeing, or tenaciously holding their ground, represent market behavior or markets characteristic of economic depression, decline, fall, or slump where there is selling at a loss by those who fear losing their investments.

taking advantage of the general demoralization, made confusion worse confounded.

The news of the panic spread in every direction down-town, and hundreds of people who had been carrying stocks in expectation of a rise, rushed into the offices of their brokers and left orders that their holdings should be immediately sold out. In this way prices fell off so rapidly that not even Vanderbilt could have stemmed the tide. * * *

Some of the men who were ruined swore, some of them wept, some of them went out of the street without saying a word; others talked of the trouble in a jovial way, and went about trying to borrow money from friends to get on the short tack with. * * *

The news of Jay Cooke's failure spread rapidly throughout the City, and in an hour or so after the announcement hundreds of people gathered about the concern, on the side-walks, and peered curiously into the windows, as if some wonderful transformation was about to be witnessed. Policemen were needed to keep the people away from the doors and it was only by the most energetic pushing and use of strong language that they were enabled to keep the way clear and the rooms of the house free from an excited crowd. Rumors of all kinds were prevalent regarding the suspension, which many could hardly believe had actually taken place. * * *

The street was not cleared of crowds waiting to discuss the serious matter of the panic until about 5 o'clock, when a grand rush was made to get dinner before the evening assembly at the Fifth Avenue Hotel.

### AT THE CLUBS

At the different clubs, last evening the all-absorbing topic was the suspension of Jay Cooke and Co., and the smaller houses, and the consequent effect on trade. After dinner the members left their accustomed haunts, and proceeded in groups to the Fifth Avenue Hotel— the goal towards which the representatives of the whole commercial and financial interest made way. The Union and Union League Clubs[2] were comparatively deserted, and the few who remained conversed eagerly on the important events of the day. Among those competent to form an opinion on such matters, it was generally conceded that although the failures and consequent depreciation of stock had been productive of much uneasiness in moneyed circles, the panic was not of a character to affect the general stability of securities, its bearing being almost entirely confined to certain railroad bonds. Later in the night those who had been at the Fifth Avenue Hotel returned and reported the feeling there.

---

2. Union and Union League Clubs: Founded in 1836, the Union Club, the oldest men's social club in New York, was considered to be the richest club in Manhattan in the 1870s; Union League Club: Begun in 1863, these clubs in northern cities were dedicated to solidifying support for the Union cause after serious losses on the battlefront and in elections suggested that support for the party of Lincoln (the nineteenth-century Republican party) was waning. The Union League Club of New York responded in the postwar era to the public's interest in viewing the private art collections displayed at the Metropolitan Fairs by helping to found the Metropolitan Museum of Art.

### The Financial Crisis: More Failures Yesterday

### The Scene in Wall Street—List of Suspensions— Government to Buy $10,000,000 of Bonds Today†

The excitement in Wall street, yesterday beggars all description. The trouble of Thursday was bad enough, but it was entirely eclipsed by that of yesterday. It is a singular coincidence that the gold corner of September, 1869, when so many persons were ruined, and the culmination of the panic in 1873, when the finances of the entire country have been placed in the same dangerous condition, happened upon the same day of the week and in the same month. Many men who appeared prominently in the first of these disturbances have also figured extensively in the last. Houses identified with the Government have been forced to succumb to the tremendous pressure brought to bear from damaging rumors and an unparalleled tightness of money. Jay Gould, too, who bullied gold in 1869 until it touched 162, is engaged in the present trouble. There have been two *Black Fridays* in the history of the country, and the sixth day of the week will be hereafter looked upon with suspicion in Wall street.

Commercial men, bankers, brokers, and the financial public generally, gathered in Wall street long before 10 o'clock yesterday morning. There was reason for it, too. The rumors which had gained currency were not at all reassuring to people who had money to invest, or who wished to borrow it. Many persons had long lines of stocks which they were carrying; a panic would swallow up their margins, and leave them—wealthy the day before—in a state of penury. Some had money deposited in banks; a panic might force these institutions to suspend. Others were in a state of indecision, and did not know what to do.

The consequence was that thousands of people who are seldom seen down-town thought it worth their while to arrive on the scene of action early in the morning, so as to be on hand for anything that might turn up. It was a universal case of looking out for "number one," and so everybody who had anything to lose, or aught to gain, was on hand.

When the hour of 10 arrived, the time for the opening of the Stock Exchange, one of the most turbulent crowds of humanity ever seen in Wall street surged about the doors eager to obtain entrance. As soon as admittance was accorded there was a general rush to reach the floor of the Long Room, and in a moment afterwards quotations for stocks were in order. No one knew what to offer, and everybody was undecided as to selling prices. It was at least 5 minutes before quotations would be made, owing to the general uncertainty regarding the situation. * * *

The Exchange closed with somewhat better prices prevailing, but with a despondent feeling concerning the policy of the Government. Brokers stood about discussing the situation until nearly 5 o'clock. * * *

† From *New York Times*, September 20, 1873: 1.

The person who finally sustained the market and kept it from break-ing to a point where half of the street would have been inevitably ru-ined was Jay Gould. He bought during the low prices several hundred thousand shares of railroad stocks, principally of the Vanderbilt stripe, and in this way put a check on the ruinous decline. These stocks were bought principally for cash, and the large clerical force of Osborn and Chapin, Gould's brokers, was employed until 5 o'clock in taking care of the deliveries and making out the checks in payment. * * *

*     *     *

*Panics*†

It is impossible to see, much less experience, a financial panic with-out an almost appalling consciousness that a new and terrible form of danger and distress has been added in comparatively recent times to the list of those by which human life is menaced or perplexed. Any one who stood on Wall Street, or in the gallery of the Stock Exchange last Thursday, and Friday, and Saturday, and saw the mad terror, we might almost say the brute terror (like that by which a horse is devoured who has a pair of broken shafts hanging to his heels, or a dog flying from a tin saucepan attached to his tail) with which great crowds of men rushed to and fro, trying to get rid of their property, almost begging people to take it from them at any price, could hardly avoid feeling that a new plague had been sent among men, that there was an impal-pable, invisible force in the air, robbing them of their wits, of which philosophy had not as yet dreamt. No dog was ever so much alarmed by the clatter of the saucepan as hundreds seemed to be by the pos-session of really valuable and dividend-paying securities; and no horse was ever more reckless in extricating himself from the *débris* of a bro-ken carriage than these swarms of acute and shrewd traders in divest-ing themselves of their possessions. Hundreds must really, to judge by their conduct, have been so confused by terror and anxiety as to be unable to decide whether they desired to have or not have, to be poor or rich. If a Roman or a man of the Middle Ages had been suddenly brought into view of the scene, he would have concluded without hes-itation that a ruthless invader was coming down the island; that his advanced guard was momentarily expected; and that anybody found by his forces in possession of Western Union, or Harlem, or Lake Shore, or any other paying stock or bond, would be subjected to cruel tor-tures, if not put to death. For neither the Roman nor the Mediæval could understand a rich man's being terrified by anything but armed violence. Seneca enumerates as the three great sources of anxiety in life the fear of want, of disease, and of oppression by the powerful, and he pronounces the last the greatest. If he had seen Wall Street brokers and bankers last week trying to get rid of stocks and bonds, he could not of course have supposed that they were poor or feared poverty; he would have judged from their physical activity that they were in perfect health, so that he would have been driven to the con-

† From "The Week," *Nation*, September 25, 1873, pp. 206–207.

clusion that some barbarian host commanded by Sitting Bull or Red Cloud[1] was entering the city, and was breathing out threatenings and slaughter against the owners of personal property. If you had tried to explain to him that there was no conqueror at the gates, that the fear of violence was almost unknown in our lives, that each man in that struggling crowd enjoyed an amount of security against force in all its forms which no Roman Senator could ever count upon, and that the terror he witnessed was caused by precisely the same agency as the flight of an army before it has been beaten, or, in other words, by "panic," he would have gazed at you in incredulous amazement. He would have said that panic in an army was caused by the sudden dissolution of the bonds of discipline, by each soldier's losing his confidence that his comrades and his officers would stand their ground; but these traders, he would have added, are not subject to discipline; they do not belong to an organization of any kind; each buys and sells for himself; he has his property there in that tin box, and if nobody is going to rob him, what is frightening him? Why is he pale and trembling? Why does he run and shout and weep, and ask people to give him a trifle, only a trifle, for all he possesses and let him go?

If you were then to set about explaining to Seneca that the way the god Pan worked confusion in our day in the commercial world was by destroying "credit" you would find yourself brought suddenly face to face with one of the most striking differences between ancient and modern, or even as we have said, mediæval society. The most prominent and necessary accompaniment or incident of property in the ancient world was possession. What a man owned, he held. His wealth was in his farm, or his house, or his granary, or his ships. He could hardly separate the idea of property from that of possession, and the state of society strengthened the association. The frugal man hoarded; and when he was terrified, he buried his money, a practice to which we owe the preservation of the greater portion of old coins now in our collections. The influence of this sense of insecurity, or the constant fear of invasion or violence, lasted long enough in all Continental countries, as Mr. Bagehot has recently pointed out, to prevent the establishment of banks of issue until very lately. The prospect of war was so constantly in men's minds that no bank could make arrangements for the run which would surely follow the outbreak of hostilities, and,

1. Seneca: Lucius Annaeus (4 B.C.E.–65 C.E.): born in what is now called Spain, this philosopher, orator, and playwright was educated in Rome where he became the ill-fated tutor and advisor of the emperor Nero; Red Cloud: Makhpiya Luta (1822–1922); here named as the feared Oglala Lakota chief who led the Sioux as they forcibly closed the Bozeman Trail, thwarting U.S. troops and prospective settlers who were invading the tribe's territory. Red Cloud signed what many Sioux continue to consider a controversial peace treaty in 1868. Sitting Bull: Tatanka-Iyotanka (1831–1890); here named as the feared Hunkpapa Lakota chief and influential Sioux spiritual leader who had been named head chief of the Lakota nation in 1868. In 1873, he would have been known for his battles against U.S. troops that had been assigned to defend railroad workers along the Yellowstone River. This article was written before gold was discovered in the Black Hills in 1874 and before Sitting Bull led the successful attack against General Custer and his troops in 1876 at the famous Battle of Little Bighorn.

in view of this contingency, nobody would be willing to hold paper promises to pay in lieu of gold and silver. It is therefore in England and America, the two countries possessing not only most commercial enterprise, but most security against invasion, that the paper money has come into earliest and wider use. To the paper of the banks have been added the checks and bills of exchange of private individuals, until money proper plays a greatly diminishing part in the operations of commerce. Goods are exchanged and debts paid by a system of balancing claims against claims, which really has almost ceased to rest on money at all. So that a man may be a very rich man in our day, and have really nothing to show for his wealth whatever. You go to his house, and you find nothing but a lot of shabby furniture. The only thing there which Seneca would have called wealth is perhaps his wife's jewels, which would not bring a few thousand dollars. You think his money must be in the bank, but you go there with him and find that all he has there is a page on the ledger bearing his name, with a few figures on it. The bank bills which you see lying about, and which look a little like money, are not only not money in the sense Seneca understood the term, but they do not represent over a third of what the bank owes to various people. You go to some safe-deposit vaults, thinking that it is perhaps there he keeps his valuables, but all you find is a mass of papers, signed by Thomas Smith or John Jones, declaring that he is entitled to so many shares of some far-off bank, or that some railroad will pay him a certain sum some thirty years hence. In fact, looked at with Roman eyes, our millionaire seems to be possessed of little or nothing, and likely to be puzzled about his daily bread.

Now, this wonderful change in the character and incidents of property may be said to be the work of the last century, and it may be said to consist in the substitution of an agency wholly moral for an agency wholly material in the work of exchange and distribution. For the giving and receiving of gold and silver, we have substituted neither more nor less than faith in the honesty, and industry, and capacity of our fellow-men. There is hardly one of us who does not literally live by faith. We lay up fortunes, marry, eat, drink, travel, and bequeath, almost without ever handling a cent; and the best reason which ninety-nine out of every hundred of us can give for feeling secure against want, or having the means of enjoyment or of charity, is not the possession of anything of real value, but his confidence that certain thousands of his fellow-creatures, whom he has never seen, and never expects to see, scattered, it may be, over the civilized world, will keep their promises, and do their daily work with fidelity and efficiency. This faith is every year being made to carry a greater and greater load. The transactions which rest on it increase every year in magnitude and complexity. It has to extend itself every year over a larger portion of the earth's surface, and to include a greater variety of race, and creed, and custom. London, and Paris, and Berlin, and Vienna now tremble when New York is alarmed. We have, in short, to believe every year in a greater and greater number of people, and to depend for our daily bread on the successful working of vast combinations, in which human character is after all the main element.

The consequence is that, when for any reason, a shade of doubt comes over men's minds that the combination is not working, that the machine is at some point going to give way, that somebody is not playing his part fairly, the solid ground seems to shake under their feet, and we have some of the phenomena resulting from an earthquake, and among others blind terror. But to any one who understands what this new social force, Credit, is, and the part it plays in human affairs, the wonder is, not that it gives way so seldom, but that it stands so firm; that these hundreds of millions of laborers, artisans, shopkeepers, merchants, bankers, and manufacturers hold so firmly from day to day the countless engagements into which they enter, and that each recurring year the result of the prodigious effort which is now put forth in the civilized world in the work of production, should be distributed with so much accuracy and honesty, and, on the whole, with so much wise adjustment to the value of each man's contributions to civilization.

There is one fact, however, which throws around credit, as around so many others of the influences by which our lives are shaped, a frightful mystery. Its very strength helps to work ruin. The more we believe in our fellow-toilers, and the more they do to warrant our belief, the more we encourage them to work, the more we excite their hopefulness; and out of this hopefulness come "panics" and "crashes." Prosperity breeds credit, and credit stimulates enterprise, and enterprise embarks in labors which about every ten years in England, and every twenty years in this country, it is found that the world is not ready to pay for. Panics have occurred in England in 1797, 1807, 1817, 1826, 1837, 1847, 1857, and there was very near being a very severe one in 1866. In this country we have had them in 1815, 1836, and 1857, and by panics we do not mean such local whirlwinds as have desolated Wall Street, but widespread commercial crises, affecting all branches of business. This periodicity is ascribed, and with much plausibility, to the fact that inasmuch as panics are the result of certain mental conditions, they recur as soon as the experience of the previous one has lost its influence, or, in other words, as often as a new generation comes into the management of affairs, which is about every ten years in the commercial world both in England and here. The fact that this country seems to be only half as liable to them as England, is perhaps due to the fact that the extent of our resources and the greater ratio of increase of population make it much harder to overdo in the work of production here than in England, and to this must be added the greater strength of nerves produced by greater hopefulness. In spite of the enormous abundance of British capital and the rashness of the owners in making investments, there hangs over the London money market a timidity and doubtfulness about the future which is unknown on this side of the water, and which very slight accidents develop into distrust and terror. If this theory be correct, our next great panic will be due about the year 1877,[2] immediately after the Centennial Exposition. Let us hope, however, that the present slight attack may inspire enough prudence and good sense to ward it off.

2. A later financial disaster, the panic in 1884 that primarily hurt the banks of New York, did occur at the appropriate time near the close of the decade from which the events of the central action of the novel were drawn. However this historical event lacked the emotional tenor that distinguishes the scene of economic betrayal described in *The Age of Innocence*. The financial fall of 1884 did not and could not evoke the personal sense of outraged innocence over the dangers of national and international speculation in stocks that characterized accounts of the "Panic of 1873." By 1884, instability in railroad corporations and banks had already become a familiar and feared part of American economic life. There were also serious depressions in 1890, 1893, and 1907, followed (nine years after the publication of the novel) by the "Great Depression" of 1929. These early depressions, often associated with questions about stock fraud and the stability of the gold standard, were also still suggestively linked to the health of the U.S. and regional agricultural economy, making autumn the season for economic falls. This was not just an issue of the market being able to speculate about the potential for crop failures; rather, as the farmers themselves waited for returns from their cash crops, this season was a time that farmers would most need to turn to banks for loans.

"**Castle Garden, New York City, 1851**," painted by Jasper F. Cropsey (1823–1900), a noted American painter identified with the Hudson River School. This particular work was painted as a gift for Jenny Lind (1820–87), the famed Swedish soprano, to commemorate her spectacular American debut there in September of 1850. Although by the time of the central events of *The Age of Innocence*, this edifice had become the country's major site for processing immigrants, Castle Garden is alluded to simply as "the old Opera-house" in the novel. (See p. 8, *n*. 5.)

**"Squatters Near Central Park"** (1869). This engraving by D. E. Wyard depicts the unpenned animals, unwatched children, and unchaperoned women of a squatters' settlement. It illustrates the populated "wilderness" (9) associated with racially and ethnically mixed communities, such as Seneca Village, that the refined landscape of Central Park was designed to replace. (From *Harper's Weekly*, June 26, 1869.)

"Rag-Pickers' Court" (1879), an engraving by William A. Rogers (*left*), and "Elizabeth Street, Water-Closets in the Yard" (published ca. 1903), a photograph by Jacob Riis (*right*), document the density of tenement populations at the time in which the novel's closing segment is set. Riis's photographs, originally taken between 1889 and 1891, became more effective social documents at the turn of the century as a result of the clarity of the image made possible by improvements in the process of half-tone printing. As both the engraving and the photograph suggest, the iconography of urban poverty in New York remained virtually the same from the late nineteenth through the early twentieth centuries.

**"Red Scare": The Lusk Committee Map (1920).** Published in the same year as *The Age of Innocence* and reproduced here in black-and-white, this detail of a hand-colored map suggests the contemporary context for the fear of foreign contamination that shapes Wharton's novel. The colors chosen were significant: The areas inhabited by Russian Jews (three years after the Bolshevik Revolution) appeared in red, while the reddest orange locates Syrians, Turks, Armenians, and Greeks. The Irish neighborhoods were dark green, the Chinese neighborhood ("Chinatown") was yellow, and those neighborhoods occupied by "Negroes" were dark brown. "Mixed" neighborhoods (places with no distinguishing ethnic concentration) were designated as "uncolored." The numbers on the map mark gathering places—settlement houses, theaters, churches—that the Lusk Legislative Committee had identified as dangerous breeding grounds for foreign ideas.

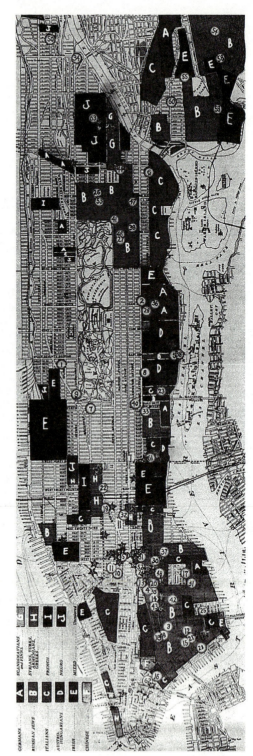

# The Business of Society: Contemporary Commentary on the New York Aristocracy

In the opening pages of *The Age of Innocence*, Wharton argues against the popular claim that Old New York was an aristocracy by insisting on the middle-class and mercantile origins of this exclusive society. While this society was not aristocratic in the European sense, the legacy of birth controlled the class-confirming rituals of family inheritance and marriage that formed the business of society. Like gentlemen in the Old World, the gentlemen of the New World of Old New York do not define themselves according to their professions; instead, these men are directed by women, ruling matriarchs such as the "Imperial" (Mrs. Manson Mingott). In Wharton's Old New York, leisure has the seriousness of a business proposition, a business that has always been driven by the investment in the propagation of heirs and the proper consolidation of property.

Not unlike the opening of a Jane Austen novel where characters weigh in according to their worth in pounds, the business of society in Old New York is to preserve this enclave threatened by those who are attempting to purchase respectability and social status through money. Established through a legacy of marital alliances and many generations of cousin-cousin marriages, the inbred world of Old New York, the New York four hundred, was said to be determined by the limited capacity of Mrs. Astor's ballroom. As one of the primary organizers of the Assemblies, the most prominent of which were the at least thrice yearly Patriarchs' Balls, Ward McAllister was both the recognized master of protocol and the official spokesman for this highly visible and fiercely private social entity. Understood to be the historical model for the novel's social arbiters, Lawrence Lefferts and Sillerton Jackson, McAllister's descriptions of social rituals in the newspaper column included here offer a suggestive parallel to the detailed explanations found in the novel itself.

Wharton chose to write about the social transformation that was taking place in this decade beginning in "the early seventies," because it was the intimate world of her childhood and because this decade encompassed an era of great change. Indeed, the world of Old New York had undergone so much change that this transformation had become highly visible in popular advice manuals that were appearing in the 1880s. Perhaps the most respected codification of the rituals of this American elite appears in Mrs. Mary Elizabeth Sherwood's *Manners and Social Usages* first published in 1884, a volume revised and reprinted through the turn of the century. Written for the newly rich and other outsiders ambitious to acquire the manners associated with the highest society, Mrs. Sherwood's revised edition of 1887 suggests that these former interlopers might actually be able to gain entry into the once-closed ballrooms of the New York elite. Mrs. Sherwood's 1887 edition includes a new chapter entitled "Fashionable Dancing," advising the mothers and daughters of the newly wealthy about the appropriateness of types of dances, insisting that dances such as the "German" are so intimate that they can only be proper when the company is well known. Following Mrs. Sherwood's advice on serving Roman Punch, this section includes four different recipes for this icy drink that declared the formality of a dinner party by establishing the cleavage between a hierarchy of dishes.

First published in the early eighties, at the close of the period from which Wharton had chosen to draw her historical events for *The Age of Innocence*, Mrs. Sherwood's manual offers a telling account of the practices of the upper class, a world once so closed that there was no need to describe these rituals to those who had imbibed them since birth. The excerpts from Mrs. Sherwood's guide included here are from the 1887 edition because this is the volume that Wharton actually used to prime her memory as she gleaned details from the social past for *The Age of Innocence*. (See p. 109 *n*.1.)

Promising in its subtitle to be "An Entrance Key to the Fantastic Life of the 400," Francis Crowninshield's *Manners for the Metropolis*, published in 1910 for those who are called "plutocrats," vowed to teach such men about how to discover the "business end of an asparagus." Radically different in tone from Mrs. Sherwood's volume, *Manners for the Metropolis* is strangely similar in its preface that also reveals social anxiety associated with the proper use of cutlery and forks. What changed by 1910 is that Edith Wharton herself had become a character to be reckoned with in Crowninshield's ostensibly humorous guide. Wharton appears here by name in the role of the famous author known for her membership in this select society. Despite its tone of satire and its penchant for making fun of social heirs, *Manners for the Metropolis* manages to give helpful advice to ambitious men and, to a lesser extent, women who are trying to break into a closed society. Just as Mrs. Sherwood's manual maintains its note of seriousness as it addresses a female audience (most pointedly mothers with marriageable daughters), *Manners for the Metropolis* takes as its audience socially climbing men who start out as dance partners in search of advice for getting invited to fine dinners and avoiding boring or unattractive women. While the social business described in these works may be contracted in the ballroom and at the dinner table, both of these seemingly disparate advice manuals are concerned with the more hierarchically informed and formal place setting to be finalized at the altar.

Even with the detailed information made available by McAllister, Sherwood, and Crowninshield, the mystery surrounding this exclusive society and the interest of the public in this private world remained high. In an 1895 article that does not fit *The Age of Innocence's* description of "newspaper rubbish" (32) about high society, *Cosmopolitan* printed a judicious piece entitled "The Myth of the New York Four-Hundred" that describes some of the forces of change that are represented in Wharton's novel. Here, Mrs. Burton Harrison discusses crucial changes such as the rise in female athleticism and the fashionable trend that has led to efforts to marry daughters of the New York elite to European aristocrats.

# "Secrets of Ball Giving": A Chat with Ward McAllister†

### *How He Came to be a Famous Ball Organizer— Reminiscences of Cotillion Dinners*

The name of the gentleman who manages the balls of the Patriarchs Society in this city is familiar to most people who read the newspapers. By many an aspirant for social elevation he is regarded as a mysterious power, whose favor is an "Open Sesame," or as an ogre who stands blocking the way to the enchanting inner circle of New-York Society.

In a social chat the other evening, Ward McAllister dispelled the idea that he was an absolute social monarch; he is only a representative of the exclusiveness that must necessarily characterize the balls which he conducts for society. His looks are certainly not terrifying. A well-knit frame supports a large head: the open forehead, genial, brilliant eyes and benevolent features, set off with mustache and imperial,[1] combine to form an expression that may be called fastidious or judicial, but by no means unkind. A representative of an old Southern family, he lives with quiet taste and easy comfort in East Sixteenth st. His lawyer's education, tact and large acquaintance stand him in good stead as a manager of estates and promoter of financial, commercial, or political enterprises where diplomacy is essential. A forenoon devoted to business, an afternoon stroll up the avenue, with an hour or two at the Union Club, a dinner party or ball in the evening, make up his routine when in town. Travel, a month or two at Newport—where he has a well-managed farm as well as a cottage—with occasional trips to the city, make up his summer schedule.

### *Beginning His Experience at Newport*

"Well, I would have to go back to the time when I was married to get at the beginning of my connection with social festivities," said Mr. McAllister, when requested to give his reminiscences. "That was in 1853. I went to Europe, came back in 1856, and spending the summer at Newport, naturally fell into the social tide there and soon began to organize the Newport picnics. Never heard of them? Well, you are young, yet. I would organize a small party, hire a steamer, and go off to some place like Rocky Point, where we would have a good luncheon, dinner, or clambake, with a frolic and dance, and a moonlight sail home."

"How did I come to manage these things? Well, I hardly know myself. I appreciated at the outset the importance of enlisting the leading men, fathers of families, who would stand by me and make failure impossible. The next great thing that I have always had to insist on is exclusiveness. A ball that anyone can gain admittance to is never

---

† From *New York Daily Tribune* March 25, 1888: 10.
1. A pointed goatee (named in honor of the French emperor Napoleon III).

attractive, while one that is rigidly exclusive will make invitations sought for by everybody. Then if I have always insisted on an attractive, and, if possible, a novel place for meeting; the best of viands, wine and service, and, you can add, the best of music and most artistic floral decorations. There you have the secret of successful ball-giving in a nutshell."

"How old is the Patriarchs Society, Mr. McAllister?"

"Let's see. The Patriarchs started in '73. Yes, but we had Cotillion dinners before that. You see I had come to New-York. The damp air at Newport did not agree with me. Well, we organized the Cotillion dinners, you know. Perhaps sixty or seventy people would meet, have a good dinner, and dance the German[2] afterward.

"Who used to lead them?"

"There were Henry Coster and James Otis and T. Burnett Baldwin. Yes, John G. Heckscher used to lead, too, and George Bend came on later. You see there were not so many millionaires in those days, and few people were spending their incomes. One of these was Mr. Belmont. I suppose he expended $60,000 or $70,000 a year. He kept a chef at $60 or $70 dollars a month, which was thought exorbitant in those days. It seems absurd in these days, when every one of pretensions keeps a chef and pays him $100 to $150 dollars a month. Then the chef often manages to get a commission of 20 per cent from tradesmen, so he makes a nice salary. You know the chefs at the Hoffman House and Delmonico's get $6,000 a year."

### Objects of the Patriarchs Society

"Well, as society grew and fortunes increased, as well as families, the leaders in society felt the need of an exclusive series of assemblies, at which to bring out their daughters and introduce to them eligible young men of good character, as well as to entertain each other and foreigners or strangers in the city. This led to the organization of the Patriarchs' balls, and I was asked to superintend their arrangements.

"You know there are fifty Patriarchs, who subscribe to pay for each season's series of three or four balls. Each Patriarch has five invitations for ladies and four for gentlemen, besides his own, to distribute, and he asks whomever he pleases. The only safeguard as to the character and exclusiveness of the guests is the high social standing of the Patriarchs themselves. This is made doubly safe by the rule that each invitation must bear the name of the guest and the name of the Patriarch issuing it, so that if any objectionable person should appear at a ball, the tickets would show who had invited him or her. But such a thing has never happened; every Patriarch knowing that he is the sponsor for the character of the guests he invites. The idea that some people have that I exercised a censorship over the list of guests invited

---

2. A dance featuring figures and waltzes (also known as the "German Cotillion"). This dance was distinguished by the ritual exchange of favors (inexpensive, playful or evocative objects) between the dancers. (See also pp. 324–28.)

is erroneous. My judgment may be sometimes requested, or I may have some tickets referred to me with discretionary power as to their distribution on special occasions, when Patriarchs are absent and cannot well send out invitations themselves."

"Might not the same person receive invitations from a half-dozen different Patriarchs?"

### Duplicate Invitations Prevented

"Certainly. There is where my work comes in, to prevent duplication. Often there is a rush of invitations offered to various popular people. The first Patriarch who sends me his list of names has the tickets issued by me with the names of his guests filled in, forwarded to him. If the next list contains names already selected, the list is returned for substitutions. I have to keep, therefore, a record of all the guests invited and who invites them. The extra tickets are usually tendered to strangers from other cities, and to foreigners of rank. It is against the rules for a Patriarch to erase the name of a guest and substitute another name. He must apply for a new card of admission. An error of this kind caused some annoyance to Miss Elsie de Wolfe[3] last winter, the tickets being irregular, and she was stopped by Johnson until the matter was satisfactorily explained.

"Only five of the original Patriarchs are now on the list. They are Robert G. Remsen, J. W. Hamersley, Maturin Livingston, G. H. Warren, and myself. Others of the original Patriarchs' were J. J. Astor, Delancey Kane, Sr., Alexander S. McComb, A. Gracie King, Louis Mason Jones, Eugene Livingston, E. T. Spelling, and W. R. Travers. Mr. Travers used to be a princely entertainer and almost rivalled Mr. Belmont in hospitality. The Patriarchs balls were begun in Delmonico's Fourteenth-st. restaurant, which I still think was the finest asembly room for the purpose that the city has had. When Delmonico moved to Fifth-ave. and Twenty-sixth st., we followed him and have had every ball since at that place except one at the Metropolitan Opera House. The difficulty of serving the supper at this last place prevented our repeating the experiment."

"Society," continued Mr. McAllister, "is an occupation in itself. Only a man who has a good deal of leisure and a taste for it can keep up with its demands and with what interests it. Say what you will, the modern leader of society must still have considerable of the old courtier and chevalier endowment to make a success of it. Numbers of people are introduced in fashionable society every season who cannot and do not make a success, and they fall out. They cannot float themselves even when some one gives them a good start. These people have not the poise, the aptitude for polite conversation, the polished and

3. Miss Elsie de Wolfe: (1865–1950), American-born stylist, known as the founder of the modern profession of interior decoration. Educated abroad, she had been presented at the court of Queen Victoria in 1883, five years before McAllister chose to share this embarrassing episode in his society column interview. Like Wharton, de Wolfe was given the highest award to foreigners by the French government for her work in World War I, in particular for her care for seriously burned soldiers.

deferential manner, the infinite capacity of good humor and the ability to entertain or be entertained that society demands.

## Society's Limits Narrowing

"Why, there are only about 400 people in fashionable New-York society. If you go outside that number you strike people who are either not at ease in a ball-room or else make other people not at ease. See the point? Of course there are any number of the most cultivated and highly respectable, even distinguished, people outside of fashionable society. When we give a large ball like the last New Year's ball for eight hundred people, we go outside of the exclusive fashionable set and invite professional men, doctors, lawyers, editors, artists, and the like. But the day has gone by. Twenty or thirty years ago it was otherwise. But now with the rapid growth of riches millionaires are too common to receive much deference; a fortune of a million is only respectable poverty. So we have to draw social boundaries on another basis; old connections, gentle breeding, perfection in all the requisite accomplishments of a gentleman, elegant leisure and an unstained private reputation count for more than newly gotten riches. You would be surprised at the number of apparently eligible men this list of requirements strikes out of consideration. The truth is we are not a nation of Chesterfields and Bayards, Sidneys and Raleighs."[4]

"Have not New-York's most brilliant entertainments often been in private houses?"

"Yes, and always will be, for various reasons. I can remember some brilliant affairs when men like Belmont and Travers entertained; when Delancey Kane had the old Bareda house, and when W. Butler Duncan entertained the first F.C.D.C. ball. You know the Family Circle Dancing Class ball was started as an overflow for the younger element when the Patriarchs' balls ceased to suffice for their entertainment. I presume that the most handsome combined dinner and cotillion ever given in New York was that of Edward Luckmeyer. It was called the 'swan dinner,' and the table had live swans floating around the green islands in a miniature lake that occupied the centre of the table.

"Leonard W. Jerome's cotillion dinner and W. R. Travers's, at Delmonico's, were memorable occasions. Of late years General Cutting's dinner for Miss Annie Cutting at Delmonico's a few years ago was remarkable for the beauty of the debutantes and the costliness of the roses, which seemed to cover the rooms and hide the walls."

## Famous Dinners of Recent Years

"The dinner which 'Cook's Bulletin' has called the finest ever served in the city for artistic cooking and appointments was that given to Attorney-General Brewster by Frederick G. Thompson at Delmonico's on February 5, 1883. It cost about $7,000, and was a remarkable af-

---

4. Distinguished British families who rose to social prominence through their enterprise and their eloquence.

fair. A Patriarch's ball followed the dinner, which all the dinner guests attended. The table was I-shaped and a mass of flowers. This was the unparalleled, brilliant season that saw the Vanderbilt fancy-dress ball. Patti and Scalchi were charming people in the old Academy with Italian melodies, and Mrs. Potter was making her first brilliant season as an amateur. This season's gayety was so remarkable that a history of it, in book form, was compiled.

"Of course, there have been handsome entertainments since. * * *

"Ah yes, there has been a great advance made of late years in the quality of suppers at our balls. Three delicacies are now considered indispensable, and they are canvasback ducks, terrapin and paté de foie gras. This season, however, it is difficult to get good canvasbacks. Either the best of them are shipped to English markets or there has been so much gunning at Havre de Gras and other points on the Chesapeake as to frighten them away from their feeding grounds of wild celery, thereby spoiling their delicacy of flavor. It seems as if something would have to be done to prevent the extinction of the canvasback ducks; or they will follow in the wake of the buffalo. Now they are so scarce as to command $7 to $9 a pair. You know that when Lord Rosebery was here, that after a dinner of canvasback, he asserted that the United States should have chosen canvasback duck as their emblem instead of a tough and worthless bald eagle.

*     *     *

# MRS. MARY ELIZABETH SHERWOOD

## From *Manners and Social Usages*†

### *Preface*

There is no country where there are so many people asking what is "proper to do," or, indeed, where there are so many genuinely anxious to do the proper thing, as in the vast conglomerate which we call the United States of America. The newness of our country is perpetually renewed by the sudden making of fortunes, and by the absence of a hereditary, reigning set. There is no aristocracy here which has the right and title to set the fashions.

But a "reigning set," whether it depend upon hereditary right or adventitious wealth, if it be possessed of a desire to lead and a disposition to hospitality, becomes for a period the dictator of fashion to a large number of lookers-on. The travelling world, living far from great centres, goes to Newport, Saratoga, New York, Washington, Philadelphia, Boston, and gazes on what is called the latest American fashion. This, though exploited by what we may call for the sake of distinction the "newer set," is influenced and shaped in some degree by people of

† From M. E. W. Sherwood. New York: Harper and Brothers, 1887, pp. 3–6; 142–58, 275, 268.

native refinement and taste, and that wide experience which is gained by travel and association with broad and cultivated minds. They counteract the tendency to vulgarity, which is the great danger of a newly launched society, so that our social condition improves, rather than retrogrades, with every decade.

There may be many social purists who will disagree with us in this statement. Men and women educated in the creeds of the Old World, with the good blood of a long ancestry of quiet ladies and gentlemen, find modern American society, particularly in New York and at Newport, fast, furious, and vulgar. There are, of course, excesses committed everywhere in the name of fashion; but we cannot see that they are peculiar to America. We can only answer that the creed of fashion is one of perpetual change. There is a Council of Trent, we may say, every five years, perhaps even every two years, in our new and changeful country, and we learn that, follow as we may either the grand old etiquette of England or the more gay and shifting social code of France, we still must make an original etiquette of our own. Our political system alone, where the lowest may rise to the highest preferment, upsets in a measure all that the Old World insists upon in matters of precedence and formality. Certain immutable principles remain common to all elegant people who assume to gather society about them, and who wish to enter its portals; the absent-minded scholar from his library should not ignore them, the fresh young farmer from the countryside feels and recognizes their importance. If we are to live together in unity we must make society a pleasant thing, we must obey certain formal rules, and these rules must conform to the fashion of the period.

And it is in no way derogatory to a new country like our own if on some minor points of etiquette we presume to differ from the older world. We must fit our garments to the climate, our manners to our fortunes and to our daily lives. There are, however, faults and inelegancies of which foreigners accuse us which we may do well to consider. One of these is the greater freedom allowed in the manners of our young women—a freedom which, as our New World fills up with people of foreign birth, cannot but lead to social disturbances. Other national faults, which English writers and critics kindly point out, are our bumptiousness, our spread-eagleism, and our too great familiarity and lack of dignity, etc.

Instead of growing angry over these criticisms, perhaps we might as well look into the matter dispassionately, and see if we cannot turn the advice in some degree to our advantage. We can, however, decide for ourselves on certain points of etiquette which we borrow from nobody; they are a part of our great nation, of our republican institutions, and of that continental hospitality which gives a home to the Russ, the German, the Frenchman, the Irishman, and the "heathen Chinee."[1] A

---

1. Russ: slang word for a Russian person; the "heathen Chinee": Slang expression coined by the writer of the American West, Bret Harte (1836–1902) in his 1870 poem, "The Heathen Chinee," that became a national sensation. Describing the pointedly named card shark, Ah Sin and his "ways that are dark," Harte's swindled character asks: "Can this be?" answering: "We are ruined by the Chinese cheap labor."

**Butterick Fashions (1872–73).** In the early 1870s clothing patterns became widely available, making it possible for the aspiring classes, who were not able to order their dresses from Worth's in Paris or buy their frock coats tailor-made from Poole on Saville Row in London, to dress fashionably. These models arranged in urban density amid a pastoral setting look as if they were depicted against the backdrop of Central Park.

somewhat wide and elastic code, as boundless as the prairies, can alone meet the needs of these different citizens. The old traditions of stately manners, so common to the Washington and Jefferson days, have almost died out here, as similar manners have died out all over the world. The war of 1861 swept away what little was left of that once important American fact—a grandfather. We began all over again; and now there comes up from this newer world a flood of questions: How shall we manage all this? How shall we use a fork? When wear a dress-coat? How and when and on whom shall we leave our cards? How long and for whom shall we wear mourning? What is the etiquette of a wedding? How shall we give a dinner-party? The young house-keeper of Kansas writes as to the manners she shall teach to her children; the miner's wife, having become rich, asks how she shall arrange her house, call on her neighbors, write her letters? Many an anxious girl writes as to the propriety of "driving out with a gentleman," etc. In fact, there is one great universal question, What is the etiquette of good society?

### The Etiquette of Balls

A hostess must not use the word "ball" on her invitation-cards. She may say,

> Mrs. John Brown requests the pleasure of the company of
> Mr. and Mrs. Amos Smith
> on Thursday evening, November twenty-second,
> at nine o'clock.
>
> Dancing.                                                    R.S.V.P.

Or,

> Mrs. John Brown
> At Home
> Thursday evening, November twenty-second,
> at nine o'clock.
>
> Cotillon at ten.                                            R.S.V.P.

But she should not indicate further the purpose of her party. In New York, where young ladies are introduced to society by means of a ball at Delmonico's, the invitation is frequently worded,

> Mr. and Mrs. Amos Smith request the pleasure
> of your company
> Thursday evening, November twenty-second,
> at nine o'clock.
>
> Delmonico's.

The card of the young débutante is sometimes (although not always) enclosed.

If these invitations are sent to new acquaintances, or to strangers in town, the card of the gentleman is enclosed to gentlemen, that of both the gentleman and his wife to ladies and gentlemen, if it is a first invitation.

A ballroom should be very well lighted, exceedingly well ventilated, and very gayly dressed. It is the height of the gayety of the day; and although dinner calls for handsome dress, a ball demands it. Young persons of slender figure prefer light, diaphanous dresses; the chaperons can wear heavy velvet and brocade. Jewels are in order. A profusion of flowers in the hands of the women should add their brightness and perfume to the rooms. The great number of bouquets sent to a débutante is often embarrassing. The present fashion is to have them hung, by different ribbons, on the arm, so that they look as if almost a trimming to the dress.

Gentlemen who have not selected partners before the ball come to their hostess and ask to be presented to ladies who will dance with them. As a hostess cannot leave her place while receiving, and people come at all hours to a ball, she generally asks two or three well-known society friends to receive with her, who will take this part of her duty off her hands, for no hostess likes to see "wall-flowers" at her ball: she wishes all her young people to enjoy themselves. Well-bred young men always say to the hostess that they beg of her to introduce them to ladies who may be without partners, as they would gladly make themselves useful to her. After dancing with a lady, and walking about the room with her for a few times, a gentleman is at perfect liberty to take the young lady back to her chaperon and plead another engagement.

A great drawback to balls in America is the lack of convenience for those who wish to remain seated. In Europe, where the elderly are first considered, seats are placed around the room, somewhat high, for the chaperons, and at their feet sit the débutantes. These red-covered sofas, in two tiers, as it were, are brought in by the upholsterer (as we hire chairs for the crowded *musicales* or readings so common in large cities), and are very convenient. It is strange that all large halls are not furnished with them, as they make every one comfortable at very little expense, and add to the appearance of the room. A row of well-dressed ladies, in velvet, brocade, and diamonds, some with white hair, certainly forms a very distinguished background for those who sit at their feet.

Supper is generally served all the evening from a table on which flowers, fruits, candelabra, silver, and glass are displayed, and which is loaded with hot oysters, boned turkey, salmon, game *pâtés*, salads, ices, jellies, and fruits, from the commencement of the evening. A hot supper, with plentiful cups of bouillon, is served again for those who dance the german.

But if the hostess so prefer, the supper is not served until she gives the word, when her husband leads the way with the most distinguished lady present, the rest of the company following. The hostess rarely goes in to supper until every one has been served. She takes the opportunity of walking about her ballroom to see if every one is happy and attended to. If she does go to supper, it is in order to accompany some distinguished guest—like the President, for instance. This is, however, a point which may be left to the tact of the hostess.

A young lady is not apt to forget her ballroom engagements, but she should be sure not to do so. She must be careful not to offend one gentleman by refusing to dance with him, and then accepting the offer of another. Such things, done by frivolous girls, injure a young man's feelings unnecessarily, and prove that the young lady has not had the training of a gentlewoman. A young man should not forget if he has asked a young lady for the cotillon. He must send her a bouquet, and be on hand to dance with her. If kept away by sickness or a death in his family, he must send her a note before the appointed hour.

It is not necessary to take leave of your hostess at a ball. All that she requires of you is to bow to her on entering, and to make yourself as agreeable and happy as you can while in her house.

Young men are not always as polite as they should be at balls. They ought, if well-bred, to look about, and see if any lady has been left unattended at supper, to ask if they can go for refreshments, if they can lead a lady to a seat, go for a carriage, etc. It is not an impertinence for a young man thus to speak to a lady older than himself, even if he has not been introduced; the roof is a sufficient introduction for any such purpose.

The first persons asked to dance by the young gentlemen invited to a house should be the daughters of the house. To them and to their immediate relatives and friends must the first attention be paid.

It is not wise for young ladies to join in every dance, nor should a young chaperon dance, leaving her protegée sitting. The very bad American custom of sending several young girls to a ball with a very young chaperon—perhaps one of their number who has just been married—has led to great vulgarity in our American city life, not to say to that general misapprehension of foreigners which offends without correcting our national vanity. A mother should endeavor to attend balls with her daughters, and to stay as long as they do. But many mothers say, "We are not invited: there is not room for us." Then her daughters should not accept. It is a very poor American custom not to invite the mothers. Let a lady give two or three balls, if her list is so large that she can only invite the daughters. If it be absolutely necessary to limit the invitations, the father should go with the daughters, for who else is to escort them to their carriage, take care of them if they faint, or look to their special or accidental wants? The fact that a few established old veterans of society insist upon "lagging superfluous on the stage" should not deter ladies who entertain from being true to the ideas of the best society, which certainly are in favor of chaperonage.

A lady should not overcrowd her rooms. To put five hundred people into a hot room, with no chairs to rest in, and little air to breathe, is to apply a very cruel test to friendship. It is this impossibility of putting one's "five hundred dear friends" into a narrow house which has led to the giving of balls at public rooms—an innovation which shocked a French woman of rank who married an American. "You have no safe-guard for society in America," she observed, "but your homes. No aristocracy, no king, no court, no traditions, but the sacred one of home.

Now, do you not run great risks when you abandon your homes, and bring out your girls at a hotel?" There is something in her wise remarks; and with the carelessness of chaperonage in cities which are now largely populated by irresponsible foreigners the dangers increase.

The first duty of a gentleman on entering a ballroom is to make his bow to the lady of the house and to her daughters; he should then strive to find his host—a very difficult business sometimes. Young men are to be very much censured, however, who do not find out their host, and insist on being presented to him. Paterfamilias in America is sometimes thought to hold a very insignificant place in his own house, and be good for nothing but to draw checks. This is indicative of a very low social condition, and no man invited to a gentleman's house should leave it until he has made his bow to the head thereof.

It is proper for intimate friends to ask for invitations for other friends to a ball, particularly for young gentlemen who are "dancing men." More prudence should be exercised in asking in behalf of ladies; but the hostess has always the privilege of saying that her list is full, if she does not wish to invite her friends' friends. No offence should be taken if this refusal be given politely.

In a majority of luxurious houses a tea-room is open from the beginning to the end of a ball, frequently on the second story, where bouillon, tea, coffee, and macaroons are in order, or a plate of sandwiches, or any such light refreshment, for those who do not wish a heavy supper. A large bowl of iced lemonade is also in this room—a most grateful refreshment after leaving a hot ballroom.

The practice of putting crash over carpets has proved so unhealthy to the dancers, on account of the fine fuzz which rises from it in dancing, that it is now almost wholly abandoned; and parquet floors are becoming so common, and the dancing on them is so much more agreeable in every way, that ladies have their heavy parlor carpets taken up before a ball rather than lay a crash.

A smoking-room, up or down stairs, is set apart for the gentlemen, where, in some houses, cigars and brandy and effervescent waters are furnished. If this provision be not made, it is the height of indelicacy for gentlemen to smoke in the dressing-rooms.

The bad conduct of young men at large balls, where they abuse their privileges by smoking, getting drunk at supper, eating unreasonably, blockading the tables, and behaving in an unseemly manner, even coming to blows in the supper-rooms, has been dwelt upon in the annals of the past, which annals ever remain a disgrace to the young fashionables of any city. Happily, such breaches of decorum are now so rare that there is no need to touch upon them here.

Many of our correspondents ask the embarrassing question, "Who is it proper to invite to a first ball?" This is a question which cannot be answered in a general way. The tact and delicacy of the host must decide it.

At public balls there should be managers, ushers, stewards, and, if possible, a committee of ladies to receive. It is very much more conducive to the elegance of a ball if there be a recognized hostess, or committee of hostesses: the very aspect of the room is thus improved. And to a stranger from another city these ladies should be hospitable, taking care that she be introduced and treated with suitable attention.

An awning and carpet should be placed at the front entrance of a house in which a ball is to be given, to protect the guests against the weather and the gaze of the crowd of by-standers who always gather in a great city to see the well-dressed ladies alight. Unfortunately, in a heavy rain these awnings are most objectionable; they are not waterproof, and as soon as they are thoroughly wet they afford no protection whatever.

The cotillion styled the German was first danced by the German court just after the battle of Waterloo, probably at the ball at Aix-la-Chapelle given to the allied sovereigns. Favors are given merely to promote enjoyment and to give variety. It is not necessary that people be matrimonially engaged to dance it. One engages his partner for it as for any other dance. It had been fashionable in Europe many years before it came to this country, but has been danced here for over forty years, first coming out at Washington.

## Fashionable Dancing

The return to quadrilles at some of the latest balls at Delmonico's in the winter of 1884 was an important epoch in the history of dancing, reiterating the well-known proverb of the dressmakers that everything comes round in fifty years. Fashion seems to be perennial in this way, for it is almost fifty years—certainly forty—since the quadrille was at the height of fashion. In Germany, where they dance for dancing's sake, the quadrille was long ago voted rococo[1] and stiff. In England and at court balls it served always as a way, a dignified manner, for sovereigns and people of inconveniently high rank to begin a ball, to open a festivity, and it had a sporadic existence in the country and at Washington even during the years when the Lancers, a much livelier dance, had chased it away from the New York balls for a long period of time.

The quadrille is a stately and conversational dance. The figures are accurate, and every one should know them well enough to respond to the voice of the leader. But inasmuch as the figures are always calling one away from his partner, the first law is to have a large supply of small-talk, so that, on rejoining, a remark and a smile may make up for lost time. A calm, graceful carriage, the power to make an elegant courtesy, are necessary to a lady. No one in these days takes steps; a sort of galop is, however, allowed in the rapid figures of the quadrille. A defiant manner, sometimes assumed by a bashful man, is out of place, although there are certain figures which make a man feel rather defiant. One of these is where he is obliged, as *cavalier seul*, to advance to three ladies, who frequently laugh at him. Then a man

1. Excessively mannered and ornate; alludes to an aesthetic style of the eighteenth century.

should equally avoid a boisterous demeanor in a quadrille, not swinging the lady round too gayly. It is never a romping dance, like the Virginia reel, for instance.

All people are apt to walk through a quadrille slowly, to music, until
they come to the "ladies' chain" or the "promenade." It is, however,
permissible to add a little swinging-step and a graceful dancing-
movement to this stately promenade. A quadrille cannot go on evenly
if any confusion arises from the ignorance, obstinacy, or inattention of
one of the dancers. It is proper, therefore, if ignorant of the figures, to
consult a dancing-master and to learn them. It is a most valuable
dance, as all ages, sizes, and conditions of men and women can join in
it. The young, old, stout, thin, lazy, active, maimed, or single, *without
loss of caste*, can dance a quadrille. No one looks ridiculous dancing a
quadrille. It is decidedly easier than the German, makes a break in a
*tête-à-tête* conversation, and enables a gentleman to be polite to a lady
who may not be a good dancer for waltz or polka. The morality of
round dances seems now to be little questioned. At any rate, young
girls in the presence of their mothers are not supposed to come to
harm from their enjoyment. Dancing is one of the oldest, the most
historical, forms of amusement. Even Socrates learned to dance.
There is no longer an excommunication on the waltz, that dance
which Byron abused.

In England the *valse à deux temps* is still the most fashionable, as it
always will be the most beautiful, of dances. Some of the critics of all
countries have said that only Germans, Russians, and Americans can
dance it. The Germans dance it very quickly, with a great deal of motion, but render it elegant by slacking the pace every now and then.
The Russians waltz so quietly, on the contrary, that they can go round
the room holding a brimming glass of champagne without spilling a
drop. This evenness in waltzing is very graceful, and can only be
reached by long practice, a good ear for music, and a natural graceful-
ness. Young Americans, who, as a rule, are the best dancers in the
world, achieve this step to admiration. It is the gentleman's duty in
any round dance to guide his fair companion gracefully; he must not
risk a collision or the chance of a fall. A lady should never waltz if she
feels dizzy. It is a sign of disease of the heart, and has brought on
death. Neither should she step flat-footed, and make her partner carry
her round; but must do her part of the work, and dance lightly and
well, or not at all. Then, again, neither should her partner waltz on the
tip of his toes, nor lift his partner too much off the floor; all should be
smooth, graceful, delicate.

The American dance of the season is, however, the polka—not the
old-fashioned "heel and toe," but the step, quick and gay, of the
Sclavonic nationalities. It may be danced slowly or quickly. It is always, however, a spirited step, and the music is undoubtedly pretty.
The dancing-masters describe the step of a polka as being a "hop,
three glides, and a rest," and the music is two-four time. In order to
apply the step to the music one must make it in four-eight time,
counting four to each measure of the music, each measure taking

about a second of time by the watch. The polka redowa and the polka mazourka are modifications of this step to different times.

The galop is another fashionable dance this winter. It is very easy, and is danced to very quick music; it is inspiriting at the end of a ball.

The *minuet de la cour* was first danced in the ancient province of Poitou, France. In Paris, in 1653, Louis XIV, who was passionately fond of it, danced it to perfection. In 1710, Marcel, the renowed dancing-master, introduced it into England. Then it went out for many years, until Queen Victoria revived it at a *bal costumé* at Buckingham Palace in 1845. In New York it was revived and ardently practised for Mrs. W. K. Vanderbilt's splendid fancy ball in 1883, and it was much admired. There seems no reason why the grace, the dignity, the continuous movement, the courtesy, the *pas grâce,* the skilfully-managed train, the play with the fan, should not commend this elegant dance to even our republican dancers; but it has not been danced this winter. It is possibly too much trouble. A dancing-master worked all winter to teach it to the performers of the last season.

To make a courtesy (or, as we are fond of saying, a *curtsy*) properly is a very difficult art, yet all who dance the quadrille must learn it. To courtesy to her partner the lady steps off with the right foot, carrying nearly all her weight upon it, at the same time raising the heel of the left foot, thus placing herself in the second position, facing her partner, counting *one*. She then glides the left foot backward and across till the toe of the left foot is directly behind the right heel, the feet about one half of the length of the foot apart. This glide commences on the ball of the left foot, and terminates with both feet flat upon the floor, and the transfer of the weight to the backward foot. The bending of the knees and the casting down of the eyes begin with the commencement of the glide with the left foot, and the genuflection is steadily continued until the left foot reaches the position required, counting *two*; then, without changing the weight from the backward foot, she gradually rises, at the same time raising the forward heel and lifting the eyes, until she recovers her full height, counting *three*; and finally transfers the weight to the forward foot, counting *four*. Such is the elaborate and the graceful courtesy. It should be studied with a master.

The "German" (the "Cotillon," as the French call it) is, however, and probably long will be, the most fashionable dance in society. It ends every ball in New York, Washington, Boston, Philadelphia, and Newport; it is a part of the business of life, and demands consummate skill in its leadership. Any number may join in it; it often reaches twice around a large ballroom. All the couples in it are regarded as introduced to each other. No lady can refuse to dance with any gentleman who is brought to her in the German. So long as she remains in the charmed circle she must dance with any one in it. Therefore the German must only be introduced at select assemblies, not at a public ball. The leader opens the German by motioning to certain couples to make a *tour de valse* round the room.

Many of our correspondents write to ask us what are the latest and the favorite figures in the German. This is a difficult question to an-swer, as the leader always has his own favorite figures. The German generally begins with *l'avant trois double*, which may be generally de-scribed thus: the leader, having performed the *tour de valse* with his partner, leaves her, and brings forward two other ladies; his lady brings forward two other gentlemen; the two *trios* place themselves opposite each other, then forward and back, and each gentleman with the lady in front of him performs a *tour de valse*. Should the company be large, two or more couples may start together, each couple choosing other ladies and gentlemen in the same manner as the first couple. Then comes *La Chaise* after the *tour de valse*. The leader places his partner in a chair in the centre of the room; he then brings forward two gen-tlemen and presents them to the lady, who chooses one of them, after which he seats the gentleman who is rejected, and brings to him two ladies: he also selects a partner, and the leader dances with the re-fused lady to her place. This figure may be danced by any number of couples.

*Les Drapeaux* is a favorite figure. Five or six duplicate sets of small flags of national or fancy devices must be in readiness. The leader takes a flag of each pattern, and his partner takes the duplicate. They perform a *tour de valse*. The conductor then presents his flags to five or six ladies, and his partner presents the corresponding flags to as many gentlemen. The gentlemen then seek the ladies having the du-plicates, and with them perform a *tour de valse,* waving the flags as they dance. Repeated by all the couples.

*Les Bouquets* brings in the favors. A number of small bouquets and boutonnières are placed upon a table or in a basket. The first couple perform a *tour de valse*; they then separate. The gentleman takes a bouquet, and the lady a boutonnière. They now select new partners, to whom they present the bouquet and boutonnière, the lady attaching the boutonnière to the gentleman's coat. They perform a *tour de valse* with their new partners. Repeated by all the couples. Other favors are frequently substituted for bouquets and boutonnières, such as rosettes, miniature flags, artificial butterflies, badges, sashes, bonbons, little bells (the latter being attached to small pieces of ribbon and pinned to the coat or dress), scarf-pins, bangles, fans, caps, imitation antique coins, breastpins, lace pins, lockets; and even gifts of great value, such as shawls, scarfs, vases, picture-frames, writing-desks, and chairs (represented, of course, by tickets) have been this winter intro-duced in the german. But the cheap, light, fantastic things are the best, and contribute more to the amusement of the company.

Some of the figures of the German border on the romp. One of these is called *La Corde*. A rope is stretched by the leading couple across the room, and the gentlemen jump over it to reach their partners. Much amusement is occasioned by the tripping of gentlemen who are thrown by the intentional raising of the rope. After all have reached their part-ners they perform a *tour de valse,* and regain their seats. This is a figure not to be commended. Still less is the figure called *Les Masques*. The gentlemen put on masques resembling "Bully Bottom" and other grotesque faces and heads of animals. They raise these heads above a screen, the ladies choosing partners without knowing them; the gentlemen remain *en masque* until the termination of the *tour de valse*. This figure was danced at Delmonico's and at the Brunswick last winter, and the mammas complained that the fun grew rather too fast and furious. *Les Rubans* is a very pretty figure. Six ribbons, each about a yard in length, and of various colors, are attached to one end of a stick about twenty-four inches in length, also a duplicate set of ribbons, attached to another stick, must be in readiness. The first couple perform a *tour de valse,* then separate; the gentleman takes one set of ribbons, and stops successively in front of the ladies whom he desires to select to take part in the figure; each of these ladies rises and takes hold of the loose end of the ribbon; the first lady takes the other set of ribbons, bringing forward the six gentlemen in the same manner. The first couple conduct the ladies and gentlemen towards each other, and each gentleman dances with the lady holding the ribbon duplicate of his own; the first gentleman dances with his partner.

We might go on indefinitely with these figures, but have no more space.

The position of a dancer should be learned with the aid of a teacher. The upper part of the body should be quiet; the head held in a natural position, neither turned to one side nor the other; the eyes neither cast down nor up. The gentleman should put his arm firmly around a lady's waist, not holding her too close, but firmly holding her right hand with his left one; the lady turns the palm of her right hand downward; her right arm should be nearly straight, but not stiff. The gentleman's left arm should be slightly bent, his elbow inclined slightly backward. It is very inelegant, however—indeed, vulgar—to place the joined hands against the gentleman's side or hip; they should be kept clear of the body. The step should be in unison; if the gentleman bends his right elbow too much, he draws the lady's left shoulder against his right, thereby drawing the lady too close. The gentleman's right shoulder and the lady's left should be as far apart as the other shoulders. If a gentleman does not hold his partner properly, thereby causing her either to struggle to be free or else to dance wildly for want of proper support, if he permits himself and partner to collide with other couples, he cannot be considered a good dancer.

### [On Serving Roman Punch]

* * * The best of these [provocatives of appetite] is the Roman punch, which, coming after the heavy roasts, prepares the palate and stomach for the canvas-back ducks or other game. Then comes the salad and cheese, then the ices and sweets, and then *cheese savourie* or *cheese fondu.* This is only toasted cheese, in a very elegant form, and is served in little silver shells, sometimes as early in the dinner as just after the oysters, but the favorite time is after the sweets.

The dessert is followed by the *liqueurs,* which should be poured into very small glasses, and handed by the butler on a small silver waiter.

When the ices are removed, a dessert-plate of glass, with a finger-bowl, is placed before each person, with two glasses, one for sherry, the other for claret or Burgundy, and the grapes, peaches, pears, and other fruits are then passed. After the fruits go round, the sugar-plums and a little dried ginger—a very pleasant conserve—are passed before the coffee.

The hostess makes the sign for retiring, and the dinner breaks up. The gentlemen are left to wine and cigars, *liqueurs* and cognac, and the ladies retire to the drawing-room to chat and take their coffee.

\* \* \*

As the dinner goes on the guest revels in unexpected surprises in the beauty of the plates, some of which look as if made of solid gold; and when the Roman punch is served it comes in the heart of a red, red rose, or in the bosom of a swan, or the cup of a lily, or the "right little, tight little" life-saving boat. Faience, china, glass, and ice are all pressed into the service of the Roman punch, and sometimes the prettiest dish of all is hewn out of ice.

\* \* \*

## Recipes for Roman Punch

### Roman Punch (Ponche Romaine).†

—(1) Put in a freezing-pot 1qt. of peach water-ice, a bottle of dry champagne, 2 wine-glassfuls of noyau, and the strained juice of four oranges. Colour it a delicate pink with a few drops of cochineal, and flavour with essence of vanilla. Work the mixture till nearly frozen, then add gradually three whites of eggs made into Italian meringue; work all together quickly till smooth, and serve.

(2) Mix together 1qt. of sherry water-ice, 1 bottle of Moselle, 2 wineglassfuls of kirschenwasser, and 1 wine-glassful of noyau; put these ingredients in a freezing-pot embedded in ice, work them thoroughly while freezing, then add the whites of three eggs of Italian meringue paste. When finished, serve the Punch in glasses.

(3) Dissolve 1½ breakfast-cupfuls of loaf sugar in 1 pint of hot water. Grate the rind of one lemon in a basin, squeeze in the juice and also that of an orange; then mix the hot syrup in with them, and let it stand till cool. Strain the Punch into a freezer, and work it till nearly frozen; beat in the whipped whites of two eggs, add 1 teacupful of either rum or wine, and serve in glasses.

### Roman Punch.†
(Ponche à la Romaine.)

3 cups lemonade;
1 cup champagne;

† From *The Encyclopedia of Practical Cookery*, ed. Theodore Francis Garrett (London: L. Upcott Gill, n.d.), p. 275.
† From Mrs. Henry Reeve, *Cookery and Housekeeping* (London: Spottiswoode & Co., 1882), p. 420.

1 cup rum;
2 oranges—juice.
Whip the whites of two eggs with $\frac{1}{2}$ lb. powdered sugar till a firm froth.
Mix with the above, and ice.


# FRANCIS W. CROWNINSHIELD

## From *Manners for the Metropolis: An Entrance Key to the Fantastic Life of the 400*†

It is undeniable that much of the pleasure in modern life is derived from social intercourse.

From time immemorial the gregarious instinct has contributed greatly to the charm of all populated regions. It is worthy of remark that, during the past decade, both in America and in England, sudden and violent changes have somewhat ruffled the placid waters of polite society. These new conditions of life have naturally necessitated new methods of social procedure. The telephone, coeducation, wireless telegraphy, motor cars, millionaires, bridge whist, women's rights, Sherry's, cocktails, four-day liners, pianolas, steam heat, *directoire* gowns, dirigible balloons, and talking machines have all contributed to an astonishing social metamorphosis.

Curiously enough no book of etiquette[1] has taken count of these violent changes. There is literally no Baedeker for this newly discovered country. Many fruitful and enchanted islands have been sighted, but have, alas, remained uncharted.

It is, therefore, with motives of generosity, charity, and kindness that this little guide has been prepared by the benevolent author.

It will be found to contain concise rules of deportment for all the more important social ceremonies—from a *tête-à-tête* to a betrothal, a picnic to a funeral, a *partie-carrée* to a divorce, an ushers' dinner to a Turkish bath, and a piano recital to a rout. It also contains excellent advice on the choice of a motor car, a summer residence, a wife, or a brand of cigar.

The author feels that it should prove of great value to those people who have been born and brought up in refined and well-bred families, and are, at the same time, desirous of entering fashionable society.

To our newer millionaires and plutocrats it should be a very present help in time of trouble, for it is undeniable that many of these captains of industry—however strong and virile their natures—become

---

† New York and London: D. Appleton and Company, 1910, pp. 3–5, 29–32, 38, 41–43, 54–55, 86–87, 122.

1. Crowninshield's call for new codifications of manners acknowledges the gap left by the death of Mrs. Sherwood (1826–1903), the recognized authority on etiquette for Victorian America. Mrs. Sherwood's frequent revisions of *Manners and Social Uses* (see pp. 317–29) were justified by the changing manners of a changing society. A successor to Mrs. Sherwood did not appear until Emily Post brought out her influential volume, *Etiquette*, published two years after *The Age of Innocence* [Editor].

utterly helpless and panic-stricken at the mere sight of a gold finger bowl, an alabaster bath, a pronged oyster fork, or the business end of an asparagus.

*   *   *

If a few people in the smart set are entertaining a stranger at lunch, it is *de rigueur* for them to converse with each other entirely in whispers and always on subjects with which he is absolutely unfamiliar.

In discussing literature at a lunch or dinner, try to remember that there are but a very few fashionable authors. They are as follows: Mrs. Wharton, Colonel Mann, Mrs. Glyn, Robert Hichens, F. Peter Dunne, John Fox, Jr., and Billy Baxter.[2]

At a dinner a gentleman sitting beside a débutante should congratulate her upon her début, and, in a few well-chosen words, should discuss the usual débutante topics—i.e., platonic love, banting, Ethel Barrymore, French dressmakers, John Drew,[3] the relative merits of Harvard and Yale, love at first sight, the football match and the matter of her great personal beauty and charm.

Try always to remember that the chief and most interesting topics of conversation are herself and yourself. *Serious* topics are very properly deemed out of place in society.

*   *   *

Whenever, at a dinner, an anecdote is narrated in French, it is always a wise precaution to laugh heartily.

Women should not complain of their husbands in public. All married women have a great deal to contend with. Everybody knows that married men make very poor husbands.

At a dinner the safest conversational opening is as follows: "Is that your bread, or mine?"

*   *   *

2. For the purposes of humor, Wharton is listed here in rather peculiar literary company. Col. Mann: Colonel William D'Alton Mann (1839–1920), Civil War hero, business magnate, writer, and publisher. Mann took over the New York weekly, *Town Topics*, from a brother who left the city after being convicted for obscenity. Col. Mann used his column, "Saunterings," to expose the indiscretions and secrets of the elite. Although he was never convicted of blackmail, Col. Mann turned his scandal sheet into a lucrative enterprise by allowing those who either felt threatened or were threatened to buy protection through the purchase of advertising in the paper or through even more formal methods. (See p. 211, *n.* 1.) Mrs. Glyn: Mrs. Elinor Glyn (1864–1943), American writer of romance novels; Robert Hichens: Robert Smythe Hichens (1864–1950), author of fiction and nonfiction, best known for his tales of the supernatural; F. Peter Dunne: Finley Peter Dunne (1867–1936), American journalist and humorist who wrote as an Irish barkeeper under the pseudonym of "Mr. Dooley"; John Fox, Jr. (1863–1919), American novelist known for his depictions of the mountain folk of his native Kentucky; Billy Baxter: Character created by William Kountz (c.1867–1899) in *Billy Baxter's Letters* (1899), a posthumously published collection of fictional letters (some previously published in various newspapers) that include, among other things, weakly humorous critiques of New York society. The plain spoken Baxter complains about his night at the opera in New York City while extolling the edifying qualities of a melodrama entitled "The White Slave."

3. banting: A technique for losing weight, based on the avoidance of sweets and carbohydrates; Ethel Barrymore: Philadelphia-born American stage and film actress (1879–1959); John Drew: Irish-born American stage actor (1827–62).

Chivalry demands that a lady's name should never be mentioned in a gentleman's club. Occasionally, however, this hard-and-fast rule may be slightly infracted, and her intimate affairs discreetly talked over— provided that the group of gentlemen be a small one and absolute privacy assured.

N.B.—A "small group" is any group of less than twelve.

*  *  *

Ladies do not call upon a bachelor, in his rooms, after attending a dinner given by him—except in Mrs. Wharton's novels.

*  *  *

In wriggling out of a dinner at the last moment in New York, it is *chic* to invent some mythical female relative in Philadelphia who has developed a sudden and alarming illness and has hastily summoned you to her bedside.

If, at a dinner, food is passed to you which you do not care to eat, it is good form to take a generous heap of it, to pat it and mess it up on your plate with a fork.

After dinner, if a lady has been asked to sing and refused, do not urge her further. It is the height of bad manners, and there is just the off chance that she may yield.

In England the matter of precedence at dinners is simplicity itself. The Sovereign precedes an ambassador, who precedes the Archbishop of Canterbury, who precedes the Earl Marshal, who precedes a duke, who precedes an earl, a marquis, a viscount, a bishop, a baron, etc.; but in America the matter is a much more perplexing one.

The author of this *brochure* respectfully suggests the following scheme of American dinner precedence: Let an opera box count 6 points; steam yacht, 5; town house, 5; country house, 4; motors, 3 each; every million dollars, 2; tiara, 1; good wine cellar, 1; ballroom in town house, 1; a known grandparent of either sex, $\frac{1}{2}$; culture, $\frac{1}{8}$. By this system, a woman of culture with four known grandparents and a million dollars will have a total of $4\frac{1}{8}$. She will, of course, be forced to follow in the wake of a lady with a town house and a tiara (6); who, in turn, will trail after a woman with a steam yacht and two motors (11). The highest known total is about 100; the lowest, about $\frac{1}{8}$. The housekeeper may arrange the totals, and the hostess can then send the guests in according to their listed quotations.

*  *  *

The valuable checks for cotillion seats are usually cornered by the cotillion leader and dealt out to the most prominent tiaras. The unhappy ladies who fail to receive one of these priceless tokens usually pass the remainder of the evening in the ultimate row of chairs wearing a granite smile and a paper cotillion favor.

A wall flower is a young lady at a dance who has not been cursed with the fatal gift. She may usually be distinguished by her wild and beseeching glances. Chloroform is the only possible way of securing a partner for her.

*   *   *

Never give a theater party in stalls. Boxes are obligatory. In seats, the men cannot go out for refreshment, and the ladies are forced to remove their hats, a tragedy usually accompanied by the most distressing and ignominious disclosures.

Ladies who have opera boxes given them at the last moment should "get on the job" at once and offer it to such of their friends as they know to be either out of town or engaged for that evening. A box has been known, under such circumstances, to pay off a dozen obligations in a single day.

*   *   *

## MRS. BURTON HARRISON

## The Myth of the Four Hundred†

When it falls to the lot of a resident of New York to go away from home westward or southward, rather than due eastward, in search of incidental studies of minor sociology, he is surprised at the extraordinary dominance of the sovereign body styled "New York Society" over the imagination of numbers of respectable people who have never seen it, or partaken in the remotest degree of "that unrest which men miscall delight" in its functions. In cities, towns, hamlets, on farms and ranches, in remote thinly settled neighborhoods throughout the length and breadth of our spacious country, men, women, and above all "young persons," are found eagerly perusing every detail obtainable in newspapers, magazines, or novels of the day, to find out what the small circle in New York, known as the "smart set," are doing—how disporting themselves, dressing, entertaining, marrying and living in marriage, building lordly pleasure-houses, and, in fine, "going the pace" of the supposed elect of good society. To meet this insatiate demand, columns of stuff are published throwing around quite every-day people a glamour as of royalty; exaggerating into importance the most trivial actions of those who have no claim whatever upon public interest; dragging into daylight the private concerns of many who are tortured by knowing themselves thus pilloried; and often deliberately falsifying the movements of unfortunates who can have no possible opportunity to set themselves right in the world's eye. Nothing is beneath the notice of the purveyors for such literature. It was recently gravely suggested to a writer upon current themes that a syndicated paper upon the feet and ankles of the feminine leaders of New York society would prove an "immense success" all over the country, and no doubt the suggester well

† From *Cosmopolitan* 19 (1895): 329–34.

knew what he was talking about. Personalities of the most intimate description are above all things craved in print, and the newspaper correspondent must often naturally feel himself at a loss to supply them. The lives of those conspicuous in society are not, as a rule, marked by originality in thought or action. Their round of everyday life is in its way as humdrum as that of the farmer's wife, who thinks there is no end of washing dishes, or the spinster who sits knitting at her window and watches the progress of life in a village street. When one reports of the favored few that they walk, or drive, or dine, or dance with the same people, more or less, until they are aweary for a change, that is pretty much all there is to say. But still the chorus extolling them goes on swelling till, against better judgment, many a reluctant ear is turned in the direction whence the pæan comes.

The comic side of this exaltation of a limited set of ultra-rich Americans, who, often to their own surprise, are made to do duty as social models for the rest of their fellow-countrymen, might be dismissed with a smile. While it is fair to some of them to say they neither seek notoriety, nor are gladdened by it, others take the affair seriously as a tribute to ruling power; as kings and queens are supposed to do, they sit complacently at meat while the proletariat looks on.

But there are deeper questions involved in the growth and expansion of the "Society" myth among us; a growth so marked and vigorous that but few sober voices question its right to represent to America at large the highest form of social progress America has attained.

Apart from the vulgarity of this perpetual blazoning, it is mischievous and hurtful to many classes of the community. The shop-girl, the bedazzled young clerk, who read of these glittering lives of their fellow-democrats, set up a false standard of the aim and end of a successful mercantile life. Their day-dream is to go on and do likewise, to be in their turn the possessors of luxury, the dispensers of social opportunity; nothing higher, more intellectual, no duty as citizens, no question of education or refinement, no claim of humanity at large, appeals to them. To amass money, to push, to strain, to stand neck-to-neck in the race with the fashionables, is the bright goal that makes toil seem worth while to them. The school-girl and -boy of the educated class are infected by the universal reverence yielded by public voice to fashion, and secretly resolve to model themselves so that they may some day be fitted to enter behind those magic portals. The young collegian who has for the first time awakened to a sense of the existence of social relations, or to their importance as a factor in his life, takes his cue from the extravagant laudation of a supposed small and superior circle in New York, and deems everything outside of it of a second quality of merit. As to the socialists, the habitual growlers against the display of wealth in a land governed by democratic theories, we are all acquainted with their resentment of this propaganda of American snobbery! If there is among us, however, one class more than another unpleasantly affected by the evils I depict, I might indicate many families of well-born, well-bred people who, feeling themselves to have every claim to position and consideration in the home of their birth and ancestry, are, through want of wealth alone, jostled out of place, made to stand in the back line, pushed against the wall, ignored and required to be content with looking on at the diversions of a favored few. To be perpetually reminded of these facts in public print, becomes in time, even to the philosophical, a blister upon their tenderest sensibilities.

I suppose—I hope—there is no place in the United States where this attitude has been assumed by so many worthy and otherwise dignified citizens, as of late years in New York. And, indeed, there is some ground for their complaint. The old order of Gotham has survived to meet the astonishing experience of an aristocracy of sudden wealth taking possession of the places once its own, and in some cases displaying toward it a stiffness of demeanor suggesting the query, "Who are you, and what do you do here."

A lady of recent fortune, newly established in Fifth avenue, chancing to meet a quick-witted young daughter of a race of statesmen and patriots who in the old days had stood before the world for the best New York could furnish, and failing to identify her by name, asked her in a casual drawl: "And, pray, how long have you been in New York?" "About two hundred years," was the girl's answer, fixing upon her interlocutor a guileless glance which, except upon a bystander who recognized and enjoyed the situation, was naturally thrown away.

"Mama," said a school-girl of ancient lineage to her mother not long ago, "what are we, really? When the girls asked me in recess to-day if you are invited to Mrs. Midas' ball, and I said no, that you do not visit Mrs. Midas, they laughed and looked at each other; and one of them said she always thought it was a mistake about our being anybody in New York, since we are never mentioned among the 'smart set'."

By such little stabs and slurs is the perhaps unconscious warfare of new against old sustained, and all the good sense, the calm indifference, the noble scorn in the world, does not suffice to ward them off entirely. The head of a family must needs exercise a control far beyond the common, to induce young people, under such circumstances, to rise superior to the idea that they are looked down upon socially. Absurd as it may and must seem to the dispassionate, this feeling exists and embitters many otherwise happy homes. There is no possible doubt that it has closed the doors of houses that might else have been in the exercise of a constant and gracious hospitality according to their means. And it has even sent wandering abroad, to seek the dull refuge of foreign cities and neighborhoods, people to the manner born who will not receive here entertainment they cannot return in kind, who, weary of the sense of inequality with current good society in their own community, and free to escape from it, have made all speed to do so.

It is no uncommon experience to hear upon the lips of one of the old régime, whose immediate predecessors have controlled opinion and social customs in New York, about one of the leaders of the new: "I don't go there; she doesn't want me; I am not rich enough."

What an extraordinary gradation of society! "Good enough—wise enough—well-born or well-mannered enough" is not considered; but "rich enough"! The thing is incredible. It is an old observation that the struggle of people on their social rise, gives opportunity for more pettiness than the ascent of any other ladder. But to be "rich enough" to cross the inner boundaries of the best society—that is an ambition left apparently to New York. A story told last season was of a plutocratic young matron who observed, "Really, now that society in New York is getting so large, one must draw the line somewhere; after this, I shall visit and invite only those who have more than five millions."

There is more of a stimulus to money-getting in this idea, than of a spur to intellectual attainment or to social agreeability. One can imagine the futility of a banquet of which the mental part is exclusively furnished by men who have made their millions, and women who have bought their crowns.

Happily, the American sense of humor, which leavens much of that mass of incongruity we call our democratic institutions, is no doubt at the bottom of the dire threat conveyed by the multi-millionairess. Somebody who looks with favor upon the social woes of his fellow-men, must have made up the story to frighten those too ambitious of amassing wealth.

So far, I have set down possibilities of an abstraction; let us lightly glance at facts. For my own part, I am an unbeliever in the body corporate which, for want of a better term, has come to be popularly known as the Four Hundred of New York. The lists for visits and invitations made out yearly by people of good position, to include their acquaintances to whom such courtesies are due, number, say, a thousand names. Of these names, who among us is equipped or prepared to say six hundred are outside the pale? So the golden circle drawn around a few wealthy and fashionable folk who are most often heard about as exchanging hospitalities with each other, exists, I truly believe, in the imagination of alarmists. The general idea that this barrier yields only by accident, or through phenomenal assiduity of push, or when distinguished talent or accomplishment are in the same scale with a light purse, to the approach of an outsider, is absurd, when the most casual observer can see the new actors every year brings forward within its arena.

Naturally, people who are clever enough to make money and to get up to the high places of the world, and even those who have spent the best years of their lives in what Walter Bagehot called "a vapid accumulation of torpid comfort," are also intelligent enough to want help in making the best display of it. It is not startling to those of us who have seen—as so many Americans have seen—the palaces and museums of the Old World, and numbers of the best private dwellings, to be bidden en masse to look at one of the many fine New York houses. Nor does a concert of great artists, hired to perform in a private drawing-room, astonish those who can for a few dollars hear the same people at the opera, if there is no social element surrounding the affair. To attract New Yorkers, and make them wish to return to the attraction, mere wealth evidently does not suffice, and this the veriest tyro in society must know. How, then, should the owners of the great fortunes who, as ball- and dinner-givers constitute, in the general mind, our present aristocracy, willingly exclude from their gatherings the clever, refined, and progressive members of a circle, larger than theirs, continually blending with it, and at points hardly to be distinguished from it. If those who compose this intellectual and artistic element of New York society, and who appear rarely in the newspapers as contributors of material gifts to the general fund of entertainment, are less known throughout the country than the others, their ranks are constantly increasing. Among them many younger women of the so-called "smart set" are now to be found. It is pleasant to see these young and active intelligences, tiring early of a round of monotonous enjoyment, yield to the impelling impulse of the times, and press forward to seek association with their own kind. To them we may look, perhaps, for future deliverance from the clog of conventionalism and timidity that seems to retard the wheels of social accomplishment among some of their elders, who, dazzled by their sudden rise, fear to transgress good form by taking advantage of it. The next generation will better understand how to bring together the diverse elements still scattered about our city; a reunion of parts that would insure general society here to be the most pleasant, sparkling, and inspiring in any great center of the world.

It is training from childhood as one of the ruling class that makes the true grande dame; she must be quick in discriminating, fearless in selecting, and gracious in retaining those she draws about her; and that sort of a social head is not so often born as made. When such qualities as these assert themselves to reinforce the natural charm of some American woman of ample means, with a house large enough to contain her friends, we may see the long-discussed salon open its portals to New York.

The homes of fashionable New Yorkers are, as a whole, the most sumptuous and comfortable in the world. Space, light, tempered warmth in every part, ventilation and every other accessory of hygiene, are here as liberally provided, as are the picturesque and decorative ideas of architects of the highest modern accomplishment; and, in numbers, these stately dwellings are like strawberries in June. From them we may go on to a wide variety of smaller and less pretentious houses, in which also may be applauded the best art of our modern decorative renaissance. Old prosaic structures of brownstone, or brick, that were made in former days to enshrine the ugly fittings and furniture of our immediate predecessors, pass under an architect's eclipse to reappear in charming and covetable guise, every corner of their renovated interiors an invitation to domestic rest and peace. But no architect has yet been found who can make New York women remain quiet in these homes. Through every keyhole, in at every chink and cranny, floats the atmosphere of unrestfulness prevailing in America, and insistent in New York. No sooner is a family installed in the new abode, than one hears of it going off to try life in some other quarter of the globe. * * *

To the impetus of the age that prompts them to constant wandering from home, New York women of the luxurious class are in process of sacrificing some of their most potent charms of personality. In New York society so many leading families are comparative strangers to each other, there is nothing of the easy interchange of sociability possible in an older, more settled, community where everybody of condition knows all about everybody else of like estate. Except for formal exchange of conventional civilities, many of the most agreeable women here live and wish to live their own lives.* * *

*     *     *

The intellectual and artistic development of fashionable society * * * is yet making good progress here in our day. Fine ladies are no longer contented to sit in their boudoirs trifling with the pages of the latest novel. They have clubs and causeries for the discussion of topics of the hour, and for the revival of classic themes. Their drawing-rooms are repeatedly thrown open for lectures by adepts in literature and the arts. The books talked of by the world are ordered in to lie upon their tables—whether to be dipped into, or studied, depending upon time and degree of earnestness. Music, as all New York has good cause to know, is largely dependent upon their liberal patronage. Paintings, more or less well selected, are bought to line the walls of their living-rooms. For their children—in some danger indeed from overtraining of the mind—the best teachers of languages and accomplishments are secured that native or foreign talent can supply. Inveterate travelers, they bring back every year, to adorn their dwellings, a host of the beautiful and dainty examples of Old World minor art, that in the Old World seem inalienable from finished homes. And, if they had accomplished nothing else, America at large would be in their debt for having made fashionable the habit of country life within the limit of one's own domain.

To this class of our community we also owe the now indispensable addition of physical culture to the education of the day. They have taken away the old reproach to American manhood and womanhood, of pale cheeks, undersize and insufficient vitality, by bringing up a race of hardy young people, the girls vying with their brothers in athletic achievements. To have made this cult the fashion is a laurel for their brows. Another example set by them for their admirers to follow, is that of simplicity in young woman's dress. It is only among those who buy cheap material to shape into garments that exaggerate the mode, that one ever sees, nowadays, a young girl overloaded with millinery or jewelry. And it is the débutante of the "smart set" who makes her first curtsey to society in a plain, high-cut frock—leaving furbelows and rich stuffs to her mother, who introduces her. The same young person goes nowhere into the great world without her mother or a substitute, and has done much to calm the agitation of foreign critics about the lawless freedom of action of American maidenhood.

A complaint common on modern lips against our fashionable girl, is her inveterate tendency to marry, when she can find him, a foreigner of rank. There are foreigners and foreigners; and perhaps it has previously fallen to the lot of some of the girls so choosing, to visit certain delightful homes abroad, created by transplanted Americans, who have proved so persistently happy with their alien husbands as to flatly disappoint their croaking countrymen. In England, certainly, there is much to console a young woman for the magnificent monotony of life in New York. Yet of all the prizes of Vanity Fair, a title without anything behind it is the one that carries least of lasting satisfaction to the winner. The woeful failure of some fusions made of late years by American plutocracy with decadent European aristocracy, needs no comment to emphasize their folly. Even among the better of these matches, a post-nuptial feature of some most extolled and glorified by the newspapers, that does not often come to American ears, is the estimate held by the groom's family of his mésalliance. It is not all plain sailing into halcyon port, on the other side, with American brides who are heralded to the world here as brilliant and successful. If they are proud and high-spirited, their own friends are the last to hear of snubs or slights put upon them by dull-witted, plain-spoken personages into whose ranks they have entered. And "noblesse" does not always "oblige" the titled husband to extend to his heiress the sympathy she might, under these circumstances, expect. Still, as the millionaires are the ones most likely to run these risks, we need not fear a general following of this example.

Of the men of what may be called our leisure class, there is less to say. The husbands and fathers of the "smart set" are most of them still in the toils; apt to leave their beautiful homes to plunge into affairs with a zest that has known no abatement after years of success. They are liberal, public-spirited, sturdy men, and loyal supporters of the metropolitan edifice; good patrons of art, givers of great gifts in charity, excellent husbands, and loving fathers; but lack of early opportunity, too much later prosperity, and a too-material present environment, have not incited them to general culture.

The real do-nothings in this busy hive, generally the inheritors of great mercantile fortunes, are of a limited class that always impresses an observer with a certain sense of sadness. To all outward appearance they are indistinguishable from the English original, after whom they model themselves in dress, and speech, and sport, and habits, and indulgences; but, lacking the Englishman's love of native soil and country, his sense of responsibility to place and politics, they seem to regard life over here as a weary show. In some respects they are to be envied. The cries of nations, the stress of the times, the waves of the great ocean of modern thought, do not reach them. Circumstances that might transform a mere ordinary man into what Carlyle called "a very unthankful, ill-conditioned, bilious, wayward, and heart-worn son of Adam," fail to disturb the even tenor of their days. But their value and success as citizens in this great democracy of ours is hardly an incentive, to the American father in general, to amass money to be left behind him for his sons to spend—as spend it they usually do. And perhaps in that fact may be found the real usefulness among us of the typical rich man's son; he can ordinarily be relied upon to correct some of the disturbing inequalities created by the prosperity and thrift of his father, and to give his best efforts to make us what the true theory of an ideal democracy requires—a people of equal fortunes, as of equal rights.

# Changing Mores in New New York: The Romance of Leisure and the Specter of Divorce

Leisure for Old New York, historically as well as in Wharton's historical novel, was already defined by a "backward glance" toward an idealized and rural past. This focus on leisure grounded in cultivated and controlled nature began to take shape in 1857 as the long process of building Central Park was begun. As May escapes from the Episcopalian Sunday devoted to prayer to take a walk with her fiancé, Newland, along the walkway called "the Mall" (52, *n.* 1) in the park, she has begun the redefinition of this day of rest that her elders already fear will become the "French Sunday" (56). While May and her family are scandalized by Mrs. Lemuel Struthers's increasingly successful efforts to force her way into society by using the lure of music and high art in the form of home entertainments to assuage the boredom associated with the New York Sunday, May herself is soon destined to become a regular guest at these Sunday soirées.

As *The Age of Innocence* suggests, Newport, Rhode Island, had long been and continued to be the summer colony of the New York four hundred. Newport, with its varieties of historic carriages ("dog-carts" and " 'vis-à-vis' " [129]), offered a relatively rural community that was known for its outdoor pleasures such as afternoon drives (344), dancing at garden parties, strolling along the famed Cliff Walk, and sailing in the protected waters of Narragansett Bay (253). The founding of the Newport Ladies Archery Society in 1873, with its celebrated archery tournaments (254), and the invention of the "fascinating new game of lawn tennis" (119) in 1874, are evidence of innovations in sports, activities that reflected the new athleticism open to the young ladies of the social elite. Later, during her family's European tours, the athletic May will prefer hiking in the Alps to seeing art in galleries or traveling to see magnificent cathedrals such as Chartre. If May's hands have become large through her physical exertions, May and Newland's daughter, with her boyish figure and large waist, reflects the "altered fashion" (208), the types of leisure that literally changed the female shape.

During the latter decades of the nineteenth century, in particular during the decade of this novel that begins "in the early seventies," wealthy men such as August Belmont Sr. kept stables in Portsmouth, the rural village to the north of Newport where Wharton's character Julius Beaufort breeds his "famous trotters" (127). These "trotters" are a sign of the increased popularity of harness racing, a trend that is visible in the many new race tracks that were built after the Civil War. Once popular among shopkeepers, harness racing became a rich man's hobby as its focus shifted to include the breeding of expensive horses. Like thoroughbred racing, the

340

popularity of polo continued to be limited to men of the elite. Long before the staging of what the novel describes as an "International Polo match" (201), this sport of kings was already an international pastime. Polo, invented in the Punjab region of present-day India, was adopted by the British as their own and brought to the United States in the 1870s as a colonial export.

Dancing and subscription balls, with their focus on finding appropriate partners, have been classified in this edition as part of the business of society, what might be called the choreography of marriage. Some of the dances like the cotillion originated in the courts of Europe, while others had their origins in popular culture. As Newland leads the newly affianced May out into the whirling circles of the waltz, they in their centrifugal embrace are participating in a pleasure associated with a modern aesthetic. Originally a daring dance, condemned by Lord Byron, the waltz, an import from Vienna, had literally set heads spinning in a euphoria that was likened to the effects of caffeine and other stimulants.

Mores associated with the idea of recreation were changing in the latter half of the nineteenth century. Historians of leisure in Manhattan have seen the mid century as a time of division, separating the classes according to their ideas of pleasure and their practices of leisure. Previously, city dwellers tended to frequent the same events, separated according to their types of seats. During this period, music halls featuring minstrel shows and other variety shows were increasingly defined not only by their bills of fare, but by their location and their assumed clientele. The *Macbeth* performed by an American actor in the Bowery was a very different type of event than the *Macbeth* performed by a British actor at the Astor Place Opera House. (This famous conjunction of the two *Macbeth*s in 1849 led to the Astor Place Riots that left 23 dead and over 100 wounded—many of whom had marched *en masse* together from the Bowery—by fire from troops. The riots suggest that this cultural transition was not entirely smooth.) While Archer notes the opening of "little musical and theatrical clubs" (65), the most specific acknowledgment of a divergence in types of amusements appears in the rumor that Mrs. Lemuel Struthers has been a performer in the "Living Wax-Works touring New England" (24), a group that has been reputedly broken up by the police.

The "Living Wax-Works" was one of the many popular traveling shows based on the fictional portrayal of "Mrs. Jarley's Waxworks," a show that appears in Dickens's novel, *The Old Curiosity Shop* (1840). Part of the American popular culture of the late nineteenth century, these performances used human actors who pretended to be wax-automatons that were being wound into jerky motions as their supposed internal mechanisms were tightened. Costumed as prominent figures from literature and history (including such macabre displays as the still-moving and bloody heads of Bluebeard's wives sticking through holes in a sheet), these performers gradually wound down into stillness, returning to their roles as inanimate wax figures. A familiar entertainment at community events and private socials, these shows featured narrators, playing Dickens's Mrs. Jarley and her employee, Little Nell, as they recited from brief scripts designed to tell each automaton's story. "King Cophetua and the Beggar Maid" has been included here as an example of these scripts that were available in published form during the 1870s. This is also the script that most closely approximates Mrs. Lemuel Struthers's own fairytale rise from poverty to aristocracy by marrying a "Shoe Polish King."

Among the romantic practices enjoyed by the rural folk and the urban elite was the use of flowers, to convey unspoken or, in *The Age of Inno-cence*, unspeakable sentiments. An ancient Persian custom, said to have been brought back to England from Turkey by the eighteenth-century woman of letters, Lady Mary Wortley Montague, "the language of flowers" gave rise to books listing flowers along with codes enumerating their corresponding sentiments. Part of the oral culture, popularly understood and used by people of all classes in Europe and the United States, these published lexicons were generally consistent in their equations but also included flowers with varying or even opposing definitions. Bouquets offered the possibility of sending complex messages that constructed their meanings through color, degree of florescence, and arrangement or juxtaposition. A sprig of the clustered small white flowers known as "candytuft" is alternately said to have meant "coldness" or "indifference." Arranged upside down in a bouquet, a sprig of candytuft is said to convey the more provocative message: "Your coldness attracts me."

Two flower dictionaries from the Victorian era are included here to provide a key to the floral messages sent in *The Age of Innocence*. Newland's daily gift of lilies-of-the-valley to May not only conveys the purity associated with lilies and whiteness, these flowers also speak to the idea of expectation by promising "return of happiness" and "future happiness." Associated in some dictionaries with "sweetness," "humility," and the proclamation "you have made my life complete," the lily-of-the-valley was the flower that Wharton carried with the Episcopal Book of Prayer in her own bridal bouquet. The yellow roses that Newland sends anonymously to the Countess Olenska (because their "fiery beauty" [51] reminds him of her) underline the sense of secrecy in his offering. While roses signify "beauty" and "love," yellow roses according to various floral lexicons may mean "jealousy," "infidelity," "adultery," "decrease of love," "love that will not last," and, much more rarely, "friendship." As a gift, these bouquets are efforts to communicate sentiments from the giver to the recipient. Just as there is no simple equivalency for the meaning of yellow roses, even as one tries to follow the idea of "infidelity" in the novel, it remains unclear whether Ellen as the estranged wife of the Count Olenski is being said to be unfaithful or whether such a gift from the engaged Archer represents an act of "infidelity" on his part. The gardenia (or "the cape jasmine") that Newland Archer wears to his wedding, often listed as meaning "transport, ecstasy" is also widely understood to signify "secret, untold love."

When the bouquet arrives from Julius Beaufort, the threat of this floral offering is unspoken but understood as Medora Manson asks Newland Archer if he "prefer[s] *that*" (101). Claiming to see this bouquet as inappropriate because she is neither "young" nor "engaged," the countess, like all the others who see this shocking bouquet, understands the language of flowers. Finally, Ellen Olenska's anger is directed toward Beaufort's bouquet not so much for the medium it uses but for the message it sends. These "crimson roses, with a knot of purple pansies at their base" (98) are shockingly explicit. While red roses signify passionate love (an emotion that was too visceral to be acknowledged in most floral lexicons of the Victorian era), the knot of pansies leaves the unsaid said, completing this message of passion by signifying "thoughts" or "thinking of you." Julius Beaufort, a married man, has sent another man's estranged wife a bouquet whose message would be inappropriate even if this token were being sent by a man to his own fiancée. The two floral dictionaries that conclude this section record some of the variations in meanings that serve to call attention to the general consistency in the language of flowers.

As these questionable floral messages sent in *The Age of Innocence* suggest, and the plethora of literary allusions to tales of marital infidelity in the novel confirm, illicit desire is an old story that crosses the boundaries of class and historical era. Laws forbidding divorce in France and severely limiting divorce among the elite in England during the nineteenth century came in reaction to public fear that morals had become lax. If divorce and remarriage to the "partner of [one's] guilt" (71, 201) were outlawed in the conservative state of New York, the abandonment of wives (practiced by Mrs. Manson Mingott's father, Bob Spicer, and by Julius Beaufort, before being threatened by Newland Archer) is one of the practices that recurs in the novel. By definition, these men have not only left town, they have lost their place in society. While marriage and divorce law have always varied according to class-based cultural and legal practice, the changing mores described in the *New York Daily Tribune* document the new challenge to legally based efforts to control marriage and to enforce monogamy during the decade from the early 1870s to the early 1880s. As this exposé of rising divorce rates laments, the New York courts could not control the laws of bordering states that allowed remarriage without regard to whether adultery had been committed. Like the spinning "social atoms" (212) described by Newland as he looks back over his own respectable life, the practical challenge to maintaining strict and punitive divorce laws is driven by the laws of motion itself as people purchase the respectability of marriage simply by taking the ferry to New Jersey. The technological changes that are invoked repeatedly in the novel will render salacious bouquets unnecessary and make the task of past chaperones nearly impossible. In this era of changing mores, the telephone became the more precise method for arranging illicit assignations and the automobile was recognized as an instrument of corruption by turn-of-the-century reformers such as Dorothea Dix who called this innovation "the devil's wagon." Indeed, the issue of divorce is central to the definintion of *The Age of Innocence* as a problem novel and the problem of divorce is linked not just to adultery but to adulteration through contact with foreigners and foreign ways. The novel's Reverend Ashmore of Grace Church with his regular jeremiads against social change has not imagined the United States of the twentieth century in which falling rates of marriage will say more about the demographics of social change than rising rates of divorce.

# JAMES MAURICE THOMPSON

## The Long Bow†

It was said of old that the twang of Diana's bowstring gave rise to a train of reflections, ending in the invention of the first stringed instrument of music. This is probably not altogether a myth. The leading idea of the story is simple, and most likely truthful, involving no more than the great antiquity of the bow as a weapon of war and the chase, and the fact that the cord of a well-strung bow gives forth, during vibration, a clear, well-defined musical note, very pleasing to most ears. For the rest, the story of the wild, beautiful hoiden goddess who, trail-

† From *Appleton's Journal* April 19, 1873: 525–26.

Edith and Teddy Wharton (Newport, ca. mid- to late-1880s).

**Bow-Shooting ( July 1877).** (Engraving from *Scribner's Monthly*, vol. XIV, no. 3.)

ing her cloud of nymphs behind her, flew over the purple hills, armed with bow and quiver, chasing the deer through cool, green groves where the winds sang songs scarcely less thrilling than the ringing note of her silken cord, and the long, low whir of her well-sent arrows—that may be too well settled by the poets to be disputed, or it may very clearly be nothing but a dream. Have it as suits your mood. But one thing admits of no contrary argument, which is, that long before the most ancient singer strung the purple shell, or even Pan had cut his "reed by the river," some person, mortal, demi-god, or god, fashioned the first bow and arrows, and became a mighty hunter. What days and nights of worrying thought it cost the inventor to mould the idea of his great missile-projector, or what hacking and hewing with stone implements, what scraping, and whittling, and rubbing, what waste of timber it required to "turn out" from the first rude manufactory the first bow and arrow, is a matter concerning which history gives no suggestions. No doubt that was a rough bit of handiwork, but the implement must have at once disclosed considerable merit, or it would most probably have been speedily abandoned, and the first bow have been the last, whereby Diana would have lost very much of her glory; for a Diana without a bow and quiver would be worse than a Bacchus without a cup.

From the most ancient times a sort of poetic halo has been seen to flicker round the head of the archer, and the bow may well be termed the poet's weapon. "Keen as an arrow," "swift as an arrow," "straight as an arrow," and a host of like expressions, are everywhere met with, even in the poetry of to-day, when, indeed, the reading public scarcely knows what an arrow really is. Somehow this peculiar glory has never invested the sling, the cross-bow, the catapult, nor the death-dealing fire-arm. If we moderns should set up a god who shouldered a double-barrelled shot-gun or a patent breech-loader—oh, fie! Even Joaquin Miller[1] dares not do such a thing. But if the long-bow is a weapon much used by the gods and greatly admired by the poets, it is because it deserves such distinction. Its antiquity, the universality of its use by all peoples for so many ages, the vast service it has rendered the human race, and the rare history through which it has sent its hissing arrows, entitle it to the immortality it enjoys.

\*    \*    \*

Archery was revived in England in 1844, and became very popular as a pastime, but I am not aware of any successful toxophilite organizations in the United States. Such organizations, however, if properly managed, would no doubt meet with success here, and be received by the people with greater favor than even base-ball companies.

Ladies may become expert archers, and the sport recommends itself to them, in that, while it gives them excellent physical exercise, it also "shows off" their form and graces to the very best advantage.

The greatest objection to archery here in America is, that we cannot

---

1. Joaquin Miller: Cicinnatus Hiner Miller (1837–1913), American-born journalist and writer of poems; a swashbuckling figure who traded as much on his image as a picturesque frontiersman as on his craft as a writer.

bear the thought of wringing any kind of pleasure out of an implement not sold to us by a patent-right agent or pedler.

# CLARENCE SATTERLEE

## [The Living Waxworks]†

### Mrs. Jarley's Lecture

Ladies and gentlemen: You are about to be favored with a view of the world-renowned and unrivaled Jarley's Wax-Works, as exhibited before the Royal Family, the nobility of England, King Kalicowhorah of the Sandwich Islands, George the Count Johannes, and the rest of the crowned heads of Europe. Also highly approved of by heads of families, and recommended by Phineas T. Barnum and Jay Gould[1] as a great moral instructor of youth. Likewise a pleasing incentive to virtue and the industrial pursuits. There are other unprincipled wax-works, but this is the real Jarley. None others are genuine. Beware of counterfeits. I am Mrs. Jarley. Contains over one hundred figures. All of the size of life. It is my pleasing duty on this occasion to explain the points of history for this highly genteel audience—admission set at the low price of twenty-five cents—special rates to schools—and to teach the young idea how to shoot—at the Creedmoor range of mingled entertainment and instruction. The collection itself is trooly stupenjous. The stage being of limited capacity, only a part of this present collection is visible; but my faithful attendants will bring them before you, one by one, and after I have described it in chaste and classic language, each will be wound up—the clock-work in its in'ards 'll be set a-going, and it will act in a highly characteristic and natural manner, so as to instruct and startle the beholders. * * *

\* \* \*

#### KING COPHETUA AND THE BEGGAR MAID[2]

His Majesty one morning was smoking a cigar at the parlor window, when a beggar girl came along with matches to sell—two boxes for five

† From William B. Dick *One hundred amusements for evening parties, picnics, and social gatherings* (New York: Dick & Fitzgerald), 1879. Dick's original collection that appeared in 1873 was enlarged in this version to incorporate a section devoted to scripts inspired by Dickens' Mrs. Jarley and her traveling show described in *The Old Curiosity Shop* (1840). Clarence Satterlee, the dramatist who scripted versions of Dickens' tale, "A Christmas Carol," wrote the scripts in which Mrs. Jarley and Little Nell narrate the notorious life stories of the costumed actors performing as wax automations.

1. P. T. Barnum, the great nineteenth-century showman, see p. 248, *n*. 9; Jay Gould: see pp. 300–307.

2. King Cophetua: A legendary African king, best known through Richard Johnson's Elizabethan ballad detailing this love-resistant figure's fall for "the beggar maid." Alluded to briefly in Shakespeare's *King Henry IV, Part II, Romeo and Juliet*, and *Love's Labour's Lost*, King Cophetua represents the archetypal passionless man who is transformed by the charms of a woman from a much lower social strata. Just a king in an earlier version of the published script, the revised script, from the 1879 printing used here, reclaims this character's racial history by linking him to the Zulu tribe.

**Original Illustration of Mrs. Jarley and Little Nell from Dickens's *The Old Curiosity Shop* (1840).** Mrs. Jarley instructs Little Nell before the unwound figures of "the stupendous collection" of mechanized waxworks. While the initials H. B. for Hablot Knight Brown (the primary illustrator of Dickens's work for a twenty-three-year period) appear on the ruffle at the bottom of the stage, the signature of G. [George] Cattermole, the artist who made many sketches for this novel, appears in the foreground near Mrs. Jarley's feet.

## [Dickens's Waxworks from *The Old Curiosity Shop*, Chapter 28]

* * * When the festoons were all put up as tastily as they might be, the stupendous collection was uncovered, and there were displayed, on a raised platform some two feet from the floor, running round the room and parted from the rude public by a crimson rope breast high, divers sprightly effigies of celebrated characters, singly and in groups, clad in glittering dresses of various climes and times, and standing more or less unsteadily upon their legs, with their eyes very wide open, and their nostrils very much inflated, and the muscles of their legs and arms very strongly developed, and all their countenances expressing great surprise. All the gentlemen were very pigeon-breasted and very blue about the beards; and all the ladies were miraculous figures; and all the ladies and all the gentlemen were looking intensely nowhere, and staring with extrordinary earnestness at nothing.

When Nell had exhausted her first raptures at this glorious sight, Mrs. Jarley ordered the room to be cleared of all but herself and the child, and, sitting herself down in an arm-chair in the centre, formally invested Nell with a willow wand, long used by herself for pointing out the characters, and was at great pains to instruct her in her duty.

'That,' said Mrs. Jarley in her exhibition tone, as Nell touched a figure at the beginning of the platform, 'is an unfortunate Maid of Honour in the Time of Queen Elizabeth, who died from pricking her finger in consequence of working upon a Sunday. Observe the blood which is trickling from her finger; also the gold-eyed needle of the period, with which she is at work.' * * *

cents. Notwithstanding her ragged dress, her face was washed and her hair combed, and she was so beautiful that all the ladies of the court, who were in the second story front window trying to find out what the butcher boy was bringing to Brown's, over the way, for dinner, were struck with envy, and began to titter. But the King, he put his cigar on the mantelpiece, and went down the front steps, and popped the question without delay, and they were married by the bishop. But there is a melancholy sequel to this touching story. She led him a dog's life after all; and when a panic came on, and stocks were down, and real estate a drug, and the King couldn't allow her more than a million a year for pin money, she ran away to Indiana, and got a divorce,[3] and married the manager of a circus troupe, and that family was broken up. It affected King Cophetua to that extent, that he broke up housekeeping and sold out, and went out among the Zulus, and was known there as King Cetewayo, and when last heard from, had changed his name to Cantgetawayo, and was out in the blackberry bushes, leading a wandering life. Wind 'em both up, George. Observe the start of pleased surprise given by the King, and the shy manner in which the maid drops her head, and then raises it again, and steals a look at the monarch. Remove the affectionate couple, George, and let them spoon at the back of the stage.

\* \* \*

# JOHN H. YOUNG

## The Language of Flowers†

How beautiful and yet how cheap are flowers! Not exotics, but what are called common flowers. A rose, for instance, is among the most beautiful of the smiles of nature. The "laughing flowers," exclaims the poet. But there is more than gayety in blooming flowers, though it takes a wise man to see the beauty, the love, and the adaptation of which they are full.

What should we think of one who had *invented* flowers, supposing that, before him, flowers were unknown? Would he not be regarded as the opener-up of a paradise of new delight? Should we not hail the inventor as a genius, as a god? And yet these lovely offsprings of the earth have been speaking to man from the first dawn of his existence until now, telling him of the goodness and wisdom of the Creative Power, which bid the earth bring forth, not only that which was useful as food, but also flowers, the bright consummate flowers to clothe it in beauty and joy!

\* \* \*

Bring one of the commonest field-flowers into a room, place it on a table, or chimney-piece, and you seem to have brought a ray of sunshine into the place. There is a cheerfulness about flowers. What a de-

---

3. In the late nineteenth century, Indiana was known for its permissive divorce laws.
† From *Our Department* (Detroit: F. B. Dickerson, 1882), pp. 410–22.

light are they to the drooping invalid! They are a sweet enjoyment, coming as messengers from the country, and seeming to say, "Come and see the place where we grow, and let your heart be glad in our presence."

There is a sentiment attached to flowers, and this sentiment has been expressed in language by giving names to various flowers, shrubs and plants. These names constitute a language, which may be made the medium of pleasant and amusing interchange of thought between men and women. A bouquet of flowers and leaves may be selected and arranged so as to express much depth of feeling—to be truly a poem. We present herewith a list of many flowers and plants, to which, by universal consent, a sentiment has become attached.

Acacia—Concealed love.
Acacia, Rose—Friendship.
Acanthus—Arts.
Adonis Vernalis—Bitter memories.
Agnus Casus—Coldness.
Agrimony—Thankfulness.
Almond—Hope.
Aloe—Superstition.
Althea—Consumed by love.
Alyssum, Sweet—Worth beyond beauty.
Amaranth—Immortality.
Amaryllis—Splendid beauty.
Ambrosia—Love returned.
Anemone—Expectation.
Anemone, Garden—Forsaken.
Angelica—Inspiration.
Apocynum (Dogbane)—Inspiration.
Apple—Temptation.
Apple Blossom—Preference.
Arbor vitæ—Unchanging friendship.
Arbutus, Trailing—Welcome.
Arum—Ardor.
Ash—Grandeur.
Ash, Mountain—Prudence.
Aspen Tree—Lamentation.
Asphodel—Regrets beyond the grave.
Aurilica—Avarice.
Azalea—Romance.
Bachelor's Button—Hope in love.
Balm—Sympathy.
Balm of Gilead—Healing.
Balsam—Impatience.
Barberry—Sharpness, satire.
Basil—Hatred.
Bay Leaf—No change till death.
Beech—Prosperity.
Bee Ophrys—Error.

Bee Orchis—Industry.
Bell Flower—Gratitude.
Belvidere, Wild (Licorice)—I declare against you.
Bilberry—Treachery.
Birch Tree—Meekness.
Black Bryony—Be my support.
Bladder-Nut Tree—Frivolous amusements
Blue Bottle—Delicacy.
Borage—Bluntness.
Box—Constancy.
Briers—Envy.
Broken Straw—Constancy.
Broom—Neatness.
Buckbean—Calm repose.
Bugloss—Falsehood.
Burdock—Importunity.
Buttercup—Riches.
Cactus—Thou leavest me.
Calla Lilly—Feminine beauty.
Calycanthus—Benevolence.
Camelia—Pity.
Camomile—Energy in action.
Candytuft—Indifference.
Canterbury Bell—Gratitude.
Cape Jasmine Gardenia—Transport, ecstasy.
Cardinal Flower—Distinction.
Carnation, Yellow—Disdain.
Catchfly (Silene), Red—Youthful love.
Catchfly, White—I fall a victim.
Cedar—I live for thee.
Cedar of Lebanon—Incorruptible.
Celandine—Future joy.
Cherry Tree—Good education.
Chickweed—I cling to thee.
Chickory—Frugality.
China Aster—I will think of thee.
China, Pink—Aversion.
Chrysanthemum, Rose—In love.
Chrysanthemum, White—Truth.
Chrysanthemum, Yellow—Slighted love.
Cinquefoil—Beloved child.
Clematis—Artifice.
Clover, Red—Industry.
Cobœa—Gossip.
Coxcomb—Foppery.
Colchium—My best days fled.
Coltsfoot—Justice shall be done you.
Columbine—Folly.
Columbine, Purple—Resolved to win.

Columbine, Red—Anxious.
Convolvulus Major—Dead hope.
Convolvulus Minor—Uncertainty.
Corchorus—Impatience of happiness.
Coreopsis—Love at first sight.
Coriander—Hidden merit.
Corn—Riches.
Cornelian Cherry Tree—Durability.
Coronilla—Success to you.
Cowslip—Pensiveness.
Cowslip, American—My divinity.
Crocus—Cheerfulness.
Crown Imperial—Majesty.
Currants—You please me.
Cypress—Mourning.
Cypress and Marigold—Despair.
Daffodil—Chivalry.
Dahlia—Forever thine.
Daisy, Garden—I share your feelings.
Daisy, Michaelmas—Farewell.
Daisy, Red—Beauty unknown to possessor.
Daisy, White—Innocence.
Daisy, Wild—I will think of it.
Dandelion—Coquetry.
Daphne Mezereon—I desire to please.
Daphne Odora—I would not have you otherwise.
Deadleaves—Sadness.
Diosma—Usefulness.
Dittany—Birth.
Dock—Patience.
Dodder—Meanness.
Dogwood Flowering (Cornus)—Am I indifferent to you?
Ebony—Hypocrisy.
Eglantine—I wound to heal.
Elder—Compassion.
Elm—Dignity.
Endine—Frugality.
Epigæa, Repens (Mayflower)—Budding beauty.
Eupatorium—Delay.
Evening Primrose—Inconstancy.
Evergreen—Poverty.
Everlasting (Graphalium)—Never ceasing memory.
Filbert—Reconciliation.
Fir Tree—Elevation.
Flax—I feel your kindness.
Flora's Bell—Without pretension.
Flowering Reed—Confide in heaven.
Forget-me-not—True love.
Foxglove—Insincerity.

Fraxinella—Fire.
Fritilaria (Guinea-hen Flower)—Persecution.
Furze—Anger.
Fuchsia—The ambition of my love thus plagues itself.
Fuchsia, Scarlet—Taste.
Gardenia—Transport; Ecstasy.
Gentian, Fringed—Intrinsic worth.
Geranium, Apple—Present preference.
Geranium, Ivy—Your hand for next dance.
Geranium, Nutmeg—I expect a meeting.
Geranium, Oak—Lady, deign to smile.
Geranium, Rose—Preference.
Geranium, Silver-leaf—Recall.
Gillyflower—Lasting beauty.
Gladiolus—Ready armed.
Golden Rod—Encouragement.
Gooseberry—Anticipation.
Goosefoot—Goodness.
Gorse—Endearing affection.
Grape—Charity.
Grass—Utility.
Guelder Rose (Snowball)—Winter.
Harebell—Grief.
Hawthorn—Hope.
Heart's Ease—Think of me.
Heart's Ease, Purple—You occupy my thoughts.
Hazel—Reconciliation.
Heath—Solitude.
Helenium—Tears.
Heliotrope, Peruvian—I love; devotion.
Hellebore—Scandal.
Henbane—Blemish.
Hepatica—Confidence.
Hibiscus—Delicate Beauty.
Holly—Foresight.
Hollyhock—Fruitfulness.
Hollyhock, White—Female ambition.
Honesty (Lunaria)—Sincerity.
Honeysuckle—The bond of love.
Honeysuckle, Coral—The color of my fate.
Honeysuckle, Monthly—I will not answer hastily.
Hop—Injustice.
Hornbeam—Ornament.
Horse-Chestnut—Luxury.
House-Leek—Domestic Economy.
Houstonia—Content.
Hoya (Wax Plant)—Sculpture.
Hyacinth—Jealousy.
Hyacinth, Blue—Constancy.

Hyacinth, Purple—Sorrow.
Hydrangea—Heartlessness.
Ice Plant—Your looks freeze me.
Indian Cress—Resignation.
Ipomaca—I attach myself to you.
Iris—Message.
Iris, German—Flame.
Ivy—Friendship; matrimony.
Jessamine, Cape—Transient joy.
Jessamine, White—Amiability.
Jessamine, Yellow—Grace; elegance.
Jonquil—Return my affection.
Judas-Tree—Betrayed.
Juniper—Perfect Loveliness.
Kalmia (Mountain Laurel)—Treachery.
Kennedia—Intellectual beauty.
Laburnum—Pensive Beauty.
Lady's Slipper—Capricious beauty.
Lagerstroema (Cape Myrtle)—Eloquence.
Lantana—Rigor.
Larch—Boldness.
Larkspur—Fickleness.
Laurel—Glory.
Laurestinus—I die if neglected.
Lavender—Distrust.
Lemon Blossom—Discretion.
Lettuce—Cold-hearted.
Lilac—First emotion of love.
Lilac, White—Youth.
Lily—Purity; modesty.
Lily of the Valley—Return of happiness.
Lily, Day—Coquetry.
Lily, Water—Eloquence.
Lily, Yellow—Falsehood.
Linden Tree—Conjugal love.
Live Oak—Liberty.
Liverwort—Confidence.
Locust—Affection beyond the grave.
London Pride—Frivolity.
Lotus—Forgetful of the past.
Love in a Mist—You puzzle me.
Love Lies Bleeding—Hopeless, not heartless.
Lucerne—Life.
Lungwort (Pulmonaria)—Thou art my life.
Lupine—Imagination.
Lychnis—Religious Enthusiasm.
Lythrum—Pretension.
Madder—Calumny.
Maiden's Hair—Discretion.

Magnolia, Chinese—Love of Nature.
Magnolia, Grandiflora—Peerless and Proud.
Magnolia, Swamp—Perseverance.
Mallow—Sweetness.
Mandrake—Horror.
Maple—Reserve.
Marigold—Cruelty.
Marigold, African—Vulgar-minded.
Marigold, French—Jealousy.
Marjoram—Blushes.
Marshmallow—Beneficence.
Marvel of Peru (Four o'clock)—Timidity.
Meadow Saffron—My best days gone.
Meadow Sweet—Usefulness.
Mignonette—Your qualities surpass your charms.
Mimosa—Sensitiveness.
Mint—Virtue.
Mistletoe—I surmount all difficulties.
Mock Orange (Syringia)—Counterfeit.
Monkshood—A deadly foe is near.
Moonwort—Forgetfulness.
Morning Glory—Coquetry.
Moss—Maternal love.
Motherwort—Secret Love.
Mourning Bride (Scabious)—Unfortunate attachment.
Mouse-ear Chickweed—Simplicity.
Mulberry, Black—I will not survive you.
Mulberry, White—Wisdom.
Mullein—Good nature.
Mushroom—Suspicion.
Mush Plant—Weakness.
Mustard Seed—Indifference.
Myosotis—Forget me not.
Myrtle—Love.
Narcissus—Egotism.
Nasturtium—Patriotism.
Nettle—Cruelty; Slander.
Night Blooming Cereus—Transient beauty.
Nightshade—Bitter truth.
Oak—Hospitality.
Oats—Music.
Oleander—Beware.
Orange—Generosity.
Orange Flower—Chastity.
Orchis—Beauty.
Osier—Frankness.
Osmunda—Dreams.
Pansy—Think of me.
Parsley—Entertainment.

Pasque Flower—Unpretentious.
Passion Flower—Religious Fervor.
Pea—Appointed meeting.
Pea, Everlasting—Wilt go with me?
Pea, Sweet—Departure.
Peach Blossom—My heart is thine.
Pear Tree—Affection.
Peony—Anger.
Pennyroyal—Flee away.
Periwinkle—Sweet memories.
Persimmon—Bury me amid nature's beauties.
Petunica—Am not proud.
Pheasant's Eye—Sorrowful memories.
Phlox—Our souls united.
Pimpernel—Change.
Pine—Time.
Pine Apple—You are perfect.
Pine, Spruce—Farewell.
Pink—Pure affection.
Pink, Clove—Dignity.
Pink, Double-red—Pure, ardent love.
Pink, Indian—Aversion.
Pink, Mountain—You are aspiring.
Pink, Variegated—Refusal.
Pink, White—You are fair.
Pink, Yellow—Disdain.
Plane Tree—Genius.
Pleurisy Root (Asclopias)—Heartache cure.
Plum Tree—Keep promise.
Plum Tree, Wild—Independence.
Polyanthus—Confidence.
Poplar, Black—Courage.
Poplar, White—Time.
Poppy—Consolation.
Poppy, White—Sleep of the heart.
Pomegranate—Foolishness.
Pomegranate Flower—Elegance.
Potato—Beneficence.
Pride of China (Melia)—Dissension.
Primrose—Early youth.
Primrose, Evening—Inconstancy.
Privet—Mildness.
Pumpkin—Coarseness.
Quince—Temptation.
Ragged-robin (Lychnis)—Wit.
Ranunculus—Radiant with charms.
Reeds—Music.
Rhododendron—Agitation.
Rose—Beauty.

Rose, Austrian—Thou art all that is lovely.
Rose, Bridal—Happy love.
Rose, Burgundy—Unconscious beauty.
Rose, Cabbage—Love's Ambassador.
Rose, Campion—Only deserve my love.
Rose, Carolina—Love is dangerous.
Rose, China—Grace.
Rose, Daily—That smile I would aspire to.
Rose, Damask—Freshness.
Rose, Dog—Pleasure and pain.
Rose, Hundred Leaf—Pride.
Rose, Inermis—Ingratitude.
Rose, Maiden's Blush—If you do love me you will find me out.
Rose, Moss—Superior merit.
Rosebud, Moss—Confessed love.
Rose, Multiflora—Grace.
Rose, Musk-cluster—Charming.
Rose, Sweetbriar—Sympathy.
Rose, Tea—Always lovely.
Rose, Unique—Call me not beautiful.
Rose, White—I am worthy of you.
Rose, White (withered)—Transient impression.
Rose, Wild—Simplicity.
Rose, Yellow—Decrease of love.
Rose, York and Lancaster—War.
Roses, Garland of—Reward of Virtue.
Rosebud—Young girl.
Rosebud, White—The heart that knows not love.
Rosemary—Your presence revives me.
Rue—Disdain.
Rush—Docility.
Saffron—Excess is dangerous.
Sage—Esteem.
Sardonia—Irony.
Satin-flower (Lunaria)—Sincerity.
Scabious, Mourning Bride—Widowhood.
Sensitive Plant—Timidity.
Service Tree—Prudence.
Snapdragon—Presumption.
Snowball—Thoughts of heaven.
Snowdrop—Consolation.
Sorrel—Wit ill-timed.
Southernwood—Jesting.
Spearmint—Warm feelings.
Speedwell, Veronica—Female fidelity.
Spindle-tree—Your image is engraven on my heart.
Star of Bethlehem—Reconciliation.
Starwort, American—Welcome to a stranger.
St. John's Wort (Hypericum)—Superstition.

Stock, Ten-week—Promptitude.
Stramonium, Common—Disguise.
Strawberry—Perfect excellence.
Strawberry Tree (Arbutus)—Esteemed love.
Sumac—Splendor.
Sunflower, Dwarf—Your devout admirer.
Sunflower, Fall—Pride.
Sweet Sultan—Felicity.
Sweet William—Artifice.
Sycamore—Curiosity.
Syringia—Memory.
Tansy—I declare against you.
Teasel—Misanthropy.
Thistle—Austerity.
Thorn Apple—Deceitful charms.
Thorn, Black—Difficulty.
Thorns—Severity.
Thrift—Sympathy.
Throatwood (Pulmonaria)—Neglected beauty.
Thyme—Activity.
Tiger Flower—May pride befriend thee.
Touch me not, Balsam—Impatience.
Truffle—Surprise.
Trumpet Flower—Separation.
Tuberose—Dangerous pleasures.
Tulip—Declaration of love.
Tulip Tree—Rural happiness.
Tulip, Variegated—Beautiful eyes.
Tulip, Yellow—Hopeless love.
Turnip—Charity.
Valerian—Accommodating disposition.
Venus's Flytrap—Caught at last.
Venus's Looking-glass—Flattery.
Verbena—Sensibility.
Vine—Intoxicating.
Violet, Blue—Love.
Violet, White—Modesty.
Violet, Yellow—Modest worth.
Virgin's Bower—Filial love.
Wall Flower—Fidelity.
Walnut—Stratagem.
Weeping Willow—Forsaken.
Wheat—Prosperity.
Woodbine—Fraternal love.
Wood Sorrel—Joy.
Wormwood—Absence.
Yarrow—Cure for heartache.
Yew—Sorrow.
Zennæ—Absent friends.

# KATE GREENAWAY

## From *Language of Flowers*†

| | |
|---|---|
| Abecedary | *Volubility.* |
| Abatina | *Fickleness.* |
| Acacia | *Friendship.* |
| Acacia, Rose or White | *Elegance.* |
| Acacia, Yellow | *Secret love.* |
| Acanthus | *The fine arts. Artifice.* |
| Acalia | *Temperance.* |
| Achillea Millefolia | *War.* |
| Aconite (Wolfsbane) | *Misanthropy.* |
| Aconite, Crowfoot | *Lustre.* |
| Adonis, Flos | *Painful recollections.* |
| African Marigold | *Vulgar minds.* |
| Agnus Castus | *Coldness. Indifference.* |
| Agrimony | *Thankfulness. Gratitude.* |
| Almond (Common) | *Stupidity. Indiscretion.* |
| Almond (Flowering) | *Hope.* |
| Almond, Laurel | *Perfidy.* |
| Allspice | *Compassion.* |
| Aloe | *Grief. Religious superstition.* |
| Althaea Frutes (Syrian Mallow) | *Persuasion.* |
| Alyssum (Sweet) | *Worth beyond beauty.* |
| Amaranth (Globe) | *Immortality. Unfading love.* |
| Amaranth (Cockscomb) | *Foppery. Affectation.* |
| Amaryllis | *Pride. Timidity. Splendid beauty.* |
| Ambrosia | *Love returned.* |
| American Cowslip | *Divine beauty.* |
| American Elm | *Patriotism.* |
| American Linden | *Matrimony.* |
| American Starwort | *Welcome to a stranger.* *Cheerfulness in old age.* |
| Amethyst | *Admiration.* |
| Anemone (Zephyr Flower) | *Sickness. Expectation.* |
| Anemone (Garden) | *Forsaken.* |
| Angelica | *Inspiration.* |
| Angrec | *Royalty.* |
| Apple | *Temptation.* |
| Apple (Blossom) | *Preference. Fame speaks him* *great and good.* |
| Apple, Thorn | *Deceitful charms.* |
| Apocynum (Dog's Vane) | *Deceit.* |
| Arbor Vitae | *Unchanging Friendship. Live* *for me.* |
| Arum (Wake Robin) | *Ardour.* |

† London: George Routledge and Sons, 1884.

| | |
|---|---|
| Ash-leaved Trumpet Flower | *Separation.* |
| Ash Tree | *Grandeur.* |
| Aspen Tree | *Lamentation.* |
| Aster (China) | *Variety. Afterthought.* |
| Asphodel | *My regrets follow you to the grave.* |
| Auricula | *Painting.* |
| Auricula, Scarlet | *Avarice.* |
| Austurtium | *Splendour.* |
| Azalea | *Temperance.* |
| Bachelor's Buttons | *Celibacy.* |
| Balm | *Sympathy.* |
| Balm, Gentle | *Pleasantry.* |
| Balm of Gilead | *Cure. Relief.* |
| Balsam, Red | *Touch me not. Impatient resolves.* |
| Balsam, Yellow | *Impatience.* |
| Barberry | *Sourness of temper.* |
| Barberry Tree | *Sharpness.* |
| Basil | *Hatred.* |
| Bay Leaf | *I change but in death.* |
| Bay (Rose) Rhododendron | *Danger. Beware.* |
| Bay Tree | *Glory.* |
| Bay Wreath | *Reward of merit.* |
| Bearded Crepis | *Protection.* |
| Beech Tree | *Prosperity.* |
| Bee Orchis | *Industry.* |
| Bee Ophrys | *Error.* |
| Belladonna | *Silence.* |
| Bell Flower, Pyramidal | *Constancy.* |
| Bell Flower (small white) | *Gratitude.* |
| Belvedere | *I declare against you.* |
| Betony | *Surprise.* |
| Bilberry | *Treachery.* |
| Bindweed, Great | *Insinuation.* |
| Bindweed, Small | *Humility.* |
| Birch | *Meekness.* |
| Birdsfoot Trefoil | *Revenge.* |
| Bittersweet; Nightshade | *Truth.* |
| Black Poplar | *Courage.* |
| Blackthorn | *Difficulty.* |
| Bladder Nut Tree | *Frivolity. Amusement.* |
| Bluebottle (Centaury) | *Delicacy.* |
| Bluebell | *Constancy.* |
| Blue-flowered Greek Valerian | *Rupture.* |
| Borus Henricus | *Goodness.* |
| Borage | *Bluntness.* |
| Box Tree | *Stoicism.* |
| Bramble | *Lowliness. Envy. Remorse.* |

| Branch of Currants | *You please all.* |
|---|---|
| Branch of Thorns | *Severity. Rigour.* |
| Bridal Rose | *Happy love.* |
| Broom | *Humility. Neatness.* |
| Buckbean | *Calm repose.* |
| Bud of White Rose | *Heart ignorant of love.* |
| Bugloss | *Falsehood.* |
| Bulrush | *Indiscretion. Docility.* |
| Bundle of Reeds, with their Panicles | *Music.* |
| Burdock | *Importunity. Touch me not.* |
| Buttercup (Kingcup) | *Ingratitude. Childishness.* |
| Butterfly Orchis | *Gaiety.* |
| Butterfly Weed | *Let me go.* |
| Cabbage | *Profit.* |
| Cacalia | *Adulation.* |
| Cactus | *Warmth.* |
| Calla Æthiopica | *Magnificent Beauty.* |
| Calycanthus | *Benevolence.* |
| Camellia Japonica, Red | *Unpretending excellence.* |
| Camellia Japonica, White | *Perfected loveliness.* |
| Camomile | *Energy in adversity.* |
| Canary Grass | *Perseverance.* |
| Candytuft | *Indifference.* |
| Canterbury Bell | *Acknowledgment.* |
| Cape Jasmine | *I'm too happy.* |
| Cardamine | *Paternal error.* |
| Carnation, Deep Red | *Alas! for my poor heart.* |
| Carnation, Striped | *Refusal.* |
| Carnation, Yellow | *Disdain.* |
| Cardinal Flower | *Distinction.* |
| Catchfly | *Snare.* |
| Catchfly, Red | *Youthful love.* |
| Catchfly, White | *Betrayed.* |
| Cedar | *Strength.* |
| Cedar of Lebanon | *Incorruptible.* |
| Cedar Leaf | *I live for thee.* |
| Calandine (Lesser) | *Joys to come.* |
| Cereus (Creeping) | *Modest genius.* |
| Centaury | *Delicacy.* |
| Champignon | *Suspicion.* |
| Chequered Fritillary | *Persecution.* |
| Cherry Tree | *Good education.* |
| Cherry Tree, White | *Deception.* |
| Chestnut Tree | *Do me justice. Luxury.* |
| Chickweed | *Rendezvous.* |
| Chicory | *Frugality.* |
| China Aster | *Variety.* |
| China Aster, Double | *I partake your sentiments.* |

| | |
|---|---|
| China Aster, Single | *I will think of it.* |
| China or Indian Pink | *Aversion.* |
| China Rose | *Beauty always new.* |
| Chinese Chrysanthemum | *Cheerfulness under adversity.* |
| Christmas Rose | *Relieve my anxiety.* |
| Chrysanthemum, Red | *I love.* |
| Chrysanthemum, White | *Truth.* |
| Chrysanthemum, Yellow | *Slighted love.* |
| Cinquefoil | *Maternal affection.* |
| Circaea | *Spell.* |
| Cistus, or Rock Rose | *Popular favour.* |
| Cistus, Gum | *I shall die to-morrow.* |
| Citron | *Ill-natured beauty.* |
| Clematis | *Mental beauty.* |
| Clematis, Evergreen | *Poverty.* |
| Clotbur | *Rudeness. Pertinacity.* |
| Cloves | *Dignity.* |
| Clover, Four-leaved | *Be mine.* |
| Clover, Red | *Industry.* |
| Clover, White | *Think of me.* |
| Cobæa | *Gossip.* |
| Cockscomb Amaranth | *Foppery. Affectation. Singularity.* |
| Colchicum, or Meadow Saffron | *My best days are past.* |
| Coltsfoot | *Justice shall be done.* |
| Columbine | *Folly.* |
| Columbine, Purple | *Resolved to win.* |
| Columbine, Red | *Anxious and trembling.* |
| Convolvulus | *Bonds.* |
| Convolvulus, Blue (Minor) | *Repose. Night.* |
| Convolvulus, Major | *Extinguished hopes.* |
| Convolvulus, Pink | *Worth sustained by judicious and tender affection.* |
| Corchorus | *Impatient of absence.* |
| Coreopsis | *Always cheerful.* |
| Coreopsis Arkansa | *Love at first sight.* |
| Coriander | *Hidden worth.* |
| Corn | *Riches.* |
| Corn, Broken | *Quarrel.* |
| Corn Straw | *Agreement.* |
| Corn Bottle | *Delicacy.* |
| Corn Cockle | *Gentility.* |
| Cornel Tree | *Duration.* |
| Coronella | *Success crown your wishes.* |
| Cowslip | *Pensiveness. Winning grace.* |
| Cowslip, American | *Divine beauty. You are my Divinity.* |
| Cranberry | *Cure for heartache.* |
| Creeping Cereus | *Horror.* |
| Cress | *Stability. Power.* |

| | |
|---|---|
| Crocus | *Abuse not.* |
| Crocus, Spring | *Youthful gladness.* |
| Crocus, Saffron | *Mirth.* |
| Crown Imperial | *Majesty. Power.* |
| Crowsbill | *Envy.* |
| Crowfoot | *Ingratitude.* |
| Crowfoot (Aconite-leaved) | *Lustre.* |
| Cuckoo Plant | *Ardour.* |
| Cudweed, American | *Unceasing remembrance.* |
| Currant | *Thy frown will kill me.* |
| Cuscuta | *Meanness.* |
| Cyclamen | *Diffidence.* |
| Cypress | *Death. Mourning.* |
| Daffodil | *Regard.* |
| Dahlia | *Instability.* |
| Daisy | *Innocence.* |
| Daisy, Garden | *I share your sentiments.* |
| Daisy, Michaelmas | *Farewell.* |
| Daisy, Party-coloured | *Beauty.* |
| Daisy, Wild | *I will think of it.* |
| Damask Rose | *Brilliant complexion.* |
| Dandelion | *Rustic oracle.* |
| Daphne Odora | *Painting the lily.* |
| Darnel (Ray grass) | *Vice.* |
| Dead Leaves | *Sadness.* |
| Dew Plant | *A Serenade.* |
| Dittany of Crete | *Birth.* |
| Dittany of Crete, White | *Passion.* |
| Dock | *Patience.* |
| Dodder of Thyme | *Baseness.* |
| Dogsbane | *Deceit. Falsehood.* |
| Dogwood | *Durability.* |
| Dragon Plant | *Snare.* |
| Dragonwort | *Horror.* |
| Dried Flax | *Utility.* |
| Ebony Tree | *Blackness.* |
| Eglantine (Sweetbrier) | *Poetry. I wound to heal.* |
| Elder | *Zealousness.* |
| Elm | *Dignity.* |
| Enchanter's Nightshade | *Witchcraft. Sorcery.* |
| Endive | *Frugality.* |
| Eupatorium | *Delay.* |
| Everflowering Candytuft | *Indifference.* |
| Evergreen Clematis | *Poverty.* |
| Evergreen Thorn | *Solace in adversity.* |
| Everlasting | *Never-ceasing remembrance.* |
| Everlasting Pea | *Lasting pleasure.* |
| Fennel | *Worthy all praise. Strength.* |
| Fern | *Fascination* |

| | |
|---|---|
| Ficoides, Ice Plant | *Your looks freeze me.* |
| Fig | *Argument.* |
| Fig Marigold | *Idleness.* |
| Fig Tree | *Prolific.* |
| Filbert | *Reconciliation.* |
| Fir | *Time.* |
| Fir Tree | *Elevation.* |
| Flax | *Domestic Industry. Fate. I feel your kindness.* |
| Flax-leaved Goldy-locks | *Tardiness.* |
| Fleur-de-Lis | *Flame. I burn.* |
| Fleur-de-Luce | *Fire.* |
| Flowering Fern | *Reverie.* |
| Flowering Reed | *Confidence in Heaven.* |
| Flower-of-an-Hour | *Delicate beauty.* |
| Fly Orchis | *Error.* |
| Flytrap | *Deceit.* |
| Fools' Parsley | *Silliness.* |
| Forget Me Not | *True love. Forget me not.* |
| Foxglove | *Insincerity.* |
| Foxtail Grass | *Sporting.* |
| French Honeysuckle | *Rustic beauty.* |
| French Marigold | *Jealousy.* |
| French Willow | *Bravery and humanity.* |
| Frog Ophrys | *Disgust.* |
| Fuller's Teasel | *Misanthropy.* |
| Fumitory | *Spleen.* |
| Fuchsia, Scarlet | *Taste.* |
| Garden Anemone | *Forsaken.* |
| Garden Chervil | *Sincerity.* |
| Garden Daisy | *I partake your sentiments.* |
| Garden Marigold | *Uneasiness.* |
| Garden Ranunculus | *You are rich in attractions.* |
| Garden Sage | *Esteem.* |
| Garland of Roses | *Reward of virtue.* |
| Germander Speedwell | *Facility.* |
| Geranium, Dark | *Melancholy.* |
| Geranium, Ivy | *Bridal favour.* |
| Geranium, Lemon | *Unexpected meeting.* |
| Geranium, Nutmeg | *Expected meeting.* |
| Geranium, Oak-leaved | *True friendship.* |
| Geranium, Pencilled | *Ingenuity.* |
| Geranium, Rose-scented | *Preference.* |
| Geranium, Scarlet | *Comforting. Stupidity.* |
| Geranium, Silver-leaved | *Recall.* |
| Geranium, Wild | *Steadfast piety.* |
| Gillyflower | *Bonds of affection.* |
| Glory Flower | *Glorious beauty.* |
| Goat's Rue | *Reason.* |

| | |
|---|---|
| Golden Rod | *Precaution.* |
| Gooseberry | *Anticipation.* |
| Gourd | *Extent, Bulk.* |
| Grape, Wild | *Charity.* |
| Grass | *Submission. Utility.* |
| Guelder Rose | *Winter. Age.* |
| Hand Flower Tree | *Warning.* |
| Harebell | *Submission. Grief.* |
| Hawkweed | *Quicksightedness.* |
| Hawthorn | *Hope.* |
| Hazel | *Reconciliation.* |
| Heath | *Solitude.* |
| Helenium | *Tears.* |
| Heliotrope | *Devotion. Faithfulness.* |
| Hellebore | *Scandal. Calumny.* |
| Helmet Flower (Monkshood) | *Knight-errantry.* |
| Hemlock | *You will be my death.* |
| Hemp | *Fate.* |
| Henbane | *Imperfection.* |
| Hepatica | *Confidence.* |
| Hibiscus | *Delicate beauty.* |
| Holly | *Foresight.* |
| Holly Herb | *Enchantment.* |
| Hollyhock | *Ambition. Fecundity.* |
| Honesty | *Honesty. Fascination.* |
| Honey Flower | *Love sweet and secret.* |
| Honeysuckle | *Generous and devoted affection.* |
| Honeysuckle Coral | *The colour of my fate.* |
| Honeysuckle (French) | *Rustic beauty.* |
| Hop | *Injustice.* |
| Hornbeam | *Ornament.* |
| Horse Chesnut | *Luxury.* |
| Hortensia | *You are cold.* |
| Houseleek | *Vivacity. Domestic industry.* |
| Houstonia | *Content.* |
| Hoya | *Sculpture.* |
| Humble Plant | *Despondency.* |
| Hundred-leaved Rose | *Dignity of mind.* |
| Hyacinth | *Sport. Game. Play.* |
| Hyancinth, White | *Unobtrusive loveliness.* |
| Hydrangea | *A boaster. Heartlessness.* |
| Hyssop | *Cleanliness.* |
| Iceland Moss | *Health.* |
| Ice Plant | *Your looks freeze me.* |
| Imperial Montague | *Power.* |
| Indian Cress | *Warlike trophy.* |
| Indian Jasmine (Ipomœa) | *Attachment.* |
| Indian Pink (Double) | *Always lovely.* |
| Indian Plum | *Privation.* |

| | |
|---|---|
| Iris | *Message.* |
| Iris, German | *Flame.* |
| Ivy | *Fidelity. Marriage.* |
| Ivy, Sprig of, with tendrils | *Assiduous to please.* |
| Jacob's Ladder | *Come down.* |
| Japan Rose | *Beauty is your only attraction.* |
| Jasmine | *Amiability.* |
| Jasmine, Cape | *Transport of joy.* |
| Jasmine, Carolina | *Separation.* |
| Jasmine, Indian | *I attach myself to you.* |
| Jasmine, Spanish | *Sensuality.* |
| Jasmine, Yellow | *Grace and elegance.* |
| Jonquil | *I desire a return of affection.* |
| Judas Tree | *Unbelief. Betrayal.* |
| Juniper | *Succour. Protection.* |
| Justicia | *The perfection of female loveliness.* |
| Kennedia | *Mental Beauty.* |
| King-cups | *Desire of Riches.* |
| Laburnum | *Forsaken. Pensive Beauty.* |
| Lady's Slipper | *Capricious Beauty. Win me and wear me.* |
| Lagerstræmia, Indian | *Eloquence.* |
| Lantana | *Rigour.* |
| Larch | *Audacity. Boldness.* |
| Larkspur | *Lightness. Levity.* |
| Larkspur, Pink | *Fickleness.* |
| Larkspur, Purple | *Haughtiness.* |
| Laurel | *Glory.* |
| Laurel, Common, in flower | *Perfidy.* |
| Laurel, Ground | *Perseverance.* |
| Laurel, Mountain | *Ambition.* |
| Laurel-leaved Magnolia | *Dignity.* |
| Laurestina | *A token. I die if neglected.* |
| Lavender | *Distrust.* |
| Leaves (dead) | *Melancholy.* |
| Lemon | *Zest.* |
| Lemon Blossoms | *Fidelity in love.* |
| Lettuce | *Cold-heartedness.* |
| Lichen | *Dejection. Solitude.* |
| Lilac, Field | *Humility.* |
| Lilac, Purple | *First emotions of love.* |
| Lilac, White | *Youthful Innocence.* |
| Lily, Day | *Coquetry.* |
| Lily, Imperial | *Majesty.* |
| Lily, White | *Purity. Sweetness.* |
| Lily, Yellow | *Falsehood. Gaiety.* |
| Lily of the Valley | *Return of happiness.* |
| Linden or Lime Trees | *Conjugal love.* |

| | |
|---|---|
| Lint | *I feel my obligations.* |
| Live Oak | *Liberty.* |
| Liverwort | *Confidence.* |
| Licorice, Wild | *I declare against you.* |
| Lobelia | *Malevolence.* |
| Locust Tree | *Elegance.* |
| Locust Tree (green) | *Affection beyond the grave.* |
| London Pride | *Frivolity.* |
| Lote Tree | *Concord.* |
| Lotus | *Eloquence.* |
| Lotus Flower | *Estranged love.* |
| Lotus Leaf | *Recantation.* |
| Love in a Mist | *Perplexity.* |
| Love lies Bleeding | *Hopeless, not heartless.* |
| Lucern | *Life.* |
| Lupine | *Voraciousness. Imagination.* |
| Madder | *Calumny.* |
| Magnolia | *Love of Nature.* |
| Magnolia, Swamp | *Perseverance.* |
| Mallow | *Mildness.* |
| Mallow, Marsh | *Beneficence.* |
| Mallow, Syrian | *Consumed by love.* |
| Mallow, Venetian | *Delicate beauty.* |
| Manchineal Tree | *Falsehood.* |
| Mandrake | *Horror.* |
| Maple | *Reserve.* |
| Marigold | *Grief.* |
| Marigold, Africa | *Vulgar minds.* |
| Marigold, French | *Jealousy.* |
| Marigold, Prophetic | *Prediction.* |
| Marigold and Cypress | *Despair.* |
| Marjoram | *Blushes.* |
| Marvel of Peru | *Timidity.* |
| Meadow Lychnis | *Wit.* |
| Meadow Saffron | *My best days are past.* |
| Meadowsweet | *Uselessness.* |
| Mercury | *Goodness.* |
| Mesembryanthemum | *Idleness.* |
| Mezereon | *Desire to please.* |
| Michaelmas Daisy | *Afterthought.* |
| Mignionette | *Your qualities surpass your charms.* |
| Milfoil | *War.* |
| Milvetch | *Your presence softens my pains.* |
| Milkwort | *Hermitage.* |
| Mimosa (Sensitive Plant) | *Sensitiveness.* |
| Mint | *Virtue.* |
| Mistletoe | *I surmount difficulties.* |
| Mock Orange | *Counterfeit.* |

| | |
|---|---|
| Monkshood (Helmet Flower) | *Chivalry. Knight-errantry.* |
| Moonwort | *Forgetfulness.* |
| Morning Glory | *Affectation.* |
| Moschatel | *Weakness.* |
| Moss | *Maternal love.* |
| Mosses | *Ennui.* |
| Mossy Saxifrage | *Affection.* |
| Motherwort | *Concealed love.* |
| Mountain Ash | *Prudence.* |
| Mourning Bride | *Unfortunate attachment. I have lost all.* |
| Mouse-eared Chickweed | *Ingenuous simplicity.* |
| Mouse-eared Scorpion Grass | *Forget me not.* |
| Moving Plant | *Agitation.* |
| Mudwort | *Tranquillity.* |
| Mugwort | *Happiness.* |
| Mulberry Tree (Black) | *I shall not survive you.* |
| Mulberry Tree (White) | *Wisdom.* |
| Mushroom | *Suspicion.* |
| Musk Plant | *Weakness.* |
| Mustard Seed | *Indifference.* |
| Myrobalan | *Privation.* |
| Myrrh | *Gladness.* |
| Myrtle | *Love.* |
| Narcissus | *Egotism.* |
| Nasturtium | *Patriotism.* |
| Nettle, Burning | *Slander.* |
| Nettle Tree | *Concert.* |
| Night-blooming Cereus | *Transient beauty.* |
| Night Convolvulus | *Night.* |
| Nightshade | *Truth.* |
| Oak Leaves | *Bravery.* |
| Oak Tree | *Hospitality.* |
| Oak (White) | *Independence.* |
| Oats | *The witching soul of music.* |
| Oleander | *Beware.* |
| Olive | *Peace.* |
| Orange Blossoms | *Your purity equals your loveliness.* |
| Orange Flowers | *Chastity. Bridal festivities.* |
| Orange Tree | *Generosity.* |
| Orchis | *A Belle.* |
| Osier | *Frankness.* |
| Osmunda | *Dreams.* |
| Ox Eye | *Patience.* |
| Palm | *Victory.* |
| Pansy | *Thoughts.* |
| Parsley | *Festivity.* |
| Pasque Flower | *You have no claims.* |

| | |
|---|---|
| Passion Flower | *Religious Superstition.* |
| Patience Dock | *Patience.* |
| Pea, Everlasting | *An appointed meeting. Lasting Pleasure.* |
| Pea, Sweet | *Departure.* |
| Peach | *Your qualities, like your charms, are unequalled.* |
| Peach Blossom | *I am your captive.* |
| Pear | *Affection.* |
| Pear Tree | *Comfort.* |
| Pennyroyal | *Flee away.* |
| Peony | *Shame, Bashfulness.* |
| Peppermint | *Warmth of feeling.* |
| Periwinkle, Blue | *Early friendship.* |
| Periwinkle, White | *Pleasures of memory.* |
| Persicaria | *Restoration.* |
| Persimmon | *Bury me amid Nature's beauties.* |
| Peruvian Heliotrope | *Devotion.* |
| Pheasant's Eye | *Remembrance.* |
| Phlox | *Unanimity.* |
| Pigeon Berry | *Indifference.* |
| Pimpernel | *Change. Assignation.* |
| Pine | *Pity.* |
| Pine-apple | *You are perfect.* |
| Pine, Pitch | *Philosophy.* |
| Pine, Spruce | *Hope in adversity.* |
| Pink | *Boldness.* |
| Pink, Carnation | *Woman's love.* |
| Pink, Indian, Double | *Always lovely.* |
| Pink, Indian, Single | *Aversion.* |
| Pink, Mountain | *Aspiring.* |
| Pink, Red, Double | *Pure and ardent love.* |
| Pink, Single | *Pure love.* |
| Pink, Variegated | *Refusal.* |
| Pink, White | *Ingeniousness. Talent.* |
| Plane Tree | *Genius.* |
| Plum, Indian | *Privation.* |
| Plum Tree | *Genius.* |
| Plum, Wild | *Independence.* |
| Polyanthus | *Pride of riches.* |
| Polyanthus, Crimson | *The heart's mystery.* |
| Polyanthus, Lilac | *Confidence.* |
| Pomegranate | *Foolishness.* |
| Pomegranate, Flower | *Mature elegance.* |
| Poplar, Black | *Courage.* |
| Poplar, White | *Time.* |
| Poppy, Red | *Consolation.* |
| Poppy, Scarlet | *Fantastic extravagance.* |
| Poppy, White | *Sleep, My bane. My antidote.* |

| | |
|---|---|
| Potato | *Benevolence.* |
| Prickly Pear | *Satire.* |
| Pride of China | *Dissension.* |
| Primrose | *Early youth.* |
| Primrose, Evening | *Inconstancy.* |
| Primrose, Red | *Unpatronized merit.* |
| Privet | *Prohibition.* |
| Purple Clover | *Provident.* |
| Pyrus Japonica | *Fairies' fire.* |
| Quaking-Grass | *Agitation.* |
| Quamoclit | *Busybody.* |
| Queen's Rocket | *You are the queen of coquettes. Fashion.* |
| Quince | *Temptation.* |
| Ragged Robin | *Wit.* |
| Ranunculus | *You are radiant with charms.* |
| Ranunculus, Garden | *You are rich in attractions.* |
| Ranunculus, Wild | *Ingratitude.* |
| Raspberry | *Remorse.* |
| Ray Grass | *Vice.* |
| Red Catchfly | *Youthful love.* |
| Reed | *Complaisance. Music.* |
| Reed, Split | *Indiscretion.* |
| Rhododendron (Rosebay) | *Danger. Beware.* |
| Rhubarb | *Advice.* |
| Rocket | *Rivalry.* |
| Rose | *Love.* |
| Rose, Austrian | *Thou art all that is lovely.* |
| Rose, Bridal | *Happy love.* |
| Rose, Burgundy | *Unconscious beauty.* |
| Rose, Cabbage | *Ambassador of love.* |
| Rose, Campion | *Only deserve my love.* |
| Rose, Carolina | *Love is dangerous.* |
| Rose, China | *Beauty always new.* |
| Rose, Christmas | *Tranquillize my anxiety.* |
| Rose, Daily | *Thy smile I aspire to.* |
| Rose, Damask | *Brilliant complexion.* |
| Rose, Deep Red | *Bashful shame.* |
| Rose, Dog | *Pleasure and pain.* |
| Rose, Guelder | *Winter. Age.* |
| Rose, Hundred-leaved | *Pride.* |
| Rose, Japan | *Beauty is your only attraction.* |
| Rose, Maiden Blush | *If you love me, you will find it out.* |
| Rose, Multiflora | *Grace.* |
| Rose, Mundi | *Variety.* |
| Rose, Musk | *Capricious beauty.* |
| Rose, Musk, Cluster | *Charming.* |
| Rose, Single | *Simplicity.* |

| | |
|---|---|
| Rose, Thornless | *Early attachment.* |
| Rose, Unique | *Call me not beautiful.* |
| Rose, White | *I am worthy of you.* |
| Rose, White (withered) | *Transient impressions.* |
| Rose, Yellow | *Decrease of love. Jealousy.* |
| Rose, York and Lancaster | *War.* |
| Rose, Full-blown, placed over two Buds | *Secrecy.* |
| Rose, White and Red together | *Unity.* |
| Roses, Crown of | *Reward of virtue.* |
| Rosebud, Red | *Pure and lovely.* |
| Rosebud, White | *Girlhood.* |
| Rosebud, Moss | *Confession of love.* |
| Rosebay (Rhododendron) | *Beware. Danger.* |
| Rosemary | *Rememberance.* |
| Rudbeckia | *Justice.* |
| Rue | *Disdain.* |
| Rush | *Docility.* |
| Rye Grass | *Changeable disposition.* |
| Saffron | *Beware of excess.* |
| Saffron Crocus | *Mirth.* |
| Saffron, Meadow | *My happiest days are past.* |
| Sage | *Domestic virtue.* |
| Sage, Garden | *Esteem.* |
| Sainfoin | *Agitation.* |
| Saint John's Wort | *Animosity. Superstition.* |
| Sardony | *Irony.* |
| Saxifrage, Mossy | *Affection.* |
| Scabious | *Unfortunate love.* |
| Scabious, Sweet | *Widowhood.* |
| Scarlet Lychnis | *Sunbeaming eyes.* |
| Schinus | *Religious enthusiasm.* |
| Scotch Fir | *Elevation.* |
| Sensitive Plant | *Sensibility. Delicate feelings.* |
| Senvy | *Indifference.* |
| Shamrock | *Light heartedness.* |
| Snakesfoot | *Horror.* |
| Snapdragon | *Presumption.* |
| Snowball | *Bound.* |
| Snowdrop | *Hope.* |
| Sorrel | *Affection.* |
| Sorrel, Wild | *Wit ill-timed.* |
| Sorrel, Wood | *Joy.* |
| Southernwood | *Jest. Bantering.* |
| Spanish Jasmine | *Sensuality.* |
| Spearmint | *Warmth of sentiment.* |
| Speedwell | *Female fidelity.* |
| Speedwell, Germander | *Facility.* |
| Speedwell, Spiked | *Semblance.* |

| | |
|---|---|
| Spider, Ophrys | *Adroitness.* |
| Spiderwort | *Esteem not love.* |
| Spiked Willow Herb | *Pretension.* |
| Spindle Tree | *Your charms are engraven on my heart.* |
| Star of Bethlehem | *Purity.* |
| Starwort | *Afterthought.* |
| Starwort, American | *Cheerfulness in old age.* |
| Stock | *Lasting beauty.* |
| Stock, Ten Week | *Promptness.* |
| Stonecrop | *Tranquillity.* |
| Straw, Broken | *Rupture of a contract.* |
| Straw, Whole | *Union.* |
| Strawberry Tree | *Esteem and love.* |
| Sumach, Venice | *Splendour. Intellectual excellence.* |
| Sunflower, Dwarf | *Adoration.* |
| Sunflower, Tall | *Haughtiness.* |
| Swallow-wort | *Cure for heartache.* |
| Sweet Basil | *Good wishes.* |
| Sweetbrier, American | *Simplicity.* |
| Sweetbrier, European | *I wound to heal.* |
| Sweetbrier, Yellow | *Decrease of love.* |
| Sweet Pea | *Delicate pleasures.* |
| Sweet Sultan | *Felicity.* |
| Sweet William | *Gallantry.* |
| Sycamore | *Curiosity.* |
| Syringa | *Memory.* |
| Syringa, Carolina | *Disappointment.* |
| Tamarisk | *Crime.* |
| Tansy (Wild) | *I declare war against you.* |
| Teasel | *Misanthropy.* |
| Tendrils of Climbing Plants | *Ties.* |
| Thistle, Common | *Austerity.* |
| Thistle, Fuller's | *Misanthropy.* |
| Thistle, Scotch | *Retaliation.* |
| Thorn Apple | *Deceitful charms.* |
| Thorn, Branch of | *Severity.* |
| Thrift | *Sympathy.* |
| Throatwort | *Neglected beauty.* |
| Thyme | *Activity.* |
| Tiger Flower | *For once may pride befriend me.* |
| Traveller's Joy | *Safety.* |
| Tree of Life | *Old age.* |
| Trefoil | *Revenge.* |
| Tremella Nestoc | *Resistance.* |
| Trillium Pictum | *Modest beauty.* |
| Truffle | *Surprise.* |
| Trumpet Flower | *Fame.* |

| | |
|---|---|
| Tuberose | *Dangerous pleasures.* |
| Tulip | *Fame.* |
| Tulip, Red | *Declaration of love.* |
| Tulip, Variegated | *Beautiful eyes.* |
| Tulip, Yellow | *Hopeless love.* |
| Turnip | *Charity.* |
| Tussilage (Sweet-scented) | *Justice shall be done you.* |
| Valerian | *An accommodating disposition.* |
| Valerian, Greek | *Rupture.* |
| Venice Sumach | *Intellectual excellence.* |
| | *Splendour.* |
| Venus' Car | *Fly with me.* |
| Venus' Looking-glass | *Flattery.* |
| Venus' Trap | *Deceit.* |
| Vernal Grass | *Poor, but happy.* |
| Veronica | *Fidelity.* |
| Vervain | *Enchantment.* |
| Vine | *Intoxication.* |
| Violet, Blue | *Faithfulness.* |
| Violet, Dame | *Watchfulness.* |
| Violet, Sweet | *Modesty.* |
| Violet, Yellow | *Rural happiness.* |
| Virginian Spiderwort | *Momentary happiness.* |
| Virgin's Bower | *Filial love.* |
| Volkamenia | *May you be happy.* |
| Walnut | *Intellect. Stratagem.* |
| Wall-flower | *Fidelity in adversity.* |
| Water Lily | *Purity of heart.* |
| Water Melon | *Bulkiness.* |
| Wax Plant | *Susceptibility.* |
| Wheat Stalk | *Riches.* |
| Whin | *Anger.* |
| White Jasmine | *Amiableness.* |
| White Lily | *Purity and Modesty.* |
| White Mullein | *Good nature.* |
| White Oak | *Independence.* |
| White Pink | *Talent.* |
| White Poplar | *Time.* |
| White Rose (dried) | *Death preferable to loss of* |
| | *innocence.* |
| Whortleberry | *Treason.* |
| Willow, Creeping | *Love forsaken.* |
| Willow, Water | *Freedom.* |
| Willow, Weeping | *Mourning.* |
| Willow-Herb | *Pretension.* |
| Willow, French | *Bravery and humanity.* |
| Winter Cherry | *Deception.* |
| Witch Hazel | *A spell.* |
| Woodbine | *Fraternal love.* |

| | |
|---|---|
| Wood Sorrel | *Joy. Maternal tenderness.* |
| Wormwood | *Absence.* |
| Xanthium | *Rudeness. Pertinacity.* |
| Xeranthemum | *Cheerfulness under adversity.* |
| Yew | *Sorrow.* |
| Zephyr Flower | *Expectation.* |
| Zinnia | *Thoughts of absent friends.* |

# Divorce and Marriage in New-York†

## *Features and Workings of an Iniquitous System*

**HOW IT IS VIEWED BY SUCH EMINENT LAWYERS AS CHIEF JUSTICE DAVIS, F. N. BANGS, F. R. COUDERT, H. B. TURNER, D. M. PORTER AND B. F. TRACY.**

An investigation of the records of the courts in New-York City having jurisdiction in divorce proceedings for the last thirteen years has disclosed the fact that there has been for five years an astonishing increase in the number of decrees of absolute divorce granted. There is only one cause for such a divorce under the statutes of the State, and the decrees, in harmony with the law, prohibit the guilty party in the case from marrying again within the life-time of the injured party. Under rulings of the Court of Appeals such marriages are valid, however, if contracted in other States, and it has been discovered that in many cases persons have contrived to have decrees entered against them in order that they might re-marry. Other causes have operated under the prevailing system to increase the number of absolute divorces and disgraceful marriages, chief among them being the secrecy with which trials are conducted.

These facts have caused consternation and alarm among persons who are brought frequently face to face with the law and its results. To obtain the views of men learned in the laws and interested in the preservation of social morality, THE TRIBUNE has sent its reporters to eminent judges and lawyers, with instructions to obtain from them their judgments on the workings of the present law as laid down in the statutes and construed by the highest tribunal of the State. The result of these inquiries and the discoveries of the records and law books are given in the appended articles. Beginning with Chief-Justice Davis, these men, with hardly an exception, speak severe criticism against the law and recommend a reform. * * *

### *The Law and its Results.*

**GREAT INCREASE IN NUMBER OF DECREES—FEATURES OF DIVORCE LAWS.**

Of late there has been a startling increase in the number of divorces granted in the courts of New-York City. As many decrees of divorce

† From *New York Tribune*, October 7, 1883, p. 9.

have been entered in the offices of the three courts that have jurisdiction in such cases during the last five years as in the preceding eight. In each case the number was about 1,400. Especially has the increase been startling since the summer of 1881. The total number in 1880 was 218; in 1881 it was 253; in 1882 it was 316; and the number of decrees already entered up to September of this year is 215. Inasmuch as the number of applications during the summer vacation was extraordinarily large, and that most of these are still before referees or untried, the entire number for this year promises to foot up more than 400—or about twice as many as were ever granted in any year preceding 1879. Following is a tabulated statement of the number of divorces that have been obtained in each of the three courts—the Supreme, Superior and Common Pleas—from 1870 to September 1, 1883, with the totals for each year:

| Years | 1870 | 1871 | 1872 | 1873 | 1874 | 1875 | 1876 | 1877 |
|---|---|---|---|---|---|---|---|---|
| Supreme | 109 | 80 | 77 | 85 | 122 | 96 | 79 | 100 |
| Superior | 70 | 70 | 47 | 27 | 26 | 27 | 14 | 26 |
| Com. Pleas | 33 | 44 | 55 | 77 | 65 | 43 | 54 | 38 |
| Total | 212 | 194 | 179 | 189 | 213 | 166 | 147 | 164 |

| Years | 1878 | 1879 | 1880 | 1881 | 1882 | 1883 to Sept. 1. |
|---|---|---|---|---|---|---|
| Supreme | 92 | 160 | 178 | 192 | 252 | 174 |
| Superior | 16 | 14 | 8 | 23 | 81 | 26 |
| Com. Pleas | 37 | 49 | 32 | 38 | 33 | 15 |
| Total | 145 | 223 | 218 | 253 | 316 | 215 |

ONE CAUSE OF THE INCREASE.

The apparent causes for this increase are several. Doubtless one of the most marked to the comparatively recent decisions of the Court of Appeals of this State, which practically remove all restraint upon the subsequent marriage of persons against whom decrees of divorce have been granted for their acts of infidelity. The case of Van Voorhis vs. Brintnall was argued in the Court of Appeals in March, 1881, and was decided in October of that year. The General Term in the Second District had held in that case (as had the General Term in this city in the case of Marshall vs. Marshall, and the General Term of the Superior Court in Thorp vs. Thorp, and as had most of the judges of the State before whom the question had come at Trial Term) that a person against whom a decree of absolute divorce had been granted could not anywhere contract a marriage that would be recognized as valid in this State during the lifetime of the person who obtained the decree. The question came before the Court of Appeals for the first time in the Van Voorhis case. The appellate court reversed the holdings of the courts below, and held that a marriage valid in the place where contracted must be considered valid here, notwithstanding any provision in the statutes of this State declaring that no such divorced person could marry during the husband's or wife's lifetime. This proposition was reaffirmed and strengthened by the decision of the same court last year in the case of Thorp vs. Thorp. The practical effect of this decision is that a person divorced for his own misconduct to-day can to-morrow step over into New-Jersey or Connecticut where there is no such restriction, and there marry the woman whom he takes with him for the purpose; when he returns to this State, its courts are bound to hold that this marriage, which the State law and the decree of the court had forbidden him to make, is valid, and that the offspring of it are legitimate. The Court of Appeals sustains this apparent inconsistency on the broad principle that no law can be so extended in its effect as to have an "extra-territorial" force unless its provisions, in terms, distinctly prescribe that it is to have such effect. But the court intimates that a law might be framed, analogous to the one to prevent duelling, that would follow the guilty divorced party out of the State and on his return to this State with his new wife.

The obvious effect of these decisions has followed. Before 1881 the severity of the divorce laws had been so firmly maintained in this State that there were few countries in Europe and scarcely any States in America where the marriage tie could not be more easily broken. But for unprincipled married persons who wish to be free from their present domestic alliances all restraint except that of public sentiment is now practically removed. A man or woman of this description can commit a flagrant act of infidelity that will be brought to the knowledge of the husband or wife, as the case may be, who will thus be forced into seeking the redress which the offending party is anxious should be obtained. When the facts are laid before the court the judge is bound to grant the divorce—there is no collusion apparent and the guilt is plain. As soon as the decree is signed the guilty individual can ride in an hour or less into another State with another, and marry, and the new consort will occupy the same position in the eyes of the law as did the innocent one who has thus been wronged. Then when the new tie becomes irksome the same operation may be repeated, and so on *ad infinitum*.

### SECRET TRIALS AND DETECTIVES' EVIDENCE.

Another source of divorce multiplication, and one that existed quite as actively before the Van Voorhis decision, is the secrecy with which decrees are obtained. This springs from the idea in the minds of many judges that the divulging of the prurient details of domestic trouble and marital infidelity before those who crowd into court-rooms to listen to such tales would have a demoralizing effect. This idea, too, is strengthened by the wish of lawyers to keep the facts in regard to their clients' cases away from public knowledge. Therefore the most of such cases are tried in the secluded offices of lawyers appointed as referees, and neither the public nor newspaper reporters know of the time or place of such hearings. Moreover, the judges make the most stringent rules, which are binding upon the clerks, forbidding them to allow the evidence in divorce cases filed with them to be made public. The unscrupulous lawyers, therefore, who advertise that they will obtain "divorces without publicity," are generally able to make good their promises in that respect. The same men have other methods to aid them in their discreditable work. Chief, and one of the worst, among these is the detective system. No home is safe from its invasion. Give to a certain class of detectives, who carry on their business in this city, a statement of the facts which it is desired shall be proven before a referee as to almost any individual in the community, and give them, also, the big fees which they will demand, and the testimony will be forthcoming.

Little, if any, of the blame can be laid upon the shoulders of the referee. In the most dangerous classes of cases—either those where the divorce is sought without the knowledge of, or service being made upon, the defendant, or where there is collusion—there is no one to cross-examine witnesses to make any investigation of the truth of statements made by them. The detectives may, therefore, tell almost any story with impunity.

* * *

Advertisement for *The Age of Innocence.* As this advertisement suggests, *The Age of Innocence* was marketed as a problem novel concerned with divorce.

# CRITICISM

# Reviews

The publication of Edith Wharton's novel *The Age of Innocence* in the year following the close of World War I was a cultural event in the United States and England. Wharton, who had published a brief novel, *Summer*, in 1917, had become an international figure based not just on her war writings but also on her extensive work helping refugees and orphans find food, clothing, and shelter during the war. Reviewed widely and in the most distinguished newspapers and journals, Wharton's novel was discussed by major literary critics and authors of the time. While some of the critics followed the tradition of maintaining their anonymity, the list of writers and scholars who reviewed *The Age of Innocence* includes such prominent figures as Henry Seidel Canby, William Lyon Phelps, Vernon L. Parrington, and Carl Van Doren. In retrospect, the most striking figure to have turned her gaze on Wharton's novel was the New Zealand–born author, Katherine Mansfield (1888–1923), who signed her review simply "K. M." Divided here according to whether they were written for a primarily American or British audience, all of these reviews provide insights into the social as well as the critical reception of the novel. While these pieces were written for newspapers and literary journals, many rise above the level of mere reviews to provide literary analysis and, as such, they are reprinted here as the early criticism of the novel.

## AMERICAN REVIEWS

## KATHARINE PERRY

### Were the Seventies Sinless?†

A new novel by Edith Wharton is by way of being an event in the literary calendar, and in this absorbing tale the almost metallic brilliance which in the "House of Mirth" dazzled the reading public hypnotizes the eager eye which would not lose one significant word. New York society in the '70's—the cynically christened "Age of Innocence"—is painted with Meissonier-like[1] clarity of detail, beginning with vast Catherine Mingott, ruler of a great family of fashionables, down to her slim, pale grand-daughter, Countess Olenska, wife of a Polish roué, seeking sanctuary with her New York kin, who prove not always kind. From the opening opera night at the old red-hung Academy of Music,

† From *The Publishers' Weekly* 98 (October 16, 1920): 1195–96.
1. See p. 128, *n.* 1.

with Nilsson singing Marguerite in "Faust," the scenes of luxury, black walnut, smug hypocrisy, formal festivities, and rampant family virtue continue in perfect sequence. Little help in such a *milieu*, for young Newland Archer, who, having married a handsome white and gold débutante of regulation inexperience, finds himself appallingly and passionately in love with her cousin, the dark, seductive Countess. Again and again, the apparent artlessness of the young wife scores as if by accident; thru her, backed by the solid phalanx of family, respectability triumphs and the smooth surface of convention is never punctured, tho all New York relishingly infers that which never really came to pass.

The plot is unobvioos [sic], delicately developed, with a fine finale that exquisitely satisfies one's sense of fitness, and as always with Mrs. Wharton, the drama of character is greater than that of event. One revels recognizingly in her clean-cut distinction of style, the inerrant aptness of adjectives, the vivisective phrase. No wonder that in the letters of Henry James his admiration for his dazzling disciple finds expression; she has a more human touch, a more vivacious humor. And in the closing scene her pen dwells lingeringly on the Paris she loves, rich in that warm atmosphere of beauty and art which New York of the '70s so crudely and coldly lacked.

# WILLIAM LYON PHELPS

## As Mrs. Wharton Sees Us†

In this present year of emancipation it is pleasant to record that in the front rank of American living novelists we find four women, who shall be named in alphabetical order—the only order that makes the world safe for democracy; much appreciated by opera impresarios, managers of stock companies and other great diplomats. The big four are Dorothy Canfield, Zona Gale, Anne Sedgwick,[1] Edith Wharton. From the first we have thus far had no new novel in 1920; but the year must be counted as a notable one in the history of American prose fiction when it has seen the appearance of three works of the distinction of *Miss Lulu Bett, The Third Window* and *The Age of Innocence.* Any modern British novelist might be proud to sign his name to each and all of these books.

Mrs. Wharton's admirable career is a progression from the external to the internal; she began as a decorator and is now an analyst. She has always been an expert in gardens and in furniture. Her first book

---

† From *New York Times Book Review* (October 17, 1920): 1, 11. Bracketed page numbers refer to this Norton Critical Edition.
1. Dorothy Canfield: Dorothy Canfield Fisher (1879–1958), popular and prolific novelist who later became an arbiter of American literary taste through her position with the Book of the Month Club; Zona Gale (1874–1938) and Anne Sedgwick (1873–1935), popular novelists. The most intriguing absence from Phelp's listing of the "big four" among American women writers is Willa Cather (1873–1947), the only figure who came close to Wharton in terms of critical recognition of the quality of her work [Editor].

was called *Decoration of Houses*, written in 1897 with O. Codman, and in 1904 she produced a work on Italian villas and their gardens. These studies of interior decorating and landscape gardening are much in evidence in her novels; I do not remember when I have read a work of fiction that gives the reader so vivid an idea of the furnishing and illuminating of rooms in fashionable houses as one will find in *The Age of Innocence*.

Those who are interested in good dinners—and who is not?—will find much to admire in these brilliant pages. Many years ago when reading about prehistoric banquets in Dickens, I determined that some day I would write an essay on novelists from the culinary point of view. I have never "got around to it"; but this story would loom large in such a disquisition. The formal and elaborate dinner parties in New York in the seventies are described here with a gusto that the steady undercurrent of irony quite fails to conceal; there were epicures in those days who sallied from their Fifth Avenue mausoleums not to talk, but to dine. They were professional diners-out, who noticed details—why does she allow her butler to cut the cucumbers with a steel knife?

It was *The House of Mirth* (1905) that gave Mrs. Wharton an international reputation; if one wishes to see how far her art has advanced since that popular book, one has merely to compare it with *The Age of Innocence*. By the side of the absolute mastery of plot, character and style displayed in her latest novel, *The House of Mirth* seems almost crude. That austere masterpiece, *Ethan Frome*, stands in a room all by itself; it is an illustration, however, of the fact that our novelist, who knows Paris and Continental urban scenes so well, was equally at home in a barren American village.

I was not at all impressed by *The Custom of the Country* (1913); the satire became burlesque, and the writer's habitual irony—most impressive when most subdued—fell into cascades of feminine shrieks. Like her idol and master, Henry James, she is forever comparing America with Europe, to the latter's advantage. I have no quarrel with her on this score, for, after all, it is simply a matter of taste, so far as questions of art are concerned; but it is only occasionally in this latest book that the direct comparison is made. Describing a hot day in Boston:

> Archer found a cab and drove to the Somerset Club for breakfast.
> Even the fashionable quarters had the air of untidy domesticity to
> which no excess of heat ever degrades the European cities.

It is a matter of no importance, but I do not believe that statement to be true. I should not like to compare my knowledge of Europe with hers; Mrs. Wharton has either missed city scenes in Europe in the dog days, or has shut her eyes.

The two previous novels in her career which most clearly foreshadow the power and technique displayed in *The Age of Innocence* are *Madame de Treymes* (1907) and *The Reef* (1912). I think, with the exception of the novel now before us, *The Reef* is her finest full-length story. In one of the many intimate letters written to her by Henry James, and now published in the already famous two-volumes, we find the following admirable remarks on *The Reef* and if one will read them immediately after finishing *The Age of Innocence* one will see how perfectly they apply to Mrs. Wharton's style at its best:

> In the key of this, with all your reality, you have yet kept the whole thing, and, to deepen the harmony and accentuate the literary pitch, have never surpassed yourself for certain exquisite *moments*, certain images, analogies, metaphors, certain silver correspondences in your *façon de dire,* examples of which I could pluck out and numerically almost confound you with, were I not stammering in this so handicapped a way. There used to be little notes in you that were like fine, benevolent finger marks of the good George Eliot—the echo of much reading of that excellent woman, here and there, that is, sounding through. But now you are like a lost and recovered "ancient" which *she* might have got a reading of (especially were he a Greek), and of whom in *her* texture some weaker reflection were to show. For, dearest Edith, you are stronger and firmer and finer than all of them put together; you go further and you say *mieux* and your only drawback is not having the homeliness and the inevitability and the happy limitation and the affluent poverty of a Country of your Own (*comme moi, par exemple!*).

The style of *The Age of Innocence* is filled with the "silver correspondences" spoken of by Henry James; and the book would be a solid satisfaction, as it is an exquisite delight, had the writer only possessed the homeliness, the rugged simplicity that is lost under the enamel of finished sophistication. The English critic, R. H. Hutton, said that Goethe was the wisest man of modern times that ever lacked the wisdom of a little child—this particular kind of wisdom is not to be found in the works of Mrs. Wharton, though we find everything but that.

Yet I am in no mood to complain. Edith Wharton is a writer who brings glory on the name America, and this is her best book. After reading so many slipshod diaries called "novels," what a pleasure it is to turn the pages of this consummate work of art. The common method today of writing a novel is to begin with the birth of the hero, shove in all experiences that the author can remember of his own childhood, most of which are of no interest to any one but himself, take him to school, throw in more experiences, introduce him to the heroine, more experiences, quit when the book seems long enough, and write the whole biography in colloquial jargon.

Here is a novel whose basis is a story. It begins on a night at the opera. The characters are introduced naturally—every action and every conversation advance the plot. The style is a thing of beauty from first page to last. One dwells with pleasure on the "exquisite moments" of passion and tragedy, and on the "silver correspondences" that rise from the style like the moon on a cloudless night.

New York society and customs in the seventies are described with an accuracy that is almost uncanny; to read these pages is to live again.

The absolute imprisonment in which her characters stagnate, their artificial and false standards, the desperate monotony of trivial routine, the slow petrifaction of generous ardours, the paralysis of emotion, the accumulation of ice around the heart, the total loss of life in upholstered existence—are depicted with a high excellence that never falters. And in the last few pages the younger generation comes in like fresh air. Mrs. Wharton is all for the new and against the old; here, at all events, here sympathies are warm. She would never, like Solness, fear youth knocking at the door.

The two young women of the story are contrasted in a manner that is of the essence of drama without being in the least artificial. The radiantly beautiful young wife might have had her way without a shadow on it, were it not for the appearance of the Countess Olenska, who is, what the other women are not, a personality. Newland Archer, between these two women, and loved by both, is not at all to be envied. The love scenes between him and Ellen are wonderful in their terrible, inarticulate passion; it is curious how much more real they are than the unrestrained detailed descriptions thought by so many writers to be "realism." Here is where Mrs. Wharton resembles Joseph Conrad and Henry James, for the love scenes in this book are fully worthy of those two men of genius. So little is said, so little is done, yet one feels the infinite passion in the finite hearts that burn. I wonder what old Browning would have thought of this frustration; for the story is not altogether unlike "The Statue and the Bust."

I do not believe I shall ever forget three scenes between Archer and Ellen—the "outing" at Boston, the night carriage drive from the ferry in New York, and the interview in the corner of the Museum of Art, with its setting of relics. These are scenes of passion that Conrad or Henry James, yes that Turgenev might have written.

I wonder if the horrible moment when Newland Archer, looking at his incomparably lovely and devoted young wife, suddenly has the diabolical wish that she were dead, is a reminiscence of Mrs. Wharton's early studies of Sudermann. In a powerful story by that writer, "The Wish," not only is that momentary impulse the root of the tragedy, but it is analyzed with such skill that no one is likely to forget it. It comes into this novel like a sudden chill—and is inexpressibly tragic. You remember what the doctor said in Sudermann's tale?

The harmony of Mrs. Wharton's management of English sentences is so seldom marred that I wish she would change the phrase, the only discord I found in the book (page 141 [89]): "varied by an occasional dance at the primitive inn when a man-of-war came in."

And is not Guy de Maupassant out of place in the early seventies?[1] Archer is unpacking some new books (page 137 [87]): "a new volume of Herbert Spencer, another collection of Guy de Maupassant's incomparable tales, and a novel called 'Middlemarch,' as to which there had lately been interesting things said in the reviews." I suppose Mrs.

---

1. Wharton later replaced Maupassant with the French writer Alphonse Daudet. For a discussion of Wharton's reaction to this discrepancy and others, see Julia Ehrhardt's essay in this volume. [Editor]

Wharton knows her Maupassant thoroughly; but unless I am quite at fault, it was not in the early seventies, but in the early eighties, that his tales began to appear.

But these are flecks. The appearance of such a book as *The Age of Innocence* by an American is a matter for public rejoicing. It is one of the best novels of the twentieth century and looks like a permanent addition to literature.

# CARL VAN DOREN

## An Elder America†

We can no more do without some notion or other of an age more golden than our own than we can do without bread. There must be, we assure ourselves, a more delectable day yet to come, or there must have been one once. The evidence of prophecy, however, is stronger than that of history, which, somehow, fails to find the perfect age. Mrs. Wharton has never ranged herself with the prophets, contented, apparently, with being the most intellectual of our novelists and surveying with level, satirical eyes the very visible world. By the "Age of Innocence" she means the seventies in New York during the past century; and the innocence she finds there is "the innocence that seals the mind against imagination and the heart against experience." To the hotter attacks which angrier critics have recently been making upon that age she does not lend herself. Her language is cool and suave. And yet the effect of her picture is an unsparing accusation of that genteel decade when the van der Luydens of Skuytercliff were the ultimate arbiters of "form" in Manhattan, and "form" was occupation and religion for the little aristocracy which still held its tight fortress in the shaggy city so soon about to overwhelm it. The imminence of the rising tide is never quite indicated. How could it be, when the characters of the action themselves do not see it, bound up as they are with walking their wintry paths and hugging their iron taboos? Newland Archer suspects a change, but that is because he is a victim of the tribal order which sentences him to a life without passion, without expression, without satisfaction. The Countess Olenska suspects it, but she too is a victim, too fine for the rougher give-and-take of her husband's careless European society and yet not conventional enough for the dull routine which in her native New York covers the fineness to which also she is native. The peculiar tragedy of their sacrifice is that it is for the sake of a person, Archer's wife, who is virtuous because she is incapable of temptation, competent because she is incapable of any deep perturbation, and willing to suit herself to the least decorum of their world because she is incapable of understanding that there is anywhere anything larger or freer. The unimaginative not only miss the flower of life themselves but they shut others from it as well.

†  From *The Nation* 111 (November 3, 1920).

Mrs. Wharton's structure and methods show no influence of the impressionism now broadening the channel of fiction; she does not avoid one or two touches of the florid in her impassioned scenes; she rounds out her story with a reminiscent chapter which forces in the note of elegy where it only partially belongs. But "The Age of Innocence" is a masterly achievement. In lonely contrast to almost all the novelists who write about fashionable New York, she knows her world. In lonely contrast to the many who write about what they know without understanding it or interpreting it, she brings a superbly critical disposition to arrange her knowledge in significant forms. These characters who move with such precision and veracity through the ritual of a frozen caste are here as real as their actual lives would ever have let them be. They are stiff with ceremonial garments and heavy with the weight of imagined responsibilities. Mrs. Wharton's triumph is that she has described these rites and surfaces and burdens as familiarly as if she loved them and as lucidly as if she hated them.

\*　\*　\*

# HENRY SEIDEL CANBY

## Our America†

America is the land of cherished illusions. Americans prefer to believe that they are innocent, innocent of immorality after marriage, innocent of dishonesty in business, innocent of incompatibility between husbands and wives. Americans do not like to admit the existence (in the family) of passion, of unscrupulousness, of temperament. They have made a code for what is to be done, and what is not to be done, and whatever differs is un-American. If their right hands offend them they cut them off rather than admit possession. They believed in international morality when none existed, and when they were made to face the disagreeable fact of war, cast off the nations of the earth, and continued to believe in national morality.

In America prostitution is tolerated in practice, but forbidden in print. All homes are happy unless there is proof to the contrary, and then they are un-American. In its wilful idealism America is determined that at all costs we shall appear to be innocent. And a novel which began with the leaders in social conformity, who keep hard and clean the code, and swept through the great middle classes that relax its rigors themselves, but exact them of others, might present the pageant, the social history, the epic of America.

Of course, Mrs. Wharton's novel does nothing of the sort. This is how Tolstoy, or H. G. Wells, or Ernest Poole would have written *The Age of Innocence*. They would have been grandiose, epical; their stories would have been histories of culture. It would have been as easy to have called their books broad as it is to call Mrs. Wharton's fine

† From the New York *Evening Post* (November 6, 1920): 3.

novel narrow. Tendencies, philosophies, irrepressible outbursts served as their protagonists, where hers are dwellers in Fifth Avenue or Waverly Place—a cosmopolitan astray, a dowager, a clubman yearning for intellectual sympathy.

And yet in the long run it comes to much the same thing. They prefer the panorama: she the drawing room canvas. They deduce from vast philosophies and depict society. She gives us the Mingotts, the Mansons, the Van der Luydens—Society, in its little brownstone New York of the seventies—and lets us formulate inductively the code of America. A little canvas is enough for a great picture if the painting is good.

The only objection I have ever heard urged against Mrs. Wharton's fine art of narrative is that it is narrow—an art of dress suit and sophistication. And this book is the answer. For, of course, her art is narrow—like Jane Austen's, like Sheridan's, like Pope's, like Maupassant's, like that of all writers who prefer to study human nature in its most articulate instead of its best or its broadest manifestations. It is narrow because it is focussed, but this does not mean that it is small. The story of *The Age of Innocence* could be set in a far broader background. It is the circumstances of the New York society which Mrs. Wharton knows so well that give it a piquancy, a reality that "epics" lack. They are like the accidents of voice, eye, gesture which determine individuality. But her subject is America.

This treating of large themes by highly personal symbols makes possible Mrs. Wharton's admirable perfection of technique. Hers is the technique of sculpture rather than the technique of architecture. It permits the fine play of a humor that has an eye of irony in it, but is more human than irony. It makes possible an approach to perfection. Behold Mrs. Manson Mingott, the indomitable dowager Catherine:

> "The immense accretion of flesh that had descended on her in middle life like a flood of lava on a doomed city had changed her . . . into something as vast and august as a natural phenomenon. She had accepted this submergence as philosophically as all her other trials, and now, in extreme old age, was rewarded by presenting to her mirror an almost unwrinkled expanse of firm pink and white flesh, in the centre of which the traces of a small face survived as if awaiting excavation. . . . Around and below, wave after wave of black silk surged away over the edges of a capacious armchair, with two tiny white hands poised like gulls on the surface of the billows."

Her art is restrained, focussed upon those points where America, in its normality and its eccentricity, has become articulate. Therefore it is sharp and convincing. Who is the central figure in this story of the leaven of intellectual and emotional unrest, working in a society that has perfected its code and intends to live by it? Is it Newland Archer, who bears the uncomfortable ferment within him? Is it his wife, the lovely May, whose clear blue eyes will see only innocence? Is it the Countess Olenska, the American who has seen reality and suffered by

it, and sacrifices her love for Newland in order to preserve his innocence? It is none of these, but rather the "family" moral according to
its lights, provincial, narrow—but intensely determined that its world
shall appear upright, faithful, courageous, in despite of facts and re-
gardless of how poor reality must be tortured into conformity. And the
"family" is just the bourgeois Puritanism of nineteenth century America.

Was May right when with the might of innocence she forced Newland to give up life for mere living? Was the Countess right when in
spite of her love for him she aided and abetted her, making him live up
to the self-restraint that belonged to his code? The story does not answer, being concerned with the qualities of the "family," not with di-
dacticism.

It says that the insistent innocence of America had its rewards as
well as its penalties. It says, in so far as it states any conclusion definitely, that the new and less trammelled generation must answer
whether it was the discipline of the parents that saved it from anarchy,
or the suppressions of its parents that made it rebellious. And the answer is not yet.

A fine novel, beautifully written, "big" in the best sense, which has
nothing to do with size, a credit to American literature—for if its author is cosmopolitan, her novel, as much as *Ethan Frome*, is a fruit of
our soil.

# R. D. TOWNSEND

## The Book Table: Devoted to Books and
## Their Makers, Novels Not for a Day†

It is said that this generation of novel readers devours everything but
remembers nothing. There is a vast crowd of mediocre stories that
sink quickly into oblivion. The competition among writers seems to be
for a merry life and a short one for their literary progeny. All the more
credit, then, to those who do not manufacture stories just to get a
laugh or a thrill, but exercise their art as the older dramatists and poets did—to deal nobly and seriously with the raw material of human
nature: passion, character and conduct, motive and action, not forgetting the spice of humor and the stress of situation.

Three recent novels[1] may be here pointed out with appreciation and
thankfulness as examples that belong to literature, that repay careful
reading because they bear the marks of careful thinking and careful
writing. They are not the only ones of the season to merit this praise,
but they are fine and welcome specimens of a class by no means too
numerous.

† From *The Outlook* (December 8, 1920): 653.
1. The other novels discussed in the original review were John Galsworthy's *In Chancery* and
Ernest Poole's *Blind: A Story of These Times*.

First in order and first in ability comes Mrs. Edith Wharton's "The Age of Innocence." The species of "innocence" prevailing in New York's fashionable society in a period now nearly half a century ago was the innocence of an artificial, conventional, and dull society. It was a little before the "Four Hundred" phrase invented by Ward McAllister obtained vogue, but there was already the idea of an exclusiveness the lines of which were those of wealth, family connection, stiff social entertainments, and patronage of the opera, rather than those having relation to the world of art, literature, brilliant talk, or intellectual impulses. What was outside of this New York self-constituted circle was considered by it as dubious; life and culture "abroad" were practically unknown quantities. This time and the people and setting for the story are described with painstaking art, from Brown of Grace Church to the few great moguls whose smile or frown made or unmade "social standing." As a picture of the "upper classes" in our metropolis as it stolidly solidified itself in the decade or so after the Civil War, the novel is curiously captivating; no one but Mrs. Wharton could have rendered the description so delicately exact. There is irony behind it all, but not the bitterness of scorn or contempt. It is an etching, not a caricature.

Into this self-satisfied and self-centered group comes a Polish countess, an American girl who has made an unhappy marriage abroad. She is regarded with suspicion, and is received only when the one family whose social supremacy is almost imperial takes her up. She is accustomed to free social interchange with writers, painters, and diplomats, to witty talk, to freedom from dulling conventionality. Contrasted with her is a charming young society girl who is loving and sweet-natured, but who simply does not conceive that "what they do" and "what they say"—"they" meaning "society"—can be disregarded. Between them hesitates the young New Yorker, Archer; he is bound by commitments to the girl of restricted nature, but longs for the woman of deeper and stronger character. In the end the bonds of convention and pledged honor prevail, but the struggle is a passionate one and leaves Archer disappointed and disillusionized.

The play of social forces and individual striving is subtle and strong. Mrs. Wharton's new novel is in workmanship equal to her very best previous work. Indeed, one is strongly inclined to declare this the best piece of American fiction of the present season. Its qualities are not superficial; its situation is led up to with admirable skill, so that the intensity of interest gradually tightens and strengthens. In its restrained art as well as its clear-sightedness the book is finely wrought. In the give and take of dialogue between the many minor characters there is ample entertainment. In its adequate dealing with a large *motif* this is a book of far more than ephemeral value.

\*　　\*　　\*

# Mrs. Wharton's Novel of Old New York†¹

Mrs. Wharton's power as a novelist has long been recognized, and the authority of her writing may lead to unquestioned acceptance of her matter. When novelists depart from pure invention and enter the realm of history they must count with an older inhabitant, who may also perhaps be jealous of his city's good report.

Sophistication has always been the keynote of Mrs. Wharton's work. It is the aspect of life that has always appealed to her, the side she has preferred to portray, and it may account for the jaundiced view she takes of New York society in the early '70s, a period which she sarcastically calls "The Age of Innocence" (Appleton).

The story is trite enough, for it deals with a young New-Yorker of the best position who marries a "nice" girl of his own set, one who measures well up to the standards of those days, and who finds himself in love with a woman who has set tradition at defiance and represents a set of ideas and opinions entirely antagonistic to those to which he is accustomed.

Newland Archer is the typical, well-bred, well-born young man, differing little from his kind of to-day. May Welland is a charming young girl, with the limitations of a careful bringing-up, which seem to excite the author's wrath as being a perversion of the truth. Countess Olenska, the disturbing element in this otherwise happy state of things, is a cousin of May's, who, having spent much of her youth abroad, has married a Pole, a man who led her such a life that, with the aid of his secretary, she managed to escape from him, and after a year spent in Switzerland concluded to return to New York, where she has many relatives. May Welland, her relations, friends, and members of her social circle, represent dulness to Mrs. Wharton, while the Countess, with her cruel husband, her contemplated divorce, her beauty and charm, stand for the larger and more intellectual life of Europe. The fact that she is more than suspected of having spent some months in the company of the young secretary only seems to add to her interest in the eyes of the author, who considers "courage" as one of the greatest virtues, especially when it defies "conventionality."

However, neither Newland nor the Countess seems to possess the requisite firmness of character to elope, and nothing happens, a fact which disturbs the reader but little, as the interest of the story lies, not with the doings of the rather wooden characters of the book, but with the picture it purports to give of New York some fifty years ago. Here the author is clearly at fault in portraying a society of such portentous dulness and also in representing the town as devoid of anything else. Winsett, a clever if unsuccessful journalist, is supposed to be withering away intellectually because he can find no congenial society. And

---

† From *Literary Digest* (February 5, 1921): 52.
1. Anonymous reviews were a common practice, ensuring that forthright views could be expressed while assuring the public that critics were not responding to the threat of recrimination or the hope of reward.

were there ever people of such wonderful social importance as the Van der Luydens? Many years ago the Astors as a family had something granted to them as to position of which no other family could boast, but as New York society expanded to take in the millionaires of every other city in the Union, such leadership disappeared, never to return.

Those whose memory of New York society takes them back fifty years will hardly agree with Mrs. Wharton as to the stupidity of those who composed it. The Century Club of those days contained men of real social brilliancy; is it to be supposed that only at their club did they find any opportunity for intelligent conversation? Did men like Clarence King, Joseph H. Choate, Judge Howland, and F. F. Marbury[1] creep back from the delights of the house in Fifteenth Street to obscure homes and inferior womenkind?

The truth is that there always has been—there is now—in New York a circle of well-born, well-bred, intelligent people, whose names, tho they convey nothing to the Pittsburgh steel-puddlers and Nevada mine-owners who throng our gates, still stand for much to those who know something of the city's social history. They do not frequent cabarets, their names are seldom in the papers, and tho they exert no visible influence on the fashionable and noisy set, they are still of social importance among the more conservative New-Yorkers. Of course the possession of great wealth may exert a stultifying effect upon the brain. It was one of the best-known society women who asked, many years ago, at an amateur performance of "Alice in Wonderland," why the Mock Turtle[2] was represented with a calf's head, but an entire ignorance of culinary affairs may have been responsible for the question.

The book is full of anachronisms which are so sure to be noticed by old New-Yorkers that we shall only mention one or two. It is claimed that there was no club box in the old Academy of Music; it was considered a distinct innovation when it was introduced, much later, in the new opera-house. Newland and the Countess could not have met at the Metropolitan Museum in the Park, for it was not until the '80's that it was moved from Fourteenth Street. De Maupassant was unknown in the early '70s and Rossetti's "House of Life" was not published until 1881. Joachim never visited America as a violinist.

1. Distinguished men who belonged to the Century Club. With the minor exception of Choate, a corporate lawyer celebrated by Mark Twain and others for his wit as a "club man," Clarence King (1842–1901), a fifth-generation scion of Newport and the first director of the Geologic Survey, is the man on this list who has remained a notable historical figure. In 1888, King secretly married a woman of African American descent with whom he had five children. Maintaining secrecy by keeping separate households, this ostensible bachelor married his wife Ada using the assumed name of James Todd and did not disclose the secret of his elite identity to his wife until just before his own death. [Editor]
2. *Alice's Adventures in Wonderland* (1865) and its sequel *Through the Looking Glass* (1872) are popular children's books written by Lewis Carroll (the pseudonym for Charles Lutwidge Dodgson (1832–98). Like the Cheshire Cat, the Mock Turtle is a character in the original story. The joke centering on the idea of the Mock Turtle requires culinary knowledge of the ingredients of a dish called "mock turtle soup," which contains not turtle flesh but small pieces of hard-boiled beef. [Editor]

# VERNON L. PARRINGTON, JR.

## Our Literary Aristocrat†

The note of distinction is as natural to Edith Wharton as it is rare in our present day literature. She belongs to the "quality," and the grand manner is hers by right of birth. She is as finished as a Sheraton sideboard, and with her poise, grace, high standards, and perfect breeding, she suggests as inevitably old wine and slender decanters. The severe ethical code which Puritanism has bequeathed to her, and the keen intellect which has made her a critical analyst, increase her native distinction; and the irony that plays lambently over her commentary, adds piquancy to her art. She belongs to an earlier age, before a strident generation had come to deny the excellence of standards. No situation which she has conceived in her novels is so ironical as the situation in which she herself is placed; shaken out of an unquestioned acceptance of the aristocratic world to which she belongs, she turns her keen analysis upon her environment, and satirizes what in her heart she loves most.

*The Age of Innocence* is perfect Whartonian. It is historical satire done with immaculate art, but though she laughs at the deification of "form" by the van der Luydens of Skuytercliff, and the tyranny of their rigid social taboos, she loves them too well to suffer them to be forgotten by a careless generation. She has painted them at full length, to hang upon our walls, where they lend historical dignity to the background of the present and utter a silent reproof to our scrambling vulgarities. New York society of the eighteen seventies, with its little clan of first families that gently simmers in its own dulness—it would be inelegant to say stews—provides a theme that exactly suits Mrs. Wharton's talent. She delights in the make-believe of the clan, in "the Pharisaic voice of a society wholly absorbed in barricading itself against the unpleasant," and she half regrets an age whose innocence "seals the mind against imagination and the heart against experience." She herself, of course, will not defend herself against reality by a decorous denial, but she likes too well many things in that world to be harsh or angry with it. Against this background of the clan she projects three figures who come perilously near to realizing a quite vulgar situation. Between May Welland, physically magnificent but mentally equipped with no more than the clan negations, and Ellen Olenska, a clan member who has freed herself from its provincialisms by a European experience that ends in separation from her Polish husband, and whose "disgrace" rocks New York society till the clan rallies to her defense, stands Newland Archer, a third member of the clan, who has played with books and ideas without liberating his mind, who is shocked into naturalness by the more vital Ellen, endeavours to break the ties of clan convention, but is held fast and ends his rebellions in a mood of ironic abnegation. There are no scenes, no vulgar jealousies

† From *The Pacific Review* 2 ( June 1, 1921): 157–60.

or accusations, nothing to offend the finest sensibility. A few frank phrases sound almost startling in their context of reticent pretense, but they do not really startle. The book unwinds slowly, somewhat meagerly, with much analysis and little vivacity of conversation. In an environment of dull and selfish respectability, how could there be vivacity; with no ideas, no spontaneity, no intellectual sincerity, it is idle to expect vivacity. The formal routine and hinting gossip wrap themselves like a boa constrictor about the characters and squeeze the naturalness out of them. Nevertheless the story never lags and is never dull. The skill with which dulness is made interesting is a triumph of art.

But when one has said that the craftsmanship is a very great success, why not go further and add that it doesn't make the slightest difference whether one reads the book or not, unless one is a literary epicure who lives for the savor of things. What do the van der Luydens matter to us; or what did they or their kind matter a generation ago? Why waste such skill upon such insignificant material. There were vibrant realities in the New York of the seventies, Commodore Vanderbilt, for example, or even Jay Gould or Jim Fiske. If Mrs. Wharton had only chosen to throw such figures upon her canvas, brutal, cynical, dominating, what a document of American history—but the suggestion is foolish. Mrs. Wharton could not do it. Her distinction is her limitation. She loathes the world of Jim Fiske too much to understand it. She is too well bred to be a snob, but she escapes it only by sheer intelligence. The background of her mind, the furniture of her habits, are packed with potential snobbery, and it is only by scrupulous care that it is held in leash. She is unconsciously shut in behind plate glass, where butlers serve formal dinners, and white shoulders go up at the mere suggestion of everyday gingham. She belongs in spite of herself to the caste which she satirizes, and she cannot make herself at home in households where the mother washes the dishes and the father tends the furnace. If she had lived less easily, if she had been forced to skimp and save and plan, she would have been a greater and richer artist, more significant because more native, more continental. But unfortunately her doors open only to the smart set; the windows from which she surveys life open only to the east, to London, Paris, Rome. She is one of our cosmopolitans, flitting lightly about and at ease with all who bear titles. And this the stay-at-home American secretly resents. What are titles to him, and for that matter, what are the vulgar rich of New York? Let the newspapers exploit them, for that becomes their vulgarity. But for Mrs. Wharton to spend her talents upon rich nobodies is no less than sheer waste.

Since we are quarreling with Mrs. Wharton let us go through with it and suggest another irritation that arises from less creditable, but quite human sources. She unconsciously irritates because she reveals so unobtrusively how much she knows and how perfect is her breeding. She pricks one's complacency with such devastating certainty; reveals so cruelly one's plebeian limitations. Her readers are always on pins and needles not to appear out of her class. It is impossible to be easy and slouchy in presence of her poise, and it is hard on us not to let down occasionally. We cannot always be mentally on the alert. It was inevitable, to fall back upon an illustration, that her dilettante hero should have gone in for Eastlake furniture, as Mrs. Wharton assures us that he did. But the easy way in which she assumes that the reader will understand her casual reference to Sir Charles's endeavour to revive a "sincere" furniture, puts one to scrambling to recall that Eastlakeism was the polite counterpart, in the seventies, of the robust rebellions of William Morris against a dowdy Victorianism. If Mrs. Wharton had only let slip the fact that she once wrote a book on household decoration, and "got up" on the Eastlake movement, it would have reassured us, and made us feel that she is a common mortal like the rest of us who have to "get up" on things. Which criticism, of course, arises from mere petulancy and self-conceit.

With her ripe culture, her clear and clean intelligence, her classical spirit, her severe standards and austere ethics, Mrs. Wharton is our outstanding literary aristocrat. She has done notable things, but she has paid a great price in aloofness from her own America. There is more hope for our literature in the honest crudities of the younger naturalists, than in her classic irony; they at least are trying to understand America as it is. "You'll never amount to anything, any of you, till you roll up your sleeves and get right down into the muck," commented the one plebeian in the book to Newland Archer, who "mentally shrugged his shoulders and turned the conversation to books." Mrs. Wharton too often mentally shrugs her shoulders over America. That she should ever roll up her sleeves and get down into the muck is unthinkable.

—V. L. P.

## British Reviews

## The Age of Innocence†

Mrs. Wharton's new book, her first "full-length" novel for some years, is perhaps a sign of the times. When the war broke in upon the settled, accepted "present day" of the novelists, it was easy to foresee the predicament in which they would find themselves before long. Since 1914 there has been no present day, in the old sense. Now we must know from the start whether we are dealing with the world before or during or since the war, and the action must be precisely timed; any and every novel, in other words, is bound to be now "historic." And since it is a hazardous venture to set about treating very recent times historically—it needs a great deal of information or a great

---

† From *Times Literary Supplement* (November 25, 1920): 775.

deal of assurance to move upon that *cineri doloso*[1]—it was probable
that a writer like Mrs. Wharton, critical of the impressions of life,
should hesitate to use the crude new material of 1920, while it is still
daily shifting and cracking before our eyes. And so she goes back—
back to the old world, and far enough into it to make the action of her
story openly historic; she goes as far back as the early seventies, in
fact, and to that New York of the early seventies which is now so much
more remote, as it happens, than even our own past of that day, over
here. Changes of the same general kind we too have seen, no doubt,
but nothing to compare in extent with the change that has turned
New York, socially speaking, from a trim and substantial old family
mansion to a resounding, glittering, promiscuous monster hotel.

The old family mansion is more than a picturesque background for
a story, though it is that too. But it is also a story in itself, or it very
easily makes one, with the elaborately composed artificiality of the life
that was led there. Nowhere, not among the most formal refinements
of the *ancien régime,* has there been seen a society more carefully and
consciously organized than that of New York a generation or so ago,
when the tide of new money, bearing new people and new standards
and new manners, was only just beginning to encroach upon the old,
and when the family in possession—it was hardly more than a family,
compactly knit together in one circle—was making its final and unsuccessful attempt to withstand it. This much is a familiar story, but
Mrs. Wharton takes it at a different aspect. A young man, Newland
Archer, belonging to the inner stock, the real right thing, finds himself
in conflict with the traditions that have made him—in conflict, that is
to say, with a very large part of himself. His traditions, working with
the smoothness of long practice, draw him remorselessly into the discreet, distinguished, airless world of his kind, into a sound profession
and a suitable marriage; while the strain of rebellion pulls on the other
side towards freedom, pulls violently, but at last has to own itself
beaten. It is easier for a stranger to get into the guarded enclosure, after all, than for a native to get out of it. For Archer freedom means
Ellen Olenska, a member of the family party like himself, but one who
has vividly (and also disastrously) succeeded in detaching herself, and
who has returned to it for support and consolation after her wanderings. Ellen is exquisite, and she and Archer are both of them much too
intelligent to underrate the virtue and the dignity of the forces opposed to them; the old order, in its way, is perfectly just and reasonable, its standards are honourable; two intelligent beings can only in
the end respect them. And so the historic setting of the story has made
the story—made it by being just what it is, strong and fine, ripely matured and absolutely sure of itself.

That is the plan of the book, and Mrs. Wharton covers it in a man-

---

1. Latin phrase from Horace's *Odes* (II, 1.7) that alludes to walking on burning coals to prove
   devotion, a practice associated with the honoring of Apollo and Diana by their respective fol-
   lowers during festivals of sacrifice. Part of a Greek proverb that was still in common use as
   an idiomatic phrase among educated British writers in the late nineteenth and early twentieth centuries, "cineri doloso" alludes to the undertaking of a dangerous task. [Editor]

ner that hardly leaves an opening for criticism. It is admirably packed; the action is clear against its background, and at the same time the background, the good family party with its perfect manners, is never a mere decoration, it takes its proper place as an essential matter in the story. It does so, at any rate, very soon; for just at first Mrs. Wharton does not quite meet the besetting difficulty of these historic studies. If you are to present what is called a "picture of the times," how are you to keep the centre of interest in your drama? The interest, if you are not very careful, falls back into the romantic or the ironic evocation of the past, and the drama is overshadowed. Necessarily Mrs. Wharton's evocation is ironic—one *must* be ironic about the seventies, they are already too far and not yet far enough to be treated otherwise—and the balance of the tone, that amusing old New York on one side, this difficult drama on the other, is insecure for a time. But it rights itself, and the slight confusion is soon forgotten, and everything goes firmly and lightly, and altogether Mrs. Wharton has accomplished one of the best pieces of her work so far.

As for her picture of the times, how is any of us over here to criticize it, beyond saying that it is full of vivacity and of character and of colour, and that there is not a point in it which *seems* to be false? (A few small anachronisms of fact are of no consequence in such things; but we interject that even the most advanced young people could not have been reading books by Vernon Lee or Huysmans or M. Paul Bourget in the early seventies). From the despotic old matriarch, Catherine Manson, outward and downward through all the ramifications of the cousinhood, through the pre-Wagnerian opera and the "Grace Church weddings" and the liturgical dinner-parties, Mrs. Wharton takes her way with what we can only believe to be a thorough mastery of the whole situation. Certainly she makes it very convincing and very entertaining. And of her dealings with the drama, and especially with the sensitive, vibrating, poetic figure of Ellen, there is no shadow of doubt. These are matters of which we can all judge, and we can all see that Mrs. Wharton's hand upon them is more skilful and felicitous than ever.

## The Innocence of New York†

For many English readers this delightful novel will be a revelation of the depths which can be sounded by international ignorance. Gentlemen of unbounded leisure and a taste for commercial probity which amounts to a disease, ladies combining the angel and the bore in a measure beyond the dreams even of a Thackeray, troops of obsequious and efficient white domestics! Not such are the inhabitants whom most of us have mentally assigned to New York—at any stage of that city's existence. But Mrs. Wharton abundantly demonstrates that this state of things obtained only in a very limited circle, to a degree

† From *The Saturday Review* 130 (December 4, 1920): 458.

inconceivable by older and more corrupt civilizations. A happy circle it cannot well be called, since to assert that happiness may be compatible with dullness is to state a contradiction in terms; by rights it should not be attractive any more than happy, but the author contrives to make it so, partly no doubt through the easy laughter called forth by its patently ludicrous standards, but partly also from admiration for the finer element contained in them.

The heroine, a daughter of this secluded aristocracy, ventures in defiance of its conventions on an exogamic alliance with a wealthy Polish nobleman, who transports her to a cosmopolitan atmosphere, where art, literature, and brilliant conversation are among the commonplaces of life. On the other hand, she is unfortunate in her husband, and the sympathy consequently bestowed upon her is of a different quality from that which under like conditions would have fallen to her share in New York. Returning, rather under a cloud, to the old home, she is received by her relations with a splendid loyalty, which she genuinely appreciates. But naturally she finds the former things insipid, and— with no evil intentions—drifts into hazardous intimacy with a young man yearning for "European culture," and for the society of women competent to discuss it. His wedded peace is gravely endangered, and only the traditional ideas intervene to hinder a tragedy from reaching its climax.

From a literary point of view, this story is on a level with Mrs. Wharton's best work. As a retrospect of the early seventies, it is less satisfactory, being marred by numerous historical lapses.

# KATHERINE MANSFIELD

## Family Portraits†

\* \* \*

In "The Age of Innocence," a novel of the early seventies in New York, we receive the same impression that here is the element in which the author delights to breathe. The time and the scene together suit Mrs. Wharton's talent to a nicety. To evoke the seventies is to evoke irony and romance at once, and to keep these two balanced by all manner of delicate adjustments is so much a matter for her skilful hand that it seems more like play than work. Like Mr. Galsworthy's novel[1] it is a family piece, but in "The Age of Innocence" the family comprises the whole of New York society. This remote, exclusive small world in itself is disturbed one day by the return of one of its prodigal daughters who begs to be taken back as though nothing had happened. What has happened is never quite clear, but it includes a fabu-

---

† From *The Athenaeum* (December 10, 1920): 810–11.
1. Refers to John Galsworthy (1867–1933), English novelist whose fiction primarily dealt with the Forsytes, an upper middle class family. *In Chancery*, the second installment in the *Forsyte Saga* trilogy, appeared in 1920 and was here and elsewhere chosen for review in the same essay with *The Age of Innocence*. [Editor]

lously rich villain of a Polish Count who is her husband and his secretary, who, rumour whispers, was all too ready to aid her escape. But
the real problem which the family has to face is that Ellen Olenska
has become that most mysterious creature—a European. She is dangerous, fascinating, foreign; Europe clings to her like a troubling perfume; her very fan beats "Venice! Venice!" every diamond is a drop of
Paris. Dare they accept her? The question is answered by a dignified
compromise, and Ellen's farewell dinner-party before she leaves for
Paris is as distinguished as she or the family could wish. These are
what one might call the outer leaves of the story. Part them, and there
is within another flower, warmer, deeper, and more delicate. It is the
love-story of Newland Archer, a young man who belongs deeply to the
family tradition, and yet at the same time finds himself wishing to
rebel. The charm of Ellen is his temptation, and hard indeed he finds
it not to yield. But that very quality in her which so allures him—what
one might call her highly civilized appreciation of the exquisite difficulty of their position—saves them from themselves. Not a feather of
dignity is ruffled; their parting is positively stately.

But what about us? What about her readers? Does Mrs. Wharton
expect us to grow warm in a gallery where the temperature is so spark-
ingly cool? We are looking at portraits—are we not? These are human
beings, arranged for exhibition purposes, framed, glazed and hung in
the perfect light. They pale, they grow paler, they flush, they raise
their "clearest eyes," they hold out their arms to each other, "extended,
but not rigid," and the voice is the voice of the portrait:

" 'What's the use—when you will go back?' he broke out, a great
hopeless *How on earth can I keep you?* crying out to her beneath his
words."

Is it—in this world—vulgar to ask for more? To ask that the feeling
shall be greater than the cause that excites it, to beg to be allowed to
share the moment of exposition (is not that the very moment that all
our writing leads to?), to entreat a little wildness, a dark place or two
in the soul?

We appreciate fully Mrs. Wharton's skill and delicate workmanship;
she has the situation in hand from the first page to the last; we realize
how savage must sound our cry of protest, and yet we cannot help but
make it; that after all we are not above suspicion—even the "finest" of
us!

# FREDERICK WATSON

## The Assurance of Art†

"The Age of Innocence" is beyond everything else a triumph of the
artistic freedom of Mrs. Wharton. It may be as good or less good than
its predecessors—it is enough that it is Mrs. Wharton's and that no

† From *The Bookman* 59 (1921): 170–72.

other living author handles with such fine ease the changing but authentic portraiture of the social aspect. She is in that respect inimitable. In this country the art of comedy flavoured by satire, never very cordial to the English palate, has fallen into neglect and disrepute.

Jane Austen is alone in her kingdom. Thackeray, in whose austere immobility is the redemption and perfection of humour, has no successor. The acceptance of the writer of great satirical comedy might almost be regarded as a proof of genius since its reception is so timorous and tardy. The capacity, moreover, to desert a familiar but never in her case down-trodden road is an example of the instinctive assurance of Art. When a novelist has scored a triumph—even a very small one—in one particular vein he is warned (should he have ideas) by his publisher that people who like stories about vicars in the country will resent vintners in the town.

The tendency, the road of the highest applause, is towards repetition until if you like a blue lagoon you know the author without any further mental strain, and if you care about the monkey house your way is clear.

So when Mrs. Wharton writes of New York in 1875 she asks for trouble. The reviewer works up a paragraph or two on the necessity of novelists to avoid the war, the public feel vaguely as though they were asked to wear bombazine (whatever that was), and those eager readers who want to know just what America is thinking about everything in these critical days are a little surprised and chilled by Mrs. Wharton.

She, unlike so many of her English contemporaries, has no religion to teach, no grievance to air, no political betrayal to reveal. Her subjects are people, of a period perhaps, but people whose characteristics of snobbery, isolation, conservatism and humbug are not peculiar to the year '75.

Into the serene, exclusive atmosphere of the miniature Dresden china New York society passes the Countess Olenska, as the leaven enters the dough. With her comes the breath of the greater world, the world on the threshold. "All the old ladies had got out their faded sables and yellowing ermines, and the smell of camphor from the front pews almost smothered the faint Spring scent of the lilies banking the altar." That was the old world waiting for the knock at the door. But no extract, no deliberate choice of all the words relegated to sounds of praise can give anything but a second-hand, musty conception of the Van der Luydens, who must be studied not in extracts but in chapters if you would possess for all time their unforgettable savour.

It is the highest compliment to an artist to say that one never questions a word or action of her characters as unnatural or frankly beyond belief. When any writer can step back half a century and write as though the people lived next door there is no more to be said.

\*   \*   \*

# Modern Criticism

As the work done by critics in the late twentieth century suggests, Wharton's *Age of Innocence* is a sophisticated historical novel, a novel that was written with a full awareness of the issues raised by World War I and the modern world that lay in its wake. Beginning with studies of the manuscript and Wharton's quandaries about the possible limits of her form and the significance of varying plots, these critical works taken together offer provocative analyses of the novel's representations of culture. As these essays argue, Wharton's seemingly elegiac novel is not apolitical; rather, *The Age of Innocence* is a masterful study of the contradictions that were implicit in the history and culture and explicit in the very cult of isolation that defined the exclusive world of Old New York. Unveiling the sexual dialectic that structures *The Age of Innocence*'s emerging narrative, linking race to fear and power, these analyses reveal the depth of Wharton's ability to represent the cultural dynamics of social change.

## JULIA EHRHARDT

## "To Read These Pages Is To Live Again": The Historical Accuracy of *The Age of Innocence*†

Writing after the armistice to her friend Bernard Berenson, Edith Wharton predicted the effect she believed World War I would have on literature: "The historical novel with all its vices, will be the only possible form for fiction."[1] When she made this pronouncement, Wharton was writing *The Age of Innocence*, the novel in which she put this philosophy into practice. The story, set in the upper echelons of New York society in the 1870s, is a testimony to the author's thorough knowledge of the period and her unparalleled ability to recreate the world of her youth in fiction. Praising Wharton's accomplishment in his review of the novel, William Lyon Phelps declared, "New York society and customs are described with an accuracy that is almost uncanny; to read these pages is to live again."[2] Phelps's comment specified what many critics deemed Wharton's most significant achievement in the novel: her literary recovery of the lost world that

---

† This essay was written specifically for this Norton Critical Edition. Parenthetical page numbers refer to this volume.
1. Quoted in R. W. B. Lewis, *Edith Wharton: A Biography* (New York: Harper and Row, 1975), p. 423. Further references to this book will be cited parenthetically.
2. William Lyon Phelps, "As Mrs. Wharton Sees Us," *New York Times Book Review* (October 17, 1920):1–11. Reprinted in this edition, p. 383.

had come to be known as "Old New York." Wharton made the past "live again" through her diverse and wide-ranging references to fashion trends, popular actors, theater productions, and venerated artists, authors, and musicians, and by setting the action in locales that comprised the social itinerary for the upper level of New York society in the 1870s and early 1880s. These places included such renowned landmarks as Wallack's Theater, Delmonico's Restaurant, and Tiffany's, as well as an obscure but actual flower shop on Fifteenth Street called Henderson's where May orders roses for the formal dinner that marks Ellen Olenska's final departure. Impressed by Wharton's vivid evocation of the period, *Nation* reviewer Carl Van Doren echoed Phelps's praise: "In lonely contrast to almost all the novelists who write about fashionable New York, she knows her world."[3] International reviewers also marveled at Wharton's "picture of the times"; as one London critic maintained, "There is not a point in it which *seems* to be false."[4] Indeed, Wharton's attention to historical detail was so painstakingly thorough that one reviewer considered it a literary liability. An obviously intimidated Vernon L. Parrington Jr. complained, "She unconsciously irritates because she reveals so unobtrusively how much she knows."[5] As he criticized the apparent ease with which the author of *The Age of Innocence* had incorporated the cultural and historical hallmarks of the era she described, Parrington acknowledged the power of the novel as a cultural document.

Although these reviews intimate that because Wharton had written about what she had lived her fictional accomplishment was an effortless endeavor, the issue of historical accuracy was one of profound concern for the expatriate author as she wrote and revised the text, and as the reception of her historical novel reveals, her obsession continued to plague her after the novel was published. The author's attempts to ensure the historical accuracy of *The Age of Innocence* and her audience's subsequent scrutiny of it reveal not only Wharton's beliefs about the writing of historical fiction but also the high expectations her readers brought to a historical novel written by a celebrated author who herself had danced in the ballrooms and breathed the air of Old New York.

The extraordinary number, depth, and breadth of the historical references in *The Age of Innocence* become even more impressive given the relatively short period of time Wharton spent composing it. The sheer frequency with which these allusions appear suggests that Wharton must have spent years researching the period and revising drafts of the novel; yet, as Shari Benstock states, the writer completed the manuscript she had started in the late summer of 1919 by the first

---

3. Carl Van Doren, "An Elder America," *Nation* 111 (November 1920): 510–11. Reprinted in this edition, p. 388.
4. "*The Age of Innocence*," *Times Literary Supplement* (November 25, 1920):775. Reprinted in this edition, p. 396.
5. Vernon L. Parrington, Jr., "Our Literary Aristocrat," *Pacific Review* 2 (June 1921): 157–60: Reprinted in this edition, p. 393.

week in April 1920.[6] Since the novel had been accepted for serial publication in *Pictorial Review*, editor Arthur Vance was anxious to have chapters as soon as Wharton had finished them so that the installments could be appropriately illustrated.[7] In addition to the magazine's strict production schedule, Rutger Jewett, Wharton's editor at Appleton-Century, urged her to complete the novel as soon as she could because he feared that a printer's strike would cause publication delays.[8]

That the manuscript was completed in just over seven months can only be read as a testament to Wharton's remarkable memory. Proclaiming her familiarity with the historical period she immortalized in the novel, Wharton declared, "Every detail of that far-off scene was indelibly stamped on my infant brain."[9] As critics have contended, Wharton's recollections most obviously surface in her descriptions of certain characters, whose striking portraits she based on her relatives and acquaintances, as well as distant but notorious figures whom she recalled from childhood. R. W. B. Lewis maintains that May Welland's talent at archery evokes the athleticism of Margaret Rutherford, a much-admired neighbor of young Edith's family; he also argues that Wharton modeled the Reverend Doctor Ashmore after the Reverend Doctor Washburn, rector of the New Calvary Episcopal Church and the father of Emylyn Washburn, Wharton's most intimate and dearest childhood friend. Lewis also identifies Mary Mason Jones, the author's great aunt, as the model for the formidable Mrs. Manson Mingott, Ellen Olenska's Granny and her most ardent female ally.[1]

In addition to using her circle of acquaintants for inspiration, Wharton also included thinly veiled and provocatively recognizable portraits of socialites in *The Age of Innocence*. While Lewis has suggested that Wharton's ne'er-do-well uncle George Alfred Jones (due to his scandalous relationship with a woman not his wife) may have served as the historical analogue for the sexually voracious banker Julius Beaufort (Lewis, *Edith Wharton*, 431), Lewis and other scholars have also linked the fictional Beaufort to the notorious financier August Belmont. In addition to noting the imperial and calendrical sources of "Julius" and "August," R. B. Dooley points out the similarities of the translated names Beaufort ("beautiful stronghold") and Bel-

6. Shari Benstock, *No Gifts from Chance: A Biography of Edith Wharton* (New York: Charles Scribner's Sons, 1994), p. 359. Further references to this book will be cited parenthetically.
7. The novel was published in four installments beginning with the July 1920 issue of *Pictorial Review*; each was accompanied by illustrations by W. B. King. The first installment concluded halfway through Chapter 9 with Newland's first visit to Ellen Olenska; the second appeared in the September 1920 issue and concluded halfway through Chapter 19, when Newland and May embark on their honeymoon. (Due to a paper shortage, the magazine did not publish a September issue.) The third installment (October 1920) concluded at the end of Chapter 29 (the scene with Newland and Ellen's discussion in the brougham), and the fourth installment (November 1920) included Chapters 30 to 34.
8. Rutger Jewett, letter to Edith Wharton, June 7, 1920 (Edith Wharton Collection, Beinecke Rare Book and Manuscript Library, Yale University). Unless otherwise noted, all Wharton correspondence cited is from this collection and used with the kind permission of the Beinecke Library.
9. Letter from Edith Wharton to Mary Cadwalader Jones, February 17, 1921. (Louis Auchincloss Collection of Edith Wharton, Beinecke Library, Yale University).
1. R. W. B. Lewis, "Introduction," *The Age of Innocence* (New York: Charles Scribner's Sons, 1968), pp. vii–viii.

mont ("beautiful mountain"). In making his case, Dooley also points out the parallels between the Belmonts' social activities and those of the fictional Beauforts. Like his counterpart in Wharton's novel, Belmont hung a Bougereau nude in his Fifth Avenue mansion that shocked the austere sensibilities of respectable New York society. Dooley also found significant the fact that the archery contest described in *The Age of Innocence* is held at the Beaufort mansion in Newport, since the annual archery parties hosted by Belmont's wife were highlights of the summer social season. Finally, Dooley recognizes parallels between Wharton's characterization of Beaufort early in the novel and Dixon Wecter's description of Belmont as "a somewhat rakish man about town" and a rumored "illegitimate scion of the house of Rothschild."[2] Certainly the traces of anti-Semitic stereotypes evident in Wharton's portrayal of Beaufort—his lack of gentlemanly discretion in his sexual affairs, his unscrupulous financial dealings, and his mysterious foreign background—correlate with contemporaneous rumors regarding Belmont's Jewish ancestry. Gossip about Belmont's mysterious provenance was common among the New York elite during the era Wharton sought to recreate, and historians have confirmed that August Belmont, who came to New York representing the interests of the Frankfurt branch of the Rothchild financial empire, was born into a German Jewish family.

Dooley has also identified Mrs. Paran Stevens, the flamboyant mother of Wharton's first fiancé and the instigator of young Edith Jones's broken engagement, as the historical model for the much derided Mrs. Lemuel Struthers, the "widow of Struthers' shoe polish," who breaks the rules of social decorum by giving parties on the Sabbath. According to Dooley (84), Mrs. Stevens consistently defied one of the most sacred social laws of her class by hosting Sunday evening soirées that featured performances by famous musicians and singers. Finally, Rhoda Nathan has proposed that Wharton modeled Sillerton Jackson and Lawrence Lefferts, the novel's authorities on "taste" and "form" respectively, on socialite Ward McAllister, the founder of the Patriarchs' Ball and the premier authority on etiquette and social ritual in the New York of Wharton's childhood.[3] Although the vast majority of readers would not grasp the references to these figures, the accretion of such subtle details in characterization indicate that Wharton may have hoped that at least part of her audience would recognize the historic figures she described, as well as enjoy the character criticisms her nuanced portraits conveyed. A month after the novel was published, Jewett informed Wharton by letter that some of her readers had begun to recognized her subtle allusions: "Society (spelled with a capital 'S') is trying to fit familiar New York names to your characters."[4]

2. R. B. Dooley, "A Footnote to Edith Wharton," *American Literature* 26 (1954): 81–82. Further references to this article will be cited parenthetically.
3. Rhoda Nathan, "Ward McAllister: Beau Nash of *The Age of Innocence*," *College Literature* 14 (1987): 276–84.
4. Rutger Jewett to Edith Wharton, November 13, 1920.

Although the expatriate author relied extensively on her voluminous memory while writing the novel, Wharton finally felt that she could not depend exclusively on her own recollections of this era to provide the deep layers of contextual details essential to her design. In addition to "steeping myself in the nineteenth century" while writing the story (Lewis, *Edith Wharton*, 424), Wharton engaged her agent and former sister-in-law, Mary Cadwalader Jones, to help her by undertaking research in America. "Minnie," as she was affectionately known to the writer, read back issues of the *New York Tribune* to verify the novelist's references about operas and plays. To confirm the dates of the first Patriarchs' ball and other social events, Minnie visited Yale to consult Ward McAllister's autobiography, *Society as I Have Found It* (Lewis, *Edith Wharton*, 430). These hours of research apparently resuscitated Minnie's own memories of the time, for when Wharton asked her assistant for a list of dramas produced in New York in the 1870s, Minnie suggested *The Shaughraun*, recalling in particular the beauty of the ribbon-kissing scene. Wharton found Jones's recommendation "positively uncanny" because she also recalled that moment in the play (having seen it at the age of thirteen) and had decided to have Newland attend Wallack's theater in spring 1875 "for the sake of that particular scene." Characteristically, Minnie Jones took no credit for the vital assistance she had provided, but instead anticipated the glowing critical response to the novel: "You bring back the time as if it were last week."[5]

Evidence suggests that Wharton fervently hoped that her story would do just that, for in addition to employing Minnie as a researcher, Wharton took a series of steps to ensure the historical accuracy of the details she presented in her narrative. In a letter written to Rutger Jewett, Wharton conceded, "There may be a few anachronisms in the first chapters of the Age of Innocence, as my childish memories are not always to be relied upon, but I will verify local colour before publication."[6] In response, Jewett assured Wharton that he would correct any errors she discovered before the book was printed, and if time permitted, he would also rectify errors in the serial version.[7] But despite her concerns about accuracy, the hastened production schedule made it impossible for Wharton to "brood over" revisions for the novel in her customary way (Benstock 359). Concerned about the high cost of paper after the war and the looming threat of a printer's strike, Jewett pushed to expedite the editorial process, and after proofreaders completed a review of the typeset pages on July 23,[8] on July 26 he sent the first set of galleys to Wharton along with the original manuscript, repeating his earlier request for her to correct and return them "at the

5. Quoted in Benstock, 360. This anecdote attests to the impression the performance must have made on both women, since the ribbon kiss is not scripted in the stage directions for the play. See James W. Gargano, "Tableaux of Renunciation: Wharton's Use of *The Shaughraun* in *The Age of Innocence*," *Studies in American Fiction* 15 (Spring 1987): 10–11.
6. Edith Wharton to Rutger Jewett, November 3, 1919.
7. Rutger Jewett to Edith Wharton, November 18, 1919.
8. Joseph Candido, "Edith Wharton's Final Alterations of *The Age of Innocence*," *Studies in American Fiction* 6 (1978): 22. Further references to this article will be cited parenthetically.

earliest possible moment."[9] Wharton completed her final revisions and returned the galleys on August 12 (Candido 22), just two weeks after she had received them.

Most of Wharton's final revisions of the manuscript consisted of simple cosmetic changes (Candido 23). In addition to rewriting some sentences, she corrected a large number of spelling and punctuation errors that the proofreader had missed. Distressed by the many typesetting mistakes, Wharton complained to Jewett, and asked him to insist that the proofreader pay closer attention to misprints: "The proof reader seems to have spent more time in making suggestions as to grammatical changes rather than attending to what, I confess, seems to me the proper business of a reader."[1] Although neither Candido nor Wharton herself mentions that she copyedited the galleys in addition to proofreading them, three pages of correction sheets appended to the manuscript in the Wharton Collection at the Beinecke Library indicate that she scrupulously reviewed the historical details in the novel before the first edition was published.[2] Determined that the story would begin with a performance of *Faust* on January 27, 1875, Wharton confirmed the dates of Ash Wednesday and Easter Sunday of that year to assure that the fictional chronology would coincide with the actual calendar. She also corroborated points of etiquette ("On p. 2, lines 12, and 13, I deled [sic] 'half past,' because I think quiet people like the Archers dined at seven") and then corrected an architectural detail in the draft. Astutely observing that if the Patroon's house (the site of a suggestive meeting between Newland and Ellen Olenska and the place where May and Newland spend their honeymoon) had been built in 1630, "[t]here wouldn't have been coal and a grate if there was a pot and crane" in the fireplace, Wharton revised a scene in which Newland had stoked the fire with coal. In the final version, her ardent hero throws a log onto the blaze.

Yet another alteration Wharton proposed on the revision sheets indicates the extent to which she had immersed herself in the period. In an early outline for the story, which she had tentatively titled "Old New York," Wharton listed "scenes at the Old Academy of Music . . . Christine Nilsson, Capoul, etc." as the most significant cultural markers that symbolized the discriminating tastes of upperclass New York society in 1875.[3] But when she proofread the manuscript, Wharton selected a new diva to set the historical stage for the novel, revising the memorable first lines to read, "On a January evening of the late seventies, Clara Louise Kellogg was singing in <u>Faust</u> at the Academy of Music in New York."[4] This radical substitution indicates that Wharton wished to invoke revolutionary changes in the performance of opera that occurred in the 1890s that paralleled the historical class conflicts that comprise one of the themes of the book. The soprano Clara

9. Rutger Jewett to Edith Wharton, June 7, 1920.
1. Edith Wharton to Rutger Jewett, August 13, 1920.
2. The sheets are located in Box 1, Folder 15, Wharton Collection, Beinecke Library.
3. The outline may be found in Box 1, Folder 1, Wharton Collection, Beinecke Library.
4. Correction sheet, Box 1, Folder 15, Wharton Collection, Beinecke Library.

Louise Kellogg (1842–1916) was the first diva trained in the United States and the first American to sing Marguerite in *Faust*. In 1873, Kellogg formed The English Opera Company, a touring opera group that translated classical operas into English and performed them in that language.[5] As Wharton's correction sheets indicate, the writer planned to substitute "Kellogg" for "Nilsson" throughout the first chapter and to replace the reference to "Capoul" with "Maas," the tenor in Kellogg's company. Furthermore, she wished to describe them as accurately as possible: "I can't find out whether Kellogg wore a light wig or not, so I deled [sic] yellow, but I fancy she did." Subsequent revisions suggest that Wharton wished to stress the enormous cultural significance of this fact and the shocking violation of tradition that it signified:

> She sang in English, since for once an unalterable and unques-
> tioned law of the musical world had been waived—a law which
> required that the text of French operas sung perhaps by Swedish
> artists should be translated into Italian for the clearer under-
> standing of English-speaking audiences.

Perhaps Wharton proposed these changes in order to accentuate the late nineteenth-century class conflict between the traditional ranks of those who comprised "Old New York" and the 'new people' that is introduced as the curtain rises on the opening scene of *The Age of Innocence*. Setting the stage for the novel's action, the narrator metonymically associates the 'new people' with the "new Opera House" that "should compete" with (and as the narrative suggests, ultimately surpass) the "costliness and splendor" of its European counterparts. Although the printed version of *The Age of Innocence* does not waive the "unalterable . . . law" (3–4) (as it opens with the Swedish soprano Nilsson in the starring role singing in Italian for her American audience), the featured diva's performance nevertheless underscores the historical competition between opposing sectors of the upper class for cultural dominance because of her own historical role in that struggle. On the evening the "new" Metropolitan Opera House opened, it was Nilsson who sang the role of Marguerite in *Faust* (Dizikes 219).

Wharton's most extensive comments on the correction sheets show that the author of *The Age of Innocence* knew that works of literature could establish the historical moment of her novel as well as provide significant allusions for her story. Checking the publication dates of many of the books mentioned in her manuscript, Wharton noted, "Page 60. I had to dele [sic] Vernon Lee's 'Euphorion' because it wasn't published until 1884; her first book, 'Studies of the Italian Renaissance' came out in 1880. Walter Pater's 'Studies of the Italian Renaissance' came out in 1873, so that's all right, and Symonds I'm pretty sure is. I had to dele [sic] 'just out' after Chastelard, as I found, rather to my surprise, it was published in 1865." Her comments con-

---

5. John Dizikes, *Opera in America: A Cultural History* (New Haven: Yale University Press, 1993), p. 203. Further references to this book will be cited parenthetically.

tinue, "It will be easy for you to find whether the 'Lettres a un Inconnue' were out in 1875—I should have guessed a little later—at the foot of page 123, you're all right about Herbert Spencer, whose 'Principles of Sociology' came out in June, 1874; and a first edition of 'The House of Life' was as early as 70. Paul Bourget, Huysmans and the Goncourts you can easily verify—I think they're safe for 1875, and of course the Brownings." Wharton concluded her corrections by quipping, "That's what I call measuring-worm exactness, but we may as well be right."

*The Age of Innocence* was published on October 15, 1920, and immediately met both commercial success and critical acclaim. However, a number of readers and reviewers were quick to point out that over the course of its journey through the pages of Wharton's manuscript, the measuring-worm had failed to traverse a number of leaves. While members of "Society" entertained themselves by guessing the identities of the characters in the roman á clef, another game had begun for "the reading public" whose "eager eye," according to Katharine Perry, "would not lose one significant word."[6] Predictably, the measuring worm's most commonly recognized "lapse" was noted by Professor Phelps, who, after praising the exquisite details of the dinner parties, interior decorations, and social rituals depicted in the novel, questioned the timeliness of Newland Archer's literary tastes. Scrutinizing the box of books the protagonist unpacks in Chapter 12, Phelps queried, "Is not Guy de Maupassant out of place in the early seventies? I suppose Wharton knows her Maupassant thoroughly, but unless I am quite at fault, it was not in the early seventies, but in the early eighties, that his tales began to appear."

Phelps dismissed the mistake as a "fleck [. . .]" in "one of the best novels of the twentieth century" but his discovery alarmed Jewett, who asked Wharton to reply to "the points he has raised."[7] Wharton replied that Phelps was "quite right" but she excused herself for the error, reminding her editor of the "high pressure" under which her novel had been written and revised. The author also added that she had asked "a clever young librarian in Paris" to verify all of the dates of the French fiction she had cited, and that he had "evidently overlooked" this reference. While Wharton confessed that "such inaccuracies annoy me very much," she insisted that the many misspelled words in the printed book caused her more worry. Momentarily shifting her concern from the historical record to the aesthetic realm, Wharton added, "Personally, I do not attach much importance to questions of exact dates in a novel of this kind, as the main thing is to render the atmosphere, and Maupassant was in the atmosphere of the young men of Archer's generation."[8] Nevertheless, Wharton urged Jewett to delete the reference in the next printing. Stating that the page layout would be ruined unless the name was replaced, Jewett inquired, "How would

6. Katharine Perry, "Were the Seventies Sinless?" *The Publishers' Weekly* 98 (October 16, 1920): 1195–96. Reprinted here, quoted p. 379.
7. Reprinted here, quoted p. 384. Rutger Jewett to Edith Wharton, October 21, 1920.
8. Edith Wharton to Rutger Jewett, November 5, 1920.

it do to substitute some of the pre-Raphaelites. Swinburne and Rossetti. Or we could add Browning or Morris. I made this suggestion as a counter proposition, as evidently you do not wish to use any French author as a substitute for de Maupassant."[9] Ultimately, Wharton substituted Alphonse Daudet for Maupassant, probably because the writers Jewett had suggested already appeared in the text.[1]

Like Phelps, most critics who identified mistakes in the novel dismissed them in light of Wharton's impressive command of her subject and her overall accomplishment. But others, such as the book critic for the *Saturday Review of London*, zealously reported with a note of self-righteous superiority the "numerous historical lapses" that "marred" Wharton's "retrospect of the early seventies."[2] In the same vein, the book reviewer for *Literary Digest* stated with a tone of disdain, "The book is full of anachronisms which are so sure to be noticed by old New Yorkers that we shall only mention one or two." Citing errors as if composing a shopping list, this reviewer found fault with the untimely presence of de Maupassant and also pointed out that the musician Joachim "had never visited America as a violinist." Noting an error that Wharton decided not to change, the reviewer also argued correctly that Newland and Ellen could not have planned their secret meeting to take place at "the Art Museum—in the Park" since the Metropolitan Museum of Art was not moved from its original location (the building on Fifth Avenue between 53rd and 54th streets that had formerly housed the Dodsworth Dancing Academy) to Fifth Avenue and Central Park until 1880.[3]

The response of a number of readers to the much-touted accuracy of Wharton's text mirrored that of the fact-checking critics. Most were more interested in reporting anachronisms and inaccuracies that they had discovered rather than noting the power of the social critique embedded in Wharton's fiction. According to a letter Jewett wrote to Wharton, several readers had discovered a flagrant (and highly telling) error in the scene depicting Newland and May's wedding in Grace Church, a mistake that her editor claimed had "added greatly to my daily correspondence."[4] A number of ministers wrote to Jewett to complain that the rector had started the Archers' wedding ceremony by quoting the opening phrases of the Episcopal funeral service: "Forasmuch as it hath pleased Almighty God."[5] After pointing out that the correct wedding rite should begin, "Dearly beloved, we are gathered together here in the sight of God," a cheeky reader recommended that the company hire an "Orthodox Episcopalian" he knew to work as a proofreader.[6]

9. Rutger Jewett to Edith Wharton, November 16, 1920.
1. This change is confirmed in Rutger Jewett to Edith Wharton, January 20, 1921.
2. "The Innocence of New York," *Saturday Review* [England] 130 (December 4, 1920): 458. Reprinted in this edition, quoted p. 397.
3. "Mrs. Wharton's Novel of Old New York," *Literary Digest* 68 (February 9, 1921): 52. References to "Joachim" appeared on pages 67 and 76 of the first edition of *The Age of Innocence*; in the third edition "Joachim" was replaced with "Sarasate." The incorrect museum location was printed on page 311 of the first edition and was never changed.
4. Rutger Jewett to Edith Wharton, January 20, 1921.
5. *The Age of Innocence* (New York: D. Appleton and Co., 1920), p. 127.
6. G. C. Fraser to Col. Howard J. Smith, November 18, 1920.

The dubious circumstances of May and Newland's union as well as the banal familiarity of the traditional wedding litany strongly suggest that Wharton committed a telling error, since this mistake adds to the repeated suggestions in the novel itself that Newland's marriage to May may constitute a version of a living death for the male protagonist. Rather than insisting he change the text, Wharton simply thanked Jewett for forwarding the reader's "most amusing" letter, claiming again that although the "unfortunate quotation" had "dreadfully distressed" her, she could not be blamed for "such accidents" because she had "no time for revision."[7] She also reiterated that the egregious misspellings and misprints in the published book "deeply troubled" her.[8] In response, Jewett assured Wharton that in the next printing he would "incorporate immediately" a list of corrections that she had sent, and in another letter the editor notified her that "the new editions will marry your hero with the correct ceremony."[9]

In addition to sending Jewett a list of corrections, Wharton prepared a three-page errata sheet listing additional mistakes that she had detected.[1] Among them were several "errors in the family tree" of "the Mingott clan" that Lillie Lamar would explore in her 1968 study of the first edition of *The Age of Innocence*. As Lamar points out, tangled genealogical roots among several characters mar the novel; the first snarl concerns the inconsistent relationship of Mrs. Welland and Mrs. Mingott. Near the beginning of the first edition, Mrs. Mingott is identified as Mrs. Welland's aunt, but much later (in Chapter 19), when the obese family matriarch proposes that the awning in front of Grace Church be removed so that her wheeled chair may clear the doorway, Mrs. Welland expresses shock at "her mother-in-law's plan."[2] On the errata sheet, Wharton changed "niece" to "daughter" to rectify the first mistake for the second printing, but did not change the second error, which an "energetic" London reader pointed out on a handwritten errata sheet he sent to Jewett. "184. Mrs. Welland's 'mother in law' should read 'mother' (see p. 3)."[3]

Wharton also corrected an error in her description of Bob Spicer, Mrs. Mingott's father. In Chapter 1, Wharton writes that Mr. Spicer abandoned his wife "a month after his marriage," but then in Chapter 17, Mrs. Mingott claims that he left much later, after she was weaned. Though Wharton recognized her mistake and changed Spicer's departure to "less than a year after his marriage" on her errata sheets, she neglected to clear up another confusion concerning consanguinity: the relationship between Mrs. Mingott and Ellen Olenska.

7. Edith Wharton to Rutger Jewett, December 22, 1920.
8. Edith Wharton to Rutger Jewett, November 5, 1920.
9. Rutger Jewett to Edith Wharton, November 16, 1920 and November 23, 1920.
1. I am indebted to Patricia Willis, Curator of American Literature at the Beinecke Library, who verified that the three-page document in Box 1, Folder 15, of the Wharton Collection was an errata sheet prepared by Wharton herself.
2. Lillie B. Lamar, "Edith Wharton's Foreknowledge in *The Age of Innocence*." *Texas Studies in Language and Literature* 8 (1996): 387. Further references to this article will be cited parenthetically.
3. Rutger Jewett to Edith Wharton, January 20, 1921. This mistake was corrected in the third edition.

Lamar notes that in Chapter 4 Ellen identifies Mrs. Mingott as her "great aunt," but in Chapter 9, both Ellen and Newland refer to her as Ellen's "Granny" (387). Interestingly, this detail was not changed in subsequent editions, nor were additional errors that Wharton—and others—had recognized. Several branches of family trees remained tangled and the incorrect reference to Vernon Lee's *Euphorion* that Wharton had detected in the proofreading stage was never deleted. In addition, in subsequent editions of the novel the Metropolitan Museum of Art was never restored to its proper location, and although the first reference to de Maupassant was corrected, a subsequent mention of this author in Chapter 20 was not.[4]

Although Wharton apparently held the publisher responsible for the many errors in the text, blaming the rushed production schedule and inattentive proofreaders for the mistakes in the first edition, by February 1921 she was ready to take the matter of what she called the "measuring-worm" into her own hands. Despite the popularity of her novel the seemingly incessant complaints from reviewers and one-upmanship from readers pointing out her lapses in historical accuracy prompted Wharton to make an unprecedented decision. In February 1921 she wrote to Jewett, "In view of the continued success of the book, and of the foolish letters which you are receiving, I am almost inclined to write a short preface to the next edition." As she outlined it, a preface would enable her to inform readers that she had been forced to revise the book with "great haste," and as well, to explain the purpose of her project to readers who, in her opinion, had missed it. She explained to Jewett:

> What I was trying to do, and what I believe every novelist who write [sic] an "historic" novel should do, was to evoke the intellectual, moral, and artistic atmosphere not of one year, but of ten years: that is to say my allusions range from, say, 1875 to 1885. Any narrower field of evocation must necessarily reduce the novel to a piece of archaeological pedantry instead of a living image of the times.[5]

Wharton also informed Minnie of her plans for the preface, which would explain "the small importance of anachronisms" to the misguided readers intent on finding them.[6] Apparently, Wharton believed that her audience, distracted by their literal-minded penchant for finding petty mistakes, was unable to appreciate the larger significance of her story. While Wharton feared that her audience needed to be taught how to read her novel, Jewett urged her "not to take the trouble," insisting that it would be impossible for an introduction to "catch up" with the errors in the first edition. Instead, Jewett advised her to ignore the "idiotic" letters from readers and urged her to begin work

4. Although time constraints or typesetting difficulties may have prevented several corrections Wharton had specified from being incorporated into the final corrected version (the sixth printing of the first edition), it is unknown why other mistakes were not rectified in subsequent editions of the novel.
5. Edith Wharton to Rutger Jewett, February 7, 1921.
6. Edith Wharton to Minnie Cadwalader Jones, February 17, 1921.

on her next two projects: a short-story collection and the novel *Glimpses of the Moon*.[7] Acceding to Jewett's wishes, Wharton never wrote a preface for the novel; the only lingering result of the experience was her adamant declaration that she would never again write a book under such demanding time constraints (Benstock 359).[8]

Jewett's reaction to Wharton's plan suggests that he recognized the primary liability of the historical novel as a genre: the more references an author includes, the more chances that some will be "wrong" for one reason or another. Perry's commentary on Wharton's text is instructive here, as it suggests a correlative "vice" of historical fiction: if readers are at all familiar with the moment the author seeks to recreate, their "eager eye[s]" will scrutinize the novel to an almost excruciating extent to determine whether the author's version—or vision—of the past squares with their own knowledge of the period, whether learned or lived. Ultimately, the fuss readers and critics made about the historical inaccuracies of *The Age of Innocence* in fact testifies once more to Wharton's extraordinary awareness of the historical moment in which she lived. That what the writer termed "the small importance of anachronisms" emerged as such controversial issues to her readership proves the incredible acuity of her statement to Berenson: the tumultuous events of recent history ensured that for ever after, the past would have a novel significance for writers—and readers—of fiction. Perhaps the best proof of her insight is evinced by Ellen and Newland's conversation in the erroneously placed "Art Museum in the Park." As the two ponder a case "crowded with small broken objects—hardly recognizable domestic utensils, ornaments and personal trifles," Ellen mourns the meaning the unidentifiable artifacts have lost over time, lamenting the fate of the insignificant "little things that used to be necessary and important to forgotten people" by remarking, "[A]fter a while nothing matters." In reply, Newland responds, "Meanwhile, everything matters—that concerns you" (185–86). This analysis of the creation and reception of *The Age of Innocence*—the author's tireless attempts to make her historical novel an unforgettable artifact of the past and the indefatigable fervor with which her readers sought to unearth her errors—demonstrate that the historical accuracy of *The Age of Innocence* ultimately concerned its audience more than Wharton herself. To be sure, the novel was the story of an age that deeply mattered to them as well as to its official chronicler.

---

7. Rutger Jewett to Edith Wharton, February 25, 1921.
8. As Candace Waid has commented, Wharton's desire to write a preface may reflect her defensiveness about her knowledge of America during this period. Though Wharton never composed a preface for *The Age of Innocence*, two years later, in her 1922 introduction to *Ethan Frome*, she vehemently defended her perspectives as reliable and true to life.

# JENNIFER RAE GREESON

## Wharton's Manuscript Outlines for
## *The Age of Innocence*: Three Versions†

Before she began to write *The Age of Innocence*, Edith Wharton sketched three brief outlines of its plot. These outlines, which are reprinted in full below, today are housed in the Beinecke Rare Book and Manuscript Library at Yale University,[1] where Wharton bequeathed all of her manuscripts after Yale named her an honorary Doctor of Letters in 1923. The process of "constructing a novel," as she termed it in *The Writing of Fiction* in 1925,[2] was of utmost concern to Wharton in the late 1910s and early 1920s, since some critics had faulted her long fiction for its lack of cohesive plot structure. In these outlines, we may observe her doing exactly that: laying out the narrative progression of her projected novel from start to finish. With these brief maps of the plot trajectory of *The Age of Innocence*, Wharton seemingly attempted to guide herself through what she called the "waterless desert"[3] of her creative process—the work of writing that fell between inspiration and completion of her fiction.

In a 1980 essay[4] Alan Price noted that Wharton's outlines for *The Age of Innocence* both confirm and deny her own account of her creative method in her 1934 memoir, *A Backward Glance*. The outlines certainly undermine Wharton's oft-cited claim that "my characters always appear with their names,"[5] since in them Newland Archer is named "Lawrence" or "Langdon," and Ellen Olenska bears the more exotic moniker "Clementine"; but at the same time the outlines bear out Wharton's declaration that from the moment of inspiration she knew the "ultimate destin[ies]" of her characters, and that her writ-

---

† This essay was written specifically for this Norton Critical Edition. Page numbers in parentheses refer to this volume.
1. Edith Wharton Collection, Yale Collection of American Literature, Beinecke Rare Book and Manuscript Library, Box 1, Folder 1, and Box 22, Folder 701.
2. "Constructing a Novel," *The Writing of Fiction* (New York: Charles Scribner's Sons, 1925), pp. 61–121.
3. "Every novelist has been visited by the insinuating wraiths of false 'good situations,' siren-subjects luring his cockle-shell to the rocks; their voice is oftenest heard, and their mirage-sea beheld, as he traverses the waterless desert which awaits him half-way through whatever work is actually in hand" ("Introduction" to *Ethan Frome* [New York: Charles Scribner's Sons, 1922], pp. ii–iii).
4. Price's article, "The Composition of Edith Wharton's *The Age of Innocence*" (*Yale University Library Gazette* 55 [1980]: 22–30) contained the first transcriptions of Wharton's sketches; he deciphered the otherwise illegible cancelled word "immoral" in the third plan. Julia Ehrhardt and Sara Gerend also provided helpful translations of these outlines written in Wharton's sometimes difficult-to-read script. Another study of Wharton's process of writing *The Age of Innocence*, based upon her revisions of the galley proofs of the novel, is Joseph Candido's, "Edith Wharton's Final Alterations of *The Age of Innocence*" (*Studies in American Fiction* 6 [1978]: 21–31).
5. "[M]y characters always appear with their names. Sometimes these names seem to me affected, sometimes almost ridiculous; but I am obliged to own that they are never fundamentally unsuitable. And the proof that they are not, that they really belong to the people, is the difficulty I have in trying to substitute other names. For many years the attempt always ended fatally; any character I unchristened instantly died on my hands, as if it were some kind of sensitive crustacean, and the name it brought with it were its shell" (*A Backward Glance* [New York: D. Appleton-Century, 1934], p. 201).

ing process then simply involved unfolding the "subsidiary action"[6] through which her characters would finally meet their predetermined fates. Yet so strikingly does the "subsidiary action" that Wharton plotted in her outlines vary from that of the finished novel, that examining the outlines can inflect our understanding of the completed text. This essay aims to begin to bring Wharton's outlines to bear on reading *The Age of Innocence*.

Indeed, it appears that Wharton herself intended that her outlines be studied by future scholars and readers interested in her creative process as she composed *The Age of Innocence*, since she preserved the outlines for posterity in her papers, carefully labeling and dating them. Like most of Wharton's working papers, the outlines were written in longhand script with pencil on ruled notebook paper or translucent copy paper. Also characteristically, Wharton struck through words she wished to omit rather than erasing them; this compositional method preserves the record of her revisions, revealing how she changed her mind and substituted one idea for another even at the earliest stages of development of the novel. Wharton's attention to recording the order in which she produced the three plans also suggests her own interest in the documentation of how her narrative developed. For instance, she clearly indicated which outline recorded her earliest conception of the novel by labeling it "1st plan" in red editor's pencil at the top of the page:

> Lawrence————sees Countess X in the Wellands' box. Horrified. The Ctess (Ellen————) had married a Polish nobleman living in Paris & Nice. Reports of his debaucheries had come home; but it was also said that <u>she</u> had been "fast," & "talked about." Vague rumours were current, & some embarrassment was felt when she came home, saying simply that she had left her husband & obtained a divorce. Still, her behavior was discreet & retiring, & she seemed so genuinely glad to be at home, in a purer atmosphere, that every one became very friendly after the first recoil, & she was used as an Awful Warning to young girls with an inclination to "marry foreigners."
>
> Gradually Archer falls in love with her, & sees that life with May Welland, or any other young woman who has not had Ellen's initiation, would be unutterably dull. It is very painful for him to break his engagement, but he finally has the courage to do so, though he does not tell May why he no longer cares for her.
>
> She gives him up magnanimously, ~~but when she finds that Ellen is the cause she is very bitter, & reproaches Ellen for Ellen too is very much distressed but still~~ because she has been taught that "ladies do not make scenes," & she continues to pretend that she does not suspect Ellen of being her rival, till the latter's en-

---

6. "But these people of mine, whose ultimate destiny I know so well, walk to it by ways unrevealed to me beforehand. Not only their speech, but what I might call their subsidiary action, seems to be their very own, and I am sometimes startled at the dramatic effect of a word or gesture which would never have occurred to me if I had been pondering over an abstract 'situation,' as yet uninhabited by its 'characters' " (*A Backward Glance*, p. 204).

gagement is announced. Even then May is heroically generous, & is among the first to bring her good wishes to her cousin.

Archer, his struggle over, is sublimely, supremely happy. He urges Ellen to marry him at once. She shocks him deeply by proposing that they should first "go off for a few weeks," so that he can be sure he is not making a mistake. He reproaches her for thinking that she "feels about her in that way," & she begins to feel ashamed of having made the suggestion, & to ~~dread the~~ say to herself that the "European corruption" has tainted her soul. To efface this impression from her own mind & his, she consents to a hasty marriage; but then, when they come back from their honeymoon, & she realizes that for the next 30 or 40 years they are going to live in Madison Ave. in winter & on the Hudson in the spring & autumn, with a few weeks of Europe or Newport every summer, her whole soul recoils, & she knows at once that she has eaten of the Pomegranate Seed & can never live without it.

She flies to Europe, & Archer consents to a separation. He realizes dimly that there is no use in struggling with her. He arranges his own life as best he can, & occasionally goes to Europe, & usually calls on his wife, & is asked to dine with her. (She is very poor, & very lonely, but she has a real life.)

He grows more & more absorbed in business, more & more subdued to "New York." He returns to live with his mother & sister. May Welland marries some one else, & nothing ever happens to him again.

The second outline appears in Wharton's 1918–23 "Subjects and Notes" workbook, where she again identified it for future readers, by adding in ink at some later date, "The Age of Innocence. (Before 1919.) <u>Finished 1920</u>":

Old New York. (in 1875–80.)
Length of action about 18 months.
Langdon Archer
May Welland
Countess Olenska (Clementine)
Clementine Olenska (cousin of May) has married young. Lived in Paris, Nice, ~~Etréat~~, Rome. Glimpses of London. ~~Gran~~ Husband charming gambler, drug-taker & debauché. Spends all her money, & marriage goes to smash. She comes back to America longing for virtue, innocence & "Old New York."

Archer is engaged to May Welland. He falls in love with Clementine. ~~She~~ but resists & marries May. (Conventional impossibility of a man's breaking his engagement in those days. Clementine enthusiastically converted to all that is "province," honour, decency, &c. ~~enth~~ applauds his resolution.) ~~& finally goes back to her husband.~~

~~In two or three years she reappears.~~

He goes on a wedding trip with May, comes back & settles down to married life in N.Y.—Clementine still there—but less enthusiastic (about New York). He sees a great deal of her. May is going to have a baby. At last he & Clementine ~~have~~ fly together (contrast between bridal night with May & <u>this</u> one). Archer is fascinated & yet terrified. They ~~go to Europe~~ go to the South together—some little place in Florida.

Arrange somehow that all this is done <u>very secretly.</u> No one knows they are together. Both get tired—she of the idea of living in America, he of the idea of a scandal & a dislocation of his life.

He cannot live without New York & respectability, nor she without Europe and emotion.

They return to N.Y. separately, & the last scene is a dinner which the happy May (who has had a boy) insists on giving to her cousin Mme Olenska before the latter sails.

          ~~Hab~~          End

Wharton laid in the third and final outline of the proposed novel, still titled "Old New York," at the beginning of her complete manuscript of *The Age of Innocence*, perhaps thereby indicating that this plan was the last she made before undertaking the writing of the book as a whole:

<u>Old New York.</u> (The scene is laid in 1875.)[7]

Langdon Archer, a young man of very good "Old New York," is engaged to May Welland, a charming young girl of the same set, with whom he is deeply in love.

Her cousin, Clementine Welland, whose parents had lived in Paris & been popular at the court of Louis Napoleon, & in fashionable French society, has been married very young to Count Olenska, ~~a very rich~~ a Polish nobleman ~~of great family~~. She has led a brilliant cosmopolitan life in Paris, London, Florence & Nice, but her husband's extravagance & dissipation have obliged her to leave him, & she returns to N.Y. at 28, disillusioned & unhappy, & thirsting (as she imagines) for "the simple life," as represented by quiet respectable "old New York" of the 'seventies.—Scenes at the Old Academy of Music, the "Assembly" balls (Christine Nilsson, Capoul, &c.)—Clementine Olenska & Langdon Archer meet & fall madly in love with each other.

He is almost carried off his feet; but in "Old New York" a girl is almost disgraced if her fiancé jilts her, & Archer dares not break with May. Mme. Olenska applauds his resolution, & with an aching heart he marries May, & they go on their tame colourless & eminently respectable wedding trip,

When they return they settle down in New York & begin to lead their life wh. is to go on till the grave. Clementine is there too, beginning to be bored with New York & virtue & renunciation, & thirsting for the freedom & variety of her European experience. She falls into Archer's arms, & they go off secretly & meet in

7. Shortly before this volume went to press, Jennifer Rae Greeson made the remarkable discovery of a handwritten or, more precisely, hand-drawn inscription that appears to be an epigraph in Arabic. Written in pencil and framed in quotations marks, this notation appears on the same line as Wharton's working title and has not previously been recognized by scholars as writing. Drawing once and marking it out, Wharton began again working from right to left copying or drawing what is as yet an indecipherable scrawl. See p. 2 for a photograph of this document, which is in the Wharton Collection housed in the Beinecke Rare Book and Manuscript Library at Yale University [Editor].

Florida, where they spend a few mad weeks. (But Mme. Olenska cannot divorce as she & her husband are Roman Catholics)

Gradually Archer realizes that he cannot break with society & live as an outcast with ~~an "immor~~ another man's wife. Mme. Olenska, on her side, is weary of their sentimental tête à tête & his scruples, & they finally go back, & ~~end~~ the story ends by Mme. Olenska's returning to Europe.

Before she goes, May (who is going to have a baby, & who suspects nothing) insists on giving her cousin a farewell dinner, at which all of Old New York is present.

Read together, Wharton's three outlines of *The Age of Innocence* demonstrate that many of the most fundamental elements of the novel were present from her earliest recorded conceptions of it. From her very "1st plan," it was clear that Wharton would engineer a social study of "Old New York" through a plot based on a love-triangle, and the basic configuration of characters in this triangle was established as well. A scion of the New York elite (Archer) would be pulled between two cousins (May and the Countess), one of whom was "his own kind," entirely enmeshed in New York tradition, and the other of whom had "had the initiation" of cosmopolitan Europe—in short, he would be torn between American "respectability" and European "emotion," as Wharton put it in the second plan. Further, Wharton in the outlines determined how she would resolve this triangulated romance: from the first sketch she was sure that the relationship between the New York heir and the Europeanized countess was doomed, and by the second sketch, she decided as well that "Old New York" society would be consolidated by the marriage of Archer and May, and would be reproduced through the birth of a son to that union. And she even identified the starting and ending points of this triangulated narrative: she began her first plan with the opening scene at the opera, and by the second plan she had visualized as well the dinner party scene that closes the central dramatic action of the book. In drafting the outlines, then, Wharton made central choices of character and plot, putting into place a great deal of the dramatic shape of the finished novel.

This being said, there are also several striking and finally telling divergences between the narratives described in the outlines and the published version of *The Age of Innocence*. Among the most crucial of these differences is the fact that Wharton's plans always allowed for the sexual consummation of the attraction between Archer and the Countess, a plot twist that would have made her novel a very different book. Including a consummated affair between the two characters would have required that Wharton focus more explicitly on sex, as we see from her inclusion in the plans of a scandalous trial marriage, an illicit rendezvous in Florida, and even a proposed comparison between the private proclivities of the rival cousins ("contrast between bridal night with May and <u>this</u> one"). In the finished novel, of course, Wharton limited her treatment of sex in "Old New York" society to asides about Lawrence Lefferts's philandering and the innuendo of the key in the unopened envelope that Ellen returns to Archer. But more important, with the consummation of the affair between Archer and the Countess in each of the plans, Wharton determined that her New York heir and Europeanized countess would be divided by their own fundamental incompatibility—not kept apart, as they are in the novel, by the social strictures of "Old New York." In the plans, Wharton had the lovers choose to leave each other because, as she put it in the second plan, "both get tired" of the other's way of life. This mutually voluntary separation of Archer and the Countess in the outlines is a resolution of plot far removed from the cruel thwarting of their seemingly ideal (and consequently impossible) love, which Wharton chose to render in the completed novel.

Wharton's assurance in these plans that Archer and the Countess would prove fundamentally incompatible always hinged upon her inclusion of the Countess's critical opinions of Archer and his restrictive "Old New York" world—perceptions that she omitted entirely from the completed text, substituting instead Ellen's admiration for the "straight-up-and-downness" (49) of New York. This observation underlines the most significant variance between the outlines and the novel: the point of view from which the story was perceived and unfolded. While Wharton finally filtered the events of *The Age of Innocence* almost entirely through the consciousness of Newland Archer, in the plans she assumed a more omniscient narrative perspective, distributing the point of view more democratically among her main characters. Although she considered May's thoughts and feelings only briefly in the first plan, and excluded them thereafter, Wharton balanced the Countess's interpretation of events against Archer's version of the narrative throughout the sketches. Indeed, in the first and second plans, the Countess's point of view threatened to take over the plot, as through her eyes Wharton illustrated the attraction of a cosmopolitan European life while criticizing the deadly dullness of life with the New York elite. Wharton's decision to privilege the Countess's thoughts in the sketches suggests the autobiographical affiliation Wharton may have felt for her character, since she, like her Countess, was estranged from elite New York society as she wrote *The Age of Innocence*. If in the early 1880s the young woman who would become Edith Wharton had suffered the embarrassment of a broken engagement that threatens May in the outlines as well as in the novel, by the late 1910s Wharton had more in common with her Europeanized countess, having become a permanent expatriate in Paris and having finally divorced her husband the year before she began to write the novel.[8] In the first sketch, Wharton's insertion between the lines of an assessment of the Countess's self exile, "She is very poor, and very lonely, but she has a real life," perhaps bespeaks her own identification with the Countess's point of view.

Fundamentally, by altering point of view between the outlines and the finished novel, Wharton changed *The Age of Innocence* from what

---

8. Several scholars have noted as well Wharton's autobiographical connection to her third main character, Archer, for Wharton herself was fifty-seven as she wrote the book that closes with a vignette of her male protagonist at fifty-seven.

she called a "psychological novel" into what she termed a "novel of manners."[9] For by restricting the worldview of the novel to Archer's consciousness, Wharton tightened her focus on the elite New York society of the 1870s and 1880s. In choosing neither to assume the twentieth-century viewpoint of an omniscient narrator, nor to contrapose and give equal weight to Archer's and the Countess's divergent interpretive views, Wharton in the finished book achieved what she considered to be the hallmark of the novel of manners, the "continual interweaving of individual with social analysis."[1] By fixing Archer, whose interpretive framework is so entirely a product of his society, as the perceiving center of her book, Wharton caused her protagonist to function symbolically in the novel as the mind of "Old New York." As she rendered Archer's judgments and interpretations of events, Wharton simultaneously depicted his society, for Archer's thoughts are as much historically preserved facets of his narrow world as are the clothes he wears. Comparing the outlines to the finished novel, noting Wharton's shift in the point of view from which she chose to tell the story of the world of her own childhood, serves notice of the extent to which Wharton tailored Archer's perceptions to tell a story of cultural constraints; reading the sketches reveals the truthfulness of Archer's desires, but also the limitation of his mind as well as his imagination. Wharton's early configurations of the Countess's interpretations of America and the events of the novel are telling, and they remain in the final silence of the novel, embodied in the unseen figure of the Countess who, like her female creator, has finally seen too much to be looked upon.[2]

Thus while the story as she outlined it is a psychological study of the incompatibility of worldviews shaped by fundamentally different experiences, Wharton's finished novel instead is an ethnography of "Old New York." In the sketches, her archetypal opposition of American and Europeanized perspectives seemingly indicated that Wharton would undertake a study of the influence of environment on individual understanding—a psychological theme reminiscent of themes in the work of her close friend Henry James, who had died in 1916. Indeed, in a genealogy of the families appearing in *The Age of Innocence*, placed in her notebook with the second outline of the novel, Wharton named May Welland's grandfather "Henry James," a choice that perhaps indicates a tribute to James or her perception of the similarity of the project she was outlining to his earlier work. But by purging the Countess's Europeanized point of view and telling the entire story from the vantage point of Archer's "Old New York," Wharton submerged much of this psychological theme and instead pushed into the

9. In *The Writing of Fiction*, Wharton distinguished among three types of novel—"manners, character (or psychology) and adventure"—and asserted that "one of the novelist's first cares is to decide which method he means to use" (pp. 66, 70).
1. *The Writing of Fiction*, p. 81.
2. Traces of this story of dissonance between Archer and the Countess do remain in the finished novel; Cynthia Griffin Wolff has charted the moments that show the distance between Newland and Ellen in *A Feast of Words: The Triumph of Edith Wharton*, 2d ed. (Reading, Mass.: Addison-Wesley, 1995), pp. 302–26.

foreground the demands made on individuals by a closed elite society. In the published version of *The Age of Innocence*, social forces rather than psychological preferences became the driving forces of Wharton's story: central to the novel, but absent from the sketches, are such material issues as the problem of divorce (which only emerges as a prohibited act parenthetically in the last outline); the problem of subsistence and status for women outside of marriage; and the problem of how an elite group disciplines and expels transgressors and interlopers. In Wharton's privileging of the social over the psychological, May's pregnancy, which had been a mere aside in the outlines, became the climactic fact on which her novel turns. Indeed, as she excluded the points of view of her female characters from *The Age of Innocence*, Wharton shifted the focus of her story to social reproduction.

Finally, then, rather than the story of psychological realism proposed in her outlines, Wharton in her forceful deptiction of cultural formation produced a novel of tragic naturalism. By purging the Countess's foreign point of view and critical distance from the pieties of "Old New York" from her finished novel, Wharton assumed a focus precisely as narrow as that of the constrained and constraining society she sought to recreate in its pages. As she told the story through Archer's eyes, Wharton's theme became the cost to individual self-fulfillment of tribalistic social reproduction. In the end, the story in Wharton's outlines carries a vastly different emotional import than the story in her novel. In her earliest conceptions of the thoughts and personalities of her characters, Wharton left no doubt that her cosmopolitan Countess would find Archer so dull that she would have to flee him, that this experienced woman who is by definition worldly would always choose Paris over Archer and the expansiveness of Europe over the "straight-up-and-downness" of "Old New York." At the close of *The Age of Innocence*, on the other hand, we are left with the thwarting of a seemingly ideal romance, a tragic sense of unfulfilled longing, and a certainty that two lives have been forever subordinated to the rigorous demands of all-powerful "Old New York."

Yet it was precisely by sacrificing Archer and the Countess to the rigors of New York society in the novel that Wharton surmounted the certainty, expressed in her outlines, that they represented fundamentally incompatible ways of life. In choosing to thwart and never to consummate the attraction between Archer and the Countess, Wharton engendered the promise of reconciliation between closed New York and cosmopolitan Europe that appears in the final chapter of *The Age of Innocence*. In this coda to the novel, never envisioned in her plans, Wharton suggested that the impossible alliance between Archer and the Countess would be achieved in the next generation through the thoroughly compatible match of Dallas, Archer's son, with Fanny Ring, the Countess's protegée. With the impending nuptials of the second generation of the love-triangle, Wharton announced that the sealed society of "Old New York," which could not admit of the marriage of Archer and the Countess, must inevitably open to modernity and to the wider world, and must thereby pass out existence. Her sense of the new social order coming into being at the end of *The Age of Innocence* is best indicated by her plans for a sequel to the novel, drafted in the same notebook in which the second outline appears. As a "continuation of 'The Age of Innocence,' " she proposed, she would tell the story of the second generation, the "[h]istory of Dallas Archer & Fanny." One possible title for the sequel, she noted in 1922, would be "The Age of Wisdom." But that, of course, would have been another story.

## CYNTHIA GRIFFIN WOLFF

## [*The Age of Innocence* as a Bildungsroman]†

\*          \*          \*

The particular traditions of old New York threaten to obscure the reader's vision, even as they threaten to suffocate the hero in *The Age of Innocence*. The crowded collage of drawing rooms and Worth gowns and opera evenings and Newport outings all evoke a compelling illusion of "place," and Wharton's eye for detail is seductive.[1] Yet to focus on place as extrinsic to character is, in the end, to miss the point of the novel. Wharton's narrative vantage is carefully chosen (it is similar to James's in *Portrait of a Lady* and even more like Austen's in *Emma*): the narrator may step outside of Newland Archer's mind to make judgments or draw conclusions; but when we see old New York, we almost always see it through his eyes. The world that seems at first a novelistic tour de force becomes, on closer examination, a mirror of Newland's mind and the very condition of his being. This is his "one segment of history"; these are the traditions that have "molded" him and "channeled his drives." The center of this novel is Newland's problem of being and becoming, given the unalterable traditions of this portion of history, this "place."

*The Age of Innocence* is Wharton's most significant *bildungsroman* (surpassing even *Summer*). In it she traces Archer's struggle to mature, to become in some continuous and authentic way—himself. She lays before us the present and the possible in such a way that the middle-aged man who concludes the novel seems an admirable and significant outgrowth of the untried youth at the beginning. Her profound acceptance of the kind of limitation described by Erikson is mirrored in the creative use to which she puts the *bildungsroman* tradition; her master was Goethe, whose works she was once again rereading in this postwar period. The theme of *The Age of Innocence* might be captured in the most famous line of *Wilhelm Meister*: "*Here or nowhere is America!*"

Newland Archer does have choices, but they have been limited by

---

† From *A Feast of Words: The Triumph of Edith Wharton* (New York: Oxford University Press), 1977; reissued (expanded) by Addison Wesley (New York, 1995) pp. 306–20. Notes have been edited. Bracketed page numbers refer to this edition.
1. Note Edmund Wilson's remark in *The Wound and the Bow* that Edith Wharton was "the poet of interior decoration" (New York: Oxford University Press, 1947), p. 163.

the nature of his one portion of history. Thus while Wilhelm's search (and that of most *bildungshelden*)[2] is pursued in a journey, Newland's search is entirely internal. He cannot flee the provincial world of old New York; he must learn to transmute it into something valuable. Newland perceives himself as alienated and without vocation; his ordeal by love teaches him the lessons that Wilhelm learned—acceptance of reality and dedication to generativity. In this novel, the ultimate place is the little rock cottage at Skuytercliff: that home stands for the values that will endure—values of family and honor. Newland is here when he decides not to become involved with Ellen, and later he spends his wedding night with May here. It is not a lofty dwelling—narrow, unaesthetic, almost primitive—it scarcely answers the visions of a romantic adolescent. Yet it is such a place as this that Newland must "find."

The journey is not an easy one. Our first glimpse of him tells us that like Ralph Marvell[3] he is, perhaps by inclination, perhaps by training, an onlooker—indeed, but one in a society that trains its young people to be no more than onlookers, members of an audience that stands to the side of life's great struggles and does not participate in them. To meet him as he prepares to watch a production of *Faust* is consummately, ironically appropriate.[4] Having no occupation sufficient to his energies, Newland has turned them to fantasy: "He was at heart a dilettante, and thinking over a pleasure to come often gave him a subtler satisfaction than its realization. This was especially the case when the pleasure was a delicate one" (2) [4]. There is a dangerous vitality in this inner life; his considerable passion, finding no satisfactory outlet, has been sublimated into extraordinary palpable fantasies (old New York gave men like Newland little else to do with their passions).

Unknown to Newland, however, the fantasies that have been nourished by the rich passional needs channeled into them slip quietly back into his perceptions of the actual world, distorting these perceptions and deluding his expectations.

> 'We'll read *Faust* together . . . by the Italian lakes,' he thought, somewhat hazily confusing the scene of his projected honeymoon with the masterpieces of literature which it would be his manly privilege to reveal to his bride. . . . If he had probed to the bottom of his vanity (as he sometimes nearly did) he would have found there the wish that his wife should be as worldly-wise and as eager to please as the married lady whose charms had held his fancy through two mildly agitated years; without, of course, any hint of the frailty which had so nearly marred that unhappy being's life, and had disarranged his own plans for a whole winter. How this miracle of fire and ice was to be created, and to sustain itself in a harsh world, he had never taken the time to think out (5) [6].

2. Hero of the *bildungsroman* (German for "education novel"), a character who undergoes moral and psychological growth [Editor].
3. The lawyer, failed poet, and ill-fated male protagonist who commits suicide in Wharton's novel *The Custom of the Country* (1913). [Editor]
4. Interestingly enough, when Newland does "get into the drama," he does so by imitating the sentimental renunciation scene of *The Shaughraun*.

Archer's naiveté about the configuration of his emotional life is coupled with an empty adherence to convention. With a little effort he might become a good man, for there is nothing vicious in his nature and much that is generous. However, never having examined the rules by which his society lives, his notion of "duty"—as in "the duty of using two silver-backed brushes with his monogram in blue enamel to part his hair" (3) [4]—is a thing easily to be confounded with Larry Lefferts' notions of "form." His reading and his active imaginative life have brought other worlds and other customs to his attention; but his reflex for conformity has been too strongly developed to permit him easily to measure his own traditions against these others. "He had probably read more, thought more, and even seen a good deal more of the world, than any other man of the number . . . but grouped together they represented 'New York,' and the habit of masculine solidarity made him accept their doctrine on all the issues called moral. He instinctively felt that in this respect it would be troublesome—and also rather bad form—to strike out for himself" (6) [6]. Thus the life of his spirit is infused with only the vaguest apprehension of purpose. There is no self-consciousness in his virtue, and he cannot be said to be "moral" because his admirable acts are informed by no continuous inner sense of conscience.

When we first meet Newland, we may be most impressed by his deficiencies—the absence of available passion and the habit but not the substance of "correct" behavior. Yet these apparently empty places in Newland's life contain the possibility of change. His innate vigor has been shaped but not hardened by the traditions of his background; the final inclinations of his character have yet to be formed, and the eighteen months of the novel's principal duration comprise the period of that transformation. Newland is nearing the conclusion of his apprenticeship in old New York. His adolescence and young adulthood have been times for experiment, for casual alliances and intellectual curiosity. Marriage represents commitment, an irrevocable assumption of his adult roles and an affirmation of the society in which he lives. Newland is not prepared for this commitment, and the moment of the crisis is complicated by "the case of the Countess Olenska" (40) [28].

Ellen is the catalyst that forces Newland's self-confrontation, for had she not appeared, he might have spent his whole life attaching his deepest emotions almost entirely to fantasy. Ellen offers him the opportunity to test his capacity to fulfill these fantasies. She draws forth his passion into a warm flesh-and-blood attachment, and she quickens his dormant emotional life. If he is ever to be the man he fancies he might become, he can be that man with Ellen Olenska. And yet, his reactions to her are deeply ambivalent.

It is typical of Newland's thinking that he should construe Ellen as a "case"; and this is of a piece with all those other habits of mind that push aside the ordinary complexities of actual human life for the grander sweep of the romantic imagination. He evaluates her exotic plight and her "foreign" appearance with nervous interest: her "pale and serious face appealed to his fancy as suited to the occasion and to her unhappy situation; but the way her dress (which had no tucker) sloped away from her thin shoulders shocked and troubled him" (12) [11]. Such a vision embodies the mystery of the unknown and represents all the world that lies beyond the familiar boundaries of Archer's experience. The "case" of a woman so intriguingly distressed appeals to his visionary sense, and his musings on her situation become fused in indefinable ways with his unutterable yearning for a larger realm of experience. Ironically, Ellen in person makes him uncomfortable (just as the fashionable nudity of her gown had unsettled his notions of propriety): her frankness, her wry sense of the absurd, and her easy assumption of intimacy all unbalance him. "Nothing could be in worst taste than misplaced flippancy" (15) [12]. Thus while the actual freedom of her manner is distasteful, the abstract "right" to "freedom" that her situation justifies is infinitely appealing to him.

Though Ellen's arrival has had the objective effect of hastening Newland's public commitment to May, it has at the same time made that commitment seem a sentence to death by asphyxiation. When Newland retreats to his study to sort out the various effects of Ellen's appearance, he finds that her case has "stirred up old settled convictions and set them drifting dangerously through his mind" (40) [28]. His image of Ellen balances conveniently and simplistically against an image of May as "the young girl who knew nothing and expected everything" (40) [28]; and the larger vistas of the twilight world from which Ellen has come diminish the appeal of a marriage that seems no more than "a dull association of material and social interests held together by ignorance on the one side and hypocrisy on the other" (41) [29]. Central to these images of the women in Archer's life is some picture of what he is to become himself. This scene in his study is but the first in a series of increasingly terrifying invocations of self; the future stretches before him, "and passing down its endless emptiness he saw the dwindling figure of a man to whom nothing was ever to happen" (228)[139]: In fearing acceptance into the "hieroglyphic world" of old New York, Archer really fears anonymity and personal insignificance.

Yet he is hindered more by his own habits of thought than by insufficiencies in the society around him, for his impatience with specific details and intractable actualities follows him in his quest for personal identity. Just as it is easier to deal with the "case" of Ellen than with Ellen herself, so it is easier to pursue an image of personal fulfillment that is uncomplicated by the details of everyday living. Throughout much of the novel Archer longs for a life that moves well beyond the charted realms of the familiar, a life of high emotional intensity and sustained moral and intellectual complexity. The kind of life he only hazily conjectures is a life that is, given the "harsh world" of human experience, available to only a very few; and Archer seems an unlikely candidate for the life that his imagination yearns toward.

Ironically, the danger that his life will be insignificant lies not so much in the probability that he will fail to fulfill these fantasies as in the more immediate possibility that, having failed to fulfill them, he will lack the capacity to give *any* aspect of his life authenticity. Not all things are possible for a man of Newland's time and place; some ways of life that are unavailable to him are, perhaps, better than any that are. But every real life involves compromises and relinquished hopes—even though some lives require more in the way of sacrifice than others. The problem that Newland faces without fully comprehending it is that his desire to create an ideal self substantially hinders him from infusing some *genuinely possible* self with meaning.

\* \* \* He might never attain the capacity for sustaining deep and meaningful bonds with others. He might become a hollow man altogether. This danger is the central problem that he faces.

And in this respect, Newland's quandary captures the quintessential problem of all who grew to maturity in the repressive society of old New York. Perhaps he will settle for a set of highly stereotyped personal relationships that serve only to mask a deep sense of isolation and incompleteness. Perhaps he will even go through his entire life never feeling that he is really "himself"—even though everyone else seems to think that he is "somebody."\* \* \*

Newland's yearning for transcendent experience is, from the very beginning, inseparable from his passion for Ellen; the longing for them suffuses the novel with an exquisite pain. And yet Wharton lets us know, though it becomes fully apparent to Newland only at the end of the novel, that precisely those capacities in Ellen that most attract him are capacities leading to behavior that his innermost being cannot tolerate. Throughout the earlier portions of the fiction, Newland drastically simplifies his notions of Ellen (indeed, as he does those of May as well) so that he need not deal with the complexities of her complete person. Newland fancies her world and the outrages she has experienced in it with convenient imprecision: it is "the society in which the Countess Olenska had lived and suffered, and also—perhaps—tasted mysterious joys" (102) [65].[5] He conjures Ellen outside of any coherent social pattern: she has the "mysterious faculty of suggesting tragic and moving possibilities outside the daily run of experience. She had hardly ever said a word to him to produce this impression, but it was a part of her, either a projection of her mysterious and outlandish background or of something inherently dramatic, passionate and unusual in herself" (113) [73]. She is the vague embodiment of all that is lacking in his own life.

Yet Archer and Ellen have not one meeting in which the deep and fundamental antipathies between their ways of life are not apparent. Archer may romanticize Ellen's past in blurred and indefinite terms, but Ellen herself has a complete and quite precise complement of habits, manners, and tastes which are the product of her world; Wharton sets the pattern for an ironic juxtaposition of these habits against Archer's in the initial chapter and continues it throughout the novel. During Archer's first visit to Ellen's home, for example, he is en-

5. The word "mysterious" occurs repeatedly in Newland's musings about Ellen. It perfectly captures her almost incorporeal quality in his life. He does not *explore* the mysteries of Ellen's world; he prefers her to remain a mystery—conveniently blurred and obscured in his perception.

chanted with the artistry of her drawing room, "intimate, 'foreign,' subtly suggestive of old romantic scenes and sentiments" (69) [45]; and in some way (the connection is surely not one of decorative affinity) he is moved to ponder his own highly "American" insistence on "'sincere' Eastlake furniture" [46]. He is charmed by her experienced, casual manner and offended by her being "flippant" (72) [48]. He is deeply outraged by her association with Beaufort, and he naively supposes that he can terminate the association by making "her see Beaufort as he really was, with all he represented—and abhor it" (75) [49]. He claims that she makes him "look at his native city objectively. Viewed thus, as through the wrong end of a telescope, it looked disconcertingly small and distant" (74) [49]; yet he leaves in a fury when she greets the Duke and Mrs. Struthers (who is not "received" by the polite world) with as much composure as she had greeted him. Each visit before Archer's marriage is tainted by Ellen's affinity for Beaufort—an attachment which he comprehends fitfully and totally detests.

Even at those times after his marriage when Archer seems most unambivalently to press Ellen to an elopement, he continues to view her more as a "case"—"the compromised woman"—than as another complex human being. Thus on the day of their outing in Boston, Archer marvels at Ellen's self-possession, and then reflects that "a woman who had run away from her husband—and reputedly with another man—was likely to have mastered the art of taking things for granted" (240) [146]. Still later, when he greets her on her return from Washington, she shocks him by asking: " 'Is it your idea, then, that I should live with you as your mistress—since I can't be your wife?' . . . The crudeness of the question startled him: the word was one that women of his class fought shy of, even when their talk flitted closest about the topic. He noticed that Madame Olenska pronounced it as if it had a recognized place in her vocabulary, and he wondered if it had been used familiarly in her presence in the horrible life she had fled from" (292–93) [174].

Unable to accept her social accommodations, Newland unrealistically rejects society altogether. " 'I want—I want somehow to get away with you into a world where words like that—categories like that—won't exist. Where we shall be simply two human beings who love each other. Who are the whole of life to each other; and nothing else on earth will matter' " (293) [174]. However, if Ellen has learned nothing else, she has learned the terrible and inexorable toll that tradition takes: "She drew a deep sigh that ended in another laugh. 'Oh, my dear—where is that country? Have you ever been there?' " (293) [174].

Ellen has a motley background; she was born of old New York, but has spent her childhood as a European vagabond. These bizarre antecedents give her more flexibility than anyone else in the novel, and though Newland is most vividly impressed with her European connections, Ellen herself is oddly imbued with an admiration for what could only be termed May's world. Ellen's view of this world is naive at first: she sees it simplistically as a place that is " 'straight up and down—like Fifth Avenue. And with all the cross streets numbered!' " (74)

[49]. But she learns of its cruel social isolations, and she learns of the loneliness of living among the " 'kind people who only ask one to pretend,' " who don't want to " 'hear anything unpleasant' " (75) [50]— and still she respects the complex morality that she (but not Archer) can so accurately calculate.

The young Newland Archer evaluates his world harshly and superficially. He sees its innocence as a stifling and destructive element— "the innocence that seals the mind against imagination and the heart against experience" (145) [91]—and it weighs insignificantly against Ellen's world of intrigue. Yet there is much in the novel that suggests intricate harmony where Archer perceives only emptiness and silence. There are silences, to be sure; but they are rich with communication—a kind of totality of understanding that is possible precisely *because* the world of old New York is small and limited. It is a world where one can understand, without being told, that Mrs. Beaufort's presence at the opera on the night of her ball indicates "her possession of a staff of servants competent to organize every detail of the entertainment in her absence" (16) [13]; a world where Archer strolling abroad in the evening can ascertain that Beaufort must be about on an errand of "clandestine nature" because "it was not an Opera night, and no one was giving a party" (64). This depth of understanding concerns grave things as well as trivial. The very first action Archer takes in the novel is that of joining May at the opera to show his support of her and the family in behalf of Ellen. It is a kind, emotionally generous gesture, and May understands it without a word's being uttered: "As he entered the box his eyes met Miss Welland's, and he saw that she had instantly understood his motive, though the family dignity which both considered so high a virtue would not permit her to tell him so. . . . The fact that he and she understood each other without a word seemed to the young man to bring them nearer than any explanation would have done" (14) [11–12]. And so, in many ways, it does.

The novel is filled with instances of May's intuitive flashes of deep understanding. Occasionally these are verbalized, but usually they are not. Her penetration into Archer's growing attachment for Ellen, for instance, is more often revealed in a failure to include him in the family's discussions or in a question that discovers him in a lie. Their relationship is filled with a profound silence, but the very limitations of the code that governs their marriage fill the silence with meaning. The most remarkable instance of this mute dialogue occurs one evening when Archer tells May he must go to Washington and May enjoins him to "be sure to go and see Ellen."

> It was the only word that passed between them on the subject; but in the code in which they had both been trained it meant: "Of course you understand that I know all that people have been saying about Ellen, and heartily sympathize with my family in their effort to get her to return to her husband. I also know that, for some reason you have not chosen to tell me, you have advised her against this course, which all the older men of the family, as well as our grandmother, agree in approving; and that it is owing to

> your encouragement that Ellen defies us all, and exposes herself
> to the kind of criticism of which Mr. Sillerton Jackson probably
> gave you, this evening, the hint that has made you so irritable.
> . . . Hints have indeed not been wanting; but since you appear un-
> willing to take them from others, I offer you this one myself, in
> the only form in which well-bred people of our kind can commu-
> nicate unpleasant things to each other: by letting you understand
> that I know you mean to see Ellen when you are in Washington,
> and are perhaps going there expressly for that purpose; and that,
> since you are sure to see her, I wish you to do so with my full and
> explicit approval—and to take the opportunity of letting her know
> what the course of conduct you have encouraged her in is likely
> to lead to." (269) [161–62]

It is true, as Ellen has observed, that old New Yorkers don't like to talk
about "unpleasant" things. But what a wealth of shared knowledge
their reticences permit!

Newland perceives May's moments of understanding as mere flick-
ers of light in an otherwise unillumined darkness. The evocation of
her as a young Diana is, in Archer's mind, a reductive vision of empty,
unknowing, unsoiled virginity. He can deal with her primitive complexity no more than he can deal with the consequences of Ellen's experiences with Old World culture. He supposes that her "faculty of
unawareness was what gave her eyes their transparency, and her face
the look of representing a type rather than a person; as if she might
have been chosen to pose for a Civic Virtue or a Greek goddess. The
blood that ran so close to her fair skin might have been a preserving
fluid rather than a ravaging element; yet her look of indestructible
youthfulness made her seem neither hard nor dull, but only primitive
and pure" (189) [115]. He doesn't hear or understand even her spoken
disclaimer: " 'You mustn't think that a girl knows as little as her parents imagine. One hears and one notices—one has one's feelings and
ideas' " (147–48) [93].

Given Archer's own abysmal innocence, he is unprepared to counter
the marshalled forces of the moral world that May commands. For Diana is the divinity of childbirth and fertility; she presides over the generation of life itself. May might well be ignorant of the more refined
customs of decadent European culture; but in her "primitive" purity,
she is committed to the most fundamental human processes, and in
this commitment she is as ruthless as nature itself. May's devotion to
an order by which the family can perpetuate itself is absolute; she is
willing to release Archer from his engagement to her (for she is a generous woman), but once he rejects that offer, she dedicates herself to
the task of holding him to the morality implicit in old New York's regulation of the process of generation.

Archer knows the rules of this morality; he recites them to Ellen
much as a child recites a catechism by rote. Old New York has
" 'rather old-fashioned ideas. . . . The individual . . . is nearly always
sacrificed to what is supposed to be the collective interest: people
cling to any convention that keeps the family together—protects the

children' " (109–10) [71]. And yet they are meaningless to him throughout much of the novel. He sees himself not as an active force in this world—indeed, it is a world whose deep moral structures he little comprehends—but as the victim of its well-mannered brutalities, "a wild animal cunningly trapped" (66) [43]. The escape that Ellen seems to offer is, given his romanticized vision of her, not the liberty to choose an alternate moral system; it is a seductively blurred vision of "freedom" in an artistically and intellectually stimulating world whose constraints and moral ambiguities he little imagines.

Ellen's view is altogether different. Her contact with Old World corruption enables her to appreciate the pious primitivism of her American cousins. Even New York's rigidities have meaning for her. " 'Under the dullness there are things so fine and sensitive and delicate that even those I most cared for in my other life look cheap in comparison. I don't know how to explain myself . . . but it seems as if I'd never before understood with how much that is hard and shabby and base the most exquisite pleasure may be paid' " (243) [147]. Much of Ellen's affection for Newland stems from her supposition that he really does embody the goodness of a society she has come to respect. She imputes to him, perhaps, a more self-consciously principled mind than he possesses; the creed he recites in attempting to dissuade her from the divorce acquires in her understanding of it a meaning that Archer cannot yet feel. The Newland Archer who is beloved of Ellen Olenska is a "self" whose emotional commitments are integrally linked to the sentiments he has uttered. " 'I felt there was no one as kind as you; no one who gave me reasons that I understood for doing what at first seemed so hard and—unnecessary. The very good people didn't convince me; I felt they'd never been tempted. But you knew; you understood; you had felt the world outside tugging at one with all its golden hands—and yet you hated the things it asks of one; you hated happiness bought by disloyalty and cruelty and indifference. That was what I'd never known before—and it's better than anything I've known' " (172) [107].

We might be tempted to judge Ellen's appraisal of Newland to be as uninformed as his is of her. Certainly she demands a kind of moral substance from him that he cannot yet recognize in himself, for the only Newland Archer that Ellen can admire is a man whose felt sense of duty would not permit him to betray those who have rested their confidence in him. Ellen has taken empty words and imputed significance to them; yet hers is not an act of such wistful longing as we might suppose. She may love a man who does not yet fully exist, but she has fixed her affections on what is potential and possible in Newland; and if he is not yet the man she judges him to be, there are clear indications that he has already committed himself to becoming that man.

The center of Newland's early pieties, the grave enduring traditions of his life, all have to do with family; when he acts without thinking, his automatic behavior affirms the bonds of kinship and familial affection. For May, and in a different way for Ellen, this loyalty is part of a coherent ethical framework; however, Newland does not feel the moral component in his behavior, probably because it is so familiar, so much a part of the "given" of his world, that he can become conscious of it only with great difficulty. The strength of his moral reflex is shown at the beginning of the novel when he rushes to May's box "to see her through whatever difficulties her cousin's anomalous situation might involve her in; this impulse had abruptly overruled all scruples and hesitations, and sent him hurrying through the red corridors to the farther side of the house" (14) [11]. The same deep instinctive tie to the norms that sustain the family can be seen in his involuntary revulsion from the "sordid" aspects of Ellen's right to "freedom." His social (and moral) inflexibility is confirmed by the splendid, parochial isolation of every European journey he makes. His inability to envision any realistic alternative to this life is captured in his groping visions of a life with Ellen—somewhere, "his own fancy inclined to Japan" (307) [182].

Yet throughout much of the novel Archer has no emotional contact with that part of his nature (by far the greater part) that is so irrevocably wedded to the customs of New York. Because so little affect attaches to this "self," he cannot experience it as truly and authentically himself; because he so little understands it, he cannot respect or admire it.

What May and Ellen do together in a remarkable unvoiced conspiracy is confront Archer with the realities of his situation and thereby confirm the integrity of his life. Ellen does this by awakening his slumbering sentient self and wrenching his passional life away from pure imagination to an actual person (however romantically construed) and a series of particular situations within which he can measure his true capacities. May does so by offering her own "innate dignity" (196) [119] as a worthy object of his emotional and moral allegiance: "Whatever happened, he knew, she would always be loyal, gallant and unresentful; and that pledged him to the practice of the same virtues. . . . She became the tutelary divinity of all his old traditions and reverences" (196–97) [119–20]. Thus his growing involvement with Ellen both awakens his deepest passions and ruthlessly outlines his personal limitations. May offers if not passion at least a "glow of feeling" (43) [29] that becomes an "inner glow of happiness" (194) [118] after the marriage; even more, she offers a way of life that is worthy of the passion he has discovered in himself. "She would not disappoint him"; she represented "peace, stability, comradeship, and the steadying sense of an unescapable duty" (208) [126]. Eventually, she offers a true and honorable life when his dreams of Ellen are confounded.[6]

6. There are many implications of this improbable cooperation between Ellen and May. For one thing, it suggests that the values that had been polarized in the depiction of the two heroines of The Reef have now been conjoined in some coherent and meaningful estimation of life. In terms of Wharton's personal development, the cooperation is even more significant.

In order to come back "for good" to the days of her childhood, Edith Wharton had to accept that part of herself that represented an internalization of Lucretia and Lucretia's values. She had to come to final terms with "Mother"—yes—but even more important, she had to accept that part of herself that imitated Mother and reflected Mother's ways.

Newland is not a stupid man, and he is to some degree aware of the emotional distance between himself and Ellen. As we have seen, all of his encounters with her are marked by the fundamental differences in their natures; and though Archer's longing for Ellen usually blinds him to these differences, he is sometimes able to put their relationship into focus. The most significant readjustment of his values occurs during and after their meeting at Skuytercliff. He is always jealous of Beaufort, consistently plagued by a desire to "correct" Ellen's views of him. When Beaufort interrupts their meeting at Skuytercliff, the old jealousy emerges. Yet this time, the outrage is tempered by an even-minded appraisal of their situation.

> Madame Olenska, in a burst of irritation, had said to Archer that he and she did not talk the same language; and the young man knew that in some respects this was true. But Beaufort understood every turn of her dialect, and spoke it fluently: his view of life, his tone, his attitude, were merely a coarser reflection of those revealed in Count Olenski's letter. This might seem to be to his disadvantage with Count Olenski's wife; but Archer was too intelligent to think that a young woman like Ellen Olenska would necessarily recoil from everything that reminded her of her past. She might believe herself wholly in revolt against it; but what had charmed her in it would still charm her, even though it were against her will. Thus, with a painful impartiality, did the young man make out the case for Beaufort and Beaufort's victim. (137) [86–87]

Having confronted this painful reassessment, Archer makes what must in part be understood as a conscious decision: he immediately journeys south to see May.

May's sympathetic understanding of his emotional conflict contrasts markedly with the distance that has just been demonstrated between himself and the Countess Olenska, and her offer to release him makes him aware, perhaps for the first time, of the depths of her basic goodness. It is a genuine offer, and when Archer refuses it, his refusal constitutes a pledge to May's world as well as to May. Once the pledge has been made, May and Ellen conspire to hold him faithful.

Terrified by the finality of his acceptance of old New York, Archer impetuously turns to Ellen for some escape, but she answers him now as she is to answer him for ever after: " 'In reality it's too late to do anything but what we've both decided on' " (171) [106]. Ellen convinces the family to hasten the marriage, and then she moves to Washington, out of Archer's sight. In every subsequent meeting, her theme is the same. She reveres the narrow pieties of old New York, and her faith in Archer's own fidelity is the significant force keeping her safely

---

We have said that in *The Reef* Wharton made a fiction out of the disparate parts of herself—and in that fiction, these parts never come together. In *The Age of Innocence*, she pursues much the same tactic: Newland Archer, Ellen Olenska, and May all represent variations of Edith Wharton's "self"; however, now they are in harmony, and now they can be made to cooperate with each other.

in America: " 'If you lift a finger you'll drive me back: back to all the abominations you know of, and all the temptations you half guess' " (245–46) [148]. She actively wills that his love for her be realized not in their union but in a continuing separation that gives substance to Archer's own moral life. She conjures him to " 'look, not at visions, but at realities' " (292) [174]. Thus when at their last private meeting he urges her to consummate their love, she protests: " 'Don't let us be like all the others' " (314) [187]. She could no longer respect him or the code of his world, and she would, as she resolutely tells him, be forced back to the indignities of life with her husband—a betrayal of her own renewed moral commitment as well. Little wonder that at that moment when they are closest to the finality of a physical union, "they looked at each other almost like enemies" (316) [188].

The news of May's pregnancy is the final force that drives the would-be lovers apart. Yet there is a real decision implicit in this penultimate act of the drama; for a man without firm moral commitments may almost as easily leave a wife and child as a wife alone. Newland is restrained from leaving not by any objective and external force—but by the deeprooted conviction that his own moral duty must ultimately be defined by family obligations. The child that May is carrying represents a felt demand that has been internalized and thus that he cannot ignore.

Wharton never supposed that Newland could find happiness with a woman like Ellen; and though there are earlier outlines of the novel in which he does break his engagement to May and marry Ellen, he and Ellen are not happy together. There is no shared sense of reality: she misses the life in Europe that she has always known; he misses the familiar amenities of old New York; and finally they separate and return to their different worlds.

Throughout the novel as finally written, Newland repeatedly tries to define the nature of his "realities." Often he presumes Ellen to have known the real world in her life outside of New York, and his own real experiences are featured as lying outside of May's world and his marriage to her. Yet just as often he finds reality in May's world: "Here was truth, here was reality, here was the life that belonged to him" (140) [88]. His renunciation of May's offer of release is a final determination of the limitations of his *real* life (though his doubts continue); and his behavior towards Ellen, especially after his marriage, betrays the fact that he has genuinely chosen to cast his life in terms of old New York morality. His yearning for Ellen is indescribably intense, yet for the most part it belongs to another world. "That vision of the past was a dream, and the reality was what awaited him" (216) [132]. He searches out the house that Ellen lives in much as one might visit the hermitage of some transfigured saint. "She remained in his memory simply as the most plaintive and poignant of a line of ghosts" (208) [126]; he sustains a private shrine to the man he might have been at a different time and in a different place, "and he had built up within himself a kind of sanctuary in which she throned among his secret thoughts and longings" (265) [159].

His passion is still deeply attached to her, and meetings with her reawaken his longing. Nevertheless, his marriage marks the beginning of a process of distancing; and for the most part Archer is more comfortable with this process as he becomes increasingly conscious of his moral estimation of any other course. "In Archer's little world no one laughed at a wife deceived, and a certain measure of contempt was attached to men who continued their philandering after marriage. In the rotation of crops there was a recognized season for wild oats; but they were not to be sown more than once" (308) [183]. The imagery suggests the degree to which Newland has actively accepted the values of May's primitive, natural order, and his humiliation when Larry Lefferts casually includes him into a fellowship of deceiving husbands is vividly acute, for "in his heart he thought Lefferts despicable" (309) [183]. In the end, he is forced to realize that there can be no *real* life for Newland Archer and Ellen Olenska together. And the magnitude of his sacrifice measures for him the value of what he has preserved. He relinquishes his Faustian dreams for the more realistic understandings of a Wilhelm Meister and turns his energies from imagination to the process of generation.

\*    \*    \*

# ELIZABETH AMMONS

## Cool Diana and the Blood-Red Muse: Edith Wharton on Innocence and Art†

\*    \*    \*

After *The Age of Innocence*, critics agree, the quality of Wharton's long fiction changes. The line of exceptional work beginning with *The House of Mirth* in 1905 and running through *The Fruit of the Tree* (1907), *Ethan Frome* (1911), *The Reef* (1912), *The Custom of the Country* (1913), and *Summer* (1917) ends in 1920. After that there is an occasional book of extraordinary accomplishment (some argue that *The Mother's Recompense*, for instance, is one), but by and large the early books greatly overshadow the novels Wharton wrote in the twenties and thirties: *The Glimpses of the Moon* (1922), *The Mother's Recompense* (1925), *Twilight Sleep* (1927), *The Children* (1928), *Hudson River Bracketed* (1929), and *The Gods Arrive* (1932). *The Age of Innocence* marks the end of Edith Wharton's major period. It also marks the end of her Progressive Era fictions; and, as I hope to explain here in my discussion of the polarized portraits of the American girl and the woman artist in *The Age of Innocence*, the novel comments significantly on its author's personal situation. *The Age of Innocence* is one of the clearest expressions we have of Edith Wharton's frustration as an American woman writer.

† From *American Novelist Revisited: Essays in Feminist Criticism*, ed. Fritz Fleischmann (Boston: Hall, 1982), pp. 209–24. Reprinted with permission of author. Bracketed page numbers refer to this volume.

Because *The Age of Innocence* culminates years of criticism on Wharton's part of America's treatment of women, it may be useful to summarize the concerns that preceded it. In *The House of Mirth*, the best-selling novel that secured her reputation as a popular yet serious writer in 1905, Edith Wharton had attacked—to use language current at the time—the "parasitism" of marriage for women. The novel is set in fashionable, wealthy New York at the turn of the century, and it studies the predicament of beautiful Lily Bart, who does not want to be anyone's wife but knows that she must nevertheless marry in order to remain financially and socially secure. Because she resists marriage, she ends up ostracized, destitute, and finally, dead.

Wharton's next three books, *The Fruit of the Tree, Ethan Frome*, and *The Reef*, are equally cheerless. *The Fruit of the Tree* (1907) is about a New Woman of exceptional intelligence and integrity, Justine Brent, who marries the liberated young man of her dreams only to have him eventually subordinate her to the memory of his dead first wife Bessy, a childish and utterly self-centered person. In *Ethan Frome* (1911), a grim modern fairy tale for adults, Wharton's two female figures finally merge into one awful image of woman as cripple; isolated from the world at large, Zeena Frome and Mattie Silver, like Ethan's mother before them, turn into invalids and madwomen—physical and mental ruins. Wharton's heroines in *The Reef* (1912), Anna Leath and Sophy Viner, attempt to change their lives: Sophy wants to find economic independence; Anna seeks erotic liberation. Each fails and not because her goal is unworthy; they fail because, as Wharton sees it, economic independence and sexual liberation are forbidden to women. Anna and Sophy end as they began: limited, unrealized people.

As if determined to write about a woman succeeding, indeed triumphing, rather than being crushed, Wharton in *The Custom of the Country* (1913) created Undine Spragg: smart, brash, ruthless. Required to marry, she plays the marriage market as skillfully as her male counterparts play the Wall Street market. Wharton loads the book with mercantile rhetoric to emphasize the crass, profit-seeking character of marriage, an institution in which women are property. Instead of resisting as Lily Bart does, Undine—aptly named for a money-making hair-curler (but also, of course, for the ancient temptress and nemesis of men, the siren)—goes through husbands like ambitious men go through jobs: with an eye on profit and advancement. She thus turns the system to her own advantage and, alone among Wharton's heroines, manages to shape her own fate. She does so, however, because she is unscrupulous; and though Wharton in many ways seems to have enjoyed charting Undine's devastating sweep through the upper reaches of old New York and sedate French society, Undine was clearly no solution to the problems Wharton had been exploring. She might be relief, vicious relief; but she was certainly no role model.

*Summer*, published in 1917, returns to the more usual, if depressing, Wharton vein. The novel, set in rural, impoverished New England, is about a very young woman's desire to escape the restrictions of village life, epitomized for her by her guardian, a man old enough to be her father. For one summer, her seventeenth, she does escape both emotionally and sexually. But the price she pays is marriage to the very person she most wanted to escape, her paternal guardian. Pregnant by another man, penniless, and without any skills to market, Charity Royall can see no alternative but to marry protective Mr. Royall. Thus, in this last book before *The Age of Innocence*, the father literally becomes the husband; there is not even the pretense of marriage as a union of equals at this primitive, and therefore unusually bold-faced, level of society.

*The Age of Innocence* brings to a close, brilliantly, this early line of fiction on what had been known in the United States for more than seventy years as "the woman question." Themes and issues that Wharton had begun exploring even before *The House of Mirth* echo and twine until *The Age of Innocence*, rich by any standard, has the unmistakable texture and depth of a masterwork. Wharton was looking backward both in historical time and in personal time when she wrote the book; she revisited in the wake of World War I the old New York of her girlhood and of America's adolescence, and, as in the world of *Summer*, the moral locale of *The Age of Innocence* has a sharp edge to it. The war had shaken Wharton. She lived in France throughout the fighting, working tirelessly on behalf of the French war effort, and she was constantly and personally aware of the devastation: the dying, the agony of widows and orphans, the razing of homes and monuments and, it seemed, culture itself. When the fighting was over, she turned, for relief no doubt, to her past and recreated in *The Age of Innocence* the New York of her youth. This is not to say that the book is nostalgic or escapist. It is rather an autopsy.

Wharton's plot is simple enough. About to announce his engagement to May Welland, who is one of old New York's loveliest virgins, Newland Archer—who is also a product of convention in the age Wharton dubs Innocent: the American 1870s—meets the Countess Olenska. She is not innocent. Originally an old New Yorker herself (though never a particularly conforming one), she has endured ten years of a miserable foreign marriage, and she has now returned to get a divorce and build a new life, one independent and wholesome, in the United States. Inevitably Archer falls in love with her. He then marries May out of duty, is unhappy, hopes to make Ellen his mistress, is disappointed. Although she loves him, the countess knows what it means to be a "kept" woman: lying, hiding, constantly hating oneself—and she would rather leave America than lead such a life. Her family, which has been trying to get rid of her is relieved to see her go. Her desire to get a divorce; her living in a Bohemian quarter of the city; her open friendships with men who are married or engaged to other women—each is an unpardonable transgression. Old New York ceremoniously sends the Countess Olenska back to Europe, and Newland Archer is left to live out his conventional life with his conventional wife, May. The book ends twenty-five years later with Newland, now a widower, gazing up at the Countess Olenska's window in Paris but deciding not to go up. He is afraid to upset his memories, afraid to see Ellen in the flesh.

As soon as Wharton named her hero Archer, she insisted upon comparison with her good friend Henry James's *The Portrait of a Lady* (1881). Both novels are set in the American 1870s, both contrast American and European values, both have as a central figure an American named Archer who is highly susceptible to Continental charm and mystery. Yet the comparison of most interest to me here is not between the two Archers, Isabel and Newland, but between the two American girls, Isabel and May, each of whom is, in a sense, the author's title character. Just as the "portrait" James paints applies most directly to Isabel Archer, so Wharton's title *The Age of Innocence*, which she took from a Reynolds portrait of a child, applies most directly to May, a character as frozen in endless childhood as the painter's little girl. As Cynthia Griffin Wolff notes, Wharton's painterly title strengthens this novel's connection to James.[1] But in its substitution of a little girl for a lady, it also, as I will go on to explain, emphasizes the great distance between them.

Henry James's American girl—adventurous, ignorant, virtuous, self-assured—was the pride of America by the time Wharton began publishing novels at the turn of the century. If the image had shocked the nation in *Daisy Miller* in the 1870s, by the late nineties the type was such a commonplace, imaginatively, that it was a staple of popular culture. The ingenuous American girl was the heroine of best-selling novels—Gertrude Atherton's *Patience Sparhawk and Her Times* (1894) is an excellent example—and she was so frequently the centerpiece of cultural analyses that in *Land of Contrasts: A Briton's View of His American Kin* (1898), James Fullarton Muirhead (author of Baedeker guides to Great Britain and the United States) could routinely remark on the type in his chapter, "An Appreciation of the American Woman":

> Put roughly, what chiefly strikes the stranger in the American woman is her candour, her frankness, her hail-fellow-well-met-edness, her apparent absence of consciousness of self or of sex, her spontaneity, her vivacity, her fearlessness. If the observer himself is not of specially refined or delicate type, he is apt at first to misunderstand the camaraderie of an American girl, to see in it suggestions of a possible coarseness of fibre. . . . But even to the obtuse stranger of this character it will become obvious—as to the more refined observer *ab initio*—that he can no more (if as much) dare to take a liberty with the American girl than with his own countrywoman. The plum may appear to be more easily handled, but its bloom will be found to be as intact and as ethereal as in the jealously guarded hothouse fruit of Europe. He will find that her frank and charming companionability is as far removed from masculinity as from coarseness; that the points in which she differs from the European lady do not bring her nearer either to a man on the one hand, or to a common woman on the other. He will find that he has to readjust his standards, to see that divergence from the best type of woman hitherto known to him does not necessarily mean deterioration; if he is of an open and sus-

1. Cynthia Griffin Wolff, *A Feast of Words: The Triumph of Edith Wharton* (New York: Oxford University Press, 1977), p. 312.

ceptible mind, he may even come to the conclusion that he prefers the transatlantic type![2]

Edith Wharton did not share Muirhead's enthusiasm. In *The Fruit of the Tree*, published thirteen years before *The Age of Innocence*, she first offered extended comment on the American girl in the character Bessy Westmore, who is vivacious, ignorant, brave, and, Wharton emphasizes, pathetically shallow. Bessy has energy but no knowledge, imagination but no depth. For all her robust self-confidence, she is an extremely limited creature. As Wharton has an attractive older woman ruefully observe, Bessy is "one of the most harrowing victims of the plan of bringing up our girls in the double-bondage of expediency and unreality . . . and leaving them to reconcile the two as best they can, or lose their souls in the attempt."[3] This description could as easily apply to Isabel Archer as to Bessy Westmore, with the major difference that, where James is fascinated to see how the reconciliation will be attempted, Wharton is disgusted by the problem's even existing. She does not see the American girl as America's noblest creation, the nation's most interesting contribution to modern civilization. She sees her as the nation's failure, the human victim of a deluded obsession with innocence.

May Welland is Wharton's rarefied version of the stereotype. Unsoiled by life, May is always connected with white: her virginity, mentally and emotionally, cannot be touched. She is permanently pure. Likewise, Wharton implies, she is permanently juvenile. She has a fresh "boyish" quality that brings to mind the "invincible innocence" of her middle-aged mother, and suggests that May too will go through life sexually unaware and armed in innocence (pp. 142, 190, 146) [89, 116, 91].[4] To be sure, she is vigorous physically—she rides, rows, plays lawn tennis, wins archery competitions—but even this healthiness is deceptive, for the allusions Wharton surrounds May with are lifeless. She walks beside Archer and "her face wore the vacant serenity of a young marble athlete" (p. 142) [88]; at another point her smile, we are told, is "Spartan"(p. 293) [176]. Elsewhere and most pointedly, Wharton says, the "faculty of unawareness was what gave her eyes their transparency, and her face the look of representing a type rather than a person; as if she might have been chosen to pose for a Civic Virtue or a Greek goddess" (p. 188) [115].

The goddess Wharton associates with May is Diana, virgin deity of the hunt. Wearing a "white dress, with a pale green ribbon about the waist and a wreath of ivy on her hat." May wins her archery match with "Diana-like aloofness" (p. 210) [128]. Later she enters a ballroom "tall and silver-shining as a young Diana" (p. 306) [183]. Similarly, at the van der Luydens' reception for Ellen Olenska, "in her dress of

2. James Fullarton Muirhead, *Land of Contrasts* (Boston: Lanson, Wolffe & Co., 1898), pp. 50–51. James was so well known on the subject that Muirhead can casually refer to him: "The American girl, as Mr. Henry James says, is rarely negative; she is either (and usually) a most charming success or (and exceptionally) a most disastrous failure" (p. 48).
3. Edith Wharton, *The Fruit of the Tree* (New York: Charles Scribner's Sons, 1907), p. 281.
4. All quotations are originally from Scribner's paperback edition of the novel: Edith Wharton, *The Age of Innocence* (New York: Charles Scribner's Sons, 1968). Notes have been edited. Bracketed page numbers refer to this edition.

white and silver, with a wreath of silver blossoms in her hair, the tall
girl looked like a Diana just alight from the chase" (pp. 65–66) [42].
In May, Wharton takes selected virtues of the American girl: her innocence, her physical vigor, her cheerfulness and vivacity, her whole-
someness and self-confidence, and links them to a forever virginal
goddess of death. Newland, with a shiver, wonders of May: "What if
'niceness' carried to that supreme degree were only a negation, the
curtain dropped before an emptiness?" (p. 211) [129]. May Welland *is*
empty. She is, in addition, living at the pinnacle of American society,
America's Dream Girl.

Wharton insists that innocent May is both ancient and artificial. In
spite of her athletic freedom and bright modern cheeriness, she is as old
as patriarchy itself. Newland is depressed as he tries to imagine a com-
radely marriage with the Wellands' daughter: "he perceived that such a
picture presupposed, on her part, the experience, the versatility, the
freedom of judgment, which she had been carefully trained not to possess" (p. 44) [29]. He realizes further that, because "of this elaborate
system of mystification" to which girls are subjected (which might well
come from one of "the books on Primitive Man that people of advanced
culture were beginning to read"), May has no depth: "she was frank,
poor darling, because she had nothing to conceal, assured because she
knew nothing to be on her guard against" (pp. 45–46) [29]. Yet Newland
knows that "untrained human nature was not frank and innocent; it was
full of the twists and defenses of an instinctive guile. And he felt himself
oppressed by this creation of factitious purity," which, ironically, has
been manufactured solely for his pleasure (p. 46) [30].

In Wharton's version, the American girl is not spontaneous. She has
been taught to be frank and self-assured as proof of her innocence
(which is simply the ancient patriarchal value of virginity served up, of
course, in nineteenth-century language). She is as manufactured an
image of femininity as any other. She may look, in the guise of Isabel
Archer or Daisy Miller, like a brand new independent creature; but
take away James's infatuation with the American girl's illusion of freedom (and that is all Isabel or Daisy has, of course: the illusion of independence), and we have May Welland. The innocent American girl
was a pernicious ideal, Wharton, looking back on the nineteenth century, felt compelled to say.

The issue here is larger, of course, than simply a difference of opinion between Edith Wharton and Henry James. Wharton was attack-
ing an entire tradition when she entered May Welland in the lists of
nineteenth-century American girls. Indeed, by the turn of the century,
William Dean Howells, the most respected man of letters in America,
was so convinced of the moral centrality of feminine virtue in fiction
and life that he devoted two volumes to the study of women in nineteenth-century novels. His *Heroines of Fiction* (1901) argues, in his
own words, "my prime position that the highest type of novelist is he
who can most winningly impart the sense of womanhood."[5] That

5. William Dean Howells, *Heroines of Fiction*, 2 vols. (New York: Harper & Brothers, 1901),
   11:43.

"sense of womanhood" most consistently admired by Howells in this book—as in his own fiction—always has the essential ingredients of the American girl. The preferred Howells heroine, who captures what *Heroines of Fiction* repeatedly calls the "Ever-Womanly," is fresh, intelligent, self-confident, and morally irradiating.

Subsequent criticism has followed Howell's lead. Paul John Eakin's *The New England Girl: Cultural Ideals in Hawthorne, Stowe, Howells and James* (1976) maintains that in the nineteenth century, "woman functioned as an all-purpose symbol of the ideals of the culture: the official repository of its acknowledged moral code, and she appears accordingly as a redemptive figure in the era.[6] Eakin is building here, by his own admission, on William Wasserstrom's earlier study, *Heiress of All the Ages: Sex and Sentiment in the Genteel Tradition* (1959), which traces images of women in American novels from James through the twenties, looking in particular at the way the American girl is used symbolically, in fact messianically, to embody American idealism. As Eakin explains the premise he shares with Wasserstrom: "As the country moved toward more secular ways, a fiction arose which explicitly proposed its heroines as cult objects. . . . The value of these young women was measured by their power to redeem the individual, to regenerate society, through love."[7] Thus Wasserstrom, for example, concludes that Maggie Verver, the American girl of James's *The Golden Bowl* (1904), is the quintessential American heroine because she miraculously "combined the qualities of a nymph and a nun [and thus] finally reconciled all antitheses; she fulfilled the American dream of love, the dream of all the ages."[8]

It should not be surprising that Edith Wharton disliked *The Golden Bowl*.[9] In *The Age of Innocence*, she argues against the sentimentality of idealizing an "innocent" American woman; she argues against the masculine tradition celebrated by James and Howells and Wasserstrom and Eakin. In the first place, she knows that the price of innocence is diminished humanity for women. In the second place, she argues that the "natural" American girl May Welland (like Bessy Westmore before her) is in fact not natural at all; she is an artificial product, a manufactured symbol of patriarchal authority. Yet in their surveys of the subject, neither Eakin nor Wasserstrom takes Wharton's criticism into account. Eakin stops with James and does not discuss Edith Wharton. Wasserstrom cites Wharton's dislike for May[1] but fails to see that May is Maggie shown from a different angle than James's. The result, as has often occurred because of superficial (or non-) treatment of women writers, is perpetuation of a distorting thesis about American literature, in this case the idea that major nineteenth and early twentieth-century Amer-

6. Paul John Eakin, *The New England Girl: Cultural Ideals in Hawthorne, Stowe, Howells and James* (Athens: University of Georgia Press, 1976), p. 5. Although Eakin's announced focus is New England's version of the American girl, his inclusion of James's girls from New York State (Daisy, Isabel) indicates that the focus is not rigid.
7. Ibid., p. 6.
8. William Wasserstrom, *Heiress of All the Ages: Sex and Sentiment in the Genteel Tradition* (Minneapolis: University of Minnesota Press, 1959), p. 98.
9. See R. W. B. Lewis, *Edith Wharton: A Biography* (New York: Harper and Row, 1975), p. 144.
1. Wasserstrom, *Heiress of All the Ages*, p. 64.

ican novelists, except for Hawthorne, idealized a virginal American girl. In fact, Edith Wharton did not.

Ironically, it may be that the tradition Edith Wharton was more in sympathy with, whether she realized it or not, is the popular one described by Nina Baym in *Woman's Fiction: A Guide to Novels by and about Women in America, 1820–1870*. The novels Baym analyzes do not celebrate innocence or idealize ignorance. Nor do they abstract women into a cultural "value." Their objective is realism and the story they tell is pragmatic: how to create for oneself a healthy adult female identity. Typically these novels "chronicle the 'trials and triumph' (as the subtitle of one example reads) of a heroine who, beset with hardships, finds within herself the abilities of intelligence, will, resourcefulness, and courage sufficient to overcome them."[2] The goal of these women's novels, like Wharton's decades later, is to examine female experience in fact and in its full social context. The difference is that where earlier women customarily offered a happy resolution to the heroine's struggle to construct an identity that mediated between the extremes of perpetual passive dependence and total (and hence antisocial) independence. Wharton, writing from the vantage point of a world no longer nineteenth-century in its basic assumptions about the primacy of family and the home, repeatedly found no happy resolution to offer. Her heroines—Ellen Olenska is a good example—seek informed active adulthoods only to find that America insists on perpetual daughterhood, eternal innocence.

Wharton's disdain for innocence as a female ideal is passionately expressed in the characterization of Ellen Olenska. She is everything May is not. She is complicated, flawed, sensual, curious, and creative. In important ways, she reflects the artist Edith Wharton trying to make a place for herself in America and failing.

Only once did Wharton make a woman writer a major character in one of her long fictions. At the beginning of her novel-writing career in *The Touchstone* (1900), she shows Margaret Aubyn, a brilliant and well-known author, being thrown over by Stephen Glennard in favor of an unthreatening, conventional young woman when it comes to marriage. Rejected, Margaret leaves America for England, where she dies. The rest of the book traces Glennard's inexcusable exploitation of Margaret after her death: in order to make money to marry, he sells the dead novelist's letters to him, which were personal. The novel condemns Glennard's dastardly behavior and ends with his remorseful confession of guilt to his wife.

As even a sketch suggests, *The Touchstone* is a melodramatic book and for that reason not very successful. Still, it is important autobiographically. Wharton had been publishing for eight years when the novel appeared, and she was not yet widely known; nevertheless, the fear of success that she invests in Margaret Aubyn's predicament is obvious. At the beginning of what would be a long and enormously

2. Nina Baym, *Woman's Fiction: A Guide to Novels by and about Women in America, 1820–1870* (Ithaca, N.Y.: Cornell University Press, 1978), p. 22.

successful career as a novelist, Wharton had chiefly fear and resentment to express about the woman writer's situation. There is nothing but discord between Margaret Aubyn's two lives. Publicly, she is brilliant, successful, and acclaimed. Personally, and in payment for that public success, she is lonely, humiliated, and punished, indeed—killed. She dies because Glennard rejects her; Glennard rejects her because she is such a brilliant and successful artist. Turn that around, and the message is clear: what a woman risks in daring to live as an artist is life itself.

As a rule, Edith Wharton avoided the subject of the woman writer. She was a proud and private person—she did not talk about her disastrous marriage to Edward Wharton; she kept her affair with Morton Fullerton so secret that not until her papers at Yale were opened in the late 1960s did biographers even know about it. She was similarly guarded about her feelings as an author. She did the ordinary things: sat for publicity photos, clipped reviews, fought with editors to get more money, wrote a memoir, *A Backward Glance* (1934), that is polite and uninformative. How she really *felt* about being a writer she expressed only very indirectly. If her first novel is remarkably direct—anger and anxiety are on the surface—it is the exception. After it, Wharton abandoned the woman writer as a character for long fiction. Perhaps she was afraid of revealing too many of her innermost feelings, perhaps she realized that writers writing about writers usually produce boring books. In any case, after *The Touchstone*, Edith Wharton continued to think about the woman artist in a few of her novels but the figure would not appear again as a writer. Sophy Viner in *The Reef* is an aspiring actress. Anne Clephane in *The Mother's Recompense* is a painter. And neither is an artist in the deepest sense. They are young, gifted women whom Wharton wishes well but in whom she does not, as she had with Margaret Aubyn, invest herself. The only artist with whom she does that again, twenty years after she started writing novels, is Ellen Olenska.

Ellen is not an artist in any narrow, sheerly production-oriented sense of the word. She does not paint, sing, write, dance, or act—although as a child she did most of those things. Indeed, old New York vividly remembers her "gaudy clothes" and

> high color and high spirits. She was a fearless and familiar little thing, who asked disconcerting questions, made precocious comments, and possessed outlandish arts, such as dancing a Spanish shawl dance and singing Neapolitan love-songs to a guitar. Under the direction of her aunt [Medora] . . . the little girl received an expensive but incoherent education, which included "drawing from the model," a thing never dreamed of before, and playing the piano in quintets with professional musicians. Of course no good could come of this. (p. 60) [38–39]

Small wonder that Ellen, who was as wild and gorgeous a child as Hawthorne's Pearl in *The Scarlet Letter,* shows up at the opera at the beginning of *The Age of Innocence* in, as Newland's grown sister describes it, a strange dress of " 'dark blue velvet, perfectly plain and flat—like a nightgown.' " Newland's mother feigns shock at her daughter's reference to a bedroom and remarks, " 'What can you expect of a girl who was allowed to wear black satin at her coming-out ball?' " (p. 40) [26]. Ellen's opera costume offends because it is dramatic and sexy (one suspects the same was true of the earlier black satin). She sits engrossed in *Faust*, "revealing, as she leaned forward, a little more shoulder and bosom than New York was accustomed to seeing" (p. 15) [10].

As an artist Ellen's medium is life itself. She moves into her aunt's dilapidated house on unfashionable West Twenty-third Street and, without commotion or a lot of money, changes it into something original. Newland looks around him and

> what struck him was the way in which Medora Manson's shabby hired house, with its blighted background of pampas grass and Rogers statuettes, had, by a turn of the hand, and the skillful use of a few properties, been transformed into something intimate, "foreign," subtly suggestive of old romantic scenes and sentiments. He tried to analyze the trick, to find a clue to it in the way the chairs and tables were grouped, in the fact that only two Jacqueminot roses (of which nobody ever bought less than a dozen) had been placed in the slender vase at his elbow, and in the vague pervading perfume that was not what one put on handkerchiefs, but rather like the scent of some far-off bazaar, a smell made up of Turkish coffee and ambergris and dried roses. (pp. 71–72) [45–46]

Ellen Olenska, receiving Newland here in an erotic red-velvet gown trimmed with black fur (p. 105) [67], is exotic and passionate. Although she is not beautiful—she is thin and pale, on occasion haggard—she creates beauty around herself, automatically. She has the visual artist's instinct for interesting statement.

Ellen's life is also fertile intellectually. She prizes good conversation even more than the heirloom jewels and priceless antiques that she married into. Stimulating talk is for her (as it was for Wharton) a necessity of life, and she settles on West Twenty-third Street because she chooses to live among writers and actors. The odd move horrifies her relatives. They "had simply, as Mrs. Welland [May's mother] said, 'let poor Ellen find her own level'—and that, mortifyingly and incomprehensibly, was in the dim depths where . . . 'people who wrote' celebrated their untidy rites. It was incredible, but it was a fact, that Ellen, in spite of all her opportunities and her privileges, had become simply 'Bohemian' " (p. 260) [158]. Unreclaimable in the opinion of conservative upper-class New York, the Countess Olenska is given a dinner— "the tribal rally around a kinswoman about to be eliminated from the tribe" (p. 334) [200]—and banished.

Her banishment, in keeping with old New York's impeccable good manners, is smooth and subtle. It even looks as if Ellen could stay in America and be happy if she wished. The family has tried to force her exit by forbidding divorce and then cutting her allowance severely—giving her no alternative but to return to her husband. Then at the last moment her grandmother, ignoring family pressure, offers Ellen a home with her. This may look appealing, but in fact, it is a sorry substitute for the freedom Ellen craved. She came to America to get a divorce, to live as an independent woman. The best she can achieve, however, is life as her grandmother's companion/dependent (with Newland propositioning her on the side). The only choice she has, in other words, is such a compromise that Wharton's point seems clear: there is no independent life available to this woman in America. The best she can do is grown-up little girlhood. Not surprisingly, Ellen turns down her grandmother's offer, and the original plan succeeds (with the help of a well-placed lie by May: she claims to be pregnant before she is positive in order to thoroughly close Ellen out of Newland's life). Forbidden a divorce and cut off from financial independence as long as she stays in the United States, Ellen is put in the position of having no good alternative but to leave. She is effectively—though politely, of course—gotten rid of.

With Ellen's exit Edith Wharton, living in France, repudiated the America of her youth and said important things about herself as an artist. Most obviously, Ellen's elimination exposes old New York as a barbaric and paranoid culture. Far from the model of genteel security that Wharton and others must have considered it during the nineteenth century, the New York of her girlhood is a frightened, primitive place in *The Age of Innocence*. And what is feared is Ellen Olenska. The woman of intellect and artistic disposition is such a threat that she must be expelled. Equally significant is the fact that Ellen is not alone. Behind her stands eccentric Aunt Medora, who raised her; behind Medora is her formidable grandmother, old Catherine Mingott. Medora is tolerated only because she lives on the fringe of society and is not as smart or creative as Ellen—also, she is no longer a sexual threat; Catherine is accepted because she has been assimilated through marriage (she has literally been incapacitated, being so fat that she can barely move without assistance). What is crucial is that these women—Catherine, Medora, Ellen (later Fanny Beaufort is added)—suggest a line of female unconventionality and vitality which has not been totally eradicated by the cultural preference for May Wellands, and one so powerful that, when irrepressible by co-option or ridicule (the methods used to keep Catherine and Medora within bounds), it requires the extreme remedy of exile. In this respect, the "matriarchal" line that Catherine Mingott heads is no sham (p. 13). There is an implication of awesome female energy and creativity that, given a chance, could explode old New York. Wharton agrees with the established order on this: Ellen Olenska, and by association Wharton herself, *is* a threat.

Biographically, the identification between Wharton and Ellen Olenska is unmistakable. Both are women and passionate. Both are alienated from their old New York roots. Both value original, inquisitive conversation above all other sorts of social intercourse and need to create around themselves physical environments that are beautiful and interesting. Both are sexually experienced women who have had love affairs in Europe with slightly younger men while still married to men totally unsuited to them (this we know of Wharton and suspect of Ellen). Both seek divorces. Both—unlike their relatives—prize the life of artistic and intellectual achievement above all other lives. Both end up leaving America (in each case for Paris). The parallels are so strong that one must believe that Wharton spoke to one degree or another of her own situation, emotionally, when she wrote of Ellen's exile. At the very least, *The Age of Innocence*, published in 1920, says that in Wharton's opinion upper-class America had long ago made it impossible for the woman of sexual, intellectual, and artistic energy— that is, the woman such as Wharton herself—to live at home.

On this subject of Ellen's expatriation, it is particularly interesting to look at certain changes Wharton made in the novel. She left three outlines for *The Age of Innocence*.[3] In the earliest, marked "1st Plan" by Wharton, Archer breaks his engagement to May and marries Ellen, who quickly finds life with him deadly. Wharton's plan says:

> When they come back from their honeymoon, & she realizes that for the next 30 or 40 years they are going to live in Madison Ave in winter & on the Hudson in the Spring & autumn, with a few weeks in Europe or Newport every summer, her whole soul recoils, & she knows at once that she has eaten of the Pomegranate Seed & can never never live without it.
>
> She flies to Europe, & Archer consents to a separation. He realizes dimly that there is no use struggling with her. He arranges his own life as best he can, & occasionally goes to Europe, & usually calls on his wife, & is asked to dine with her. She is very poor, & very lonely, but she has a real life.[4]

In this first plan, Ellen leaves Archer and America of her own free will. Likewise, in the next prospectuses, she leaves instead of being expelled. In each, Archer marries May out of duty, as in the published book, but then has an affair with Ellen, who eventually leaves because she is bored. In the second plan, "both get tired—she of the idea of living in America, he of the idea of a scandal & a dislocation of his life."[5] In the third plan, "Mme. Olenska, on her side, is weary of their sentimental tête à tête & his scruples, & they finally go back [from Florida, where they have their affair], & the story ends by Mme. Olenska's returning to Europe."[6] In all three prospectuses, Ellen decides she is tired both of Archer and of living in America. She rejects the United States, not the other way around.

In the published novel, Wharton discarded all three plans by having America reject Ellen more than vice versa; and I want to suggest that

3. This manuscript material, available in the Edith Wharton Collection at the Beinecke Library, Yale University, is conveniently summarized and quoted by Alan Price in "The Composition of Edith Wharton's *The Age of Innocence*," *Yale University Library Gazette* 55 (July 1980): 22–30. [See Jennifer Rae Greeson's article, pp. 412–19. Editor.]
4. Ibid., p. 24.
5. Ibid., p. 26.
6. Ibid., p. 27.

both the plans and the finished version, although they conflict, reflect the author's own estrangement from the land of her birth. Wharton left America early in the twentieth century of her own free will, much like the Ellen Olenska of the prospectuses, presumably because she found her native land dull and confining personally and artistically— not unlike James before her and Hemingway after her. In this respect Hawthorne's famous complaint that the United States was too young, too traditionless to foster great art was Wharton's as well; so she left. She did not hate her country or feel aggrieved; she simply needed an older, richer environment in which to live and work. Having spent large portions of her youth in Europe, she settled abroad. This, I think, is the Wharton who planned *The Age of Innocence*, who in three different prospectuses had Ellen leaving America because it was too shallow for her.

Added to this idea of mere discontent in the finished book, however, is the idea that Ellen leaves because she is forced to leave: the idea that the new world, at least in its upper reaches, actively conspires against the woman of intellect and artistic talent. Between the prospectus and the published novel, Wharton changed the fable at the center of *The Age of Innocence*. The plan was to say that the woman artist finds America narrow, confining. But the book goes further and offers another and more profound criticism, namely that America finds the creative woman dangerous *because* she is female and there-fore ostracizes her. In the finished novel, Wharton does not make Ellen simply bored—simply a victim of stultifying upper-class Ameri-can culture; rather, in Ellen's tragedy, she specifically links American contempt for art and the life of the mind to the national fear of female independence. In the remembered America of *The Age of Innocence*— the America of Wharton's "formative" years—May Welland's forays into the world of athletic achievement are applauded while Ellen Olenska's desire to live among artists and writers is met with horror. This is a fundamental split. The realm of Diana, chaste and rule-bound, is open to women. The world of art, dangerously sexual and full of mystery and adult knowledge, is denied. Wharton's America is not the land of liberty when it comes to the woman of artistic and in-tellectual disposition. Ironically, Europe, the "old world," though hardly perfect, offers more freedom.

How accurate this criticism is objectively is debatable. One could point out that Willa Cather and Ellen Glasgow developed and pros-pered at the same time as Wharton and neither expatriated (Glasgow even came from much the same social class as Wharton). One could also point out, though, that Cather's *A Lost Lady*, published just three years after *The Age of Innocence*, wages much the same criticism as Wharton's novel, and Kate Chopin, another white contemporary, clearly did feel censured—indeed exiled—for her art twenty years ear-lier, as did the African American fiction writer Pauline Hopkins. But whatever the large historical truth for women,[7] the subjective truth for

7. American women writers as a group at the turn of the century are the subject of my book *Conflicting Stories: American Writers at the Turn into the Twentieth Century* (New York: Ox-

Edith Wharton in 1920 seems to have been that the woman artist was exiled, banished, from her homeland.

Edith Wharton had no story to rival Ellen's in the remaining decade of her career. The idea that America had rejected the woman artist—expressed in *The Touchstone* but then buried for twenty years—surfaced in her work at the same time that she began to deteriorate as an artist. True, the deterioration is partially explained by the fact that Edith Wharton, born in 1862, was getting old by 1920; also, as I explain at length elsewhere, she was permanently changed by the war, as was America.[8] But added to those facts and raising questions for American women writers in general is the fable of ceremonial death at the heart of *The Age of Innocence*. Ellen's banishment means that the woman artist is despised by ruling-class America. It means that the woman of unusual intellect and talent is rejected, symbolically killed.

The image that opens *The Age of Innocence* perfectly anticipates Wharton's theme. The novel begins with a performance of *Faust*, and it is the soprano Christine Nilsson, not any of the male artists, that Wharton asks us to imagine on stage. We are required to enter the novel with a real woman artist in mind. To reinforce the point, we later watch Wharton's fictional characters attend a production of Boucicault's *The Shaughraun* with Ada Dyas in the female lead. Still later, it is *Romeo and Juliet* with Adelaide Neilson as Juliet. These references to opera and theater serve the obvious purpose of strengthening realism in the novel. Christine Nilsson, Ada Dyas, and Adelaide Neilson did play New York in the 1870s. At the same time, the inclusion of real women who made their living as artists is, in this particular book, revealing. These women are independent. They are not American. Finally (and most complicated), they are actresses—not writers or painters or sculptors. They are women who make their living playing roles. Wharton emphasizes in each case that there is a real woman on stage pretending to be a woman she is not, pretending to be a *naif*. The only women artists valued in *The Age of Innocence* are those who act out—literally—the culture's insistence on feminine innocence. The irony, of course, is that while old New York plots the punishment of Ellen Olenska, it pays to see these other unconventional women masquerade as ingenues. Clearly, magnificent Christine Nilsson playing Marguerite parallels Ellen Olenska trying to "play" May Welland—with the differ-

---

ford University Press, 1992). Also see Ammons, Elizabeth, "Edith Wharton and Race," in *The Cambridge Companion to Edith Wharton*, Millicent Bell, ed. (New York: Cambridge University Press, 1995). [Editor's note: See Cather, p. 381, *n.* 1. Ellen Glasgow: (1873–1945) American-born novelist who set her novels of female struggle amidst the fallen aristocracy of her home state of Virginia. Awarded the Pulitzer prize in 1942, Glasgow's finest work includes her novel *The Sheltered Life* (1932). Kate Chopin: Kate O'Flaherty Chopin (1850–1904), American writer born into a French-speaking home, best known for her tales of Creole life and her celebrated feminist masterpiece, *The Awakening* (1899). Pauline Hopkins: (1859–1930) American-born writer of socially telling and politically resonant fiction who was a significant literary force in her role as editor of *The Colored Magazine* (1900–1904), which provided a major venue for gifted African American writers. In addition to her novel, *Contending Forces: A Romance Illustrative of Negro Life North and South* (1900), Hopkins assured the sales of her magazine by writing three other compelling novels in serial form between 1901 and 1903.]

8. See Ammons, *Edith Wharton's Argument with America* (Athens: University of Georgia Press, 1980), Chs. 6 and 7.

ence that Nilsson, by all accounts, was brilliant at the task. Dressed all in white, she was able to make audiences believe that she was innocent, artless. Ellen Olenska could not. Seen in this light, she is exiled for choosing to identify herself with the artist rather than the role—for making the same inevitably alienating choice that Edith Wharton made. On stage, in the world of make-believe, female passion and feminine innocence might be one. In real life, the two, like Ellen and May in *The Age of Innocence*, were enemies.

## NANCY BENTLEY

## [Realism, Relativism, and the Discipline of Manners]†

\*    \*    \*

Wittgenstein's[1] attention to the production of anthropology through its "tone" invites us to see the history of culture as a history of the discourse of culture. Viewed in this way, we could say that anthropological culture is a variant of fictional realism and that the archives of tribal discipline are not a preserved history but a literature produced by a new imagining of manners.

Culture, as Tylor described it, holds the key to "the remarkable tacit consensus that induces populations to unite in the use of the same language, same religion, and settle to the same general level of art and knowledge." Malinowski dubbed this cohesion the "Mystery of the Social."[2] In *Folkways*, William Graham Sumner insisted that only an impartial scrutiny of the widest range of human customs could yield knowledge about the social.

> When, therefore, the ethnographers apply condemnatory or depreciatory adjectives to the people whom they study, they beg the most important question which we want to investigate; that is, what are standards, codes, and ideas of chastity, decency, propri-

† From *The Ethnography of Manners: Hawthorne, James, Wharton* (New York: Cambridge University Press, 1995), pp. 98–113. Reprinted with permission of Cambridge University Press. Notes have been edited. Bracketed page numbers refer to this edition.
1. Ludwig Wittgenstein (1889–1951), Austrian philosopher noted for his theory concerning the conventional basis of language [Editor].
2. [Editor's note: "Tylor": Sir Edward Burnett Tylor (1832–1917), English anthropologist, noted for his work on primitive religious beliefs. Tylor, *Primitive Culture*, 1:10. "Malinowski": Bronislaw Malinowski (1884–1942), Polish-born English anthropologist, regarded as the founder of the functionalist school of social anthropology.] Malinowski's phrase appears in manuscript materials held at the London School of Economics. George Stocking quotes from the manuscript in his article "Malinowski's Encounter with Freudian Psychoanalysis," in *Malinowski, Rivers, Benedict and Others: Essays on Culture and Personality*, ed. George W. Stocking, Jr. (Madison: University of Wisconsin Press, 1986), pp. 13–49. Introducing the notebook passage, Stocking writes, "His goal—as suggested in some undated early notes toward his never realized theoretical book on kinship—was to solve 'the fundamental Mystery of the Social': 'When we understand how this system [kinship] comes into being, how it imposes the prototype values of future social morals: respect for authority, personal loyalty, subordination of impulses to feelings—when we discover that, we have really answered (in a concrete instance, but one which allows of a simple generalization by extension) the main question: how does society impress its norms on the individual?' "

ety, modesty, etc. and whence do they arise? The ethnographical
facts contain the answer to this question, but in order to reach it
we want a colourless report of the facts.[3]

Here the question of manners and conduct is no longer a matter of
their propriety, or even of their "stage" of civilization. It is rather a
question of social "codes" themselves, what they are and how they
work. Through unbiased global comparison, manners become an objective "report of the facts." Even as the great encyclopedic works like
*The Golden Bough*[4] reached their largest audience (around 1910),
ethnographers began to turn from evolutionary comparisons to more
concrete analyses of particular tribal societies. Increasingly, the object
of ethnographic works in this period was not the reconstruction of a
grand "scale of civilization" but analysis of closely observed and fully
realized rites and manners. This shift brought a heightened realism—
the reporting of actual field observations, attention to detail and
everyday behavior—and at the same time an increased relativism—a
representation of multiple realities born of a universe of multiple cultures. For the ethnographic observer, Malinowski insists, "the culture
of his tribe" must be grasped and presented "as a self-contained reality."[5] The mystery of the social is to be discovered in writing the special realism of culture.

What did it mean at the turn of the century to recognize the "reality" of cultural manners, to scrutinize and record them in books? Nor-
bert Elias[6] notes that the social manners of Western cultures have
long been observed and recorded, from the Renaissance books of
courtesy to etiquette manuals that guided the rise of the middle
classes. A "direct line of tradition" connects such texts to the courtly
portraits of Saint-Simon and the English character writers, and later
to the realist novels of the nineteenth century: all are genres created
out of a keen "lucidity of human observation" and a "capacity to see
people in their entire social context and understand them through it."[7]
Elias shows that the lucidity of observation that fosters realism was itself a tactic for bourgeois advancement, a practical skill for perceiving
and judging nuances of social relations and distinctions crucial for
success in increasingly interdependent societies. The realist novel,
then, is an artifact of what could be called "realist observation," a
practice central to the ascendance of the middle class and necessary
for any individual who wanted to rise. But with the advent of profes-

---

3. William Graham Sumner, *Folkways* (1907; rpt. New York: Arno Press, 1979), p. 418.
4. Influential book by Scottish classicist Sir James George Frazer (1854–1941), which examines parallels between early pagan and Christian folklore and rituals, first published in 1890
   [Editor].
5. Malinowski, *Argonauts of the Western Pacific* (1922; rpt. Prospect Heights, Ill.: Waveland
   Press, 1984), p. lxix. James Boon argues Malinowski introduced literary realism into ethnography. Unlike Frazer's massive collection of rites from all parts of the globe, "Malinowski's
   prose accounts adopt mechanistic models and conventions of space-time isolates that are associated with realist and naturalist novels (and literary theories)." *Other Tribes, Other Scribes*
   (Cambridge: Cambridge University Press, 1982), p. 11.
6. German-born sociologist who fled to England (1897–1990), known for his analyses of the
   construction of civilization through his studies of manners and mores, in particular *The Civ-
   ilizing Process* (1939) [Editor].
7. Elias, *Power and Civilization*, 2:275–6.

sional anthropology, manners had become the special concern of more than just of the socially ambitious and the novelists who chronicled them. Manners were also the business of scientists. Customs and rules of behavior were not merely a canon transmitted to the young but an object of reflection from which to extract rational knowledge about culture. Indeed, for anthropologists and sociologists, the customs and conventionalized wisdom Sumner called "folkways" held the ultimate keys to social power. "The folkways are the widest, most fundamental, and most important operation by which the interests of men in groups are served."[8]

As anthropology was organized into a professional discipline, the realist observation embedded in a field of private social praxis moved into public institutions of knowledge and social administration. A view of culturally constructed self, a *homo habitus*, became an academic truth. John Dewey's axiom that "Man is a creature of habit, not of reason nor yet of instinct" is echoed decades later when Lévi-Strauss remarks that "between the instincts inherited from our genotype and the rules inspired by reason, the mass of unconscious rules remains more important and more effective."[9] At the same time, cultural customs interested makers of public policy. Folkways are "the dominating force in history," Sumner[1] writes, and "a condition as to what can be done, and as to the methods which can be employed." A study of folkways was the necessary groundwork for any systematic regulation of society. The 1878 silver agitation or the "mob gathered in the slums of a great city" could only be understood in a global context that included the rise of Moslem prophets and the power of the Mahdis in Africa. "What is the limit to the possibilities of fanaticism and frenzy which might be produced in any society by agitation skillfully addressed to the fallacies and passions of the masses? The answer lies in the mores."[2] Mediating between mobs and etiquette manuals, the folkways are the basis for establishing a professional "lucidity" of cultural observation.

The realism of James[3] and Wharton, I have argued, is similarly situated at the intersection where private social life becomes the province of institutions of cultural knowledge. * * * It is these minute aspects of manner, rooted in details of speech, clothing, carriage, and taste, that constitute an invisible force keeping "different social strata from mixing."

> Hardly ever can a youth transferred to the society of his betters unlearn the nasality and other vices of speech bred in him by the

---

8. Sumner, *Folkways*, p. 34.
9. John Dewey, American philosopher and educator (1859–1952), best known as the founder of a pragmatic philosophy called instrumentalism [Editor]. Dewey's remarks, from his *Human Nature and Conduct*, are cited in an epigraph to Malinowski's *Sex and Repression in Savage Society* (1927; rpt. Chicago: University of Chicago Press, 1985). Claude Lévi-Strauss, (b. 1908), French anthropologist, founder of structuralist anthropology [Editor]. Claude Lévi-Strauss, "The Anthropologist and the Human Condition," in *The View from Afar*, trans. Joachim Neugroschel (New York: Basic Books, 1985), p. 34.
1. William Graham Sumner (1840–1910), American sociologist and political economist who coined the term "ethnocentrism" [Editor].
2. Sumner, *Folkways*, pp. 36, 38, 52.
3. James: Henry James (1843–1916), expatriate American novelist and man of letters who was also one of Wharton's closest friends [Editor].

association of his growing years. Hardly ever, indeed, no matter how much money there be in his pocket, can he even learn to *dress* like a gentleman-born. The merchants offer their wares as eagerly to him as to the veriest "swell," but he simply cannot buy the right things. An invisible law, as strong as gravitation, keeps him within his orbit, arrayed this year as he was the last; and how his better-bred acquaintances contrive to get the things they wear will be for him a mystery till his dying day.[4]

The rich parvenu who attempts to enter "society," the subject of so many stories by Henry James and Edith Wharton, is here transposed to a social science textbook. As manners enter the discourses of social science, they are analyzed explicitly as signs of a silent network of social power rather than inherent propriety. The "mystery" of clothing and taste, the mute manners of the body, all heed an "invisible law" that governs society and its interlocking orbits. * * *

Edith Wharton's realism is even more clearly articulated through what Ruth Benedict[5] called "culture consciousness" and the institutions that fostered and codified it. As in ethnography, representing a reality of manners for Wharton rests on a principle of relativism, a principle that brings about her own version of a crisis of manners. But the "culture consciousness" in Wharton's fiction, I want to argue, allows her fiction both to critique and to preserve the authority of the turn-of-the-century leadership class, a double strategy that finally serves to accommodate the very changes that the class appeared to oppose. Like Benedict in her essay "The Science of Custom," Wharton presents culture as a "flexible instrument" for "divesting" a society of rigid absolutes while "reinstating and reshaping" the local values that sustain a particular social existence.[6]

To Wharton, scientific knowledge is indispensable for discovering our "inward relation to reality." She immersed herself in what her contemporary Marcel Mauss called "the science of manners." Favorite works included the volumes of Spencer, Frazer's *Golden Bough*, E. A. Westermarck's[7] *History of Primitive Marriage*, and the "remarkable books on tribal life in Melanesia" by Malinowski (whom she came to know socially). Like these authors, however, Wharton had discovered that the reality of manners contains a crucial relativism: the real includes not only material forces and human instincts but the irre-

---

4. William James, *The Principles of Psychology* (1890; rpt. New York: Dover, 1950), 1:121–2. William James (1842–1910) was an American philosopher known for *Principles of Psychology* (1890), *The Varieties of Religious Experience* (1902), and *Pragmatism* (1907). He was the brother of the noted novelist, Henry James [Editor].
5. American anthropologist (1887–1948), whose studies of culture worked against racist constructions inherent in ethnocentrism [Editor].
6. Ruth Benedict, quoted in Margaret M. Caffrey, *Ruth Benedict: Stranger in This Land* (Austin: University of Texas Press, 1989), p. 161; Ruth Benedict, "The Science of Custom: The Bearing of Anthropology on Contemporary Thought," *Century Magazine* 117 (April 1929): 641–9.
7. Marcel Mauss (1872–1950), French sociologist and anthropologist well known for his study of gift-giving customs; Herbert Spencer (1820–1903), English philosopher whose evolutionary arguments greatly influenced Darwin; E. A. Westermarck (1862–1939), Finnish-born and Swedish-educated social anthropologist best known for his three volume study, *The History of Human Marriage* (1889–1891) [Editor].

ducible reality of social forms, a reality that is always both essential and equivocal. For although there is no human life outside of a web of mutual relations ("man is human only because he is socialized," Durkheim[8] writes), still no particular social feature—this form of marriage, that division of labor or gender roles—is in itself either necessary, unalterable, or permanent. Wharton's *Age of Innocence* explores precisely this tension between the real and the conventional—or, in terms that Wharton grafts onto her novel, between nature and culture, the submerged faultline that was also at the heart of anthropological studies.[9]

Interestingly, anthropologists helped to construct the idea of culture in the "wide" sense by calling upon drawing-room manners. In their effort to present tribes as complex, full-bodied societies, anthropologists turned to the domain of Western taste, etiquette, and civility, creating an ironic register of cross-cultural manners. Franz Boas[1] made class etiquette a touchstone for his attempt to frame ethnological questions in terms of cultural history rather than racial capacity. What is "purely traditional," like our rules of modesty or table manners, Boas writes, nevertheless constitutes our whole social and moral equilibrium: "to eat with people having table manners different from our own seems to us decidedly objectionable and causes feelings of displeasure which may rise to such intensity as to cause qualmishness." Our taboo on eating dogs, Boas argues, is no different from the southwestern tribes' taboo on eating fish: "the customary action is the ethical action, a breach of custom is everywhere considered as essentially unethical."[2] Manners here locate the modern sense of relative culture: no longer a monolithic scale with a succession of stages stretching from savagery to civilization, culture is the whole body of local explanations and rules, historically rooted sentiment and feeling, customs, and habits of thought.

"The savage rules of etiquette are not only strict, but formidable," Robert Lowie writes, "nevertheless, to us their table manners are shocking." In ethnography, all manners and rules of custom carry a doubleness; they are simultaneously proper and strange. Lèvi-Strauss, in *Tristes Tropiques*, describes this structure of feeling when he writes that "for the first time in my life, I was on the other side of the equator in the tropics, and, I felt I was in a drawing room."[3] In his

8. Émile Durkheim (1858–1917), French sociologist who is credited (along with Max Weber) with having founded sociology as a discipline [Editor].

9. On Wharton's reading, see R. W. B. Lewis, *Edith Wharton: A Biography* (New York: Fromm, 1985), pp. 56, 108, 230. Wharton's description of Malinowski's work and her comment on the "inward relation to reality" appear in *The Letters of Edith Wharton*, ed. R. W. B. Lewis and Nancy Lewis (New York: Simon & Schuster, 1988), pp. 546, 102. The quotation from Durkheim is taken from Émile Durkheim, *Selected Writings*, trans. Anthony Giddens (Cambridge: Cambridge University Press, 1972), p. 232.

1. German-born anthropologist (1858–1942), who developed and disseminated theories concerning cultural relativism; Boas became the father of anthropology as an academic discipline in the United States [Editor].

2. Franz Boas, "Psychological Problems in Anthropology," in *A Franz Boas Reader*, ed. George W. Stocking (Chicago: University of Chicago Press, 1974), pp. 252–3.

3. Robert Lowie, *Are We Civilized?: Human Culture in Perspective* (New York: Harcourt, Brace, 1929), p. 48; Claude Lévi-Strauss, *Tristes Tropiques*, trans. John Weightman and Doreen Weightman (New York: Atheneum, 1984), p. 85.

*Argonauts of the Western Pacific*, Malinowski mocks the colonial magistrate who, when "asked about the manners and customs of the natives answered, 'Customs none, manners beastly.' " The joke depends on the magistrate's priggish confusion of the category of culture with bourgeois cultivation. But Malinowski's aim is to take this confusion seriously, to show Western readers that the natives possess "excellent manners in the full meaning of this word"—to show, that is, that within the foreign customs of a savage tribe are all the internally differentiating codes that articulate the complex fabric of Trobriand reality: the tacit rules that define propriety for men and women, the value attached to possessions and gifts, the boundaries that separate the ceremonious from everyday life, the internal codes of decorum, prestige, and "glamour."[4]

It is in fact the glamor of the elaborate *kula* gift-exchange system that Malinowski is most concerned to convey and analyze, even as he concedes that *kula* objects are, to European eyes, little more than "greasy trinkets." By drawing upon the disparity within the meaning of manners, Malinowski opens up a new way of representing the real: neither glamorous nor greasy, the *kula* treasures belong to a new "ethnographic reality" that is founded on precisely the difference between the two views. Like fiction writers, Malinowski writes in a space that mediates between the real and the imaginary:

> The objective items of culture, into which belief has crystallized in the form of tradition, myth, spell and rite are the most important source of knowledge. In them, we can face the same realities of belief as the native faces in his intimate intercourse with the magical, the same realities which he not only professes with his tongue, but lives through partly in imagination and partly in actual experience.[5]

Claiming to have discovered the "full meaning" of manners, Malinowski establishes a kind of writing that combines a dimension of cultural strangeness and arbitrariness we perceive in customs not our own with a structure of realism in which those same customs appear inevitable, natural, and necessary, as they do to native inhabitants. "Ideas, feelings, and impulses," Malinowski writes, are "an ethnic peculiarity of the given society."[6] Through relativism, ethnographic realism transforms the most immediate texture of subjectivity into an "ethnic" signature.

By holding itself out as a special realist register of subjectivity, ethnography was poaching on the territory of the novel. Lionel Trilling,[7] in his essay "Manners, Morals and the Novel," described the novel as the leading agent of "moral realism" in the two-hundred-year history of the bourgeois transformation of literature: from Cervantes onward, the novel pursues its "quest for reality" beneath the illusions

4. Malinowski, *Argonauts of the Western Pacific*, p. 156.
5. Ibid., pp. 106, 397.
6. Ibid., p. 22.
7. American literary critic and author (1905–75), especially noted as an essayist [Editor].

generated by "snobbery" and money, with "manners as the indication of the direction of man's soul."[8] Within ethnographic realism, however, a gap opens up between manners and morals: there is no way to read the canons of behavior as moral imperatives, no way to place taste and grace within a universal aesthetics, no measurement of sensibility against an irreducible common sense. Similarly, in Wharton's fiction the novel has become a vehicle of what might be described as a "realism of custom," writing that represents through a fine-grained verisimilitude of social detail a world that is nevertheless relative and ungrounded, while still claiming to uncover and display the essential workings of culture. In their novels both Wharton and James often seem to expose, even to flaunt, a loss of what Trilling calls the genre's accumulated "moral realism"; to many contemporary observers this fact was further proof of an erosion of civilized values. But the loss of a universal moral ground in their fiction, I have argued, is answered and composed in the novels in a way that corresponds closely to the *composure of culture* in social theory: the construction of a culture concept based precisely on a recognition of both the reality and the relativism of different social worlds. To trace this in greater detail, I want to analyze Wharton's *Age of Innocence* for the way it constructs a new realism of culture out of the discovery of ungrounded and competing social realities. Invoked by a crisis of relativism, the novel's culture concept is founded upon "tribal discipline," a class power that is at once tragic (for its own members) and effective (against class outsiders) and finally adaptive (to the new conditions that the discipline of manners is designed to oppose).

Until the arrival of Ellen Olenska, Newland Archer accepts even the most baroque observance and distinction of his circle as a natural, almost "congenital" inheritance (1021) [7].[9] But when he falls in love with Ellen, the New York "tribal" life and its worship of " 'Taste', that far-off divinity," (1026) [10] begin to appear as an archaic formalism, a "parody of life." A gulf opens between the world of social convention and a private, alternative world he calls "reality":

> he had built up within himself a kind of sanctuary in which she throned among his secret thoughts and longings. Little by little it became the scene of his real life, of his only rational activities. . . . Outside it, in the scene of his actual life, he moved with a growing sense of unreality and insufficiency, blundering against familiar prejudices and traditional points of view as an absent-minded man goes on bumping into the furniture of his own room. (1224) [159].

Newland's crisis is a personal and emotional one, of course, but its repercussions have the broadest possible social range. His illicit desire triggers an estrangement at the level of the smallest details of social life and spreads into the very "structure of his universe" (1097) [64].

8. Cervantes: Miguel de Cervantes (1547–1616), Spanish author of the picaresque novel, *Don Quixote* (1607–1615) [Editor]. Trilling, "Manners, Morals, and the Novel," p. 212.
9. References to *Age of Innocence* are indicated by page numbers in brackets in the text.

As the larger contours of the novel make clear, Newland's sense of "unreality" dramatizes the forces of dislocation pressuring a whole social group. The Archer family, for instance, feels keenly the changes in New York society, vigilantly tracing "each new crack in its surface" (1210) [155]. The novel provides hints about the sources of the ruptures—new technologies, a changing cityscape, novel ideas about woman and marriage, the perception of "a country in possession of the bosses and the emigrant" (1115) [79]. The characters themselves, however, say almost nothing about these large-scale changes. Instead, they focus on small, discrete adjustments in their own social habits, a slight increase in "extravagance" of dress or a shift in the customary round of leisure entertainments.

For the reigning clans of Old New York, though, change and heterogeneity do not prompt a perceived erosion of reality as they do for Newland. Instead, change is understood as a threatening challenge to universal standards of propriety and taste. What is more, the elders absorb the very marks of change into their patterns of social ritual: without fail, Mrs. Archer will ceremoniously "enumerate the minute signs of disintegration" during the mid-October "household ritual" (1219) [155] of assembling the proper carpets and curtains. Like the rector's jeremiad, delivered every year in his Thanksgiving sermon, Mrs. Archer's laments about social decline become part of the linked institutions that actually foster continuity and strength for her social circle. On one side, therefore, even the effects of a crisis in manners becomes a process by which New York "managed its transitions" (1222) [157]. Social energies marshaled under the banner of "disintegration" help to convert the very arbitrariness of manners into a continuing source of meaning and cohesion.

On another side, however, exposing the contingency of culture produces a different kind of energy, a restlessness represented by Newland's agitated sense of "unreality." For Newland, we have seen, manners are no longer a matter of natural decorum. Performing the round of social calls expected of a fiancé, he feels "trapped" as they "rolled from one tribal doorstep to another" and wonders if "his readings in anthropology caused him to take such a coarse view of what was after all a simple and natural demonstration of family feeling" (1069–70) [43]. Here anthropological allusions make vivid Newland's sense of estrangement: what was natural is now hollow, even coercive. Newland seems to be directly at odds with his family on the question of social "form" and manners. Through ritual repetition, the Archers and their circle confirm their customs as a "natural demonstration" of feeling, while for Newland repetition serves to empty those customs of any inherent meaning. The novel stages a clash between two versions of culture, between drawing-room culture ("decent people had to fall back on sport or culture" [1115] [79], in one of the Old New York axioms) and anthropological culture (Tylor's "culture in the wide ethnographic sense"). The conflict is between manners as inherent values of propriety and manners as local forms of human society. But although these paradigms are at odds, the conflict actually belongs to the novel's larger solution to the problem of social change. By displaying the tension, Wharton makes visible the particular "crisis of cultural authority" among the educated classes. Yet the tension itself, as we will see, is put into the service of cultural continuity. By illuminating the difference between absolute and relative manners, the novel provides for a heightened "culture consciousness" that finally serves to revitalize the world of the Archers and the social power of their kin and kind.

What is real in the novel becomes intelligible precisely through a dialectic of the traditional and the personal, the arbitrary and the actual. And the medium for this dialectic is custom, the locally rooted but contingent forms that can be disowned or disobeyed but never transcended. When Newland Archer calls his very real passion for Ellen the "only reality," Ellen confronts him with the reality of bourgeois kinship: "Is it your idea, then, that I should live with you as your mistress—since I can't be your wife?" Newland's answer resists these social classifications: "I want somehow to get away with you into a world where words like that—categories like that—won't exist" (1245) [174]. But Ellen's reply, "Where is that country? Have you ever been there?" returns the novel to its foundation in the cultural—the variable but irreducible categories of countries, classes, regions, and urban castes. Ellen's response acknowledges both their mutual desire and their mutual relation to New York kinship (we are "Newland Archer, the husband of Ellen Olenska's cousin," she recounts for him, "and Ellen Olenska, the cousin of Newland Archer's wife"), and the novel's poignancy comes from the inevitable tension between the unassimilable realities of kinship and illicit passion. Wharton thus uses a love story to install a certain space of culture, the same space Malinowski represents in the Trobriands, where an ethnographic reality emerges out of "the power of tribal law, and of the passions which work against and in spite of these."[1]

Wharton underscores this double structure of culture, at once conventional and actual, in the scene that places Newland and Ellen within the "queer wilderness of cast-iron and encaustic tiles known as the Metropolitan Museum," in front of the glass cases housing the "Cesnola antiquities" (1261) [185]. As the lovers struggle with a painful recognition of the real force of New York kinship taboos, Wharton balances the scene's emotion with a cooler, detached view of culture itself, represented by the fragments of a now-vanished ancient community. "It's glass shelves were crowded with small broken objects—hardly recognizable domestic utensils, ornaments and personal trifles—made of glass, of clay, of discoloured bronze and other time-blurred substances" (1262) [185]. Gazing on the display, Ellen points to the tension that Wharton has built into the novel as a whole, noting that these reified, frozen pieces of an exotic world carry a life and meaning now inaccessible but once as real as her own: "these little things, that used to be necessary and important to forgotten people,

---

1. Malinowski, *Sexual Lives of Savages* (1929; rpt. Boston: Beacon Press, 1987), p. 13.

and now have to be guessed at under a magnifying glass and labelled: 'Use unknown.' " While Ellen dwells on the historical contingency of experience, Archer returns the dialectic to its opposite pole of immediacy—"Meanwhile everything matters"—though this declaration is ultimately framed by a "vista of mummies and sarcophagi" (1263) [186], another reminder of the mutability of cultures and their customs. Shifting rapidly between the two perspectives, Wharton creates a wider consciousness of culture out of the reader's heightened sense of the difference. By juxtaposing the exotic and the immediate, Wharton turns the "unreality" of the New York scene into the permanence of culture, converting the drawing-room crisis into the authority of the museum. The "queer wilderness" of the Metropolitan Museum becomes the field for securing the real. It is precisely the decentered nature of museum culture, its relativism of customs and manners, that recovers reality and authenticity.

Examining the "strange organized disorder" of museums, Paul Valéry[2] would critique that authority in an essay, published one year after *The Age of Innocence*, entitled "The Problem of the Museum." But Valéry's very challenge illuminates both the logic and the strength of the culture concept that had begun its ascendancy during the years of Wharton's story (proleptically, Wharton has Newland inscribe the dominant authority of museums like the Metropolitan: "Some day, I suppose, it will be a great Museum"). Valéry complained of the "abuse of space known as the collection," a disorder created in museums by the radically decontextualized objects reassembled and competing for attention in the same rooms. But the process of collection and display that Valéry calls "abuse" had been established as the most powerful means to sanction cultural value and authenticity, and his attack is in part a reflection of the now-dominant authority of the museum model, which had been extended from art and antiquities to ethnographic collections. The logic of the museum collection is based precisely on an "organized disorder," on a coordination of disjunctions and juxtapositions—objects from vastly different worlds—that by their very disparateness are made witnesses to a larger continuity: the wholeness of art, and the authenticity of culture, broadly conceived.[3] A similar logic governs Wharton's fiction, ordering the textual juxtaposition of "Old New York" with prehistoric antiquities and tribal metaphors. Taken together, the very gaps and discrepancies between utterly different social worlds produce a coherent discursive space unified under the concept of "culture."

Writing of the social function of museums in this era, Philip Fisher

2. Distinguished French poet and man of letters, (1871–1945) [Editor].
3. Valéry quoted in Philip Fisher, *Making and Effacing Art: Modern American Art in a Culture of Museums* (New York: Oxford University Press, 1991), pp. 10–11. I have drawn from Fisher's discussion of the authenticity invested in museum objects from "alien societal, religious, and artistic communities" (p. 20). Alan Trachtenberg discusses the establishment of American museums during this period in *The Incorporation of America: Culture and Society in the Gilded Age* (New York: Hill & Wang, 1982). On the socializing function of museums as "civic temples," see Pierre Bourdieu, "Artistic Taste and Cultural Capital," in *Culture and Society: Contemporary Debates*, ed. Jeffrey C. Alexander and Steven Seidman (Cambridge: Cambridge University Press, 1990), pp. 205–15.

analyzes the new role of the museum in creating authenticity for societies now fully committed to industrial mass production. In the age of factories, "the British Museum in London and the Metropolitan Museum in New York represent a new kind of institution. No longer do they provide a visible history of the culture itself: that is, a display of objects rich with symbolic, local significance. Instead they are storage areas for authenticity and uniqueness per se, for objects from any culture or period whatever that were said to be irreplaceable."[4] It is not just the choice of the Metropolitan as a setting in *The Age of Innocence*, then, that links Wharton's fiction to the new institution of the museum. Wharton shares the assumptions that made modern museums possible, assumptions that the authentic and the real are in some sense precarious, in need of preservation, and that they reveal their purest meaning in the form of collections and the apparatus of archival representation. "The compact world of my youth has receded into a past from which it can only be dug up in bits by the assiduous relic-hunter," Wharton writes in *A Backward Glance*, "and its smallest fragments begin to be worth collecting and putting together before the last of those who knew the live structure are swept away with it."[5] Here culture is that which is "worth collecting." Conceived as "relics" and "fragments," the past is reassembled according to new dual principles of "worth": cultural wholeness, and cultural extinction—on the one hand a comprehensive "live structure" analogous to Tylor's definition of culture as a "complex whole" and, on the other, the imminent loss of that living whole.

Collected and displayed as "relics," the manners of the New York circle in *The Age of Innocence* are vested with a rich realism even as they signify what Malinowski calls an "ethnic peculiarity." But the novel also asserts that the "real" is held in place by subtle yet highly effective techniques of social force. The plot of *The Age of Innocence* shows that the very boundaries that determine cultural identity and meaning are silently—and in times of crisis, actively—policed. Had the plot line allowed Archer and Ellen to escape the claims of kinship, the narrative would have swerved from its terms of realism into romance, the utopia of a "country" without cultural categories—the husband, the wife, the mistress. Keeping the realist plot in place, however, requires every resource of the families' "tribal discipline," not only the ritual sacrifice of Ellen but the imprisonment and surveillance of Archer.

May's elaborate dinner party, the narrator says, is a "tribal rally around a kinswoman about to be eliminated from the tribe" (1281) [200]. As Ellen is ceremoniously expelled, Archer realizes that he is also being subjected to the same forces that Pierre Bourdieu has called the "symbolic or euphemized violence" of custom.[6] Dinner con-

4. Fisher, *Making and Effacing Art*, p. 29.
5. Edith Wharton, *A Backward Glance*, in *Edith Wharton: Novellas and Other Writings*, ed. Cynthia Griffin Wolff (New York: Library of America, 1990), p. 781.
6. [Editor's note: Pierre Bourdieu (1930– ), French anthropologist and sociologist, known primarily as a cultural theorist concerned with value and cultural production, in particular the concept of "cultural capital".] "Symbolic violence is that form of domination which, transcending the opposition usually drawn between sense relations and power relations, communication and domination, is only exerted *through* the communication in which it is disguised." Bourdieu, *Outline of a Theory of Practice*, p. 237.

versation dwells on the recently exiled Beauforts, cast out for a financial scandal, and by the "inexorableness" of its tone Archer knows the discussion is a collective threat issued to him: " 'It's to show me,' he thought, 'what would happen to me—' " (1282) [201]. The family has issued what anthropologists in their fondness for classifying species of magic termed a "conditional curse," a protective spell that calls down in advance the punishment that will befall anyone who transgresses it. Like Wharton, Malinowski presents conditional curses as part of an implicit legal structure that serves to enforce the tribal code. Where Western law requires separate institutions of courts and prisons, Malinowski sees tribal law is part of an entire "social machinery of binding force."[7] Archer realizes that the unspoken ceremony enacted at the dinner is merely the culmination of forces of daily, ongoing tribal regulation: "He guessed himself to have been, for months, the centre of countless silently observing eyes and patiently listening ears, he understood that, by means as yet unknown to him, the separation between himself and the partner of his guilt had been achieved, and that now the whole tribe had rallied about his wife on the tacit assumption that nobody knew anything" (1282) [200]. As Bourdieu notes of euphemized violence, its power lies in the collective denial that any coercion is taking place, making direct resistance inappropriate or even absurd. Archer knows that the conspiracy to ignore the crime, a "tissue of elaborate mutual dissimulation" (1285) [203], is the family's most effective way of subduing him. He eats Florida asparagus and smokes with the men in the drawing room, but by these very acts knows he is a "prisoner in the centre of an armed camp" (1282) [201].

By presenting the silent punishment enacted through the conventions of a dinner party, Wharton addresses what Malinowski singled out as one of the "riddles of Culture" that most intrigued anthropologists: the power of tribal discipline. Once the myth of the wild savage was dismissed and "it became plain that hypertrophy of rules rather than lawlessness is characteristic of primitive life," the savage came to represent "a model of the law-abiding citizen." As Malinowski wryly notes, this did not prevent ethnologists from being drawn to sensational cases of "blood-curdling crime, followed by tribal vendetta, in accounts of criminal sorcery with retaliation, of incest, adultery, breach of taboo or murder." But such acts of violent retribution were now seen as contributing to a "transcending solidarity of the kindred group." (Malinowski himself was at pains to disprove the notion of a "mysterious 'group-sentiment' " that he imputed to Rivers,[8] Durkheim, and others, but he too saw in tribal life remarkable "forces of cohesion.")[9] Wharton borrows from this literature of savage crime and ceremonial discipline to represent acts of power inherent in the genteel

7. Malinowski, *Crime and Custom in Savage Society*, p. 55. Malinowski discusses conditional curses in chapter 12, "Specific Legal Arrangements," pp. 60–2, and in *Sexual Lives*, chapter 11, "The Magic of Love and Beauty," pp. 290–318.
8. W. H. R. Rivers (1864–1922), British anthropologist, psychologist, and psychiatrist considered to be a pioneer in what came to be known as "the talking cure" as he worked with the physically and psychically damaged soldiers who fought in World War I [Editor].
9. Malinowski, *Crime and Custom in Savage Society*, pp. 72, 9, 73, 11.

decorum of New York society. The anthropological perspective not only accepts the fundamental reality of custom, it also perceives custom as an active always-present web of force. This represents a considerable transformation of the traditional novel of manners. Although the genre had always recognized the pressures of social and sexual politics, it rarely if ever pictured those pressures as a machinery of punishment and coercion. Retaining the drawing-room settings and the portraits of sensibility of a Jane Austen novel, Wharton adds a subtext of crime, surveillance, and punishment more likely in a Dostoyevsky novel, or, more to the point, in a work like Malinowski's *Crime and Custom in Savage Society.*

Although duplicitous, May's dinner is a ceremony of "rehabilitation and obliteration," carried out in much the same way as the Trobrianders' "magic of oblivion," ritual spells that restore marital happiness after the wounds of adultery. For Malinowski, what is real in a "fetching back" rite is its effectiveness: "This formula is said to be very powerful, and to have restored married happiness to scores of broken households."[1] The same is true of the New Yorkers' willful denial of the love affair: what matters is not the denial's falsity but its power. By resolving the novel as she does, Wharton completes the work of "obliteration." After the climactic sacrifice, Ellen Olenska is never again seen or heard from in the narrative. Even after thirty years of social change and moderation, the ritual act holds: when Newland gazes at Ellen's Paris house in the book's final scene, unexplained forces keep him from crossing the threshold. The magic of the Welland's "fetching back" rite is as strong as ever.

Once manners are recast as performative ritual rather than a measurable propriety, the novel has transformed an analysis of moral meaning into an anatomy of social power. Questions of social discipline, of course, have always been implicit in the novel of manners. But by detaching manners from any definitive set of moral imperatives and binding them to a complex machinery of decorous force, Wharton's realism comes to match the vision of contemporary social theorists, who saw manners not as immanent values but as a permeating "system," like trade or law or government. The result, for James as well as Wharton, is the creation of an "extraordinary discourse" to register perceived ruptures in the substance of ordinary social life. But if descriptions of drawing-room sacrifice and other civilized blood sports bespeak cultural disruption, we should see in the same language a discourse of mastery—not only the intellectual mastery of "laws of culture," but a language of social mastery "discovered" in tribal life itself. The novelists are members of the "body of specialists" Bourdieu describes as necessary in times of cognitive crisis, experts charged with formulating in new kinds of discourse all of the practices and beliefs that were once accepted as natural and unremarkable phenomena, and thereby transforming them into objects of a new cognitive mastery.

---

1. Malinowski, *Sexual Lives of Savages,* p. 323.

Thus if rewriting the novel of manners is an act of preservation directed against the threat of an exhausted tradition and a menacing modernity, it is an act that renews the genre for the world it appears to resist, sharing and circulating through the institution of fiction the authority of modern institutions—museums, social sciences, popular discourses of primitivism.[2] *The Age of Innocence* displays the paradoxical modernity that could issue from the "relics" of culture. Archer's ultimate surrender to the tribal ways brings a restored sense of reality, yet at the same time it provides the basis for a transition to a modern society of technology and a liberal hegemony. Ellen's expulsion, at once a stunning tribal sacrifice and a tribal "victory," is the emotional center of the novel; Wharton's aesthetic energies have their most brilliant play in this scene, perfectly harmonizing drawing-room and ethnographic manners. But it is the novel's final chapter, set twenty-six years later in Paris, that reveals the full implications of Wharton's realism. In modern Paris, Newland himself is now a relic ("Don't be prehistoric!" his son tells him). But it is precisely as an antiquarian object that Newland achieves a poignant sense of reality, though a reality now recognized as customary, fragile, and in need of preservation. Newland finds himself unable to cross the threshold to Ellen's apartment: " 'It's more real to me here than if I went up,' he suddenly heard himself say; and the fear lest that last shadow of reality should lose its edge kept him rooted to his seat as the minutes succeeded each other" (1302) [217].

The moment is preserved in museumlike stillness. But with a precious reality "rooted" with Archer in this scene, the chapter also embraces the opposing forces of modernity that had produced the extinction of Old New York. Telephones and electric lighting, Roosevelt's politics, and rapid overseas travel have been integrated into the life of the next generation of leading New Yorkers. Even more importantly, the taboos against exogamous marriage to the sons and daughters of business and politics have been lifted. Now society is a "huge kaleidoscope where all the social atoms spun around on the same plane" (1296) [211], but the disorder is an energy harnessed by Archer's children. Wharton's portrait of a class that in fact retained and strengthened its claim to power and wealth through the tumultuous social changes of fin-de-siècle America is demographically correct. In spite of a pervasive sense of WASP[3] decline—indeed, in part through that very sense—the northeastern elite expanded its social influence and helped to acculturate the American polity to a new society of consumption and corporate capitalism. Newland Archer's story is a story of culture consciousness and the new social life it produced in the name of cultural preservation.

2. Though I do not classify James and Wharton unreservedly with Lears's antimodernists, I do claim that the enterprise of writing about manners as they practiced it was revitalized and redefined for a modern order that both writers faced with real reservations. Lears argues that "American antimodernism unknowingly provided part of the psychological foundation for a streamlined liberal culture appropriate to twentieth-century consumer capitalism." Jackson Lears, *No Place of Grace* (New York: Pantheon, 1981), p. 6.
3. Popular twentieth-century acronym standing for "White Anglo-Saxon Protestant" [Editor].

# ANNE MACMASTER

## Wharton, Race, and *The Age of Innocence*: Three Historical Contexts†

*The Age of Innocence*, manifestly about a narrow slice of American society at a particular moment in history, the swan song of that would-be aristocracy called Old New York, actually registers the central crux of American identity. Wharton's novel maps a paradox located at the intersection of several ironies: the history of slavery in the land of the free, the fear of the foreign in a nation of immigrants, the drive toward conformity behind the creed of individualism. Racial difference is a latent topic in *The Age of Innocence*, a topic at first invisible beside the obvious topic of Old New York, but—once discovered—never far from the narrative's central concerns. At work in this novel we find what Toni Morrison in *Playing in the Dark* identifies as "American Africanism" or the "Africanist presence" in American literature.[1] With the phrase "Africanist presence," Morrison refers to those black characters created by white writers who thus embody the "blackness that African peoples have come to signify" in the European-American imagination (*Dark*, 6). Rather than presenting the views of African-Americans, such characters "enable white writers to think about themselves" (*Dark*, 51). Through the use of such characters of color, Wharton expresses her main characters' rebellions, fantasies, and displays of power. Her use of dark characters both records and questions the construction of whiteness at her own cultural moment.[2]

Before turning to the Africanist presence in *The Age of Innocence*, however, I want to set the novel within the contexts in which it was produced: the intersection, that is, between Wharton's life and the history of race relations in America and France between 1870 and 1920. Three historical moments matter to *The Age of Innocence*, two in which its action occurs and another in which the novel was written. In the first of these three periods, which Wharton calls "the age of innocence," the body of the story takes place; in the mid 1870s, the young Newland Archer attempts to choose between his duty to May Welland and his desire for Ellen Olenska. In Wharton's life, the 1870s

---

† From *A Forward Glance: New Essays on Edith Wharton*, eds. Clare Colquitt, Susan Goodman, and Candace Waid (Newark: University of Delaware Press, 1999), pp. 188–205. Reprinted with permission of Associated University Presses.

1. [Editor's note: Toni Morrison: (b. 1931), American-born writer known for her haunting novels that bring together specters of race, desire, and human longing. A distinguished literary figure, whose works such as *Song of Solomon* (1977) and *Beloved* (1987) join the historical with the profoundly spiritual, Morrison in 1993 became the first African American to win the Nobel Prize.] Toni Morrison, *Playing in the Dark: Whiteness and the Literary Imagination* (Cambridge: Harvard University Press, 1992). References to this work are hereafter cited in the text with the abbreviation *Dark* and the page number in parentheses.

2. For a different but not opposing approach to ethnicity in Wharton's works, see Nancy Bentley's *The Ethnography of Manners: Hawthorne, James, Wharton* (New York: Cambridge University Press, 1995). In addition to the sections on Wharton, Bentley's second chapter, "Nathaniel Hawthorne and the Fetish of Race," is relevant to my approach to *The Age of Innocence* (24–67).

constitute the decade in which Edith Newbold Jones moved through childhood and adolescence to come of age in the style of Old New York. But while the young Edith lived in New York, Newport, and Europe, her view remained limited. Exposed to various national cultures in Europe, Wharton knew only the uppermost strata of her native New York. While in New York, Wharton's associations were only with "that tiny fraction of the city" that "extended along Fifth Avenue from Washington Square to 'the' Central Park";[3] meanwhile, in other parts of the city, waves of immigrants from abroad and blacks from the South arrived to change the city's racial dynamics. It is unlikely that these changes registered much on young Edith's consciousness, even though her family employed a black cook and coachman and a number of Irish servants, and even though her friend Emmeline Washburn explored various portions of the city, observing street life and speaking to all kinds of people.[4] According to R. W. B. Lewis, of the other New Yorks beyond Wharton's narrow strip, the sheltered debutante caught no more than "a fleeting glimpse" (22).

Such "innocence" was no longer possible a quarter-century later in the period of increased immigration that constitutes the second of the novel's three contexts. The novel's coda is set around the turn of the century: Newland Archer, now fifty-seven years old, looks back on his renunciation of Ellen and its consequences for his life, only to renounce her again. In Wharton's own life at the same time, the society matron broke out of her inherited role to transform herself into a professional novelist. Circulating between New York, her country home in the Berkshires, and Europe, Wharton gradually established France as her permanent home yet maintained her American identity. While Wharton came into her powers as a woman and a novelist, New York City's immigrant and African-American populations burgeoned, and across the nation white insecurities flared up in race riots, lynchings, and eugenics societies. At the end of "the age of innocence," a shift also occurred in the origin of the immigrants from abroad; around 1880, immigrants from Southern and Eastern (rather than Northern) Europe began to arrive in New York. A sharp increase in immigration since the 1870s and an economic downturn in the 1890s fueled a growing anti-immigrant sentiment among white native-born Americans.

By the close of the century, American notions of race were reconstructed to reflect new hostilities. According to Susan S. Lanser, "the common nineteenth-century belief in three races—black, white, yellow—each linked to a specific continent, was reconstituted so that 'white' came to mean only 'Nordic' or Northern European, while 'yellow' applied not only to the Chinese, Japanese, and light-skinned African Americans but also to Jews, Poles, Hungarians, Italians, and

3. R. W. B. Lewis, *Edith Wharton: A Biography* (1975; New York: Harper Colophon Books, 1987), 21. References to Lewis's work are hereafter cited in the text with the author's last name and page number in parentheses.
4. Shari Benstock, *No Gifts from Chance: A Biography of Edith Wharton* (New York: Scribner's, 1994), 3, 34.

even the Irish. Crusaders warned of 'yellow inundation.' "[5] In this cli-mate, in the first decade of the new century, Wharton's career took off just as her social acquaintance with Theodore Roosevelt deepened into friendship. Roosevelt not only was Wharton's friend, but also a fellow member of her "set" and a distant relative by marriage.[6] As pres-ident, Roosevelt urged women of the "proper sort" to abjure birth con-trol lest America lose its national identity. In 1905, the same year that Wharton lunched at the White House with Roosevelt (Lewis, 6), her distinguished lunch companion ended one public speech by intoning, "race purity must be maintained." The following year, in his State of the Union Address, Roosevelt warned against "willful sterility"—the practice of birth control by middle-class whites—"the one sin for which the penalty is national death, race suicide."[7] When Wharton has New-land Archer, at the age of fifty-seven, weigh his gains against his losses, she throws into the balance her character's friendship with Roosevelt: Although Newland is grateful to have had "one great man's friendship to be his strength and pride," he also perceives, "[s]omething he knew he had missed: the flower of life" [207, 208].[8] Set in the era of Roo-sevelt's presidency, the coda of *The Age of Innocence* both condemns and mourns the loss of a vanished social order.

The third historical moment relevant to *The Age of Innocence* con-sists of those years during and right after World War I when the novel was conceived, written, and published. During the war, Wharton was mostly in Paris, witnessing the general upheaval, organizing relief for refugees, and at long last welcoming American troops. Soon after the war's end, she began to write *The Age of Innocence*, and within a year, the novel was complete. In the United States during the same years, race relations changed forever. In New York City, the war years created plentiful employment for black men and marked the start of the African-American move uptown to Harlem.[9] At the same time, African-American men in the military received decent treatment from the French and encountered from the U.S. military a variety of official and unofficial forms of discrimination based on race. African-American vet-

5. Susan S. Lanser, "Feminist Criticism, 'The Yellow Wallpaper,' and the Politics of Color in America," *Feminist Studies* 15, no. 3 (fall 1989): 415–41. For connections between African peoples and the Irish "race," whom British imperialists labeled "white Negroes," see Vincent J. Cheng, *Joyce, Race, and Empire* (Cambridge: Cambridge University Press, 1995). Cheng refers the reader to several historians and theorists of "race."
6. On Wharton's relation to Roosevelt, R. W. B. Lewis reports, "Within the community of cousins to which she belonged, Edith was distantly related to the second Mrs. Roosevelt, the former Edith Carow" (112).
7. Quoted in Angela Y. Davis, *Women, Race, and Class* (New York: Vintage Books, 1983), 209. All the phrases I quote from Roosevelt's speeches are cited by Davis except the phrase "the proper sort," which appears in Jane Sherron DeHart and Linda K. Kerber, *Women's America: Refocusing the Past* (New York: Oxford University Press, 1991), 340. Davis cites Melvin Steinfeld, *Our Racist Presidents* (San Ramon, Calif.: Consensus Publishers, 1972), 212; and Bonnie Mass, *Population Target: The Political Economy of Population Control in Latin Amer-ica* (Toronto, Canada: Women's Educational Press, 1977), 20. De Hart and Kerber do not cite the sources of their quotations from Roosevelt.
8. Edith Wharton, *The Age of Innocence* (New York: Macmillan, 1986), 346, 347 [207, 208]. All further references to this work are cited in the text with the abbreviation *Age* in paren-theses. Bracketed page references refer to this volume.
9. See John Hope Franklin and Alfred A. Moss, *From Slavery to Freedom: A History of African Americans*, 7th ed. (New York: McGraw Hill, 1994), 323–60.

erans, on their return from France, confronted heightened discrimination that they met with a new spirit of resistance. During the summer of 1919, while Wharton was at work in France on a novel about a more innocent age in an American city, "race riots transformed twenty-six U.S. cities into war zones, where black citizens, many still in uniform, were lynched with impunity and their homes were burned because they dared to organize to demand job opportunities."[1]

In New York City itself, African-American troops were initially welcomed home by large crowds, but their situation rapidly worsened as many whites blamed rising unemployment on the city's expanding black population. Even without major riots, New York City itself arguably underwent greater changes in race relations than any other U.S. city during 1919 and 1920. According to historians Moss and Franklin, it was the new prosperity of Harlem that made New York the site from which African-Americans voiced "their most eloquent demands for equality during and after World War I."[2]

By 1919, it must have been harder than it was at the turn of the century, even for someone of Wharton's class living abroad, to see New York and its dramas as contained within the area along Fifth Avenue from Washington Square to Central Park. In 1919, it would have been difficult to avoid the American implications of race, even in a novel set in earlier ages, even for a writer who could assume the "Americanness" of her own ethnicity. To view The Age of Innocence as a novel about race in the United States is not to diminish its focus on the disillusion with European civilization brought on by the Great War; it is rather to set the national context within the international one. Wharton's novel captures the inseparability for Americans of the social changes brought about by the Great War which led to the stirrings of a civil rights movement.

In The Age of Innocence, Wharton addresses her class's anxieties about race after World War I not only by contrasting two earlier time periods—the 1870s and the century's turn—but also by making racial doubling into a narrative strategy. Race enters the novel through Ellen Olenska's status as the novel's dark heroine. In her characteristic style, Wharton subverts the convention of paired heroines by making May Welland, the fair heroine, turn out again and again to be more knowing than Newland realizes, and Ellen, the dark heroine, to be more naive, vulnerable, and moral than Newland expects. Still, May remains the fair heroine and Ellen the dark, each according to her respective devotion to or defiance of convention, and Wharton emphasizes this polarity through the heroines' contrasting colorings. Repeatedly, Wharton poses Ellen's tight brown curls and dusky cheeks against May's fair hair, blue eyes, and skin as white as marble. Ellen, true to her nature as a dark heroine, rebels from her social role and sees through its conventions. Her vision sets her apart from all the other Society women except her grandmother, Catherine Mingott.

1. Blanche Wiesen Cook, *Eleanor Roosevelt: 1884–1933*, vol. 1 (New York: Penguin, 1992), 251.
2. Franklin and Moss, *From Slavery to Freedom*, 364.

And it is here, in this connection between Ellen and Catherine, that the Africanist presence enters the novel.

Ellen and Catherine, the only two unconventional women in this society, are the only New Yorkers who eagerly employ dark-skinned servants. Ellen, who is herself described as a "dark lady," travels with an Italian maid named Nastasia who is "swarthy," "foreign-looking," and, for Newland, "vaguely . . . Sicilian" (*Age*, 68) [77, 44]; Catherine relies upon "the mulatto maid," a character who, although not even honored with a name, asserts a conspicuous presence in Catherine's house and Newland's consciousness (*Age*, 271) [179]. Other members of Society, by contrast, employ dark-skinned servants only with the greatest displeasure. May's parents, wintering in Florida, view the hiring of black servants as one of the "insuperable difficulties" of "rough[ing] it" in a fashionable Southern resort (*Age*, 142) [89]. In the houses of Catherine and Ellen, on the other hand, swarthy maids not only serve, but seem to preside, embodying the spirits of these unconventional households. Each servant, as gatekeeper to her mistress's private rooms and uncanny abettor of her designs, braces her mistress's stand against convention.

Ellen, Catherine, and their servants fit into a configuration of characters that associates the dark heroine with women of color and aligns darkness (or color) with resistance to conformity, with passion, courage, and vitality. In the darker toned minor characters of this novel—the mulatto maid, the swarthy Nastasia, the anonymous black man for whom the intellectual Sillertons throw a party (*Age*, 220) [135]—we have instances of what Morrison calls "the strategic use of black characters to define the goals and enhance the qualities of white characters" (*Dark*, 52–53). In *The Age of Innocence*, the presence of the darker servants not only marks the defiance of the central female characters, but also reveals the desires and fears of the major male characters and, by extension, of the dominant culture. Newland Archer, Julius Beaufort, Larry Lefferts, and the rest of "masculine New York" find the dark Ellen more desirable (and less marriageable) than the fair May (*Age*, 11) [87]. In the context of Ellen's associations with Nastasia and the mulatto maid, this sexual preference for Ellen is implicated in certain American myths of race and realities of privilege and oppression. In the myths, white male culture projects its own lusts onto the black woman's body, exaggerating the black woman's sexuality while downplaying that of the white woman in some misguided pursuit of racial or sexual purity.[3]

In such a scheme, white women become associated with marriage, with legitimate offspring, with Theodore Roosevelt's cry that "race purity must be maintained." Making an appropriate match assures one's position in the tribe and fortifies the tribe's position in America. Engaged to May, Newland desires Ellen. He oscillates between wanting to escape his ties to May and "thank[ing] heaven that he was . . . to

---

3. For a discussion of this trend, see Ann DuCille, *The Coupling Convention: Sex, Text, and Tradition in Black Women's Fiction* (New York: Oxford University Press, 1993), 72–74, 85.

ally himself with one of his own kind" (*Age*, 31) [21]. In its immediate context, "his own kind" means someone of the same social "set" (*Age*, 31) [21]; in the context of the chapter that it concludes, however, the phrase might just as well mean someone of the same skin tone. In this chapter, which places repeated emphasis on the whiteness of skin, Catherine tellingly albeit inadvertently links marriage with color (as well as with class) when, admiring May's engagement ring, she comments: "Her hand is large . . . but the skin is white.—And when's the wedding to be?" (*Age*, 29) [19]. Ellen Olenska, whom Newland is glad not to be marrying even though he desires her more than he desires May, has "foreign" ways, "dusky" skin, and calls to mind "the bold brown Ellen Mingott of his boyhood" (*Age*, 59, 64, 31) [[26], 38, 21]. Ellen's darkness aligns her with Nastasia, the mulatto, and a series of dark-skinned and colorfully dressed women who seem to constitute, from the perspective of "masculine New York," a fantasy of extramarital sex. In this scheme, the class difference between the women men marry and the women men enjoy sexually outside of marriage is highlighted by a difference in pigmentation.

The tones of Ellen's skin and hair and the shades of her clothing thus connect her with an array of vividly garbed and darkly hued women. Recalling the mulatto in her "bright turban" and Nastasia in her "gay neckerchief," Ellen is associated with gypsies, Neapolitans, and the "beautiful Spanish dancer" with whom her great grandfather disappeared to Cuba (*Age*, 214, 68, 10) [131, 44, 8]. These associations have their origins in Ellen's first appearance in New York as an orphan with "an air of gaiety that seemed unsuitable in a child who should still have been in black for her parents. . . . [Instead of mourning], Ellen was in crimson merino and amber beads, like a gipsy founding . . . and possessed outlandish arts, such as dancing a Spanish shawl dance and singing Neapolitan love songs to a guitar" (*Age*, 59) [38]. The references here to the groups whom Wharton later calls "the southern races" (*Age*, 69) [44], in the context of Ellen's "gaudy clothes[,] . . . high color and high spirits," show that she has been unfit for the monotony of Old New York; at the same time, these references exaggerate the erotic in Ellen's portrait. Any allusion to skin darker than May's works as what Morrison calls a "metaphorical shortcut" to suggest the erotic (*Dark*, x).

Drawing on a related series of race-based myths, Newland heightens the erotic aspects of Ellen's character by projecting the mystique of the "Orient" onto her drawing room. To Newland, the room's "vague pervading perfume" calls to mind "some far-off bazaar, a smell made up of Turkish coffee and ambergris and dried roses" (*Age*, 70) [45–46]. Nourished by Western myths of the Orient as a romantic, timeless realm, Newland's imagination transforms Ellen's room and his own desire into the elements of high Romance. Newland finds "the atmosphere of the room . . . so different from any he had ever breathed" that it arouses in him "the sense of adventure" (*Age*, 70) [45]. Like the young narrator of James Joyce's "Araby," Newland projects onto the object of his desire and the prosaic settings associated with her a sense of the Orient as a world elsewhere. Newland endows Ellen with the exotic qualities of a Westerner's fantasy of "Oriental woman."[4] Such links between Ellen and women of various "colors" imbue the Countess with the primitive sexuality that Western culture, in the late nineteenth century and on into the 1920s, projected onto dark bodies.[5]

To heighten the polarity between Ellen and May, Wharton uses what Morrison calls "the Africanist character as surrogate" (*Dark*, 51). At the moments in the novel when Newland seeks out Ellen, the dark-toned servants make their appearances. Again and again in scenes of subtle replacement, Newland encounters a dark servant at times and in places where he expects to find Ellen. When the Archers, recently returned from their honeymoon, visit Catherine's house at Newport, both are disconcerted to learn that Ellen is staying there; yet when Catherine calls Ellen, the mulatto maid appears in Ellen's stead, entering the novel just as Nastasia has done before her to explain Ellen's absence. In the most telling of these instances of the dark servant's standing in for the dark heroine, Newland counts on finding Ellen at Catherine's house when he answers the sick woman's summons. Anticipating a private interview with Ellen, Newland arrives expecting a climactic encounter: "Archer's heart was beating violently when he rang old Mrs. Mingott's bell. . . . here he was on the doorstep. Behind the door, behind the curtains of the yellow damask room . . . , [Ellen] was surely awaiting him; in another moment he would see her, and be able to speak to her before she led him to the sick-room" (*Age*, 297–98) [179]. Wharton builds these expectations only to dash them: Newland expects Ellen, "but in the yellow sitting-room it was the mulatto maid who waited. Her white teeth shining like a keyboard" (*Age*, 298) [179]. This image recalls Nastasia's "welcom[ing] him with all her white teeth" (*Age*, 68) [44] on Newland's first visit to Ellen's house, and the image—in all of its "economy of stereotype" (*Dark*, 58)—registers white America's simultaneous desire for and fear of a racial Other. Here American Africanism appears in what Morrison calls "its lush and fully blossomed existence in the rhetoric of dread and desire" (*Dark*, 64). The dark-skinned servants, in marking Ellen's difference from the other Society women, indicate that Newland desires not a particular person, but an Other, a romanticized or demonized version of his self.

4. See Shari Benstock, *No Gifts from Chance*, on how Wharton's view of non-Western cultures grew more realistic between 1888 and 1917 (the year before she wrote *The Age of Innocence*). In 1888, "Edith Wharton revels in the otherness and exoticism" of "Africa, Asia Minor, and the Aegean islands [whereas] . . . thirty years later, visiting Morocco, . . . her perspective was still Western, Christian, and colonialistic, but her attitudes had changed toward the circumstances in which Arab women and children lived" (65–66).
5. See Sander L. Gilman, "Black Bodies, White Bodies: Toward an Iconography of Female Sexuality in Late Nineteenth Century Art, Medicine, and Literature," *Critical Inquiry* 12, no. 1 (autumn 1985): 204–42. Gilman shows that, by the end of the nineteenth century, the black woman had become–in art, literature, and medicine–an icon for sexuality. Most relevant to Wharton's novel is Gilman's tracing of the use of the black servant to mark the sexuality of white characters in European art and music from the eighteenth to the twentieth century. Works probably familiar to Wharton—William Hogarth's *A Rake's Progress* (1733–34), Edouard Manet's *Olympia* (1865), and Hugo von Hofmannsthal's *Der Rosenkavalier* (1911)—use black servants to mark the illicit sexuality of main characters who are white (206–9). "It is this iconography," according to Anne DuCille in *The Coupling Convention* "that helped make a bare-breasted Josephine Baker the rage in Paris in the twenties" (73)— just after Wharton completed *The Age of Innocence*.

Wharton's linking of Ellen and the mulatto maid in this way also clarifies Newland's later suggestion that Ellen become his mistress. The novel's association between dark heroine and dark servant points to an actual connection between mistresses and mulattas—a legacy from America's antebellum past. Under the American institution of slavery, sexual abuse of female slaves by their owners tended to take different forms according to the shade of the slave woman's skin. Whereas darker skinned slaves were often forced to have sex and children against their wills, mulatta women such as Linda Brent in Harriet Jacob's *Incidents in the Life of a Slave Girl* were often compelled to submit to what Lauren Berlant describes as "white men's parodic and perverse fantasies";[6] owners could pretend that these lightskinned women were not their slaves but their mistresses. Masking the reality that the mulatta lacks the power to resist her master's sexual advances, such fantasies transformed her into a mistress: one who comes to a man not because she is forced like a slave or legally obligated (and protected) like a wife, but out of her own desire for him and/or financial dependence on him. Such a mistress can be "kept on the side," in addition to a wife. With these fantasies, Berlant points out, slave owners "set up a parallel universe" that "involved dressing up the beautiful mulatta and playing white-lady-of-the-house with her."[7] Viewed against this historical role of the mulatta, Ellen's association with the mulatto maid unmasks the insult behind Newland's desire to make Ellen his lover after he has married May. In this light, his earlier casting of Ellen's drawing room as "something intimate, . . . suggestive of old romantic scenes and sentiments," already envisions Ellen as the kept woman. Against Newland's perception of "what May's drawing-room would look like" (*Age*, 70) [46], Ellen's house, with its boudoir-like drawing room, "parodie[s] the big one."[8] Juxtaposed with Ellen's connections to the mulatta, Newland's vision of Ellen's *bordello*like house anticipates Faulkner's depiction of the house where Charles Bon's octoroon mistress/wife in *Absalom, Absalom!* is kept.

The Africanist presence in *The Age of Innocence*, by serving as a marker of both white male privilege and white female defiance, seems to express two meanings that might cancel each other out. Such a paradoxical use of darkness conforms to its function in American fiction in general. As Morrison observes, darkness can carry two contradictory meanings at the same time: "Images of blackness can be evil *and* protective, rebellious *and* forgiving, fearful *and* desirable—all of the self-contradictory features of the self" (*Dark*, 59; author's emphasis). Darkness, color, difference, variety: All these, in the collective psyche of masculine New York, threaten the integrity of the old order even as they embody its "darkest" desires.

While Ellen's status as dark heroine points in different directions at once, May's status as fair heroine leads, through a string of associa-

---

6. Lauren Berlant, "The Queen of America Goes to Washington City: Harriet Jacobs, Frances Harper, Anita Hill," *American Literature* 65, no. 3 (September 1993): 554.
7. Ibid., 555.
8. Ibid.

tions, nowhere at all. Whereas blackness has double meanings in this scheme, whiteness is drained of meaning. Among images in American literature, Morrison writes, "Whiteness, alone, is mute, meaningless, unfathomable, pointless, frozen, veiled, curtained, dreaded, senseless, implacable" (*Dark*, 59). The whitest characters in *The Age of Innocence*, both metaphorically and literally, exemplify these qualities and are associated with images of ice, snow, shrouds, and a living death. Henry and Louisa van der Luyden, in their fair coloring and identicalness to each other, resemble "bodies caught in glaciers [that] keep for years a rosy life-in-death" (*Age*, 52) [34]. With the van der Luydens, Wharton creates a sense of *fin-de-race* exhaustion, of the inbred lines collapsing in on themselves as in Poe's "The Fall of the House of Usher." Whiteness or blue blood, taken to an extreme, is revealed here as self-annihilating. The blue blood of the van der Luydens, in all the imagery that characterizes the couple—from the snowscape of their estate on the frozen Hudson to the sheet-draped furniture of their house in town, from their faded coloring and unaging features to their own chilly response to human contact—connects their racial purity to May's sexual purity and suggests that their whiteness is no more an innate essence than May's innocence.

When Newland acknowledges that May's "abysmal purity" is a carefully cultivated artifice, he pictures her innocence in images that recall the whiteness of the glacial van der Luydens: "[H]e returned discouraged [from his fantasy of initiating May sexually] by the thought that all this frankness and innocence were only an artificial product[,] . . . so cunningly manufactured . . . because it was supposed to be what he wanted, what he had a right to, in order that he might exercise his lordly pleasure in smashing it like an image made of snow" (*Age*, 7, 45) [5, 29–30]. More disturbing to Newland than May's "snow-like" artifice is his suspicion that May's innocence conceals nothing. Predictably, then, during the archery match, Beaufort's derisive comment about May's purity sends "a shiver through [Newland's] heart": "What if 'niceness' carried to that supreme degree were only a negation, the curtain dropped before an emptiness?" (*Age*, 212) [129]. Through curtains, veils, ice, and snow, the novel's imagery connects this possibility that nothingness lies behind the façade of May's innocence with the likelihood that emptiness underlies the van der Luydens' "whiteness."

However we define "whiteness"—as an historically changing variable;[9] as a curtain/veil to mask one's own color and privilege;[1] or a

---

9. See Ruth Frankenberg, *White Women, Race Matters: The Social Construction of Whiteness* (Minneapolis: University of Minnesota Press, 1993): "Jewish Americans, Italian Americans, and Latinos have, at different times and from varying political standpoints, been viewed as both 'white' and 'nonwhite.' And as the history of 'interracial' marriage and sexual relationships also demonstrates, 'white' is as much anything else an economic and political category maintained over time by a changing set of exclusionary practices, both legislative and customary" (11–12). (See map on p. 310.)

1. Ibid., 1. Here, I combine three of Frankenberg's definitions of "whiteness": "First, whiteness is a location of structural advantage, of race privilege. Second, it is a 'standpoint,' a place from which white people look at ourselves, at others, and at society. Third, 'whiteness' refers to a set of cultural practices that are usually unmarked and unnamed" (1).

racist "artifice" that promotes "racial cleansing"—whiteness, with its claims to blankness, is often harder to see than darkness. Darkness or "color" is often defined as ethnicity itself; whiteness, in turn, is assumed to be the norm and signifies an absence of ethnicity. Like female innocence, whiteness in this novel is a curtain before an emptiness. Old New York's strategy for preserving whiteness, the practice of marrying "one's own kind," "carried to a supreme degree" may result in "a negation." That Old New York may be headed down an evolutionary cul-de-sac is implied when Newland draws an analogy between May's culturally inherited blindness and the biological blindness of "the Kentucky cave-fish, which had ceased to develop eyes because they had no use for them" (*Age*, 82) [53]. Whether the struggle for existence here is cast in Darwinian or Spencerian terms, the analogy can portend no good for Old New York.

But this self-selective and selected group does not die out.[2] Instead, the New York society represented in *The Age of Innocence* gets a transfusion of "new blood and new money," and this change registers significantly on the color imagery of the novel (*Age*, 30) [20]. Of the characters trying to "lay siege to" Society's "tight little citadel" in the beginning, one (Mrs. Lemuel Struthers) is associated with darkness and another (Fanny Ring of the canary yellow carriage) with bright color. Initially, these colors brand these characters as outsiders (*Age*, 30) [20]. Early in the novel, Mrs. Struthers's tainted sexual past and lower class origins make Ellen's attendance at one of her gatherings a damning social move. Mrs. Struthers's disreputable status is emphasized by her "intensely black" hair, the cut of which, in "the Egyptian style," links her (through racist etymology) to the "gypsy" Ellen (*Age*, 36) [24]. Over the time traversed in the novel, however, eventually even the decorous May can attend Mrs. Struthers's entertainments without a qualm. Mrs. Struthers's entry into New York Society represents the beginning of a real but relatively small demographic change that occurs between "the age of innocence" and the turn of the century: the infiltration of Old New York by new money. Her conquest calls to mind larger demographic changes and, more importantly, changes of thought occurring at the same time. Wharton figures Mrs. Struthers's entree into Society as the conversion of a darker element into a lighter one: "Once people had tasted of Mrs. Struthers's easy Sunday hospitality they were not likely to sit at home remembering that her champagne was transmuted Shoe-Polish" (*Age*, 260) [157]. Viewed against Progressive-era fear of "race suicide," this image betrays a nativist fantasy of averting "national death" by absorption of the ethnic Other. Mrs. Struthers's champagne anticipates Ralph Ellison's symbol of the paint factory in *Invisible Man* ("Keep America Pure with Liberty Paints"): When ten black drops are stirred into each can

2. Nancy Bentley in *The Ethnography of Manners* observes: "Wharton's portrait of a class that in fact retained and strengthened its claim to power and wealth through the tumultuous social changes of fin-de-siècle America is demographically correct. In spite of a pervasive sense of WASP decline—indeed, in part through that very sense—the northeastern elite expanded its social influence and helped to acculturate the American polity to a new society of consumption and corporate capital" (113).

of Optic White paint, they simply disappear, not diluting but intensifying the paint's whiteness.[3] Aside from the obvious economic alchemy, Wharton's image of "transmuted Shoe-Polish" points to a process of ethnic alchemy similar to the one Ellison satirizes. In Wharton's trope for the move from "the age of innocence" to the twentieth century, the Africanist presence, already necessary to the definition of "whiteness," revitalizes an aged and dying "race" by being absorbed into it and thereby disappearing itself. Wharton emphasizes the vampirishness of Society here by referring to Catherine as "the carnivorous old lady" when she calls for "new blood" (*Age*, 30) [20].

Wharton's image of shoe-polish-into-champagne also points to a change in thinking about race that began around the time this novel was written and published. After the Great War, according to Ruth Frankenberg, thinking about race was gradually moving away from the old "essentialist racism" to a view that Frankenberg labels "color evasiveness" and "power evasiveness."[4] This change complemented a shift toward "an 'assimilationist' analysis of what would and should happen to people of color in the United States."[5] Wharton's image of something dark transmuted into something light stands thus poised at an ideological shift that would ultimately lead to assimilationist racism. The failure of the dark and light elements to blend implies that they are essentially different; the tendency of Society to absorb newcomers by blanching them suggests assimilation.

The change set in motion by Mrs. Struthers's invitation to the Beauforts' ball and carried forward when her shoe polish turns to champagne culminates in another "assimilationist" event: the fulfillment of Lawrence Lefferts's prophecy that "If things go on at this pace . . . we shall see our children . . . marrying Beaufort's bastards" (*Age*, 338) [202]. In the approaching marriage of Newland's son Dallas to Fanny Beaufort, daughter of Julius Beaufort and his mistress Fanny Ring, the Archer family accepts the child of both the colorful (or sexual) woman and the Jew.[6] Because Beaufort himself, who "passed for an Englishman," was not fully accepted into "the clan" a generation before in spite of his marriage to Regina Dallas (Regina, in fact, had jeopardized her own standing in Society by marrying him), his daughter's marriage to Newland's son amounts to an act of assimilation (*Age*, 19) [13]. Everything objectionable to Society in the Jew Beaufort and his mistress Fanny Ring is dissociated from their daughter who, like a second-generation immigrant, assimilates into "the tribe" by leaving her parents' identities behind. Indeed, Dallas does not marry a "dark lady."

---

3. Ralph Ellison, *Invisible Man* (New York: Random House, 1972), 192, 195–97.
4. Frankenberg, *White Women, Race Matters*, 13.
5. Ibid., 14, 13.
6. Shari Benstock in *No Gifts from Chance* reports that Wharton "based Beaufort on financier August Belmont (rumored to be Jewish), who kept a mistress . . . and provided her with a canary-yellow carriage" (358). Annette Zilversmit informed me at the Edith Wharton at Yale Conference (in honor of R. W. B. Lewis, April 1995) that Belmont was a Schoenberg and the only Jew in Old New York during the 1870s. Susan Meyer interpreted Beaufort's Jewish identity in quite interesting ways in "Jews, Sex, and Edith Wharton" (session on Edith Wharton and Taboo, annual meeting of the Modern Language Association, Washington, D.C., December 28, 1996).

By the time Fanny is engaged to Dallas, her identity has already been detached from her father's status as "a 'foreigner' of doubtful origin" and from her mother's place among "[s]uch 'women' (as they were called)" (*Age*, 44, 84) [29, 54]. Although Newland's family welcomes Fanny, in her it admits neither Jew nor "dark lady." Her acceptance by Newland's family shows not that America embraces difference, but rather that admission to the ruling class requires the surrender of "ethnicity."[7] The upcoming name change from Fanny Beaufort to Mrs. Dallas Archer suggests how the new concept of assimilation could itself, like the old Progressive Era concept of essential difference between the races, constitute a form of racism.

But even as *The Age of Innocence* registers multiple theories of race, it disrupts racist "logic" as well. Much in the novel works against both essentialist and assimilationist concepts of race. Wharton, who could analyze so astutely how culture constructs gender, seems sometimes to be on the verge of a similar historicizing of race. The novel embodies a tension between viewing the absorption of difference as desirable and seeing such dilution as a loss. Although the images of absorbed others reveal the racist anxieties and fantasies of Wharton's class, gaps in the text uncover the illogic of such fantasies for Americans.

In a novel in which there is much talk of America and "Americanness," America is ostensibly contrasted with Europe, but Wharton repeatedly subverts the international theme to question American claims to freedom, individualism, and originality. As Ellen points out to Newland, New York parrots European forms. Far from encouraging individuality and freedom, "America" in this novel enforces conformity to convention, and this way of life at times constitutes Newland's main antagonist. One day during his engagement to May, Newland decides not to stop at his club on the way home from work because "a haunting horror of doing the same thing every day at the same hour besieged his brain" (*Age*, 83) [54]. As he looks in on the "familiar tall-hatted figures" inside his club, Newland voices what seems to be his argument with America: " 'Sameness—sameness!' he muttered, the word running through his head like a persecuting tune" (*Age*, 83) [54] Later, married to May, Newland "wonder[s] if the deadly monotony of their lives had laid its weight on her also" (*Age*, 293) [176]. Wharton connects the monotony of Newland's life, this deadly dullness of "see[ing] the same people every day" (*Age*, 106) [68], with his people's all being the same. Their sameness, given the novel's color coding, takes on ethnic/racial significance.

Wharton, moreover, exposes New York's fear of difference as the nation's problem. Washington, D.C., "where one was supposed to meet more varieties of people and of opinion" (*Age*, 240) [146] than else-

---

7. For an opposing view of Fanny's marriage, assimilation, and the changes in thinking about race of the 1920s, see Walter Benn Michaels, *Our America: Nativism, Modernism, and Pluralism* (Durham, N.C.: Duke University Press, 1995), 110–12. Nancy Bentley's interpretation of this marriage in *The Ethnography of Manners*, on the other hand, supports my sense of it as one of the events in which Old New York absorbs the vitality of outsiders without taking on their "color." Although in Bentley's words "the taboos against exogamous marriage . . . have been lifted, . . . the disorder is an energy harnessed by Archer's children" (113).

where in America, fails to stimulate Ellen. In Boston, a city associated with American individualism, Newland is struck by the lack of variety among Americans. Strangely, Newland deplores the sameness of American faces immediately after noticing ethnic diversity in the features of people on the streets. These juxtaposed moments unveil a contradiction: the paradox that everyone looks alike in a land of immigrants. While Newland waits for Ellen outside her hotel, "A Sicilian youth with eyes like Nastasia's offer[s] to shine his boots, and an Irish matron to sell him peaches" (*Age*, 236) [144]. The next moment, Newland watches the people coming out of the hotel and "marvel[s] . . . that all the people . . . should look so like each other, and so like all the other hot men who, at that hour, through the length and breadth of the land, were passing continuously in and out of the swinging doors of hotels" (*Age*, 236) [144]. For whatever reason these hotel patrons resemble one another, the other Bostonians who might provide some relief from this uniformity—the Irish matron, the Sicilian youth—are excluded from the image of Americans moving across the length and breadth of the land. Newland is conveniently colorblind.

On a less-conscious level, however, Newland is not colorblind, because it is his encounter with the excluded immigrants that triggers his exasperation with the sameness of "American" faces. His exasperation, in turn, heightens the contrast between the one European face he sees in Boston, that of M. Rivière, and all the identical American faces. The moment after Newland notices the immigrants, he notes the similarity of "American" faces; the next moment, his glimpse of M. Rivière's face conveys to him all that America lacks: "And then, suddenly, came a face that . . . was so many more things at once, and things so different[,] . . . somehow, quicker, vivider, more conscious; or perhaps seeming so because he was so different" (*Age*, 236–37) [144]. Here, clearly, difference is good, and lack of difference is an American failing. To all America, then, Wharton extends Catherine's complaint about "the tribe": "Ah, these Mingotts—all alike! . . . No, no; not one of them wants to be different; they're as scared of it as the small pox" (*Age*, 152) [95]. Newland, too, perceives fear of difference as a national failing (and seems to equate the valuing of difference with national integrity) when, staring at a "row of stark white village houses" outside of Boston, he concedes to Ellen: "We're damnably dull. We've no character, no colour, no variety" (*Age*, 241) [147].

While the racial difference of M. Rivière—his "sallow skin" is repeatedly contrasted with Newland's skin (especially when both men blush)—and that of other middle-class Europeans comes to stand in the conscious minds of Newland and the narrator for the variety that America lacks, the racial difference of the immigrants lacks this saving power (*Age*, 201, 250) [123, 151]. These characters impinge upon Newland's senses, but not on his colorblind consciousness. They are not, in his view, candidates for inclusion in America. Similarly ironic is Newland's juxtaposition of "heat-prostrated and *deserted* Boston" with his perception that "a shirt-sleeved populace . . . moved through the streets near the station" (*Age*, 229, 228 emphasis added) [140, 140].

Although typically the narrator is more perceptive than Newland, the irony of this description is left unremarked.

But while Bostonians like the Irish matron and the Sicilian youth are, in some ways, invisible to Newland and to the narrator, they nevertheless are connected to the differently colored and cultured characters associated with Ellen and to alternatives to America's deadening lack of "colour." The novel's logic of image and character, which aligns courage with color and vitality with variety, undermines Newland's narrow definition of what "American" means.

True to the contradictions of Newland's time and class, he can be dying of sameness in one of the world's most diverse cities. This paradox captures one important aspect of "whiteness" characteristic of his time and place (though not exclusive to either). Whiteness includes unexamined acceptances of the system of advantage that maintains one's privilege. Added up, these acts of acceptance constitute a "cunningly manufactured" ignorance of how one's own identity is "raced." To borrow a phrase from another of Wharton's novels, Newland's people possess "a force of negation which eliminated everything beyond their own range of perception."[8] One of Wharton's gifts as a novelist is her ability to depict such a force of negation from its own point of view, even as she indicates the extent of what it negates, wastes, destroys. *The Age of Innocence*, which is so incisive about social constructions of gender, also apprehends some of the ways society constructs racial categories. It is a short step from realizing the artificiality of May's sexual innocence to realizing the limitations of "whiteness" as a point of view. Between her fine sense of irony and her good eye for the cultural construction of identity, Wharton is able to record some of the complexities of American identity where race, gender, and class intersect. *The Age of Innocence*, written during an upwelling of anti-immigrant sentiment and during a nascent movement for racial equality, depicts whiteness as an active, artificial "innocence." However attractive this ignorance may appear against the alternative of facing the nation's racial problems, Wharton's novel marks the cultural moment at which this "age of innocence" must begin to give way.

# DALE M. BAUER

## [Whiteness and the Powers of Darkness in *The Age of Innocence*]†

\* \* \*

As Claudia Koonz argues in "Genocide and Eugenics," the prevailing sentiment after World War I was inspired by the wide support for the

---

8. Edith Wharton, *The House of Mirth*, ed. Elizabeth Ammons, Norton Critical Edition (New York: W. W. Norton, 1990), 40.
† From *Edith Wharton's Brave New Politics*, (Madison: The University of Wisconsin Press, 1994. 170–79). Reprinted with permission of the University of Wisconsin Press. Notes have been edited. Bracketed page numbers refer to this volume.

1926 law stipulating forced sterilization laws: "Oliver Wendell Holmes wrote the majority decision—declaring that after so many of the nation's finest had sacrificed their lives in World War I, it would not represent a great sacrifice if the least qualified gave up their potential to reproduce"(156). Such a bio-political dimension of modern science was central to the theory behind Nazism in particular, and modern culture in general. Marked by instability in established religious, familial, and communal life, the culture sought radical bio-political solutions, like sterilization of the "unfit," while growing nostalgic for the past. Wharton's solutions, however, did not take a reactionary form. Instead, she tried to divest authoritative mass-produced culture of its alienating control over individuals. Whether the threat was a standardized beauty (as it was in *The Children*) or the more blatant class argument for twilight sleep[1] and eugenic legislation, Wharton blasted the simplification in such measures and the state regulation of the individual. As Nancy Stepan and Sander Gilman argue in "Appropriating the Idioms of Science: The Rejection of Scientific Racism," the rhetorical power of late nineteenth-century science rested in its claims of objectivity, neutrality, and universality; in order to present an intellectual resistance to these claims, one had to appropriate scientific idioms to subvert them. "From 1870 to 1920, science became more specialized and authoritative as a cultural resource and language of interpretation. . . . The outcome was a narrowing of the cultural space within which, and the cultural forms by which, the claims of biological determinism could be effectively challenged" (80). In *The Age of Innocence*, Wharton begins to revise the ethical and political claims of the new sciences and their explanatory force. In doing so, she posits fiction's moral force against the determinism of science by subverting science's own terms and theories. In taking up the contradictions of human nature, she suggested that desire is more variegated than the movements for birth control, marriage, or family studies policy were allowing for.

Ultimately, Wharton sought to unravel the implicit ties between the early twentieth-century campaign for racial purity and the cult of feminine purity she herself inherited as a legacy of nineteenth-century domestic life. Almost every Wharton novel of the twenties centers on divorce (engineered by a New Woman), with divorce serving as Wharton's dominant trope for the disruption of the bourgeois family. Unlike contemporary writers such as Charlotte Perkins Gilman and Gertrude Atherton,[2] Wharton resisted the call of eugenics schemes as a bulwark against changes in the social "trend."[3]

1. "twilight sleep": Anesthetic composed of scopolamine and morphine used from 1902 through the early 1960s to block the memory of pain in childbirth. Controversial from its inception, this drug provided the title for Wharton's 1927 novel, a work that links the shallowness of modern society to society's and science's efforts to disconnect the maternal role from its origins in suffering [Editor].
2. Gertrude Atherton (1857–1948), American-born writer of historical and social fiction, known for her feminist views and her novels of California life. Of interest here is *Black Oxen* (1923), her sensational novel about a glandular treatment that she had actually benefited from in life. Charlotte Perkins Gilman (1860–1935), American-born feminist and social theorist, who in addition to her prose critiques, wrote *Herland* (1915), a utopian novel about a society of women who live without men, reproducing by means of parthenogenesis [Editor].
3. For instance, on Sinclair Lewis's advice, she refused to join the Literary Council of the Authors' League of America (see letter to Minnie of January 29, 1929, Beinecke Library).

Appearing in 1920, the year that saw a great wave of anti-foreign incidents culminating in the second wave of the KKK and the Anti-
Immigration Act of 1924, but set in the 1870s, Wharton's *Age of
Innocence* links two central preoccupations, women's purity and
hereditary purity—concerns that come unnervingly together in the
person of Ellen Olenska. What critics have called May Wellandism is
less nostalgia for the cult of true womanhood and more the fantasy of
women's freedom from such demands. Throughout the novel, Wharton links Ellen to the fears of racial impurity and even to the anti-
immigrationist sentiment contemporaneous to this novel. May
Welland, on the other hand, is associated with a no less disquieting social blindness. Newland Archer contemplates May's ambiguous
"abysmal purity" (7) [5], and what marriage to "that terrifying product
of the social system he belonged to and believed in" might mean: "the
young girl who knew nothing and expected everything, looked back at
him like a stranger through May Welland's familiar features; and once
more it was borne in on him that marriage was not the safe anchorage
he had been taught to think, but a voyage on uncharted seas" (43)
[28]. As much as anything, Archer's "readings in anthropology" affect
his view of this situation (69) [43–44]. Indeed, the 1870s witnessed a
passion for social science, especially anthropology, matched only in
Wharton's time by the twenties' consequent fascination for the primitive. The anthropology that people would have been reading in the
1870s was hereditarianist in kind, drawing on theories of instinct to
describe human nature, and Archer himself is learning to see the
world through his new anthropological framework.

Marriage becomes more complicated for Archer precisely because
he interprets it as a ritual function, exorcising impure and threatening
social elements. Newland's rumored adultery with Ellen is also much
more complex than it appears, in that, for him, their love affair threatens the ritual transmission of American cultural values. The anxiety
over foreign contamination and amalgamation guarantees the ritual
exclusion of Ellen from the family. Not only is she married to a foreigner, but she is also likened to gipsies and aligned with Mediterranean stock, and with an Eastern European stock as embodied in the
Polish Count Olenski.

Archer's worry merely renders small the novel's claims about intermarriage and how its dangers clarify the perceived threat to cultural
transmission: the Albany Chiverses had "insanity recurring in every
second generation" (10) [7] and Ellen Olenska's Uncle Thorley
Chivers dies in a madhouse (60) [39]. The lessons of intermarriage
and eugenics are clear: marriage is much less an affair of the heart
and more a social cement, one which could be used to yield "blameless stock" (12) [9]. The "family," as the critical backdrop of Wharton's
novel, is something to be investigated and guarded to preserve its purity. When Newland Archer's mother worries that the "trend" was
changing Old New York, she sees it embodied not only in Ellen's bohemianism but also in that professor of archeology, Emerson Sillerton,
a member of "a venerable and venerated family tree" (219) [134]. Mrs.

Welland especially objects to the professor's giving a party for a "black man," but it is impossible to tell whether she objects to the guest of honor or the party's timing, since the party coincides with Julia Mingott's *thé dansant* (220) [135]. For the Wellands, blacks appear only as a supply of house servants in St. Augustine or as Mrs. Mingott's maid. Mrs. Welland expects the professor to know that her *kind* does not mix socially in the black man's society: "No one in the Mingott set could understand why Amy Sillerton had submitted so tamely to the eccentricities of a husband who filled the house with long-haired men and short-haired women, and, when he traveled, took her to explore tombs in Yucatan instead of going to Paris or Italy. But there they were, set in their ways, and apparently unaware that they were different from other people" (220) [134].

At every turn, Wharton parodies the good breeding of her characters, whose genetic lines are assumed to assure "congenital" supremacy. When describing Lawrence Lefferts, she trivializes the character traits phrenology was once assumed to reveal: "One had only to look at him, from the slant of his bald forehead and the curve of his beautiful fair moustache to the long patent-leather feet at the other end of his lean and elegant person, to feel that the knowledge of 'form' must be congenital in any one who knew how to wear such good clothes so carelessly and carry such height with so much lounging grace" (8) [6–7]. With little more than a knowledge of form to promote himself, Lefferts gossips and snipes. Personal qualities seem to have been purged from the leisure classes, and Archer wonders about May whether " 'niceness' carried to that supreme degree were only a negation, the curtain dropped before an emptiness?" (211) [129]. Repeating a fear she had first expressed in *French Ways and Their Meaning*, Wharton has Archer liken May Welland to the Kentucky cavefish, blind and able only to "look out blankly at blankness" (83) [53]. In this way, Archer comes to realize that the good breeding he once believed in is little more than "factitious purity" (46) [30].

Arguably the most famous passage from *The Age of Innocence*, * * * concerns the "arbitrary signs" of the "hieroglyphic world" Wharton depicts [in the novel]. Following that passage is another which suggests how anthropology, one of the new social sciences popularized in the late nineteenth century, had begun to influence "advanced culture": one of those arbitrary signs is Mrs. Welland's "air of having had her hand forced [in the announcement of her daughter's engagement], quite as, in the books on Primitive Man that people of advanced culture were beginning to read, the savage bride is dragged with shrieks from her parents' tent" (45) [29]. Books about Primitive Man were the rage; they kindled in Wharton the sense that the line between primitive and advanced was as arbitrary, but no less powerful, than any other sign in culture. Preserved in the rite of marriage is the "elaborate system of mystification" Newland Archer recognizes as cultural lore about the exchange of the young girl in marriage, which is the subject of at least one of [Bronislaw] Malinowski's books and of several other contemporaneous anthropological texts, and of the new sexology that Havelock Ellis and Sam Schmalhausen[4] codified. Here Archer fears that May cannot survive in his world, since social purity demands that women become blind to passion and that the power of "insight" be bred out of them (83) [53].

To this extent the commonly-held functionalist view of the family as regulatory force is the object of Wharton's criticism. The family's irregularities and permutations interested the writer as important human and familial variations. In this regard, a key word in *The Age of Innocence* is "bohemianism" with which Ellen is associated: even as a child she is dressed as a "gipsy foundling" instead of in black American mourning clothes for her parents (60) [38]; she is linked to the "gipsy-looking people" Wharton had first discussed in Charity's lineage in [her 1917 novel] *Summer*. Katherine Joslin reads "the Bohemian Peril" embodied in Ellen as a threat to Old New York and to Newland, since bohemia is "a world of independent ideas and artistic expression" (Joslin 106–7). Yet the reference to the bohemian in this novel is not to the artistic world of the 1920s but to the influx of Bohemian immigrants of the 1870s. The "Bohemian" in the novel refers first to the largely peasant immigrants from Eastern Europe, not the few spirited inhabitants of the social and sexual enclaves of New York. This confusion may well be deliberate, significantly so because it illustrates the connections Wharton makes between European immigration and the artistic and intellectual freedom that followed. Reading the "Bohemian" in the novel simply as a sexual threat, then, ignores the 1870s anthropological influence. That Wharton creates an amalgam of 1870s and 1920s cultures is telling: the bohemian life represented a threat to culture not because of its sexual permissiveness per se but because of what it suggested about heredity and radical thought. Remember that the "Bohemian" is associated with Mediterranean stock: Marchioness Manson's Spanish shawls, Nastasia's Sicilian accent and "swarthy foreign-looking" demeanor (70) [44], and Ned Winsett's radical intellectualism are all distrusted as expressions of inferior ancestry compared to Nordic roots, not to mention the failed European revolutions of 1848–49: "Archer, who dressed in the evening because he thought it cleaner and more comfortable to do so, and who had never stopped to consider that cleanliness and comfort are two of the costliest items in a modest budget, regarded Winsett's attitude as part of the boring 'Bohemian' pose that always made fashionable people who changed their clothes without talking about it, and were not forever harping on the number of servants one kept, seem so much simpler and less self-conscious than the others. Nevertheless, he was always stimulated by Winsett . . ." (124) [78]. Winsett's greatest wish is to emigrate, and he addresses his radical bent to a sympathetic but ironic Archer: "You'll never amount to anything, any of you, till you roll up your sleeves and get right down into the muck" (126) [79]. Winsett

4. Havelock Ellis (1868–1935), English physician who studied sex, best known for his work *Sexual Inversion* (1897) on homosexuality. Samuel D. Schmalhausen (b. 1890), New York psychologist whose books include *Why We Misbehave* (1928); he was also co-editor of *Sex in Civilization* (1929), for which Ellis wrote the introduction [Editor].

implies that Archer might end up like the social gadfly Larry Lefferts, shallow and smug, unless he commits himself to radical change, namely politics. Where Winsett fails, Ellen succeeds in compelling Archer to be "once more conscious of the curious way in which she reversed his values" (104) [66].

Ned Winsett lives in the same bohemian neighborhood as Ellen, which Ellen's family dislikes. It was "not the peril but the poverty" to which her family objected, the relative squalor of "a 'Bohemian' quarter given over to 'people who wrote' " (104) [66]. "People who wrote" as the neighborhood's principle of inclusion suggests that intellect and inclination, and temperament and talent, would presumably distinguish who belonged and who didn't much better than heredity or money—and this was a situation not to be abided. Yet its poverty is explicity linked to a self-consciousness, to the extent that writing and privation were closely associated with peril, both in politics and waning culture. Wharton is quick to undermine this danger, however, since Winsett's and Ellen's lives are intertwined by an act of kindness Ellen does for Ned's little boy, whose leg she bandages when she sees him hurt in the street outside her house. Here Ellen's foreign threat is domesticated by one democratic act of kindness. The subtler impact of the scene is also part of Wharton's strategy: the maternal instinct, seen as a universal trait binding all women together, served to show how all women held the same values of family and home that Americans did. By appealing to a kind of universal motherhood, Ellen Olenska—"bare-headed, carrying [the son] in her arms, with his knee all beautifully bandaged, and . . . so sympathetic and beautiful"—represents the "better" sort of immigrant, the maternal symbol of the universal family (123) [77].

Or does she? This image of Ellen is almost immediately reversed when she appears out of the "armor" ladies usually wore in the evening. Wharton's ambivalence about Ellen is never so clear as when Ellen appears as the Venus in Furs, the figure for whom Leopold von Sacher-Masoch named his 1870 novel. Wharton's depiction of Ellen's attire—"heedless of tradition"—closely recalls Sacher-Masoch's icon of masochism: "But Madame Olenska . . . was attired in a long robe of red velvet bordered about the chin and down the front with glossy black fur. Archer remembered, on his last visit to Paris, seeing a portrait by the new painter, Carolus Duran, whose pictures were the sensation of the Salon, in which the lady wore one of these bold sheath-like robes with her chin nestling in fur. There was something perverse and provocative in the notion of fur worn in the evening in a heated drawing room, and in the combination of a muffled throat and bare arms; but the effect was undeniably pleasing" (105–6) [67]. Sacher-Masoch's hero Severin, who becomes the love slave of the masochist Wanda in the 1870 novel, feels the same about seeing his mistress draped in furs: at various points, Severin (whom Wanda renames Gregor) associates the furs with cruelty, despotism, and tyranny (108). Their symbolic meaning is tied to masochistic love, as Severin declares: "I have repeatedly told you that suffering has a peculiar attraction for me. Nothing can intensify my passion more than tyranny, cruelty, and especially the faithlessness of a beautiful woman" (75).

Why does Wharton identify her heroine with the sensational confessions of the masochist? One could argue that she merely employs this reference as a cultural market for the historical setting, just as she refers to *Middlemarch* and books by Herbert Spencer and Alphonse Daudet (Archer's impatiently awaited books from London) to give her novel the social texture that the realist novel required. Yet the comparison is more deliberate since the novel concerns Ellen's erotic control over Archer, with one lover as the hammer, the other as the anvil, as Sacher-Masoch has it. Drawing as it does on the contemporaneous images of sadomasochism, Ellen's appearance as the Venus in Furs gives the lie to Wharton's ironic title, "age of innocence," since the age was not innocent but embroiled in new sexological debates about sadomasochism and perversion. The "age" of the novel is not innocent; rather, it is the "age" that lost the struggle to preserve innocence and that set in motion the corruptions to come. In this context, Wharton's matriarch, Catherine the Great, the nickname of old Catherine Mingott, is also ironic: as Sacher-Masoch, among others, suggests, she was history's first sadist. The heroine of *Venus in Furs*, Wanda, instructs her slave Severin about the moral of his punishment: "I may confess to you that I loved you deeply. You yourself, however, stifled my love by your fantastic devotion and your insane passion. From the moment that you became my slave, I knew it would be impossible for you ever to become my husband . . ." (238). Ellen's lesson to Archer is no different: Archer is willing to abandon himself to his ideal of Ellen, without making her his equal. He wants to be her slave, to be dominated by her worldliness. Archer's abjection at Ellen's hands supplants the fantasy of cultural purity underwriting the age's pretense of innocence and taste, in a novel where divorce and default are the most popular topics of conversation.

If passion is instinctual and inherited, as some sociologists argued, then those who would give themselves over to it—like Ellen and like Archer—must be disciplined from within the familial ranks. May's pregnancy proves to be just such a retaliatory function, reining in Archer just as he is about to stray. May prematurely assures Ellen that the Newland Archers are about to have a baby, an announcement that in clinching Ellen's allegiance to familial order proves to be an internally motivated regulation by the family. As a weapon against Ellen, May's intimation of her pregnancy takes on an unethical cast; in miniature, this act harbingers the state regulation of families through eugenics, which was portentous for Wharton. Nevertheless, that Newland and May's three children are studies in human variation and heredity—Mary and Bill like their mother, but Dallas ready to marry the exiled Julius Beaufort's daughter, Fanny—suggests that these human variations are necessary to revitalize culture and to establish "more tolerant views. There was good in the new order too" (349) [208–09], Archer reflects.

At the end of the novel, Archer contemplates the scientific changes of technological modernity in this new order: "There would one day be a tunnel under the Hudson through which the trains of the Pennsylvania railway would run straight into New York. They were of the brotherhood of visionaries who likewise predicted the building of ships that would cross the Atlantic in five days, the invention of a flying machine, lighting by electricity, telephonic communication without wires, and other Arabian Night marvels" (284) [171]. He conjectures that these modern inventions would propel changes in social behavior and compel human adaptability to them. Yet Wharton represents the antimodern impulse, too, in *The Age of Innocence*, in a group whose nostalgia for simpler, less self-conscious life leads them to recreate it. A brotherhood of visionaries, Dr. Carver's Community offered spiritual antidotes to the general fears of a disintegrating society. While Archer fosters his alienation as his refuge from Family, Carver's meetings try to combat such feelings in their outward search for meaning and simplification of life. At the same time, one response to the new anthropology is suggested by the vague transcendentalism of Dr. Carver's "Valley of Love Community," his theories of "Direct Contact," and his "Inner Thought" meetings (158–60, 184, 208) [98, 99, 127]. These are antidotes to the general sense of cultural decline the Wellands name the "trend." But they are also, as Jackson Lears suggests, ballast for antimodernism. For Lears these communities arose in opposition to the new ethnic and class-divided laborer societies in urban centers. What the "overcivilized bourgeoisie" needed was a self-improvement community of their own, derived from the Protestant evangelical tradition and with a certain antimodern appeal (see Lears 1981, 71–73).

Even so, Wharton distances herself—and Archer—from these radical antimodernists in that she returns to Ned Winsett's claim for sustained, however tentative, political engagement. Archer's own refusal as a "gentleman" to enter politics early in life is drawn from his indifference to collective politics and a belief—as his above rumination suggests—in technological and scientific progress. That he later enters politics under the mentorship of Teddy Roosevelt suggests how shaken his vision of innocence has been. For Archer, the new society has courage, but he has no conviction in it: "The young men nowadays were emancipating themselves from the law and business and taking up all sorts of new things. If they were not absorbed in state politics or municipal reform, the chances were that they were going in for Central American archaeology" (345) [206]. Once again, South America serves as Wharton's dystopia of political evasion, as it had in *The Reef* and *The Children* in particular.

The contradiction between Wharton's professed interest in the new anthropology and her hatred of the so-called primitive such as Harlem life—or, here, her scorn for antimodern primitives—cannot be overemphasized. She writes approvingly of the discoveries of anthropology at the same time that she relegates blacks to "the local African supply" of servants (143) [89]. Franz Boas's 1911 *The Mind of Primitive Man* changed social science in its insistence on the complexity of the "primitive," arguing for the equality of mind between primitive and civilized—a tack Wharton also seems to take in *The Age of Innocence* by showing how primitive the rituals of bloodshedding, potlatch, and fetishism were in New York society. On the other hand, while Wharton launches an attack on the neo-primitivism of the Simple Lifers in Dr. Carver's communities and brotherhoods, she objects to the representation of the primitive as Van Vechten celebrates it in *Nigger Heaven*,[5] since its simplifications seem to her to glorify primitive over civilized consciousness. Wharton knew that civilization could not return to such profound "innocence," and saw in the worship of the primitive in modern jazz the same distorted and misguided resistance to the enervation and commercialization of modern life that she did in Carver's Valley of Love Communities. The way to salvation and happiness, for Wharton, led through the much more complex terrain of cultural contradictions, by embracing the ambivalence that was so much a part of modern life for her. * * *

\* \* \*

## References

Joslin, Katherine. *Edith Wharton.* New York: St. Martin's Press, 1991.
Koonz, Claudia. "Genocide and Eugenics." In *Lessons and Legacies: The Meaning of the Holocaust in a Changing World*, ed. Peter Hayes. Evanston: Northwestern University Press, 1991: pp. 155–77.
Lears, Jackson. *No Place of Grace.* N.Y.: Pantheon, 1981.
Sacher-Masoch, Leopold von. *Venus in Furs.* Rahnghild Ed. New York: William Faro, 1932 [1870].
Stepan, Nancy Leys, and Sander Gilman. "Approaching the Idioms of Science: The Rejection of Scientific Racism." In *The Bounds of Race*, ed. Dominick LaCapra. Ithaca: Cornell University Press, 1991, pp. 72–103.
Van Vechten, Carl. *Nigger Heaven.* New York: Grosset and Dunlap, 1926.

## BRIAN T. EDWARDS

## The Well-Built Wall of Culture: Old New York and Its Harems†

> *The past is a foreign country; they do things differently there.*
> —*L. P. Hartley* (1953)[1]

### Marvels of the Arabian Nights

As Newland Archer paces the railway platform in Jersey City, awaiting Ellen Olenska's arrival from Washington, D.C., his thoughts transport him, as if on a magic carpet: "[H]e remembered that there were people who thought there would one day be a tunnel under the Hudson through which the trains of the Pennsylvania railway would run straight into New York. They were of the brotherhood of visionaries

---

5. Provocative novel published in 1926 by Carl Van Vechten (1880–1964) establishing this writer and photographer as one of the most influential among the white figures associated with the African American creative movement known as the Harlem Renaissance [Editor].
† This essay was written specifically for this Norton Critical Edition. Parenthetical page numbers refer to this volume.
1. L. P. Hartley, *The Go-Between* (London: Hamish Hamilton, 1953), 9.

who likewise predicted the building of ships that would cross the Atlantic in five days, the invention of a flying machine, lighting by electricity, telephonic communication without wires, and other Arabian Nights marvels" (171). Since such technological marvels as airplanes, telephones, and electric lighting had come to exist by 1920, the year of the novel's publication, this passage places the early readers of *The Age of Innocence* among the fraternity of prescient "visionaries"; it is Wharton's wink of complicity with the citizens who inhabit this literally preposterous modern world. Still, the passage is odd, almost awkward as Newland prophetically "remember[s]" that which the future will indeed bring. The final phrase is both familiar and curious: what is it about such technological advances that suggest the *Tales of the Arabian Nights*? At first, the reference to the *Arabian Nights* seems merely a felicitous turn of phrase, the completion of Wharton's metaphor of a "brotherhood of visionaries" who through the magic of the historical novel are able to see into the future. However, in the context of Wharton's broader concerns as she composed *The Age of Innocence*, her allusion is a clue to the complexity of her thinking amid the ruins of the post-war era and suggests the multiple levels of cultural experience on which Wharton's novel is based. The allusion transports the reader outside the world of Old New York, into a place where space and time are radically altered—beyond America and Europe to a foreign world of strange tales and exotic visions. From this distance, we are offered a vantage from which to see Old New York with its varying and multiple layers of manufactured innocences, as if New York itself were indeed a foreign country. Perhaps most important, for Wharton, New York in its "age of innocence" was not merely a place that had become a time for which to be nostalgic; this past world of her own childhood was also the key to much that distressed her about America in the modern age. Just as Newland's mind wanders to the *Arabian Nights* while he stands in Jersey City waiting for Ellen's train, Wharton herself assumed the distance essential to an acute observer of culture as she composed *The Age of Innocence* in her villa outside Paris. By viewing New York from a foreign perspective, from a distance, Wharton placed New York's "primitive" attitudes, particularly those limiting the freedom of women, into relief and was able to connect these proscriptive attitudes to the nation's equally backward policy of isolationism. This policy of isolationism, separatism, and noninterference, as Wharton repeatedly argued, was part of America's national naïveté, a destructive pose of innocence that had nearly destroyed Wharton's beloved France and with it her ideal of what she considered to be the highest form of Western civilization.

Despite the medieval provenance of the *Tales of the Arabian Nights*, in nineteenth- and early twentieth-century America the *Tales* were often associated with the marvels of new technologies, most likely because of the frequent manipulation of space found there in secret doorways that conceal chthonic worlds and enormous *djinns* that emerge from small bottles. Four years after Wharton's *Age of Innocence* appeared, *The Thief of Baghdad* (1924) thrilled crowds of film goers with its modern special effects (including a flying carpet ride); this classic film was just one of several early films that employed new cinematic technologies to represent tales from the *Arabian Nights* and the Arab world more generally. Such a film makes a cameo appearance in Wharton's 1917 novel *Summer* in which the naïve female protagonist is overwhelmed as "all the world has to show seemed to pass before her in a chaos of palms, minarets, charging cavalry regiments. . . ."[2] In the 1910s and 1920s, links were commonly made between the new art of cinema and the ancient Middle East, because of their mutual "hieroglyphic structure."[3] Still earlier, Edgar Allan Poe, one of Wharton's favorite authors, had directly connected the *Arabian Nights* with the wonders of the future. In Poe's 1845 story "The Thousand-and-Second Tale of Scheherazade," the crafty heroine of the *Arabian Nights* attempts to entertain her murderous monarch-husband by telling him, among other oddities, of the latest discoveries of Poe's own time (the King does not believe her, fulfilling Poe's epigraph "truth is stranger than fiction").[4] Wharton clearly associated Poe with the *Arabian Nights*. In yet another mention of the telephone in *The Age of Innocence*, this time by Ellen Olenska, the new technology garners a reference to the author of the 1002d night: "This struck from all three allusions to Edgar Poe and Jules Verne, and such platitudes as naturally rise to the lips of the most intelligent when they are talking against time, and dealing with a new invention in which it would seem ingenuous to believe too soon" (85). But if Poe is linked to fantasies of the future, he is also for Wharton deeply associated with claustrophobia, suffocation, and premature burial, among her deepest personal fears;[5] indeed, the fear of entrapment and of forced enclosure is a recurring theme in *The Age of Innocence*. Such a theme, of course, also motivates the *Arabian Nights*, which are after all the intertwined tales a female narrator conjures each evening to delay execution in the morning by her husband the King.

Wharton's mention of the *Arabian Nights*, which opposes travel and claustrophobia, technologies of movement and premature burial, re-

2. Edith Wharton, *Summer* (N.Y.: Signet, 1993), p. 91. Examples of silent films set in the Arab world are Cecil B. DeMille's *The Arab* (1915), Ernst Lubitsch's *Eyes of the Mummy* (1916), Douglas Fairbanks' *Bound in Morocco* (1918), *Sahara* (1919), and the blockbuster *The Sheik* (1921). The last spurred on a series of sequels and spoofs throughout the 1920s. Long considered never even to have seen a motion picture (Wharton chose not to see the two cinematic translations of *The Age of Innocence* produced in her lifetime), Wharton saw at least one moving picture in Spain during the summer of 1914, a few months after her return from a springtime trip to Tunisia.
3. Discussing the proliferation of mummy films in the 1910s, the influence of Egyptian architecture on early cinema theaters, and those who wrote about film in the 1920s, Antonia Lant writes: "It became almost a commonplace . . . to explain the newest art in terms of the oldest, to attribute to it a hieroglyphic structure and thus to describe it not only as a universal language but as an originating language" (Lant, "The Curse of the Pharaoh, or How Cinema Contracted Egyptomania," *Visions of the East: Orientalism in Film*, ed. Matthew Bernstein and Gaylyn Studlar [New Brunswick, N.J.: Rutgers University Press, 1997], p. 89).
4. Wharton may have been thinking specifically of this tale, which also includes a reference to the fish of the Mammoth Cave of Kentucky; Newland associates the Kentucky cave fish with May in *The Age of Innocence* (53). Compare Edgar Allan Poe, *The Complete Tales and Poems* (N.Y.: Vintage, 1975), p. 111.
5. See Candace Waid, *Edith Wharton's Letters from the Underworld* (Chapel Hill: University of North Carolina Press, 1991), pp. 177–78ff.

calls the book that immediately preceded *The Age of Innocence* in Wharton's litany of publications: her travelogue *In Morocco* (1920), which had been published earlier in the same year. Just one week prior to her husband Carl Van Doren's review of *The Age of Innocence* for *The Nation*, Irita Van Doren reviewed Wharton's *In Morocco* for the same publication: "All the properties of an Arabian Nights tale are here—camels and donkeys, white-draped riders, palmetto deserts, camel's hair tents, and veiled women."[6] Confusing contemporary Morocco with the classic tales from the Middle East, Van Doren followed Wharton herself, who had described the "untouched" portions of Morocco as having "[e]verything that the reader of the Arabian Nights expects to find."[7] It is one of the peculiarities of the popular Western view of the lands of the Near and Middle East that an allusion to the *Arabian Nights* with its aura of mystery and the inexplicable could signify both the unbelievable technologies of the future and the sand covered realm of the "primitive" past. In either case, the *Arabian Nights* is associated with travel through time, which is always an experience of the *étrange*—the strange and the foreign. And as the novelist L. P. Hartley notes so efficiently, the past is strange in the way that the foreign is strange: "The past is a foreign country; they do things differently there." Newland's "Arabian Nights marvels" of the future similarly play on this double sense of the *étrange*, particularly the idea that the future might make rapid communication across continents possible.

In *The Age of Innocence*, Wharton brings her experience of three continents together. By having Newland refer to the *Arabian Nights*, Wharton was not simply making an allusion to her previous book.[8] Rather, the mention of the *Arabian Nights* suggests the powerful associations Wharton herself made between Old New York society and a colonized North African country ostensibly far beyond the scope of the notoriously exclusive, excluding, and as Wharton's novel suggests limited realm. Such cultural comparison would not be possible for Newland, who is well read, but finally provincial. Newland speaks of wanting "to go away . . . on a long trip, ever so far off—away from everything" (205), suggesting India and Japan, even at one point, Egypt (46), countries all associated with the vaguely defined "Orient." Newland tries to locate himself in a future defined by places that he

6. Reprinted in James Tuttleton, Kristin O. Lauer, Margaret P. Murray, eds., *Edith Wharton: The Contemporary Reviews* (N.Y.: Cambridge University Press, 1992), pp. 300–01.
7. Edith Wharton, *In Morocco* (1920; N.Y.: Ecco, 1996), p. 24. Further references noted in text, with the prefix "IM."
8. Helen Killoran, *Edith Wharton: Art and Allusion* (Tuscaloosa: University of Alabama Press, 1996), p. 131. Killoran sees an allusion here to Horace Walpole's *Hieroglyphic Tales* (1764), in particular to his tale "A New Arabian Nights Entertainment," and more generally through the novel to Washington Irving's *The Alhambra*. While she does catch a reference to Morocco in Wharton's novel *The Children* (1928), there are no mentions of the allusions in *The Age of Innocence* to Wharton's own two preceding books. When she refers to the near robbery of Wharton in Algeria in 1914 as a near rape in Morocco in 1917 (202 n. 11), Killoran makes a grievous error since it plays directly into racist attitudes toward Arab sexuality typical of American Orientalism. Wharton herself is unambiguous about the attempted robbery and also takes pains to specify that the intruder was "I think *not* an Arab" (*The Letters of Edith Wharton*, ed. R. W. B. Lewis and Nancy Lewis [N.Y.: Charles Scribner's Sons, 1998], pp. 318–19).

imagines to be far away from his own "world" and its restrictions. But of course Newland Archer does not take such trips. The European trips Newland does make take place within his own carefully circumscribed world defined by his immediate family. Part of the comic representation of the extreme isolationism of Americans abroad consists in explaining the series of innocent events that led Newland's mother and his sister to break their rule of not "exchang[ing] a word with a 'foreigner' other than those employed in hotels and railway-stations" (117) in order to become friends with the Carfrys, two entirely innocuous British women. Such is Newland's isolation that he and May are compelled to see the Carfrys in London, their only acquaintance in a city that is a "desert" for them socially (117). After May and Newland have been married for a long time and are traveling abroad with their three children, May offers her husband the chance to go off to Paris (the place where Ellen Olenska has made her home). Here, Newland chooses to remain with the family amid the natural scenery of the Alps rather than enter the more imbricated cultural, aesthetic, and erotic temptations associated with Paris (210). Newland can only travel afield through literature, shut up "at home with his spoils" (81), the latest crop of books from his London bookseller, which includes books of anthropology and evolutionary science (43–44, 87).

Wharton herself had traveled extensively, and she had learned to view New York from a perspective that Newland lacks. By the time she wrote *The Age of Innocence*, she had lived in Europe for nearly a decade, had traveled across Tunisia and Algeria in 1914, and visited Morocco. As the imagery of the novel itself underlines, Wharton's 1917 trip to Morocco was fresh in her mind, as she turned from composing her essays on Morocco to another remembered place in her story of Old New York. Wharton's experience of visiting the French protectorate of Morocco was marked strongly by her visit to several harems, representatives of a cultural institution that, by her own account, terrified her. As Wharton had learned, Moroccan harems were not the sensual playgrounds of Western fantasy, nor were they distinguished by any particular architectural enclosure. Rather, the harem— from the Arabic word meaning "the forbidden"—existed by common consent; and like the rigid boundaries of Old New York, seen in the hieroglyphic world of Newland and May's marriage as well as in the realm of Wharton's childhood where rules remained unspoken, the harem's boundaries were invisible and self-imposed. Indeed, Wharton's experience of Morocco clearly informs her retrospective view of the past recreated in *The Age of Innocence*, a novel in which marriage insists on the withdrawal of women from circulation (Newland means for May to be admired by the young men of the best society, but seen from a distance as unattainable). In Wharton's backward glance from the East, she was able to see that she too had come from a closed society, an exclusive society regulated by tribal rites and ceremonies, rituals that had arisen from the fundamental understanding that marriage and renunciation are essential structures in a clan in which kinship is finally everything.

Wharton's deep interest in cultural anthropology encouraged her to compare North Africa, a part of the world she considered "primitive," with the circumscribed world of the New York of her childhood and youth. Wharton's extended use of anthropological metaphors in *The Age of Innocence* has been discussed by such critics as Nancy Bentley and Walter Benn Michaels, who have pointed out Wharton's participation in a general reassessment of the meanings of "culture" in the modern age.[9] Wharton's readings in anthropology were her entrée to a wider perspective on her world and New York "culture." Referring to the work of some of the same anthropologists Newland reads in *The Age of Innocence*, Wharton wrote in her autobiography: it is "hopeless to convey to a younger generation the first overwhelming sense of cosmic vastnesses which such 'magic casements' let into our little geocentric universe."[1] But Wharton did more than simply borrow metaphors and concepts from a newly developing academic field. Rather, she used the observations she had made in Morocco as fieldwork, one of the crucial journeys that allowed her to locate her own past as an exotic world made visible to her through the act of comparing Morocco and New York. While Wharton does not announce this comparison in *The Age of Innocence*, her previous book *In Morocco*, a travel guide of sorts written for English speakers, is structured around the necessity of cultural comparison. For Wharton, the "primitive" aspects of Moroccan culture in the teens had their explicit corollary in the rites and ceremonies of upper-class New York, a world that Wharton and her American readers would have considered nearer to the other end of the cultural hierarchy, nearer to what was still called "civilization." Wharton could borrow the method and vocabulary of ethnographic studies of "primitive" culture with the certainty that Old New York would be considered primitive only in the realm of metaphor. With such confidence, Wharton could distance herself from the material realities of colonized Morocco and adapt lessons learned there in order to critique the ritually constructed walls of isolation and ignorance veiled as innocences in Old New York. Like the Moroccans who maintained the suffocating institution of the harem, New York society had cordoned itself off. For Wharton, the walls that separated men from women in Old New York were repeated in the isolationist walls that kept America apart from the greater world. In 1920, Wharton suggests, America still kept women and men apart in all but sexual commerce, a sign and symptom of the inherent lack of social maturity characteristic of her home nation, which had remained isolationist for far too long during World War I. As *The Age of Innocence* argues, both sets of walls—those constructed by the clans of the elite in Old New York and those that had become part of the edifice of a national identity—were "primitive" innocences that a postwar United States would have to disassemble.

9. Nancy Bentley, " 'Hunting for the Real': Wharton and the Science of Manners," *The Cambridge Companion to Edith Wharton*, ed. Millicent Bell (N.Y.: Cambridge University Press, 1995), pp. 47–67; Walter Benn Michaels, *Our America: Nativism, Modernism, and Pluralism* (Durham, N.C.: Duke University Press, 1995), pp. 110–12.
1. Edith Wharton, *A Backward Glance* (N.Y.: Appleton-Century, 1934), p. 94.

Readers of *The Age of Innocence* have long disagreed about whether Wharton's vision in the novel is one that opposes the modernizing forces at which the younger Newland hesitantly sneers. Surely the novel is marked by Wharton's nostalgia for her own past, the lost world of Old New York and her childhood, yet we should be careful not to misread this recognizable nostalgia for a reactionary reluctance to move forward into what the novel calls the "new state of things." As Dale Bauer has pointed out, Wharton's underappreciated post–World War I fiction is marked by a reorientation of the aging author's earlier concerns and an engagement with "the most heated and fractious arguments concerning the rise of social scientific discourse, the power of mass culture, and the replacement of the cult of personality over 'character.' "[2] Indeed, when we consider *The Age of Innocence* in the context of Wharton's two previous books—*French Ways and Their Meaning* (1919) and *In Morocco*—we are better able to appreciate the layers of cultural comparison at work in Wharton's postwar novel. For Wharton, contemporary French society offered an example to America in how it should conduct itself. American women could learn from their French counterparts, while the United States as a nation might benefit from the example of France's internationalism, an internationalism displayed in, among other things, its management of its colony in Morocco. As *The Age of Innocence* demonstrates, links between such seemingly disparate topics as contemporary French society, Moroccan harems and ritual ceremonies, and Old New York of the 1870s were not arbitrary. Fluent in so many discourses (social, scientific, literary and aesthetic), cosmopolitan, and fiercely political, Wharton brought her experience of France, French North Africa, and her postwar vision for U.S. society to her writing of this seemingly "innocent" novel. In Bauer's words: "Politics and sexuality were topics that Wharton could rarely, if ever, separate" (Bauer, 19). Wharton could move between projects and genres fluidly, but she did not check her international experience at the door when she came to examine the multiple layers, the hierarchical levels of "innocences," that *The Age of Innocence* sought to expose and ultimately to critique.

The younger Newland of *The Age of Innocence* is only able to glimpse such a politics, and usually does not recognize what he is seeing. For the moment, on the train platform, Newland savors the current state of things, particularly the ferry ride across the Hudson that will allow him extra time alone with the desired and ultimately unattainable Ellen. There is an edge of panic in his ruminations on a future in which the train will continue directly to Manhattan. " 'I don't care which of their visions comes true,' " Newland decides, " 'as long as the tunnel isn't built yet.' " How could a romance such as Newland and Ellen's, a romance structured on distance and difference, survive in such an age, in a world fused by time-collapsing technologies? While the young Newland of the 1870s scoffs at "the brotherhood of

2. Dale Bauer, *Edith Wharton's Brave New Politics* (Madison: University of Wisconsin Press, 1994), pp. xiv–xv.

visionaries" who "predicted" such things, the middle aged Newland of the novel's final chapter has come to see those space-collapsing inventions erase time through the direct lines of wires and wirelessness. The inventions that brought disparate places and peoples into closer communication had come to be a part of "the new state of things" (207) with which the novel ends, the dawn of a new century, with a president named Theodore Roosevelt leading the charge of an America with greater international ambitions than those of Newland's youth. Yet even with such changes, America had left itself too walled in, in Wharton's view. After seven years expatriation in Paris, she was deeply disappointed with her native country. In domestic matters, she was critical of the way in which women of her class were "withdrawn from circulation" after marriage; on the international level, she felt betrayed by the long hesitance of the U.S. government to involve the country in World War I, a hesitation nearly fatal to the world and the values Wharton considered to be the highest form of "civilization." Newland's reference to ships that might cross the Atlantic in five days is, from Wharton, a pointed one, further evinced by its repetition in the final chapter, when they have become a "matter of course" (209). Although such ships could traverse the ocean in less than a week, Wharton knows that it took three full years of war (1914–17) before the United States finally joined the struggle. Technology by itself would not break down walls of national isolationism.

Even while seducing us with the story of Ellen and Newland's impossible affair, the novel examines the ways in which the constricted social space of Old New York suffocates its characters. The novel is deeply concerned with the ways in which New York society constructs invisible boundaries everywhere. To have one's "horizon . . . bounded by the Battery and the Central Park" (86) has a much more profound effect on New Yorkers than merely being stifled in love: it makes those Americans, despite all claims to wealth and worldliness, unquestionably provincial. Newland senses the ways in which New York's self-constructed boundaries limit his own possibilities. As he tells Ellen: "I want—I want somehow to get away with you into a world where words like that—categories like that—won't exist"; to which the more worldly countess offers a pessimistic response: "Oh, my dear—where is that country? Have you ever been there?" (174). Wharton knows, of course, that such a "country" is to be found in the future. Her anthropological eye, however, allowed her to see all the more clearly how the categories with which Old New York understood itself were indeed repeated in the "wayside places" that Newland can only conceive of in passion-driven fantasies. Her own recent foray in North Africa provided her with a disturbing experience—the fear of entombment in a harem—and a metaphor by which to understand New York's primitive innocences. These innocences, founded on the sanctity of marriage and the silence of women, would have demanded Wharton's own sacrifice of herself had she not (like Scheherazade) narrated herself into a more cosmopolitan world, acquiring what she herself called "citizenship" in "[t]he Land of Letters" (Wharton, BG, p. 119).

## Morocco Bound

Although she visited Morocco for only three weeks in 1917, Edith Wharton took home a vivid snapshot of the country.[3] If French hosts carefully framed Wharton's sights, her experience of Morocco was nevertheless telling and the lessons she learned in North Africa contained contradictions. While Wharton deplored the Moroccan institution of the harem, which she claimed condemned Moroccan culture never to "grow up" (IM, 205), she praised French efforts to "protect" what she saw as Morocco's "primitive" aspects. The French emphasis on preservation included the maintenance of the historic walls that surrounded the Moroccan *medina* (city). Placing their own administrative buildings on the outskirts of the walled cities, the French made certain that their own roads did not break through what they considered living monuments to the past. The great irony of Wharton's ability to see how harems are constructed by invisible walls that work to contain the individual's subjectivity through internalized boundaries is that she failed to appreciate the ways in which the French colonization of Morocco maintained a similarly debilitating hold on the country. She failed to note how French preservation reversed the direction of the *medina* walls: those walls that had formerly kept foreign intruders out of Moroccan cities, now held Moroccans in. Such an apparent contradiction is explained by Wharton's deep admiration for France, her implicit acceptance of French colonialism, and her inability to imagine Morocco governing itself effectively. And while Wharton was not alone of course in supporting colonialism, her admiration for General Lyautey's "sympathetic" (IM, 213) approach to governing Morocco helps clarify her post–World War I vision for America.

Despite Wharton's precise observation of the architecture of the harems, she took away a sense of the visible effect of a segregation based more in culture than architectural construction. After all, the Arabic word *harim* translates as "an inviolable place," and is derived from the verb *haruma*, "to be forbidden."[4] Thus in Moroccan culture, the "harem" need not refer solely to a physical enclosure, but also (and more generally) to an internalized set of invisible borders, as the Moroccan feminist sociologist Fatima Mernissi has shown.[5] For Wharton, not only did the harem enfeeble Moroccan women, but it was a "stifling" (IM, 204) institution that restrained Morocco from maturing as a nation. Even if she ignored France's own role in "stifling" the Moroccan people, Wharton's intended lesson for America was that national maturity is impossible without a reconsideration of its own

3. Clifford Geertz, the important American anthropologist who did fieldwork in Morocco during the 1960s and 1970s, calls Wharton in Morocco "distant, superior, but marvelously observant" (Geertz, *After the Fact* [Cambridge, Mass.: Harvard University Press, 1995], p. 84).
4. Hans Wehr, *A Dictionary of Modern Written Arabic*, ed. J. Milton Cowan (Beirut: Librairie du Liban, 1980).
5. Fatima Mernissi connects the "harem" with the concept of *huddud* (borders, "sacred frontiers") and argues that the idea of the harem is internalized by Moroccan women and men. Its architectural component is only secondary. Thus Mernissi is able to call the French protectorate over Morocco, "the French Harem" (Mernissi, *Dreams of Trespass: Tales of a Harem Girlhood* [Reading, Mass.: Addison-Wesley, 1994]).

internalized walls, its own harem structures. In her 1919 book *French Ways and Their Meaning*, Wharton was explicit: "No nation can have grown-up ideas till it has a ruling caste of grown-up men and women; and it is possible to have a ruling caste of grown-up men and women only in a civilisation where the power of each sex is balanced by that of the other."[6] If France offered Wharton a model, she elided any sense she may have had of the harem structure of French colonialism and focused on the French metropole's international and sexual cosmopolitanism. By so doing, Wharton suppressed the metropole's reliance on its subjugated colonies for that very cosmopolitanism. French "civilization" positioned itself as "grown-up" precisely by making certain that its colonial subjects remained children.

Since 1912, Morocco had been a French "protectorate," the name by which the colonization of Morocco went. Under Resident-General Hubert Lyautey's influential administration (1912–25), Moroccan "primitiveness" was guarded through the construction of a network of highways, railroads, airports, ports, and schools outside and around Moroccan towns and cities. After France's more direct colonization of Algeria (1830) and Tunisia (1881), Lyautey's project for Morocco revised French techniques for administering a country it could not hope fully to understand. Yet Lyautey's complex technologies of control, derived from an avowed sense of what Paul Rabinow calls his *démophilie*, or love for the Moroccan "children" he felt it was his duty to protect, effectively framed an essentialist idea of Moroccan "culture."[7] Wharton's description of Lyautey's approach demonstrates her admiration: "A sympathetic understanding of the native prejudices, and a real affection for the native character, made him try to build up an administration which should be, not an application of French ideas to African conditions, but a development of the best native aspirations" (IM, 213). Both Wharton and Lyautey shared an idea of Moroccan "culture" that relied on French Orientalist scholarship and a literary and pictorial tradition of depicting Morocco as a sensual and unpredictable fantasyland, forever trapped in the past. Nevertheless, for Wharton, even the "best native aspirations" were hopelessly far from "French ideas."

Wharton, both well-known writer and respected social activist in war-ravaged Paris, was invited to Morocco by Resident-General Lyautey as an official guest of the French Protectorate, most likely with the hope that she would publicize his efforts to the Anglophone world. The trip was a vacation from Wharton's wartime duties in Paris, and she clearly was a willing participant in Lyautey's fantasy that Morocco might be kept outside of time's way, a journey into the past that served as a prelude to her historical foray in *The Age of Innocence*.[8]

6. Edith Wharton, *French Ways and Their Meaning* (N.Y.: D. Appleton-Century Co., 1919), p. 113. Further references noted in text, with the prefix "FW."
7. Paul Rabinow, "Techno-Cosmopolitanism: Governing Morocco," in *French Modern: Norms and Forms of the Social Environment* (Cambridge, Mass.: MIT Press, 1989), p. 283.
8. Earlier in his career, Lyautey had enlisted the efforts of the Swiss writer Isabelle Eberhardt in the aid of his political projects in Algeria, despite Eberhardt's putative anticolonial politics. See Ali Behdad, *Belated Travelers: Orientalism in the Age of Colonial Dissolution* (Durham: Duke University Press, 1994), pp. 113–32.

Chauffeured around by government limousine—"the next best thing to a Djinn's carpet" (IM, viii)—Wharton felt that she had returned to the imagined space of the *Arabian Nights*. Writing to Mary Cadwalader Jones, her confidante and former sister-in-law, Wharton declared: "I write from a fairy world, where a motor from the 'Résidence' stands always at the door to carry us to new wonders, & where every expedition takes one straight into Harun-al-Raschid land."[9] Wharton decided that time was a Western concept with little meaning in Morocco. Remarking on Fez, the cultural capital of Morocco, Wharton writes: "[O]ur pink-saddled mules carried us at once out of the bounds of time. How associate anything so precise and Occidental as years or centuries with these visions of frail splendor seen through cypresses and roses?" (IM, 83–84) Everywhere she looked, she saw evidence for her theory: "The passion for clocks and other mechanical contrivances is common to all unmechanical races, and every chief's palace in North Africa contains a collection of time pieces which might be called striking if so many had not ceased to go" (IM, 172).

With Morocco safely ensconced in the timeless past, it could be served up to her as a museum, easily delivered data for her cultural analysis. And she was particularly interested in the "spectacle" (IM, 170) of the Moroccan harem. A celebrated American woman and an official guest of the Resident General, Wharton was invited to pass through doorways whose points of egress were barred to Moroccan women. Yet she did not—perhaps could not—imagine that by doing so she mirrored France's own colonial invasion, a forcible entry into once private places. Indeed, Wharton summons a particularly rapacious vocabulary to describe the occasions on which she "penetrated" (IM, 165) spaces from which other Moroccans were kept: "The eunuch delivered us to other negresses, and we entered a labyrinth of inner passages and patios, all murmuring and dripping with water" (IM, 171). Wharton's narrative of her visits to Moroccan harems mixes the sexualized language of nineteenth-century exploration narratives with the polite language of the Victorian drawing room. Although Wharton knew the double function of doorways—that a door's purpose is as much to exclude as it is to admit—she never questioned her right to enter the doorways of Moroccan harems. As Wharton had written over thirty years earlier, in *The Decoration of Houses*, "Under ordinary circumstances, doors should always be kept shut."[1] But when doors are opened, Wharton advised, they should leave little doubt as to the importance of visitors: "Doors should always swing *into* a room. This facilitates entrance and gives the hospitable impression that everything is made easy to those who are coming in" (DH, 61). Wharton traversed those otherwise closed harem doors with the confidence that her privileged position would leave her unaffected. Yet if Wharton's invited visits to the harem of the Moroccan Sultan, and those of three high dignitaries in Rabat, Fez, and Marrakech, were conducted with

9. *Letters*, ed. Lewis and Lewis, p. 399.
1. Edith Wharton and Ogden Codman, Jr., *The Decoration of Houses* (1897; N.Y.: W. W. Norton, 1978), p. 49. Further references noted in text, with the prefix "DH."

all the hospitality of a door that swings inward, once inside Wharton felt herself threateningly closed in. The harem, Wharton decided, was a stifling prison, a claustrophobic tomb, in which "both sexes live till old age in an atmosphere of sensuality without seduction" (IM, 195). Wharton's visits to the harems of the Moroccan elite brought her into uncomfortable proximity with women whose social class she recognized, even if the comparison to their Western counterparts left her with a relieved sense of her own ability to escape. Nonetheless, Wharton's sense of claustrophobia in the Moroccan harem intensified markedly when she realized the effect of enclosure—both literal and figurative—on *herself* and a moment of sympathy with the harem women was sufficient to break off her narrative.

Visiting the home of a high government official, "a Moroccan dignitary of the old school," Wharton is received by several women of the household. Sitting in a modestly appointed room, Wharton allows herself a cultural comparison:

> They all wore sober dresses, in keeping with the simplicity of the house, and but for the vacuity of their faces the group might have been that of a Professor's family in an English or American University town, decently costumed for an Arabian Nights' pageant in the college grounds. I was never more vividly reminded of the fact that human nature, from one pole to the other, falls naturally into certain categories, and that Respectability wears the same face in an Oriental harem as in England or America. (IM, 184–85)

The women's elevated social class—their "Respectability"—is important to Wharton and permits her to compare these upper-middle-class Moroccan women to their American and British contemporaries. The image of American women and men costuming themselves for an "Arabian Nights' pageant" allows Wharton to suggest the existence of the Moroccan harem in her home country's "decent" society. Even if dressing up as harem women relies on an assumed cultural distance of the United States from the "Orient," Wharton claims that the Anglo-American women have successfully replicated the harem—their performance of the harem is, she suggests, accurate. All that separates the Anglo-American women from their Moroccan counterparts is the "vacuity" of the Moroccan faces. But Wharton removes even this distinction in the following sentence: the fact that the Western women wear costumes masks the observation that both Moroccan and Anglo-American women "wear the same face." By bringing American and Moroccan women into the same equation, Wharton produces the sort of cultural comparison of which the male protagonist of *The Age of Innocence* is incapable. Wharton's performs her cosmopolitanism; in the Moroccan harem, she alone is able to compare Moroccan and American society. Such an international perspective is in distinction to the isolationism that she explicates in *The Age of Innocence*, where Newland's inability to make international analogies reflects the isolationist policies of the United States.

The exclusion of French women from Wharton's comparison here is significant. In *French Ways and Their Meaning*, Wharton had argued at length that American women must attempt to learn about "the new Frenchwoman" (FW, 99; see pp. 288–96 in this volume). The superiority of the French woman was not new at all, Wharton claims, but France's successful carrying of the burden of World War I was due in no small part to the role of its women, a success that should compel American women to "try to find out what she is, and why she is what she is" (FW, 102). For Wharton, the comparison is clear. American women are "like children in a baby-school," but "like the men of her race, the Frenchwoman is *grown up*" (FW, 100). According to Wharton, this maturation is due to French women's direct and integral role in the business activities of their husbands, whereas American women "are each other's only audience, and to a great extent each other's only companions."

If, according to Wharton, American women are cloistered—or put into a figurative harem—the walls of that harem are established through the institution of marriage: "It is precisely at the moment when her experience is rounded by marriage, motherhood, and the responsibilities, cares and interests of her own household, that the average American woman is, so to speak, 'withdrawn from circulation'" (FW, 115). In the Moroccan harem, Wharton offers an exaggerated example of women removed from circulation. A brief conversation with the women ensues, with the host's brother-in-law fielding Wharton's more pointed questions. The discussion continues awkwardly, not only because of the brother-in-law's intervention, but also because the Moroccan women remind Wharton of the parallel between themselves and their American sisters. They ask the divorced Wharton whether she has children, and Wharton responds "alas," telling them that "in the western world also childless women were pitied." The comment is a caustic reminder for her American readers, and in the context of her argument regarding French women, an instruction for those American women who would sympathize with Moroccan women without critically examining their own cultural constriction.[2]

Wharton's chapter on harems substitutes a domestic idea of the harem for the romantic idea of concubinage that was prevalent in contemporary Western representations of North African female captivity. As she writes: the "word [concubine] evokes to occidental ears images of sensual seduction which the Moroccan harem seldom realizes" (IM, 192).[3] If Wharton's analysis of marriage as captivity was not rare, Wharton's departure from a romantic reinscription of the harem

2. Compare the sympathy of the "radical" American writer Mary Heaton Vorse, who after a visit to Tangier, Morocco, in 1909, concluded: "When the East and the West meet, two women can more easily bridge the gulf of religion and language and custom if they are both mothers of small boys" (Vorse, "The Infidel City," *Harper's Monthly*, 120 [May 1910]: 821).

3. Fatima Mernissi distinguishes between the imperial harems of the Muslim imperial dynasties (from the Damascus-based Omayyads of the seventh century through the Ottoman Empire, which stretched from the sixteenth century until 1909) and the domestic harems that existed well into the twentieth century. The former is that which "has fascinated the West almost to the point of obsession"; the latter, which is the type that Wharton visited and that Mernissi discusses, is the more mundane and, in Mernissi's words, has "hardly any erotic dimension to speak of" (Mernissi, *Dreams of Trespass*, 34–35 *n*).

was rare in contemporary English-language representations of North Africa.[4] One need only compare the history of Lady Diana in the wildly popular American film *The Sheik* (1921). The would-be feminist Diana (played by Agnes Ayres) begins an unaccompanied desert journey by refusing a suitor: "Marriage is captivity—the end of independence. I am content with my life as it is." But confronted by a tempting and powerful chieftain (played by Rudolph Valentino), Diana revises her ideas about her need of or desire for freedom.[5] Unlike *The Sheik*'s romanticization of the idea of female captivity via a fantasy of North Africa—"When an Arab sees a woman that he wants, he takes her!" exclaims the Sheik in one of the silent film's titles—Wharton's portrait of the North African harem demonstrates the lack of appeal in cordoning off women, whether literally or through social and legal codes.

Wharton's discussion of Moroccan harems ends the travelogue portion of her book, and the text breaks off, wondering at the future of a Morocco that sustains the harem. As she makes clear in her discussion of the French woman, the perils of sexual segregation endanger more than women; the nation itself is imperiled. Even while Moroccan women are made passive and pathetic by the harem, Wharton understands Moroccan men to be enfeebled as well by the boundaries separating the sexes. The men in the harems Wharton visited include eunuchs and "hermaphrodite" boy dancers, an "aloof" Sultan, and the Caïd of Marrakech, who seems "great" and "enlightened" to Wharton, until she remembers his concubines in the context of "all the shadowy evils of the social system that hangs like a millstone about the neck of Islam" (IM, 201). Wharton's final image in her description of the Moroccan harem is of a fragile male infant in Marrakech, the diminutive child of the powerful Caïd, and the heir to the spiritual leadership of the Moroccan south: "The weak little body hung with amulets and the heavy head covered with thin curls pressed against a brocaded bosom. . . . No precaution had been neglected to protect him from maleficent influences and the danger that walks by night, for his frail neck and wrists were hung with innumerable charms" (IM, 204–5). For Wharton, the image of the ghostly child is a harbinger of cultural degradation. "Would all his pretty mothers, his eyes seemed to ask, succeed in bringing him to maturity in spite of the parched summers of the south and the stifling existence of the harem?" (IM, 204–5). Wharton's narrative concludes wistfully, as she leaves behind a culture she has condemned to childhood, destined never to mature. The moment of

4. I am indebted to Elizabeth Ammons's discussion of Wharton's position in regards to "New Woman" debates and definitions. Ammons dedicates only one paragraph to *In Morocco*, however, and does not interrogate the relationship of Wharton's experience of the Moroccan harem to patriarchal structures in American society. See Ammons, *Edith Wharton's Argument with America* (Athens: University of Georgia Press, 1980). For powerful studies of the relationship of British travel discourse on harems to domestic debates about women, see Inderpal Grewal, *Home and Harem: Nation, Gender, Empire and the Cultures of Travel* (Durham: Duke University Press, 1996), and Anne McClintock, *Imperial Leather: Race, Gender and Sexuality in the Colonial Contest* (N.Y.: Routledge, 1995).

5. See Miriam Hansen, "Male Stars, Female Fans" for a reading of female identification with the captivity narrative in *The Sheik* (Hansen, *Babel & Babylon: Spectatorship in American Silent Film* [Cambridge, Mass.: Harvard University Press, 1991]).

sympathy passes—too much cultural comparison would be unthinkable—and Wharton's next chapter champions the ways in which General Lyautey has saved Morocco from self-destruction.

It is particularly significant that Wharton breaks off the account of her travels in the harem, for it is there that she feels most threatened by the effect of proscribed invisible boundaries on individual subjectivity. The painful surprise that, after too much time in a Moroccan harem, Wharton herself felt bound—"I felt my own lips stiffening into the resigned smile of the harem"—informs Wharton's recognition that her New York, particularly the New York of her youth, also walled off its women. On the national level, post–World War I restrictions on immigration and xenophobia satirized the "Open Door" of U.S. imperial policy toward Central and South America, a policy that Wharton's former lover Morton Fullerton had written about in his *Problems of Power* (1913). Wharton brought her experience of the harem as a debilitating enclosure into her analysis of Old New York in *The Age of Innocence*. By recognizing the interconnectedness of sexual politics and international relations, Wharton's texts of the early 1920s contribute to the postwar environment an argument for a more fluid understanding of gendered and national spaces. Although she confesses not to understand fully the option for America that she would propose three years after the publication of *The Age of Innocence* in her novel *A Son at the Front* (set in Paris during World War I), Wharton senses that France can instruct the United States in an internationalism without boundaries. If such an internationalism included a disregard for the self-determination of less powerful nations such as Morocco, so be it; for Wharton, such countries had doomed themselves to outside intervention by refusing to remove their own "primitive" structures. Moving from one literary project to the next in quick succession, Wharton's fiction suggests that she was viewing her past as both a familiar and a foreign country; and, seeing harems all over Old New York in *The Age of Innocence*, Wharton recalls the difficult lessons she learned during her journey to "Harun-al-Raschid land."

### Here and There

*The Age of Innocence* begins with a figurative harem. In the novel's opening scene, New York society is tucked away in opera boxes, looking out from them and being looked upon. Under the watchful eyes of such social arbiters as Lawrence Lefferts and Sillerton Jackson, Old New York is contained as surely by the rules of "form" and the lines of "family" as it is by the enclosure of the prestigious boxes themselves. With such boundaries in place, any variance is immediately visible, as it is when the Mingott family announces the return of the long-absent Ellen Olenska (estranged from her foreign husband) by bringing her into their box. Making such a public statement strikes Newland as inappropriate, a violation of form, since Ellen is shown "in the very box" (9) where his future fiancée is also visible. Opera boxes here are like domestic harems, with the women of a family grouped in careful arrangements, and the problem for Newland is that the women of his own prospective family are so much on display: "It was annoying that the box which was thus attracting the undivided attention of masculine New York should be that in which his betrothed was seated between her mother and aunt" (8). He is bothered to such an extent that he can think of nothing to do but enter that female space himself, and thus he enacts the part of a jealous harem keeper. In response to the opera glasses turned upon his women folk, Newland decides to "be the first man to enter Mrs. Mingott's box," in order "to see [May] through" her difficulties (11). If the Mingott women are to be seen, he will make sure that he is seen with them. Intent on asserting his masculine presence and his role as a protector of female and family virtue, Newland increasingly becomes a powerless emissary of these women who recognize his usefulness as an enforcer of boundaries, a man who fulfills the classic function of the eunuch, pledged to the service of boxed-in women.

Throughout *The Age of Innocence*, Wharton represents the limited horizon of what is permissible in New York society with architectural motifs, suggesting again the doubled meaning of *harim* (the inviolable place). Newland's own mother and sister Janey live in a sort of harem themselves, "squeezed . . . into narrower quarters below" (22) to accommodate his own more spacious apartments on a separate floor; such an arrangement is repeated by Janey's "springs of suppressed romance" (23) and the pretense maintained even at home that because unmarried, she can not speak of "grown-up" matters. Similarly the eccentric "ancestress," Mrs. Manson Mingott, is considered radically unconventional because she keeps the doorway to her bedroom "always open," startling her visitors by "the foreignness of this arrangement, which recalled scenes in French fiction, and architectural incentives to immorality such as the simple American had never dreamed of" (19). Mrs. Mingott recalls the Empress Mother described in *In Morocco*, an exceptional elderly woman who advises her son the sultan and whom Wharton portrays as having "air and daylight" in the "depth of her soul" (IM, 178). Both Mrs. Mingott and the Moroccan Empress Mother are anomalous in their societies precisely because the doors of communication they have opened let "air and daylight" into their souls; and of course the exceptions here prove Wharton's rule. Newland speaks of his society "wholly absorbed in barricading itself against the unpleasant" (62), a society that is "narrow" (71). His conversations with his writer-friend Ned Winsett lead Newland to the conclusion that literary New York "turned out, in the end, to be a smaller box, with a more monotonous pattern, than the assembled atoms of Fifth Avenue" (79). Even if Fifth Avenue comes out ahead here, both upper-class New York and literary New York are, in Newland's metaphor, constricting and monotonous boxes. The image repeats the novel's opening scene at the opera, with New York society separated into diorama-like boxes, classified and put on display, flanked by others of what the novel calls their own "kind." The metaphor of a society that keeps itself in boxes is extended throughout the novel. In church, Newland looks out and sees his circle seated "in the same boxes (no, pews)" (110), and in Newport, the Wellands' house is referred to as "one of the square boxes on the cliffs" (126). As the novel progresses, such boxes become vaults in Wharton's imagery, as doors and windows close and asphyxiate.

If the social and spatial arrangements of New York are stifling, it is not surprising that Newland frequently employs metaphors of burial to describe New York's unwritten social codes. In a moment of clarity, as he is confronted with rumors about Countess Olenska's affair, Newland blurts out: "I'm sick of the hypocrisy that would bury alive a woman . . . if her husband prefers to live with harlots"; it is "a discovery of which he was too irritated to measure the terrific consequences" (27, 27). The image of a premature burial recalls the "painted sepulchre at the harem" in Morocco (IM, 188), a signal that Wharton associates New York's restrictive codes with the living death of Moroccan harem life. Newland's "discovery" also looks forward to another of Wharton's writings set in North Africa, her Poe-like tale "A Bottle of Perrier" (1926), in which a long-awaited character is found to have been buried in the well of his own desert home. As Candace Waid has argued regarding "A Bottle of Perrier," Wharton's story about a feminized man entrapped within the timelessness of the desert is more than merely a ghost story: "[It] depicts Wharton's fears about the dangers of stasis and her anxieties about the stagnation she associated with the place of women."[6] Wharton's experience of North Africa continued to resonate for her throughout the 1920s; her memory of the harem representing the ways in which societal forms could suffocate the individual.

*The Age of Innocence* is deeply informed by Wharton's interest in the incipient field of cultural anthropology, which at the moment of her writing was developing the new practice of "fieldwork" in order to study the "ways and their meaning" of peoples in other corners of the world. Indeed, it is the anthropological trope that allows Wharton to make the otherwise unnamed comparison between Moroccan harems and New York ones. Paradoxically, Wharton's attention to developments in twentieth-century anthropology connects her novel to modern intellectual currents even while it allowed her to keep contemporary New York culture at a distance. Dale Bauer points out a contradiction in Wharton's interest in contemporary anthropology and her "hatred of the so-called primitive such as Harlem life," what Bauer calls elsewhere "Wharton's repressed racial unconscious."[7] Wharton preferred to keep her primitives at a distance, in their place, which is precisely the reason that her portrait of Old New York is so blanched. Thus even while North Africa is on her mind, African-American culture appears as only a shadowy presence in Wharton's vision of Amer-

---

6. Candace Waid, *Edith Wharton's Letters from the Underworld*, p. 184. This tale, first published in March 1926 in the *Saturday Evening Post* under the title "A Bottle of Evian," was included in Wharton's collection *Certain People* (N.Y.: D. Appleton, 1930).
7. Bauer, *Edith Wharton's Brave New Politics*, pp. 178, 167. (See pp. 474–82 in this volume [Editor].)

ica, thrown off in a phrase, a dismissive reference to the Wellands' Florida servants "drawn from the local African supply" (89) or reappearing suggestively, as Anne MacMaster has pointed out, in the form of Mrs. Mingott's "mulatto" maid who more than once enters the room when Newland is expecting the dark and sexually provocative Ellen.[8] Wharton's novel mentions Emerson Sillerton, the archeologist who prefers to "explore tombs in Yucatan instead of going to Paris or Italy," and who does such "revolutionary things" as give a "party for a black man" (134), demonstrating her association of African and African-American culture with the study of the "primitive"; but the novel leaves Professor Sillerton as well as his celebrated colleague of color off stage. Similarly, Wharton keeps Morocco and the harem at a distance, an implicit and structuring metaphor about the restrictive structures of New York society. Wharton's choice to keep the Moroccan harem off stage while critiquing harem structures in American society replicates a move authorized by the work of modern American anthropologists such as Franz Boas, soon to be joined by Margaret Mead and Ruth Benedict, whose studies of cultures at a remove from Anglo America implied and justified arguments about shortcomings in Anglo-American culture.

In this way, *The Age of Innocence*'s combination of nostalgia and an anthropological perspective—both of which might be considered technologies of looking[9]—reveal the marked modernism of the novel and suggest Wharton's understanding of the tangled relationship of culture, writing, and place in what was then a new world order, a cultural landscape in which the meanings of the "world" and "America" had recently, rapidly, and irrevocably changed. As Newland's wife's new carriage carries the temporarily joined, but ultimately divided couple up Fifth Avenue, Ellen reminds Newland of their place in the clan-ordained scheme of things: "[W]e're only Newland Archer, the husband of Ellen Olenska's cousin, and Ellen Olenska, the cousin of Newland Archer's wife" (175). Throughout *The Age of Innocence*, Wharton charts the genealogical relationships between characters almost obsessively, with branches overlapping and intertwining; given names are usually family names, and thus they bear meaning. Such careful attention to kinship reflects her admiration for the anthropology of Bronislaw Malinowski, who during the teens had argued for the importance of first-hand fieldwork in his studies of aboriginal Australian and Melanesian kinship patterns and the relationship of the social institution of the family to "the general structure of society."[1] Following *French Ways and Their Meaning* and *In Morocco*, Wharton

---

8. See MacMaster's essay in this volume, pp. 461–74 [Editor].
9. For discussions of the changes in understanding time and space in relation to technological developments during the modern period see Jonathan Crary, *Techniques of the Observer: On Vision and Modernity in the Nineteenth Century* (Cambridge, Mass.: MIT Press, 1990); Anne Friedberg, *Window Shopping: Cinema and the Postmodern* (Berkeley and Los Angeles: University of California Press, 1993); Stephen Kern, *The Culture of Time and Space: 1880–1918* (Cambridge, Mass.: Harvard University Press, 1983).
1. Bronislaw Malinowski, *The Family among the Australian Aborigines* (1913), quoted in George W. Stocking, Jr., *The Ethnographer's Magic* (Madison: University of Wisconsin Press, 1992), p. 41. See also Nancy Bentley, "Hunting for the Real."

turned to a novel that would study the tribal patterns and ritual meanings of Old New York and locate within those ornate patterns of upper- and upper-middle-class society the "general structure" of the society of the United States. The crucial importance of Wharton's complex use of anthropological perspective is in how the novel allows us to read Wharton's deeply inscribed interest in what lay beyond the boundaries of Old New York even in a book that seems to be so firmly ensconced within them. Wharton's *Age of Innocence* becomes her own study, in the form of a work of fiction, of the rituals and ceremonies of New York's elite, an explication of the clans of American aristocracy.

In *The Age of Innocence*, Wharton's cultural comparisons of "primitive" and "respectable" society, then, contribute to a larger argument against American naïveté, a strong argument against cultural and political isolation. As E. B. Tylor argued at the end of his influential book of 1871, *Primitive Culture* (no doubt one of the books on "Primitive Man" to which the novel alludes), anthropology could indeed be a "reformer's science."[2] The frequency and ingenuousness with which Newland Archer employs the seemingly innocent phrases "not for the world" and "nothing in the world" marks one of the many "innocences" left behind by World War I. Wharton, whose wartime work in Paris was motivated by a deep concern for the future of the "world" and "civilization" in the face of the German threat and whose frustration with the long period of isolationism in U.S. policy is dramatized in her war novel *A Son at the Front*, was arguably, as she stood amid the uncleared rubble of 1920, as critical of such an international innocence as she was nostalgic for it.[3]

Although Wharton makes scant reference to the subject matter of her preceding book, her experience in Morocco clearly informs her rendering of the "hieroglyphic world" (29) of Old New York. What Wharton brings from her trip to Morocco to *The Age of Innocence* is a sense that harems (both literal and figurative) leave their powerful imprint on a culture and threaten the future of a nation. Wharton's ironic association of the Arabian Nights with the future of the American infrastructure—in Newland's Jersey City ruminations about the technological advances that are soon to come to pass—plays on her larger vision of the harem structures, the walls of the culturally for-

2. Nancy Bentley, *The Ethnography of Manners: Hawthorne, James, Wharton* (N.Y.: Cambridge University Press, 1995), p. 76.

3. Nostalgia is most often understood as motivated by conservative and reactionary social forces, particularly in the context of imperialism and colonialist nostalgia. See, for example, Renato Rosaldo, "Imperialist Nostalgia," in *Culture & Truth* (Boston: Beacon Press, 1989); Edward Said, "Overlapping Territories, Intertwined Histories," in *Culture and Imperialism* (N.Y.: Knopf, 1993). For an argument resuscitating the political possibilities of nostalgia, see Stuart Tannock, "Nostalgia Critique," *Cultural Studies* 9 (Oct. 1995): 453–64. See also Susan Stewart's challenging and rewarding study, *On Longing: Narratives of the Miniature, the Gigantic, the Souvenir, the Collection* (Durham, N.C.: Duke University Press, 1993). On Wharton's involvement with wartime charities, see Alan Price, *The End of the Age of Innocence* (N.Y.: St Martin's Press, 1996). On her political arguments against German eugenics and a reading of her understanding of "culture," see Bauer, *Edith Wharton's Brave New Politics*. Chapter 4, "The War," of Ammons' *Edith Wharton's Argument with America*, argues that World War I encouraged Wharton to revisit her "argument" regarding the "new woman" in America. Shari Benstock's introduction to *A Son at the Front* (1923; DeKalb, Ill.: Northern Illinois University Press, 1995) points out the relationship between Wharton's war work and frustration about American isolation.

bidden that were framing, restraining, and infantilizing American society. When Newland looks back on his career at the end of the novel, when all those Arabian Nights marvels have come true, he notes that "even his small contribution to the new state of things seemed to count, as each brick counts in a well-built wall" (207). That metaphorical "well-built wall" of American society suggests the double function of a Whartonian door—it excludes and divides as much as it protects. As *The Age of Innocence* suggests, the wall of international isolationism that divided America from the world is, for Wharton, inextricably linked to the culturally constructed and equally infantilizing wall dividing American men and women.

Earlier, standing at the altar waiting for his bride, May Welland, "still, in look and tone, the simple girl of yesterday," Newland Archer reflects that a New York wedding was "a rite that seemed to belong to the dawn of history" (109). Its ceremonial rituals give him comfort, as he recalls the debate over whether the wedding presents should be "shown" and looks forward to a private evening, "concealment of the spot in which the bridal night was to be spent being one of the most sacred taboos of the prehistoric ritual" (110). New York, after all, decides carefully when to exhibit and when to conceal. Yet as he casts his anthropological eye on the event—standing both outside it and inside it like a modern ethnographer—Newland senses the limitation of his own perspective. Caught up in the most celebrated rite of his own culture, the groom speculates on the "real things" happening elsewhere: "[T]here was a time when . . . everything concerning the manners and customs of his little tribe had seem to him fraught with world-wide significance. 'And all the while, I suppose,' he thought, 'real people were living somewhere, and real things happening to them . . .'" (111). When Ellen's final departure is secured, and her troublesome role in New York society is concealed in order to give her a proper send off, a "tribute," Newland recognizes a "tribal rally around a kinswoman about to be eliminated from the tribe" (200).

Newland's anthropological view of New York society recognizes its circumscribed boundaries, the space within which its "codes" and "meanings" exist. Newland reads anthropology, keeping up with the latest developments through his London bookdealer (87). His interest in the developing science not only provides him with a vocabulary with which to understand the "manners and customs of his little tribe" (111) but also distances him from a more immediate emotional involvement with his society. As Newland reflects in a moment of self-consciousness, before returning to his role as a participant observer: "He supposed that his readings in anthropology caused him to take such a coarse view of what was after all a simple and natural demonstration of family feeling" (43). For Newland, anthropology is a form of perspective, a set off space from which to "take . . . a coarse view" or even to view the coarseness of his contemporaries. One of the dramatic arcs of *The Age of Innocence* is, then, how Newland recognizes that New York has always been bound by such codes of conduct and how those codes rely upon firmly laid albeit invisible borders and cultural walls. Such a society has "placed its powerful imprint" upon Newland, and like the girl in the Rabat harem, Newland can only look at his surroundings with "remote and passive eyes" (IM, 187).

Ellen Olenska, of course, is a woman in a different sort of a harem, unhappily married to a roguish count kept ever off stage in a forbiddingly libertine Europe. But Newland, as her influential cousin, her legal counselor, and her lover, persuades her to abide by the New York codes of conduct, to remain legally bound: "Our legislation favours divorce—our social customs don't" (70). Stuttering, he separates her from any legitimate contact with him or any other man as he argues that a woman who "has exposed herself" to insinuation is in effect a woman who cannot afford to leave the harem (70). "But my freedom—is that nothing?" she asks. "But aren't you free as air as it is?" he replies. By accepting Newland's analysis, Ellen moves from one harem—Count Olenski's—to another. If Newland realizes the constrictedness of Old New York's codes of conduct as he both participates in and observes the social hypocrisies of this rigidly defined world, Ellen becomes aware of her haremification only as she grasps that she cannot remain forever an observer in New York and has unwittingly become a participant. In other words, once Newland, the self-styled anthropologist, instructs her to read that space *between* legislation and customs, Ellen is trapped, as if by the very line on the page (—), the dash that questions the equation of a woman's "freedom" with "nothing." As Wharton had underlined in "The New Frenchwoman," "the growth and the maturing take place *in the intervals between*" (FW, 109) the material realities of living. That interval for Ellen is taken away when liberal legislation cedes to restrictive customs. As Ellen asks earlier: "Is New York such a labyrinth? I thought it so straight up and down—like Fifth Avenue. And with all the cross streets numbered!" (49). The escape to New York, which Ellen initially and seemingly without irony called "heaven," gradually becomes an incarceration, the grid of straight streets and avenues turns from Cartesian plane to the crosshatch of what is increasingly linked in the novel to the interment in family vaults and life sentences behind closed prison windows.

Wharton saves her most direct allusion to the harem for her description of Ellen's home on West 23d Street, the unfashionable place where she has gone to escape the prying eyes that want *not* to see her transgressions. Ellen's home, her hideaway, becomes only more visible by its "Bohemian" location in a neighborhood associated with artists and "people who wrote" (66). Here, the countess is visited by those society gentlemen who go out of their way to see her. Secluding herself only highlights Ellen's boundedness within New York's harem, and her drawing room appropriately conjures up the East: "the atmosphere . . . was so different from any [Newland] had ever breathed that self-consciousness vanished in the sense of adventure" (45); the room had "been transformed into something intimate, 'foreign,' subtly suggestive of old romantic scenes and sentiments" (45). Newland is titillated and disoriented: "He tried to analyze the trick, to find a clue in the way the chairs and tables were grouped, . . . in the vague pervading perfume that was not what one put on handkerchiefs, but rather like the scent of some far-off bazaar, a smell made up of Turkish coffee and amber-gris and dried roses" (46). Although the house is "shabby" (45) with a startling piece of red damask "nailed on discoloured wallpaper" (44), and as in the Moroccan palaces and harems, Ellen's clock has stopped, Newland cannot help but be seduced by this place that re-minds him of the Orient: "New York seemed much farther off than Samarkand" (49). But in being seduced by the woman who is so clearly trapped in a web of social and legal codes, Newland himself is prey to the popular misconception of the harem as bordello, the New Woman as "vamp."[4] Precisely every detail that demonstrates Ellen's suffocation—her claustrophobia—is stimulating to Newland. Ellen goes out to dinner not in white silk, "slightly open in the neck" like New York ladies, but "attired in a long robe of red velvet bordered about the chin and down the front with glossy black fur" (67). And just as he is excited by her interior decoration, Newland is excited by Ellen's clothing: "There was something perverse and provocative in the notion of fur worn in the evening in a heated drawing-room, and in the combination of a muffled throat and bare arms; but the effect was undeniably pleasing" (67). Ellen's clothing exaggerates, or satirizes, the suffocation of her own marital harem, and her refusal to wear the white of the supposedly innocent May and her decision to wear red re-minds her suitors that she is a woman of experience. After all, this [is] a scene where ornate red fabric only partially covers the "discoloured" and stained walls underneath. Yet the image of heat—and suffoca-tion—proves sexually provocative to Newland. Framed and at the same time muffled by her fur collar, the woman of experience, of course, will be "eliminated" by the dominant tribe. Newland's inability to "analyze the trick" and to recognize the harem for what it is—a "painted sepulchre" (IM, 188)—figures his larger inability to break down the walls, the harem-structures that surround him.

As Wharton had recently suggested in her description of the harems in *In Morocco*, the removal of women from circulation was debilitating for both men and women. If Newland himself is a sort of harem keeper, guarding the opera box that contains his wife and her female relations, advising Ellen against the scandal of divorce, he too is en-closed by the walls of Old New York culture. "I shall never be happy unless I can open the windows!" he gasps to May when she tells him he'll "catch [his] death" with them open (178). He does not speak the words that throng in his suffocating body: "But I've caught it already. I *am* dead—I've been dead for months and months." The suggestion of Poe again recalls the sepulchral harem. Like the bejeweled son of the Moroccan caïd, whose maturity is threatened by "the stifling existence

---

4. The vamp was a popular character type in U.S. films of the teens and twenties. According to Gaylyn Studlar, the vamp allowed female consumers and fan-magazine readers to explore a fantastical exaggeration of the New Woman, whose challenge derived from an alleged per-version of gendered power relations, while borrowing freely from the idea of sexual chaos at-tributed to the "Orient." Studlar, " 'Out-Salomeing Salome': Dance, the New Woman, and Fan Magazine Orientalism," in *Visions of the East: Orientalism in Film*, ed. Matthew Bern-stein and Gaylyn Studlar (New Brunswick, N.J.: Rutgers University Press, 1997).

of the harem," Newland's future development is in question. As May humors him in the same managerial manner in which he has seen both her and her mother humor Mr. Welland, May's hypochondriacal father, Newland's future health and his potential for development is clearly being called into question. Newland's final inability to visit Ellen Olenska in her Paris apartment is the enactment of those very codes he struggled against, but ultimately helped to uphold, the wall New York constructed between women and men. Looking up at the window he imagines to be that of Ellen Olenska, Newland Archer watches until a manservant comes to close the window.

If Wharton's political lesson seems clear, her manner is complex. In the final chapter of *The Age of Innocence*, a quarter century after the rest of the novel, Dallas Archer says to his father Newland: "Dash it, Dad, don't be prehistoric!" (213). For the novel ends with Newland's own nostalgia, as he looks back on the 1870s and muses on "his small contribution to the new state of things," whether or not "men like himself *were* what his country needed, at least in the active service to which Theodore Roosevelt had pointed" (207). Newland takes comfort in the "well-built wall" that he helped establish, a wall that seems to be a foundation, such as for the museums and opera houses and apartments that dot Wharton's New York landscape. Yet for Wharton, the wall is more problematic. Writing in her notebook in 1918, Wharton declared: "I want the idols broken, but I want them broken by people who understand why they were made."[5] Newland's "well-built wall" is a wall of tradition, but it is also the seemingly impermeable wall dividing and suffocating those stuck in Old New York's harem, an isolating and isolationist wall. Although *The Age of Innocence* can imagine a new generation, a "new state of things," represented by Newland's son Dallas, the well-built wall of modern America still stands. The novel's passionate ending thus offers a challenge. As Dallas visits Ellen, Newland "wondered if the people were right who said that his boy 'took after him' " (216). Returning to the past in the present, Wharton poses the question of whether such a wall—the wall of national isolation—may be dismantled. The thwarted love story is obviously being rewritten by the next generation. Dallas is marrying his Fanny, the protégé of Ellen Olenska, the illegitimate daughter of Julius Beaufort: Newland and May's son is going beyond the once-forbidden walls that confined his parents in a "deaf-and-dumb asylum" (213) by marrying the woman he loves, even if she is someone whom Old New York had called one of "Beaufort's bastards" (202).

If *The Age of Innocence* is, among other things, an anthropological study of the "ways and their meaning" of American cultural isolation—both from World War I, in the crucial years of the conflict, and the isolation of the sexes—this elegiac novel offers a complex revision of Wharton's idea of "culture" itself. The anthropological trope is too extended in *The Age of Innocence* to be merely an addendum to Wharton's excoriation of the conventional rites and rituals of marriage in

---

5. Quoted in Bentley, " 'Hunting for the Real,' " 64.

America, as powerfully explored by her earlier New York novels *The House of Mirth* and *The Custom of the Country*. Rather, the anthropological perspective in *The Age of Innocence* allows Wharton to expand on her comparison of Moroccan women in their harem to the American upper-middle class. What is at stake here is the concept of "culture," the meaning of which was being contested by American anthropologists and sociologists when Wharton wrote *The Age of Innocence*. The year before *The Age of Innocence* was published, the prominent anthropologist Edward Sapir had fused two popular meanings of "culture" that had been in conflict: that of the ethnologist, for whom "all human groups are cultured, though in vastly different manners and grades of complexity"; and that of the "conventional idea of individual refinement."[6] Arguing for a joining of these concepts, Sapir contended that an idea of culture could be derived that would "embrace in a single term those general attitudes, views of life, and specific manifestations of civilization that give a particular people its distinctive place in the world."[7]

Wharton's idea of culture as developed in *The Age of Innocence* could accommodate both the ethnographer's concept of culture and the Arnoldian idea that it is the cultured who are in possession of culture. Yet Wharton's delineation of the various haremlike structures in Old New York—in her argument for an end to the age of (international) innocence—ultimately relied on at least two elisions. First, as I have mentioned above, Wharton's use of the Moroccan harem as a metaphor for gender relations in the United States kept women of non-Anglo races and of the lower classes in a hierarchically subjugated role and maintained an idea that the white upper-middle-class woman stood at the top of an international hierarchy. Such an impulse in Wharton's writing has been explored by Elizabeth Ammons and can be found elsewhere in Wharton's fiction, such as in Lily Bart's decision (in *The House of Mirth*) not to costume herself as Tiepolo's North African Cleopatra, but rather as Reynolds' Mrs. Lloyd, "unquestionably, purely white."[8] Second, in pushing forward the "idea" of France as a model for America as it moved out of isolation in the interests of commerce—a commerce, Wharton argued, that should include women as well as men—Wharton neatly adapted the French "idea" of France, an idea that relied on a colonial empire.

Despite the geographical circumscription of its action, *The Age of Innocence* is not an isolationist novel; rather it is a novel about what happens to individual subjectivity when a culture wills itself into isolation. In *The Age of Innocence*, Wharton's understanding of contemporary France and of French-administered Morocco are translated into telling

---

6. Edward Sapir, *Culture, Genuine and Spurious* (1924), a revision of his *Civilization and Culture* (1919). Quoted in George W. Stocking, Jr., "The Ethnographic Sensibility of the 1920s," in *Romantic Motives: Essays on Anthropological Sensibility*, ed. George W. Stocking, Jr., *History of Anthropology* vol. 6 (Madison: University of Wisconsin Press, 1989), 216. See also Nancy Bentley, " 'Hunting for the Real,' " and Walter Benn Michaels, *Our America*.
7. Stocking, "Ethnographic Sensibility," p. 216.
8. Elizabeth Ammons, "Wharton and Race" in *The Cambridge Companion to Edith Wharton*, p. 79. For another reading of the *tableau vivant* in *The House of Mirth* see Waid, *Edith Wharton's Letters from Underground*, pp. 27ff.

and, at times, explicit critique of American culture. In *The Age of Inno-cence*'s anthropological rendering of Old New York, Wharton makes use of a new critical vocabulary gleaned from her trip to French North Africa. In doing so, she associates the haremlike segregation of Ameri-can women and the childlike "innocence" of American ideas about the "world" in her critique of U.S. illusions of international innocence, an illusory separation from the concerns of the world that resulted in the nation's long-deferred entry into World War I. Harem structures, as Wharton realized, are ultimately invisible and internalized structures that exist multiply in the unspoken rites of culture. In order for Whar-ton's America to move beyond its age of innocence, sexual segregation *and* national isolation would have to be relegated to the past. As she of-fered France as a model for postwar America, Wharton was herself lim-ited by the assumption that American women as a whole were best represented by the example of the French women who inhabited pro-gressive drawing rooms, a population limited to white women from the privileged classes, and she exchanged one set of walls for other walls as she proposed that the alternative to national isolationism was some-thing closer to French imperialism. While Wharton was ambivalent about the impact of colonialism on Moroccan culture—primarily wor-rying over how French modernization would steal the mystery and romance from Morocco's "Arabian Nights" spectacle—she did not question France's right to overstep national boundaries. Indeed, Whar-ton's sense of Moroccan "primitiveness" not surprisingly reflects a gen-eral refusal on her part to move beyond the accepted codes of color, the racial hierarchization of the early twentieth century, in which "white-ness" was assumed to be the invisible standard by which the rest of America and the world could be measured. But despite these limita-tions, it is possible to recognize Wharton's achievement in *The Age of Innocence*. What she would later call "the idea of France" (in her war novel *A Son at the Front*, published in 1923) necessarily foregrounded and merged a rejection of international isolation and its troubling corollary—sexual isolationism. As *The Age of Innocence* makes the in-visible visible, this novel opens the door to reveal a great deal about postwar conversations that tied the fate of women as a class to the question of the manifest destiny of the nation.

## BRIGITTE PEUCKER

## Scorsese's *Age of Innocence*: Adaptation and Intermediality†

While she approved of the adaptations of her fiction to the theater, Edith Wharton, we are told, had little or no use for the cinema. Whar-

† Revised from the essay entitled "Rival Arts? Filming *The Age of Innocence*," which appeared in *Edith Wharton Review* 13.1 (1998): 19–22, eds. Clare Colquitt, Susan Goodman, and Candace Waid. Reprinted with permission of author and of *The Edith Wharton Review*. Bracketed page numbers refer to this volume. Notes have been edited.

ton's experience of the movies was probably limited to one visit in Bilbao, Spain, in 1914, a visit that may have given rise to the brief rendering of cinematic spectatorship we find in Wharton's novella *Summer*, published three years later. Insofar as *Summer*'s evocation of cinematic experience emphasizes visual sensations such as "swimming circles of heat and blinding alternations of light and darkness" (97), it participates in an attitude of the times that sees the moving images of cinema as waging an assault upon the human sensorium.[1] From this point of view, cinema constitutes one aspect of the "chaos" of urban experience, of which the crowds constitute another: in *Summer*, interestingly, Charity Royall's act of spectatorship merges the images on the screen with those of the crowd around her, whose faces "became part of the spectacle, and danced on the screen with the rest" (139). Wharton may have absorbed this contemporary attitude toward cinematic images, but it is also likely that this traumatic merging of screen images with those of real world experience has its origin in Wharton's personal abhorrence for a "spectacle shared by a throng of people."[2] In any case, in 1917 Wharton shared the American attitude towards cinema that stressed its entertainment rather than its artistic values. It would not be until D. W. Griffith released *Broken Blossoms* as a European art film in 1919 that the expectations of the public would begin to change.

But Wharton's attitude towards the cinema remained constant. Though not averse to the income derived from screen adaptations of her work, Wharton had no interest in what Hollywood now calls "the product" and did not see either of the two movie versions of *The Age of Innocence* that were released during her lifetime.[3] Had Wharton been able to see Martin Scorsese's 1993 adaptation of her novel, however, she might have experienced a conversion. Shot with the most minute attention to visual surface, Scorsese's film is suffused with "high art" values and subtleties: it is, as he has put it, shot and composed for "the purists."[4] Scorsese seems intuitively to grasp that the intriguing issue of cinematic adaptation is most appropriately viewed against the backdrop of a broader approach to the interrelation of the arts in cinema, since it is that interrelation that determines film as a medium. Scorsese's *Age of Innocence* substantiates the claim that, as a latecomer among the arts, film alludes to, absorbs, and undermines the

1. See Scott Marshall's excellent compendium, "Edith Wharton on Film and Television: A History and Filmography," *Edith Wharton Review* 13.2 (spring 1995): 15–26.
2. Walter Benjamin's "Work of Art in the Age of Mechanical Reproduction" (1935) later famously theorized this attitude. See *Film Theory and Criticism: Introductory Readings*, ed. Leo Braudy and Marshall Cohen (N.Y.: Oxford University Press, 1999), pp. 731–51.
3. For that matter, she did not see the stage version starring Katherine Cornell, either. Scott Marshall notes that *The Age of Innocence* was first filmed in 1924 by Wesley Ruggles, with Beverly Bayne as Countess Olenska and Eliot Dexter as Newland Archer. Unfortunately, this silent film is lost. In 1934, Wharton's novel was filmed again. This film was directed by Philip Moeller, with Irene Dunne as the Countess and John Boles as Archer. Although it is generally unavailable, this film was shown during the Wharton Conference at Yale University in April of 1995, where I had an opportunity to screen it. (For further information, see Scott Marshall, 17, 22.)
4. From "Martin Scorsese Interviewed by Gavin Smith," 22. For a detailed account of the making of the film, see Martin Scorsese and Jay Cocks, *The Age of Innocence: A Portrait of the Film* (New York: Newmarket, 1993).

language of the other arts in order to create its own idiom.[5] Borrowing from literature and painting equally, the medium of film is an amalgam of image and narrative that renders film heterogeneous, a hybrid that emerges out of traditionally sanctioned cultural forms. Seen in this light, as the convergence of literary and painterly concerns, film as a medium might very well have appealed to Wharton, for the conjoining of image and narrative is figured in Wharton's fiction: a preoccupation with the visual is central to her writing.

In *The Age of Innocence* as elsewhere, Wharton frequently makes use of painting in order to delineate her characters. It tells us a great deal about the dashing Julius Beaufort, that he "ha[s] the audacity to hang 'Love Victorious' "—a painting Wharton calls "the much-discussed nude of Bouguereau"—in his drawing room [15]. It is telling, too, that the portrait executed of Mrs. Henry van der Luyden twenty years ago is still "a 'perfect likeness' " of this lady who, as Wharton puts it, "ha[s] been rather gruesomely preserved in the airless atmosphere of a perfectly irreproachable existence," entombed like the image of the portrait in a kind of "life-in-death" [34]. And Newland Archer, one of Wharton's "collectors" and a man of sensibility, escapes from the strict decorum and from what he takes to be the stifling lack of imagination of New York society into a world of literature and painting. Somewhat predictably, then, Newland falls in love with the Countess Olenska, in part because she represents the "decadent" European world of culture and also because, as her grandmother notes, she is a woman whose portrait has been painted nine times. For Newland, art is both the suppressed realm of the imagination and the erotic; it is not at all surprising, therefore, that he chooses the art museum as the setting of their tryst.

In keeping with these concerns, Scorsese frames Wharton's characters in painterly effects: in the profilmic,[6] of course, actors are arranged in painterly compositions, but Scorsese goes far beyond these arrangements. Using color in film as though it were paint, Scorsese tells us in a compelling interview by Gavin Smith, "the camera moves in on the back of Newland's head, music comes up, and the wall goes red, like a blush" (16). The film's syntax, paying homage to the syntax of silent cinema with its irises, masking, and fades, was also made to reinforce Scorsese's painterly aesthetic: instead of fading to black at the end of scenes, he chose to fade to red and to yellow because, as he says, he "was interested in the use of color like brushstrokes throughout the film" (16). Editing procedures also contributed to the painterly look of this film, Scorsese tells us, as when he chose to shorten many of its shots "sort of like a brush coming through and painting bits and pieces of color, swishing by" (18). And sometimes camera movement suggests the sweep of the artist's paintbrush, as when a slow tracking shot from left to right gradually reveals the long

---

5. I make this argument about the nature of film at greater length in *Incorporating Images: Film and the Rival Arts* (Princeton: Princeton University Press, 1995).
6. profilmic: That which appears on the screen itself; the profilmic includes scenes that have been arranged, constructed, and selected to appear before the camera's lens [Editor].

landscape painting that hangs in the Countess's drawing room to Newland's eye.

Literary concerns also inform the film. Its visual surface, its minute attention to detail, have been termed "fetishistic" by critics,[7] and Scorsese's style does indeed mirror the attention to objects and ceremonies that we find in Wharton's novel. But this almost slavish recreation of detail is clearly not simply a bow to realism and period style or a recognition of importance of mise-en-scène in Wharton, be its function fetishistic or not. It is also a deliberate attempt to transpose novelistic description into the imagistic terms of film, an attempt to bridge the "schism" between novelistic and filmic description.[8] Further, the use of the third-person voiceover, Joanne Woodward's voice, is designed to give the impression of the narrator's voice—or actually Wharton's voice, Scorsese tells us—and thus to simulate the experience of reading the novel (18). Thus the voice of a woman is superimposed upon our experience of the film, constituting an aural dimension that both distances and draws the spectator in, and reinforces the spectatorial position that Scorsese strove to create. The emotional power of melodrama to entangle the spectator is to be tempered, according to the director, by the distance achieved through the conscious aestheticization of the film's surface. (This is a balancing act that is familiar to us from the films of Rainer Werner Fassbinder to whom we shall recur below.) Scorsese's critics, however, have tended primarily to fix upon the impression of distance that the film conveys.[9] Amy Taubin puts it aptly when she suggests that "Scorsese's desire was somehow 'to present' Wharton's novel" (12).

Film understood as a medium in which different representational systems—specifically those of painting and writing—at times collide, at times replace, but always supplement one another make film a medium particularly congenial to the artistic concerns of Wharton, whose work not only manifests a pronounced interest in the visual, but whose mode of allusion is so frequently intermedial—so frequently involves, that is, the multiple layering of painterly and writerly references. As Cynthia Griffin Wolff has pointed out, *The Age of Innocence* derives its title from the Reynolds portrait of that name and is connected by this means—"a private pun"—to James's *Portrait of a Lady*, thus making Newland Archer the subject of Wharton's "Portrait of a Gentleman" (312). Candace Waid has allowed us to see

7. Amy Taubin, "Dread and Desire," *Sight and Sound* 3 (Dec. 1993): 6. Also Pam Cook, *Review of* The Age of Innocence by Martin Scorsese, *Sight and Sound* 4 (Feb. 1994): 45.

8. See Gavin Smith's interview, 21. It should be noted that Scorsese made one major visual, and hence, perhaps, ideological, change in his film: May Welland, as played by Winona Ryder, is not a blonde and blue-eyed athlete, just as the Countess Olenska, as played by Michelle Pfeiffer, is not dark and frail. Scorsese does not code these women as convention would dictate, with the "dark lady" (the Countess Olenska) as literally dark-haired, as well as "aesthetic," and dangerously alluring. While one might read this choice as intending to undermine these conventions, it seems more likely that Scorsese was paying more attention in his choice of actress to the emotional power—and sense of "decadence"—that maturity can confer than to coloring.

9. It is interesting that the *New York Times* critic of Moeller's earlier film adaptation of the novel also makes the point that *his* "photoplay" "leaves the spectator curiously cold and detached from the raging emotions of the story," *New York Times Film Reviews, 1932–38,* vol. 2 (New York: New York Times Press, 1970), p. 1105.

that *The House of Mirth*, another novel that has recourse to a Reynolds portrait, alludes via Reynolds's painting both to Ariosto's story of Angelica and Medoro[1] and to the many other artists—Tiepolo among them—who have chosen to depict it (29). Both of these instances of intertextuality—and there are many similar moments in Wharton's writing—draw simultaneously upon painting and literature, creating a textual overlay, a palimpsest of sorts, that is at once imagistic and verbal.

Any filmmaker who, in adapting Wharton's text to film, had done his or her homework carefully—and Martin Scorsese has—would certainly have noticed this method of layering representational systems in Wharton's work. It is precisely this stylistic feature that makes adapting Wharton's work to film cinematically challenging, a working out of what it means to transpose one medium into another, for this layering of allusions necessitates a conscious working-through of the relation of film to writing and painting. Indeed, the manner in which Scorsese addresses these concerns makes it quite evident that, in preparation for shooting *The Age of Innocence*, Scorsese had not only seen Philip Moeller's 1934 adaptation,[2] but Eric Rohmer's *Marquise of O . . .* , another film that is notable for the manner in which it approaches a literary text suffused with references to the visual arts—the novella of that title by Heinrich von Kleist. The relation of the visual to the literary and their transumption by film is the central preoccupation of Rohmer's *Marquise*. And Rohmer, like other French New Wave directors a writer on film as well as a filmmaker, in his turn learned a great deal from the films of F. W. Murnau, a German art historian-turned-filmmaker of the 1920s, from whose work the French New Wave directors developed their theory of the filmmaker as auteur. Indeed, Rohmer himself wrote a book about Murnau that remains one of the most sustained meditations upon the relation of painting to cinema (see Rohmer, *L'organisation*).

But what do these relationships have to do with Scorsese's adaptation of Wharton? By my next example, I'd like to suggest that they have a great deal to do with it. At one decisive moment in Wharton's novel—in Newport, after the honeymoon that marks his marriage to May Welland—Newland Archer is sent down to the water to fetch Ellen, the Countess Olenska, who is standing immobile near a "pagoda-like summerhouse" facing the bay [132]. Newland pauses at a distance, contemplating Ellen as a spectator might view a sculpture, and decides that he will go to her only if she turns before a certain sailboat reaches Lime Rock. He will go to her only, that is, if her inan-

1. In the romantic epic "Orlando Furioso" by Italian poet Ludovico Ariosto (1474–1533), Angelica, a princess of Cathay, marries a humble Moor named Medoro. Orlando, a knight who has fallen in love with Angelica, goes mad after seeing the couple together in the woods [Editor].
2. Scorsese mentions other filmic influences upon his film, among these a lot of early New York City films, some very early Otoscope rolls whose images were reminiscent of the pages of a flipbook; Dreyer's *Gertrud*; Max Ophuls's *Lola Montes* and *Letter from An Unknown Woman*; William Wyler's *The Heiress* (based on Henry James's *Washington Square*). See Gavin Smith and also Ian Christie, "The Scorsese Interview" *Sight and Sound* 4 (Feb. 1994): 10–15.

imate figure—her body as "sculpture"—will, like Pygmalion's Galatea, magically come to life. (Pygmalion, the sculptor of classical antiquity, fell in love with his own work of art and, as Ovid tells us, took the sculpture of Galatea to bed with him.) But the moment in which Newland watches Ellen by the bay takes on an additional significance in Scorsese's film. In imitation of Wharton, Scorsese uses painting to evoke social position, taste, and the historical moment that he is representing. But he uses it also to say something about his chosen medium of film as when, for instance, the camera sweeps across the long canvas that hangs in Ellen's house as though in imitation of a brushstroke, emphasizing by this means the diegetic[3] flexibility of film the director's involvement with Wharton's writing and its complicated conjunction of literature with painting. Film, too, has an abiding interest in tableau vivant,[4] for tableau vivant moments in film—moments of arrested motion—remind us by contrast that the "motion picture" is the first medium that is able to animate visual representation, that is able to make painting "come to life." From the point of view of the human perceptual apparatus, it is motion that confers the impression of three-dimensionality upon the image. Tableau vivant moments in film set up a tension between the two- and three-dimensional, between stasis and movement, between the "death" of the human body in painting and its "life" in cinema.

Siegfried Kracauer, the noted film theorist, has contended that there are no films on the subject of art in which the camera is not featured (ix). And, indeed, flashy camerawork is everywhere apparent in Scorsese's film. Interestingly, it is Michael Ballhaus, Fassbinder's cameraman, who is Scorsese's cinematographer. The German director Fassbinder, also very much concerned with the conjunction of literature, painting, and theater, is a director in whose films artifice and formal arrangements can be understood as erotic display. The ostentatious movement of the camera in *The Age of Innocence*, so typical of films Ballhaus shot for Fassbinder, calls attention to itself, underlining the way in which the camera virtually generates space and gestures toward the three-dimensionality of that cinematic space in the process. Camera motion also affects our perception of the human body in film: in *The Age of Innocence*, the camera's striking mobility forms a pronounced contrast to the relative immobility of the characters as when, for instance, they are seated at table in shots that almost suggest tableaux vivants. At such times the camera zooms in and moves in circles, tracking around the actors as though to expose the painterly stasis in which they are entrapped.

But Ballhaus's prominent camerawork has yet another point of connection to Wharton. The film's credit sequence, designed by Saul and Elaine Bass, superimposes a text in cursive over the image, thus figur-

3. Adjectival form of *diegesis* (Greek for "a recounted story"); here it means the world shaped by the film, including what is implied by the action of the story. For example, the source of a sound may be seen in the film or the sound may either suggest or further articulate the story of the world being evoked, a world that can lie outside the filmic frame [Editor].
4. French, literally "living painting." A form of entertainment in which participants assume static poses to enact well-known paintings, using costumes, props, and scenery [Editor].

ing the conjunction of the literary with the imagistic.[5] With its operatic soundtrack and the repeated (erotic) image of an unfolding flower
shot in stop-action photography first opening, then finally going to
seed, this credit sequence is followed by the first diegetic shot of the
film, a close-up of a chrysanthemum. The camera then tracks back to
reveal a bunch of chrysanthemums, part of the stage set of Gounod's
*Faust.* One of these flowers is plucked, and the camera draws back to
reveal the garden scene with Marguerite holding the flower by means
of which she will symbolically deflower and dismember herself. After
this operatic "defloration," the camera, in what we discover to be an
extreme close-up of Newland Archer's evening attire—the frame is
black—pans to the left to focus on his boutoniere, on the white gardenia in his lapel. A few shots later, Newland's gaze through opera
glasses (another famous cinematic citation),[6] followed by shots from
his point of view, ally the camera with Newland's gaze. This sequence
of shots establishes Newland's gaze and the sensibility of the connoisseur and spectator as the determining sensibility of the camera. The
shots that follow, of several other men looking through opera glasses—
Larry Lefferts, arbiter of style in Wharton's novel, is the most prominent among them—confirm the conjunction of camera and opera
glass in joint connoisseurship. Under such a gaze the woman as flower
must ever be aestheticized and, like Marguerite and her model, Ophe-
lia, consigned to death—if not to an actual death, then to a death in
art.

A brief look at the other extant film version of *Age of Innocence,* a
film to which Scorsese referred while planning his own, provides additional insight into the trope of the woman dying into art. Like Scorsese's film, Philip Moeller's 1934 adaptation simultaneously addresses
concerns of Wharton's writing and of filmmaking, perhaps most
clearly in the scene in the Metropolitan Museum. This scene begins in
a room that contains a few classical sculptures of male and female
nudes among which the Countess Olenska and Newland Archer wander: in this film too, there is a suggestion of Pygmalion and Galatea.
Soon the couple enters the room containing the Egyptian collection,
where they converse among Egyptian sculptures and encounter a
mummy, labeled "A Woman Who Lived in Egypt." The label functions
as an interesting diversion from the factuality of the female corpse and
its "mummification," its preservation in art. In Egyptian culture, of
course, art and the preservation of the body go hand in hand: Egyptian
art at once defies and is in complicity with death, expressing, as André
Bazin has put it, "the mummy complex," or what Bazin has called the
"psychological ambition" of all art to "embalm time" (9–11). By means
of this Egyptian Room setting, the film version of 1934 addresses the
issues implicit in Scorsese's summerhouse sequence in which Ellen
stands immobile—the issues posed by the Galatea story and in tableau

5. Saul Bass is notable as a designer of evocative credit sequences for the films, among others,
of Alfred Hitchcock.
6. Most notably it occurs in Fritz Lang films, but it is more generally a self-conscious reference
to another lens, that of the camera.

vivant, which may be read either as the "bringing to life" of painting or as the "killing off" of the living body into the stasis of art. Again the fate of Lily Bart in *The House of Mirth* looms large. Displayed in death, her corpse is a still life or, as Candace Waid has pointed out, a *tableau* mort (38).

But in what sense is this scene in the Egyptian collection to be understood as self-consciously cinematic? On the one hand, it probably alludes to an early Hitchcock film, *Blackmail*, released in 1929, which includes an astonishing chase sequence through the Egyptian collection of the British Museum. *Blackmail* contains the first of several museum sequences in Hitchcock's films, many of which are concerned with precisely the issues which we have been discussing, with the delineation of film, narrative, and painting, and with the "killing off" of the female body into the aesthetic: *Vertigo* is a prime instance of this obsession. On the other hand, it is important to understand that for early writers on film such as Vachel Lindsay, film images are best understood as "hieroglyphics": Lindsay develops his notion of "photoplay-hieroglyphics" as analogous to Egyptian picture writing (203). The scene in the Egyptian collection, then—somewhat surprising to the spectator as that may be—serves as a reminder that film is indeed a "mixed medium," a form of "picture writing." Finally, as the term "picture writing" could reasonably serve as another metaphor for the simultaneously verbal and imagistic allusions in Wharton, a metaphor for what I earlier called the "multiple layering" of visual and verbal allusion, it seems a particularly resonant choice. Paradoxically, in this scene "hieroglyph" is "the word which makes all clear."[7]

I will conclude by briefly recalling to mind the scene at the end of Scorsese's film, the moment at which the golden light shining on the Countess's window in Paris recalls Newland Archer's "decisive moment" at Newport to his memory. Wharton tells her readers that for Newland "by some queer process of association, that golden light became for him the pervading illumination in which she lived" [215]. Wharton's readers recognize that light as the auratic glow of the aesthetic: this moment in Paris serves as Wharton's private tribute to James (Wolff, 333–34). But in his film Scorsese elaborates on this moment to play once again on the painterly quality of his earlier, multivalent scene. When, this time, in Pygmalion-like fashion, Newland Archer succeeds in making his Galatea come to life—she turns, if only briefly, in his imagination—we realize that at this moment, for Scorsese, film has triumphed over painting by means of its capacity for movement and for the representation of *life*.

## Works Cited

Astrue, Alexandre. "Fire and Ice." *Càhiers du Cinéma in English* 1 (1966): 69–73.
Bazin, André. "The Ontology of the Photographic Image." *What is Cinema?* Vol. 1. Berkeley: University of California Press. 1967.
Christie, Ian. "The Scorsese Interview," *Sight and Sound* 4 (Feb. 1994): 10–15.

7. Edith Wharton, *The House of Mirth* (N.Y.: Charles Scribner's Sons, 1905). These are the concluding words of the novel.

Cook, Pam. "Review of *The Age of Innocence* by Martin Scorsese," *Sight and Sound* 4 (Feb. 1994): 45–46.

Kracauer, Siegfried. *Theory of Film: The Redemption of Physical Reality.* Oxford: Oxford University Press, 1960.

Lindsay, Vachel. *The Art of the Moving Picture.* New York: Liveright, 1970.

Marshall, Scott. "Edith Wharton on Film and Television: A History and Filmography," *Edith Wharton Review* 13 (spring 1996): 15–26.

*New York Times Film Reviews, 1932–38.* Vol. 2. New York: New York Times Press, 1970, p. 1105.

Rohmer, Eric. *L'organisation de l'espace dans le "Faust" du Murnau.* Paris: Union Générale d'Editions, 1977.

Smith, Gavin. "Martin Scorsese Interviewed by Gavin Smith," *Film Comment* 29 (Nov–Dec 1993): 15–26.

Taubin, Amy. "Dread and Desire," *Sight and Sound* 3 (Dec. 1993): 6–9.

Waid, Candace. *Edith Wharton's Letters from the Underworld: Fictions of Women and Writing.* Chapel Hill: University of North Carolina Press, 1991.

Wharton, Edith. *Summer.* New York: Appleton, 1917.

———*The Age of Innocence.* New York: W. W. Norton, 2000.

Wolff, Cynthia Griffin. *A Feast of Words: The Triumph of Edith Wharton.* New York: Oxford University Press, 1977.

# Edith Wharton: A Chronology

1862    Edith Newbold Jones born into a family with two significantly older progeny, her brothers Frederic (b. 1846) and Harry (b. 1850) on January 24, in New York City.

1866    Moves to Europe with family for an extended period, reaping the financial advantages of renting their properties at home.

1872    Returns with family from Europe.

1877    Completes secretly written novella, "Fast and Loose," just after turning fifteen.

1878    Her collection of poetry, *Verses*, is privately published; a poem appears in the *Atlantic Monthly*.

1879    Makes her debut into society a year earlier than New York social custom dictated.

1880    Jones' family returns to Europe for her father's health.

1882    Her father, George Frederic Jones, dies in France at Cannes; returns with her mother to the United States in March; engaged to Harry Leyden Stevens in August; wedding postponed (engagement broken) in October.

1885    Marries Edward ("Teddy") Wharton on April 29; former fiancé, Harry Stevens, dies of tuberculosis a few weeks later.

1890    Short story, "Mrs. Manstey's View," published in *Scribner's*.

1897    *The Decoration of Houses*, written with Ogden Codman, is published.

1899    First collection of short stories, *The Greater Inclination*, published.

1900    *The Touchstone*, a short novel, published.

1901    Her mother, Lucretia Rhinelander Jones, dies; second collection of short stories, *Crucial Instances*, issued.

1902    *The Valley of Decision*, Wharton's first long novel, published; Wharton and her husband move into The Mount, the house she designed in western Massachusetts.

1903    *Sanctuary*, a short novel, published.

1904    Third volume of short stories, *The Descent of Man*, published.

1905    *The House of Mirth* published.

1907    *The Fruit of the Tree*, a novel, published.

1908    Love affair with Morton Fullerton, which will last about two years, begins; *A Motor-Flight through France*, a book of travel writing, published.

1909    *Artemis to Actaeon*, a collection of poems, published; Wharton becomes a permanent resident of France.

1911    *Ethan Frome*, a short novel, published.

1912    *The Reef*, a novel, published.
1913    Divorce from Teddy Wharton; *The Custom of the Country*, a novel, published.
1914    Permanently residing in France, Wharton becomes actively involved in war relief work.
1915    *Fighting France*, describing devastation witnessed during her eight trips to the French front, published.
1916    *The Book of the Homeless*, edited by Wharton and designed to raise money for war-relief work, published; *Xingu and Other Stories* appears.
1917    *Summer*, short novel, published.
1918    *The Marne*, a war novel, published.
1919    *French Ways and Their Meanings*, essays written to describe French culture to American soldiers entering World War I, published.
1920    *The Age of Innocence*, novel, published; *In Morocco*, travel work emphasizing cultural comparisons between the civilizations of Northern Africa and the Western world, published.
1921    Awarded the Pulitzer Prize for *The Age of Innocence*.
1922    *The Glimpses of the Moon*, novel, published.
1923    Receives honorary degree from Yale University; last visit to the United States; *A Son at the Front*, a war novel, appears.
1924    *Old New York*, a collection of four novellas, published; honored with Gold Medal from the National Institute of Arts and Letters.
1925    *The Mother's Recompense*, a novel, published; *The Writing of Fiction*, a collection of theoretical pieces, issued.
1926    Selected for membership in the National Institute of Arts and Letters.
1927    *Twilight Sleep*, a novel, published.
1928    Teddy Wharton dies; *The Children*, a novel, published.
1929    The novel *Hudson River Bracketed* appears.
1930    *Certain People*, short stories, brought out.
1932    Sequel to *Hudson River Bracketed*, *The Gods Arrive*, published.
1934    *A Backward Glance*, memoirs, published; at work on *The Buccaneers*, novel left unfinished at her death.
1937    Dies on August 11; buried in the Cimetiere des Gonards in Versailles, France; *Ghosts*, a collection of what she considered to be her best supernatural tales, published posthumously.
1938    Unfinished novel, *The Buccaneers*, edited and published posthumously by her literary executor, Gaillard Lapsley.

# Selected Bibliography

## WORKS BY WHARTON

### NOVELS AND NOVELLAS

*The Touchstone.* New York: Scribner's, 1900.
*The Valley of Decision.* 2 vols. New York: Scribner's, 1902.
*Sanctuary.* New York: Scribner's, 1903.
*The House of Mirth.* New York: Scribner's, 1905.
*The Fruit of the Tree.* New York: Scribner's, 1907.
*Madame de Treymes.* New York: Scribner's, 1907.
*Ethan Frome.* New York: Scribner's, 1911.
*The Reef.* New York: Appleton, 1912.
*The Custom of the Country.* New York: Scribner's, 1913.
*Summer.* New York: Appleton, 1917.
*The Marne.* New York: Appleton, 1918.
*The Age of Innocence.* New York: Appleton, 1920.
*The Glimpses of the Moon.* New York: Appleton, 1922.
*A Son at the Front.* New York: Scribner's, 1923.
*Old New York: False Dawn, The Old Maid, The Spark, New Year's Day.* New York: Appleton, 1924.
*The Mother's Recompense.* New York: Appleton, 1925.
*Twilight Sleep.* New York: Appleton, 1927.
*The Children.* New York: Appleton, 1928.
*Hudson River Bracketed.* New York: Appleton, 1929.
*The Gods Arrive.* New York: Appleton, 1932.
*The Buccaneers.* New York: Appleton-Century, 1938.
*Fast and Loose, a Novelette by David Olivieri.* Viola Hopkins Winner. ed. Charlottesville: University Press of Virginia, 1977.

### SHORT STORY COLLECTIONS

*The Greater Inclination.* New York: Scribner's, 1899.
*Crucial Instances.* New York: Scribner's, 1901.
*The Descent of Man and Other Stories.* New York: Scribner's, 1904.
*The Hermit and the Wild Woman and Other Stories.* New York: Scribner's, 1908.
*Tales of Men and Ghosts.* New York: Scribner's, 1910.
*Xingu and Other Stories.* New York: Scribner's, 1916.
*Here and Beyond.* New York: Appleton, 1926.
*Certain People.* New York: Appleton, 1930.
*Human Nature.* New York: Appleton, 1933.
*The World Over.* New York: Appleton-Century, 1936.
*Ghosts.* New York: Appleton-Century, 1937.
*The Collected Short Stories of Edith Wharton.* 2 vols. Ed. R. W. B. Lewis. New York: Scribner's, 1968.

### POETRY

*Verses.* Newport, R.I.: C. E. Hammett, 1878.
*Artemis to Actaeon and Other Verse.* New York: Scribner's, 1909.
*Twelve Poems.* London: The Medici Society, 1926.

### AUTOBIOGRAPHIES

*A Backward Glance.* New York: Appleton-Century, 1934.
"A Little Girl's New York." *Harper's Magazine,* CLXXVI (March, 1938): 356–64.

"Life and I" (previously unpublished autobiography). In *Novellas and Other Writings by Edith Wharton*. Ed. Cynthia Griffin Wolff. New York: Library of America, 1990.

### LETTERS

*The Letters of Edith Wharton*. Ed. R. W. B. Lewis and Nancy Lewis. New York: Scribner's, 1988.
Henry James and Edith Wharton, *Letters: 1900–1915*. Ed. Lyall H. Powers. New York: Scribner's, 1990.

### TRAVEL WRITINGS

*Italian Backgrounds*. New York: Scribner's, 1905.
*A Motor-Flight through France*. New York: Scribner's, 1908.
*In Morocco*. New York: Scribner's, 1920.

### WAR WORKS

*Fighting France, from Dunkerque to Belfort*. New York: Scribner's, 1915.
*The Book of the Homeless* (editor). New York: Scribner's, 1916.
*French Ways and Their Meaning*. New York: Appleton, 1919.

### CRITICAL PROSE ON ART AND AESTHETICS

*The Decoration of Houses* (with Ogden Codman, Jr.). New York: Scribner's, 1897.
*Italian Villas and Their Gardens*. New York: Century, 1904.
*The Writing of Fiction*. New York: Scribner's, 1925.
*The Uncollected Critical Writings*. Ed. Frederick Wegener. Princeton: Princeton University Press, 1996.

### TRANSLATION

*The Joy of Living*, by Hermann Sudermann. New York: Scribner's, 1902.

### SELECTED BOOKS ON WHARTON

Ammons, Elizabeth. *Conflicting Stories: American Women Writers at the Turn into the Twentieth Century*. New York: Oxford University Press, 1992.
Ammons, Elizabeth. *Edith Wharton's Argument with America*. Athens: University of Georgia Press, 1980.
Auchincloss, Louis. *Edith Wharton*. Minneapolis: University of Minnesota Press, 1961.
Auchincloss, Louis. *Edith Wharton: A Woman in Her Time*. New York: Viking, 1971.
Bauer, Dale M. *Edith Wharton's Brave New Politics*. Madison: University of Wisconsin Press, 1994.
Bauer, Dale M. *Female Dialogics: A Theory of Failed Community*. Albany: State University of New York Press, 1988.
Beer, Janet. *Kate Chopin, Edith Wharton, and Charlotte Perkins Gilman: Studies in Short Fiction*. New York: St. Martin's Press, 1997.
Bell, Millicent. *Edith Wharton and Henry James: The Story of Their Friendship*. New York: George Braziller, 1965.
Bell, Millicent, ed. *The Cambridge Companion to Edith Wharton*. New York: Cambridge University Press, 1995.
Bendixen, Alfred and Annette Zilversmit, eds. *Edith Wharton: New Critical Essays*. New York: Garland, 1992.
Benstock, Shari. *No Gifts from Chance: A Biography of Edith Wharton*. New York: Scribner's, 1994.
Benstock, Shari. *Women of the Left Bank: Paris, 1900–1940*. Austin: University of Texas Press, 1986.
Bentley, Nancy. *The Ethnography of Manners: Hawthorne, James, Wharton*. New York: Cambridge University Press, 1995.
Bloom, Harold, ed. *Modern Critical Views: Edith Wharton*. New York: Chelsea, 1986.
Brown, E. K. *Edith Wharton: Études Critiques*. Paris: Librarie Droz, 1935.
Colquitt, Clare, Susan Goodman, and Candace Waid, eds. *A Forward Glance: New Essays on Edith Wharton*. Newark: University of Delaware Press, 1999.
Coolidge, Olivia. *Edith Wharton, 1862–1937*. New York: Scribner's, 1964.
Donovan, Josephine. *After the Fall: The Demeter-Persephone Myth in Wharton, Cather, and Glasgow*. University Park: Pennsylvania State University Press, 1989.

Dwight, Eleanor. *Edith Wharton: An Extraordinary Life*. New York: Henry A. Abrams, 1994.

Erlich, Gloria C. *The Sexual Education of Edith Wharton*. Berkeley: University of California Press, 1992.

Fedorko, Kathy A. *Gender and the Gothic in the Fiction of Edith Wharton*. Tuscaloosa: University of Alabama Press, 1995.

Fracasso, Evelyn E. *Edith Wharton's Prisoners of Consciousness*. New York: Greenwood Press, 1994.

Fryer, Judith. *Felicitous Space: The Imaginative Structures of Edith Wharton and Willa Cather*. Chapel Hill: University of North Carolina Press, 1986.

Gilbert, Sandra M. and Susan Gubar. *No Man's Land*. Vol. 2: *Sex Changes*. New Haven, Conn: Yale University Press, 1989.

Gimbel, Wendy. *Edith Wharton: Orphancy and Survival*. New York: Praeger, 1984.

Goodman, Susan. *Edith Wharton's Inner Circle*. Austin: University of Texas Press, 1994.

Goodman, Susan. *Edith Wharton's Women: Friends and Rivals*. Hanover, N.H.: University Press of New England, 1990.

Goodwyn, Janet Beer. *Edith Wharton: Traveller in the Land of Letters*. New York: St. Martin's Press, 1990.

Griffith, Grace Kellogg. *The Two Lives of Edith Wharton, The Woman and Her Work*. New York: Appleton-Century, 1965.

Hadley, Kathy Miller. *In the Interstices of the Tale: Edith Wharton's Narrative Strategies*. New York: Peter Lang, 1993.

Holbrook, David. *Edith Wharton and the Unsatisfactory Man*. New York: St. Martin's Press, 1991.

Howe, Irving, ed. *Edith Wharton, A Collection of Critical Essays*. Englewood Cliffs, N.J.: Prentice-Hall, 1962.

Jessup, Josephine Lurie. *The Faith of Our Feminists: A Study in the Novels of Edith Wharton, Ellen Glasgow, Willa Cather*. New York: Smith, 1950.

Joslin, Katherine. *Edith Wharton*. New York: St. Martin's Press, 1991.

Joslin, Katherine, and Alan Price, eds. *"Wretched Exotic": Essays on Edith Wharton in Europe*. New York: Peter Lang, 1993.

Joslin-Jeske, Katherine. *The Social Thought and Literary Expression of Jane Addams and Edith Wharton*. Ann Arbor: University of Michigan Press, 1984.

Kaplan, Amy. *The Social Construction of American Realism*. Chicago: University of Chicago Press, 1988.

Killoran, Helen. *Edith Wharton: Art and Allusion*. Tuscalosa: University of Alabama Press, 1996.

Lawson, Richard H. *Edith Wharton*. New York: Ungar, 1976.

Lewis, R. W. B. *Edith Wharton: A Biography*. New York: Harper & Row, 1975.

Lindberg, Gary H. *Edith Wharton and the Novel of Manners*. Charlottesville: University Press of Virginia, 1975.

Lubbock, Percy. *Portrait of Edith Wharton*. New York: Appleton-Century, 1947.

Lyde, Marilyn. *Edith Wharton: Convention and Morality in the Work of a Novelist*. Norman: University of Oklahoma Press, 1959.

McDowell, Margaret. *Edith Wharton*. Boston: Twayne, 1976 (rev. 1990).

Montgomery, Maureen E. *Displaying Women: Spectacles of Leisure in Edith Wharton's New York*. New York: Routledge, 1998.

Nettels, Elsa. *Language and Gender in American Fiction: Howells, James, Wharton, and Cather*. Charlottesville: University Press of Virginia, 1997.

Nevius, Blake. *Edith Wharton: A Study of Her Fiction*. Berkeley: University of California Press, 1953.

Preston, Claire. *Edith Wharton's Social Register*. New York: St. Martin's Press, 1999.

Price, Alan. *The End of the Age of Innocence: Edith Wharton and the First World War*. New York: St. Martin's Press, 1996.

Rae, Catherine M. *Edith Wharton's New York Quartet*. Lanham, MD: University Press of America, 1984.

Raphael, Lev. *Edith Wharton's Prisoners of Shame*. New York: St. Martin's Press, 1991.

Singley, Carol J. *Edith Wharton: Matters of Mind and Spirit*. New York: Cambridge University Press, 1995.

Tuttleton, James. *The Novel of Manners in America*. Chapel Hill: University of North Carolina Press, 1972.

Tuttleton, James W., Kristin O. Lauer, and Margaret P. Murray, eds. *Edith Wharton: The Contemporary Reviews*. New York: Cambridge University Press, 1992.

Vita-Finzi, Penelope. *Edith Wharton and the Art of Fiction*. London: Pinter, 1990.

Wagner-Martin, Linda. *The Age of Innocence: A Novel of Ironic Nostalgia*. New York: Twayne, 1996.

Waid, Candace. *Edith Wharton's Letters from the Underworld*. Chapel Hill: University of North Carolina Press, 1991.

Walton, Geoffrey. *Edith Wharton: A Critical Interpretation*. Rutherford, N.J.: Farleigh Dickinson University Press, 1970.

Wershoven, Carol. *The Female Intruder in the Novels of Edith Wharton*. Rutherford, N.J.: Fairleigh Dickinson University Press, 1982.

White, Barbara A. *Edith Wharton: A Study of the Short Fiction*. Boston: Twayne, 1991.

Wiser, William. *The Great Good Place: American Expatriate Women in Paris*. New York: W. W. Norton, 1991.

Wolff, Cynthia Griffin. *A Feast of Words: The Triumph of Edith Wharton*. New York: Addison Wesley, 1995.

Wright, Sarah Bird. *Edith Wharton A to Z: The Essential Guide to the Life and Work of Edith Wharton*. New York: Facts on File, 1998.

Wright, Sarah Bird. *Edith Wharton's Travel Writing: The Making of a Connoisseur*. New York: St. Martin's Press, 1997.

## SELECTED ESSAYS ON *THE AGE OF INNOCENCE*

Aaron, Daniel. "Three Old Women," *Queens Quarterly* 102 (1995): 633–39.

Ammons, Elizabeth. "Cool Diana and the Blood-Red Muse: Edith Wharton on Innocence and Art." In *American Novelists Revisited: Essays in Criticism*, ed. Fritz Fleischmann. Boston: G. K. Hall, 1982. 209–24.

Asya, Ferda. "Resolutions of Guilt: Cultural Values Reconsidered in *Custom of the Country* and *The Age of Innocence*," *Edith Wharton Review* 14 (1997): 15–20.

Bentley, Nancy. " 'Hunting for the Real': Wharton and the Science of Manners." In *The Cambridge Companion to Edith Wharton*. Ed. Millicent Bell. New York: Cambridge University Press, 1995. 47–67.

Blackall, Jean Frantz. "Edith Wharton's Art of Ellipsis," *Journal of Narrative Technique* 17 (1987): 145–61.

Blackall, Jean Frantz. "The Intrusive Voice: Telegrams in *The House of Mirth* and *The Age of Innocence*," *Women's Studies* 20 (2): 163–68 (1991).

Boydston, Jeanne. " 'Grave Endearing Traditions': Edith Wharton and the Domestic Novel." In *Faith of a (Woman) Writer*. Ed. Alice Kessler-Harris and William McBrien. Westport, Connecticut: Greenwood, 1988. 31–40.

Candido, Joseph. "Edith Wharton's Final Alterations of *The Age of Innocence*," *Studies in American Fiction* 6–7 (1978–79): 21–31.

Castellitto, George P. "Imagism and Martin Scorsese: Images Suspended and Extended," *Literature-Film Quarterly* 26.1 (1998): 23–29.

Celly, Anu. "Barricaded by Banalities of Evasion: Women in *The Age of Innocence*," *Indian Journal of American Studies* 28.1–2 (1998): 37–47.

Christie, Ian. "The Scorsese Interview." *Sight and Sound* (February 1994): 10–15.

Colquitt, Clare. "Unpacking Her Treasures: Edith Wharton's 'Mysterious Correspondence' with Morton Fullerton," *Library Chronicle of the University of Texas* 31 (1985): 73–107.

Cuddy, Lois A. "Triangles of Defeat and Liberation: The Quest for Power in Edith Wharton's Fiction," *Perspectives on Contemporary Literature* 8 (1982): 18–26.

Das, Dilip K. "The American Family in Transition: Some Turn-of-the-Century Images," *Indian Journal of American Studies* 21 (1991): 47–54.

Davis, Linette. "Vulgarity and Red Blood in *The Age of Innocence*," *Journal of the Midwest Modern Language Association* 20 (fall 1987): 1–8.

Dessner, Lawrence Jay. "Edith Wharton and the Problem of Form," *Ball State University Forum* 24.3 (1983): 54–63.

Durczak, Joanna. "America and Europe in Edith Wharton's *The Age of Innocence*." In *Polish-American Literary Confrontations*. Ed. Joanna Durczak and Jerzy Durczak. Lublin: Maria Curie-Sklodowska University Press, 1995. 35–47.

Eby, Clare Virginia. "Silencing Women in Edith Wharton's *The Age of Innocence*," *Colby Library Quarterly* 28 (1992): 93–104.

Evans, Elizabeth. "Musical Allusions in *The Age of Innocence*," *Notes on Contemporary Literature* 4 (1974): 4–7.

Fracasso, Evelyn E. "The Transparent Eyes of May Welland in Wharton's *The Age of Innocence*," *Modern Language Studies* 21.4 (1991): 43–48.

Fryer, Judith. "Purity and Power in *The Age of Innocence*," *American Literary Realism* 17 (2): 153–68.

Gargano, James W. "Tableaux of Renunciation: Wharton's Use of *The Shaughran* in *The Age of Innocence*," *Studies in American Fiction* 15 (spring 1987): 1–11.

Gibson, Mary Ellis. "Edith Wharton and the Ethnography of Old New York," *Studies in American Fiction* 13 (1985): 57–69.

Gilbert, Sandra M., and Susan Gubar. "Angel of Devastation: Edith Wharton on the Arts of the Enslaved." In *No Man's Land: The Place of the Woman Writer in the Twentieth Century*, vol 2. New Haven: Yale University Press, 1989.

Godfrey, David A. " 'The Full and Elaborate Vocabulary of Evasion': The Language of Cowardice in Edith Wharton's Old New York," *Midwest Quarterly: A Journal of Contemporary Thought* 30 (autumn 1988): 27–44.

Hadley, Kathy Miller. "Ironic Structure and Untold Stories in *The Age of Innocence*," *Studies in the Novel* 23 (1991): 262–72.

Hatch, Ronald B. "Edith Wharton: A Forward Glance." In *The Twenties*. Ed. Barbara Smith Lemeunier. Aix-en-Provence: University of Provence, 1982. 7–20.

Helmetag, Charles H. "Recreating Edith Wharton's New York in M. Scorsese's *The Age of Innocence*" *Literature-Film Quarterly* 26.3 (1998): 162–65.

Jacobson, Irving F. "Perception, Communication, and Growth as Correlative Theme in Edith Wharton's *The Age of Innocence*," *Agora: A Journal in the Humanities and Social Sciences* 2.2 (1973): 68–82.

Knights, Pamela. "Forms of Disembodiment: The Social Subject in *The Age of Innocence*." In *The Cambridge Companion to Edith Wharton*. Ed. Millicent Bell. New York: Cambridge University Press, 1995. 20–46.

Lamar, Lillie B. "Edith Wharton's Foreknowledge in *The Age of Innocence*," *Texas Studies in Literature and Language: A Journal of the Humanities* 8 (1966): 385–89.

Lee, Robert A. "Watching Manners: Martin Scorsese's *The Age of Innocence*, Edith Wharton's *The Age of Innocence*." In *The Classic Novel: From Page to Screen*. Ed. Robert Giddings. New York: St. Martin's Press, 2000. 163–78.

Mayne, Gilles. "About the Displacement of Certain Words in *The Age of Innocence*: A Bataillian Reading," *Edith Wharton Review*. 14.2 (1997): 8–14.

McWilliams, Jim. "Wharton's *The Age of Innocence*," *Explicator* 48.4 (1990): 268–70.

Miller, D. Quentin. " 'A Barrier of Words': The Tension between Narrative Voice and Vision in the Writings of Edith Wharton," *American Literary Realism* 27.1 (1994): 11–22.

Mizener, Arthur. *Twelve Great American Novels*. New York: New American Library, 1967.

Morgan Gwendolyn. "The Unsung Heroine—A Study of May Welland in *The Age of Innocence*." In *Heroines of Popular Culture*. Ed. Pat Browne. Bowling Green, Ohio: Bowling Green University Popular Press, 1987. 32–40.

Murphy, John J. " 'Filters, Portraits, and History's Mixed Bag': *A Lost Lady* and *The Age of Innocence*," *Twentieth-Century Literature: A Scholarly and Critical Journal* 38.4 (1992): 476–85.

Nathan, Rhoda. "Ward McAllister: Beau Nash of *The Age of Innocence*," *College Literature* 14 (fall 1987): 277–84.

O'Neal, Michael J. "Point of View and Narrative Technique in the Fiction of Edith Wharton," *Style* 17 (1983): 270–79.

Orlando, Emily J. "Rereading Wharton's 'Poor Archer': A Mr. 'Might-Have-Been' in *The Age of Innocence*," *American Literary Realism* 30.2 (1998): 56–77.

Peucker, Brigitte. "Rival Arts? Filming *The Age of Innocence*." *Edith Wharton Review* 13 (1): 19–22.

Pimple, Kenneth D. "Edith Wharton's 'Inscrutable Totem Terrors': Ethnography and *The Age of Innocence*," *Southern Folklore* 51.2 (1994): 137–52.

Pizer, Donald. "American Naturalism in Its 'Perfected' State: *The Age of Innocence* and *An American Tragedy*." In *Edith Wharton: New Critical Essays*. Ed. Alfred Bendixen and Annette Zilversmit. New York: Garland, 1992. 127–41.

Poder, Elfriede. "Concepts and Visions of 'the Other': The Place of 'Woman' in *The Age of Innocence, Melanctha*, and *Nightwood*." In *Women in Search of Literary Space*. Ed. Gudrun M. Grabher and Maureen Devine. Tubingen, Ger., Narr., 1992. 113–33.

Price, Alan. "The Composition of Edith Wharton's *The Age of Innocence*," *Yale University Library Gazette* 55 (July 1980): 22–30.

Richards, Mary Margaret. " 'Feminized Men' in Wharton's Old New York," *Edith Wharton Newsletter* 3 (fall 1986): 2–3, 12.

Robinson, James A. "Psychological Determinism in *The Age of Innocence*," *Markham Review* 5 (1975): 1–5.

Salecl, Renata. "I Can't Love You Unless I Give You Up." In *Gaze and Voice as Love Objects*. Ed. Renata Salecl and Slavoj Zizek. Durham: Duke University Press, 1996. 179–209.

Saunders, Judith P. "Becoming the Mask: Edith Wharton's Ingenues," *Massachusetts Studies in English* 7.4 (1982): 33–39.

Scheick, William J. "Cupid without Bow and Arrow: *The Age of Innocence* and *The Golden Bough*," *Edith Wharton Newsletter* 2 (1): 2–5 (1985).

Sensibar, Judith. "Edith Wharton Reads the Bachelor Type: Her Critique of Modernism's Representative Man," *American Literature* 60 (4): 575–90 (1988).

Strout, Cushing. "Complementary Portraits: James' *Lady* and Wharton's *Age*," *Hudson Review* 35 (1982): 405–15.

Tintner, Adeline R. "Jamesian Structures in *The Age of Innocence* and Related Stories," *Twentieth Century Literature* 26 (1980): 332–47.

Tintner, Adeline R. "The Narrative Structure of Old New York: Text and Pictures in Edith Wharton's Quartet of Linked Short Stories," *Journal of Narrative Technique* 17 (winter 1987): 76–82.

Trumpener, Katie, and James M. Nyce. "The Recovered Fragments: Archeological and Anthropological Perspectives in Edith Wharton's *The Age of Innocence*." In *Literary Anthropology: A New Interdisciplinary Approach to People, Signs and Literature*. Ed. Fernando Poyatos. Amsterdam: Benjamins, 1988. 161–69.

Tuttleton, James W. "Edith Wharton: The Archeological Motive," *The Yale Review* 61.4 (1972): 562–74.

Updike, John. "Archer's Way," *New York Review of Books* 14 (Nov. 30, 1995): 16, 18.

Van Gastel, Ada. "The Location and Decoration of Houses in *The Age of Innocence*," *Dutch Quarterly Review of Anglo-American Letters* 20.2 (1990): 138–53.

Vidal, Gore. "Of Writers and Class: In Praise of Edith Wharton," *Atlantic* 241 (February 1978): 64–67.

Wagner, Linda W. "A Note on Wharton's Use of Faust," *Edith Wharton Newsletter* 3.1 (1986): 1, 8.

Wegener, Frederick. "Edith Wharton and the Difficult Writing of *The Writing of Fiction*," *Modern Language Studies* 25 (spring 1991): 3–12 and 8 (fall 1991): 3–10, 32.

Wershoven, Carol. "America's Child Brides: The Price of a Bad Bargain." In *Portraits of Marriage in Literature*. Ed. Anne C. Hargrove and Maurine Magliocco. Macomb, Il.: Essays in Literature, 1984. 151–57.

Widmer, Eleanor. "Edith Wharton: The Nostalgia for Innocence." In *The Twenties: Fiction, Poetry, Drama*. Ed. Warren French. Deland, Florida: Everett/Edwards, Inc., 1975. 27–38.

Wilson, Edmund. "Justice to Edith Wharton" in *The Wound and the Bow*. New York: Oxford University Press, 1947. 195–213.

Wolff, Cynthia Griffin. "The Age of Innocence: Wharton's 'Portrait of a Gentleman.' " *Southern Review* 12 (1976): 640–58.

Wynne-Davies, Marion. " 'All by Myself in the Moonlight': Edith Wharton's *Age of Innocence*." *Kobe College Studies* 41.2 (1994): 1–14.

## SELECTED BIBLIOGRAPHIES ON WHARTON

Bendixen, Alfred. "A Guide to Wharton Criticism, 1976–1983," *Edith Wharton Newsletter* 2 (1985): 1–8. (Comments by others included.)

Bendixen, Alfred. "New Directions in Wharton Criticism: A Bibliographic Essay," *Edith Wharton Review* 10 (2): 20–24.

Bendixen, Alfred. "Recent Wharton Studies: A Bibliographic Essay," *Edith Wharton Newsletter* 3 (1986): 5, 8–9.

Bendixen, Alfred. "Wharton Studies, 1986–1987: A Bibliographic Essay," *Edith Wharton Newsletter* 5 (1988): 5–10.

Bendixen, Alfred. "The World of Wharton Criticism: A Bibliographic Essay," *Edith Wharton Review* 7 (1): 18–21.

Brenni, Vito J. *Edith Wharton: A Bibliography*. Morgantown, Va.: McClain Printing Co., 1966.

Garrison, Stephen, ed. *Edith Wharton: A Descriptive Bibliography*. Pittsburgh: University of Pittsburgh Press, 1990.

Lauer, Kristin O., and Margaret P. Murray, eds. *Edith Wharton: An Annotated Secondary Bibliography*. New York: Garland Publishing, 1990.

Schriber, Mary Suzanne. "Edith Wharton and the French Critics, 1906–1937," *American Literary Realism* 13 (1980): 61–72.

Springer, Marlene, ed. *Edith Wharton and Kate Chopin: A Reference Guide*. Boston: G. K. Hall, 1976.

Springer, Marlene, and Joan Gilson, eds. "Edith Wharton: A Reference Guide Updated," *Resources in American Literary Study* 14 (spring/autumn 1984): 85–111.

Tuttleton, James W. "Edith Wharton." In *American Women Writers: Bibliographical Essays*. Eds. Maurice Duke, Jackson R. Bryer, and M. Thomas Inge. Westport, Conn.: Greenwood Press, 1983. 71–107.

Tuttleton, James W., Kristin O. Lauer, and Margaret P. Murray, eds. *Edith Wharton: Contemporary Reviews*. New York: Cambridge University Press, 1992. 296.

Zilversmit, Annette. "Appendix, Bibliographical Index," *College Literature* 14 (1987): 305–9.

## SELECTED BIBLIOGRAPHY OF SOURCES

Adelman, Melvin L. *A Sporting Time: New York City and the Rise of Modern Athletics, 1820–1870*. Urbana: University of Illinois Press, 1986.

Ammons, Elizabeth. *Conflicting Stories: American Women Writers at the Turn into the Twentieth Century*. New York: Oxford University Press, 1992.

Auchincloss, Louis. *The Vanderbilt Era: Profiles of a Gilded Age*. New York: Charles Scribner's Sons, 1989.

Auerbach, Nina. *Woman and the Demon: The Life of a Victorian Myth*. Cambridge: Harvard University Press, 1982.

Baxter, Raymond and Arthur G. Adams. *Railroad Ferries of the Hudson, and Stories of a Deckhand*. Woodcliff Lake, N.J.: Lind, 1987.

Bender, Thomas. *New York Intellect: A History of Intellectual Life in New York City from 1750 to the Beginnings of Our Own Time*. New York: Knopf, 1987.

Burrows, Edwin G. and Mike Wallace. *Gotham: A History of New York City to 1898*. New York: Oxford University Press, 1998.

Burt, Nathaniel. *Palaces for the People: A Social History of the American Art Museum*. Boston: Little, Brown, and Co., 1977.

Caldwell, Mark. *A Short History of Rudeness: Manners, Morals, and Misbehavior in Modern America*. New York: Picador, 1999.

Chauncey, George. *Gay New York: Gender, Urban Culture, and the Making of the Gay Male World, 1890–1940*. New York: Harper Collins, 1994.

Crouthamel, James L. *Bennett's New York Herald and the Rise of the Popular Press*. Syracuse, N.Y.: Syracuse University Press, 1989.

Dizikes, John. *Opera in America: A Cultural History*. New Haven: Yale University Press, 1993.

Gilfoyle, Timothy J. *City of Eros: New York City, Prostitution, and the Commercialization of Sex, 1790–1920*. New York: W. W. Norton, 1992.

Jackson, Kenneth T., ed. *The Encyclopedia of New York City*. New Haven: Yale University Press, 1995.

Lankevitch, George J. *American Metropolis: A History of New York City*. New York: New York University Press, 1998.

Lott, Eric. *Love and Theft: American Blackface Minstrelsy and the American Working Class*. New York: Oxford University Press, 1993.

McNickle, Chris. *To Be Mayor of the City of New York: Ethnic Politics in the City*. New York: Columbia University Press, 1993.

Michaels, Walter B. *Our America: Nativism, Modernism & Pluralism*. Durham, N.C.: Duke University Press, 1995.

Rosenzsweig, Roy, and Elizaqbeth Blackmar. *The Park and the People: A History of Central Park*. Ithaca, N.Y.: Cornell University Press, 1992.

Sobel, Robert. *Panic on Wall Street: A History of America's Financial Disasters*. Frederick, Md: Beard Books, Inc., 1999.

Trachtenberg, Alan. *The Incorporation of America: Culture and Society in the Gilded Age*. New York: Hill & Wang, 1982.

Vella, Christina. *Intimate Enemies: The Two Worlds of the Baroness Pontalba*. Baton Rouge: Louisiana State University, 1977.

Wicker, Elmus. *Banking Practices of the Gilded Age*. New York: Cambridge University Press, 2000.

# Illustration Credits

Wharton's Outline for *The Age of Innocence*. Courtesy of The Beinecke Rare Book and Manuscript Library, Yale University.

Interior of Lucretia Rhinelander Jones's Home in New York. Courtesy of The Beinecke Rare Book and Manuscript Library, Yale University.

Mary Mason Jones's home, Madison Avenue looking Northwest from 55th Street, ca. 1870. Courtesy of The Museum of the City of New York.

Close-up view of Mary Mason Jones's home on Fifth Avenue, 1875. Courtesy of The Museum of the City of New York.

The Old Academy of Music, corner of 14th Street and Irving Place, 1886. Courtesy of The New York Historical Society. Negative number 41226.

The Metropolitan Opera House. Courtesy of The Metropolitan Opera Archives.

"The Shaugraun," Harry Montague and Ada Dyas, 1874. Museum of the City of New York. Gift of Mrs. McCoskry Butt, 33.94.237.

Bird's-Eye Map of Newport (1888). Courtesy of The Newport Historical Society (P1704).

Watching the Regatta at Castle Hill, ca. 1890. Courtesy of The Newport Historical Society. Negative number P1749.

The Newport Young Ladies' Archery Society, ca. 1872. Courtesy of The Newport Historical Society.

Christine Nilsson, 1871. Courtesy of The Metropolitan Opera Archives.

Edith Newbold Jones, 1874. Courtesy of The Lilly Library, Indiana University. Wharton mss. Box 9, f.2, no. 3.

"Castle Garden, New York City, 1851," by Jasper Cropsey. Copyright © Collection of The New York Historical Society.

"Squatters Near Central Park," 1869. Courtesy of The New York Historical Society.

"Red Scare": The Lusk Committee Map, 1920. Courtesy of The New York Historical Archive, Albany, New York.

Butterick Fashions, 1872–73. Courtesy of The New York Historical Society. The Landauer Collection, Negative numbers 48291 and 48295.

Edith and Teddy Wharton (Newport, ca. mid- to late-1880s) Courtesy of the Clifton Waller Barrett Library, University of Virginia Library. Negative # 1724-AC.

Bow-Shooting, July 1877. Courtesy of The Davidson Library Special Collections.